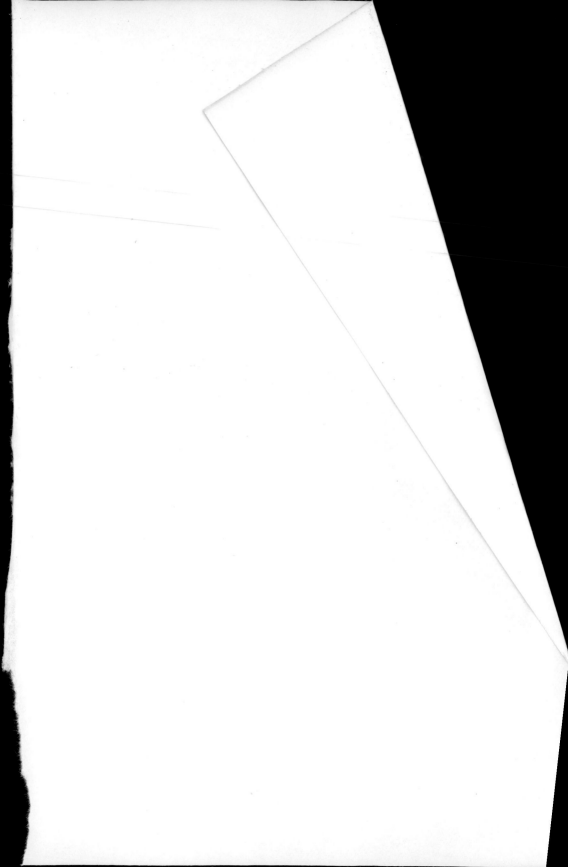

A BIBLIOGRAPHY OF
MODERN HISTORY

A BIBLIOGRAPHY OF MODERN HISTORY

EDITED BY

JOHN ROACH

Professor of Education in the University of Sheffield and
Fellow of Corpus Christi College, Cambridge

CAMBRIDGE
AT THE UNIVERSITY PRESS
1968

Published by the Syndics of the Cambridge University Press
Bentley House, 200 Euston Road, London, N.W. 1
American Branch: 32 East 57th Street, New York, N.Y. 10022

© Cambridge University Press 1968

Library of Congress Catalogue Card Number: 67–11528

Printed in Great Britain
at the University Printing House, Cambridge
(Brooke Crutchley, University Printer)

Other works for reference

General Survey

The most convenient single-volume reference book and bibliography is the American Historical Association's *Guide to Historical Literature* (1961), which cites books, periodicals, and the major printed collections of sources. Among brief bibliographies which are easily accessible, the *Helps for Students of History* series, published by the Historical Association, should be particularly mentioned. Recent titles include no. 58, *English Constitutional History*, Chrimes, S. B. and Roots, I. A. (eds.) (1958); no. 60, *Modern European History 1789–1945*, Medlicott, W. N. (ed.) (1961); no. 61, *British History since 1926*, Mowat, C. L. (ed.) (1961); no. 63, *British Overseas Expansion and the History of the Commonwealth*, Morrell, W. P. (ed.) (1961); no. 66, *The History of the Church*, Chadwick, O. (ed.) (1962). Two other very useful surveys are *A Select List of Works on Europe and Europe Overseas 1715–1815*, Bromley, J. S. and Goodwin, A. (eds.) (Oxford, 1956), and *A Select List of Books on European History 1815–1914*, Bullock, A. and Taylor, A. J. P. (eds.) (Oxford, 1957). The Historical Association also publishes an extremely useful *Annual Bulletin of Historical Literature* (1911–). A more elaborate publication of a similar type is the *International Bibliography of Historical Sciences* (1926–) (published for the International Committee of Historical Sciences, Lausanne).

A number of the principal series of historical works include valuable bibliographical information. The first *Cambridge Modern History* (1907–1912) contains very full bibliographies. Among more recent works the American series, *The Rise of Modern Europe*, Langer, William L. (ed.) is especially useful as each volume contains a bibliographical essay. Two French series should also be mentioned: (*a*) *Peuples et civilisations, histoire générale*, Halphen, L. and Sagnac, P. (eds.) and (*b*) *Clio: introductions aux études historiques*. The first of these is a series of studies of successive historical periods; the volumes of the latter are both advanced textbooks and bibliographical studies.

There are many bibliographies of the history of the various states, and only a very brief selection for the major countries can be given here; for fuller information see the American Historical Association's *Guide* already mentioned.

Great Britain

The volumes of the *Oxford History of England*, Clark, G. N. (ed.) contain extensive bibliographies. For surveys of recent work see *Writings on British History 1934–45*, Milne, A. T. (ed.) (8 vols.), (published by the Royal Historical Society); *Bibliography of Historical Works issued in the United Kingdom 1946–56*, Lancaster, J. C. (ed.) (1957) and *Bibliography of Historical Works issued in the United Kingdom 1957–60*, Kellaway, W. (ed.) (1962), (both published by University of London, Institute of Historical Research).

France

The volumes in the two series edited by Lavisse, E., *Histoire de France depuis les origines jusqu'à la Révolution* and *Histoire de France contemporaine depuis la*

CONTENTS

Révolution jusqu'à la Paix de 1919 both contain bibliographies. For more recent work see *Répertoire bibliographique de l'histoire de la France* (annually from 1920 1) (published by Centre national de la recherche scientifique).

Germany

Dahlmann-Waitz, *Quellenkunde der deutschen Geschichte* (9th ed., Leipzig, 1931). Annual surveys appear in *Jahresberichte für deutsche Geschichte* (published by Deutsche Akademie der Wissenschaften, Berlin) (under various titles since 1878).

Italy

Hassall, W. O. *A Select Bibliography of Italy* (London, 1946) is a very brief survey only. There are useful historical articles and bibliographies in *Enciclopedia italiana di scienze, lettere ed arti*, 36 vols. (Rome, 1929–39); Appendices, 5 vols. (1938–61).

Spain and Spanish America

Fuentes de la historia española e hispano-americana, Sánchez Alonso, B. (ed.) (3rd ed., 3 vols., Madrid, 1952). *Latin American History. A Guide to the Literature in English*, Humphreys, R. A. (ed.) (Royal Institute of International Affairs, 1958). For recent work see *Indice Histórico Español* (Barcelona), quarterly since 1953.

United States

Harvard Guide to American History, Handlin, O. and others (eds.) (Cambridge, Mass., 1954). For new literature see *Writings on American History* (from 1906), forming vol. II of the *Annual Report* of the American Historical Association.

Russia

A Select Bibliography of Works in English on Russian History, Shapiro, D. (ed.) (Blackwell, Oxford, 1962). *Books on Soviet Russia 1917–42*, a *Bibliography and a Guide to Reading*, Grierson, P. (ed.) (London, 1943); for annual supplements to this see *Slavonic and East European Review* (1946–).

LIST OF CONTRIBUTORS

Allen, G. C.
Andersen, N. K.
Anderson, M. S.
Andersson, I.
Armstrong, C. A. J.
Aubenas, R.
Ballhatchet, K. A.
Barber, W. H.
Baron, H.
Beaglehole, J. C.
Beasley, W. G.
Beer, E. S. de
Beller, E. A.
Beloff, M.
Bertier de Sauvigny, G. de
Betts, R. R.
Bizer, E.
Boas, M.
Borah, W.
Bosher, J. F.
Brock, W. R.
Brogan, D. W.
Bromley, J. S.
Bruford, W. H.
Bruun, G.
Bury, J. P. T.
Butler, R. D'O.
Campbell, A. E.
Carr, R.
Carsten, F. L.
Carter, A. C.
Chandler, D. G.
Clark, G. N.
Coleman, D. C.
Conze, W.
Cooper, J. P.
Craig, G.
Crawley, C. W.
Crombie, A. C.
Dakin, D.
Darby, H. C.
Davidson, J. W.
Davies, C. C.
Derry, T. K.
Deutscher, I.
Dickson, P. G. M.
Elliott, J. H.
Elton, G. R.

Evennett, H. O.
Fage, J. D.
Fennell, J. L. I.
Fitzgerald, C. P.
Foot, M. R. D.
Gillispie, C. C.
Godechot, J.
Goodwin, A.
Greaves, R. W.
Griffin, C. C.
Gulick, E. V.
Habakkuk, H. J.
Hale, J. R.
Hall, A. R.
Hall, D. G. E.
Hamilton, B.
Hargreaves, J. D.
Hartwell, R. M.
Hatton, R. M.
Hay, D.
Heaton, H.
Heller, E.
Horn, D. B.
Houtte, J. A. van
Hoskin, M. A.
Howard, M. E.
Humphreys, R. A.
Hurstfield, J.
Jablonowski, H.
Joll, J.
Jones, M. A.
Judges, A. V.
Keep, J. L. H.
Knaplund, P.
Koenigsberger, H. M. G.
Kossmann, E. H.
Laffan, R. G. D.
Langdon, F. C.
Lewis, B.
Lewis, M.
Lewitter, L. R.
Leyden, W. von
Lindsay, J. O.
Livermore, H. V.
Livet, G.
Lloyd, C. C.
Longmore, A.
Lossky, A.

Lough, J.
Lütge, F.
Lynch, J.
Macartney, C. A.
McKie, D.
Mack Smith, D.
McManners, J.
Magalhães Godinho, V.
Markham, F. M. H.
Mathiex, J.
Matthews, W. R.
Mattingly, G.
Medlicott, W. N.
Miles, G. J. A.
Miles, W.
Mosse, G. L.
Mousnier, R.
Murray, A. V.
Néré, J.
Ogg, D.
Palmer, R. R.
Parry, J. H.
Parry, V. J.
Payne, E. A.
Philipp, W.
Potter, D. M.
Potter, G. R.
Pouthas, C.
Price, J. M.
Purcell, V.
Quinn, D. B.
Ramm, A.
Ramsay, G. D.
Roach, J. P. C.
Roberts, J. M.
Roberts, M.

Rothkrug, L.
Rudé, G. E.
Rupp, E. G.
Ryan, A. N.
Schenk, H. G.
Shennan, J. H.
Skalweit, S.
Skwarczynski, P.
Smith, W. H. C.
Spear, T. G. P.
Spini, G.
Spooner, F. C.
Stark, W.
Stoye, J. W.
Tapié, V. L.
Taylor, A. J. P.
Thomson, D.
Thorlby, A. K.
Thornton, A. P.
Tooley, M. J.
Trevor-Roper, H. R.
Veenendaal, A. J.
Vyvyan, J. M. K.
Walsh, J. D.
Wangermann, E.
Ward, W. R.
Wernham, R. B.
Western, J.
Whiteman, A.
Wijn, J. W.
Williams, T. H.
Williams, T. I.
Wilson, C. H.
Wright, E.
Young, I.

commonly cited in the *Bibliography* are
ed in full.

les, and their

59; III,

Review

ociétés, civilisations

. ii). page 1   *view*

2   *Review*

3   *Historical Review*

5

6   *ift*

tory of Ideas

8   *n History*

l. I,

ii).

10   *philologie et d'histoire*

12   *e*

15   *ora*

an Economic History Review

19   *nd East European Review*

w   *ions of the Royal Historical Society*

e

e

e

SYNOPSIS

(Giving the *New Cambridge Modern History* volume and chapter ti
subsection numbers within the Bibliography.)

SECTION A: 1493–1648 (vols. I, 1493–1520; II, 1520–
1559–1610; IV, 1609–48)

Economic and Social Conditions

1 The face of Europe on the eve of the great discoveries (vol. I, cl
2 Economic change. 1. Agriculture (vol. II, ch. ii).
3 Economic change. 2. The greatness of Antwerp (vol. II, ch. ii).
4 The economy of Europe 1559–1609 (vol. III, ch. ii).
5 The European economy (vol. IV, ch. ii).

Intellectual Life, Education and Science

6 Fifteenth-century civilisation and the Renaissance (vol. I, ch. iii).
   Learning and education in Western Europe from 1470 to 1520 (vo
   ch. v).
7 Intellectual tendencies. 1. Literature: the printed book (vol. II, ch. x
8 Schools and universities (vol. II, ch. xiii).
   Education and learning (vol. III, ch. xiv).
9 Intellectual tendencies. 2. Science (vol. II, ch. xii).
   Science (vol. III, ch. xv).
   Science and philosophy (vol. IV, ch. iv).
10 The theatre (vol. IV, ch. viii).

Constitutional History, Political Theory and International La

11 Constitutional development and political thought in Western Europ
   (vol. II, ch. xiv).
12 Constitutional development and political thought in Eastern Europ
   (vol. II, ch. xv).
13 Social structure, office-holding and politics, chiefly in Western Europ
   (vol. III, ch. v).
14 International diplomacy and international law (vol. III, ch. vi).
15 Political thought and the theory and practice of toleration (vol. III
   ch. xvi)
16 The exponents and critics of absolutism (vol. IV, ch. iii).

The Art of War: armies and navies

17 International relations in the West: diplomacy and war (vol. I, ch. ix).
   Armies, navies and the art of war (vol. II, ch. xvi).
   Armies, navies and the art of war (vol. III, ch. vii).
   (a) Armies and warfare (vol. IV, ch. vi).

Religion: (a) Roman Catholicism to 1550

18 The Papacy and the Catholic church (vol. I, ch. iv).
19 Italy and the Papacy (vol. II, ch. viii).
20 The New Orders (vol. II, ch. ix).

(b) Protestantism to c. 1555

(c) The Churches 1555–1648

The Politics of the European States

The Histories of separate countries
France

Spain

Italy

England

The Netherlands

Germany and the Empire

Eastern and Northern Europe

Europe Overseas

SECTION B: 1648–1793 (vols. V, 1648–88; VI, 1688–1713; VII, 1713–63; VIII, 1763–93)

Economic and Social Conditions

France: the revolutionary generation to 1793

Spain, Portugal and their Empires

Italy and the Mediterranean

The British Isles

The Netherlands

Germany and the Habsburg Lands

Eastern and Northern Europe

Europe Overseas

America before the revolution: Spanish America

The United States

Asia and Africa

SECTION C: 1793–1945 (vols. IX, 1793–1830; X, 1830–70; XI, 1870–98; XII, 1898–1945)

Economic and Social Conditions

Intellectual Life, Literature, Science and Education

Religion, Social and Political Thought and Institutions

The Art of War: armies and navies

The Politics of the European States

The Histories of separate countries

France

Spain

Italy

The Mediterranean and the Near East

Britain and the British Commonwealth

The Netherlands

Germany

Austria–Hungary and the Balkans

Eastern and Northern Europe

The Americas

Asia and Africa

SECTION A: 1493–1648

The volumes of the *New Cambridge Modern History* covered in this section are: I (1493–1520); II (1520–59); III (1559–1610); IV (1609–48). The book-lists for each chapter normally deal with the period of time embraced by the volume in which they appear; exceptions are noted in the synopsis. There are a few cases where particular lists overlap the general division into sections, but these are noted both in the synopsis and in the text.

Other points to note in using the bibliography are:

(1) Each entry is numbered, with a separate series of numbers for each section. The first reference to any book is to be considered the master reference, and normally only the first reference gives the full details about that work. Thereafter it appears as a number reference with the appropriate section letter added and with the author's name, e.g. B 995, Clough, S. B. Therefore, in using any list, it must be remembered that important references may be contained in these number references at the end, and these should be looked up in each case. This is particularly true of books which appear many times, such as, for the sixteenth-century chapters, F. Braudel, *La Méditerranée et le monde méditerranéen à l'époque de Philippe II.*

(2) There is a brief list of some of the chief historical bibliographies and of some of the chief historical series on pp. x–xi. In general, where a book contains a useful bibliography, this is noted in the chapter list.

(3) There are no lists on music or the visual arts, though lists have been provided for the literary chapters where this was thought appropriate. In very few other cases only has no chapter list been provided.

(4) It is assumed that English books have been published in London and French books in Paris, unless otherwise stated. Other places of publication and all dates of publication are given.

ECONOMIC AND SOCIAL CONDITIONS

1   The Face of Europe on the Eve of the Great Discoveries (vol. I, ch. ii)

An account of the geography of Europe is given in the first eleven volumes of the *Géographie Universelle*, produced under the direction of Vidal de la Blache, P. and Gallois, L. (1927–48). The titles of these volumes are as follows:

A 1   Demangeon, A. *Les Iles Britanniques* (1927).
A 2   —— *Belgique. Pays-Bas. Luxembourg* (1927).
A 3   Zimmerman, M. *États scandinaves. Régions polaires boréales* (1933).
A 4   de Martonne, E. *Europe centrale* (2 vols., 1930–1).
A 5   d'Almeida, P. C. *États de la Baltique. Russie* (1932).
A 6   de Martonne, E. and Demangeon, A. *La France* (3 vols., 1946–8).

A 7   Sorre, M., Sion, J. and Chataigneau, Y. *Méditerranée. Péninsulés Méditerranéenes* (2 vols., 1924).
A 8   Shackleton, M. R. *Europe: a regional geography* (6th ed., 1958); a convenient one-volume summary.

Maps in the following historical atlases will be found helpful:

A 9   Freeman, E. A. *The historical geography of Europe*, with the accompanying *Atlas* (1881); there is a 3rd ed. by Bury, J. B. (1903).
A 10   Poole, R. L. (ed.), *Historical atlas of modern Europe* (Oxford, 1902).
A 11   Spruner, K. von and Menke, Th., *Spruner–Menke Hand-Atlas für die Geschichte des Mittelalters und der neueren Zeit* (Gotha, 1880); this is the 3rd ed. of K. v. Spruner's *Hand-Atlas*, ed. Menke, Th.

The medieval background is discussed at length in the first three volumes of *The Cambridge economic history of Europe* (with full and classified bibliographies).

A 12   Clapham, J. H. and Power, E. (eds.), vol. 1. *The agrarian life of the middle ages* (Cambridge, 1941).
A 13   Postan, M. and Rich, E. E. (eds.), vol. 2. *Trade and industry in the middle ages* (Cambridge, 1952).
A 14   Postan, M. M., Rich, E. E. and Miller, E. (eds.), vol. 3. *Economic organisation and policies in the middle ages* (Cambridge, 1963).

These constitute the main bibliographical guide to the material used in the preparation of the chapter. The following studies may also be noted:

A 15   Hoskins, W. G. 'English provincial towns in the early sixteenth century', *TRHS* 5th series, 6 (1956), pp. 1–19.
A 16   Lynam, E. W. O. F. *The Carta Marina of Olaus Magnus*, Venice 1539 and Rome 1572 (Tall Tree Library, Jenkintown, Pa., U.S.A., 1949).
A 17   Pohlendt, H. *Die Verbreitung der mittelalterlichen Wüstungen in Deutschland* (Göttinger geographische Abhandlungen, no. 3, Göttingen, 1950).

For the background of the Age of Discovery see:

A 18   Beazley, C. R. *The Dawn of modern geography*, vol. 3 (Oxford, 1906).
A 19   Newton, A. P. (ed.). *Travel and travellers of the middle ages* (1926).
A 20   Williamson, J. A. *Maritime enterprise, 1485–1558* (Oxford, 1913).

2   Economic Change. 1. Agriculture (vol. II, ch. ii)

A 21   Abel, W. *Agrarkrisen und Agrarkonjunkturen in Mitteleuropa vom 13. bis 19. Jahrhundert* (Berlin, 1935).
A 22   —— *Die Wüstungen des ausgehenden Mittelalters* (2nd ed., Stuttgart, 1955).
A 23   Ashley, W. J. *Introduction to English economic history and theory* (2 vols., 1888 and 1893).
A 24   Bateman, J. *The great landowners of Great Britain and Ireland* (4th ed. 1883).

A 25   Bloch, M. *Les Caractères originaux de l'histoire rurale française*, vol. 1, Oslo, 1931; vol. 2 (Dauvergne, R., ed., 1956).

A 26   Campbell, M. L. *The English yeoman under Elizabeth and the early Stuarts* (New Haven, 1942).

A 27   Doren, A. *Italienische Wirtschaftsgeschichte* (Jena, 1934).

A 28   Franklin, T. B. *A history of Scottish farming* (1952).

A 29   Goodwin, A. (ed.), *European nobility in the eighteenth century* (1953).

A 30   Habakkuk, H. J. 'Economic functions of English landowners in the seventeenth and eighteenth centuries', *Explorations in Entrepreneurial History*, **6**, 1953.

A 31   Hoskins, W. G. 'The Leicester farmer in the sixteenth century', *Transactions of the Leicestershire Archaeological Society*, **22**, pt. 1, (1942).

A 32   Klaveren, J. van. *Europäische Wirtschaftsgeschichte Spaniens im 16. und 17. Jahrhundert* (Stuttgart, 1960).

A 33   Leicher, R. 'Historische Grundlagen der landwirtschaftlichen Besitz- und Betriebsverhältnisse in Italien', *Vierteljahrschrift für Sozial- und Wirtschaftsgeschichte*, **47**, 1960; good bibliography.

A 34   Lütge, F. 'Das 14/15. Jahrhundert in der Sozial- und Wirtschafts-geschichte', *Jahrbücher für Nationalökonomie und Statistik*, **162**, 1952.

A 35   —— *Die mitteldeutsche Grundherrschaft und ihre Auflösung* (2nd ed., Stuttgart, 1957).

A 36   —— *Deutsche Sozial- und Wirtschaftsgeschichte* (2nd ed., Berlin–Göttingen–Heidelberg, 1960).

A 37   Medici, G. *I tipi d'impressa nell'agricoltura italiana* (Rome, 1951).

A 38   Pino-Branca, A. *La vita economica degli stati italiani nei secolo XVI, XVII, XVIII* (Catania, 1938).

A 39   Ricci, R. *Compendio storico dell'agricoltura italiana* (Catania, 1920).

A 40   Rostow, W. W. *The process of economic growth* (Oxford, 1953).

A 41   Roupnel, G. *Histoire de la campagne française* (new ed. 1955).

A 42   Sée, H. *Esquisse d'une histoire économique et sociale de la France* (1929).

A 43   —— *Französische Wirtschaftsgeschichte* (2 vols., Jena, 1930–6).

A 44   Tawney, R. H. *The agrarian problem in the sixteenth century* (1912).

A 45   Thirsk, J. *Fenland farming in the sixteenth century* (Leicester, 1953).

A 46   —— *English peasant farming. The agrarian history of Lincolnshire from Tudor to recent times* (1957).

A 47   Woodroffe, T. *The enterprise of England* (1958).

3   Economic Change. 2. The Greatness of Antwerp (vol. II, ch. ii)

General Studies

SIXTEENTH-CENTURY ECONOMIC HISTORY

A 48   Clough, S. B. and Cole, C. W. *Economic history of Europe* (3rd ed., Boston, 1952).

A 49   Haussherr, H. *Wirtschaftsgeschichte der Neuzeit* (Cologne, 1960).

A 50   Heaton, H. *Economic history of Europe* (New York, 1948).

A 51   Houtte, J. A. van. *Esquisse d'une histoire économique de la Belgique* (Louvain, 1943).

SIXTEENTH-CENTURY BELGIAN HISTORY

A 52 Houtte, J. A. van, in *Algemene Geschiedenis der Nederlanden*, vol. 4, 1477–1567 (Houtte, J. A. van, Niermayer, J. F., Presser, J., Romein, J., Werveke, H. van, eds.) (Utrecht, 1952).

A 53 Pirenne, H. *Histoire de Belgique*, vol. 3 (Brussels, 1923).

A 54 Wee, H. van der. *The growth of the Antwerp market and the European economy (fourteenth to sixteenth centuries)* (3 vols., Louvain, 1963); is a very important general survey of the economic history of these centuries.

A 55 Bindoff, S. T. *The Scheldt question in 1839* (1945); useful for a wide period.

A 56 Prims, F. *Geschiedenis van Antwerpen* (10 vols. and register, Antwerp, 1927–49); vol. 7 (1938) covers the years 1477–1555.

A 57 Sabbe, E. *Anvers, métropole de l'occident (1492–1566)* (Brussels, 1952).

A 58 Wegg, J. *Antwerp 1477–1559, from the battle of Nancy to the treaty of Cateau Cambrésis* (1916).

A 59 For Lodovico Guiccardini, see *The Description of the Low Countreys gathered into an epitome out of the Historie of L.G.* (Engs. trans. 1593).

Detailed Studies

COMMERCE

A 60 Coornaert, E. *Les Français et le commerce international à Anvers: fin de XVe–XVIe siècle* (2 vols., 1961).

A 61 Craeybeckx, J. *Un Grand Commerce d' importation; les vins de France aux anciens Pays-Bas, XIIIe–XVIe siècles* (1958).

A 62 Edler, F. 'The Van Der Molen, commission merchants of Antwerp: trade with Italy, 1538–1544', *Medieval and Historiographical Essays in Honour of James Westfall Thompson* (Cate, J. L. and Anderson, E., eds.) (Chicago, 1938).

A 63 Goris, J. A. *Étude sur les colonies marchandes méridionales (portugais, espagnols, italiens) à Anvers de 1488 à 1567* (Louvain, 1925).

A 64 Houtte, J. A. van. 'La genèse du grand marché international d'Anvers à la fin du moyen age', *RBPH*, **19** (1940).

A 65 ——— 'Bruges et Anvers, marchés "nationaux" ou "internationaux" du XIVe au XVIe siècle', *RN*, **33–4** (1952).

A 66 ——— 'Anvers au XVe et XVIe siècles: avènement et apogée', *AESC*, **16** (1961).

A 67 Jeannin, P. *Les Marchands au XVIe siècle* (1957).

A 68 Smedt, O. de. *De Engelse natie te Antwerpen in de 16e eeuw (1496–1582)* (2 vols., The Hague, 1950, 1954).

A 69 Werveke, H. Van. *Bruges et Anvers: huit siècles de commerce flamand* (Brussels, 1944).

CREDIT AND BANKING

A 70 Ehrenberg, R. *Capital and finance in the age of the Renaissance: a study of the Fuggers and their connections* (Eng. trans., 1928). An abridged French edition, *Le siècle des Fugger* (1955).

A 71   Roover, R. de. 'Anvers comme marché monétaire au XVIe siècle', *RBPH*, **31** (1953).
A 72   —— *L'Evolution de la lettre de change, XIVe–XVIIIe siècles* (1953).
A 73   Tawney, R. H. *Introduction to Thomas Wilson's A Discourse upon Usury* (1925).

INDUSTRY

A 74   Coornaert, E. 'Draperies rurales, draperies urbains. L'évolution de l'industrie flamande au Moyen Age et au XVIe siècle', *RBPH*, **28** (1950).
A 75   Nef, J. U. 'Industrial Europe at the time of the Reformation ca. 1515–ca. 1540', *Journal of Political Economy*, **49** (1941).
A 76   —— 'Mining and metallurgy in medieval civilisation', *Cambridge Economic History of Europe*, vol. 2 (Cambridge, 1952); this goes down to the mid-sixteenth century.

4   The Economy of Europe, 1559–1609 (vol. III, ch. ii)

General Studies

A 77   Braudel, F. *La Méditerranée et le monde méditerranéen à l'époque de Philippe II* (1949).
A 78   Hauser, H. *Le Prépondérance espagnole 1559–1660* (1933).
A 79   Kulisher, J. *Allgemeine Wirtschaftsgeschichte des Mittelalters und der Neuzeit* (2 vols., Munich, 1928–9).
See also:
A 48 Clough, S. B. and Cole, C. W.; A 50 Heaton, H.

Detailed Studies

A 80   Borah, W. W. *New Spain's century of depression* (Berkeley, 1951).
A 81   Boxer, C. R. *The great ship from Amaçon* (Lisbon, 1959).
A 82   Brésard, M. *Les Foires de Lyon aux XVe et XVIe siècles* (1914).
A 83   Chaunu, H. and P. *Séville et l'Atlantique* (12 vols., 1955–9); indispensable statistics on Spanish trade and economy.
A 84   Cole, C. W. *French mercantilist doctrines before Colbert* (New York, 1931).
A 85   Collier, R. and Billioud, J. *Histoire du commerce de Marseille* (Rambert, G., ed., vol. 3, 1949–54).
A 86   Fisher, F. J. 'Commercial trends and policy in sixteenth-century England', *Econ. HR*, 1st ser., **10** (1940).
A 87   Girard, A. *Le Commerce français à Séville et Cadix au temps des Habsbourgs* (1932).
A 88   Grice-Hutchinson, M. *The school of Salamanca* (Oxford, 1952).
A 89   Haebler, K. *Die wirtschaftliche Blüte Spaniens im 16 Jahrhundert und ihr Verfall* (Berlin, 1888).
A 90   Hamilton, E. J. *American treasure and the price revolution in Spain 1501–1650* (Cambridge, Mass., 1934).
A 91   Haring, C. H. *Trade and navigation between Spain and the Indies in the time of the Hapsburgs* (Cambridge, Mass., 1918).
A 92   Hauser, H. (ed.). *La Response de Jean Bodin à M. de Malestroit (1568)* (1932).
A 93   Heckscher, E. *An economic history of Sweden* (Eng. trans., Cambridge, Mass., 1954).

A 94   Klein, J. *The Mesta* (Cambridge, Mass., 1920).
A 95   Lane, F. C. *Venetian ships and shipbuilders of the Renaissance* (Baltimore, 1934).
A 96   Lubimenko, I. 'Les marchands anglais en Russie au XVIe siècle', *RH*, **109** (1912).
A 97   —— 'Les relations de l'Angleterre et de la Russie au XVIe siècle', *RH*, **121** (1916).
A 98   Lyashchenko, P. I. *History of the national economy of Russia* (New York, 1949).
A 99   Mols, R. *Introduction à la démographie historique des villes d'Europe du XIVe au XVIIIe siècle* (3 vols., Louvain, 1954–6); bibliography.
A 100   Nef, J. U. *Industry and government in France and England 1540–1640* (Philadelphia, 1940).
A 101   Phelps Brown, E. H. and Hopkins, S. 'Wages and prices; evidence for population pressure in the sixteenth century', *Economica*, new series no. **24** (1957).
A 102   Poelnitz, G. von. *Anton Fugger* (2 vols., Tübingen, 1958–).
A 103   Sella, D. 'L'industrie lainière à Venise', *AESC*, **12** (1957).
A 104   Spooner, F. C. *L'Economie mondiale et les frappes monétaires en France 1493–1680* (1956).
A 105   Tawney, R. H. *Religion and the rise of capitalism* (1947).
A 106   Unwin, G. *Industrial organization in the sixteenth and seventeenth centuries* (Oxford, 1904).
A 107   Usher, A. P. *The history of the grain trade in France 1400–1710* (Cambridge, Mass., 1913).
A 108   —— *The early history of deposit banking in the Mediterranean* (Cambridge, Mass., 1943).
A 109   Weber, M. *The protestant ethic and the spirit of capitalism* (Eng. trans., 1930).

See also:

A 73 Tawney, R. H.

5   The European Economy (vol. IV, ch. ii)

General Studies

A 110   Clark, G. N. *The seventeenth century* (2nd ed., Oxford, 1947).

See also:

A 48 Clough, S. B. and Cole, C. W.; A 50 Heaton, H.; A 78 Hauser, H.; A 79 Kulisher, J.

Detailed Studies

A 111   Barbour, V. 'Dutch and English maritime shipping in the seventeenth century', *Econ. HR*, 1st. ser., **2** (1930).
A 112   —— *Capitalism in Amsterdam during the seventeenth century* (Baltimore, 1950).
A 113   Beloch, K. J. *Bevölkerungsgeschichte Italiens* (3 vols., Berlin, 1937–61).

A 114   Bergasse, L. and Rambert, G. *Histoire du commerce de Marseille* (Rambert, G., ed., vol. 4, 1954).
A 115   Blok, P. J. *A history of the people of the Netherlands* (Eng. trans., 5 vols., New York, 1898–1912).
A 116   Bloom, H. I. *The economic activities of the Jews in Amsterdam in the seventeenth and eighteenth centuries* (Williamsport, 1937).
A 117   Boissonade, P. *Le Socialisme d'état* (1927).
A 118   Cipolla, C. M. 'The decline of Italy', *Econ. HR*, 2nd ser., 5 (1952).
A 119   Christensen, A. *Dutch trade to the Baltic about 1600* (Copenhagen, 1941).
A 120   Coleman, D. 'Labour in the English economy of the seventeenth century', *Econ. HR*, 2nd ser., 8 (1956).
A 121   Coornaert, E. *Un centre industriel d'autrefois, la draperie-sayetterie d'Hondschoote (XVe–XVIIIe siècles)* (1930).
A 122   Davies, R. Trevor. *Spain in decline 1621–1700* (1957).
A 123   Dillen, J. G. van (ed.). *History of the principal public banks* (The Hague, 1934).
A 124   Edmundson, G. *Anglo-Dutch rivalry during the first half of the seventeenth century* (Oxford, 1911).
A 125   Egerton, H. E. *A short history of British colonial policy 1606–1909* (1932).
A 126   Elsas, M. J. *Umriss einer Geschichte der Preise und Löhne in Deutschland vom ausgehenden Mittelalter bis zum Beginn des neunzehnten Jahrhunderts* (2 vols., Leiden, 1936–49).
A 127   Franz, G. *Der Dreissigjährig Krieg und das deutsche Volk* (Stuttgart, 1961).
A 128   Glamann, K. *Dutch–Asiatic trade 1620–1740* (Copenhagen, 1958).
A 129   Hamilton, E. J. 'Spanish mercantilism before 1700', *Facts and figures in economic history*, Cole, A. H. and others (eds.) (Cambridge, Mass., 1932).
A 130   —— 'The decline of Spain', *Econ. HR*, 1st ser., 8 (1938).
A 131   Hauser, H. *La Pensée et l'action économique du Cardinal de Richelieu* (1944).
A 132   Heckscher, E. *Mercantilism* (Eng. trans., 2nd ed., 2 vols., 1956).
A 133   Hobsbawm E. J. 'The general crisis of the European economy in the seventeenth century', *PP*, nos. 5, 6 (1954).
A 134   Nef, J. U. *The rise of the British coal industry* (2 vols., 1932).
A 135   —— *War and human progress* (Cambridge, Mass., 1950).
A 136   Posthumus, N. *De geschiedenis van de Leidsche Lakenindustrie* (3 vols., The Hague, 1908–39).
A 137   Pribram, A. *Materialien zur Geschichte der Preise und Löhne in Österreich* (vol. 1, Vienna, 1938).
A 138   Scott, W. R. *The constitution and finance of English, Scottish and Irish joint-stock companies to 1720* (3 vols., Cambridge, 1910–12).
A 139   Supple, B. *Commercial crisis and change in England 1600–1642* (Cambridge, 1959).
A 140   Tawney, R. H. *Business and politics under James I* (Cambridge, 1958).
A 141   Utterstroem, G. 'Climactic fluctuations and population problems in early modern history', *SEHR*, 3 (1955).
A 142   Viner, J. *Studies in the theory of international trade* (New York, 1937).
A 143   Wittrock, G. *Svenska handelskompaniet och kopparhandeln under Gustaf II Adolf* (Uppsala, 1919).

See also:

A 83 Chaunu, H. and P.; A 84 Cole, C. W.; A 90 Hamilton, E. J.; A 99 Mols, R.; A 103 Sella, D.; A 104 Spooner, F. C.; A 106 Unwin, G.

INTELLECTUAL LIFE, EDUCATION AND SCIENCE

6   Fifteenth-Century Civilisation and the Renaissance (vol. I, ch. iii)
     Learning and Education in Western Europe from 1470 to 1520 (ch. v)

General Studies

A 144 'Recent literature of the Renaissance.' Very complete annual bibliography, published in the April issues of *Studies in Philology* since 1939. Starts with the beginnings of Renaissance and Humanism in the fourteenth century.

A 145 Allen, P. S. *The age of Erasmus* (Oxford, 1914).

A 146 Ferguson, W. K. *The Renaissance in historical thought: five centuries of interpretation* (Boston, 1948); discusses the nature of fourteenth- to sixteenth-century civilization in all European countries. A basic historiographical and bibliographical introduction.

A 147 Gilmore, M. P. *The world of humanism 1453–1517* (New York, 1952); best general survey. Annotated bibliography.

A 148 Hassinger, E. *Das Werden des neuzeitlichen Europa, 1300–1600* (Braunschweig, 1959); annotated bibliography.

A 149 Naef, W. *Die Epochen der neueren Geschichte*, vol. I (2nd ed., Aarau, 1959).

A 150 Renaudet, A. *Humanisme et Renaissance* (Geneva, 1958); collection of articles.

A 151 Sandys, J. E. *History of classical scholarship*, vols. I and 2 (Cambridge, 1921).

A 152 Voigt, G. *Die Wiederbelebung des classischen Alterthums* (3rd. ed. by Lehnerdt, M., 2 vols., Berlin, 1893); still valuable.

National Studies

ENGLAND

A 153 Allen, P. S. and H. M. *Letters of Richard Fox 1486–1527* (Oxford, 1929).

A 154 Ferguson, A. B. *The Indian summer of English chivalry. Studies in the decline and transformation of chivalric idealism* (Durham, N.C., 1960).

A 155 Hay, D. *Polydore Vergil: Renaissance historian and man of letters* (Oxford, 1952); the problems of the influence of Italian humanistic historiography.

A 156 Jayne, S. R. *John Colet and Marsilio Ficino* (Oxford, 1963).

A 157 Kingsford, C. L. *Prejudice and promise in XVth century England* (Oxford, 1925).

A 158 Lupton, J. H. *Life of John Colet* (1887 and later reprints).

The titles of the periodicals most ⸻
abbreviated as below. Others are cit⸻

AHR	*American Historical*
AESC	*Annales: économies.*
AS	*Annals of Science*
Econ. HR	*Economic History*
EHR	*English Historical Review*
HAHR	*Hispanic American Historical Review*
HZ	*Historische Zeitschrift*
Hist.	*History*
JHI	*Journal of the History of Ideas*
JMH	*Journal of Modern History*
PP	*Past and Present*
RBPH	*Revue Belge de philologie et d'histoire*
RH	*Revue Historique*
RN	*Revue du Nord*
SEHR	*Scandinavian Economic History Review*
SEER	*Slavonic and East European Review*
TRHS	*Transactions of the Royal Historical Society*

(Giving the ⸻
subsection ⸻   S⸻

A 159   Schirmer, W. F. *Der englische Frühhumanismus* (Leipzig, 1931).
A 160   Weiss, R. *Humanism in England during the fifteenth century* (2nd ed., Oxford, 1957).

FRANCE

Coville, A. *Gontier et Pierre Col et l'humanisme en France au temps de Charles VI* (1934).
⸻ruelle, L. *Guillaume Budé* (1907).
⸻, R. L. *The decline of chivalry as shown in the French literature of ⸻ddle ages* (Cambridge, Mass., 1937).
⸻ *Guillaume Budé* (1468–1540) *et les origines de l'humanisme*
⸻*forme et humanisme à Paris* (2nd ed., 1953); standard
⸻*d scholasticism at the University of Paris.*
⸻*imento francese* (Turin, 1961); discusses earlier
⸻*he French Renaissance* (Cambridge, 1918).

⸻UNDY–NETHERLANDS

⸻*f Burgundy; studies in the history of civilisation*
⸻*ion of the aristocracy in the Renaissance*',
⸻*for Burgundian fifteenth-century nobility.*
⸻*the middle ages, a study of the forms of life,*
⸻*d the Netherlands in the XIVth and XVth*
⸻*many languages and editions; the first in*
⸻*orical significance of Burgundian courtly*
⸻*2nd ed., Zürich, 1942); supplementary*
⸻*al background of Burgundian culture.*
⸻*, or Christian Renaissance, 1380–1520*
⸻*e* (Grand Rapids, Michigan, 1950).
⸻*common life*', in his *Essays in the*
⸻*r, 1953).*
⸻Y
⸻*mation* (5th ed., Stuttgart, 1948);
⸻*ginning with the late fifteenth*
⸻*r Humanist Johannes Cuspinian*
⸻*Spätmittelalters*', *Der* ⸻
⸻*e* (Götting⸻

A 179   Rupprich, H. *Humanismus und Renaissance in den deutschen Städten und an der Universitäten* (same series, VIII, 2, 1935); the introductions to these two volumes contain the only satisfactory recent survey of German humanism from its fifteenth-century beginnings; geographically arranged.

A 180   Spitz, L. W. *Conrad Celtes, the German archhumanist* (Cambridge, Mass., 1957).

See also:

A 34 Lütge, F.

ITALY

A 181   Baron, H. *The crisis of the early Italian Renaissance: civic humanism and republican liberty in an age of classicism and tyranny* (Princeton, N.J., 1955); bibliographies.

A 182   Burckhardt, J. *Die Kultur der Renaissance in Italien* (1st ed., 1860); many editions and translations, Eng. trans. as *The civilization of the Renaissance in Italy*. Created the modern conception of the Renaissance. For its significance after a century see D. Hay, *History Today*, **10** (1960) and H. Baron, *Renaissance News*, **13** (1960).

A 183   Chabod, F. *Machiavelli and the Renaissance* (1958); Eng. trans. of fundamental papers on Machiavelli together with one of the best discussions of the 'concept of the Renaissance' and the most complete bibliography of the Italian Renaissance.

A 184   Cochrane, E. W. 'Machiavelli: 1940–1960', *JMH*, **33** (1961); historical revision, supplementing Chabod.

A 185   Douglas, R. M. *Jacopo Sadoleto, 1477–1547, humanist and reformer* (Cambridge, Mass., 1959).

A 186   Garin, E. *Der italienische Humanismus* (Bern, 1947); revised Italian ed., *L'umanesimo italiano: filosofia e vita civile nel rinascimento* (Bari, 1952); excellent characterisation of the attitudes of fifteenth-century humanists.

A 187   Hay, D. *The Italian Renaissance in its historical background* (Cambridge, 1961).

A 188   Kristeller, P. O. *The classics and Renaissance thought* (Cambridge, Mass., 1955).

A 189   Mattingly, G. *Renaissance diplomacy* (Boston, 1955).

A 190   Rice, W. F. *The Renaissance idea of wisdom* (Cambridge, Mass., 1958); complementary to Garin.

A 191   Valeri, N. *L'Italia nell'età dei principati 1343–1516* (Milan, 1949); annotated bibliography.

A 192   Whitfield, J. H. *Petrarch and the Renascence* (Oxford, 1943); includes the development of humanism to about 1450.

7   Intellectual Tendencies. 1. Literature: the Printed Book (vol. II, ch. xii)

General Studies

A good selection of topics and comprehensive, brief bibliographies are to be found in:

A 193   Steinberg, S. H. (ed.). *Cassell's encyclopaedia of world literature* (2 vols., 1953).

There are no adequate studies of European literature as a whole for this period, but the following are worth reading:

A 194 Hallam, H. *Introduction to the literature of Europe in the XV, XVI and XVII centuries* (1837–9 and many reprints).

A 195 Tieghem, P. van. 'La littérature latine de la Renaissance', *Bibliothèque d'humanisme et renaissance*, 4 (1944), pp. 177–411; surveys the enormous bulk of neo-Latin writing.

Printing

Early printing has an enormous bibliography. The following will be found useful introductions:

A 196 Febvre, L. and Martin, H. J. *L'Apparition du livre* (1958).
A 197 Goldschmidt, E. P. *The printed book of the Renaissance* (Cambridge, 1950).
A 198 McMurtrie, D. C. *The Book* (New York, 1938).
A 199 Winship, G. P. *Gutenberg to Plantin* (Cambridge, Mass., 1926).

National Studies

ITALY

A 200 Sanctis, F. de. *Storia della letteratura italiana* (2 vols., Milan, 1934); written between 1869 and 1871.

A 201 Tiraboschi, G. *Storia della letteratura italiana* (1772–82); still indispensable.

A 202 Toffanin, G. *Il cinquecento*, 'Storia letteraria d'Italia' (3rd ed., Milan, 1945).

FRANCE

A 203 Bédier, J. and Hazard, P. *Histoire de la littérature française illustrée* (2nd ed., 2 vols., 1948–9).

A 204 Tilley, A. *The literature of the French Renaissance* (2 vols., Cambridge, 1904).

SPAIN

A 205 Brenan, G. *The literature of the Spanish people* (Cambridge, 1951).
A 206 Fitzmaurice-Kelly, J. *A new history of Spanish literature* (1926).

GERMANY

A 207 Robertson, J. G. *A history of German literature* (3rd ed., Purdie, E., ed., Edinburgh, 1962); bibliography and chronological table.

A 208 Stammler, W. *Von der Mystik zum Barock, 1400–1600* (Epochen der deutschen Literatur, vol. 2, i, 2nd ed., Stuttgart, 1950).

BRITAIN

A 209 Bennett, H. S. *English books and readers, 1475 to 1557* (Cambridge, 1952).

A 210 Lewis, C. S. *English literature in the sixteenth century, excluding drama* (Oxford, 1954); a brilliant book, valuable for its awareness of European influences.

Selected Writers

A 211 Caprariis, V. de. *Francesco Guiccardini* (Bari, 1950).
A 212 Chambers, R. W. *Thomas More* (1935).
A 213 Phillips, M. M. *Erasmus and the northern Renaissance* (1949).
A 214 Plattard, J. *La Vie et l'œuvre de Rabelais* (1939).
A 215 Ridolfi, R. *N. Machiavelli* (Rome, 1954).
A 216 Smith, P. *Erasmus* (New York, 1923).
A 217 Villey, P. *Les Sources italiennes de la 'Deffense et illustration de la langue françoise' de J. du Bellay* (1908).
A 218 —— *Les sources et l'évolution des essais de Montaigne* (Bordeaux, 1933).

8   Schools and Universities (vol. II, ch. xiii)
     Education and Learning (vol. III, ch. xiv)

Scholarship and Scholars: General Studies

A 219 Armstrong, E. *Robert Étienne—royal printer* (Cambridge, 1954).
A 220 Bataillon, M. *Érasme et l'Espagne* (1937).
A 221 Bolgar, R. R. *The classical heritage and its beneficiaries* (Cambridge, 1954).
A 222 Clarke, M. L. *Classical education in Britain 1500–1900* (Cambridge, 1959).
A 223 Febvre, L. *Le Problème de l'incroyance au XVIe siècle—La religion de Rabelais* (rev. ed., 1947).
A 224 Fueter, E. *Geschichte der neueren Historiographie* (Munich, 1936).
A 225 Millar, D. A. (ed.). *George Buchanan—a memorial 1509–1906* (St Andrews/London, 1906).
A 226 Miller, P. *The New England mind* (New York, 1939); for Petrus Ramus.
A 227 Ong, W. J. *Ramus. Method, and the decay of dialogue* (Cambridge, Mass., 1958).
A 228 *Ramus and Talon inventory. A short-title inventory of the published works of Peter Ramus (1515–1572) and of Omer Talon (ca. 1510–62)* (Cambridge, Mass., 1958).
A 229 Taylor, H. O. *Thought and expression in the sixteenth century* (2 vols., 2nd ed., New York, 1930); a general survey of the intellectual history of the century.
A 230 Viard, P. E. *André Alciat 1492–1550* (1926).

See also:

A 146 Ferguson, W. K.; A 151 Sandys, J. E.; A 188 Kristeller, P. O.

The Universities

A 231 d'Irsay, S. *Histoire des universités* (2 vols., 1933–5).
A 232 Rashdall, H. (Powicke, F. M. and Emden, A. B., eds.). *The universities of Europe in the middle ages* (3 vols., Oxford, 1936); often deals with sixteenth-century developments.

ENGLAND

A 233   Costello, W. T. *The scholastic curriculum at early seventeenth-century Cambridge* (Cambridge, Mass., 1958).

A 234   Curtis, M. H. *Oxford and Cambridge in transition 1558–1642* (Oxford, 1959).

A 235   Mallet, C. E. *History of the University of Oxford* (3 vols., 1924–7).

A 236   Mullinger, J. B. *The University of Cambridge* (3 vols., Cambridge, 1873–1911).

A 237   Porter, H. C. *Reformation and reaction in Tudor Cambridge* (Cambridge, 1958).

GERMANY

A 238   Friedensburg, W. *Geschichte der Universität Wittenberg* (Halle, 1917).

A 239   Paulsen, Fr. *Geschichte des gelehrten Unterrichts* (2 vols., 3rd ed., Leipzig, 1919–21).

SPAIN

A 240   Raynier, G. *La Vie universitaire dans l'ancienne Espagne* (1902).

A 241   Ajo G. y Sáinz de Zúñiga, C. M. *Historia de las universidades hispánicas*, vol. 2, *El siglo de oro universitario* (Ávila, 1958).

Humanism

A 242   Garin, E. *L'educazione in Europa (1400–1600)* (Bari, 1957).

A 243   Garin, E. (ed.). *L'educazione umanistica in Italia, testi scelti* (Bari, 1949).

A 244   Lefranc, A. *Histoire du collège de France* (1893).

A 245   Maylender, M. *Storia delle accademie d'Italia* (5 vols., Bologna, 1926–30).

A 246   Vocht H. de. *History of the Collegium Trilingue Lovaniense 1517–50* (4 vols., Louvain, 1951–5).

A 247   Woodward, W. H. *Studies in education during the age of the Renaissance 1400–1600* (Cambridge, 1906).

A 248   —— *Vittorino da Feltre and other humanist educators* (Cambridge, 1905); contains translations of important essays.

A 249   Yates, F. A. *The French academies of the sixteenth century* (London, 1947).

See also:

A 145 Allen, P. S.

Educational Change and its social consequences

A 250   Casa, G. della. *Galateo* (Pine-Coffin, R.S. trans.) (Harmondsworth, 1958).

A 251   Castiglione, B. (Cian, V., ed.). *Il Cortegiano* (Florence, 1947); there are many translations of this very influential book.

A 252   Lehmberg, S. E. *Sir Thomas Elyot* (Austin, Texas, 1960).

A 253   Zeeveld, W. G. *Foundations of Tudor Policy* (Cambridge, Mass., 1948).

See also:

A 169 Hexter, J. H.

Religious Education

THE JESUITS

A 254 Dainville, F. de. *Les Jésuites et l'éducation de la société française: la naissance de l'humanisme moderne* (2 vols., 1940).

A 255 Dupont-Ferrier, G. *Du Collège de Clermont au lycée Louis-le-Grand* (2 vols., 1923).

A 256 Schimberg, A. *L'Education morale dans les collèges de la compagnie de Jésus en France sous l'ancien régime* (1913).

THE PROTESTANTS

A 257 Borgeaud, C. *Histoire de l'université de Genève. L'Académie de Calvin 1559-1798* (Geneva, 1900).

A 258 Hartfelder, K. *Philipp Melancthon als Praeceptor Germaniae* (Berlin, 1889) (Monumenta Germaniae Paedagogica, vii).

A 259 Knox, J. *First book of discipline, Works* (Laing, D., ed.), vol. 2 (Edinburgh, 1848).

A 260 Richard, J. W. *Philipp Melancthon. The protestant preceptor of Germany 1497-1560* (New York, 1898).

A 261 Sohm, W. *Die Schule Johann Sturms und die Kirche Strassburgs* (Munich, 1912).

Education in England

A 262 Baldwin, T. W. *William Shakspere's petty school* (Urbana, 1943).

A 263 —— *William Shakspere's small Latine and less Greeke* (2 vols., Urbana, 1944).

A 264 Brown, J. H. *Elizabethan schooldays* (Oxford, 1933).

A 265 Conybeare, John. *Letters and exercises of the Elizabethan schoolmaster* . . . (Conybeare, F. C., ed.) (1905).

A 266 Leach, A. F. *English schools at the Reformation 1546-8* (Westminster, 1896); Leach's views are still the subject of controversy. For a note on this see *British Journal of Educational Studies*, **12**, pp. 184-94.

A 267 Watson, Foster. *English grammar schools to 1660* (1908); a useful but undigested compilation.

A 268 Wood, N. *The Reformation and English education* (1931).

A 269 Wright, L. B. *Middle-class culture in Elizabethan England* (Ithaca, 1958).

Education in France

A 270 Ariès, Ph. *L'Enfant et la vie familiale sous l'ancien régime* (1960).

A 271 Barnard, H. C. *The French tradition in education. Ramus to Mme. Necker de Saussure* (Cambridge, 1922).

A 272 Compayré, G. *Histoire critique des doctrines de l'éducation en France depuis le seizième siècle*, vol. 1 (1879).

A 273 Gaullieur, E. *Histoire du collège de Guyenne* (1874).

A 274 Hodgson, G. E. *Studies in French education from Rabelais to Rousseau* (Cambridge, 1908); contains essays on Rabelais and Montaigne.

9   Intellectual Tendencies. 2. Science (vol. II, ch. xii)
        Science (vol. III, ch. xv)
        Science and Philosophy (vol. IV, ch. iv)

        The primary sources for the history of science are the works of the great
scientists themselves. There is insufficient space here to list these;
reference should be made to the general works cited below and to the
following bibliographies:

A 275   Russo, F. *Histoire des sciences et des techniques: Bibliographie* (1954).
A 276   Sarton, G. *Horus. A guide to the history of science* (Waltham, Mass., 1952).
A 277   Daumas, M. (ed.). *Histoire de la science* (Encyclopédie de la Pléiade, 5, 1957).
A 278   Taton, R. (ed.). *Histoire générale des Sciences*, vol. 2, *La Science moderne* (1958); both these books contain good bibliographies.

General studies of the history of Science

Many of the histories of the separate sciences cover much longer periods
than are dealt with here; among these see:

ASTRONOMY, NAVIGATION AND CARTOGRAPHY

A 279   Brown, L. A. *The story of maps* (Boston, Mass., 1950).
A 280   Dreyer, J. L. E. *A history of the planetary systems from Thales to Kepler* (repr. New York, 1953).
A 281   Taylor, E. G. R. *The haven-finding art* (New York, 1957); bibliography.

BIOLOGY AND MEDICINE

A 282   Castiglioni, A. *History of medicine* (New York, 1941); bibliography.
A 283   Cole, F. J. *History of comparative anatomy* (London, 1949).
A 284   Foster, M. *Lectures on the history of physiology* (Cambridge, 1924).
A 285   Franklin, K. J. *Short history of physiology* (1933).
A 286   Needham, J. *History of embryology* (2nd ed., Cambridge, 1959).
A 287   Nordenskiold, E. *History of biology* (New York, 1946); the most useful survey.
A 288   Singer, C. *Short history of anatomy from the Greeks to Harvey* (2nd ed., New York, 1957).
A 289   —— *A history of biology* (3rd ed., New York, 1959).
A 290   Singer, C. and Underwood, E. A. *A short history of medicine* (2nd ed., Oxford, 1962).

CHEMISTRY

A 291   Partington, J. R. *History of chemistry* (1961).
A 292   Stillman, J. M. *The story of early chemistry* (1924).

MATHEMATICS

A 293   Montucla, J. F. *Histoire des mathématiques* (2nd ed., 4 vols., 1799–1802).
A 294   Scott, J. F. *A history of mathematics* (2nd ed., 1960).

PHYSICS

A 295 Crew, H. *The rise of modern physics* (1928).
A 296 Dugas, R. *History of mechanics* (1957).
A 297 Ronchi, V. *Histoire de la lumière* (1956).

TECHNOLOGY

A 298 Singer, C., Holmyard, E. J., Hall, A. R. and Williams, T. I. *A history of technology*, vol. 3: *From the Renaissance to the Industrial Revolution* (1957).

General studies of sixteenth- and seventeenth-century science

A 299 Boas, M. *The scientific Renaissance 1450–1630* (1962).
A 300 Crombie, A. C. *Augustine to Galileo*, vol. 2: *Science in the later middle ages and early modern times, thirteenth to seventeenth centuries* (1961); bibliography.
A 301 Hall, A. R. *From Galileo to Newton, 1630–1720* (1963).
A 302 —— *The scientific revolution, 1500–1800* (1954); bibliography.
A 303 Sarton, G. *The appreciation of ancient and medieval science during the Renaissance* (Philadelphia, 1955).
A 304 —— *Six wings: men of science in the Renaissance* (1958); Sarton's two books are the fullest bibliographical guides to Renaissance science.
A 305 Thorndike, L. *History of magic and experimental science*, vols. 5 and 6 (New York, 1941).

Much factual information is to be found in:

A 306 Wolf, A. *A history of science, technology and philosophy in the sixteenth and seventeenth centuries* (corrected ed., 1950).

An outline of the general intellectual history of the period is in:

A 307 Smith, P. *A history of modern culture*, vol. 1: *The great renewal, 1543–1687* (1930).

Detailed studies of sixteenth-century science

ASTRONOMY, NAVIGATION, CARTOGRAPHY

A 308 Dreyer, J. L. E. *Tycho Brahe* (Edinburgh, 1890).
A 309 Johnson, F. R. *Astronomical thought in Renaissance England* (Baltimore, 1937); bibliography.
A 310 Koyré, A. *From the closed world to the infinite universe* (Baltimore, 1957).
A 311 Kuhn, T. S. *The Copernican revolution* (Cambridge, Mass., 1957).
A 312 Prowe, L. *Nicolaus Copernicus* (Berlin, 1883–4); standard biography.
A 313 Rosen, E. *Three Copernican treatises* (New York, 1939); with Kuhn, above, the two most useful recent books in English; bibliographies.
A 314 Singer, D. W. *Giordano Bruno, his life and thought* (New York, 1950).
A 315 Taylor, E. G. R. *Tudor geography, 1485–1583* (1930).
A 316 —— *Late Tudor and early Stuart geography* (1934).
A 317 —— *The mathematical practitioners of Tudor and Stuart England* (Cambridge, 1954).

A 318 Waters, D. W. *The art of navigation in England in Elizabethan and early Stuart times* (1958), bibliography.

A 319 Zinner, E. *Entstehung und Ausbreitung der Coppernicanischen Lehre* (Erlangen, 1943).

BIOLOGY AND MEDICINE

A 320 Arber, A. *Herbals* (2nd ed., Cambridge, 1938).

A 321 Callot, E. *La Renaissance des sciences de la vie au XVIe siècle* (1951).

A 322 Cushing, H. *A bio-bibliography of Andreas Vesalius* (New York, 1943).

A 323 O'Malley, C. D. and Saunders, J. B. de C. *Leonardo da Vinci on the human body* (New York, 1952).

A 324 Pagel, W. *Paracelsus; an introduction to philosophical medicine in the era of the Renaissance* (Basel, 1958).

A 325 Raven, C. E. *English naturalists from Neckham to Ray* (Cambridge, 1947).

A 326 Roth, M. *Andreas Vesalius Bruxellensis* (Berlin, 1892).

A 327 Singer, C. and Rabin, C. *A prelude to modern science* (Cambridge, 1946).

Detailed studies of early seventeenth-century science

SCIENTIFIC SOCIETIES IN GENERAL

A 328 Ornstein, M. *The role of scientific societies in the seventeenth century* (Chicago, 1938).

ITALY

A 329 Carutti, D. *Breve storia dell'Accademia dei Lincei* (Rome, 1883).

FRANCE

A 330 Brown, H. *Scientific organizations in seventeenth-century France (1620–80)* (Baltimore, 1934).

ENGLAND

A 331 Johnson, F. R. 'Gresham College: precursor of the Royal Society', *JHI*, **1**, 4 (1940).

A 332 McKie, D. 'The origins and foundations of the Royal Society of London', *The Royal Society—its origins and founders*, Hartley, H. (ed.) (1960).

UNIVERSITIES, EDUCATION AND TRAINING

A 333 Allen, P. 'Medical education in seventeenth century England', *Journal of the History of Medicine*, **1**, 1 (1946).

A 334 —— 'Scientific studies in the English universities of the seventeenth century', *JHI*, **10**, 2 (1949).

PHILOSOPHY AND CONCEPT OF NATURE

A 335 Anderson, F. H. *The philosophy of Francis Bacon* (Chicago, 1948).

A 336 Burtt, E. A. *The metaphysical foundations of modern physical science* (rev. ed., 1932).

A 337 Lenoble, R. *Mersenne, ou la naissance du mécanisme* (1943).

A 338 Milhaud, G. *Descartes savant* (1921).

SPREAD OF IDEAS

A 339 Ascoli, G. *La Grande-Bretagne devant l'opinion française au XVIIe siècle* (2 vols., 1930).

A 340 Brunot, F. *Histoire de la langue française*, vol. 6, i, *Le mouvement des idées et les vocabulaires techniques* (fasc. 2, 'La langue des sciences', 1930).

MECHANICS AND ASTROMONY

A 341 Caspar, M. *Kepler* (1959).

A 342 Dijksterhuis, E. J. *Simon Stevin* (The Hague, 1943).

A 343 Dugas, R. *Mechanics in the seventeenth century* (Neuchâtel, 1958).

A 344 Koyré, A. *Études galiléennes* (Actualités scientifiques et industrielles, 852–4, 1939).

A 345 —— *La Révolution astronomique* (1961).

A 346 Scott, J. F. *The scientific work of René Descartes* (1952).

A 347 Taylor, F. S. *Galileo and the freedom of thought* (1938).

MATHEMATICS

A 348 Hofmann, J. E. *Geschichte der Mathematik*, vol. 2: *Von Fermat und Descartes bis zur Erfindung des Calculus und bis zum Ausbau der neuen Methoden* (Berlin, 1957).

SCIENTIFIC INSTRUMENTS

A 349 Daumas, M. *Les Instruments scientifiques au XVIIe et XVIIIe siècles* (1953).

OPTICS

A 350 Sabra, A. I. *Theories of light from Descartes to Newton* (1964).

MAGNETISM AND ELECTRICITY

A 351 Daujat, J. *Origine et formation de la théorie des phénomènes electriques et magnetiques* (Actualités scientifiques et industrielles 989–91, 1945).

CHEMISTRY

A 352 Metzger, H. *Les doctrines chimiques en France du début du XVIIe siècle à la fin du XVIIIe siècle*, vol. 1 (1923).

BIOLOGY

A 353 Bayon, H. P. 'William Harvey, physician and biologist', *AS*, **3**, 1 (Jan. 1938); 4 (Oct. 1938); **4**, 1 (Jan. 1939); 4 (Oct. 1939).

A 354 Gilson, E. *Études sur le rôle de la pensée médiévale dans la formation du système cartésien* (Études de la philosophie médiévale, vol. 13, 1930).

MEDICINE

A 355 Delaunay, P. *La Vie médicale au XVIe, XVIIe et XVIIIe siècles* (1935).

10   The Theatre (vol. IV, ch. viii)

General Studies

A general sketch of European drama in this period is to be found in vols. 2 and 3 of:

A 356   Dubech, L. *Histoire générale illustrée du théâtre* (5 vols., 1931–4).

A certain number of documents relating to this period are reproduced (where necessary, in translation) in:

A 357   Nagler, A. M. *Sources of theatrical history* (New York, 1959).

The most up-to-date and detailed work on European drama in this period (omitting France) is:

A 358   Kindermann, H. *Theatergeschichte Europas*, vol. 3, *Das Theater der Barockzeit* (Salzburg, 1959); profusely illustrated and extensive bibliography.

Detailed Studies

ENGLAND

A 359   Bentley, G. E. *The Jacobean and Caroline stage* (5 vols., Oxford, 1941–56).
A 360   Boas, F. S. *An introduction to Stuart drama* (Oxford, 1946).
A 361   Chambers, E. K. *The Elizabethan stage* (4 vols., Oxford, 1923).
A 362   Harbage, A. B. *Cavalier drama* (New York, 1936).
A 363   —— *Shakespeare's audience* (New York, 1941).
A 364   —— *Shakespeare and the rival traditions* (New York, 1952).
A 365   Reyher, P. *Les Masques anglaises* (1909).
A 366   Sisson, C. J. *Le Goût public et le théâtre élisabéthain jusqu'à la mort de Shakespeare* (Dijon, 1921).
A 367   Welsford, E. *The court masque* (Cambridge, 1927).

See also:

A 269   Wright, L. B.

FRANCE

A 368   Adam, A. *Histoire de la littérature française au XVIIe siècle*, vols. 1 and 2 (1949–51).
A 369   Baschet, A. *Les Comédiens italiens à la cour de France sous Charles IX, Henri III, Henri IV et Louis XIII* (1882).
A 370   Fransen, J. *Les Comédiens français en Hollande aux XVIIe et XVIIIe siècles* (1925).
A 371   Lacour, L. *Richelieu dramaturge* (n.d.).
A 372   Lancaster, H. C. *A history of French dramatic literature in the seventeenth century* (9 vols., Baltimore, 1929–42).
A 373   Liebrecht, H. *Histoire du théâtre français à Bruxelles aux XVIIe et XVIIIe siècles* (Brussels, 1923).
A 374   Lough, J. *Paris theatre audiences in the seventeenth and eighteenth centuries* (1957).
A 375   Prunières, H. *Le Ballet de cour en France avant Benserarde et Lully* (1913).
A 376   Scherer, J. *La Dramaturgie classique en France* (1950).

GERMANY

A 377 Baesecke, A. *Das Schauspiel der englischen Komödianten in Deutschland* (Halle, 1935).

A 378 Creizenach, W. *Die Schauspiele der englischen Komödianten* (Berlin–Stuttgart, 1889).

A 379 Flemming, W. *Geschichte des Jesuitentheaters in den Landen deutscher Zunge* (Berlin, 1923).

A 380 —— *Das Barockdrama*, vols. 1–5 (Leipzig, 1930–3), in *Deutsche Literatur in Entwicklungsreihen: 1. Das schlesische Kunstdrama; 2. Das Ordensdrama; 3. Das Schauspiel der Wanderbühne; 4. Die Komödie; 5. Die Oper.*

A 381 Gryphius, A. *Carolus Stuardus*, (Powell, H., ed.) (Leicester, 1955); the long introduction gives useful information about German drama in this period.

ITALY

A 382 Lea, K. M. *Italian popular comedy. A study in the Commedia dell'Arte, 1560–1620* (2 vols., Oxford, 1934).

The influence of Italian theatres and stage settings is well brought out in:

A 383 Nicoll, A. *The development of the theatre* (4th ed., 1958), and see also: A 358 Kindermann, H. (see above).

For the rise of the opera see:

A 384 Grout, D. J. *A short history of opera* (2 vols., Oxford, 1947).

SPAIN

A 385 Mérimée, H. *Spectacles et comédiens à Valencia (1580–1630)* (Toulouse and Paris, 1913).

A 386 Pérez Pastor, C. *Nuevos datos acerca del histrionismo español en los siglos XVI y XVII* (2 vols., Madrid, 1901; Bordeaux, 1914).

A 387 Rennert, H. A. *The Spanish stage in the time of Lope de Vega* (New York, 1909).

A 388 Valbuena Prat, A. *Historia del teatro español* (Barcelona, 1956).

A 389 Wardropper, B. W. *Introducción al teatro religioso del siglo de oro (la evolución del auto sacramental: 1500–1648)* (Madrid, 1953).

CONSTITUTIONAL HISTORY, POLITICAL THEORY AND INTERNATIONAL LAW

11 Constitutional Development and Political Thought in Western Europe (vol. II, ch. xiv)

Constitutional Development

SPAIN

A 390 Koenigsberger, H. *The government of Sicily under Philip II of Spain* (1951); contains an introduction by J. M. Batista i Roca describing Spanish government.

A 391   Merriman, R. B. *The rise of the Spanish Empire in the old world and the now* (3 vols., 1918); chs. xiv and xv deal with late medieval changes and ch. xxiii with the reign of Charles V.

A 392   Walther, A. *Die Anfänge Karls V* (1911); on Burgundian influences.

FRANCE

A 393   Doucet, R. *Les Institutions de la France au XVIe siècle* (2 vols., 1948).
A 394   Russell Major, J. *The Estates General of 1560* (Princeton, 1951); analyses the history of the estates in the previous eighty years.

ENGLAND

A 395   Elton, G. R. *The Tudor constitution: documents and commentary* (Cambridge, 1960); contains in effect a full guide to the bibliography.
A 396   —— *The Tudor revolution in government* (Cambridge, 1953).
A 397   Pickthorn, K. W. M. *Early Tudor government* (2 vols., Cambridge, 1934).
A 398   Richardson, W. C. *Tudor chamber administration* (Baton Rouge, 1952).

GERMANY

A 399   Carsten, F. L. *Princes and parliaments in Germany from the fifteenth to the eighteenth century* (Oxford, 1959).
A 400   Hartung, F. *Deutsche Verfassungsgeschichte* (6th ed., Stuttgart, 1954).
A 401   Salomien, M. *Die Pläne Karls V für eine Reichsreform mit Hilfe eines allgemeinen Bundes* (Helsinki, 1953).

COVERING MORE THAN ONE COUNTRY

A 402   Hintze, O. 'Typologie der ständischen Verfassungen des Abendlandes', *HZ*, **141** (1929).
A 403   Lord, R. H. 'The parliaments of the middle ages and the early modern period', *Catholic Historical Review*, **16** (1930).

See also:

A 148 Hassinger, E.; A 189 Mattingly, G.

Political Thought

A 404   Allen, J. W. *Political thought in the sixteenth century* (1928); except for misleading treatment of Luther, still the best general account.
A 405   Church, W. F. *Constitutional thought in sixteenth-century France* (Harvard, 1941).
A 406   Elton, G. R. 'The political creed of Thomas Cromwell', *TRHS*, 5th ser., **6** (1956).
A 407   Hexter, J. H. *More's Utopia: the biography of an idea* (Princeton, 1952).
A 408   Janelle, P. (ed.). *Obedience in church and state* (Cambridge, 1930).
A 409   Morris, G. C. *Political thought in England from Tyndale to Hooker* (1953); bibliography.
A 410   Soder, J. *Die Idee der Völkergemeinschaft: Francisco de Vitoria* (Frankfurt, 1955).

A 411 Törnvall, G. *Geistliches und weltliches Regiment bei Luther* (German trans. from Swedish, Munich, 1947).

See also:

A 253 Zeeveld, W. G.

12 Constitutional Development and Political Thought in Eastern Europe (vol. II, ch. xv)

Something about the constitutional development of Poland, Bohemia and Hungary may be learned from the books by Seton-Watson, Harrison Thomson, Denis, Brecholz, Sinor, Kosary, and Eckhardt cited in the bibliography (Sec. A, 25).

There is much of relevance in:

A 412 *Cambridge History of Poland*, vol. 1 (Reddaway, W. F., Penson, J. H., Halecki, O., Dyboski, R., eds.) (Cambridge, 1950), chs. xiva, xv, xvii.

The text of Frycz Modrzewski's treatise is in:

A 413 *Andreae Fricii Modrevii commentarium de Republica Emendanda* (Kumaniecki, C., ed.) (Warsaw, 1953).

A 414 Chrzanowski, I. and Kot, S. *Humanizm a Reformacja w Polsce* (Lwow, 1927); contains the text of Orzechowski's 'Ad equites polonos oratio'. His tract 'Subditus Fidelis' is in:

A 415 —— *Subditus fidelis Stanislai Orzechowski* (Radzynski, P. A., ed.) (Warsaw, 1698).

The best account of the constitutional development of Bohemia in this period is:

A 416 Rezek, A. *Geschichte der Regierung Ferdinands I in Böhmen* (Prague, 1878).

The text of V. Kornel ze Vsehrd's *De iuribus terrae bohemicae libri decem* was edited by Jirecek, H. in:

A 417 *Codex juris bohemici*, vol. 3, part iii (Prague, 1874).

For the constitutional history of Hungary in the sixteenth century the best account and the best bibliography are in:

A 418 Hóman, B. and Szekfű, G. *Magyar törtenét* (Magyar History), vol. 3 (Budapest, 1935).

The most recent edition of Verbőczy's treatise is:

A 419 Werbőcz, S. de. *Opus Tripartitum* (7 vols., Leipzig, 1902).

13 Social Structures, Office-holding and politics, chiefly in Western Europe (vol. III, ch. v)

General Studies

GREAT BRITAIN

A 420 Bindoff, S. T., Hurstfield, J., Williams, C. H. (eds.). *Elizabethan government and society* (1961); contains a number of essays on the social and constitutional problems of the age.

A 421   Dietz, F. C. *English public finance 1558–1641* (New York, 1932).
A 422   Holdsworth, W. S. *A history of English law*, vols. 4 and 5 (2nd ed., 1937).
A 423   McIlwain, C. H. *The High Court of parliament and its supremacy* (New Haven, 1910).
A 424   —— *The political works of James I* (1918); has a valuable introduction.
A 425   Mosse, G. L. *The struggle for sovereignty in England, from the reign of Queen Elizabeth to the petition of right* (East Lansing, Michigan, 1950).

The best examination of the structure of the House of Commons, as well as of the provincial society which furnished its members is:

A 426   Neale, J. E. *The Elizabethan House of Commons* (1949).
A 427   —— *Elizabeth I and her parliaments* (1953, 1957); deals with the political, ecclesiastical and constitutional issues fought out in that assembly.
A 428   Notestein, W. *The winning of the initiative by the House of Commons* (repr. 1949); an important essay, originally published in the *Proceedings of the British Academy*.
A 429   Rowse, A. L. *The England of Elizabeth. The structure of society* (1950).
A 430   Tawney, R. H. 'The rise of the gentry', *Econ. HR*, 1st ser., **11** (1941); the continuing controversy may be followed in the same journal, and see especially:
A 431   Trevor-Roper, H. R. *The gentry, 1540–1640* (Cambridge, 1953); a supplement to it.
A 432   Willson, D. H. *King James VI and I* (1956).

THE ADMINISTRATION

A 433   Bell, H. E. *An introduction to the history and records of the Court of Wards and Liveries* (Cambridge, 1953); analyses its administration from 1540 to 1660.
A 434   Evans, F. M. G. (Mrs. C. S. S. Higham). *The principal secretary of state* (Manchester, 1923).
A 435   Hurstfield, J. *The Queen's wards: wardship and marriage under Elizabeth I* (1958); deals with the effect of feudal survivals on the economy and government of the period.
A 436   Reid, R. R. *The King's Council in the north* (1921).
A 437   Williams, P. *The Council in the Marches of Wales under Elizabeth I* (Cardiff, 1958).

SCOTLAND

A 438   Lee, M., Jr. *John Maitland of Thirlestane and the foundations of the Stewart despotism in Scotland* (Princeton, 1959).
A 439   Rait, R. S. *The parliaments of Scotland* (Glasgow, 1924).

OTHER COUNTRIES

A 440   Davies, R. Trevor. *The golden century of Spain* (1937).
A 441   Mitchell, J. H. *The Court of the Connétablie* (1947).
A 442   Mousnier, R. *La Vénalité des offices sous Henri IV et Louis XIII* (Rouen, 1945).

4

A 443   Sutherland, N. *The French secretaries of state in the age of Catharine de Medicis* (1962).

See also:

A 77 Braudel, F.; A 100 Nef, J. U.; A 390 Koenigsberger, H. G.; A 393 Doucet, R.; A 405 Church, W. F.

14   International Diplomacy and International Law (vol. III, ch. vi)

General Studies

A 444   Adair, E. R. *The extraterritoriality of ambassadors in the sixteenth and seventeenth centuries* (New York, 1929).
A 445   Calmette, J. *L'élaboration du monde moderne* (1934).
A 446   Hill, D. J. *A history of diplomacy* (1921); dated but still useful.
A 447   Hrabar, V. E. *De legatis et legationibus tractatus varii* (Dorpat, 1906); an indispensable guide to fifteenth- and sixteenth-century writings about diplomacy.
A 448   Oman, C. *The art of war in the sixteenth century* (1937).
A 449   Zeller, G. *Histoire des relations internationales; les temps modernes* (1954).

See also:

A 189 Mattingly, G.

Detailed Studies

A 450   Altamira y Crevea, R. *Ensayo sobre Felipe II, hombre de estado* (Mexico City, 1950).
A 451   Fernández Álvarez, M. *Tres embajadores de Felipe II* (Madrid, 1951).
A 452   Geisendorf, P-F. *Théodore de Bèze* (Geneva, 1949).
A 453   Kingdon, R. M. *Geneva and the coming of the wars of religion in France* (Geneva, 1956).
A 454   Martin, C. *Les protestants anglais refugiés à Genève...1555–60* (Geneva, 1915).
A 455   Merriman, R. B. *The rise of the Spanish Empire*, vol. 4, *Philip the Prudent* (New York, 1934).
A 456   Meyer, A. O. *Die englische Diplomatie im Deutschland zur Zeit Edwards VI und Mariens* (Breslau, 1900).
A 457   Meyer, O. A. *England and the Catholic Church under Elizabeth* (1916).
A 458   Romier, L. *La Conjuration d'Amboise* (1923).
A 459   —— *Origines politiques des guerres de religion* (1913).
A 460   Rowse, A. L. *The expansion of Elizabethan England* (1955).
A 461   Ruble, J. E. A. de. *Le Traité de Cateau-Cambrésis* (1889).
A 462   Scott, J. B. *The Spanish origins of international law* (Oxford, 1934).
A 463   Torne, P. O. de. *Don Juan d'Autriche et les projets de conquête de l'Angleterre* (2 vols., Helsinki, 1915–28).
A 464   Vaughan, D. *Europe and the Turk* (Liverpool, 1954).
A 465   Willan, T. S. *Early history of the Russia Company, 1553–1603* (Manchester, 1956).
A 466   Zeller, G. *La Réunion de Metz à la France 1552–1648* (in two parts, 1926).

See also:

A 77 Braudel, F.

15   Political Thought and the Theory and Practice of Toleration (vol. III, ch. xvi)

General Studies

A 467   Acton, Lord. *The history of freedom and other essays* (ed. with an introduction by Figgis, J. N. and Lawrence, R. V., 1909).
A 468   Bury, J. B. *A history of freedom of thought* (1920).
A 469   Figgis, J. N. *Political thought in the sixteenth century* (Cambridge, 1907).
A 470   Mataquin, A. *Histoire de la tolérance religieuse* (1905).

See also:

A 404 Allen, J. W.

Detailed Studies

Constructive thinking about both religious toleration and politics largely developed in England and France in the second half of the sixteenth century, and most particular studies are focused on one or other of these countries.

A 471   Baudrillart, H. J. L. *Jean Bodin et son temps* (1853).
A 472   Buisson, F. *Sébastien Castellion: sa vie et son œuvre* (1892).
A 473   Chauviré, R. *Jean Bodin, auteur de la République* (1914).
A 474   Davies, E. T. *The political ideas of Richard Hooker* (1949).
A 475   Jordan, W. K. *The development of religious toleration in England* (4 vols., 1932–40).
A 476   Munz, P. *The place of Richard Hooker in the history of thought* (1952).
A 477   Pearson, A. F. S. *Church and State: political aspects of sixteenth-century puritanism* (Cambridge, 1928).
A 478   Reynolds, B. *Proponents of limited monarchy in sixteenth-century France: F. Hotman and J. Bodin* (Columbia University Studies in History, no. 534) (New York, 1931).
A 479   Shirley, F. J. *Richard Hooker and contemporary political ideas* (1946).
A 480   Weill, G. *Théories sur le pouvoir royal en France pendant les guerres de religion* (1892).

Texts

The subject is best studied in contemporary sources, and a number of the most important texts have been made available in modern editions and in translations.

A 481   Acontius, J. *Satanae Strategemata libri octo* (Basle, 1565); trans. *Satan's Strategems, or the Devil's Cabinet-Council Discovered* (1648).
A 482   Bilson, T. *The True Difference between Christian Subjection and Unchristian Rebellion* (Oxford, 1585).
A 483   Bodin, J. *Heptaplomeres* (first full text published in Schwerin, 1857. An incomplete French version was published by Chauviré, 1914).
A 484   —— *Six Livres de la République* (1576). Trans. Tooley, M. J. *The Six Books of the Commonwealth by Jean Bodin* (Oxford, 1955).
A 485   Browne, R. *A Treatise of Reformation* (Middleburgh, 1582); reprinted in *The Writings of Robert Harrison and Robert Browne* (Peel, A. and Carlson, L. H., eds.) (1953).

A 486   Buchanan, G. *De Jure Regni apud Scotos* (Edinburgh, 1579). Trans.
        Macfarlan, R. Presbyterian's Armoury, vol. 3 (Edinburgh, 1863).
A 487   Burleigh, Lord. *The Execution of Justice in England* (1583); reprinted
        Harleian Miscellany, vol. 3.
A 488   Calvin, J. *Instituts de la religion Chrétienne* (Geneva, 1541); Lefranc, A.,
        Chatelain, H., and Pannier, J. (eds.) (1911).
A 489   Castellion, S. *De Hereticis an sint persequendi* (Basle, 1554); trans. Olivet,
        A. *Traité des Hérétiques* (1913).
A 490   Hooker, R. *Laws of Ecclesiastical Polity*, books 1 and 8 (1666); reprinted
        with introduction (Everyman ed.) (1907).
A 491   Hotman, F. *Franco-Gallia* (Geneva, 1573); trans. Robert, Viscount
        Molesworth, *Franco-Gallia: the ancient free state of France* (1738).
A 492   *Vindiciae contra tyrannos* (1578); trans. Laski, H., *A Defence of Liberty
        against Tyrants* (1924).
A 493   Whitgift, J. *An Answer to a certain Libel intituled An Admonition to
        Parliament* (1572).
A 494   —— *Defence of the Answer* (1572); ed. in vol. 1 of the *Works* for the
        Parker Society (1851), together with Cartwright's *Admonition to Parlia-
        ment*.

16   **The Exponents and Critics of Absolutism (vol. IV, ch. iii)**

        This bibliography is limited to works dealing expressly with political
        theory in order not to overlap with the chapters on the histories of the
        various states. For works published up to 1947 reference may be made to:

A 495   Préclin, E. and Tapié, V. L. *Le XVIIe siècle: Monarchies centralisées,
        1610–1715 (Clio, Introduction aux études historiques*, vol. 7, 2nd ed.,
        1947).

        In general, works cited here were published after this date, though some
        earlier works are also mentioned.

General Studies

A 496   Battaglia, F. *Lineamenti di storia delle dottrine politiche* (2nd ed., Milan,
        1952); bibliography.
A 497   Friedrich, C. J. *The Philosophy of Law in historical perspective* (Chicago,
        1958).
A 498   Jaszi, O. L. *Against the tyrant. The tradition and theory of tyrannicide*
        (Glencoe, Ill., 1957).
A 499   Meinecke, Fr. *Die Idee der Staatsräson in der Geschichte* (4th ed., Berlin,
        1957); a classic treatment of the theme.
A 500   Mesnard, P. *L'Essor de la philosophie politique au XVIe siècle* (2nd ed.,
        1952); valuable for the early part of the seventeenth century.

        For the papalist point of view:

A 501   Arnold, Fr. X. *Die Staatslehre des Kardinals Bellarmin* (Munich, 1934).
A 502   Rommen, H. *La teoría del estado y de la comunidad internacional en
        Francisco Suárez* (Buenos Aires, 1951).
A 503   Suarez, Fr. *Selections* (2 vols., Oxford, 1944).

Detailed Studies

GREAT BRITAIN

Some of the major texts are:

A 504 Cromwell, Oliver. *Writings and Speeches* (Abbott, W. C., ed.) (4 vols., Cambridge, Mass., 1937–47).

A 505 Filmer, Robert. *Patriarcha* (Laslett, P., ed.) (Oxford, 1949).

A 506 Hobbes, Thomas. *Leviathan* (Oakeshott, M., ed.) (Oxford, 1946).

A 507 Allen, J. W. *English political thought 1603–60*, vol. 1, *1603–44* (1938).

A 508 Frank, J. *The Levellers* (Cambridge, Mass., 1955).

A 509 Gough, J. W. *Fundamental law in English constitutional history* (Oxford, 1955).

A 510 Judson, M. A. *The crisis of the constitution...1603–45* (New Brunswick, N.J., 1949).

A 511 Pocock, J. G. A. *The ancient constitution and the feudal law* (Cambridge, 1957).

A 512 Warrender, H. *The political philosophy of Hobbes* (Oxford, 1957).

A 513 Zagorin, P. *A history of political thought in the English Revolution* (1954).

FRANCE

A 514 Mousnier, R. 'Comment les Français voyaient la Constitution', *XVIIe siècle, Bulletin de la société d'étude du XVIIe siècle*, nos. 25–6 (1955); and see also bibliography on 'France 1610–61' (Sec. A, **39**).

SPAIN

A 515 Maravall, J. A. *La Philosophie politique espagnole au XVIIe siècle dans ses rapports avec l'esprit de la contre-réforme* (Cazes, L. and Mesnard, P., eds. and trans.) (1955).

UNITED PROVINCES

A 516 Knight, W. S. M. *The life and works of Hugo Grotius* (1925).

A 517 Nobbs, D. *Theocracy and toleration. A study of the disputes in Dutch Calvinism from 1600 to 1650* (Cambridge, 1938).

A 518 Oestreich, G. 'Justus Lipsius als Theoretiker des neuzeitlichen Machtstaates', *HZ*, **181** (1956).

GERMANY

A 519 Gierke, O. von. *Johannes Althusius und die Entwicklung des naturrechtlichen Staatstheorien* (3rd ed., Breslau, 1913).

A 520 Friedrich, C. J. *Constitutional reason of state. The survival of the constitutional order* (Providence, R.I., 1957).

ITALY

A 521 Botero, G. *Della Ragione di Stato* (Firpo, L., ed.) (Turin, 1948); an important text.

A 522 Bozza, T. *Scrittori politici italiani dal 1550 al 1650* (Rome, 1949).

RUSSIA

A 523   Medlin, W. K. *Moscow and East Rome. A political study of the relation of church and state in Moscovite Russia* (Geneva, 1952).

THE ART OF WAR: ARMIES AND NAVIES

17   International Relations in the West: Diplomacy and War (vol. I, ch. ix)

Armies, Navies and the Art of War (vol. II, ch. xvi)
Armies, Navies and the Art of War (vol. III, ch. vii)
(a) Armies and Warfare (vol. IV, ch. vi)

General Studies

A 524   Bouthoul, G. *Les guerres, éléments de polémologie* (1951).
A 525   Preston, R. A., Wise, S. F. and Werner, H. O. *Men in arms* (1955); very extensive bibliography.
A 526   Sombart, W. *Studien zur Entwicklungsgeschichte des modernen Kapitalismus. 2. Krieg und Kapitalismus* (Munich, 1913).
A 527   Steinmetz, S. R. *Die Philosophie des Krieges* (Leipzig, 1907).
A 528   Toynbee, A. J. *War and civilisation* (1950).
A 529   Wright, Q. *A study of war* (2 vols., Chicago, 1947).

War on land

BIBLIOGRAPHIES

A 530   Cockle, M. *Bibliography of military books up to 1642* (repr. 1957); for contemporary works.
A 531   Jähns, M. *Geschichte der Kriegswissenschaften*, vol. 3 (Munich, 1889); a massive account of contemporary literary (non-archival) sources.
A 532   Ropp, T. *War in the modern world* (rev. ed., New York, 1962); excellent, up-to-date bibliographies.

GENERAL

For the late fifteenth century:

A 533   Erben, W. *Kriegsgeschichte des Mittelalters* (Munich, 1929).
A 534   Lot, F. H. *L'Art militaire et les armées au moyen age*, vol. 2 (1946).

For the sixteenth century:

A 535   Delbrück, H. *Geschichte der Kriegskunst im Rahmen der politischen Geschichte*, vol. 4 (Berlin, 1920).

See also:

A 448 Oman, C.

For the seventeenth century:

A 536 Clark, G. N. *War and society in the seventeenth century* (Cambridge, 1958).

National Studies

ENGLAND

A 537 Cruickshank, C. G. *Elizabeth's army* (1946).
A 538 Firth, C. H. *Cromwell's army* (1921).
A 539 Fortescue, J. W. *History of the British army*, vol. 1 (1899).

FRANCE

A 540 Barre-Duparcq, E. de la. 'L'art militaire pendant les guerres de religion, 1562–98', *Séances et Travaux de l'academie des sciences morales et politiques* (1863).
A 541 Boutaric, E. *Institutions militaires de le France avant les armées permanantes* (1863).
A 542 Colin, J. and Reboul, J. *Histoire militaire et navale* (1925).
A 543 Dickinson, G. (ed.). The *'Instructions sur le faict de la guerre' of Raymond de Beccarie de Pavie Sieur de Forquevaux* (1954); the introduction describes the army under Francis I.
A 544 Hanotaux, G. and La Force, Duc de. *Histoire du Cardinal de Richelieu*, vols. 1–6 (1893–1947); deals with the war 1635–42.

GERMANY

A 545 Frauenholz, E. von. *Entwicklungsgeschichte des deutschen Heerwesens*, vols. 2 and 3 (part i) (Munich, 1936–8).
A 546 Klopp, O. *Der dreissigjährige Krieg bis zum Tode Gustav Adolfs 1632* (3 vols., Paderborn, 1891–6).
A 547 Opitz, W. *Die Schlacht bei Breitenfeld 1631* (Leipzig, 1892).
A 548 Schulz, H. *Wallenstein* (Monographien zur Weltsgeschichte III) (Bielefeld/Leipzig, 1898).
A 549 Struck, W. *Die Schlacht bei Nördlingen im Jahre 1643* (Stralsund, 1893).
A 550 Wedgwood, C. V. *The Thirty Years War* (1938); the best account in English.

ITALY

A 551 Pieri, P. *Il Rinascimento e la crisi militare italiana* (Turin, 1952); a weighty and original book, relating war to economic and political factors.
A 552 Taylor, F. L. *The art of war in Italy 1494–1529* (Cambridge, 1921).

SPAIN

A 553 Essen, L. van der. *Alexandre Farnese Prince de Parme, Gouverneur-Général des Pays-Bas, 1542–92* (5 vols., Brussels, 1933–7); especially vol. 2, ch. i.

SWITZERLAND

A 554 Kohler, C. *Les Suisses dans les guerres d'Italie 1506–12* (1897).

THE LOW COUNTRIES

A 555   Frederick Henry, Prince of Orange. *Mémoires, qui contiennent ses ex-
péditions militaires...de 1621 à 1646* (2 vols., Amsterdam, 1733); with
plans and portraits.

A 556   Hahlweg, W. *Die Heeresreform der Oranier und die Antike* (Berlin, 1941).

A 557   Lonchay, H. *La Rivalité de la France et de l'Espagne aux Pays-Bas 1635–
1700* (Brussels, 1896).

A 558   Roloff, G. 'Moritz von Oranien und die Begründung des modernen
Heeres', *Preussische Jahrbücher*, **3** (1903).

NORTHERN AND EASTERN EUROPE

A 559   Roberts, M. *Gustavus Adolphus* (2 vols., 1953, 1958); important for the
art of war under Gustav Adolf II.

A 560   —— *The military revolution, 1560–1660* (Belfast, 1956); excellent
bibliographical notes.

A 561   *Revue internationale d'histoire militaire*, **12** (1952); contains two articles
on Poland: Laskowsky, O. 'L'art militaire polonais au XVIe et XVIIe
siècles', and Sawczynski, A. 'Les institutions militaires polonaises'.

THE TURKS

A 562   Lybyer, A. *The government of the Ottoman Empire in the time of Suleiman
the Magnificent* (Cambridge, Mass., 1913).

ARMAMENT

A 563   Jähns, M. *Handbuch einer Geschichte des Kriegswesens von der Urzeit bis
zur Renaissance. Technischer Theil: Bewaffnung, Kampfweise, Befestigung,
Belagerung, Seewesen* (Leipzig, 1880); a general classified survey.

BIBLIOGRAPHIES

A 564   Dean, B. *The Metropolitan Museum of Art. Handbook of arms and armor*
(New York, 1930); a simple general account.

A 565   Mann, J. G. *Wallace collection catalogues. European arms and armour*,
part iii (1945), pp. 644 ff.

ARMOUR

A 566   Blair, C. *European armour* (1958).

HAND FIREARMS

A 567   Hayward, J. F. *European firearms. Victoria and Albert Museum* (1955);
short bibliography.

ARTILLERY

A 568   Lewis, M. 'Armada guns', *Mariners' Mirror*, **28**, 1942–3.

A 569   Montu, C. *Storia della artiglieria italiana*, vol. 1 (Rome, n.d.).

A 570   Susane, Le général. *Histoire de l'artillerie française* (1874).
A 571   Vigón, J. *Historia de la artillería española*, vol. 1 (Madrid, 1947).

FORTIFICATIONS

The best short survey of the influence of gunpowder is still:

A 572   Engels, F. 'Fortification', *The New American Cyclopaedia* (Dana and Ripley, eds.), 1858–63.

The only work on a single country is:

A 573   O'Neil, B. H. St J. *Castles and cannon. A study of early artillery fortification in England* (Oxford, 1960).

The best study of a military architect during the sixteenth century is:

A 574   Langenskiöld, E. *Michele Sanmicheli, the Architect of Verona* (Uppsala, 1938).

For the relationship between fortification and town-planning see:

A 575   Lavedan, P. *Histoire de l'urbanisme. Renaissance et temps modernes* (new ed., 1959).

ECONOMIC ASPECTS

A 576   Redlich, F. *De Praeda Militari. Looting and booty 1500–1815* (Wiesbaden, 1956); a specialised study, showing the richness of the almost unexploited economic approach to war in this period.

See also:

A 135   Nef, J. U.

INTERNATIONAL LAW

A 577   Elbe, J. von. 'The evolution of the concept of the just war in international law', *American Journal of International Law*, **33** (1939).
A 578   Jessup, P. C. and Deák, F. *Neutrality. Its history, economics and law*, vol. 1 (New York, 1935).

LITERARY IMPACT OF WAR

A 579   Jorgensen, P. A. *Shakespeare's military world* (Berkeley/Los Angeles, 1956); excellent bibliographical notes.

CHIVALRY

A 580   Huizinga, J. 'The political and military significance of chivalric ideas in the late middle ages', *Men and Ideas* (1960).

See also:

A 154 Ferguson, A. B.

War at sea

GENERAL STUDIES

A 581   Anderson, R. and R. C. *The sailing-ship* (1926).
A 582   Clowes, G. S. L. *Sailing ships, their history and development as illustrated by the collection of ship models in the Science Museum* (2 parts, 1936, 1948).

A 583 Corbett, J. S. *Drake and the Tudor navy* (2 vols., 1898); contains much general information about ship design, tactics, etc.

A 584 Rodgers, W. L. *Naval warfare under oars fourth to sixteenth century. A study of strategy, tactics and ship design* (Annapolis, 1939).

NATIONAL STUDIES

ENGLAND

A 585 Corbett, J. *The successors of Drake* (1933).

A 586 Lewis, M. *The Armada* (1960).

A 587 Mattingly, G. *The defeat of the Spanish Armada* (1959); Mattingly is fuller on the diplomatic background, Lewis on the details of the fleets.

A 588 Oppenheim, M. *A history of the organisation of the royal navy and of merchant shipping in relation to the navy 1590 to 1660* (1896).

A 589 Richmond, Sir Herbert. *The navy as an instrument of policy 1558–1727* (Cambridge, 1953).

FRANCE

A 590 La Roncière, C. de. *Histoire de la marine française*, vols. 2–4 (1900–10).

ITALY

A 591 Guglielmotti, A. *Storia della marina pontificia*, vols. 3–7 (Rome, 1886–92).

A 592 Manfroni, C. *Storia della marina italiana dalla caduta di Constantinopoli alla battaglia di Lepanto* (Rome, 1897).

See also:

A 95 Lane, F. C.

EASTERN MEDITERRANEAN

A 593 Anderson, R. C. *Naval wars in the Levant 1559–1853* (Liverpool, 1952).

A 594 Jurien de la Gravière, E. *Les Corsaires barbaresques et la marine de Soliman le grand* (1887).

NORTHERN EUROPE

A 595 Anderson, R. C. *Naval wars in the Baltic during the sailing-ship epoch 1522–1850* (1910).

SPAIN

A 596 Fernández Duro, C. *Armada española desde la unión de los reinos de Castilla y de León*, vols. 1–3 (9 vols., Madrid, 1895–1903).

NAVIGATION

See also:

A 318 Waters, D. W.

INTERNATIONAL LAW

A 597 Kulsrud, C. J. *Maritime neutrality to 1780* (Boston, 1936).

A 598 Marsden, R. G. (ed.). *Documents relating to the law and custom of the sea*, vol. 1 (Naval Records Society, 1915).

RELIGION: (a) CATHOLICISM TO 1550

18   The Papacy and the Catholic Church (vol. i, ch. iv)

A 599   Aubenas, R. and Ricard, R. *L'Église et la Renaissance* (*Histoire de l'Église*) (Fliche, A. and Martin, V., eds., vol. 15, 1951); gives a detailed bibliography.

The Papacy: General Studies

The two principal works, one written from the Lutheran, the other from the Catholic point of view, are:

A 600   Ranke, L. von. *The history of the popes during the last four centuries* (revised English trans., 3 vols., 1908); there is also a revised Italian translation (Florence, 1959).

A 601   Pastor, L. von. *The history of the popes from the close of the middle ages* (vols. 1–40, Eng. trans., 1891–).

A 602   Seppelt, F. X. *Das Papsttum im Spätmittelalter und in der Renaissance*; vol. IV of *Geschichte der Päpste* (2nd ed., Munich, 1957).

Detailed Studies

A 603   Bauer, C. 'Studi per la storia delle finanze papali durante il pontificato di Sisto IV', *Archivio della società romana di storia patria* (1927).

A 604   Brezzi, P. *La politica di Callisto III* (Studi romani, 1959).

A 605   Lea, H. C. 'The taxes of the papal penitentiary', *EHR*, **8** (1893).

On Savonarola:

A 606   Bedoyère, M. de la. *The meddlesome friar. The story of the conflict between Savonarola and Alexander VI* (1957).

A 607   Klein, R. *Le Procès de Savonarole* (1957).

A 608   Renaudet, A. *Le Procès de Savonarole* (1957).

A 609   Ridolfi, R. *The life of Savonarola* (Eng. trans., 1959).

On the Alexandrine bulls:

A 610   García Gallo, A. *Las bulas de Alejandro VI y el ordenamiento jurídico de la expansión portuguesa y castellana en Africa e Indias* (Madrid, 1958).

A 611   Weckmann, L. *Las bulas alejandrinas de 1493 y la teoría política del papado medieval. Estudio de la supremacía papal sobre islas* (Mexico, 1949).

On the Concordat of Bologna of 1516:

A 612   Thomas, J. *Le Concordat de 1516, ses origines, son histoire au XVIe siècle* (3 vols., 1910).

On papal indulgences:

A 613   Paulus, N. *Geschichte des Ablasses am Ausgang des Mittelalters* (Paderborn, 1923).

On the reform of the regular clergy:

A 614   Beltrán de Heredia, V. *Historia de la reforma de la provincia de España* (*1450–1550*) (Rome, 1939).

A 615 Debongnie, P. *Jean Mombaer de Bruxelles* (Louvain-Toulouse, 1927).
A 616 Godet, M. 'La congrégation de Montaigu', (fascic. 198, *Bibliothèque Ecole Hautes Etudes, Sciences histor. et philol.*, 1912).

The religious life of the Time

GERMANY

A 617 Janssen, J. *History of the German people at the close of the middle ages* (Eng. trans., 17 vols., 1896–1925).

See also:

A 175 Andreas, W.

FRANCE

A 618 Febvre, L. 'Les origines de la Réforme française et le problème générale des causes de la Réforme', *RH*, **161** (1929).
A 619 Imbart de la Tour, P. *Les Origines de la Réforme*, vol. 2 (2nd ed., Lanhers, Y., ed., Melun, 1946).
A 620 Maulde-la-Clavière, M. A. R. de. *Les Origines de la révolution française au commencement du XVIe siècle* (1889).

See also:

A 150 Renaudet, A.; A 165 Renaudet, A.

BELGIUM

A 621 Moreau, E. de. *Histoire de l'Église en Belgique*, vol. 4 (*1378–1559*) (Brussels, 1949); bibliography.

ENGLAND

A 622 Capes, W. *The English Church in the fourteenth and fifteenth centuries* (1920).
A 623 Coulton, G. G. *Life in the middle ages* (Cambridge, 1928–30).
A 624 Hamilton Thompson, A. *The English clergy and their organization in the later middle ages* (Oxford, 1937).
A 625 *Visitations of the diocese of Lincoln (1517–31)* (Lincoln Record Society, 1940–4).
A 626 Judd, A. F. 'The episcopate of Thomas Bekynton, bishop of Bath and Wells, 1443–63', *Journal of Ecclesiastical History*, **8** (1957).

19 Italy and the Papacy (vol. II, ch. viii)

The political and social background is dealt with in:

A 627 Croce, B. *La Spagna nella vita italiana durante la Rinascenza* (Bari, 1917); the intellectual relations between Spain and Italy.
A 628 Gothein, E. *Staat und Gesellschaft des Zeitalters der Gegenreformation* (Berlin/Leipzig, 1908).
A 629 Simeoni, L. *Le signorie* (2 vols., Milan, 1950).
A 630 Visconti, A. *L'Italia dell'epoca della controriforma dal 1516 al 1713* (Milan, 1958); the most complete recent synthesis.

The Papacy

The two standard works have already been mentioned, see:

A 600 Ranke, L. von; A 601 Pastor, L. von.

Other studies include:

A 631   Capasso, C. *Paolo III* (2 vols., Messina, 1924).

A 632   Friedensburg, W. *Kaiser Karl V und Papst Paul III 1534–49* (Leipzig, 1932).

A 633   Jedin, H. *History of the Council of Trent*, vols. 1, 2 (Eng. trans., 1957, 1961); takes the story only to 1547.

See also, by the same author:

A 634   —— *Das Konzil von Trient; ein Überblick über die Erforschung seiner Geschichte* (Storia e Letteratura 19, Rome, 1948).

A 635   —— *Girolamo Seripando* (Eng. trans., 1956).

A 636   —— *Tommaso Campeggio: tridentinische Reform und kuriale Tradition* (Münster, 1958).

A 637   Bainton, R. H. *Bernardino Ochino, esule e riformatore senese del cinquecento 1487–1563* (Florence, 1940).

A 638   Brown, G. K. *Italy and the Reformation to 1550* (Oxford, 1933).

A 639   Cantimori, D. *Eretici italiani del cinquecento, ricerche storiche* (Florence, 1939); the standard work on the religious radicals. German trans. *Italienische Haeretiker des Spätrenaissance* (Basel, 1949).

A 640   Chabod, F. *Per la storia religiosa dello stato di Milano durante il dominio di Carlo V* (2nd ed., Rome, 1962).

A 641   Church, F. C. *The Italian reformers 1534–64* (New York, 1932).

A 642   Clone, E. *Juan de Valdes. La sua vita e il suo pensiero religioso* (Bari, 1938).

A 643   Croce, B. *Un calvinista italiano. Il Marchese de Vico Galeazzo Caracciolo* (Bari, 1933).

A 644   Ferrara, O. *Gasparo Contarini et ses missions* (trans. from Spanish, 1956); semi-popular.

A 645   Lemmi, F. *La riforma in Italia e i riformatori italiani all'estero nel secolo XVI* (Milan, 1939).

See also:

A 185 Douglas, R. M.

20   The New Orders (vol. II, ch. IX)

General Studies

A 646   Cistellini, A. *Figure della Riforma Pretridentina* (Brescia, 1948); an excellent modern work dealing with Catholic reformers and the foundation of new orders in Italy in the early sixteenth century.

A 647   Heimbucher, M. *Die Orden und Kongregationen der katholischen Kirche* (2 vols., enlarged ed., Paderborn, 1933–4); the standard general book on the history of the religious orders and congregations. There are bibliographies for each order.

A 648   Schmitz, P. *Histoire de l'ordre de Saint Benôit*, vol. 3 (Maredsous, 1948); covers the first half of the sixteenth century.

Individual Orders

THE CAPUCHINS

A 649   *Monumenta Historica Ordinis Fratrum Minorum Capuccinorum* (Assisi, 1937–40, Rome, 1941, etc.); gives the sources for the beginnings and early history of the Capuchins.

A 650   *A Capuchin chronicle* (Capuchin Classics III, Father Cuthbert, ed., New York, 1931); an English trans. of an attractive early Capuchin chronicle.

A 651   Cuthbert, Father. *The Capuchins* (2 vols., 1928); an excellent book in every respect.

A 652   Melchior a Pobladura, Father. *Historia Generalis Ordinis Fratrum Minorum Capuccinorum* in *Biblioteca Seraphico-Capuccina, Sectio Historica* (vol. 1, Rome, 1947, covers the period up to 1618); the most complete and systematic modern account of the order's earlier years and has full bibliographies.

THE EARLY CLERKS REGULAR

A 653   Chiminelli, P. *San Gaetano da Tiene* (Vicenza, 1928); long, uncritical, and highly hagiographical.

A 654   Maulde-la-Clavière, M. A. R. de. *St Cajetan*. Eng. trans., by Ely, G. H. in the series, *The saints* (1902); the revised ed. in the Italian translation of Salvadori, G. (Rome, 1911), though incomplete, contains additional material of great value.

A 655   Paschini, P. *San Gaetano Thiene, Gian Pietro Carafa e le origini dei chierici regolari Teatini* (Rome, 1926); essential for understanding the origins of the Theatines.

A 656   Premoli, O. *Storia dei Barnabiti* (3 vols., Rome, 1913–25); the standard work.

THE SOCIETY OF JESUS

The sources for the life of St Ignatius and the foundation and early years of the Society are published in the *Monumenta Historica Societatis Jesu* (1903 onwards, first published in Madrid, now in Rome). Among the more important volumes are:

A 657   *Fontes Narrativi de S. Ignatio de Loyola et de Societatis Jesu Initiis* (vols. 66, 73 and 85 in the series as a whole, Rome, 1943, 1951 and 1960).

A 658   The *Constitutiones Societatis Jesu* (vols. 63, 64 and 65, Rome, 1934, 1936 and 1938).

In addition:

A 659   *Archivum Historicum Societatis Jesu* (Rome), a periodical containing very full information about new works on every aspect of the Society's history and activities.

The early history of the Society in Spain, France, Germany and the Low Countries is fully treated in the large histories by Astrain, A., S.J., Fouqueray, H., S.J., Duhr, B., S.J. and Poncelet, P., S.J. respectively. Some other countries are similarly treated.

A 660 Böhmer, H. *Les Jésuites* (French trans. from the German, with additional notes by Monod, G.) (1910).

A 661 Brodrick, J., S.J. *The origins of the Jesuits* (1940).

A 662 —— *St. Ignatius Loyola: the pilgrim years* (1956); vivid, learned and highly readable.

A 663 Dudon, P., S.J. *Saint Ignace de Loyola* (1934); a leading biography.

A 664 Dyke, P. van. *Ignatius Loyola* (New York, 1926).

A 665 Farrell, A. P., S.J. *The Jesuit code of liberal education* (Milwaukee, 1938); contains much interesting information about early Jesuit schools.

A 666 Gothein, E. *Ignatius von Loyola und die Gegenreformation* (Halle, 1895).

A 667 Guibert, J. de, S.J. *La spiritualité de la Compagnie de Jésus* (Rome, 1953); full history of Jesuit spiritual writings up to 1940.

A 668 Ignatius, St. *The spiritual exercises* (trans. and ed. Keane, H., S.J., 5th ed., 1952); another ed. by Longridge, W. H. (4th ed., 1950).

A 669 Leturia, P., S.J. *El gentilhombre Iñigo López de Loyola* (Barcelona, 1941); the best study up to 1522.

A 670 Sedgwick, H. D. *Ignatius Loyola* (New York, 1923).

A 671 Tacchi Venturi, P., S.J. *Storia della Compagnia di Gesù in Italia* (2 vols., Rome, 2nd ed., 1950, 1951); very full and essential for the serious scholar.

OTHER ORDERS

A 672 Leclerq, J. *Un Humaniste erémite, le bienheureux Paul Giustiniani* (Rome, 1951).

A 673 Lugano, P. *La congregazione camaldolese degli eremiti di Monte Corona* (Rome-Frascati, 1908).

A 674 Marie de Chantal Gueudré, Mère. *Histoire de l'Ordre des Ursulines en France*, vol. I (1957); deals more with the expansion of the Ursulines in France than the early beginnings in Brescia and other Italian towns.

A 675 Monica, Sister. *Angela Merici and her teaching idea* (1927).

(b) PROTESTANTISM TO *c.* 1555

21   Luther and the German Reformation to 1529 (vol. II, ch. iii)
       The German Reformation to 1555 (vol. II, ch. vi. 1)

Luther

PRIMARY SOURCES

A 676 *Luthers Werke*, kritische Gesamtausgabe (Weimar, 1883–); the great standard edition, nearing completion.

A 677 *Luthers Werke in Auswahl* (6 vols., Clemen, O., ed., Berlin, 1950); the handiest edition for a student to possess.

A 678 *Luther's Works* (American ed., 6 vols., Philadelphia, 1915–32).

A 679   *Reformation Writings of Martin Luther* (2 vols., 1956).

A 680   Aland, K. *Hilfsbuch zu Luther studium* (Gütersloh, 1956); a valuable collation of the many German editions of Luther's works.

A 681   Kidd, B. J. *Documents illustrating the continental Reformation* (Oxford, 1911); still very useful.

SECONDARY STUDIES

A 682   Bainton, R. H. *Here I stand* (New York, 1950).

A 683   Bohmer, H. *The road to Reformation* (Philadelphia, 1946).

A 684   Fife, R. H. *The revolt of Martin Luther* (New York, 1957).

A 685   Holl, K. *Gesammelte Aufsätze. Luther* (Tubingen, 1927); still very valuable.

A 686   Kooiman, W. J. *By faith alone* (1954).

A 687   Mackinnon, J. *Luther and the Reformation* (4 vols., London, 1925–30); ample but dull.

A 688   Schwiebert, E. G. *Luther and his times* (St Louis, 1950).

A 689   Tappert, T. G. *Luther: letters of spiritual counsel* (Library of Christian Classics, 1955).

For accounts of Luther's doctrines see:

A 690   Rupp, E. G. *The righteousness of God* (1953).

A 691   Watson, P. S. *Let God be God* (1947).

A 692   Wingren, G. *The Christian's calling* (1958).

The German Reformation: General studies, sources, bibliography

A 693   Franz, G. *Bibliographie de la Réforme 1450–1648*, I/II (Leiden, 1958).

A 694   Lortz, J. *Die Reformation in Deutschland* (2 vols., Freiburg, 1949); a distinguished modern Catholic interpretation.

A 695   Müller, K. *Kirchengeschichte* II/I (Tübingen, 1911).

A 696   Schottenloher, K. *Bibliographie zur deutschen Geschichte im Zeitalter der Glaubensspaltung 1517–85* (Leipzig, 1933–58).

A 697   Wolf, G. *Quellenkunde der deutschen Reformationsgeschichte*, I/II 1.2 (Gotha, 1915–22).

Detailed Studies

A 698   Bizer, E. *Analecta Brentiana* (*Blätter für Württembergische Kirchengeschichte*, supplement, Leube, M., ed., 1957–8).

A 699   —— *Studien zur Geschichte des Abendmahlsstreites im 16. Jahrhundert* (Gütersloh, 1940).

A 700   Born, K. E. 'Moritz von Sachsen und die Fürstenverschwörung gegen Karl V', *HZ*, **191** (1960).

A 701   Bornkamm, H. 'Das Ringen der reformatorischen Motive in den Anfängen der sächsischen Kirchenverfassung', *Archiv für Reformationsgeschichte*, **41** (1948).

A 702   Brandi, K. (ed.). *Der Augsburger Religionsfrieden vom 25 September 1555* (2nd ed., Göttingen, 1927).

A 703   Brunner, P. 'Nikolaus von Amsdorf als Bischof von Naumburg', *Schriften des Vereins für Reformationsgeschichte*, **179** (1961).

A 704   Franz, G. *Der deutsche Bauernkrieg* (4th ed., Darmstadt, 1956).
A 705   Hasenclever, A. *Die kurpfälzische Politik in der Zeit des Schmalkaldischen Krieges* (Heidelburg, 1905).
A 706   Heidrich, P. *Karl V und die deutschen Protestanten am Vorabend des Schmalkaldischen Krieges* I/II (Frankfurt, 1911–12).
A 707   Hirsch, E. *Die Theologie des Andreas Osiander* (Göttingen, 1918).
A 708   Lipgens, W. *Kardinal Johannes Gropper 1503–59* (Münster, 1951).
A 709   Maier, P. L. *Caspar Schwenkfeld on the person and work of Christ* (Assen, 1959).
A 710   Rautenberg, W. *Johann Bugenhagen* (Berlin, 1958).
A 711   Redlich, O. *Staat und Kirche am Niederrhein zur Reformationszeit* (Leipzig, 1938).
A 712   Roth, F. *Augsburger Reformationsgeschichte* (4 vols., Munich, 1901–11).
A 713   Richter, L. *Die evangelischen Kirchenordnungen des 16. Jahrhunderts* (Uckeley, A., ed.) (Marburg, 1939).
A 714   Spitz, L. W. 'Particularism and peace, Augsburg 1555', *Church History*, 25 (1956).
A 715   Stupperich, R. 'Der Humanismus und die Wiedervereinigung der Konfessionen', *Schriften des Vereins für Reformationsgeschichte*, **160** (1936).
A 716   —— *Der unbekannte Melancthon* (Stuttgart, 1961).

See also:
A 632 Friedensburg, W.; A 633 Jedin, H.

22   The Reformation in Zürich, Strassburg and Geneva (vol. II, ch. iv. 1)
Zürich and Basel

A 717   Bromiley, G. W. *Zwingli and Bullinger* (Library of Christian Classics, 1953).
A 718   *Dictionnaire de théologie catholique:* 'Zwingli', 'Zwinglianisme'.
A 719   Farner, O. *Huldrych Zwingli* (4 vols., Zürich, 1943–60).
A 720   —— *Zwingli, the Reformer* (1952).
A 721   Köhler, W. *Huldrych Zwingli* (2nd ed., Leipzig, 1954).
A 722   —— *Zwingli und Luther*, I/II (Leipzig, 1924, Gütersloh, 1953); compresses the great eucharistic controversy.
A 723   Staehelin, E. *Briefe und Akten zum Leben Oekolampadius* (2 vols., Leipzig, 1927–34).
A 724   —— *Das theologische Lebenswerk Johannes Oekolampadius* (Leipzig, 1939).

Strassburg

A 725   *Martini Buceri Opera* (Wendel, F. and Stupperich, R., eds.) (Paris, Gütersloh, 1956–, in progress).
A 726   Hopf, C. *Martin Bucer and the English Reformation* (Oxford, 1946).
A 727   Poll, J. van der. *Martin Bucer's liturgical ideas* (Assen, 1954).
A 728   Pollet, J. V. *Martin Bucer* (Paris, 1958).

Geneva

A 729 Calvin, Jean. *Opera Selecta* (Barth, P., ed.) (5 vols., Monachii, 1952–63).
A 730 Hall, B. *Calvin* (Historical Association pamphlet, 1956, with bibliography).
A 731 Niesel, W. *The theology of Calvin* (1956).
A 732 Strohl, H. *La Pensée de la réforme* (Neufchatel, 1951); a most useful essay.
A 733 Wendel, F. *Calvin* (Paris, 1950); a most useful introduction.

23   The Anabaptists (vol. II, ch. iv. 2)

Bibliographies

A 734 *The Mennonite Encyclopedia*, vols. i–iv (Scottdale, Pa., 1955–9); this incorporates much material from *Die Mennonitischen Lexikon* (Frankfurt a. M., 1914–).
A 735 Wilbur, E. M. *A bibliography of the pioneers of the Socinian-Unitarian movement in modern Christianity in Italy, Switzerland, Germany, Holland, Rome* (Rome, 1950).
A 736 Williams, G. H. 'Studies in the radical Reformation (1517–1618). A bibliographical survey of research since 1939', *Church History*, **37** (1958).

Primary Sources

A 737 Lumpkin, W. L. *Baptist confessions of faith* (Philadelphia, 1959); includes the Schleitheim Confession (1527), the Waterland Confession (1580) and the Dordrecht Confession (1632).
A 738 Menno Simons, *Complete works* (Eng. trans., Wenger, J. C., ed. with bibliography by Bender, H. S.) (Scottdale, Pa., 1956).
A 739 Williams, G. H. (ed.). *Spiritual and anabaptist writers* (Library of Christian Classics, vol. 25 (Philadelphia and London, 1957). Contains extracts from Blaurock, Müntzer, Grebel, Hübmaier, Denck, Hofmann, Obbe and Dietrich Philips, Menno Simons, etc. and 'A bibliography of material in English translation written by representatives of the Radical Reformation (1524–75)'.

Detailed Studies: Biographical and General

A 740 Bainton, R. H. *David Joris. Wiedertäufer und Kämpfer für Toleranz* (Leipzig, 1937).
A 741 —— *Hunted heretic. The life and death of Servetus* (Boston, 1953).
A 742 Bender, H. S. *Conrad Grebel* (Goshen, Ind., 1950).
A 743 Brandt, O. *Thomas Müntzer, sein Leben und seine Schriften* (Jena, 1933).
A 744 Coutts, A. *Hans Denck, 1495–1527* (Edinburgh, 1927).
A 745 Fischer, H. G. *Jakob Huter. Leben, Frömmigkeit, Briefe* (Newton, Kansas, 1956).
A 746 Goeters, J. F. G. *Ludwig Hätzer* (Gütersloh, 1957).
A 747 Kiewiet, J. J. *Pilgram Marbeck* (Kassel, 1957).
A 748 Krahn, C. *Menno Simons* (Karlsruhe, 1936).

A 749   Krajewski, E. *Leben und Sterben der Zürcher Täuferführers Felix Mantz* (Kassel, 1957).

A 750   Lohmann, A. *Zur geistigen Entwicklung Thomas Müntzers* (Leipzig, 1931).

A 751   Moore, J. A. *Der starke Jorg* (Blaurock) (Kassel, 1955).

A 752   Schultz, S. G. *Caspar Schwenkfeld von Ossig* (Norriston, Pa., 1946).

A 753   Teufel, E. *Landräumig Sebastian Franck; ein Wanderer an Donau, Rhein und Neckar* (Neustadt a.d. Aisch, 1954).

A 754   Vedder, H. C. *Balthasar Hübmaier* (New York/London, 1905).

A 755   Wiswedel, W. *Bilder und Führergestalten aus dem Täufertum* (3 vols., Kassel, 1928, 1930, 1952).

A 756   Barclay, R. *The inner life of the religious societies of the Commonwealth* (1876).

A 757   Bergsten, T. *Pilgram Marbeck und seiner Auseinandersetzung mit Caspar Schwenkfeld* (Uppsala, 1958).

A 758   Blanke, F. *Brüder in Christo. Die Geschichte der ältesten Täufergemeinde* (Zürich, 1955).

A 759   Fast, H. *Heinrich Bullinger und die Täufer* (Weierhof, 1959).

A 760   Friedmann, R. *Mennonite piety through the centuries* (Goshen, Ind., 1949).

A 761   Hershberger, G. F. (ed.). *The recovery of the anabaptist vision* (Scottdale, 1957).

A 762   Heyer, F. *Der Kirchenbegriff der Schwärmer* (Leipzig, 1929).

A 763   Hinrichs, C. *Luther und Müntzer; ihre Auseinandersetzung über Obrigkeit und Widerstandsrecht* (Berlin, 1952).

A 764   Horsch, H. J. *The Hutterian brethren, 1528–1931* (Goshen, Ind., 1931).

A 765   Jenny, B. *Das Schleitheim Täuferbekenntnis 1527* (Thayngen, 1951).

A 766   Jones, R. *The spiritual reformers of the sixteenth and seventeenth centuries* (1914).

A 767   Kot, S. *The social and political ideas of the Polish Antitrinitarians in the sixteenth and seventeenth centuries* (Eng. trans., Boston, 1957).

A 768   Kuhn, J. *Toleranz und Offenbarung* (Leipzig, 1923).

A 769   Littell, F. H. *The anabaptist view of the Church* (revised ed., Boston, 1958).

A 770   Müller, L. *Der Kommunismus der Mährischen Wiedertäufer* (Leipzig, 1927).

A 771   Peachey, P. *Die soziale Herkunft der Schweizer Täufer in der Reformationszeit* (Karlsruhe, 1954).

A 772   Schoeps, H. J. *Vom himmlischen Fleisch Christi: eine dogmengeschichtliche Untersuchung* (Tübingen, 1952).

A 773   Smirin, M. M. *Die Volksreformation des Thomas Münzer und der grosse Bauernkrieg* (German trans., Berlin, 1952).

A 774   Smithson, R. J. *The anabaptists, their contribution to our protestant heritage* (1935).

A 775   Wilbur, E. M. *A history of Unitarianism: Socinianism and its antecedents* (Cambridge, Mass., 1946).

A 776   Wolkan, R. *Die Lieder der Wiedertäufer* (Berlin, 1903).

See also:

A 639 Cantimori, D.; A 685 Holl, K.

24   The Reformation in Scandinavia and the Baltic (vol. II, ch. v)

A 777   Johanneson, G. 'Die Kirchenreformation in den nordischen Ländern', *Rapports,* **4,** 11th International Congress of Historical Sciences, pp. 148–83 (Stockholm, 1960); bibliography, including all recent books and important articles.

A 778   Andersen, J. O. *Der Reformkatholizismus und die dänische Reformation* (Studien der Luther-Akademie no. VII, Gütersloh, 1934).

A 779   Andersen, N. K. *Confessio Hafniensis. Den københavnske Bekendelse af 1530* (Copenhagen, 1954).

A 780   Arbusov, L. *Die Einführung der Reformation in Liv-, Est- und Kurland* (Leipzig, 1921).

A 781   Bang, A. C. *Den norske kirkes historie i det 16. aarhundrede* (Kristiania, 1895).

A 782   Bergendorff, C. *Olavus Petri and the ecclesiastical transformation in Sweden (1521–52). A study in the Swedish Reformation* (New York, 1928).

A 783   Dunkley, E. H. *The Reformation in Denmark* (1948).

A 784   Fabricius, L. P. *Reformationstiden* (L. P. Fabricius Danmarks Kirkehistorie II., Copenhagen, 1936).

A 785   Gummerus, J. *Michael Agricola, der Reformator Finnlands, sein Leben und sein Werk* (Schriften der Luther-Agricola Gesellschaft in Finnland 2, Helsinki, 1941).

A 786   Helgason, J. *Islands Kirke fra Reformationen til vore Dage* (Copenhagen, 1922).

A 787   Holmquist, Hj. *Reformationstidevarvet,* Svenska kyrkans historia, 3 (Holmquist, Hj. and Pleijel, H., eds.) (Stockholm, 1933).

A 788   Johannesson, G. *Den skånska kyrkan och reformationen* (Lund, 1947).

A 789   Svalenius, I. *Gustav Vasa* (Stockholm, 1950).

A 790   Westmann, K. B. *Reformationens genombrottsår i Sverige* (Uppsala, 1918).

25   The Reformation in Difficulties: Poland, Bohemia and Hungary (vol. II, ch. vi. 2)

There is nothing which deals with the Reformation in central Europe as a whole. For each of the three countries there is an extensive monographic literature in the vernacular. Apart from that the following books can be recommended:

Poland

A 791   Fox, P. *The Reformation in Poland* (Baltimore, 1924) and the same author's briefer and more recent account in:

A 412   —— *Cambridge History of Poland,* vol. I, ch. xiv (Cambridge, 1950).

A 792   Krasinski, V. *The Reformation in Poland* (2 vols., 1838); can still be read with pleasure and profit if it is remembered that Krasinski was a Protestant Polish exile.

A 793   Völker, K. *Kirchengeschichte Polens* (Berlin/Leipzig, 1930); is impartial and fairly adequate, with book-lists at the end of each chapter.

There are many Latin documents relating to the subject in:

A 794 Theiner, A. *Vetera monumenta Poloniae et Lithuaniae* (Rome, 1860–4).
A 795 *Monumenta Reformationis Polonicae et Lithuanicae* (Wilno, 1925).
A 796 Tazbir, J. *Reformacja a problem chłopski w Polsce XVI w.* (Wrocław, 1953) (The Reformation and the peasant problem in Poland in the sixteenth century); has an extensive and up-to-date bibliography.

Bohemia

There is no single book which deals with the religious history of Bohemia in the sixteenth century exclusively. There are relevant sections in:

A 797 Harrison Thomson, S. *Czechoslovakia in European history* (2nd ed., Princeton, 1953).
A 798 Seton-Watson, R. W. *A history of the Czechs and Slovaks* (1943); and a somewhat more old-fashioned account in:
A 799 Denis, E. *La Fin de l'indépendance bohème* (2 vols., 1890).
A 800 Frind, A. *Kirchengeschichte Böhmens*, vol. 4 (Prague, 1878); still has some value. Another more modern account can be found in:
A 801 Bretholz, B. *Neuere Geschichte Böhmens*, vol. 1 (Gotha, 1920).

A full bibliography can be found in:

A 802 Hrejsa, F. *Dějiny křest'anství v Československu* (History of Christianity in Czechoslovakia) (Prague, 1948, 1950); vols. 4 and 5 of which are devoted to the religious history of the Czechoslovak lands, 1526–76.

Hungary

There is no history of the Reformation in Hungary in a west European language. Brief accounts are to be found in such general histories of Hungary as:

A 418 Hóman, B. and Szekfű, G. *Magyar történet* (Hungarian history), vol. 3 (Budapest, 1935); has a very large but unhandy bibliography.
A 803 Eckhardt, F. *A short history of the Hungarian people* (1931).
A 804 Kosary, D. G. *A history of Hungary* (Cleveland, Ohio, 1941).
A 805 Léger, L. *Histoire de l'Autriche-Hongrie* (6th ed., 1920).
A 806 Sinor, D. *History of Hungary* (1959).

For bibliography see also:

A 807 Horváth, J. *A reformáció jegyében* (In the sign of the Reformation) (Budapest, 1953).

There are many documents in Latin and German in a most valuable collection of sources:

A 808 *Egyháztörténelmi emlékek a magyországi hiújítás karából* (Monumenta ecclesiastica tempora innovatae in Hungaria religionis illustrantia) (Bunyitay, V., Rapaics, R. and Karácsonyi, I., eds.) (Budapest, 1902–12).

For the history of Lutheranism in Transylvania there is:

A 809 Teutsch, F. *Geschichte der evangelischen Kirche in Siebenbürgen* (2 vols., Hermanstadt, 1921, 1922).

See also, on the anti-Trinitarian movement:

A 775 Wilbur, E. M.

26   The Reformation in Difficulties: France, 1519–59 (vol. II, ch. vi. 3)
General Studies

The standard bibliography is:

A 810 Hauser, H. *Les Sources de l'histoire de France depuis les origines jusqu'en 1815*, 2e partie, *Le XVIe siècle (1494–1610)* (2 vols., 1906–15).

For the biographies of personalities:

A 811 Haag, E. and E. *La France protestante* (10 vols., 1846–59). (A second edition by Bordier, H., 8 vols., 1877–92.)
A 812 Duby, G. and Mandrou, R. *Histoire de la civilisation française* (2 vols., 1958).
A 813 Lemonnier, H. *Les Guerres d'Italie; la France sous Charles VIII, Louis XII et François I*, vol. 5 of *Histoire de France* (Lavisse, E., ed.) (1903).
A 814 Leonard, E. G. *Histoire générale du protestantisme* (2 vols., 1961).
A 815 Renaudet, A. and Hauser, H. *Les Débuts de l'âge moderne, la renaissance et la réforme* (1929).
A 816 Vienot, J. *Histoire de la réforme française des origines à l'édit de Nantes* (2 vols., 1926).

See also:

A 619 Imbart de la Tour, P.

Detailed Studies

A 817 Autin, A. *L'Echec de la réforme en France au XVIe siècle* (1918).
A 818 Bourrilly, V. L. *Guillaume du Bellay* (1904).
A 819 Busson, H. *Les Sources et le développement du rationalisme dans la littérature française de la Renaissance 1533–1601* (new ed., 1957).
A 820 Carrière, Abbé V. *Les Epreuves des églises de France au XVIe siècle* (1936).
A 821 Chamberland, A. and Hauser, H. 'La banque et les changes au temps de Henri II', *RH*, **160** (1929).
A 822 Christiani, L. *L'Eglise à l'époque du concile de Trente* (1948).
A 823 Doucet, R. *Etude sur le gouvernement de François I dans ses rapports avec le Parlement de Paris* (2 vols., 1921).
A 824 Febvre, L. *Un destin: Martin Luther* (1928).
A 825 —— *Autour de l'Heptaméron, amour sacré, amour profane* (1944).
A 826 —— *L'Origine des placards de 1534* (1945).
A 827 —— *Au Cœur religieux du XVIe siècle* (1957).
A 828 Fouqueray, H. *Histoire de la compagnie de Jésus en France des origines à la suppression, 1528–1762* (3 vols., 1910–21).
A 829 François, M. *Le Cardinal François de Tournon* (1951).

A 830   Hauser, H. *Etudes sur la réforme française* (1909).
A 831   —— *La Naissance du Protestantisme* (1940).
A 832   Hautecœur, L. *Histoire de l'architecture classique en France*, vol. 1 (1943).
A 833   Haydn, H. *The Counter Renaissance* (New York, 1950).
A 834   Jacqueton, G. 'Le trésor de l'Epargne sous François I', *RH*, **56** (2 parts) (1894).
A 835   Lognon, A. *La Formation de l'unité française* (1922).
A 836   Mollat, M. *Le Commerce de la Haute Normandie au XVe siècle et au début du XVIe siècle* (1952).
A 837   Moore, W. G. *La Réforme allemande et la littérature française* (Strassburg, 1930).
A 838   Raveau, P. 'Le pouvoir d'achat de l'argent et de la livre tournois en Poitou du règne de Louis XI à celui de Louis XIII', *Bulletin de la Société des Antiquités de l'Ouest* (1922).
A 839   Romier, L. *Le Royaume de Catherine de Médicis* (2 vols., 1922).
A 840   Spont, A. *Semblançay (?–1527): la bourgeoisie financière au début du XVIe siècle* (1895).
A 841   Weiss, C. (ed.). *Les Papiers d'Etat du Cardinal de Granvelle*, vol. 1 (1844).
A 842   Weiss, N. *La Chambre Ardente* (1889).
A 843   —— and Bourrilly, V. L. 'L'affaire des placards', *Bulletin de la Société de l'Histoire du Protestantisme français* (1903).

See also:

A 223 Febvre, L.; A 244 Lefranc, A.; A 393 Doucet, R.; A 459 Romier, L.; A 612 Thomas, J.

27   The Reformation in England (vol. II, ch. vii)
General Studies

The following two books, which treat the subject from slightly different angles, contain fairly full select bibliographies:

A 844   Elton, G. R. *England under the Tudors* (1955).
A 845   Parker, T. M. *The English Reformation to 1558* (1950).

Various points of view are represented in:

A 846   Hughes, P. *The Reformation in England* (3 vols., 1950, 1953, 1954); Roman Catholic: vol. 2 carries more bias than vol. 1.
A 847   Maynard Smith, P. *Henry VIII and the Reformation* (1948); some useful discussion of theological points.
A 848   —— *Pre-Reformation England* (1938).
A 849   Powicke, F. M. *The Reformation in England* (1941).

Detailed Studies

A 850   Chambers, R. W. *Thomas More* (1935).
A 851   Darby, H. S. *Hugh Latimer* (1953).
A 852   Dickens, A. G. *Lollards and Protestants in the diocese of York 1509–58* (Oxford, 1959).

A 853 Dickens, A. G. *Thomas Cromwell and the English Reformation* (1959).

A 854 Harbison, E. H. *Rival ambassadors at the court of Queen Mary* (1940).

A 855 Knappen, M. M. *Tudor Puritanism* (Chicago, 1939); the earlier chapters concern this period.

A 856 Knowles, D. *The religious orders in England,* vol. 3 (Cambridge, 1959); supersedes all earlier accounts of the dissolution of the monasteries.

A 857 Muller, J. A. *Stephen Gardiner and the Tudor reaction* (1926).

A 858 Pollard, A. F. *Henry VIII* (1902; repr. 1905, etc.).

A 859 —— *Thomas Cranmer and the English Reformation* (1905).

A 860 —— *Wolsey* (1929).

A 861 Rupp, E. G. *Studies in the making of the English protestant tradition* (1947).

A 862 Smyth, C. H. *Cranmer and the Reformation under Edward VI* (Cambridge, 1926).

See also:

A 726 Hopf, C.

(*c*) THE CHURCHES 1555–1648

28 The Papacy, Catholic Reform, Christian Missions (vol. III, ch. iii) Protestantism and Confessional Strife (vol. III, ch. iv)

General studies dealing with both Protestantism and Roman Catholicism:

A 863 Grimm, H. J. *The Reformation Era 1500–1650* (New York, 1954); useful bibliography.

A 864 Smith, Preserved. *The age of the Reformation* (1920).

A 865 Whitney, J. P. *History of the Reformation* (revised ed., 1920).

On the social teaching of the churches:

A 866 Troeltsch, E. *The social teaching of the Christian Church* (Eng. trans., 2 vols., 1931).

See also:

A 105 Tawney, R. H.; A 109 Weber, M.

On the idea of toleration:

A 867 Bainton, R. H. *The travail of religious liberty* (1953); a collection of studies covering the sixteenth and seventeenth centuries.

A 868 Lecler, J. *Toleration and the Reformation* (Eng. trans., 2 vols., New York, 1960).

See also:

A 475 Jordan, W. K.

The Roman Catholic Church

GENERAL STUDIES

A 869 Cristiani, L. *L'Eglise à l'époque du Concile de Trente* (1948).

A 870 Willaert, L. *Après le Concile de Trente. La restauration catholique 1563–1648* (1960); these form vol. 17 and 18 of *Histoire de l'Eglise depuis les origines jusqu'à nos jours* (Fliche, A. and Martin, V., eds.).

A 871   Eder, K. *Geschichte der Kirche im Zeitalter des konfessionellen Absolutismus*
        (1555–1648) (Vienna, 1949).
A 872   Janelle, P. *The Counter Reformation* (1949).
A 873   Kidd, B. J. *The Counter Reformation 1550–1600* (1933).

See also:

A 600 Ranke, L. von; A 601 Pastor, L. von; A 602 Seppelt, F. X.

DETAILED STUDIES

For the Council of Trent see:

A 633 Jedin, H.; and also:

A 874   Hefele, C. J. *Histoire des Conciles:* vols. 9.i (1930) and 9.ii by Richard,
        P. and 10.i (1938) by Michel, A.
A 875   Evennett, H. O. *The Cardinal of Lorraine and the Council of Trent*
        (Cambridge, 1930).
A 718   *Dictionnaire de théologie catholique,* 'Trente, Concile de', by Michel, A.
A 876   Schreiber, G. (ed.). *Das Weltkonzil von Trient, sein Werden und Wirken*
        (2 vols., Freiburg, 1951); a collection of studies.

On the Counter-Reformation in Italy:

A 877   Brodrick, J. *Robert Bellarmine, saint and scholar* (revised ed., 1961).
A 878   —— *The progress of the Jesuits 1556–79* (1946); continues the history of
        the Society of Jesus.
A 879   Paschini, P. *Cinquecento romano e riforma Cattolica. Scritti raccolti in
        occasione dell'ottantesimo compleanno dell'autore* (Rome, 1958); also
        contains a bibliography of Paschini's own studies on the religious history
        of Italy.
A 880   Ponnelle, L. and Bordet, L. *St Philip Neri and the Roman society of his
        times 1515–95* (Eng. trans., 1932).
A 881   Yeo, M. *A Prince of Pastors; St Charles Borromeo* (1938).

For Germany see the general histories by K. Brandi and M. Ritter cited
elsewhere, and also:

A 882   Brodrick, J. *Saint Peter Canisius, S.J.* (1935).
A 883   Petry, L. *Die Gegenreformation in Deutschland* (Braunschweig, 1952).

For the English Recusants:

A 884   Hughes, P. *Rome and the Counter Reformation in England* (1942).
A 885   Pollen, J. H. *The English Catholics in the reign of Elizabeth* (1920).
A 886   Watkin, E. I. *Roman Catholicism in England from the Reformation to 1950*
        (1957).

See also:

A 457 Meyer, O. A.

For the Orthodox Church:

A 887   Halecki, O. *From Florence to Brest 1439–1596* (Rome, 1958).

Two general works on the missions of the Church are:

A 888 Delacroix, S. *Histoire universelle des missions catholiques* (3 vols., 1956–8). See vols. 1 and 2; good bibliographies and illustrations.

A 889 Latourette, K. S. *A history of the expansion of Christianity*, vol. 3 (1940); see also p. 261.

On St Francis Xavier:

A 890 *Epistolae S. Francisci Xavierii aliaque ejus scripta*, Schurhammer, G. and Wicki, J. (eds.) (2 vols., Rome, 1944–5); is an edition of his letters.

For biographies see:

A 891 Brodrick, J. *Saint Francis Xavier 1506–1552* (1952).

A 892 Schurhammer, G. *Franz Xavier, sein Leben und seine Zeit*, vol. 1 (1506–41) (Freiburg, 1955).

Other works on the Church in Asia include:

A 893 Bernard, H. *Le père Matthieu Ricci et la société chinoise de son temps, 1552–1610* (2 vols., Tientsin, 1937).

A 894 Boxer, C. R. *The Christian century in Japan 1549–1650* (Berkeley, 1951).

A 895 Costa, H. de la. *The Jesuits in the Philippines 1581–1768* (Cambridge, Mass., 1961).

A 896 Cronin, V. *The wise man from the West* (2nd ed., 1959).

A 897 —— *A pearl to India* (1959); two popular lives of Ricci and of Robert de Nobili.

A 898 Maclagan, E. D. *The Jesuits and the Great Mogul* (1932).

On the struggle to save the American Indians see:

A 899 Hanke, L. U. *Aristotle and the American Indians* (1959).

A 900 —— *The Spanish struggle for justice in the conquest of America* (Philadelphia, 1949).

A 901 Ricard, R. *La conquête spirituelle du Mexique 1523–72* (1933).

The Protestant churches

GENERAL STUDIES

A 902 Bainton, R. H. *The Reformation of the sixteenth century* (1953).

Two older studies are:

A 903 Beard, C. *The Reformation of the sixteenth century in relation to modern thought and knowledge* (1883).

A 904 Lindsay, T. M. *History of the Reformation* (2 vols., Edinburgh, 1906–7); vol. 2 covers countries other than Germany.

See also:

A 814 Leonard, E. G.

DETAILED STUDIES

On Calvinism and Geneva:

A 905　McNeill, J. T. *The history and character of Calvinism* (1954).
A 906　Schelven, A. A. van. *Het calvinisme gedurende zijn bloeitijd; zijn uitbreiding en cultuurhistorische beteekenis*. Part ii, *Schotland-England-Noord Amerika* (Amsterdam, 1951).
A 907　Beza, Theodore. *Correspondance* (Aubert, H., ed., 1960–).
A 908　Choisy, E. *L'état chrétien calviniste à Genève au temps de Théodore de Bèze* (1902).

See also:

A 452 Geisendorf, P. F.

On the French Protestants:

A 909　Armstrong, E. *The French wars of religion* (2nd ed., Oxford, 1904).
A 910　Baird, H. M. *History of the rise of the Huguenots* (2 vols., 1880).
A 911　——— *The Huguenots and Henry of Navarre* (2 vols., 1886).
A 912　Grant, A. J. *The Huguenots* (1934).
A 913　Romier, L. *Catholiques et Huguenots à la cour de Charles IX* (1924).

See also:

A 453 Kingdon, R. M.; A 839 Romier, L.

On Germany see the works by Karl F. F. Müller, J. Lortz, G. Mecenseffy cited elsewhere. A recent general work is:

A 914　Holborn, H. *A history of modern Germany: the Reformation* (New York, 1961).

On the Netherlands see:

A 52　Vol. 5 of *Algemene Geschiedenis der Nederlanden* (Houtte, J. A. van, and others, eds.) already cited.

A useful general work is:

A 915　Geyl, P. *The revolt of the Netherlands* (Eng. trans., 2nd ed., 1958).

On England, for a guide to the very extensive literature see:

A 916　Read, Conyers (ed.). *Bibliography of British history. Tudor period 1485–1603* (2nd ed., Oxford, 1959).

Some books covering various aspects of the subject are:

A 917　Burrage, C. *Early English dissenters* (2 vols., Cambridge, 1912).
A 918　Frere, W. H. *A history of the English church in the reigns of Elizabeth and James I* (1904).
A 919　Gee, H. and Hardy, W. J. *Documents illustrative of English church history* (1896).
A 920　Haller, W. *The rise of Puritanism* (New York, 1938).
A 921　Hart, A. T. *The country clergy in Elizabethan and Stuart times 1558–1660* (1958).
A 922　Jordan, W. K. *The charities of London 1480–1660* (1960).

A 923 Jordan, W. K. *The charities of rural England 1480–1660* (1961).
A 924 —— *Philanthropy in England 1480–1660* (1959).
A 925 Maitland, F. W. 'The Anglican settlement and the Scottish Reformation', *Cambridge modern history*, vol. II (1903).
A 926 Paget, F. *An introduction to the fifth book of Hooker's treatise of the laws of ecclesiastical polity* (Oxford, 1907).

See also:

A 237 Porter, H. C.; A 490 Hooker, R.; A 846 Hughes, P.; A 855 Knappen, M. M.

On Scotland there is a modern edition of:

A 927 Knox, John. *History of the Reformation in Scotland* (Dickinson, W. C., ed.) (2 vols., 1949).

Modern studies include:

A 928 Burleigh, J. H. S. *A church history of Scotland* (1960).
A 929 Donaldson, G. *The Scottish Reformation* (Cambridge, 1960).
A 930 Macgregor, J. G. *The thundering Scot; a portrait of John Knox* (1958).
A 931 Mathieson, W. L. *Politics and religion; a study in Scottish history from the Reformation to the Revolution* (2 vols., Glasgow, 1902).
A 932 Percy, Lord Eustace. *John Knox* (1937).

29 Religion (vol. IV, ch. V)
General Studies

The fullest general sketch is:

A 695 Müller, K. *Kirchengeschichte*, II/2 (Tübingen, 1923).

For a comprehensive analysis of the religious trends of the early seventeenth century see:

A 933 Tholuck, D. A. *Vorgeschichte des Rationalismus* (2 vols., Halle, 1853).
A 934 Weber, H. E. *Reformation, Orthodoxie und Rationalismus* (2 vols., Gütersloh, 1951).

Other important studies include:

A 935 Bremond, H. *A literary history of religious thought in France* (Eng. trans., 3 vols., 1928–36).
A 936 Elert, W. *Morphologie des Luthertums* (2 vols., Munich, 1952).
A 937 Schnürer, G. *Katholische Kirche und Kultur der Barockzeit* (Paderborn, 1937).

See also:

A 517 Nobbs, D.
Detailed Studies

A 938 Abercrombie, N. *The origins of Jansenism* (Oxford, 1936).
A 939 Adam, A. *Sur le problème religieux dans la première moitié du XVIIe siècle* (Oxford, 1959); this Zaharoff lecture is a short general interpretation.
A 940 Busson, H. *La Pensée religieuse française de Charron à Pascal* (1933).

A 941   Dagens, J. *Bérulle et les origines de la restauration catholique* (Bruges, 1952).

A 942   D'Angers, J-E. *Pascal et ses précurseurs* (1954).

A 943   Harrison, A. W. *Arminianism* (1937).

A 944   Knox, R. A. *Enthusiasm* (Oxford, 1950); contains most stimulating chapters on Anabaptism and Jansenism.

A 945   Pintard, R. *Le Libertinage érudit dans la première moitié du XVIIe siècle* (2 vols., 1934).

A 946   Schreiber, G. *Deutsche Mirakelbücher* (Düsseldorf, 1938).

A 947   —— *Deutschland und Spanien* (Düsseldorf, 1936); these two books are the best analysis of the popular piety of the period.

A 948   Spini, G. *Ricerca dei libertini* (Rome, 1950); indispensable for the history of unbelief.

A 949   Tulloch, J. *Rational theology and Christian philosophy in England in the seventeenth century* (Edinburgh and London, 1874).

See also:

A 767 Kot, S.; A 768 Kuhn, J.

THE POLITICS OF THE
EUROPEAN STATES

30   The Invasions of Italy (vol. I, ch. xii)

On the background before 1494:

A 950   Ady, C. M. *Lorenzo dei Medici and Renaissance Italy* (1956).

A 951   Delaborde, H-F. *L'Expédition de Charles VIII en Italie* (1888).

A 952   Palmarocchi, R. *La politica italiana di Lorenzo de' Medici* (Florence, 1933).

See also:

A 187 Hay, D.; A 189 Mattingly, G.

General Studies

A 953   Guiccardini, F. *Storia d'Italia*, Panigada, C. (ed.) (Bari, 1929); the best contemporary source.

A 954   Ranke, L. von. *History of the Latin and Teutonic peoples* (1824; Eng. trans., 1909); an early work which remains useful as a careful narrative of the period 1494–1514.

More recent works include:

A 955   Bridge, J. S. C. *A history of France* (Oxford, 1924–9); vols. 2–4 cover, in considerable detail, French activities in Italy, 1494–1514.

A 956   Ercole, F. *Dal Carlo VIII al Carlo V* (Florence, 1932).

A 957   Jacob, E. F. (ed.). *Italian Renaissance studies* (1960); contains a number of important essays.

See also:
A 191 Valeri, N.; A 629 Simeoni, L.

For military history see:
A 551 Pieri, P.; A 552 Taylor, F. L.

Local histories

A 601 *The history of the popes* by L. von Pastor, already mentioned, is useful for Italy as a whole.

VENICE

A 958 Brown, H. F. 'Venice', *Cambridge modern history*, vol. 1 (Cambridge, 1902); remains the most useful political narrative in English.
A 959 Cessi, R. *Storia della repubblica di Venezia*, vol. 2 (Milan, 1946).
A 960 Romanin, S. *Storia documentata di Venezia*, vol. 5 (Venice, 1856).

MILAN

A 961 Ady, C. M. *A history of Milan under the Sforza* (1907).
A 962 *Storia di Milano*, vols. 7 and 8 (Milan, Fondazione Treccani degli Alfieri, 1956–7); various authors, well illustrated.

FLORENCE

A 963 Hale, J. R. *Machiavelli and Renaissance Italy* (1961).
A 964 Schevill, F. *A history of Florence* (2nd ed., New York, 1961).

CENTRAL ITALY

A 965 Pepe, G. *La politica dei Borgia* (Naples, 1946).

NAPLES

A 966 Pontieri, E. *Per la storia del Regno di Ferrante d'Aragona* (Naples, 1947).

There is, however, no satisfactory treatment of Southern Italy in this period.

31   The Empire of Charles V in Europe (vol. II, ch. x)
General Studies

The fullest guide to both the sources and the secondary authorities is:

A 967 Brandi, K. *Kaiser Karl V*, vol. 2, *Quellen und Erörterungen* (Munich, 1941); vol. 1 (Munich, 1937) is the best general biography. English trans. by C. V. Wedgwood, *The emperor Charles V* (1939).

A 968 Armstrong, E. *The emperor Charles V* (2 vols., 2nd ed., 1910); accurate and readable.

A 969 *Mémoires de Charles Quint*, Morel-Fatio, A. (ed.) (1913); from a sixteenth-century Portuguese translation. The original French and Latin versions are lost.

A 970   Ranke, L. von. *Die Osmanen und die spanische Monarchie* (Sämtliche Werke, vol. 35/36, Leipzig, 1877). English trans., by W. K. Kelly from the 1st ed., *The Ottoman and the Spanish Empires* (1843); still very suggestive.

A 971   Rassow, P. *Die Kaiser-Idee Karls V* (Historische Studien, vol. 217, Berlin, 1932).

A 972   —— *Die politische Welt Karls V* (Munich, 1946); these two books are fundamental contributions to the subject.

A 973   Sandoval, P. de. *Historia de la Vida y Hechos del Emperador Carlos V* (Valladolid, 1604–6 and many later editions). Abridged trans. by J. Stevens, *The history of Charles the Vth* (1703); prints much contemporary material, but is not always reliable.

A 974   Santa Cruz, A. de. *Crónica del Emperador Carlos V* (Madrid, 1920–5); best contemporary history.

A 975   Schwarzenfeld, G. von. *Charles V: father of Europe*, trans. by R. M. Bethell (1957); popular biography, not always accurate.

A 976   Tyler, R. *The emperor Charles V* (1956); extensive bibliography; otherwise good only on finance and on relations with England.

Symposia on the occasion of the quattro-centenary of Charles V's abdication and death:

A 977   *Charles-Quint et son temps* (Exposition organisée par l'Administration communale de Gand, Musée des Beaux-Arts, Ghent, 1955); excellent illustrations, especially portraits of many of the important persons of the period.

A 978   *Charles-Quint et son temps* (Centre National de la Recherche Scientifique, Paris, 1959).

A 979   *Karl V. Der Kaiser und seine Zeit* (Rassow, P. and Schalk, F., eds.) (Cologne, 1960).

The two last mentioned works contain many excellent articles.

Detailed Studies

For Germany and the Empire see the chapters on these subjects and on the German Reformation.

THE NETHERLANDS

A 52   *Algemene Geschiedenis der Nederlanden*, vol. 4.

A 53   Pirenne, H. *Histoire de Belgique*, vol. 3, have already been mentioned.

A 980   Boom, G. de. *Marie de Hongrie* (Brussels, 1956).

A 981   Iongh, I. de. *Margaret of Austria* (Eng. trans., 1954).

A 982   Rosenfeld, P. *The provincial governors from the minority of Charles V to the revolt* (Ancien Pays et Assemblées d'Etats, vol. 17, Louvain, 1959); good monograph.

A 983   Walther, A. *Die burgundischen Zentralbehörden unter Maximilian I und Karl V* (Leipzig, 1909); excellent history of administrative structure of the Netherlands.

See also:

A 392   Walther, A.

ITALY

A 984   Chabod, F. *Lo stato di Milano nell'impero di Carlo V* (Rome, 1934); very illuminating about the whole problem of government in the sixteenth century.

A 985   Coniglio, G. *Il regno di Napoli al tempo di Carlo V* (Naples, 1951); very good on the economic side.

A 986   Titone, V. *La Sicilia spagnuola* (Palermo, 1948).

A 987   —— *La Sicilia dalla dominazione spagnuola all'unità d'Italia* (Bologna, 1955); both volumes contain illuminating essays and cover a longer period than the reign of Charles V.

SPAIN

A 988   Albèri, E. *Relazioni degli ambasciatori Veneti*, ser. I, vols. 1, 2 and 3 (Florence, 1839).

A 989   Carande, R. *Carlos V y sus banqueros* (2 vols., in progress, Madrid, 1943, 1949); indispensable but very difficult.

A 990   Maravall, J. A. *Carlos V y el pensamiento político del renacimiento* (Madrid, 1960).

A 991   Seaver, H. L. *The great revolt in Castile* (1929); good account of the revolt of the *comuneros*.

See also:

A 220 Bataillon, M.; A 391 Merriman, R. B.; A 440 Davies, R. Trevor.

32   The Habsburg–Valois Struggle (vol. II, ch. xi)
General Studies

A 992   Fueter, E. *Geschichte des europäischen Staatensystems von 1492–1559* (Munich, 1919).

A 993   Mignet, A. *La Rivalité de François I et de Charles-Quint* (2 vols., 1875).

See also:

A 813 Lemonnier, H.; A 815 Renaudet, A. and Hauser, H.

Detailed Studies

A 994   Brandi, K. *Die deutsche Reformation und Gegenreformation* (Leipzig, 1927–30).

A 995   Carrera Pujal, J. *Historia de la economía española*, vol. 1 (Barcelona, 1943).

A 996   Gachard, L. P. *La Captivité de François I et le traité de Madrid* (Brussels, 1860).

A 997   Gossaert, E. E. *Charles-Quint et Philippe II* (Brussels, 1896).

A 998   Hauser, H. *Le Traité de Madrid et la cession de la Bourgogne à Charles-Quint* (1912).

A 999   Kalkoff, P. 'Zur Kaiserwahl Franz I und Karl V', *Zeitschrift für die Geschichte des Oberrheins*, new series, **40** (1926).

A 1000 Merriman, R. B. *Suleiman the Magnificent* (Cambridge, Mass., 1944).

A 1001   Schick, L. *Un Grand Homme d'affaires au début de XVIe siècle: Jacob Fugger* (1957).
A 1002   Strieder, J. *Jacob Fugger the rich 1459–1523* (Eng. trans., New York, 1931).
A 1003   Zeller, G. *Le Siège de Metz par Charles-Quint* (Nancy, 1943).

See also:

A 70 Ehrenberg, R.; A 189 Mattingly, G.; A 466 Zeller, G.; A 551 Pieri, P.; A 562 Lybyer, A.; A 829 François, M.; A 835 Lognon, A.; A 967 Brandi, K.; A 968 Armstrong, E.; A 971 Rassow, P.; A 978 *Charles-Quint et son temps*; A 989 Carande, R.

33 The British Question, 1559–69 (vol. III, ch. viii)

The best bibliographical guide is:

A 916   Read, Conyers. *Bibliography of British history: Tudor period, 1485–1603* (2nd ed., Oxford, 1959); this, while not exhaustive, gives a very full and systematic survey of the printed material, with occasional comment, down to the end of 1956 and includes much of the material published in 1957–8. This work makes it unnecessary to mention here any but a few more recent publications. An excellent but briefer bibliography is contained in:

A 1004   Black, J. B. *The reign of Elizabeth* (2nd ed., Oxford, 1959).

Other relevant works are:

A 1005   Dickinson, W. C. and Pryde, G. S. *A new history of Scotland*, vol. I (1961).
A 1006   Lythe, S. G. E. *The economy of Scotland in its European setting, 1550–1625* (Edinburgh, 1960).

See also:

A 453 Kingdon, R. M.; A 929 Donaldson, G.

34 Western Europe and the Power of Spain (vol. III, ch. ix)

There is no entirely satisfactory guide to both the sources and the secondary authorities for the whole of this chapter.

A 77   Braudel, F. *La Méditerranée et le monde méditerranéen à l'époque de Philippe II;* an extensive guide to MS sources.
A 455   R. B. Merriman's *The rise of the Spanish Empire*, vol. 4, *Philip the Prudent* (New York, 1934, repr. 1962); still the best general history of Spain and her empire with extensive guide to sources and literature.
A 988   Albèri, E. *Relazioni degli ambasciatori Veneti;* provides brilliant contemporary observations.

The best of the near-contemporary historians is:

A 1007   Cabrera de Córdova, L. de. *Filipe Segundo, Rey de España* (4 vols., Madrid, 1876–77).

Spain

A 1008   Elliott, J. H. *Imperial Spain 1469–1716* (1963); the best modern history of this period in English.

A 1009   Gonçalez de Cellorigo, M. *Memorial de la política necessaria, y util restauración a la República de España* (etc.) (Valladolid, 1600); brilliant contemporary analysis of Spain's economic and social weaknesses.

A 1010   Marañón, G. *Antonio Pérez* (2 vols., Mexico, 1947); abbreviated Eng. trans. by Ley, C. D. (1954); good on Philip II's court.

A 1011   Reglá Campistol, J. *Felip II i Catalunya* (Barcelona, 1956).

A 1012   Sánchez-Albornoz, C. *España un enigma histórico*, vol. 2 (Buenos Aires, 1956); suggestive.

A 1013   Vicens Vives, J. (ed.). *Historia social y económica de España y América*, vol. 3 (Barcelona, 1957).

See also:

A 83   Chaunu, H. and P.

Portugal

A 1014   Franchi Conestaggio, I. de. *The Historie of the Uniting of the Kingdom of Portugal to the Crowne of Castile*, Eng. trans. by Blount, F. (1600); best contemporary account.

A 1015   Queiroz Velloso, J. M. de. *O Reinado do Cardeal D. Henrique* (Lisbon, 1946).

A 1016   —— *O Interregno dos Governadores* (Lisbon, 1953); the best modern accounts of the conquest of Portugal.

Italy

See bibliography for vol. II, ch. x (p. 54) and, of books already mentioned:

A 390   Koenigsberger, H. G. *The government of Sicily under Philip II of Spain*, which contains an extensive guide to sources and literature.

A 962   *Storia di Milano*, vol. 10.

A 1017   Albertini, R. von. *Das florentinische Staatsbewusstsein im Übergang von der Republik zum Prinzipat* (Berne, 1955).

A 1018   Catalano, G. *Controversie giurisdizionali tra chiesa e stato nell'età di Gregorio XIII e Filippo II* (Palermo, 1955).

A 1019   *Civiltà Veneziana del Rinascimento, La* (Fondazione Giorgio Cini, Venice, 1958); essays on different aspects of Venetian history by different authors.

A 1020   Cozzi, G. *Il Doge Nicolò Contarini* (Venice, 1958); excellent, especially on the intellectual history of the Venetian aristocracy.

A 1021   Cramer, L. *La Seigneurie de Genève et la Maison de Savoie de 1559 à 1593* (4 vols., Geneva, 1912–1958).

A 1022   Davis, J. C. *The decline of the Venetian nobility as a ruling class* (Baltimore, 1962); covers a much longer period than the later sixteenth century.

A 1023   Koenigsberger, H. G. 'The parliament of Piedmont during the Renaissance', *IXᵉ Congrès international des sciences historiques. Studies presented to the International Commission for the History of Representative and Parliamentary Institutions*, vol. 11 (Louvain, 1952).

A 1024   Segre, A. and Egide, P. *Emanuele Filiberto* (2 vols., Turin, 1928); conventional.

The Netherlands

The best accounts have already been mentioned:

A 52   *Algemene Geschiedenis der Nederlanden* (Houtte, J. A. van, and others, eds.) vol. 5; is the most comprehensive up-to-date work.

A 915   Geyl, P. *The revolt of the Netherlands* is the best modern account in English.

A 1025   Delfos, L. *Die Anfänge der Utrechter Union 1577–87* (Berlin, 1941); excellent political and constitutional analysis.

A 1026   Griffiths, G. *William of Hornes, Lord of Hèze and the revolt of the Netherlands, 1576–80* (Berkeley/Los Angeles, Univ. of California Publications in History, vol. 51 (1954)); good monograph.

A 1027   Koenigsberger, H. G. 'The organisation of revolutionary parties in France and the Netherlands during the sixteenth century', *JMH*, **27** (1955).

A 1028   Motley, J. L. *The rise of the Dutch Republic* (3 vols., 1855; many later editions).

A 1029   —— *History of the United Netherlands, from the death of William the Silent to the Synod of Dort* (4 vols., 1860–7; many later editions); the classic statement of the liberal and protestant view.

A 1030   Smit, J. W. 'The present position of studies regarding the revolt of the Netherlands', *Britain and the Netherlands* (Bromley, J. S. and Kossmann, E. H., eds.) (1960); historiographical essay.

A 1031   Wedgwood, C. V. *William the Silent* (1944); readable.

See also:

A 553   Essen, L. van der.

France

A 1032   Mariéjol, J. H. *La Réforme et la Ligue—l'édit de Nantes (1559–98).*

A 1033   —— *Henri IV et Louis XIII*, vol. 6, parts i and ii of Lavisse, E. *Histoire de France* (1904–11); still the best political history of the period.

A 1034   Drouot, H. *Mayenne et la Bourgogne* (2 vols., 1937).

A 1035   Fagniez, G. *L'Economie sociale de la France sous Henri IV 1589–1610* (1897).

A 1036   Lamar Jensen, D. *Diplomacy and dogmatism. Bernardino de Mendoza and the French Catholic league* (Cambridge, Mass., 1963).

A 1037   L'Estoile, P. de. *Journal...pour la Reigne de Henri III* (1943).

A 1038   —— *Journal...pour la Reigne de Henri IV* (2 vols., 1948, 1958); biased but vivid contemporary diary.

A 1039   Neale, J. E. *The age of Catherine de Medici* (1943); short version of Romier (see below).

A 1040   Wilkinson, M. *A history of the league* (Glasgow, 1929).

See also:

A 442 Mousnier, R.; A 443 Sutherland, N.; A 453 Kingdon, R. M.; A 458 Romier, L.; A 459 Romier, L.; A 839 Romier, L.; A 913 Romier, L.

The War with England

A 1041   Falls, C. *Elizabeth's Irish Wars* (1950).

See also:

A 587 Mattingly, G.

35   The Policy of Spain and the Years of Truce (vol. IV, ch. ix)

There are few published sources and few good modern works on Spanish policy in Europe under Philip III.

A 1042   *Colección de Documentos Inéditos para la Historia de España* (Madrid, 1842–95); this includes correspondence of the Archduke Albert (vols. 42–3), of the Duke of Osuna (vols. 44–7) and of the Marquis of Villafranca, governor of Milan, 1616–18 (vol. 96).

A 1043   *Correspondance de la Cour d'Espagne sur les affaires des Pays-Bas, 1598–1700* (Lonchay, H. and Cuvelier, J., eds.) (Brussels, vol. 1 (1923) and vol. 6 (1937)).

A 1044   *Archivo Histórico Español*, vols. 3, 4, *Consultas del Consejo de Estado*, Alcocer y Martínez, M. (ed.) (Valladolid, 1930); dealing mainly with the Netherlands, 1603–6.

A 1045   *Archivo General de Simancas, Catálogo IV Secretaría de Estado*, Paz, J. (ed.) (1914); for relations with France.

A 1046   *Documentos Inéditos para la Historia de España*, vols. 1–4 (Madrid, 1936–45), 'Correspondencia Oficial de D. Diego de Sarmiento de Acuña, conde de Gondomar'.

A 1047   *Correspondencia Inédita de Guillén de San Clemente, embajador en Alemania de los Reyes don Felipe II y III...1581–1608* (Zaragoza, 1892).

General Studies

A 1048   Cánovas del Castillo, A. *Historia de la decadencia de España* (2nd ed., Madrid, 1910).

A 1049   Weiss, Ch. *L'Espagne depuis le Règne de Philippe II jusqu'à l'avènement des Bourbons* (1844).

See also:

A 970 Ranke, L. von.

For particular aspects of Spanish policy see:

A 1050   Brown, H. F. *Studies in Venetian history* (1907); contains a good essay on the Spanish conspiracy of 1618.

A 1051   —— 'The Valtelline', *Cambridge modern history*, vol. IV (Cambridge, 1906); excellent.

A 1052   Callegari, E. *Storia politica d'Italia, Preponderanze straniere 1530–1790* (Milan, 1895); valuable.
A 1053   Chudoba, B. *Spain and the Empire 1519–1648* (Chicago, 1952); makes use of unpublished Czech sources.
A 1054   Coniglio, G. *Il Viceregno di Napoli nel sec. XVII* (Rome, 1955); valuable.
A 1055   Corbett, J. *England in the Mediterranean 1603–1713* (1904).
A 1056   Fernández Duro, C. *El Gran Duque de Osuna y su marina* (Madrid, 1885).
A 1057   Gardiner, S. R. *History of England*, vols. 1–4 (2nd ed., 1883–4).
A 1058   Geyl, P. *The Netherlands divided* (Eng. trans., 1936).
A 1059   Gindely, A. *The Thirty Years War* (Eng. trans., New York, 1884).
A 1060   Lefèvre, J. *Spinola et la Belgique* (Brussels, 1947).
A 1061   Lyon, F. H. *El Conde de Gondomar* (Oxford, 1916); brief but useful.
A 1062   Philippson, M. *Heinrich IV und Philipp III, die Begründung des französischen Übergewichts in Europa* (Berlin, 1870); detailed and valuable.
A 1063   Quazza, R. *Storia Politica d'Italia, Preponderanza spagnuola 1559–1700* (2nd ed., Milan, 1950); useful bibliographies.
A 1064   Rodríguez Villa, A. *Ambrosio Spínola, primer Marqués de Los Balbases* (Madrid, 1904); valuable.
A 1065   Tocco, V. di. *Ideali d'Indipendenza in Italia durante la Preponderanza spagnuola* (Messina, 1926).

See also:

A 53 Pirenne, H. vol. 4.

36   The Thirty Years War (vol. IV, ch. xi)

General Studies

A 1066   Gardiner, S. R. *The Thirty Years War* (1874).
A 1067   Gebhardt, B. *Handbuch der deutschen Geschichte*, vol. 2, pp. 133–56 (Stuttgart, 1955); bibliography.
A 1068   Pagès G. *La Guerre de trente ans* (1949); particularly good on French diplomacy.
A 1069   Ritter, M. *Deutsche Geschichte im Zeitalter der Gegenreformation und des dreissigjährigen Krieges*, vol. 3 (Stuttgart/Berlin, 1908).
A 1070   Ward, A. W. in *Cambridge modern history*, vol. IV (Cambridge, 1906).

See also:

A 550 Wedgwood, C. V.; A 1059 Gindely, A.

Detailed Studies

THE BOHEMIAN REVOLT

A 1071   Green, M. A. E. *Elizabeth, Electress Palatine and queen of Bohemia*, revised by Lomas, S. C. (1909).
A 1072   Tapié, V. L. *La Politique étrangère de la France et le début de la guerre de trente ans* (1934); particularly valuable for its use of Czech historical literature.

A 1073 Weiss, J. G. 'Die Vorgeschichte des böhmischen Abenteuers Friedrichs V. von der Pfalz', *Zeitschrift für die Geschichte des Oberrheins* (new series), **53** (1939–40); an account of Frederick V's acceptance of the Bohemian crown.

THE DANISH WAR

A 1074 Opel, J. O. *Der niedersächsisch-dänische Krieg* (3 vols., Halle/Magdeburg, 1872–94).

A 1075 Schäfer, D. *Geschichte von Dänemark*, vol. 5 (Gotha, 1902).

THE SWEDISH PERIOD

A 1076 Ahnlund, N. G. *Gustav Adolf the Great* (Eng. trans., Princeton, 1940).

A 1077 Kretzschmar, J. R. *Der Heilbronner Bund, 1632–35* (3 vols., Lübeck, 1922).

A 1078 Paul, J. *Gustaf Adolf* (3 vols., Leipzig, 1927–32).

See also:

A 559 Roberts, M.

FRANCE

A 1079 Fagniez, G. C. *Le père Joseph et Richelieu (1577–1638)* (2 vols., 1894); study of Richelieu's chief adviser and collaborator.

A 1080 Leman, A. *Richelieu et Olivarès, leurs négociations secrètes de 1638 à 1642 pour le rétablissement de la paix* (Lille, 1938).

A 1081 Mommsen, W. *Richelieu, Elsass und Lothringen* (Berlin, 1922).

See also:

A 544 Hanotaux, G. and La Force, Duc de; A 1068 Pagès, G.; A 1072 Tapié, V. L.

WALLENSTEIN

A 1082 Pekař, J. *Wallenstein 1630–1634, Tragödie einer Verschwörung* (2 vols., Berlin, 1937); a great work of scholarship—anti-Wallenstein. In the first chapter the author surveys the most important literature.

A 1083 Srbik, Heinrich Ritter von. *Wallensteins Ende* (revised ed., Vienna, 1952); more favourable to Wallenstein than Pekař.

A 1084 Watson, F. *Wallenstein, soldier under Saturn* (New York, 1938).

PEACE OF WESTPHALIA

A 1085 Braubach, M. *Der Westphälische Friede* (Münster, 1948); a brief survey of the negotiations and the significance of the final peace.

37 **The Aims of France and International Relations, 1648–59 (vol. IV, ch. xiv)**

The first printed source to be consulted is the well-known collection:

A 1086 *Instructions données aux ambassadeurs et ministres de France depuis les traités de Westphalie jusqu'à la révolution française*, especially:

A 1087 Hollande, André, L. (ed.) (vol. 21/1, 1922).

A 1088   *Angleterre*, Jusserand, J. J. (ed.) (vol. 24/1, 1929).
A 1089   *Diète germanique*, Auerbach, B. (ed.) (vol. 18, 1912).
         Also important are:
A 1090   Cardinal Mazarin, J. *Lettres pendant son ministère*, Chéruel, A. and
         d'Avenel, G. (eds.) (1883–1906).
A 1091   The *Memoirs* of the Maréchal de Gramont, duke and peer of France
         (Coll. Michaud et Poujoulat, 3rd ser., vol. 7, 1839).
A 1092   The *Memoirs* of the comte de Brienne, minister and secretary of state
         (*ibid.*, 3rd ser., vol. 3, 1838).
         Official documents are to be found in:
A 1093   Vast, H. *Les Grands Traités du règne de Louis XIV*, vol. 1 (1893).

General Studies

A 1094   Platzhoff, W. *Geschichte des europäischen Staatensystems 1559–1660*
         (Munich/Berlin, 1928).

See also:

A 446 Hill, D. J.; A 449 Zeller, G.

For bibliographies see:

A 78 Hauser, H.; A 495 Préclin, E. and Tapié, V-L. *Le XVIIe siècle.
Monarchies centralisées (1610–1715)*.

Detailed studies of the major themes
RELATIONS BETWEEN FRANCE AND THE EMPIRE

A 1095   Chéruel, A. *Etudes sur la Ligue ou Alliance du Rhin*, Comptes-rendus des
         travaux de l'académie des sciences morales et politiques (1885); a little
         old-fashioned, but still useful.
A 1096   Dickmann, F. *Der Westfälische Friede* (Munster, 1959); excellent
         bibliography.
A 1097   Livet, G. *L'Intendance d'Alsace sous Louis XIV (1648–1715)* (1956);
         elucidates a disputed topic.
A 1098   Waddington, A. *Le Grand Electeur Frédéric Guillaume de Brandebourg.
         Sa politique extérieure (1640–1688)*, vol. 1 (1640–60) (1905–8).

RELATIONS WITH THE MARITIME POWERS

A 1099   Ballhausen, C. *Der erste englisch-holländische Seekrieg 1652–1654* (The
         Hague, 1923).
A 1100   Edmundson, G. *Anglo-Dutch rivalry 1600–1653* (Oxford, 1911).
A 1101   Fulton, T. W. *The sovereignty of the seas* (1911).
A 1102   Gardiner, S. R. 'Cromwell and Mazarin 1652', *EHR*, 11 (1896).
A 1103   Waddington, A. *La République des Provinces-Unies, la France et les Pays-
         Bas espagnols de 1630 à 1650*, vol. 2 (1642–50) (2 vols., 1895–7).

See also:

A 339 Ascoli, G.

THE WAR BETWEEN FRANCE AND SPAIN

A 1104 Dollot, R. *Les Origines de la neutralité de la Belgique et le système de la barrière, 1609–1830* (1902).

A 1105 Masson, P. *Histoire du commerce français dans le Levant au XVIIe siècle* (1896).

A 1106 Valfrey, J. *Hugues de Lionne. Ses ambassades en Espagne et Allemagne* (1881).

A 1107 —— *Hugues de Lionne. Ses ambassades en Italie 1642–56* (1877).

See also:

A 557 Lonchay, H.

THE NORTHERN WAR

A 1108 Haumant, E. *La guerre du Nord et la paix d'Oliva (1655–60)* (1893).

A 1109 Hill, C. E. *The Danish sound dues and the command of the Baltic* (Durham, N.C., 1926).

A 1110 Konopczynski, L. 'Le problème baltique dans l'histoire moderne', *RH*, **172** (1929).

A 1111 Waliszewski, K. *Les relations diplomatiques entre la France et la Pologne au XVIIe siècle, 1644–67* (Cracow, 1889).

THE HISTORIES OF SEPARATE COUNTRIES

These bibliographies refer only to specific chapters of the *New Cambridge modern history*. For general bibliographical works or the history of the countries concerned see the Introduction.

FRANCE

38   France under Charles VIII and Louis XII (vol. I, ch. x)

The standard bibliography is to be found in the work by H. Hauser:

A 810 *Les Sources de l'histoire de France*...which has already been mentioned, and in:

A 1112 Molinier, A. *Les Sources de l'histoire de France des origines aux guerres de l'Italie (1494)*, 1st part *Les Valois (suite), Louis XI et Charles VIII*, vol. 5 (1904).

General Studies

A 955 Bridge, J. S. C. *A history of France from the death of Louis XI 1483–1515* (5 vols., Oxford, 1921–36) and also:

A 812 Duby, G. and Mandrou, R.; A 813 Lemonnier, H.; A 815 Renaudet, A. and Hauser, H.

Detailed Studies

A 1113   Cherrier, C. de. *Histoire de Charles VIII* (2 vols., 1868).

A 1114   Dupont-Ferrier, G. *Etudes sur les institutions financières de la France à la fin du moyen-âge* (2 vols., 1930–2).

A 1115   Helton, T. (ed.). *The Renaissance* (Madison, 1961).

A 1116   Kristeller, P. O. *Studies in Renaissance thought and letters* (Rome, 1956).

A 1117   Luzzatto, G. *An economic history of Italy; from the fall of the Roman Empire to the beginning of the sixteenth century* (1961).

A 1118   Michel, A. (ed.). *La Renaissance*, vol. 4 of *Histoire de l'Art* (1911).

A 1119   Pelissier, L. G. *Louis XII et Ludovic Sforza* (2 vols., 1896).

A 1120   Plattard, J. *La Renaissance des lettres en France de Louis XII à Henri IV* (1925).

A 1121   Sanudo, M. (Fulin, R., ed.). *La spedizione di Carlo VIII* (Venice, 1873–83).

See also:

A 70 Ehrenberg, R.; A 146 Ferguson, W. K.; A 165 Renaudet, A.; A 170 Huizinga, J.; A 189 Mattingly, G.; A 393 Doucet, R.; A 551 Pieri, P.; A 554 Kohler, C.; A 612 Thomas, J.; A 835 Lognon, A.; A 836 Mollat, M.; A 838 Raveau, P.; A 951 Delaborde, H. F.

For other works on the history of France in the sixteenth century, see the bibliographies, Sec. A, **26, 28, 34**.

---

39   France (vol. IV, ch. xvi)

For works published up to 1947 see:

A 495   Préclin, E. and Tapié, V. L. *Le XVIIe siècle, Monarchies centralisées 1610–1715*, already mentioned.

General Studies

A 1122   Mousnier, R. 'L'âge classique, 1598–1715', *Histoire de France*, Reinhard, M. (ed.), vol. i (1954).

A 1123   Préclin, E. and Jarry, E. *Les Luttes politiques et doctrinales aux XVIIe et XVIIIe siècles (Histoire de l'Eglise, xix)* (2 vols., 1955–6).

A 1124   Tapié, V. L. *La France de Louis XIII et de Richelieu* (1952).

A 1125   Touchard, J. and others. *Histoire des idées politiques* (2 vols., 1959).

See also:

A 449 Zeller, G.

Detailed Studies

POLITICAL INSTITUTIONS AND ADMINISTRATION

A 1126   Mousnier, R., Bluche, F. and others, 'Serviteurs du Roi. Quelques aspects de la fonction publique dans la société française du XVIIe siècle', *XVIIe siècle, Bulletin de la société d'étude du XVIIe siècle*, **42–3** (1959); bibliography.

A 1127 Olivier-Martin, Fr. *Histoire du droit français des origines à la Révolution* (1948).

A 1128 Petot, J. *Histoire de l'administration des Ponts et Chaussées (1599–1815)* (1958).

A 1129 Vaille, E. *Histoire générale des postes françaises*, vol. 3 (*1477–1630*) (1949).

See also:

A 441 Mitchell, J. H.; A 442 Mousnier, R.; A 1097 Livet, G.

SOCIAL AND ECONOMIC HISTORY

A 1130 Boiteux, L. A. *Richelieu, grand maître de la navigation et du commerce de la France. La marine et l'histoire* (1955).

A 1131 Bouvier-Ajam, M. *L'Histoire du travail en France des origines à la Révolution* (1957).

A 1132 Lousse, E. *La Société d'ancien régime—organisation et représentation corporatives* (1943).

A 1133 Olivier-Martin, Fr. *L'Organisation corporative de la France d'ancien régime* (1938).

See also:

A 104 Spooner, F. C.; A 114 Bergasse, L. and Rambert, G. vol. iv; A 131 Hauser, H.

RELIGIOUS HISTORY

A 1134 Blet, P. *Le Clergé de France et la monarchie. Etude sur les assemblées générales du clergé de 1615 à 1666* (2 vols., Rome, 1959).

A 1135 Catta, E. *La Vie d'un monastère sous l'ancien régime. La visitation Sainte Marie de Nantes (1630–1792)* (1954).

A 1136 Cognet, L. *Relation écrite par la Mère Angélique Arnaud sur Port-Royal* (1949).

INTELLECTUAL HISTORY

A 1137 Adam, A. *Histoire de la littérature française au XVIIe siècle* (5 vols., 1948–56); to be used with care for the relationship between literature and economic and social development.

A 1138 Pottinger, D. T. *The French book trade in the ancien régime, 1500–1791* (Cambridge, Mass., 1958).

See also:

A 945 Pintard, R.

REGIONAL HISTORIES

A 1139 Ford, F. L. *Strasburg in transition 1648–1789* (Cambridge, Mass., 1958).
A 1140 Rebillon, A. *Histoire de Bretagne* (1957); bibliography.
A 1141 Richard, J. *Histoire de la Bourgogne* (1957); bibliography.

A 1142   Amiguet, P. *La Grande Mademoiselle et son siècle* (1957).
A 1143   Carré, H. *The early life of Louis XIV (1638–1661)* (Eng. trans. 1951).
A 1144   Delpech, J. *Madame de Longueville* (1957).
A 1145   Mongredien, G. *Le Grande Condé, l'homme et son œuvre* (1959).

See also:

A 544 Hanotaux, G. and La Force, Duc de, vol. 6.

POPULAR RISINGS

A 1146   Kossmann, E. H. *La Fronde* (Leiden, 1954).
A 1147   Mousnier, R. 'Quelques raisons de la Fronde. Les causes des journées révolutionnaires parisiennes de 1648', *XVIIe siècle. Bulletin de la Société d'étude du XVIIe siècle,* 1949, nos. 2–3.

SPAIN

40   **The Hispanic Kingdoms and the Catholic Kings (vol. I, ch. xi)**
General Studies

The fullest general history of Spain published in this century:

A 1148   Ballesteros y Beretta, A. *Historia de España y su influencia en la historia universal* (12 vols., 2nd ed., Barcelona, 1943–8); contains detailed bibliographies of both contemporary and modern works. These may be supplemented by the references in:
A 1149   Soldevila, F. *Historia de España* (8 vols., Barcelona, 1952–9).

Other general works covering the reigns of the Catholic Kings are:

A 1150   Hume, M. A. S. *Spain, its greatness and decay (1479–1788)* (3rd ed., Cambridge, 1913).
A 1151   Mariéjol, H. *L'Espagne sous Ferdinand et Isabelle* (1892), Eng. trans. by Keene, B., *The Spain of Ferdinand and Isabella* (Rutgers, 1961); with preface and bibliographical survey of recent work on the reign.
A 1152   Prescott, W. H. *History of the reign of Ferdinand and Isabella* (1838); still has many merits.

See also:

A 391 Merriman, R. B.; A 440 Davies, R. Trevor; A 1008 Elliott, J. H.

On international politics see:

A 1153   Doussinague, J. M. *La política internacional de Fernando el Católico* (Madrid, 1944).

See also:

A 189 Mattingly, G.; A 392 Walther, A.

Detailed Studies

THE BACKGROUND BEFORE THE REIGN OF THE
CATHOLIC KINGS

A 1154   Calmette, J. L. *La Formation de l'unité espagnole* (1946).
A 1155   Vicens Vives, J. *Historia crítica de la vida y reinado de Fernando II de Aragón* (Zaragoza, 1962).
A 1156   —— *Juan II de Aragón: monarquía y revolucion en la España del siglo XV* (Barcelona, 1935).
A 1157   Vilar, P. *La Catalogne dans l'Espagne moderne*, vol. 1 (1962); an analysis of the decline of Catalonia.

STATE AND ADMINISTRATION

A 1158   Cepeda Adán, J. *En torno al concepto del estado en los reyes católicos* (Madrid, 1956); a study of political beliefs and theories.
A 1159   Gounon-Loubens, J. *Essai sur l'administration de la Castille au XVIe siècle* (1860).
A 1160   Maravall, J. A. 'The origins of the modern state', *Journal of World History*, 6 (1961).
A 1161   Vicens Vives, J. 'Estructura administrativa estatal en los siglos XVI y XVII', vol. 4 of *Rapports*, XIe Congrès International des Sciences Historiques (Stockholm, 1960).
A 1162   —— *Politica del Rey Católico en Cataluña* (Barcelona, 1940).

RELIGIOUS POLICY

A 1163   Lea, H. C. *A history of the Inquisition in Spain*, (4 vols., New York, 1906–7); the fundamental work.
A 1164   Longhurst, J. E. *Erasmus and the Spanish Inquisition: the case of Juan de Valdés* (Albuquerque, 1950).
A 1165   Tarsicio de Azcona, P. *La elección y reforma del episcopado español en tiempo de los Reyes Católicos* (Madrid, 1960).
A 1166   Turberville, A. S. *The Spanish Inquisition* (1949); a good brief account.

See also:

A 220   Bataillon, M.

THE MOORS AND THE JEWS

A 1167   Caro Baroja, J. *Los Moriscos del reino de Granada* (Madrid, 1957).
A 1168   Lea, H. C. *Moriscos of Spain, their conversion and expulsion* (Philadelphia, 1901).
A 1169   Lepeyre, H. *Géographie de l'Espagne Morisque* (1959); a statistical survey of the Morisco population with bibliography.
A 1170   Neuman, A. A. *The Jews in Spain* (2 vols., Philadelphia, 1948).
A 1171   Roth, C. *A History of the Marranos* (1959).

ECONOMIC LIFE

A 1172   Ibarra y Rodríguez, E. *El problema cerealista en España durante el reinado de los Reyes Católicos* (Madrid, 1944).

A 1173   Smith, R. S. *The Spanish Guild Merchant: a history of the Consulado 1250–1700* (Durham, N.C., 1940).

A 1174   Vicens Vives, J. *Manual de historia económica de España* (Barcelona, 1959); with a good bibliography.

See also:

A 32 Klaveren, J. van; A 83 Chaunu, H. and P.; A 94 Klein, J.

For overseas expansion, refer to bibliographies on Europe overseas and to:

A 1175   Konetzke, R. *Das Spanische Weltreich: Grundlagen und Entstehung*, trans. into Spanish as *El Imperio Español. Orígenes y Fundamentos* (Madrid, 1946).

For other works on the history of Spain in the sixteenth and early seventeenth centuries, see the bibliographies, Sec. A, **31, 34, 35.**

41   Spain and Portugal 1598–1648 (vol. IV, ch. xv)
        Spain and her Empire (vol. V, ch. xv)
        (See Sec. B, **37**)

General Studies

A helpful general survey of recent work on the period is:

A 1176   Vicens Vives, J., Reglá, J. and Nadal, J. 'L'Espagne aux XVIe et XVIIe siècles', *RH*, **220** (1958).

The only book in English of any value on the decline of Spain remains:

A 1177   Hume, M. A. S. *The Court of Philip IV* (2nd ed., n.d.); although it is in many ways inadequate.

The classic statement by an economic historian on the causes of the decline is:

A 130   Hamilton, Earl J. 'The decline of Spain', *Econ. HR*, 1st ser., **8** (1938); which has formed the basis of most recent interpretations, but now itself needs to be revised and supplemented.

Valuable suggestions towards a new and wider synthesis can be found in:

A 1178   Vilar, P. 'Le Temps de Quichotte', *Europe*, **34** (1956); and a re-formulation of the problems in the light of recent work is attempted in:

A 1179   Elliott, J. H. 'The decline of Spain', *PP*, no. 20 (1961).

Detailed Studies

THE SPANISH ECONOMY

Two Spanish works have already been mentioned:

A 995   Carrera Pujal, J. *Historia de la economía española* (5 vols.); an indiscriminate compilation of much important contemporary material.

A 1174   Vicens Vives, J. *Manual de historia económica de España.*

Two fundamental works on wages, prices and monetary policy are:

A 90   Hamilton, Earl J. *American treasure and the price revolution in Spain* (Cambridge, Mass., 1934).

A 1180 —— *War and prices in Spain, 1651–1800* (Cambridge, Mass., 1947).

The first documented study to appear on the Spanish Crown finances in the reign of Philip IV is:

A 1181 Domínguez Ortiz, A. *Política y Hacienda de Felipe IV* (Madrid, 1960).

A 1182 Kellenbenz, H. *Unternehmerkräfte im Hamburger Portugal- und Spanien-handel, 1590–1625* (Hamburg, 1954); deals admirably with economic relations between Spain and northern Europe.

The vitally important subject of the agrarian history of Castille has been almost entirely neglected, apart from the brief sketch:

A 1183 Viñas Mey, C. *El problema de la tierra en la España de los siglo XVI–XVII* (Madrid, 1941).

See also:

A 83 Chaunu, H. and P.

Since: GOVERNMENT AND SOCIETY

A 1048 Cánovas del Castillo, A. *Historia de la decadencia de España* (2nd ed., Madrid, 1910).

A 1184 —— *Estudios del reinado de Felipe IV* (2 vols., 2nd ed., Madrid, 1927); extraordinarily little of lasting value has appeared on the government of Spain under Philip III and Philip IV.

A 1185 Marañón, G. *El Conde-Duque de Olivares* (3rd ed., Madrid, 1952); an important biography of the leading statesman of the period.

The reign of Charles II has been studied in detail in:

A 1186 Maura, Duque de. *Vida y reinado de Carlos II* (2 vols., 2nd ed., Madrid, 1954).

There is an illuminating contemporary account of Charles's court in:

A 1187 Villars, Marquis de. *Mémoires de la cour d'Espagne* (Morel-Fatio, A., ed., 1893). The Spanish nobility in this period remains unstudied, but some light is thrown on the causes of aristocratic discontent by Marañón's life of Olivares and:

A 1188 Ezquerra Abadía, R. *La conspiración del Duque de Híjar, 1648* (Madrid, 1934).

THE EXPULSION OF THE MORISCOS

The Valencian Moriscos have been studied by:

A 1189 Halperin Donghi, T. 'Les Morisques du royaume de Valence au XVIe siècle', *AESC*, **11** (1956), and the Moriscos of the Crown of Aragon as a whole by:

A 1190 Reglá, J. 'La expulsión de los moriscos y sus consecuencias', *Hispania*, **13** (1953).

See also:

A 1169 Lepeyre, H.

CATALONIA

A 1191   Nadal, J. and Giralt, E. *La Population catalane de 1553 à 1717* (1960); is a meticulous study of Catalan demographic problems, and in particular of the French migration into Catalonia.

The origins of the revolution of 1640 are traced in:

A 1192   Elliott, J. H. *The revolt of the Catalans. A study in the decline of Spain (1598–1640)* (Cambridge, 1963).

For the course of the revolution and Catalonia's relations with France, see:

A 1193   Sanabre, J. *La acción de Francia en Cataluña* (Barcelona, 1956).

PORTUGAL

(See also bibliography to Sec. B, **38**.)

A 1194   Mauro, F. *Le Portugal et l'Atlantique (1570–1670)* (1960); is a comprehensive survey of Portugal's Atlantic economy.

There is no adequate study of the Portuguese revolution of 1640, but the activities of Richelieu's agents are studied in:

A 1195   Révah, I. S. *Le Cardinal de Richelieu et la restauration du Portugal* (Lisbon, 1950).

ITALY

For works on the history of Italy in the sixteenth century, see the bibliographies, Sec. A, **19, 28, 30, 31** and **34**.

ENGLAND

For works on the history of England in the sixteenth century, see the bibliographies, Sec. A, **27, 28, 33** and Sec. B, **44**.

THE NETHERLANDS

42   The Burgundian Netherlands 1477–1521 (vol. I, ch. viii)

See: **General Studies**

A 53   Pirenne, H. *Histoire de Belgique*, vol. 3 already mentioned.

A 52   *Algemene Geschiedenis der Nederlanden*, vol. 4 already mentioned; the bibliographical notes appended to each of the chapters, when taken together, provide a select bibliography in various languages covering every aspect of the period.

A 967   Brandi, K. *Kaiser Karl V* (2 vols.) already mentioned; the opening chapters of each volume offer a brilliant sketch of the transition in the Netherlands from the period of Charles the Bold to that of the Emperor Charles V.

Source material is dispersed and frequently not available in up-to-date editions. See:

A 1196 *Actes des Etats-Généraux des anciens Pays-Bas* (Académie royale de Belgique, Commission royale d'histoire), quarto series, in progress: vol. 1, *Actes, 1427–77*, Cuvelier, J., Dhondt, J. and Doehard, R. (eds.) (Brussels, 1948); invaluable for the assemblies of 1477.

Detailed Studies

A 1197 Boom, G. de. *Marguérite d'Autriche-Savoie et la pré-Renaissance* (1935).
A 1198 Dansart, G. *Guillaume de Croÿ-Chièvres* (Brussels, n.d.); these two books contain useful material for the rivalry of Chièvres and Margaret.
A 1199 Dhondt, J. 'Ordres ou Puissances: l'exemple des états de Flandre', *AESC,* 5 (1950); of exceptional value for the territorial estates of the provinces.
A 1200 Enno van Gelder, H. and Hoc, M. *Les monnaies des Pays-Bas bourguignons et espagnols 1434–1713* (Amsterdam, 1960).
A 1201 Hirschauer, H. *Les États d'Artois* (2 vols., 1923); also very valuable on the territorial estates.
A 1202 Holder, J. H. and others (eds.). *Geschiedkundige Atlas van Nederland,* vol. 1 (Utrecht, 1921); excellent maps accompanied by historical commentaries.
A 1203 Post, R. R. *Kerksgeschiendenis van Nederland in de middeleeuwen* (2 vols., Utrecht, 1959); goes up to 1559.

See also:

A 55 Bindoff, S. T.; A 58 Wegg, J.; A 61 Craeybeckx, J.; A 99 Mols, R.; A 621 Moreau, E. de; A 982 Rosenfeld, P.; A 983 Walther, A.

For other works on the history of the Netherlands in the sixteenth century see the bibliographies, Sec. A, **31** and **34**.

43 The Netherlands (vol. IV, ch. xii)
General Studies
The standard works remain:

A 52 *Algemene Geschiedenis der Nederlanden,* vol. 6; deals with both the Northern and the Southern Netherlands and provides the most up-to-date information.
A 53 Pirenne, H. *Histoire de Belgique,* vol. 4; describes the history of the Southern Netherlands from 1567 to 1648.

The best general work in English covering the Northern Netherlands and the Flemish-speaking parts of the Southern Netherlands is:

A 1058 Geyl, P. *The Netherlands divided, 1609–48* (1936).

An original interpretation of Dutch history in the seventeenth and eighteenth centuries is given in:

A 1204 Renier, G. J. *The Dutch Nation* (1944).

For the Northern Netherlands see:

A 115   Blok, P. J. *History of the people of the Netherlands*, vols. 3 and 4 (Eng. trans., New York and London, 1900–7); this remains useful.

Detailed Studies

NORTHERN NETHERLANDS

POLITICAL HISTORY

A 1205   Blok, P. J. *Frederik Hendrik. Prins van Oranje* (Amsterdam, 1926).
A 1206   Haak, S. P. 'De wording van het conflict tusschen Maurits en Oldenbarneveldt', *Bijdragen voor Geschiedenis en Oudheidkunde*, 5th series, vol. 6 (1919) and vol. 10 (1923).
A 1207   Kernkamp, G. W. *Prins Willem II* (Amsterdam, 1943).
A 1208   Poelhekke, J. J. *De vrede van Munster* (The Hague, 1948).
A 1209   Raa, F. G. J. ten and Bas, F. de. *Het staatsche Leger*, vol. 4 (1625–48) (Breda, 1918).

See also:

A 1103 Waddington, A.

ECONOMIC AND SOCIAL HISTORY

A 1210   Brakel, S. van. *De Hollandsche handelscompagnieën der 17e eeuw* (The Hague, 1908).
A 1211   Elias, J. E. *De vroedschap van Amsterdam 1758–95* (2 vols., Haarlem, 1903–5).
A 1212   Kooy, T. P. van der. *Hollands stapelmarkt en haar verval* (Rotterdam, 1931).
A 1213   Kranenburg, H. A. H. *De zeevisserij van Holland in den tijd der Republiek* (Rotterdam, 1946).
A 1214   Pringsheim, O. *Beiträge zur wirtschaftlichen Entwickelungsgeschichte der Vereinigten Niederlande im 17. und 18. Jahrhundert* (Leipzig, 1890).

See also:

A 112 Barbour, V.; A 119 Christensen, A.; A 136 Posthumus, N.

RELIGIOUS HISTORY

A 1215   Gelder, H. A. Enno van. *De levenbeschouwing van C. P. Hooft* (Amsterdam, 1918).
A 1216   Itterzon, G. P. van. *Franciscus Gomarus* (Leiden, 1929).
A 1217   Rogge, H. C. *Johanes Wtenbogaert en zijn tijd* (3 vols., Leiden, 1874–6).
A 1218   Winkelman, P. H. *Remonstranten en Katholieken in de eeuw van Hugo de Groot* (Nijmegen, 1945).

SOUTHERN NETHERLANDS

POLITICAL HISTORY

A 1219   Brants, V. *La Belgique au XVIIe siècle. Albert et Isabelle* (Louvain, 1910).

A 1220 Villermont, M. de. *L'infante Isabelle, gouvernante des Pays-Bas* (2 vols., 1912).

See also:

A 557 Lonchay, H.

ECONOMIC AND SOCIAL HISTORY

A 1221 Cosemans, A. *De bevolking van Brabant in de 17e en 18e eeuw* (Brussels, 1939).
A 1222 Houtte, J. A. van. *Onze 17e eeuw 'Ongelukseeuw'?* (Mededelingen Koninklijke Vlaamse Academie voor Wetenschappen, Klasse der Letteren, jaargang 15, nummer 8, Brussels, 1953).
A 1223 Jouret, G. *Histoire économique de la Belgique*, vol. 2 (Mons, 1939).
A 1224 Lindemans, P. *Geschiedenis van de landbouw in België* (2 vols., Antwerp, 1952).
A 1225 Sabbe, E. *De Belgische vlasnijverheid:* vol. 1, *De Zuidnederlandsche vlasnijverheid tot het verdrag van Utrecht* (Bruges, 1943).

See also:

A 51 Houtte, J. A. van.

RELIGIOUS HISTORY

A 621 Moreau, E. de. *Histoire de l'Eglise en Belgique*, vol. 5, *L'Eglise des Pays-Bas (1559–1633)* (Brussels, 1952).
A 1226 Pasture, A. *La Restauration religieuse aux Pays-Bas catholiques sous les archiducs Albert et Isabelle* (Louvain, 1929).
A 1227 Willaert, L. *Les Origines du Jansénisme dans les Pays-Bas catholiques:* vol. 1, *Le milieu. Le Jansénisme avant la lettre* (Brussels, 1948).

GERMANY AND THE EMPIRE

44   **The Empire under Maximilian I (vol. 1, ch. vii)**

A 1228 Kaser, K. *Deutsche Geschichte zur Zeit Maximilians I, 1486–1519* (Stuttgart/Berlin, 1912); an outstanding work on the empire as a whole.

See also:

A 175 Andreas, W.

Detailed Studies

ECCLESIASTICAL HISTORY

A 1229 Hashagen, J. *Staat und Kirche vor der Reformation* (Essen, 1931); contains much material on lay control of the clergy.

See also:

A 694 Lortz, J.

ECONOMIC HISTORY

A 1230   Strieder, J. *Zur Genesis des modernen Kapitalismus* (2nd ed., Munich and Leipzig, 1935); with considerable bibliography.

See also:

A 1002 Strieder, J.

AUSTRIA

A 1231   Kaindl, R. F. *Geschichte und Kulturleben Deutsch-Österreichs...bis 1526* (Vienna, 1929).

THE NORTH-EAST

A 1232   Carsten, F. L. *The Origins of Prussia* (Oxford, 1954); chs. vii to xii cover the fifteenth and sixteenth centuries.

OTHER TERRITORIES

A 1067   Gebhardt, B. *Handbuch der Deutschen Geschichte*, vol. 2 (8th ed., Stuttgart, 1955), sections iv–vi.

THE SWISS

A 1233   Bonjour, E., Offler, H. S. and Potter, G. R. *A short history of Switzerland* (Oxford, 1952); with select bibliography.

A 1234   Guggenbühl, G. *Geschichte der Schweizerischen Eidgenossenschaft*, vol. 1 (Zürich, 1947).

Biographical

A 1235   Hartung, F. 'Berthold von Henneberg', *HZ*, **103** (1909).

A 1236   Jansen, M. *Kaiser Maximilian I* (Munich, 1905); favourable to Maximilian.

A 1237   Walther, A. 'Die neuere Beurteilung Kaisers Maximilians I', *Mitteilungen des Instituts für Österreichische Geschichtsforschung*, **33** (1912).

Good popular biographies of the emperor are:

A 1238   Breitner, E. *Maximilian I* (Bremen, 1939).

A 1239   Hare, C. *Maximilian the Dreamer* (1913).

A 1240   Seton-Watson, R. W. *Maximilian I* (Westminster, 1902).

See also:

A 102 Poelnitz, G. von.

45   Austrian Habsburgs and the Empire (vol. III, ch. x)
The State of Germany (to 1618) (vol. IV, ch. x)
(See also the bibliographies, Sec. A, **21** and **46**).

General Studies

Several of the principal works on this period have already been mentioned.

A 1069   Ritter, M. *Deutsche Geschichte im Zeitalter der Gegenreformation und*

des Dreissigjährigen Krieges (1555–1648), Bibliothek deutscher Geschichte, vols. 1–3 (Stuttgart, 1889–1908); the standard narrative of
political events, though very weak on the social and economic side.

In English there are:

A 617　　Janssen, J. *History of the German people at the close of the middle ages*,
　　　　　already mentioned.

A 1070　　Ward, A. W. in *Cambridge Modern History*, already mentioned, vols.
　　　　　III and IV (Cambridge, 1904, 1906).

A 1241　　Brandi, K. *Gegenreformation und Religionskriege* (Leipzig, n.d.); the
　　　　　best short narrative.

Detailed Studies

A 1242　　Aubin, G. 'Bartolomäus Viatis. Ein Nürnburger Grosskaufmann
　　　　　vor dem Dreissigjährigen Kriege', *Vierteljahrschrift für Sozial- und
　　　　　Wirtschaftsgeschichte*, **33** (1940); an illuminating study of the outstanding
　　　　　merchant of the pre-war period.

A 1243　　Aubin, G. and Kunze, A. *Leinenerzeugung und Leinenabsatz im ostlichen
　　　　　Mitteldeutschland zur Zeit der Zunftkaufe. Ein Beitrag zur industriellen
　　　　　Kolonisation des deutschen Ostens* (Stuttgart, 1940); a remarkable work,
　　　　　vital for the industrial history of Germany.

A 1244　　Beutin, L. *Hanse und Reich im handelspolitischen Endkampf gegen Eng-
　　　　　land* (Berlin, 1929); throws light on the methods used by Rudolf II in
　　　　　exerting his authority.

A 1245　　—— *Der deutsche Seehandel im Mittelmeergebiet bis zu den Napoleonis-
　　　　　chen Kriegen* (Neumünster in Holstein, 1933); deals mainly with the
　　　　　late sixteenth and early seventeenth centuries.

A 1246　　Bibl, V. *Maximilian II, der rätselhafte Kaiser* (Hellerau bei Dresden,
　　　　　1929); scholarly, though not beyond controversy.

A 1247　　Ehrenberg, R. *Hamburg und England im Zeitalter der Königin Elisabeth*
　　　　　(Jena, 1896); very useful for the Hanseatic towns.

A 1248　　Hagedorn, B. *Ostfrieslands Handel und Schiffahrt im 16. Jahrhundert*
　　　　　(Berlin, 1910).

A 1249　　—— *Ostfrieslands Handel und Schiffahrt vom Ausgang des 16. Jahr-
　　　　　hunderts bis zum Westfälischen Frieden (1580–1648)* (Berlin, 1912);
　　　　　Hagedorn's are excellent monographs and are useful for the spread of
　　　　　Protestantism as well as for trade.

A 1250　　Lütge, F. 'Die wirtschaftliche Lage Deutschlands vor Ausbruch des
　　　　　Dreissigjährigen Krieges', *Jahrbücher für Nationalökonomie und Statistik*,
　　　　　170 (1958); a very important essay by a leading economic historian which
　　　　　challenges the view that the German economy was declining before
　　　　　1618.

A 1251　　Mecessennfy, G. *Geschichte des Protestantismus in Österreich* (Graz,
　　　　　1956); largely late sixteenth century.

See also:

A 882 Brodrick, J.; A 1182 Kellenbez, H.; A 1232 Carsten, F. L.

16   The Habsburg Lands (vol. IV, ch. xvii)
          (See also bibliography, Sec. A, 45.)

General Studies

A 1252   Domanovsky, A. *Die Geschichte Ungarns* (Munich/Leipzig, 1923).
A 1253   Hantsch, H. *Die Geschichte Österreichs* (2 vols., Vienna, 1947–50).
A 1254   Mayer, F. M. *Geschichte Österreichs* (Vienna, 1909).
A 1255   Pekař, J. *Dějiny Československé* (Czechoslovak history) (Prague, 1921).
A 1256   Szekfű, G. *Der Staat Ungarn* (Stuttgart/Berlin, 1918).

Detailed Studies

THE HISTORY OF INSTITUTIONS

A 1257   Bidermann, H. I. *Geschichte der österreichische Gesamt-Staatsidee 1526–1804* (Innsbruck, 1867).
A 1258   Fellner T. and Kretschmayr, H. *Die Österreichische Zentralverwaltung.* Part i—*Von Maximilian I bis zur Vereinigung der Österreichische und Böhmische Hofkanzlei (1749)*: vol. 1, *Geschichtliche Übersicht* (Vienna, 1907); vol. 2, *Aktenstücke (1491–1681)* (Vienna, 1907); (Veröffentlichungen der Kommission für neuere Geschichte Österreichs, nos. 5, 6, 7, 18, 29, 32, 35, 36, 42, 43, Vienna, 1907–).
A 1259   Hellbling, E. C. *Österreichische Verfassungs- und Verwaltungsgeschichte* (Vienna, 1956).
A 1260   Huber, A. *Geschichte Österreichs*, vol. 5 (Gotha, 1896).

See also:
A 400 Hartung, F.

DEMOGRAPHY AND SOCIETY

A 1261   Janáček, J. *Dějiny obchodu v předbělohorské Praze* (Prague, 1955); history of commerce at Prague before the battle of the White Hill.
A 1262   Keyser, E. *Die Bevölkerungsgeschichte Deutschlands* (3rd ed., Leipzig, 1943).
A 1263   Placht, O. *Lidnatost a společenská skladba českého státu v 16.–18. století* (Prague, 1957); population and social structure of the kingdom of Bohemia from the sixteenth to the eighteenth centuries.

See also:
A 127 Franz, G.

POLITICAL, ECONOMIC AND INTELLECTUAL DEVELOPMENT

A 1264   Coreth, A. *Österreichische Geschichtsschreibung in der Barockzeit 1620–1740* (Vienna, 1950).
A 1265   Denis, E. *La Bohême depuis la Montagne Blanche* (2nd ed., 1930); a now outdated work.
A 1266   Leitich, A. T. *Vienna gloriosa, Weltstadt des Barock* (Vienna, 1944).
A 1267   Novak, A. *Prague Baroque* (French trans., Prague, 1920).

A 1268 Redlich, O. 'Über Kunst und Kultur des Barocks in Österreich', *Archiv für österreichische Geschichte*, 115 (1943).

A 1269 Sturmberger, H. *Aufstand in Böhmen* (Munich/Vienna, 1959).

A 1270 Tapié, V-L. *The age of grandeur. Baroque art and architecture* (Eng. trans., New York, 1960); bibliography.

A 1271 Tibal, A. *L'Autrichien* (1936).

A 1272 Wandruska, A. *Das Haus Habsburg* (Vienna, 1956).

EASTERN AND NORTHERN EUROPE

47   Eastern Europe (vol. I, ch. xiii)

Many of the relevant books on the history of Poland, Bohemia and Hungary are referred to in the bibliographies, Sec. A, 12, 25 (pp. 22, 42–4). For Russia see bibliography, Sec. A, 49 (p. 80).

See also: Bohemia

A 1273 Bretholz, B. *Geschichte Böhmens und Mährens* (4 vols., Reichenberg, 1921–4).

A 1274 Prokeš, J. *Histoire Tchécoslovaque* (Prague, 1927).

                          Czechoslovakia
The best history is still:

A 1275 *Vlastivěda* (Czech Encyclopaedia), vol. 4, parts i and ii: Dějiny (History) (Prague, 1932–3).

Monographs on the period:

A 1276 Brock, P. *The political and social doctrines of the unity of Czech Brethren in the fifteenth and early sixteenth centuries* (The Hague, 1957).

A 1277 Truhlář, J. *Humanismus a humanisté v Čechách za krále Vladislava II (1471–1516)* (Prague, 1894).

                          Hungary

A 418   Hóman, B. and Szekfű, G. *Magyar történet*, vol. 2.

The most solid work on the period was done in the nineteenth century by V. Fraknói. Two of his works have been translated into German:

A 1278 V. Fraknói. *Matthias Corvinus, König von Ungarn* (Freiburg im Breisgau, 1891).

A 1279 —— *Ungarn vor der Schlacht bei Mohács* (Budapest, 1886).

48   The Ottoman Empire (1481–1520) (vol. I, ch. xiv)
        The Ottoman Empire (1520–66) (vol. II, ch. xvii)
        The Turkish Danger (vol. III, ch. xi)
        The Revival of Ottoman Power 1617–48 (vol. IV, ch. xx)
        The Ottoman Empire under Mehmed IV (vol. V, ch. xxi)
        The Retreat of the Turks 1683–1730 (vol. VI, ch. xix)

                          Bibliographies

A 1280 Pearson, J. D. *Index Islamicus 1906–55* (Cambridge, 1958), pp. 568–99.

A 1281   Pearson, J. D. *Index Islamicus Supplement 1956–60* (Cambridge, 1962), pp. 178 90.
These list articles and monographs relating to the Ottoman Turks.

A 1282   Sauvaget, J. *Introduction à l'histoire de l'Orient Musulman. Eléments de bibliographie*, Corrections et Supplément, Juillet 1946 (Initiation à l'Islam, no. 1. Institut d'Etudes Islamiques de l'Université de Paris), new and augmented issue, Cahen, C. (ed.) (1961), pp. 195 ff.

A 1283   Spuler, B. and Forrer, L. *Der Vordere Orient in Islamischer Zeit* (Wissenschaftliche Forschungsberichte, Geisteswissenschaftliche Reihe: Orientalistik, III. Teil) (Bern, 1954), pp. 193–233.

A 1284   Stavrianos, L. S. *The Balkans since 1453* (New York, 1958), pp. 873–946; will also serve as a bibliographical guide.

A 1285   *The Encyclopaedia of Islam* (4 vols., and supplement, Leiden and London, 1913–38); an indispensable work of reference containing numerous articles which, though uneven in quality, offer a rich store of information about the Ottoman Turks. A new and augmented edition has been in process of publication since 1954.

These provide useful guidance to the literature of travel in Ottoman lands:

A 1286   Weber, S. H. *Voyages and travels in Greece, the Near East and adjacent regions made previous to the year 1801* (Princeton, 1953).

A 1287   Ebersolt, J. *Constantinople Byzantine et les Voyageurs au Levant* (1918); an older work.

General Studies

A 1288   Hammer-Purgstall, J. von. *Geschichte des osmanischen Reiches* (10 vols., Pesth, 1827–35). (*Histoire de l'Empire Ottoman depuis son origine, jusqu'à nos jours* (18 vols., 1835–43); this work based in the main on Ottoman sources is still indispensable. The French translation corrects some errors.

A 1289   Jorga, N. *Geschichte des osmanischen Reiches* (5 vols., Gotha, 1908–13); at times confused and innacurate, but makes use of numerous Balkan sources.

A 1290   Zinkeisen, J. W. *Geschichte des osmanischen Reiches in Europa* (7 vols., Gotha, 1840–63); an excellent narrative.

See also:

A 464 Vaughan, D. M.; A 988 Albèri, E. *Le relazioni degli ambasciatori veneti al Senato* (ser. 3, 3 vols., Florence, 1840, 1844, 1855 and Appendix (vol. 15), Florence, 1863); the reports of the Venetian ambassadors are rich in acute observation and analysis.

Detailed Studies

1481–1520

A 1291   Ayalon, D. *Gunpowder and firearms in the Mamluk kingdom. A challenge to a mediaeval society* (London, 1956); the decline of the Mamluk sultanate in Syria and Egypt.

A 1292   Fisher, S. N. *The foreign relations of Turkey 1481–1512* (Illinois Studies in the Social Sciences, vol. 30, no. 1) (Urbana, Ill., 1948).

A 1293   Hinz, W. *Irans Aufsteig zum Nationalstaat im fünfzehnten Jahrhundert* (Berlin/Leipzig, 1936).

A 1294   Jansky, H. 'Die Eroberung Syriens durch Sultan Selim I', *Mitteilungen zur osmanischen Geschichte*, **2** (1926).

A 1295   Sanuto, M. *I Diarii* (Barozzi, N., Berchet, G., Fulin, R. and Stefani, F., eds.) (58 vols., Venice, 1879–1903); summarises a large number of Venetian documents relating to Ottoman affairs, 1496–1535.

A 1296   Stripling, G. W. F. *The Ottoman Turks and the Arabs 1511–74* (Illinois Studies in the Social Sciences, vol. 26, no 4) (Urbana, Ill., 1942).

1520–1566

A 1297   Charrière, E. *Négociations de la France dans le Levant* (Collection de documents inédits sur l'histoire de France, no. 29) (4 vols., 1848–60).

A 1298   *H. Dernschwams Tagebuch einer Reise nach Konstantinopel und Klein-asien (1553–5)* (Babinger, F., ed.) (Munich/Leipzig, 1923).

A 1299   Egli, E. *Sinan, der Baumeister osmanischer Glanzzeit* (Zürich, 1954).

A 1300   Forster, C. T. and Daniell, F. H. B. *The life and letters of Ogier Ghiselin de Busbecq* (1881).

A 1301   Fischer-Galati, S. A. *Ottoman imperialism and German protestantism 1521–53* (Harvard Historical Monographs, 43) (Cambridge, Mass., 1959).

A 1302   Gévay, A. von. *Urkunden und Actenstücke zur Geschichte der Ver-hältnisse zwischen Osterreich, Ungarn, und der Pforte im XVI und XVII Jahrhunderte* (3 vols., Vienna, 1838–42).

See also:

A 562 Lybyer, A.; A 1000 Merriman, R. B.

1566–1617

A 1303   Barozzi, N. and Berchet, G. *Relazioni degli stati Europei lette al Senato dagli Ambasciatori Veneti nel secolo XVII*, ser. 5 (Venice, 1866–72).

A 1304   Baumer, F. L. 'England, the Turk and the common corps of Christen-dom', *AHR*, **50** (1944).

A 1305   Berchet, G. *Relazioni dei Consoli Veneti nella Siria* (Turin, 1866).

A 1306   Hill, Sir George. *A history of Cyprus*, vol. 3 (Cambridge, 1948); on the Ottoman conquest of 1570–1.

A 1307   Lewis, B. 'Some reflections on the decline of the Ottoman Empire', *Studia Islamica*, **9** (Paris, 1958).

A 1308   Sanderson, John. *The Travels of…in the Levant 1584–1602*, Foster, Sir William (ed.) (Hakluyt Society, 2nd ser., vol. 67) (1931).

A 1309   Wood, A. C. *A history of the Levant Company* (Oxford, 1935).

See also:

A 77 Braudel, F.

The troubles inside Persia which gave the Ottomans a favourable prospect of success in the long Ottoman-Persian war of 1578–90 can be studied in:

A 1310 Bellan, L. *Chah 'Abbas Ier: sa vie, son histoire* (1932).
A 1311 Hinz, W. 'Schah Esma 'il II', *Mitteilungen des Seminars für orientalische Sprachen zu Berlin*, **36** (1933).
A 1312 Roemer, H. *Der Niedergang Irans nach dem Tode Isma 'ils des Grausamen (1577–81)* (Würzburg, 1939).

1617–1648

A 1313 Danon, A. 'Contributions à l'histoire des sultans Osman II et Mouçtafâ I', *Journal Asiatique*, 2nd ser., **14** (1919).
A 1314 Roe, Sir Thomas. *The Negotiations of...in his Embassy to the Ottoman Porte from the year 1621 to 1628 inclusive* (1740).
A 1315 Tongas, G. *Les Relations de la France avec l'empire ottoman durant la première moitié du XVIIe siècle* (Toulouse, 1942).

See also:

A 1105 Masson, P.

1648–1730

For bibliographical information see:

A 1316 Böhm, B. *Bibliographie zur Geschichte des Prinzen Eugen von Savoyen und seiner Zeit* (Vienna, 1943); useful for Eugene's campaigns against the Turks.
A 1317 Uhrlitz, K. *Handbuch der Geschichte Österreichs und seiner Nachbarländer Böhmen und Ungarn* (4 vols., Graz and Vienna, 1927–44).
A 1318 Arneth, A. von. *Prinz Eugen von Savoyen* (3 vols., Vienna, 1858).
A 1319 Bigge, W. *Der Kampf um Candia in den Jahren 1667–9* (Kriegsgeschichtliche Einzelschriften, Heft 26) (Berlin, 1899).
A 1320 d'Arvieux, L. *Mémoires...contenant ses voyages à Constantinople, dans l'Asie, la Syrie, la Palestine, l'Egypte et la Barbarie...* (Labat, J. B., ed.) (6 vols., 1735).
A 1321 *Conrad Jacob Hiltebrandts dreifache schwedische Gesandtschaftsreise nach Siebenbürgen, der Ukraine und Constantinopel, 1656–8* (Babinger, F., ed.) (Leiden, 1937).
A 1322 Jacob, I. *Beziehungen Englands zu Russland und zur Türkei in den Jahren 1718–27* (Basel, 1945).
A 1323 *Kara Mustafa vor Wien. Das türkische Tagebuch der Belagerung Wiens 1683* (Osmanische Geschichtsschreiber, Band 1), Kreutel, R. F., trans. (Graz, 1955).
A 1324 Klopp, O. *Das Jahr 1683 und der folgende grosse Türkenkrieg bis zum Frieden von Carlowitz 1699* (Graz, 1882).
A 1325 Mantran, R. *Istanbul dans la seconde moitié du XVIIe siècle. Essai d'histoire institutionelle, économique et sociale* (1962).
A 1326 Marsigli, L. F. *Stato Militare dell'Impero Ottomanno* (text in Italian and French, 2 parts (The Hague, 1732); a work of the first order,

indispensable for a sound knowledge of Ottoman military institutions in the times of the Köprülü viziers.

A 1327   Montagu, M. W. *Letters (1717–18)* (1934).

A 1328   Montecuccoli, R. *Opere* (Foscolo, U., ed.) (Milan, 1807–8), (Grassi, G., ed.) (Turin, 1821) (see also *Ausgewählte Schriften des Raimund Fürsten Montecuccoli* (Veltzé, A., ed.) (4 vols., Wien/Leipzig, 1899–1900); Montecuccoli gives in his 'Memorie' or 'Aforismi dell'Arte Bellica' much valuable information about the armies of the sultan.

A 1329   Osman Aga, *Leben und Abenteuer des Dolmetschers...Eine türkische Autobiographie aus der Zeit der grossen Kriege gegen Österreich* (Bonner Orientalische Studien, Neue Serie, Band 2) (Kreutel, R. F. and Spies, O., trans.) (Bonn, 1954).

A 1330   Pallis, A. A. *In the days of the Janissaries* (1951); based on the travel book of Evliyā, who journeyed far and wide through the Ottoman Empire in the middle of the seventeenth century.

A 1331   Redlich, O. *Weltmacht des Barock; Österreich in der Zeit Kaiser Leopolds I* (4th ed.) (Vienna, 1961); gives a full account of the wars between the Ottoman Empire and Austria.

A 1332   Roeder von Diersburg, P. *Des Markgrafen Ludwig Wilhelm von Baden Feldzüge wider die Türken* (2 vols., Carlsruhe, 1839–42).

A 1333   Rycaut, P. *The present state of the Ottoman Empire* (1668).

A 1334   —— *History of the Turkish Empire (1623–77)* (1679–80) (vol. 2 of R. Knolles, *The Turkish history* (1687–1700)).

A 1335   —— *The history of the Turks (1679–99)* (1700) (vol. 3 of R. Knolles, *op. cit.*).

The works of Rycaut, based on contemporary sources and on his own experiences in the Levant, offer even now the fullest account available in English of Ottoman affairs during the seventeenth century.

A 1336   Shay, M. L. *The Ottoman Empire from 1720 to 1734 as revealed in the despatches of the Venetian Baili* (Illinois Studies in the Social Sciences, vol. 27, no. 3) (Urbana, Ill., 1944).

A 1337   Sumner, B. H. *Peter the Great and the Ottoman Empire* (Oxford, 1949).

A 1338   Vandal, A. *Les Voyages du Marquis de Nointel (1670–80)* (1900).

A 1339   Veltzé, A. 'Die Hauptrelation des kaiserlichen Residenten in Constantinopel Simon Reniger von Reningen 1649–66', *Mittheilungen des k. und k. Kriegs-Archivs*, new series, 12 (1900).

A 1340   Wright, W. L. *Ottoman statecraft. The book of counsel for Vizirs and Governors of Sari Mehmed Pasha* (Princeton, 1935).

49   Russia 1462–1583 (vol. II, ch. xviii)
Russia (vol. IV, ch. xix (*b*))

General Studies

Students are recommended to consult such general histories of Russia as:

A 1341   Florinsky, M. T. *Russia. A history and an interpretation* (2 vols., New York, 1953).

A 1342   Milyoukov, P. N. and others. *Histoire de Russie* (3 vols., 1932–3).
A 1343   Platonov, S. F. *History of Russia* (Bloomington, Ind., 1964).
A 1344   Stählin, K. *Geschichte Russlands* (Stuttgart, 1961).
A 1345   Vernadsky, G. V. *A history of Russia* (New Haven, 1961).
A 1346   Klyuchevsky, V. O. *A History of Russia* (Eng. trans., 5 vols., 1911–31); the collected works of this most famous of Russian historians have recently been republished:
A 1347   —— *Sochincniya* (8 vols., Moscow, 1956–9); vol. 7 contains two important articles: *Proiskhozhdenie krepostnogo prava v Rossii* and *Podushnaya podat i otmena kholopstva v Rossii*, and vol. 8 his *Sostav predstavitelstva na Zemskikh Soborakh drevneĭ Rusi* (on the sixteenth-century sobors); the earlier volumes contain his famous lectures.

Two more recently published works are:

A 1348   Clarkson, J. D. *A history of Russia* (New York, 1960); lively and scholarly.
A 1349   Rimscha, H. von. *Geschichte Russlands* (Sammlung Wissen und Leben, 8) (Wiesbaden, 1960); an excellent account from the earliest times to the present.

The fifteenth and sixteenth centuries

A 1350   *Ocherki istorii SSSR* (Period feodalizma IX–XV vv. part 2; Period feodalizma konets XV v.—nachalo XVII v. (Moscow, 1953–5); the standard Soviet history, gives much attention to social and economic aspects.
A 1351   Solov'ev, S. M. *Istoriya Rossii s drevneishikh vremen*, vols. 5, 6 (2nd ed., St Petersburg, 1897); straightforward factual account, now somewhat out of date.
A 1352   Vernadsky, G. *Russia at the dawn of the modern age* (Yale, 1959); the reigns of Ivan III and Vasily III, also describes West Russia in the sixteenth century; useful bibliography.

DETAILED STUDIES

A 1353   Bazilevich, K. V. *Vneshnyaya politika Russkogo tsentralizovannogo gosudarstva vtoraya polovina XV veka* (Leningrad, 1952); the best Russian account of Ivan III's foreign policy.
A 1354   Cherepnin, L. V. *Russkie feodal'nye arkhivy XIV–XV vekov* (2 vols., Moscow/Leningrad, 1946–51); valuable information on treaties signed by Ivan III.
A 1355   Fennell, J. L. I. *Ivan the Great of Moscow* (1961); the most detailed account of Ivan III's reign in English.
A 1356   —— *The Correspondence between Prince A.M. Kurbsky and Tsar Ivan IV of Russia 1564–79* (Cambridge, 1955); Russian text and English translation of the famous correspondence.
A 1357   Forsten, G. V. *Bor'ba iz-za gospodstva na Baltiĭskom more v XV i XVI stoletiyakh* (St Petersburg, 1884); for Russian–Scandinavian relations.
A 1358   Herberstein, Baron, S. von. *Rerum Moscoviticarum Commentarii* (Eng. trans. Hakluyt Society, 1851); invaluable description of life in Muscovy under Vasily III.

A 1359   Jablonowski, H. *Westrussland zwischen Wilna und Moskau* (Leiden, 1955); excellent account of position of Lithuania's Ruthenian subjects.

A 1360   Kazakova, N. A. and Lur'e, Ya. S. *Antifeodal'nye ereticheskie dvizheniya na Rusi XIV-nachala XVI veka* (Moscow/Leningrad, 1955); the best work on the heresy of the Zhidovstvuyushchie.

A 1361   Korolyuk, V. D. *Livonskaya Voĭna* (Moscow, 1954); straightforward description of Ivan IV's Livonian war.

A 1362   Leontovich, V. *Die Rechtsumwälzung unter Iwan dem Schrecklichen* (Frankfurt, 1951).

A 1363   Maslennikova, N. N. *Prisoedinenie Pskova k russkomu tsentralizovan-nomu gosudarstvu* (Leningrad, 1955); the best work on the annexation of Pskov.

A 1364   Philipp, W. *Iwan Peresvetov und seine Schriften zur Erneuerung des Moskauer Reiches* (Osteurop. Forschungen, Hoetzsch, O. (ed.), new series, 20) (Königsberg/Berlin, 1935).

A 1365   Sadikov, P. A. *Ocherki po istorii oprichniny* (Moscow/Leningrad, 1950); the most detailed Soviet account of Ivan IV's *Oprichnina*.

A 1366   Schaeder, H. *Moskau, das dritte Rom: Studien zur Geschichte der politischen Theorien in der slawischen Welt* (Hamburg, 1929).

A 1367   Smirnov, I. I. *Ocherki politichsekoĭ istorii Russkogo gosudarstva 30–50-kh godov XVI veka* (Moscow/Leningrad, 1958); the most detailed Soviet account of the first three decades of Ivan IV's reign.

A 1368   —— 'Vostochnaya Politika Vasiliya III', *Istoricheskie Zapiski*, no. 27; the best account of Vasily III's Tartar policy.

A 1369   Waliskewski, K. *Ivan le Terrible* (1904); has the defects of the rest of his work but is useful as an introduction for non-Russian readers.

The seventeenth century

A 1350   *Ocherki istorii SSSR*, the relevant volume in this series is: Period feodalizma: XVII v. (Moscow, 1955).

The writings of N. I. Kostomarov, though almost a hundred years old, are still not devoid of interest. See:

A 1370   Kostomarov, N. I. *Sobranie sochineniĭ* (8 vols., St Petersburg, 1903–6); *Cherty narodnoĭ yuzhno-russkoĭ istorii* and *Bunt Stenki Razina* (vol. 1), *Smutnoe Vremya v. Mosk. gosudarstve* (vol. 2), his biography of Bogdan Khmelnitsky (vol. 4), and more material on the annexation of the Ukraine in vol. 5, and two useful articles in vol. 8: *Ocherk domashneĭ zhizni i nravov velikorusskago naroda v XVI–XVII vv.* and *Ocherk torgovli mosk. gosudarstva.*

A 1371   Nolde, Baron, B. *La formation de l'empire russe; études, notes et docu-ments* (Collection historique de l'institut d'études slaves, XV) (2 vols., 1952–3); a fundamental work on Russian expansion in Asia, the Ukraine and the Caucasus, which the author did not live to complete. Most of it deals with the eighteenth century, but in the first volume there is a good deal of material on eastward expansion in the seventeenth century.

S. F. Platonov is the author of a number of most useful works on the Muscovite period. See:

A 1372   Platonov, S. F. *Sochineniya* (published in 2 vols., St Petersburg, 1913); the first volume contains a large number of useful articles, the second his *Drevnerusskiya skazaniya i povesti o smutnom vremeni XVII v.*, an examination of the sources available for the Time of Troubles.

Platonov produced a definitive history of this period which has become the standard work:

A 1373   —— *Ocherki po istorii smuty v moskovskom gosudarstve XVI–XVII vv.* (4th ed., Moscow, 1937).

Useful introductory works by him are:

A 1374   —— *Ivan Grozny* (Berlin, 1924); in Russian.
A 1375   —— *Boris Gudonov* (Prague, 1924); in Russian.
A 1376   —— *La Russie Moscovite* (1923); in French.
A 1377   Stashevsky, E. D. *Ocherki po istorii tsarstvovaniya Mikhaila Fedorovicha*, part i (Kiev, 1913).
A 1378   Waliszewski, K. *Le Crise révolutionnaire en Russie 1584–1614* (1906).
A 1379   —— *Le Berceau d'une dynastie: Les premiers Romanovs* (1909); has a useful bibliography of the older literature. See comment on A 1369 for Waliszewski's work in general.

DETAILED STUDIES

TIME OF TROUBLES

A 1380   Fleischhacker, H. *Russland zwischen 2 dynastien (1598–1613): eine Untersuchung über die Krise in der obersten Gewalt* (Studien zur Osteurop. Geschichte, herausgegeben von Prof. Dr H. Ubersberger, N.F., vol. 1) (Baden bei Wien, 1933).
A 1381   Zolkiewski, Hetman S. *Expedition to Moscow: a Memoir* (Giertych, J., trans. and ed.) (Polonica series, no. i) (London, 1959); an important source.

FOREIGN POLICY

A 1382   Fleischhacker, H. *Die staats- und völkerrechtlichen Grundlagen der moskauischen Aussenpolitik, 16–17 Jhd.* (Jahrbücher für Geschichte Ost-europas, Beiheft 1) (Breslau, 1938); a fundamental study.
A 1383   Hrushevsky, M. *A history of Ukraine* (Frederiksen, O. J., ed.) (New Haven, 1941).

For Anglo-Russian relations see:

A 1384   Lubimenko, I. *Les Relations commerciales et politiques de l'Angleterre avec la Russie avant Pierre le Grand* (French trans. 1933).

A 1385   Konovalov, S.; in several articles in *Oxford Slavonic Papers*, vol. 1 (1950), 2 (1951), 4 (1953), 8 (1958), 10 (1960).

Two important works in Russian are:

A 1386 Novosel'sky, A. A. *Bor'ba moskovskogo gosudarstva s tatarami v I-oĭ polovine XVII v.* (Moscow/Leningrad, 1948).

A 1387 Vaĭnshteĭn, O. L. *Rossiya i 30-letnyaya voĭna 1618–48 gg.* (Leningrad, 1947).

CHURCH AND CULTURAL AFFAIRS

A 1388 Ammann, A. M. *Abriss der ostslawischen Kirchengeschichte* (Vienna, 1950); the standard work.

On the raskol see:

A 1389 Avvakum, *The life of the archpriest...by himself* (Eng. trans. 1924); an important source.

A 1390 Conybeare, F. C. *Russian dissenters* (Harvard Theological Studies, x) (Cambridge, Mass., 1921).

A 1391 Pascal, P. *Avvakum et les débuts du raskol* (1938).

A 1392 Platonov, S. F. *Moskva i zapad* (Berlin, 1926); Russia and the West.

See also:

A 523 Medlin, W. K.

ECONOMIC AND SOCIAL HISTORY

A 1393 Kulisher, J. *Russische Wirtschaftsgeschichte* (German trans., Jena, 1925); an excellent introduction.

A 1394 Amburger, E. *Die Familie Marselis: Studien zur russischen Wirtschafts-geschichte* (Giessener Abhandlungen zur Agrar- und Wirtschafts-forschungen des europäischen Ostens, vol. 4) (Giessen, 1957); contains much interesting material.

A 1395 Miller, A. *Essai sur l'histoire des institutions agraires de la Russie centrale du XVIe au XVIIIe siècle* (1926); valuable for the genesis of the commune.

Two important works in Russian:

A 1396 Got'e, Yu. V. *Zamoskovny kraĭ v XVII v.* (2nd ed., Moscow, 1937).

A 1397 Smirnov, P. P. *Posadskie lyudi i ikh klassovaya bor'ba do serediny XVII v.* (2 vols., Moscow/Leningrad, 1947–8).

POLITICAL HISTORY

A 1398 Keep, J. H. L. 'The regime of Filaret, 1619–33', *SEER*, **38** (1960); discusses the policies of the Patriarch Filaret.

A 1399 —— 'The decline of the Zemsky Sobor' [medieval representative assembly], *ibid.* **36** (1957).

ASIAN EXPANSION

There are two first-class works on this subject:

A 1400 Fisher, R. H. *The Russian fur trade, 1550–1700* (Berkeley, Calif., 1943).

A 1401 Lantzeff, G. V. *Siberia in the seventeenth century: a study of the colonial administration* (Berkeley, Calif., 1943).

These are vols. 31 and 30 respectively of the University of California Publicationo in Hiotory.

See also:

A 1402   Kerner, R. J. *The urge to the sea: the course of Russian history* (Berkeley/ Los Angeles, Calif., 1946).

CONTEMPORARY ACCOUNTS

The most instructive of these is by the German traveller:

A 1403   Olearius, A. *Vermehrte newe Beschreibung der Muscowitischen und Persischen Reyse...*(Schleswig, 1656); this is available in a modern German edition, published in East Berlin, 1959; there is also a seventeenth century English translation.

50   **Poland and Lithuania (vol. III, ch. xii)**

General Studies

General works on the history of Poland, covering much longer periods, include:

A 412   *Cambridge History of Poland*, vol. 1, Reddaway, W. F., and others (eds.) (Cambridge, 1950).

A 1404   *Encyklopedia staropolska* (Encyclopaedia of Poland before the partitions), vols. 1–2 (Warsaw, 1939); supplies the most important information on various topics and contains about 4000 illustrations.

A 1405   Lipiński, E. *Studia nad historią polskiej myśli ekonomicznej* (Studies on the history of economic ideas in Poland) (Warsaw, 1956); bibliography. Marxist point of view, but contains valuable information.

A 1406   Konopczyński, W. *Dzieje Polski nowożytnej* (Modern History of Poland), vol. 1 (1506–1648) (Cieszyn, 1936); contains bibliographies with books in languages other than Polish.

A 1407   Kutrzeba, S. and Vetulani, A. *Historia ustroju Polski* (Constitutional History of Poland (Warsaw, 1949); very useful bibliography. See also in German, *Grundriss der polnischen Verfassungsgeschichte* (Berlin, 1912).

A 1408   Rutkowski, J. *Historia gospodarcza Polski* (Economic history of Poland) (Warsaw, 1953); most useful bibliography of books in various languages, which also covers primary sources. French trans. of an earlier ed.: *Histoire économique de la Pologne avant les partages* (1928).

See also:

A 793 Völker, K.

For Polish culture see:

A 1409   Barycz, H. *The development of university education in Poland* (Warsaw, 1957).

A 1410   Brückner, A. *Dzieje kultury polskiej* (History of Polish culture), vols. 1–4 (Cracow, 1930–1, 1946).

A 1411   Kot, S. *Historia wychowania* (History of education), vols. 1, 2 (Lwów, 1934); bibliography.

A 1412 Kot, S. *Rzeczpospolita Polska w literaturze politycznej Zachodu* (Poland in the political literature of the West) (Cracow, 1919).

Detailed Studies

DOMESTIC POLITICS AND FOREIGN AFFAIRS

A 1413 Biaudet, H., Karttunen, K. J., Pårnånen, J. A. deal with the election of Zygmunt Wasa and Swedo-Polish relations in excellent studies published in French in: *Annales Academiae Scientiarum Fennicae*, ser. B. vols. 2, 5, 8, 10, 12, 28 (1910–15, 1934).

A 1414 Champion, P. *Henri III roi de Pologne, 1573–5*, vols. 1–2 (1943, 1951); valuable, though the author is not familiar enough with the Polish sources.

A 1415 *Etienne Báthory, roi de Pologne, prince de Transylvanie* (Académie des sciences Hongroises, Académie Polonaise des sciences et des lettres (Cracow, 1935); by Hungarian and Polish historians, exhaustive bibliography.

A 1416 Herbst, S. *Wojna inflancka, 1600–2* (The war in Livonia, 1600–2) (Warsaw, 1938); very useful bibliography.

A 1417 Lechicki, C. *Mecenat Zygmunta III i życie umysłowe na jego dworze* (Zygmunt as a patron of the arts and the intellectual life of his court) (Warsaw, 1932).

A 1418 Lepszy, K. *Walka stronnictw w pierwszych latach panowania Zygmunta III* (The struggle of the parties during the early years of the reign of Zygmunt III) (Cracow, 1929).

A 1419 —— *Rzeczpospolita Polska w dobie sejmu inkwizycyjnego* (The Commonwealth of Poland during the period of the Parliament of the Inquisition) *1589–92* (Cracow, 1939).

A 1420 Noailles, H. de. *Henri de Valois et la Pologne en 1572*, vols. 1–3 (1867); still contains much valuable information.

A 1421 Skwarczyński, P. discusses the election of Henry of Valois in *SEER*, **88** (1958) and in:

A 1422 *Revue internationale d'histoire politique et constitutionnelle* (1955). He deals with the next two elections in:

A 1423 *Teki historyczne*, **10** (London 1959).

A 1424 Sobieski, W. *Pamiętny sejm 1606 roku* (The parliament of 1606) (Warsaw, 1913).

A 1425 Szelągowski, A. *Der Kampf um die Ostsee, 1544–1621* (Munich, 1916); the Polish edition of 1921 has useful footnotes.

A 1426 Tyszkowski, K. *Poselstwo Lwa Sapiehy w Moskwie 1600 roku* (Embassy of L. Sapieha to Moscow in 1600) (Lwów, 1927).

A 1427 Vetulani, A. *Polskie wpływy polityczne w Prusiech książęcych* (Polish political influences in Ducal Prussia) (Gydnia, 1939).

A 1428 Zakrzewski, W. *Po ucieczce Henryka, dzieje bezkrólewia* (After the flight of Henry: the history of the interregnum) *1574–5* (Cracow, 1878); still valuable.

See also:

A 561 *Revue internationale d'histoire militaire* 1952, no. 12.

CHURCH AFFAIRS

A 1429 Chodynicki, K. *Kościół prawosławny a Rzeczpospolita polska* (The Orthodox Church and the Polish Commonwealth) *1370–1632* (Warsaw, 1934); excellent, with useful bibliography.

A 1430 Jorgensen, K. *Oekumenische Bestrebungen unter den polnischen Protestanten bis zum Jahre 1645* (Copenhagen, 1942).

A 1431 Lewicki, K. *Książę Konstanty Ostrogski a unja brzeska* (Prince K. Ostrogski and the Union of Brest) *1596* (Lwów, 1933).

A 1432 Sobieski, W. *Nienawiść wyznaniowa tłumów za rządów Zygmunta III* (Mass religious hatred in the reign of Zgymunt III) (Warsaw, 1902).

A 1433 —— *Polska a Hugonoci po nocy św. Bartłomieja* (Poland and the Huguenots after the Massacre of St Bartholomew) (Cracow, 1910).

See also:

A 767 Kot, S.; A 775 Wilbur, E. M.; A 887 Halecki, O.

ECONOMIC AND SOCIAL HISTORY

A 1434 Hinton, R. W. K. *The eastland trade and the common weal in the seventeenth century* (Cambridge, 1959).

A 1435 Hoszowski, S. *Handel Gdańska w okresie 15–18 wieku* (Danzig's trade between the fifteenth and eighteenth centuries) (Cracow, 1960).

A 1436 —— 'The revolution of prices in Poland in the sixteenth and seventeenth centuries', *Acta Poloniae Historica*, II (Warsaw, 1959).

A 1437 Małowist, M. 'The economic and social development of the Baltic countries from the fifteenth to the seventeenth centuries'. *Econ. HR*, 2nd ser., **12** (1959).

A 1438 Pawiński, A. *Skarbowość w Polsce i jej dzieje za Stefana Baterogo* (Finance in Poland and its history in the reign of King Stephen Báthory), Źródła dziejowe, vol. 8 (Warsaw, 1881).

A 1439 Rybarski, R. *Handel i polityka handlowa Polski w 16 stuleciu* (The trade and trade policy of Poland in the sixteenth century), vols. 1–2 (Poznań, 1928–9).

A 1440 —— *Wielickie żupy solne w latach 1497–1694* (The Wielicka salt mines in the years 1497–1594) (Warsaw, 1932).

A 1441 Szelągowski, A. *Z dziejów wspolzawodnictwa Anglii i Niemiec, Rosyi i Polski* (History of economic rivalry between England and Germany, Russia and Poland) (Lwów, 1910), and his article:

A 1442 Szelągowski, A. and Gras, N.S.B., 'The Eastland Company in Prussia 1579–85', *TRHS*, 3rd ser., **6** (1912).

A 1443 —— *Pieniądz i przewrót cen w 16 i 17 wieku w Polsce* (Currency and the price revolution in the sixteenth and seventeenth centuries in Poland) (Lwów, 1902).

A 1444 Tarnawski, A. *Działalność gospodarcza Jana Zamoyskiego, kanclerza i hetmana wielkiego koronnego* (The economic enterprises of J. Zamoyski, crown chancellor and hetman) *1572–1605* (Lwów, 1935).

51   Poland (vol. IV, ch. xix (a))
          Poland to the death of John Sobieski (vol. V, ch. xxiv)
                              General Studies
          There are few books dealing with this period in languages other than
          Polish. For bibliographical material see the following articles:

A 1445   Dobrowolska, W. 'Czasy Zygmunta III. Bibliografja, stan badań,
          postulaty', *Księga pamiątkowa ku czci profesora dra W. Sobieskiego*, I
          (Cracow, 1932), 72–113.
A 1446   Herbst, S. 'Czasy Zygmunta III', *Przegląd historyczny*, 34 (1937–8),
          215–23.
A 1447   Tomkiewicz, W. 'Czasy Władysława IV i Jana Kazimierza w historio-
          grafii ostatnich lat dwudziestu', *Przegląd historyczny*, 34 (1937–8),
          224–39.
A 1448   Woliński, J. 'Czasy Sobieskiego (1674–96) w historiografii XX w.',
          Przegląd historyczny, 30 (1932), 133–45.
A 1449   —— 'Czasy Sobieskiego (1674–96) w historiografii ostatniego cztero-
          lecia (1932–6)', *Przegląd historyczny*, 34 (1937–8), 240–4.

          Studies of leading figures of the century:

A 1450   Czapliński, Wł. 'Władysław IV. (Próba charakterystyki)', *Roczniki
          historyczne*, 17 (1948), 126–42.
A 1451   Czermak, W. 'Jan Kazimierz. Próba charakterystyki', *Kwartalnik
          historyczny*, 3 (1889), 1–27.
A 1452   Forst-Battaglia, O. 'Michał Wiśniowiecki. Ein Kapitel aus einer
          politische Geschichte Polens', *Festschrift zur Feier des zweihundert
          jährigen Bestandes des Haus-, Hof- und Staatarchivs*, II (Vienna, 1951),
          339–48.
A 1453   —— *Jan Sobieski, König von Polen* (Einsiedeln/Zürich, 1946).
A 1454   Laskowski, O. *Sobieski, King of Poland* (Glasgow, 1944).

                              Detailed Studies

A 1455   Godziszewski, Wł. *Polska a Moskwa za Władysława IV* (Cracow, 1930).
A 1456   Konopczyński, L. *Le liberum veto. Etude sur le développement du principe
          majoritaire* (1930).
A 1457   Kubala, L. *Jerzy Ossoliński*, (2nd ed., Warsaw, 1924); Ossoliński was
          one of the major Polish statesmen of the seventeenth century.
A 1458   Lepszy, K. (ed.). *Polska w okresie drugiej wojny północnej 1655–60*,
          vols. 1–3 (Warsaw, 1957); vol. 3 contains a comprehensive bibliography.
A 1459   Lorenz, R. *Türkenjahr 1683. Das Reich im Kampf um den Ostraum*
          (2nd ed., Vienna, 1934).
A 1460   Ogonowski, Zb. *Z zagadnień tolerancji w Polsce XVII wieku* (Warsaw,
          1958).
A 1461   Piwarski, K. 'Osłabienie znaczenia międzynarodowego Rzeczypospolitej
          w drugiej połowie XVII w.', *Roczniki historyczne*, 23 (1957), 221–58.
A 1462   Prochaska, A. *Hetman Stanisław Żółkiewski* (Warsaw, 1927); deals with
          the war of 1609–11 with Russia.

A 1463 Rybarski, R. *Skarb i pieniądz za Jana Kazimierza, Michała Korybuta i Jana III* (Warsaw, 1939).
A 1464 Sobieski, W. *Nienawiść wyznaniowa tłumów za rządów Zygmunta III* (Warsaw, 1902).
A 1465 Suwara, F. *Przyczyny i skutki klęski cecorskiej 1620 r.* (Cracow, 1930).
A 1466 Tyszkowski, K. *Wojna o Smoleńsk 1613–15* (Lwów, 1932).
A 1467 Wójcik, Zb. *Traktat andruszowski 1667 roku i jego geneza* (Warsaw, 1959).

See also:
A 1078 Paul, J.; A 1425 Szelągowski, A.

52   Sweden and the Baltic (vol. III, ch. xiii)
        Sweden and the Baltic (vol. IV, ch. xiii)
        (On the Reformation in Scandinavia, see Sec. A, 24.)

For bibliographical guides see:
A 1468 Bring, S. E. *Bibliografisk handbok till Sveriges historia* (Stockholm, 1934).
A 559   Roberts, M. *Gustavus Adolphus* (2 vols., 1953, 1958).
A 1469 Tham, W. *Den svenska utrikespolitikens historia*, 1:2 (1560–1648) (Stockholm, 1960).

General Studies

SWEDEN

A 1470 Andersson, I. *A history of Sweden* (Eng. trans. 1955).
A 1471 Hecksher, E. F. *Sveriges ekonomiska historia från Gustav Vasa*, I:I (Stockholm, 1933).
A 1472 Hildebrand, E. *Gustav Vasas Söner* (*Sveriges historia till våra dagar*, V) (Stockholm, 1926).
A 1473 —— (revised by Jacobson, G.), *Kristina och Karl X Gustav* (*Sveriges historia till våra dagar*, VII) (Stockholm, 1926).
A 1474 Rosén, J. and Carlsson, St. *Svensk historia*, I (Stockholm, 1962).
A 1475 Wittrock, G. *Gustav II Adolf* (*Sveriges historia till våra dagar*, VI) (Stockholm, 1927).

DENMARK

A 1476 Arup, E. *Danmarks Historie*, II (Copenhagen, 1932).
A 1477 Engelstoft, P. *Det Danske Folks Historie*, IV: *Christian IVs Tidsalder* (Copenhagen, 1928).
A 1478 Fridericia, J. A. *Danmarks Riges Historie*, IV (1588–1699) (Copenhagen, n.d.).
A 1479 Friis, A., Linvald, A. and Mackeprang, M. (eds.), *Schultz Danmarkshistorie*, II–III (Copenhagen, 1941–2).

Detailed Studies

1560–1611

A 1480 Almquist, H. *Sverige och Ryssland 1595–1611* (Uppsala, 1907).
A 1481 Andersson, I. *Erik XIV* (4th ed., Stockholm, 1951).

A 1482 Andersson, I. *Erik XIV:s engelska underhandlingar. Studier i svensk diplomati och handelspolitik.* Eng. summary (Lund, 1935).

A 1483 —— 'Om Hamletsdramats nordiska miljö', in *Svenskt och europeiskt femtonhundratal.* German summary (Lund, 1943).

A 1484 Arnell, S. *Die Auflösung des Livländischen Ordensstaates. Das schwedische Eingreifen und die Heirat Johanns von Finnland 1558–62* (Lund, 1937).

A 1485 Attman, A. *Den ryska marknaden i 1500-talets baltiska politik 1558–95* (Lund, 1944).

A 1486 Dalgård, S. *Dansk-Norsk Hvalfangst 1615 60. En Studio ovor Danmark-Norges Stilling i Europæisk Merkantil Expansion,* Eng. summary (Copenhagen, 1962).

A 1487 Federley, B. *Kunglig Majestät, svenska kronan och furstendömet Estland 1592–1600* (Helsinki, 1946).

A 1488 Friis, A. *Alderman Cockayne's project and the cloth trade. The commercial policy of England in its main aspects* (Copenhagen, 1927).

A 1489 Hermansson, Å. *Karl IX och ständerna. Tronfrågan och författningsutvecklingen i Sverige 1598–1611.* German summary (Stockholm/ Uppsala, 1962).

A 1490 Lepszy, K. 'The Union of the Crowns between Poland and Sweden in 1587', *Poland at the XIth International Congress of Hist. Sciences in Stockholm* (Warsaw, 1960).

A 1491 Nilsson, S. A. *Kampen om de adliga privilegierna 1526–94,* German summary (Lund, 1952).

A 1492 Odén, B. *Rikets uppbörd och utgift. Statsfinanser och finansförvaltning under senare 1500-talet,* German summary (Lund, 1955).

A 1493 —— *Kopparhandel och statsmonopol. Studier i svensk handelshistoria under senare 1500-talet,* German summary (Stockholm, 1960).

A 1494 Palme, S. U. *Sverige och Danmark 1596–1611* (Uppsala, 1942).

A 1495 Rauch, G. von. 'Zur Geschichte des schwedischen Dominium Maris Baltici. Ein Forschungsbericht', *Die Welt als Geschichte* 1952, Heft 2; with bibliographical notes.

A 1496 *Riketsvapen och flagga* (The arms and flag of the realm) (Stockholm, 1960).

A 1497 Tham, W. *Axel Oxenstierna. Hans ungdom och verksamhet intill år 1612* (Stockholm, 1935).

See also:

A 119 Christensen, A.

1611–1654

For Gustavus Adolphus see:

A 559 Roberts, M.; A 1076 Ahnlund, N.; A 1078 Paul, J.; already mentioned.

For the Baltic question in general:

A 1498 Hornborg, E. *Kampen om Östersjön* (Stockholm, 1945).

A 1499 Schäfer, D. 'Der Kampf um die Ostsee im 16. und 17. Jahrhundert', *Sybels Historische Zeitschrift,* **83** (N.F. 47) (1889).

See also:

A 1109 Hill, C. E.; A 1425 Szelągowski, A.

On Swedish foreign policy:

A 1500 Ahnlund, N. *Gustaf Adolf inför tyska kriget* (Stockholm, 1918); definitive account of Swedish policy in the years before 1630.

A 1501 Arnoldsson, S. *Svensk-fransk krigs- och fredspolitik i Tyskland 1634–6* (Göteborg, 1937).

A 1502 Lindqvist, Å. *Politiska förbindelser mellan Sverige och Danmark 1648–55* (Lund, 1944).

A 1503 Lorents, Y. *Efter Brömsebrofreden. Svenska och danska förbindelser med Frankrike och Holland 1645–9* (Uppsala, 1916).

A 1504 Lundgren, S. *Johan Adler Salvius. Problem kring freden, krigsekonomien och maktkampen* (Lund, 1945).

A 1505 Olofsson, S. I. *Efter Westfaliska freden. Sveriges yttre politik 1650–4* (Stockholm, 1957).

A 1506 Schybergson, M. G. *Sveriges och Hollands diplomatiska förbindelser 1621–30* (Helsingfors, 1881); large collection of documents.

A 1507 Thyresson, B. *Sverige och det protestantiska Europa från Knäredfreden till Rigas erövring* (Uppsala, 1928).

A 1508 Voges, U. *Der Kampf um das Dominium Maris Baltici 1629–45. Schweden und Dänemark vom Frieden zu Lübeck bis zum Frieden vom Brömsebro* (Zeulenroda, 1938).

On Danish foreign policy see in addition:

A 1509 Fridericia, J. A. *Danmarks ydre politiske Historie i Tiden fra Freden i Lybek til Freden i Prag* (Copenhagen, 1876); a magisterial study.

A 1510 —— *Danmarks ydre politiske Historie i Tiden fra Freden i Prag til Freden i Brömsebro* (Copenhagen, 1881).

A 1511 Schweitzer, V. 'Christian IV von Dänemark und die niederdeutschen Städte i. d. J. 1618–25'. *Historisches Jahrbuch*, 25 (1904).

A 1512 Schybergson, M. G. *Underhandlingarna om en evangelisk allians åren 1624–5* (Helsingfors, 1880).

A 1513 Willmans, E. *Der Lübecker Friede 1629* (Bonn, 1904).

For Dutch foreign policy in the baltic see:

A 1514 Kernkamp, G. W. *De sleutels van de Sont. Het aandeel van de Republiek in den Deensch-Zweedschen oorlog van 1644–5* (The Hague, 1890).

A 1515 Kolkert, W. J. *Nederland en het Zweedsche Imperialisme* (Deventer, 1908); ch. i deals with this period.

A 1516 Wiese, E. *Die Politik der Niederländer während des Kalmarkrieges...und ihr Bündnis mit Schweden (1614) und den Hansestädten (1616)* (Heidelberg, 1903).

For French interest in the Baltic see:

A 1517 Tongas, A. *L'Ambassadeur Louis Deshayes de Cormenin* (1937); should be used with caution, and also:

A 131 Hauser, H.

EUROPE OVERSEAS

53   Expansion as a concern of all Europe (vol. I, ch. xvi)

Many of the books in this bibliography cover topics in the expansion of Europe overseas during the whole of the sixteenth and early seventeenth centuries, and this list should be used in conjunction with the later lists in this section.

General Studies

A 1518   *Die überseeische Welt und ihre Erschliessung* (Historia Mundi, viii, Valjavac, F. ed.) (Bern/Munich, 1959); the most useful collection of brief studies of national expansion, with some comparative material.

A 1519   Baker, J. N. L. *A history of geographical discovery and exploration* (2nd ed., 1937); the standard textbook.

A 1520   Panikkar, K. M. *Asia and western dominance* (1953); essential for the Asiatic approach to European expansion.

A 1521   Parry, J. H. *The Age of reconnaissance* (1963).

A 1522   Penrose, B. *Travel and discovery in the Renaissance 1420–1620* (Cambridge, Mass., 1960); the most useful general narrative, good on the literature of travel.

Detailed Studies

CARTOGRAPHY AND NAVIGATION

A 1523   Anthiaume, A. *Evolution et enseignement de la science nautique en France* (2 vols., 1920).

A 1524   Cortesão, A. *Cartografia e cartógrafos portugueses dos séculos XV e XVI* (2 vols., Lisbon, 1935); an indispensable collection.

A 1525   Crone, G. R. *Maps and their makers* (1953).

A 1526   Franco García, S. *Historia del arte y ciencia de navegar* (2 vols., Madrid, 1947).

A 1527   Nordenskiöld, A. E. *Facsimile-atlas to the early history of cartography* (Stockholm, 1889, repr. 1961).

A 1528   —— *Periplus* (Stockholm, 1897, repr. 1962); these two works remain the starting point for the study of the maps of the period.

A 1529   Skelton, R. A. *Explorers' maps* (1958).

See also:

A 318 Waters, D. W.

CULTURAL INFLUENCES

For the effects of the discoveries on literature see:

A 1530   Atkinson, G. *Les Nouveaux Horizons de la Renaissance française* (1935).

A 1531   Chinard, G. *L'exotisme américain dans la littérature française au XVIe siècle* (1911); the best introduction to the subject.

A 1532   Gonnard, R. *La Légende du bon sauvage* (1946).

A 1533   Romeo, R. 'Le scoperte americane nella coscienza italiana del cinquecento', *Rivista storica italiana*, 65 (1953).

For the impact of the discoveries on geography see:

A 1534 Atkinson, G. *La Littérature géographique française de la Renaissance* (1927), *Supplément* (1936); an annotated bibliography.

A 1535 Barlow, R. *A brief summe of geographie* [1541] (Hakluyt Society, 1932).

A 1536 Dainville, F. de. *La Géographie des humanistes* (1940); deals mainly with the Jesuits.

A 1537 Dupront, A. 'Espace et humanisme', Bibliothèque d'Humanisme et Renaissance, *Travaux et Documents*, 8 (1946).

A 1538 Gallois, L. *Les Géographes allemands de la Renaissance* (Lyons, 1890).

See also:

A 315 Taylor, E. G. R.; A 316 Taylor, E. G. R.

CONTACTS BETWEEN ORIENTAL AND WESTERN CILIVIZATIONS

A 1539 Boxer, C. R. *Fidalgos in the Far East, 1550–1770* (The Hague, 1948).

A 1540 Boxer, C. R. (ed.). *South China in the sixteenth century* (Hakluyt Society, 1953).

A 1541 Chew, S. C. *The crescent and the rose* (New York, 1937); cultural contacts between England and the Middle East.

A 1542 Hudson, G. F. *Europe and China* (1931, repr. Boston, 1961); the only systematic outline, going down to 1800.

A 1543 Kammerer, A. *La Découverte de la Chine par les Portugais au XVIe siècle* (Leyden, 1944).

A 1544 Morales Padrón, F. *Fisonomía de la conquista Indiana* (Seville, 1955); useful as a brief Spanish approach to the problems presented by the barbarian peoples overseas.

A 1545 Penrose, B. *Urbane travellers* (Philadelphia, 1942).

A 1546 Sansom, G. B. *The western world and Japan* (1950); the early chapters form the best introduction to the renewed cultural and other contacts of the Renaissance.

See also:

A 894 Boxer, C. R.; A 896 Cronin, V.; A 899 Hanke, L. U.; A 900 Hanke, L. U.

THE PRICE REVOLUTION

A 90 Hamilton, E. J. *American treasure and the price revolution in Spain 1501–1650;* the basic monograph.

A 1547 —— 'The history of prices before 1750', *Rapports du Congrès international des Sciences Historiques*, 1 (Uppsala, 1960), pp. 144–64; provides a guide to the literature since 1934.

THE MAJOR CHANNELS OF TRADE

A 1548 Chaunu, P. *Les Philippines et le Pacifique des Ibériques* (1960); complementary to: A 83 Chaunu, H. and P.

A 1549 Gentil da Silva, J. (ed.). *Stratégie des affaires à Lisbonne entre 1595 et 1607* (1956).

A 1550 Kernkamp, J. H. *De handel op den vijand, 1572–1609* (2 vols., Utrecht, 1931–4); shows how the Dutch commerce with Spain continued throughout the war.

A 1551 Magalhães-Godinho, V. *L'Economie de l'empire portugais aux XVe et XVIe siècles* (1959).

A 1552 Ramsay, G. D. *English overseas trade in the centuries of emergence* (1957); the only recent general survey, deals with the overseas world only slightly.

A 1553 Schurz, W. L. *The Manila galleon* (New York, 1939).

See also:

A 70 Ehrenberg, R.; A 77 Braudel, F.; A 81 Boxer, C. R.; A 1194 Mauro, F.

INTERACTIONS BETWEEN INDIVIDUAL COUNTRIES AND THE OVERSEAS WORLD

ITALY

A 1554 Almagiá, A. *Gli italiani primi esploratori dell'America* (Rome, 1937); the best general account of the Italian contribution.

A 1555 Morison, S. E. *Christopher Columbus, admiral of the ocean sea* (1 and 2 vol. eds.) (Boston, 1942).

A 1556 Verlinden, C. *Précédents médiévaux de la colonie en Amérique* (Pan-American Institute of Geography and History, Mexico City, 1954); mainly uses Italian instances, but their application is general. More specific is:

A 1557 —— 'Italian influences in Iberian colonisation', *HAHR*, **33** (1953).

FRANCE

A 1558 *Les Classiques de la colonisation*, vol. 1. Les Français en Amérique pendant la première moitié du XVIe siècle, Julien, C. A., Herval, R. and Beauchesne, T. (eds.) (1946); vol. 2. Les Français en Amérique pendant la deuxième moitié du XVIe siècle, part i, Le Brésil et les Brésiliens, Lussagnet, S. (ed.) (1953), part ii, Les Français en Floride, Julien, C. A. and Lussagnet, S. (eds.) (1958); vol. 3, Les voyages de Samuel Champlain, Deschamps, H. (ed.) (1951).

A 1559 Biggar, H. P. *The precursors of Jacques Cartier* (Ottawa, 1911).

A 1560 —— *The voyages of Jacques Cartier* (Ottawa, 1924).

A 1561 —— *A collection of documents relating to Jacques Cartier and the Sieur de Roberval* (Ottawa, 1930), and the Champlain Society's editions of Champlain and Lescarbot, see A 1768, A 1769 below, cover all the major documents.

A 1562 Anthiaume, A. *Cartes marines, constructions navales, voyages de découverte chez les Normands, 1500–1650* (2 vols., 1920); illustrates development in a characteristic centre.

A 1563 Bishop, M. *Champlain. The life of fortitude* (1949); a sympathetic biography.

A 1564 Guenin, E. *Ango et ses pilotes* (1901); illustrates the beginnings of French overseas maritime activity.

A 1565   Julien, C. A. *Les Voyages de découverte et les premiers établissements* (1947), an excellent general treatment.

ENGLAND

Contemporary works, re-published, for instance, by the Hakluyt Society, appear under the name of the editor, not of the original author.

A 1566   Andrews, K. R. (ed.). *English privateering voyages to the West Indies, 1588–95* (Hakluyt Society, 1959).
A 1567   Connell-Smith, G. *Forerunners of Drake* (1954); deals with England's earliest participation in the Spanish-American trade.
A 1568   Foster, Sir W. *England's quest of eastern trade* (1933); the various indirect methods attempted to tap the oriental trade and the early history of the East India Company.
A 1569   Foster, Sir W. (ed.). *The voyages of Sir James Lancaster to Brazil and the East Indies, 1591–1603* (Hakluyt Society, 1940).
A 1570   Hakluyt, Richard, *Principall navigations* (1589, re-published in facsimile (Hakluyt Society, 1962) and *Principal navigations* (the edition of 1598–1600) (12 vols., Glasgow, 1903–4).
A 1571   Harlow, V. T. (ed.). *The discoverie of Guiana* (1928).
A 1572   —— *Ralegh's last voyage* (1932); documents on the Gilbert–Raleigh ventures.
A 1573   Parks, C. B. *Richard Hakluyt and the English voyages* (2nd ed., New York, 1961); very good on the literature of the voyages.
A 1574   Quinn, D. B. *Raleigh and the British Empire* (2nd ed., 1962); a brief outline.
A 1575   —— 'The argument for the English discovery of America between 1480 and 1494', *Geographical Journal*, **127** (1961); introduces the new perspectives on North American discovery made possible by documentary finds.
A 1576   Quinn, D. B. (ed.). *The voyages and colonising enterprises of Sir Humphrey Gilbert* (2 vols., Hakluyt Society, 1940).
A 1577   —— *The Roanoke voyages 1584–90* (2 vols., Hakluyt Society, 1955). These two works contain documents on the Gilbert–Raleigh ventures.
A 1578   Rowse, A. L. *Sir Richard Grenville* (1937).
A 1579   Stefansson, V. *The three voyages of Martin Frobisher* (2 vols., 1938).
A 1580   Taylor, E. G. R. (ed.). *The writings and correspondence of the two Richard Hakluyts* (2 vols., Hakluyt Society, 1935); prints the main documents relating to them, but see also: A 1570 *Principall navigations* above.
A 1581   Taylor, E. G. R. (ed.). *The troublesome voyage of Captain Edward Fenton 1582–3* (Hakluyt Society, 1959).
A 1582   Wagner, H. R. *Sir Francis Drake's voyage round the world* (San Francisco, 1926).
A 1583   Willan, T. S. *The Muscovy Merchants of 1555* (Manchester, 1953); deals with the economic history of a new branch of English commerce.
A 1584   —— *Studies in Elizabethan foreign trade* (Manchester, 1959); includes a full treatment of the English trade with Morocco.

A 1585   Willan, T. S. 'Some aspects of English trade with the Levant in the sixteenth century', *EHR*, **70** (1955).

A 1586   Williamson, J. A. *The age of Drake* (3rd ed., 1952); the best general account.

A 1587   —— *The Cabots and the Bristol voyages under Henry VIII* (Hakluyt Society, 1962); discussion and documents. This does not supersede:

A 1588   —— *The voyages of the Cabots and English discovery under Henry VII and Henry VIII* (1929); for the years 1509–47.

A 1589   —— *Hawkins of Plymouth* (1949); does not entirely supersede:

A 1590   —— *Sir John Hawkins* (Oxford, 1927); important for naval as well as colonial developments.

A 1591   Wright, I. A. (ed.). *Spanish documents concerning English voyages to the Caribbean, 1527–68* (1929).

A 1592   —— *Documents concerning English voyages to the Spanish Main, 1569–80* (1932).

A 1593   —— *Further English voyages to Spanish America 1583–94* (1951).

(All three edited for the Hakluyt Society).

See also:

A 460 Rowse, A. L.; A 465 Willan, T. S.; A 587 Mattingly, G.; A 1309 Wood, A. C.

THE NETHERLANDS

Contemporary works appear under the name of their modern editors (see 'England' above).

A 1594   Boxer, C. R. *The Dutch in Brazil 1624–54* (Oxford, 1957); a valuable monograph.

A 1595   —— *Salvador de Sá and the struggle for Brazil and Angola 1602–86* (1952).

A 1596   Burnell, A. C. and Tiele, P. A. *The voyage of Jan Huyghen van Linschoten to the East Indies* (2 vols., Hakluyt Society, 1885); the English trans. of 1598.

A 1597   Clark, Sir, G. N. and Eysinga, W. J. M. van. *The colonial conferences between England and the Netherlands in 1613–15* (2 vols., Bibliotheca Visseriana, xv, xvii (Leyden, 1940–51)); illustrative of the difference between Dutch and English views of expansion.

A 1598   Colenbrander, H. T. *Koloniale Geschiedenis* (3 vols., The Hague, 1925–6); the standard history, with:

A 1605   Stapel, F. W., below.

A 1599   Davies, D. W. *A primer of Dutch seventeenth century overseas trade* (The Hague, 1961).

A 1600   Elias, J. E. *Het voorspel van den eersten engelschen oorlog* (2 vols., The Hague, 1920).

A 1601   Hall, D. G. E. *A history of South-east Asia* (rev. ed. 1958).

A 1602   Hyma, A. *The Dutch in the Far East* (Chicago, 1942); with A 1606 Vlekke, B. H. M., below, the only survey from the Dutch side available in English.

A 1603   Keuning, J. (ed.). *De tweede schipvaart der Nederlanders naar Oost-Indie onder Jacob Cornelis van Neck en Wybrant Warwijck* (Linschoten Vereeniging, in 3 parts, The Hague, 1938–51).
A 1604   Mollema, J. C. (ed.). *De eerste schipvaart der Hollanders naar Oost-Indie 1595–7* (Linschoten Vereeniging, The Hague, 1935).
A 1605   Stapel, F. W. (ed.). *Geschiedenis van Nederlandsch Indië* (5 vols., Amsterdam, 1938–40).
A 1606   Vlekke, B. H. M. *Nusantara* (2nd ed., New York, 1960). See A 1602 Hyma, A. above.

See also:
A 128 Glamann, K.

54   The New World: 1. Portuguese Expansion (vol. i, ch. xv)
                              General Studies
          Two general histories of Portugal are:
A 1607   Livermore, H. V. *History of Portugal* (Cambridge, 1947).
A 1608   Peres, D. *História de Portugal. Edição monumental* (9 vols., Barcelos, 1928–54).

A 1609   Prestage, E. *The Portuguese pioneers* (1933); the best general survey in English.

          The essential works in Portuguese include:
A 1610   Cortesão, A. Z. *Portugaliae monumenta cartographica* (Lisbon, 1960).
A 1611   Cortesão, J. *Os descobrimentos portugueses* (2 vols., Lisbon, 1960–1).
A 1612   Peres, D. *História dos descobrimentos portugueses* (Oporto, 1943).

          The documents are collected in:
A 1613   Magalhães Godinho, V. *Documentos sôbre a expansão portuguesa* (3 vols., Lisbon, 1956).
A 1614   Silva Marques, J. M. da. *Descobrimentos portugueses* (vol. 1 and supplement) (Lisbon, 1944).

          For bibliographical indications see:
A 1615   Walsh, D. V. *Catalog of the Wm. B. Greenlee collection* (Newberry Library, Chicago, 1953).

                              Detailed Studies
                         HENRY THE NAVIGATOR
A 1616   Axelson, E. 'Prince Henry the navigator and the discovery of the searoute to India', *Geographical Journal*, **127** (1961).
A 1617   Beazley, Sir C. R. *Prince Henry the navigator* (New York, 1895).
A 1618   Major, R. H. *Prince Henry the navigator* (1868); now much dated.
A 1619   Martins, O. *The golden age of Prince Henry* (1914).

THE EXPLORATION OF AFRICA

A 1620 Blake, J. W. *European beginnings in West Africa 1454–1578* (1937).
A 1621 Blake, J. W. (trans. and ed.). *Europeans in West Africa 1450–1560, documents...* (2 vols., Hakluyt Society, 1941–2).
A 1622 Crone, G. R. *The voyages of Cadamosto* (Hakluyt Society, 1937).
A 1623 Kimble, G. H. T. (ed.). Duarte Pacheco Pereira, *Esmeraldo de Situ Orbis* (Hakluyt Society, 1937).
A 1624 Peres, D. *Os mais antigos roteiros da Guiné* (Lisbon, 1952).
A 1625 —— *Viagens de Luis de Cadamosto e Pedro de Sintra* (Lisbon, 1948).

THE FIRST VOYAGES TO INDIA AND BRAZIL

A 1626 Greenlee, W. B. *The Voyage of Pedro Alvares Cabral to Brazil and India* (Hakluyt Society, 1937).
A 1627 Ravenstein, E. G. *A Journal of the first voyage of Vasco da Gama, 1497–99* (Hakluyt Society, 1898).

THE PORTUGUESE IN BRAZIL

A 1628 Malherio Dias, C. *História da colonização portuguesa do Brasil* (3 vols., Oporto, 1921–4).

55   **Europe and the East (vol. II, ch. xx)**

The best sources for this period are undoubtedly the Portuguese. The following titles represent a selection of works available in other languages, though some titles in Portuguese are also given.

A 1629 Barros, J. de. *Ásia*, vols. 1–8 in the editions of Barros and Couto (Lisbon, 1777–88).
A 1630 Boxer, C. R. *Three historians of Portuguese Asia* [Barros, Couto, Bocarro] (Macau, 1948); a masterly evaluation of the work of three major contemporary Portuguese historians.
A 1631 —— 'The Portuguese in the Far East 1500–1800', in *Portugal and Brazil, an introduction* (Livermore, H. V. and Entwistle, W. J., eds.) (1953); contains invaluable references and a bibliography.
A 1632 Castanheda, F. Lopes de. *História do descobrimento e conquista da Índia pelos Portugueses* (4 vols., Coimbra, 1924–33).
A 1633 Couto, D. de. *Ásia*, vols. 10–24 of the edition of Barros and Couto (Lisbon, 1777–88).
A 1634 Galvão, A. *Tratado dos Descobrimentos* (Oporto, 1944).
A 1635 Jann, A. *Die katholischen Missionen in Indien, China und Japan, ihre Organisation und das portugiesische Patronat vom 15. bis ins 18. Jahrhundert* (Paderborn, 1915); the standard work, but the author is hostile to the Portuguese. See also A 1640 Silva Rego's work below.
A 1636 Pereira, S. G. *The temporal and spiritual conquest of Ceylon* (3 vols., Colombo, 1930).
A 1637 Pieris, P. E. *Ceylon: the Portuguese era* (2 vols., Colombo, 1923–4).

A 1638   Pieris, P. E. and Fitzler, H. *Ceylon and Portugal* (Leipzig, 1927).

A 1639   Prestage, E. *Afonso de Albuquerque, Governor of India. His life, conquests, and administration* (Watford, 1929).

A 1640   Silva Rego, A. da. *História das Missões do Padroado Português do Oriente*, vol. I (India, 1500–42) (Lisbon, 1949); see A 1635 Jann, A. above.

A 1641   Whiteway, R. S. *Rise of the Portuguese power in Asia, 1497–1550* (1899); critical of Portuguese policy.

A 1642   Winstedt, R. O. *History of Malaya* (Singapore, 1935); contains an account of the Portuguese arrival and settlement in Malaya.

See also:

A 894 Boxer, C. R.; A 1540 Boxer, C. R.; A 1546 Sansom, G. B.; A 1609 Prestage, E.

**56   Colonial Development and International Rivalry outside Europe: Asia and Africa (vol. III, ch. xvii b)
The European Nations in the East (vol. IV, ch. xxi)
Europe and Asia (vol. V, ch. xvii, 1 and 2)**

Asia and the Pacific

EXPLORATION AND TRAVEL

A 1643   *Abel Janszoon Tasman and the discovery of New Zealand*, with an introduction by Beaglehole, J. C. (Wellington, N.Z., 1942).

A 1644   Beaglehole, J. C. *The exploration of the Pacific* (2nd ed., 1947); bibliography.

A 1645   Foster, Sir W. (ed.). *Early travels in India 1583–1619* (Oxford, 1921).

A 1646   Heawood, E. *A history of geographical discovery in the seventeenth and eighteenth centuries* (Cambridge, 1912).

A 1647   Heeres, J. E. *The part borne by the Dutch in the discovery of Australia 1606–1765* (Leiden and London, 1899).

A 1648   Oaten, E. F. *European travellers in India during the fifteenth, sixteenth and seventeenth centuries* (1909).

GENERAL STUDIES, COVERING THE ACTIVITIES OF SEVERAL POWERS

A 1649   Ballard, G. A. *Rulers of the Indian ocean* (1927); deals with the maritime rivalries of Portuguese, Dutch and English.

A 1650   Lannoy, C. de and Linden, H. Vander. *Histoire de l'expansion coloniale des peuples européens* (3 vols., Brussels, 1907–21); vol. 1 covers Spain and Portugal, vol. 2 the Netherlands and Denmark.

ON PORTUGAL

A 1651   Boxer, C. R. *Four centuries of Portuguese expansion 1415–1825: a succinct survey* (Johannesburg, 1961).

A 1652   Duffy, J. *Shipwreck and empire* (Cambridge, Mass., 1955); an account of Portuguese maritime disasters 1550–1650.

A 1653   Faria y Sousa, M. de. *Ásia portuguesa* (6 vols, Oporto, 1945–7); reprint
         of a seventeenth-century work.
A 1654   Jayne, K. G. *Vasco da Gama and his successors 1460–1580* (1910).

See also:

A 81 Boxer, C. R.; A 1642 Winstedt, R. O.

THE ENGLISH IN INDIA

A 1655   *Cambridge history of the British Empire*, vol. IV, *British India 1497–1858*,
         Dodwell, H. H. (ed.) (Cambridge, 1929) [also published as *Cambridge
         history of India*, vol. V]; extensive bibliographies.
A 1656   Hunter, Sir W. W. *A history of British India* (2 vols., 1899–1900);
         covers the period up to the union of the companies in 1708.
A 1657   Rawlinson, H. G. *British beginnings in western India 1579–1657* (Oxford,
         1920).
A 1658   Wilbur, M. E. *The East India Company and the British Empire in the
         Far East* (Stanford, 1945); a general survey of the history of the English
         company.

Source material is contained in:

A 1659   Birdwood, Sir G. and Foster, W. (eds.). *The first letter book of the
         East India Company* (1893).
A 1660   Foster, Sir W. (ed.). *The English factories in India: a calendar of docu-
         ments* (13 vols., Oxford, 1906–27); covers the years 1618–69. A new
         series, edited by Sir Charles Fawcett (4 vols., Oxford 1936–55) covers
         the years 1670–84.
A 1661   Sainsbury, E. B. (ed.). *A calendar of the court minutes of the East India
         Company 1635–70* (8 vols., Oxford, 1907–29).

On the economic history of India see:

A 1662   Khan, Sir Shafaat Ahmad. *The East India trade in the seventeenth
         century* (Oxford, 1923).
A 1663   Krishna, Bal. *Commercial relations between India and England (1601 to
         1757)* (London, 1924).
A 1664   Moreland, W. H. *India at the death of Akbar* (1920).
A 1665   —— *From Akbar to Aurangzeb* (1923).

Both Moreland's books deal with the indigenous economies of India.

A 1666   Morse, H. B. *The chronicles of the East India Company trading to
         China 1635–1834* (5 vols., Oxford, 1926–9); vol. I (1926) goes up to
         the mid-eighteenth century.
A 1667   Mukerjee, Radhakamal. *The economic history of India 1600–1800*
         (London and New York, 1955).

See also:

A 1568 Foster, Sir W.

THE DUTCH

A 1668   Boxer, C. R. *Jan Compagnie in Japan 1600–1850* (2nd ed., The Hague, 1950).
A 1669   Graaf, H. J. de. *Geschiedenis van Indonesië* (The Hague, 1949).
A 1670   Klaveren, J. J. van. *The Dutch colonial system* (Rotterdam, 1953).
A 1671   Klerck, E. S. de. *History of the Netherlands East Indies* (2 vols., Rotterdam, 1938).
A 1672   Leur, J. C. van. *Indonesian trade and society. Essays in Asian social and economic history* (The Hague, 1955).

Important source material is contained in:

A 1673   Colenbrander, H. T. (ed.). *Jan Pietersz. Coen: Bescheiden omtrent zijn bedrijf in Indië* (6 vols., The Hague, 1919–34); vol. 6 is a biography of Coen by Colenbrander.
A 1674   Jonge, J. K. J. de, and others. *De Opkomst van het Nederlandsche gezag in oost-Indië* (15 vols., The Hague, 1862–1909: 2nd series, 3 vols., 1886–95).

Contacts between Europe and the East

A 1675   Charles, Père. 'Europe and the Far East', in *European civilization, its origin and development*, Eyre, E. (ed.), vol. 7 (*The relations of Europe with non-European peoples*) (Oxford, 1939).
A 1676   Clark, Sir G. N. *Science and social welfare in the age of Newton* (2nd ed., Oxford, 1949); has a brief treatment.

See also:
A 889 Latourette, K. S.

CHINA AND JAPAN

See:
A 1542 Hudson, G. F.; A 1546 Sansom, G. B.; and A 1668 Boxer, C. R. already mentioned.

A 1677   Appleton, W. W. *A cycle of Cathay. The chinese vogue in England during the seventeenth and eighteenth centuries* (New York, 1951).
A 1678   Fitzgerald, C. P. *China. A short cultural history* (rev. ed., 1950).
A 1679   Needham, J. *Science and civilisation in China*, vol. 3 (Cambridge, 1959); deals with the scientific contribution of the Jesuits.
A 1680   Pinot, V. *La Chine et la formation de l'esprit philosophique en France (1640–1740)* (1932).
A 1681   Reichwein, A. *China and Europe. Intellectual and artistic contacts in the eighteenth century* (Eng. trans., 1925).
A 1682   Soothill, W. E. *China and the West* (Oxford, 1925).

See also:
A 1543 Kammerer, A.

On Christian missions see:

A 1683   Bernard, H. *Aux portes de la Chine. Les missionaires du seizième siècle 1514–88* (Tientsin, 1933).

A 1684   Jenkins, R. C. *The Jesuits in China and the legation of Cardinal de Tournon* (1894).
A 1685   Latourette, K. S. *History of christian missions in China* (1929).
A 1686   Rowbotham, A. H. *Missionary and mandarin. The Jesuits at the court of China* (Berkeley, Calif., 1942).

Trade between England and China is dealt with in:

A 1687   Eames, J. B. *The English in China 1600–1843* (1909).
A 1688   Pritchard, E. H. *Anglo-Chinese relations during the seventeenth and eighteenth centuries* (Univ. of Illinois studies in the social sciences, xvii) (Urbana, Ill., 1929).

For travellers in India and Central Asia see:

A 1689   Bernier, F. *Travels in the Mogul Empire 1656–68* (Constable, A. and Smith, V. A., trans. and eds.) (2nd ed., 1914).
A 1690   Fryer, J. *A new account of East India and Persia* (Crooke, W., ed.) (2 vols., Hakluyt Society, 1909, 1912).
A 1691   Manucci, N. *Storia do Mogor or Mogul India 1653–1708* (Irvine, W., trans. and ed.) (4 vols., Indian Texts series, 1907–8).
A 1692   Tavernier, J. B. *Travels in India* (Crooke, W., ed.) (2 vols., Oxford, 1925).
A 1693   Wessels, C. *Early Jesuit travellers in central Asia 1603–1721* (The Hague, 1924).

AFRICA
General Studies

A 1694   Bovill, E. W. *Caravans of the old Sahara* (Oxford, 1933).
A 1695   —— *The golden trade of the Moors* (Oxford, 1958). Both deal with the trans-Saharan caravan trade.
A 1696   Donnan, E. *Documents illustrative of the history of the slave trade to America*, vol. 1 (1441–1700) (Washington, D.C., 1930).
A 1697   Duffy, J. *Portuguese Africa* (Cambridge, Mass., 1959); a full study.
A 1698   Wyndham, H. A. *The Atlantic and slavery* (1935).

WEST AFRICA

A 1699   Claridge, W. W. *A history of the Gold Coast and Ashanti* (2 vols., 1915).
A 1700   Fage, J. D. *Ghana. A historical interpretation* (Madison, Wisc., 1961).
A 1701   —— *An introduction to the history of West Africa* (3rd ed., Cambridge, 1962).
A 1702   Gray, J. M. *A history of the Gambia* (Cambridge, 1940).
A 1703   Ward, W. E. F. *A history of the Gold Coast* (1949).

See also:

A 1620 Blake, J. W.; A 1621 Blake, J. W. (ed.).

EAST AFRICA

A 1704   Oliver, R. and Mathew, G. (eds.). *History of East Africa*, vol. 1 (Oxford, 1963); has chapters on both the coast and the interior and a bibliography.

A 1705   Boxer, C. R. and Azevedo, C. de. *Fort Jesus and the Portuguese in Mombasa 1593–1729* (1960).
A 1706   Coupland, Sir R. *East Africa and its invaders from the earliest times to... 1856* (2nd ed., Oxford, 1956).
A 1707   Gray, J. M. *History of Zanzibar from the middle ages to 1856* (1962).

ETHIOPIA

A 1708   Mathew, D. *Ethiopia. The study of a polity, 1540–1935* (1947).
A 1709   Beckingham, C. F. and Huntingford, G. W. B. *Some records of Ethiopia 1593–1646* (Hakluyt Society, 1954).
A 1710   —— *The Prester John of the Indies...being the narration of the Portuguese Embassy to Ethiopia in 1520...*by Father Francisco Alvares (2 vols., Hakluyt Society, 1961).

SOUTHERN AFRICA

A 1711   Axelson, E. *South-east Africa 1488–1530* (1940).
A 1712   —— *Portuguese in South-east Africa 1600–1700* (Johannesburg, 1960); both these works have bibliographies.
A 1713   Lobato, A. *A expansão portuguesa em Moçambique de 1498 a 1530* (2 vols., Lisbon, 1954).
A 1714   Theal, G. M. *History and ethnography of South Africa before 1795* (3 vols., 2nd ed., 1910).
A 1715   —— *Records of South-eastern Africa* (9 vols., 1898–1903).

There are several books on South Africa before 1806 by S. R. Welch (published between 1935 and 1951); for these see:

A 1716   Boxer, C. R. in *Journal of African History*, 1 (1960).

57   The New World: Spaniards in the New World (vol. 1, ch. xv, 2.)

The most comprehensive guide to the many bibliographies on Spain in America is:

A 1717   Jones, C. K. *A bibliography of Latin American bibliographies* (2nd ed., rev., Washington, Govt. Printing Office, 1942); contains more than 3,000 items.

A very full critical list of current publications is contained in:

A 1718   *Handbook of Latin American Studies* (Harvard Univ. Press, 1936–50, Univ. of Florida Press, 1951–); published annually.
A 391   Merriman, R. B. *The rise of the Spanish Empire...* (4 vols.), already mentioned and A 455, covers the whole story from the reign of Ferdinand and Isabella to that of Philip II.

Of the many published collections of documents relating to the discovery of America by Europeans, and to the early Spanish expeditions there, the most important are:

A 1719   Cortés Society, *Documents and narratives concerning the discovery and conquest of Latin America* (5 vols., New York, 1917–24).

A 1720   Fernández de Navarette, M. *Colección de los viages y descubrimientos que hicieron por mar los Españoles* (5 vols., Madrid, 1825–37).

A 1721   Reale Commissione Colombiana, *Raccolta di documenti*, pubblicati dalla R.C.C. nel quarto centenario dalla scoperta dell'America (Rome, 1892).

The cartographical results of the discoveries can best be seen in the great collection of reproductions published by the duke of Alba:

A 1722   *Mapas españoles de América, siglos xv–xvii* (Madrid, 1951).

On Columbus himself see:

A 1555   S. E. Morison, *Christopher Columbus admiral of the ocean sea* (1942).

A 1723   Loven, S. *Origins of the Tainan Culture* (Göteborg, 1935); describes the native peoples whom Columbus found.

On the Bulls of Demarcation there are two outstanding articles:

A 1724   Linden, H. Vander. 'Alexander VI and the demarcation of the maritime and colonial domains of Spain and Portugal 1493–4', *AHR*, **22** (1916).

A 1725   Staedler, E. 'Die *Donatio Alexandrina* und die *Divisio Mundi* von 1493', *Archiv für Katholisches Kirchenrecht* (Mainz, 1937).

The best sources of information on Vespucci are:

A 1726   Markham, C. R., trans. and ed. *Letters of Amerigo Vespucci* (Hakluyt Society, 1894).

A 1727   Vignaud, H. *Améric Vespucci* (1917).

Standard works on the peoples of the middle-American mainland are:

A 1728   Morley, S. G. *The ancient Maya* (Stanford, 1947).

A 1729   Vaillant, G. C. *The Aztecs of Mexico* (New York, 1944).

On the activities of the Spaniards down to the fall of Mexico:

A 1730   Anderson, C. L. G. *Life and letters of Vasco Núñez de Balboa* (New York, 1941).

A 1731   Kirkpatrick, F. A. *The Spanish Conquistadores* (1946); a very able brief summary.

A 1732   Maudslay, A. P., trans. and ed., Díaz del Castillo, B. *The true history of the conquest of New Spain* (5 vols., Hakluyt Society, 1908–16); the best of all contemporary *relaciones*, by a soldier in Cortés' army.

A 1733   McNutt, F. A. (ed.). *The letters of Cortés* (2 vols., New York, 1908).

A 1734   Prescott, W. H. *History of the conquest of Mexico* (3 vols., New York, 1842 and many later editions); a famous classic, outmoded in many details but still valuable.

A 1735   Wright, I. A. *The early history of Cuba 1492–1586* (New York, 1916).

58   The New World 1521–1580 (vol. II, ch. xix)

The largest and most authoritative history of Spanish imperial rule in America is:

A 1736   Ballesteros y Beretta, A. (ed.). *Historia de América y de los pueblos americanos* (25 vols. in course of publication, Barcelona, 1946–).

The best account in English of the economy and administration of the Indies under the Hapsburgs is:

A 1737 Haring, C. H. *The Spanish Empire in America* (rev. ed.) (New York, 1953).

Two major seventeenth-century publications, one a treatise, the other a code of legislation, describe the whole government of the Indies and contain much sixteenth-century information:

A 1738 Solórzano Pereira, J. de. *Política Indiana* (Madrid, 1647).
A 1739 *Recopilación de leyes de los reynos de las Indias* (4 vols., Madrid, 1681).

There are two published collections of particular importance for the sixteenth century:

A 1740 *Colección de documentos inéditos relativos al descubrimiento, conquista y colonización de las posesiones españolas en América y Oceanía* (42 vols., Madrid, 1864–84).

A 1741 *Colección de documentos inéditos relativos al descubrimiento, conquista y organización de las antiguas posesiones españolas de ultramar* (21 vols., Madrid, 1884–1932).

On the native peoples of South America the principal work of reference is:

A 1742 Steward, J. H. (ed.). *Handbook of South American Indians* (6 vols., Smithsonian Institution, Washington, 1946–50).

On the high civilisations see:

A 1743 Means, P. A. *Ancient civilisations of the Andes* (New York, 1931).
A 1744 —— *The fall of the Inca Empire and the Spanish rule in Peru* (New York, 1932).
A 1745 Prescott, W. H. *History of the conquest of Peru* (2 vols., New York, 1847); the best known account of this subject. Most of the contemporary *relaciones* of the conquest of Peru, and of the wars which followed, have been published in translation by the Hakluyt Society.

On the various aspects of settlement and organisation the following are useful:

A 1746 Chevalier, F. *La Formation des grandes domaines au Mexique* (1952); an excellent account of early colonial economics.
A 1747 Kubler, G. *Mexican architecture of the sixteenth century* (2 vols., New Haven, 1948); the theme is wider than the title implies.
A 1748 Parry, J. H. *The audiencia of New Galicia in the sixteenth century* (Cambridge, 1948).
A 1749 Schäfer, E. *El consejo real y supremo de las Indias* (2 vols., Seville, 1935, 1947).
A 1750 Simpson, L. B. *The encomienda in New Spain* (Berkeley, Calif., 1929).
A 1751 —— *Studies in the administration of the Indians in New Spain*, vols. 1–4 (Berkeley, Calif., 1934–40); the best accounts of the Indian economy and Indian administration in general.

See also:

A 901 Ricard, R.

The theoretical aspects of Spanish imperialism are discussed in:

A 1752 Parry, J. H. *The Spanish theory of empire in the sixteenth century* (Cambridge, 1941).
A 1753 Zavala, S. *Las instituciones jurídicas en la conquista de América* (Madrid, 1935).

See also:

A 900 Hanke, L. U.

On trade and economic life generally see:

A 1754 Borah, W. W. *Early colonial trade and navigation between Mexico and Peru* (Berkeley, Calif., 1954).

See also:

A 83 Chaunu, H. and P.; A 90 Hamilton, E. J.; A 91 Haring, C. H.

The literature on early settlement in Brazil is much less extensive than that on Spanish America. The following articles contain the best summaries of what little is known:

A 1755 Greenlee, W. B. 'The first half-century of Brazilian history', *Mid-America*, **25** (1943).
A 1756 Marchant, A. 'Feudal and capitalistic elements in the Portuguese settlement of Brazil', *HAHR*, **22** (1942).
A 1757 Nowell, C. E. 'The French in sixteenth-century Brazil', *Americas*, **5** (1949).

59   **Colonial Development and International Rivalry outside Europe: A. America (vol. III, ch. xvii a)**
        (for vol. IV, ch. xxiii, see Sec. B, **37**)

General Studies

Besides the bibliographies and general works which have already been mentioned, much information about the development of the Spanish Empire in the later sixteenth century and later is to be found in the viceregal memorials:

A 1758 *Instrucciones que los vireyes de Nueva España dejaron a sus sucesores* (2 vols., Mexico, 1867–73).
A 1759 *Memorias de los vireyes que han governado el Perú durante el tiempo del coloniaje español* (6 vols., Lima, 1859).

Many general surveys of the Indies were compiled under Philip II and Philip III. Perhaps the best, and the only one available in English, is:

A 1760 Vázquez de Espinosa, A. (Clark, C. U., trans.). *Compendium and description of the West Indies* (Smithsonian miscellaneous collections, vol. 102, Washington, 1942).

Many contemporary accounts of European expeditions have been published in English by the Hakluyt society. Much information about the irruption of other European maritime powers into the New World is contained in works which have already been mentioned:

A 590 La Roncière, C. de; A 596 Fernández Duro, C.; A 1570 Hakluyt, R.

Detailed Studies

The evidence of economic and demographic decline has been carefully studied for New Spain:

A 1761 Cook, S. F. *Soil erosion and population in central Mexico* (Berkeley, 1949).
A 1762 Cook, S. F. and Simpson, L. B. *The population of central Mexico in the sixteenth century* (Berkeley, 1948).
A 1763 Simpson, L. B. *Exploitation of land in central Mexico in the sixteenth century* (Berkeley, 1952).

See also:
A 80 Borah, W. W.

The only comparable work for Peru is:

A 1764 Rowe, J. H. 'The Incas under Spanish colonial institutions', *HAHR*, 37 (1957).

For Brazil in the same period:

A 1765 Butler, R. L. 'Mem de Sá, third Governor-General of Brazil, 1557–72', *Mid-America*, 26 (1944).
A 1766 Jacobsen, J. V. 'Jesuit founders in Portugal and Brazil', *Mid-America*, 24 (1942).

Two important works have already been mentioned:

A 83 Chaunu, H. and P. *Séville et l'Atlantique*; on the Spanish convoy system.
A 318 Waters, D. W. *The art of navigation in England in Elizabethan and early Stuart times*; this contains information about Spanish, Portuguese and Dutch methods and theories.

On the activities of other European nations in the Americas:

A 1767 Andrews, C. M. *The colonial period of American history* (vol. 1 of 4 vols., New Haven, 1934).
A 1768 Biggar, H. P., trans. and ed. *The works of Samuel de Champlain* (6 vols., Toronto, 1922–).
A 1769 Lescarbot, M. (Grant, W. L. trans., and ed.). *The history of New France* (2 vols., Toronto, 1907–14); a lively contemporary account.
A 1770 Newton, A. P. *The European nations in the West Indies 1493–1688* (1933).
A 1771 Parkman, F. *Pioneers of France in the New World* (rev. ed.) (1905); tells the story of the Florida Huguenots.
A 1772 Parry, J. H. and Sherlock, P. M. *A short history of the West Indies* (1957).

A 1773   Sluiter, E. 'Dutch maritime power and the colonial *status quo* 1585–1641', *Pacific Historical Review*, **11** (1942).

A 1774   —— 'Dutch–Spanish rivalry in the Caribbean area, 1594–1609', *HAHR*, **28** (1948).

See also:

A 1559 Biggar, H. P.; A 1560 Biggar, H. P.; A 1571 Harlow, V. T.; A 1576 Quinn, D. B.; A 1577 Quinn, D. B.; A 1586 Williamson, J. A.; A 1589 Williamson, J. A.; A 1591 Wright, I. A.; A 1592 Wright, I. A.; A 1593 Wright, I. A.

SECTION B: 1648–1793

The volumes of the *New Cambridge Modern History* covered in this section are: V (1648–88); VI (1688–1713); VII (1713–63); VIII (1763–93). The book-lists for each chapter normally deal with the period of time embraced by the volume in which they appear; exceptions are noted in the synopsis. There are a few cases where particular lists overlap the general division into sections, but these are noted both in the synopsis and in the text.

Other points to note in using the bibliography are:

(1) Each entry is numbered, with a separate series of numbers for each section. The first reference to any book is to be considered the master reference, and normally only the first reference gives the full details about that work. Thereafter it appears as a number reference with the appropriate section letter added and with the author's name, e.g. B 995, Clough, S. B. Therefore, in using any list, it must be remembered that important references may be contained in these number references at the end, and these should be looked up in each case. This is particularly true of books which appear many times, such as, for the sixteenth-century chapters, F. Braudel, *La Méditerranée et le monde méditerranéen à l'époque de Philippe II.*

(2) There is a brief list of some of the chief historical bibliographies and of some of the chief historical series on pp. x–xi. In general, where a book contains a useful bibliography, this is noted in the chapter list.

(3) There are no lists on music or the visual arts, though lists have been provided for the literary chapters where this was thought appropriate. In very few other cases only has no chapter list been provided.

(4) It is assumed that English books have been published in London and French books in Paris, unless otherwise stated. Other places of publication and all dates of publications are given.

ECONOMIC AND SOCIAL CONDITIONS

Some of the general economic histories, which have already been mentioned in Section A, are also useful for this period:

A 48   Clough, S. B. and Cole, C. W. *Economic history of Europe.*
A 50   Heaton, H. *Economic history of Europe.*
A 79   Kulisher, J. *Allgemeine Wirtschaftsgeschichte*, vol. 2.

Another useful work is:

B 1   Sée, H. *Les Origines du capitalisme moderne* (1930).

1   Economic Problems and Policies (vol. v, ch. ii)

Countries and Topics. It is impossible to provide even approximately equal bibliographical coverage for both the main topics and the main countries. That the topics listed below are included separately is largely the result of the availability of certain general books; for other topics it is necessary to consult particular works on particular countries.

National Studies

ENGLAND

B 2   Clapham, Sir J. H. *A concise economic history of England to 1750* (Cambridge, 1951); a recent and fluent survey.

B 3   Harper, L. A. *The English navigation laws* (New York, 1939); bibliography.

B 4   Lipson, E. *Economic history of England*, vols. 2, 3 (4th ed., 1947); full of useful information but awkwardly arranged.

See also:

A 1552 Ramsay, G. D.

FRANCE

B 5   Cole, C. W. *Colbert and a century of French mercantilism* (2 vols., New York, 1939).

B 6   Martin, G. and Besançon, M. *L'Histoire du crédit en France sous le règne de Louis XIV* (1913).

B 7   Sée, H. *Histoire économique de la France*, vol. 1 (1939).

See also:

A 25 Bloch, M.; A 104 Spooner, F. C.; A 107 Usher, A. P.

GERMANY AND NORTHERN EUROPE

On Germany see:

B 8   Bechtel, H. *Wirtschaftsgeschichte Deutschlands vom Beginn des 16. bis zum Ende des 18. Jahrhunderts* (Munich, 1953).

B 9   Ergang, R. R. *The myth of the all-destructive fury of the Thirty Years' War* (Pocono Pines, Pa., 1956).

See also:

A 127 Franz, G.; A 1232 Carsten, F. L.

For Sweden see:

A 93 Hecksher, E. F. *An economic history of Sweden.*

For Poland:

A 1408 Rutkowski, J. *Histoire économique de la Pologne avant les partages.*

ITALY

A 118 Cipolla, C. M. 'The decline of Italy', *Econ. HR*, 2nd ser., 5, 2 (1952).

THE NETHERLANDS

A 53   Pirenne, H. *Histoire de Belgique*, vols. 4 and 5 cover the southern Netherlands. For the northern see:

B 10   Baasch, E. *Holländische Wirtschaftsgeschichte* (Jena, 1927).

B 11   Wilson, C. H. *Profit and power: a study of England and the Dutch wars* (1957); has much which is useful on the Dutch economy as well as on the English.

See also:

A 111 Barbour, V.; A 112 Barbour, V.

SPAIN AND PORTUGAL

B 12   Girard, A. *Le Commerce français à Seville et Cadiz* (1932); Valuable also for certain aspects of Spanish commercial arrangements.

B 13   Shillington, V. M. and Chapman, A. B. W. *The commercial relations of England and Portugal* (1908).

See also:

A 94   Klein, J.; A 130 Hamilton, E. J.; A 1180 Hamilton, E. J.

Detailed Studies

BANKING AND FINANCE

A 123 Dillen, J. G. van (ed.). *History of the principal public banks* (The Hague, 1934).

B 14   Judges, A. V. 'Money, finance and banking from the Renaissance to the eighteenth century', *European Civilization: its origin and development*, Eyre, E. (ed.), vol. 5, part ii (Oxford, 1935).

MERCANTILISM

A 132 Heckscher, E. F. *Mercantilism* (2nd ed., 2 vols., 1956); full of ingenious ideas and valuable information, but the approach, essentially that of an economist, has been much criticised in recent years. For examples of such criticism see:

B 15   Coleman, D. C. 'Eli Heckscher and the idea of mercantilism', *SEHR*, 5, I (1957).

B 16   Wilson, C. H. *Mercantilism* (Historical Association pamphlet, no. 37, 1958); an admirable and concise survey.

POPULATION

B 17   Carr-Saunders, Sir A. V. 'The growth of the population of Europe', *European Civilization: its origin and development*, Eyre, E. (ed.), vol. 5, part i (Oxford, 1937).

See also:

A 99   Mols, R.

2   The Map of Commerce 1683–1721 (vol. VI, ch. xiii (1))

Many of the books referred to in the previous bibliography also cover this period. Others are:

General Studies

B 18   Clark, G. N. *The Dutch alliance and the war against French trade, 1688–97* (1923).
B 19   —— 'War trade and trade war, 1701–13', *Econ. HR*, I (1927–8).
B 20   Davis, R. 'English foreign trade, 1660–1700', *Econ. HR*, 2nd ser., 7 (1954).
B 21   Levasseur, E. *Histoire du commerce de la France* (2 vols., 1911–12).
B 22   Wilson, C. H. 'The economic decline of the Netherlands', *Econ. HR*, 1st ser., 9 (1939).

See also:

A 138 Scott, W. R.

Detailed Studies

TRADE AND SHIPPING

B 23   Albion, R. G. *Forests and sea power: the timber problem of the royal navy 1652–1862* (Cambridge, Mass., 1926).
B 24   Charliat, P. J. *Trois siècles d'économie maritime française* (1931).
B 25   Davies, K. G. *The royal African company* (1957); especially valuable for the years 1672–1712.
B 26   Davis, R. 'Merchant shipping in the economy of the late seventeenth century', *Econ. HR*, 2nd ser., 9 (1956).
B 27   Deerr, N. *The history of sugar* (2 vols., 1949–50).
B 28   Enjalbert, H. 'Comment naissent les grands crus: Bordeaux, Porto, Cognac', *AESC*, 8 (1953).
B 29   Gras, N. S. B. *The evolution of the English corn market from the twelfth to the eighteenth centuries* (Cambridge, Mass., 1915).
B 30   Innis, H. A. *The cod fisheries* (rev. ed., New Haven, Conn., 1954).
B 31   —— *Fur trade in Canada* (rev. ed., Toronto, 1956).
B 32   Kaeppelin, P. *Les Origines de l'Inde française: la compagnie des Indes orientales et François Martin* (1908).
B 33   Lawson, M. G. *Fur: a study in British mercantilism, 1700–75* (Toronto, 1943).
B 34   Magalhães Godinho, V. 'Problèmes d'économie atlantique: Le Portugal, les flottes du sucre et de l'or, 1670–1770', *AESC*, 5 (1950).
B 35   Masson, P. *Histoire du commerce français dans le Levant au XVIIIe siècle* (1911).
B 36   Romano, R. *Commerce et prix du blé à Marseille au XVIIIe siècle* (*Monnaie-Prix-Conjoncture*, III) (1956).

See also:

A 128 Glamann, K.; A 1105 Masson, P.; A 1309 Wood, A. C.; A 1663 Krishna, Bal.

INDUSTRY

B 37 Coleman, D. C. *British paper industry, 1495–1860* (Oxford, 1958).
B 38 Court, W. H. B. *The rise of the Midland industries, 1600–1838* (1938).
B 39 Dutil, L. 'L'industrie de la soie à Nîmes jusqu'en 1789', *Revue d'histoire moderne et contemporaine*, **9** (1908).
B 40 Flinn, M. W. 'Revisions in economic history, xvii: The growth of the English iron industry 1660–1760', *Econ. HR*, 2nd ser., **11** (1958); with bibliography.
B 41 Gill, C. *The rise of the Irish linen industry* (Oxford, 1925).
B 42 Hamilton, H. *The English brass and copper industries to 1800* (1926).
B 43 Heaton, H. *Yorkshire woollen and worsted industries* (Oxford, 1920).
B 44 Hecksher, E. F. 'Un grand chapitre de l'histoire du fer: le monopole suédois', *Annales d'histoire économiques et sociales*, **4** (1932).
B 45 Horner, J. *The linen trade of Europe during the spinning-wheel period* (Belfast, 1920).
B 46 Léon, P. *La Naissance de la grande industrie en Dauphiné* (2 vols., 1954).
B 47 Nef, J. U. *The rise of the British coal industry* (2 vols., 1932); also contains good chapters on European production.
B 48 Sagnac, P. 'L'industrie et le commerce de la draperie en France à la fin du XVIIe siècle et au commencement du XVIIIe', *Revue d'histoire moderne et contemporaine*, **9** (1907–8).
B 49 Scoville, W. C. *Capitalism and French glass making 1640-1789* (Berkeley, Calif., 1950).

3   War Finance 1689–1714 (vol. VI, ch. ix)

General Studies

The history of public finance has been relatively neglected in recent years, while most of the secondary works published in the nineteenth century ignore the wider economic aspects of the subject and are of doubtful accuracy.

B 50 Cohen, B. *A compendium of finance* (1822); a general survey of the problem of long-term borrowing.
B 51 Baxter, R. D. *National debts* (1871); drawn on B. Cohen above.

For France there is a detailed bibliography of printed works:

B 52 Stourm, R. *Bibliographie historique des finances de la France au XVIIIe siècle* (1895).

A number of works bearing on this subject are mentioned in the other bibliographies on economic history in this part, and reference should also be made to them.

National Studies

GREAT BRITAIN

A great deal of material about the development of British government finance has been published as Parliamentary Papers. Particularly useful are:

B 53   *PP* 1857–8, **33** (return of the national debt of Great Britain and Ireland 1691–1857).

B 54   *PP* 1868–9, **35** (accounts of public income and expenditure from 1688).

B 55   *PP* 1890–1, **48** (report on the national debt from 1786 to 1890).

B 56   *PP* 1898, **52** (history of the earlier years of the funded debt from 1694 to 1786).

A mass of original Treasury and Exchequer records is printed in:

B 57   *Calendar of Treasury books and papers* (32 vols., 1904–62); the introductions by W. A. Shaw must, however, be treated with caution.

Other useful works are:

B 58   Binney, J. E. D. *British public finance and administration 1774–92* (Oxford, 1958); the best modern survey of the financial machine, which is useful, even though concerned with a later period.

B 59   Clapham, Sir J. *The Bank of England, a history* (2 vols., Cambridge, 1944).

B 60   Ewen, C. L. *Lotteries and sweepstakes in the British Isles* (1932).

B 61   Hughes, E. *Studies in administration and finance* (Manchester, 1934); contains much information about the excise.

B 62   Richards, R. D. *The early history of banking in England* (1929).

THE UNITED PROVINCES

The original materials for the history of Dutch public finance have been little used by historians. There is a great deal of information in:

B 63   *Resolutien van de Heeren Staaten van Holland en Westvriesland* (278 vols. of text and 17 of indices, The Hague, 1772–98).

B 64   *Secreete Resolutien van de Edele Groot Mog. Heeren Staaten van Holland en Westvriesland* (16 vols. of text and 2 of indices, The Hague, 1791).

Other works which may be consulted are:

B 65   Bloom, H. I. *The economic activities of the Jews of Amsterdam in the seventeenth and eighteenth centuries* (Williamsport, Pa., 1937).

B 66   Buijs, M. T. *De Nederlandsche Staatschuld sedert 1814* (Leiden, n.d.).

B 67   Fruin, R. *Geschiedenis der Staatsinstellingen in Nederland* (2nd ed., The Hague, 1922).

FRANCE

All subsequent writers about the history of French public finance have drawn extensively on:

B 68   Véron de Forbonnais, M. *Recherches et Considérations sur les finances de France* (2 vols., Basel, 1758).

B 69   *Comptes rendus des Finances de...France...ouvrage posthume de M. Mallet* published in London in 1789 is also very useful. Mallet was *premier commis* to Desmaretz, controller-general of finance 1708–15.

A masterly contemporary analysis of the evils of the financial system is:

B 70   Le Prestre de Vauban, S. *Project d'une dixme royale* (?Paris, 1707 and later editions).

Apart from these books the most valuable source is:

B 71   Boislisle, A. M. de. *Correspondance des Contrôleurs généraux des finances avec les Intendants des Provinces* (3 vols., 1874–97).

Other works include:

B 72   Antoine, M. *Le Fonds du Conseil d'État du Roi aux Archives Nationales* (1955).

B 73   Cans, A. *La Contribution du clergé de France à l'impôt pendant la seconde moitié du règne de Louis XVI* (1910).

B 74   Luthy, H. *La Banque protestante en France* (2 vols., 1959–61); vol. 1 (1959); an invaluable contribution to the financial history of the period, based on extensive research.

B 75   Mathews, G. T. *The royal general farms in the eighteenth century* (New York, 1958).

B 76   Saint-Germain, J. *Samuel Bernard, le banquier des rois* (1960); an interesting account of Bernard's many-sided activities.

B 77   Seligman, A. *La Première Tentative d'émission fiduciaire en France* (1925); a study of the 'Billets de trésor'.

B 78   Vührer, A. *Histoire de la dette publique en France* (2 vols., 1886); chronological treatment with little analysis.

THE HABSBURG MONARCHY

Much material on the finances of the monarchy is printed in books which have already been mentioned:

A 1258   Fellner, T. and Kretschmayr, H. *Die österreichische Zentralverwaltung* (vols. 5–7); vol. 5 is a useful general guide to the administrative and financial history of the period up to 1749.

A 1318   Arneth, A. von. *Prinz Eugen von Savoyen*.

Other works include:

B 79   Braubach, M. *Die Bedeutung der Subsidien für die Politik im spanischen Erbfolgekriege* (Bonn, 1923).

B 80   Mensi, F. von. *Die Finanzen Österreichs von 1701 bis 1740* (Vienna, 1891); the most complete work, though confused and inaccurate in places.

B 81   Srbik, H. von. *Der staatliche Exporthandel Österreichs von Leopold I bis Maria Theresia* (Vienna, 1907); useful for Habsburg borrowing in Holland.

4   The Growth of Overseas Commerce and European Manufacture (vol. VII, ch. ii)

Once again reference should be made to the earlier bibliographies of this section. The list which follows covers the principal countries of Europe and some special topics.

National Studies

BRITAIN AND HER EMPIRE

The books and selected chapters refer especially to the framework of legislation and ideas within which government sought to stimulate trade and industry. Industry is covered with particular reference to the part it played in overseas trade.

B 82   Andrews, C. M. *The colonial period* (London and New York, 1912).

B 83   —— 'The acts of trade', *Cambridge history of the British Empire*, vol. I (Cambridge, 1929), ch. ix.

B 84   Beer, G. L. *British colonial policy 1754–65* (New York, 1922).

B 85   Clark, G. N. *The wealth of England from 1496 to 1760* (Oxford, 1946).

B 86   McLachlan, J. O. *Trade and peace with Old Spain 1667–1750* (Cambridge, 1940).

B 87   Pares, R. *War and trade in the West Indies 1739–63* (Oxford, 1936).

B 88   —— *A West India fortune* (1950).

B 89   Rees, J. F. 'Mercantilism and the colonies', *Cambridge history of the British Empire*, vol. I (Cambridge, 1929) ch. xx.

B 90   Wadsworth, A. P. and Mann, J. *The cotton trade and industrial Lancashire 1600–1780* (Manchester, 1931).

SPAIN

Professor Hamilton's price studies (see: A 90; A 129; A 130; A 1180) have influenced opinion strongly on Spanish economic history, but no reliable modern study of the Spanish economy as a whole exists for this period. Judgment must necessarily be suspended on some of Professor Hamilton's suggested explanations for Spanish decline. An illuminating criticism of eighteenth-century economic policy in Spain is:

B 91   Uztariz, Don G. de. *The theory and practice of commerce and maritime affairs* (Eng. trans., 1957).

FRANCE

B 92   Bamford, P. 'Entrepreneurship in seventeenth and eighteenth century France', *Explorations in Entrepreneurial History* (April, 1957).

B 93   Grassby, R. B. 'Social status and commercial enterprise under Louis XIV', *Econ. HR*, 2nd ser., **13** (1960).

B 94   Hauser, H. 'The characteristic features of the French economic history from the middle of the sixteenth to the middle of the eighteenth centuries', *Econ. HR*, 1st ser., **4** (1933).

B 95   Paris, R. *Histoire du commerce de Marseille*, vol. 5 (*1660–1789; Le Levant*) (1957).
B 96   Sée, H. *La Vie économique et les classes sociales en France au XVIIIe siècle* (1924).

HOLLAND AND HER EMPIRE

No good study of the eighteenth-century economy in decline exists in English.

B 10   Baasch, E., *Holländische Wirtschaftsgeschichte* contains much useful information of a factual kind. The best account is that of de Vries, below. It is admirably equipped with bibliographies, notes and statistical appendices, but unfortunately does not contain the English summary that is a welcome feature of many Dutch works, nor an index.

B 97   Dillen, J. G. van. *Algemene Geschiedenis der Nederlanden*, ch. vii (1648–1748) (Utrecht, 1954).
B 98   Vries, J. de. *De economische achteruitgang der Republiek in de achttiende eeuw* (Amsterdam, 1959).
B 99   Wilson, C. H. *Anglo-Dutch commerce and finance in the eighteenth century* (Cambridge, 1941).

See also:
A 1606 Vlekke, B. H. M.

For Belgium and Germany respectively see:
B 100   Dechesne, L. *Histoire économique et sociale de la Belgique* (1932).
A 36   Lütge, F. *Deutsche Sozial- und Wirtschaftsgeschichte* (2nd ed., 1960).

Detailed Studies

SEA POWER

B 101   Richmond, Sir H. *Statesmen and sea power* (Oxford, 1946); valuable for its comments on the relationships of sea power, economic growth and the balance of power.

COLONIALISM

B 102   Pares, R. 'Economic factors in the history of empire', *Econ. HR*, 1st ser., 7 (1937).

INTERNATIONAL TRADE AND PAYMENTS

B 103   Wilson, C. H. 'Treasure and trade balances; the mercantilist problem', *Econ. HR*, 2nd ser., 2 (1949–50).
B 104   Morini-Comby, J. *Mercantilisme et protectionnisme* (1930).

POPULATION

B 105   Carr-Saunders, A. M. *World population: past growth and present trends* (Oxford, 1936).
B 106   Habakkuk, H. J. 'English population in the eighteenth century', *Econ. HR*, 2nd ser., 6 (1953–4).

ECONOMIC THOUGHT

B 107   Gray, A. *The development of economic doctrine* (1931).
B 108   MacGregor, D. H. *Economic thought and policy* (Oxford, 1949).

MAPS

B 109   Zeissig, H. *Neuer Geschichts- und Kultur-Atlas* (Frankfurt, 1954).

5   **Population, Commerce and Economic Ideas (vol. VIII, ch. ii)**

General Studies

On population the most comprehensive history is:

B 110   Reinhard, M. E. and Armengaud, A. *Histoire générale de la population mondiale* (1961).

There is considerable bibliographical material in:

A 99   Mols., R. *Introduction à la démographie historique des villes d'Europe du XIVe au XVIIIe siècles*; already mentioned. There is no single volume covering the growth of international commerce in this period.
For France:

B 21   Levasseur, E. *Histoire du commerce de la France*; already mentioned.

For England the chief modern works are:

B 111   Scholte, W. *British overseas trade from 1700 to the 1930s* (Eng. trans., Oxford, 1952).
B 112   Schumpeter, B. *English overseas trade statistics 1697–1808* (Oxford, 1960).

On economic ideas the best modern survey is:

B 113   Schumpeter, J. A. *History of economic analysis* (New York, 1955).

Detailed Studies

There are several books on the population history of individual countries, but in many cases these need to be supplemented by more recently published articles.

AUSTRIA

B 114   Gürtler, B. *Die Volkszählungen Maria Theresias und Josefs II. 1753–90* (Innsbruck, 1909).

ENGLAND AND WALES

B 115   Griffith, G. T. *Population problems in the age of Malthus* (Cambridge, 1926).

FRANCE

B 116   Levasseur, E. *La Population française*, I (1889).

IRELAND

B 117   Connell, K. H. *The population of Ireland, 1750–1845* (Oxford, 1950).

B 118   Gille, H. 'The demographic history of the northern European countries in the eighteenth century', *Population Studies*, 3 (1949–50).

See also:

A 113 Beloch, K. J.; A 1221 Cosemans, A.; A 1262 Keyser, E.

COMMERCE

Some studies on commerce which contain information on this period have been already mentioned earlier in the section. The following are also important:

B 119   Halm, H. *Habsburgischer Osthandel im 18. Jahrhundert* (Munich, 1954).
B 120   Rambert, G. *Histoire du commerce de Marseille*, vol. 6 (*1660–1789; les colonies*) (1959).
B 121   Svoronos, N. G. *Le Commerce de Salonique au XVIIIe siècle* (1956).

See also:

A 1245 Beutin, L.

THE PHYSIOCRATS

On the Physiocrats there are a series of authoritative works by G. Weulersse:

B 122   Weulersse, G. *Le Mouvement physiocrate en France de 1756 à 1770* (2 vols., 1910).
B 123   —— *Les Physiocrates* (1931).
B 124   —— *La Physiocratie sous les ministères de Turgot et de Necker, 1774–81* (1950).
B 125   —— *La Physiocratie à la fin du règne de Louis XV* (1959).

On the cameralists see:

B 126   Small, A. W. *The Cameralists* (Chicago, 1909).
B 127   Sommer, L. *Die österreichischen Kameralisten* (2 vols., Vienna, 1920–5).

The Spanish economic ideas of the period are discussed in:

B 128   Sarrailh, J. *L'Espagne éclairée de la seconde moitié du XVIIIe siècle* (1954).

SCIENCE, INTELLECTUAL LIFE, LITERATURE AND EDUCATION

Bibliographies of the history of science and the general histories of the various sciences have already been referred to in section A. A number of the more detailed studies which are mentioned there also cover this period.

6   The Scientific Movement (vol. v, ch. iii)

Works which are important for the background to specific scientific advances. Most of them have ample bibliographies.

B 129   Boas, M. 'The establishment of the mechanical philosophy', *Osiris*, **10** (1952).

B 130   Burtt, E. A. *The metaphysical foundations of modern physical science* (2nd ed., 1932).

B 131   Jones, R. F. *Ancients and moderns* (St Louis, 1936).

B 132   Lenoble, R. *Mersenne ou la naissance du mécanisme* (1943).

B 133   Merton, R. K. 'Science, technology and society in seventeenth-century England', *Osiris*, **4** (1938).

B 134   Mouy, P. *Le développement de la physique cartésienne, 1646–1712* (1934).

B 135   Westfall, R. S. *Science and religion in seventeenth-century England* (New Haven, 1958).

B 136   Wiener, P. P. and Noland, A. (eds.). *Roots of scientific thought* (New York, 1957); a collection of important papers from *JHI*.

Detailed Studies

ASTRONOMY

B 137   MacPike, E. F. *Correspondence and papers of Edmond Halley* (1932).

BIOLOGY

B 138   Guyénot, E. *Les sciences de la vie aux XVIIe et XVIIIe siècles* (1941).

B 139   Raven, C. E. *John Ray, naturalist* (Cambridge, 1950).

CHEMISTRY

B 140   Boas, M. *Robert Boyle and seventeenth-century chemistry* (Cambridge, 1958).

EMBRYOLOGY

B 141   Cole, F. J. *Early theories of sexual generation* (Oxford, 1930).

B 142   Meyer, A. W. *An analysis of the 'De Generatione Animalium' of William Harvey* (Stanford, 1936).

MATHEMATICS

B 143   Boyer, C. *The history of the calculus and its conceptual development* (New York, 1959).

B 144   Turnbull, H. W. *The mathematical discoveries of Newton* (London/Glasgow, 1945).

MECHANICS AND PHYSICS

B 145   Bell, A. E. *Christian Huygens and the development of science in the seventeenth century* (1947).

B 146   Dijksterhuis, E. J. *The mechanisation of the world picture* (Eng. trans., Oxford, 1961).

B 147   More, L. T. *Isaac Newton* (New York/London, 1934); the best, though not definitive, biography of Newton.

MEDICINE

B 148   Comrie, J. D. *Selected works of Thomas Sydenham* (1922).

OPTICS

B 149   Roberts, M. and Thomas, E. R. *Newton and the origin of colours* (1934).
B 150   Scott, J. F. *Scientific work of René Descartes* (1952).

7   **The Scientific Movement and the diffusion of Scientific ideas 1688–1751 (vol. VI, ch. ii)**
        General Studies
        In addition to the general works already mentioned see:
B 151   Ferguson, A. (ed.). *Natural philosophy through the eighteenth century, and allied topics* (Philosophical Magazine commemoration number, 1948).
B 152   Wolf, A. *A history of science, technology and philosophy in the eighteenth century* (rev. ed., 1952); contains much factual information.

Detailed Studies
THE ROYAL SOCIETY

B 153   Cochrane, R. C. 'Francis Bacon and the rise of the mechanical arts in eighteenth-century England', *Annals of Science*, **12** (1956).
B 154   Lyons, H. G. *The Royal Society 1660–1940* (Cambridge, 1944).
B 155   Weld, C. R. *A history of the Royal Society*, vol. I (1848).

THE FRENCH ACADEMY OF SCIENCES

B 156   Gauja, P. *L'Académie des sciences* (1934).
B 157   —— 'L'académie royale des sciences (1666–1793)', *Revue d'histoire des sciences*, **2** (1949).
B 158   Maindron, E. *L'Académie des sciences* (1888).

THE PRUSSIAN ACADEMY

B 159   Bartolmess, C. *Histoire philosophique de l'académie de Prusse depuis Leibnitz jusqu'à Schelling*, vol. I (1950).

EDUCATION

B 160   Hans, N. *New trends in education in the eighteenth century* (1951).

POPULARISATION

B 161   Brunet, P. *Maupertuis* (2 vols., 1929).
B 162   Daumas, M. *Les Cabinets de physique au XVIIIe siècle* (ed. Palais de la Découverte, Paris, 1951).
B 163   *L'Encyclopédie et les progrès des sciences et des techniques* (P.U.F., Paris, 1952).
B 164   Lanson, G. *Voltaire* (4th ed., 1922).
B 165   Marsak, L. M. 'Bernard de Fontenelle: the idea of science in the French Enlightenment', *Transactions of the American Philosophical Society*, new ser., **49** (December, 1959).
B 166   Torlais, J. *L'Abbé Nollet* (1955).
B 167   Wade, I. O. *Voltaire and Madame du Châtelet* (Princeton, 1951).

MECHANICS

B 168   Cohen, I. B. *Franklin and Newton* (Philadelphia, 1956).

B 169   Koyré, A. 'Pour une édition critique des œuvres de Newton', *Revue d'histoire des sciences*, 8 (1955).

CHEMISTRY

B 170   Metzger, H. *Newton, Stahl, Boerhaave et la doctrine chimique* (1930).

B 171   White, J. H. *History of the Phlogiston theory* (1932).

SCIENTIFIC INSTRUMENTS

B 172   Clay, R. S. and Court, T. H. *History of the microscope* (1932).

B 173   King, H. C. *The history of the telescope* (1956).

BIOLOGY

B 174   Ashley Montagu, M. F. *Edward Tyson, M.D., F.R.S., 1650–1708, and the rise of human and comparative anatomy in England* (Philadelphia, 1943).

B 175   Baker, J. R. *A. Trembley of Geneva* (1952).

B 176   Canguilhem, G. *La Formation du concept de réflexe aux XVIIe et XVIIIe siècles* (1955).

B 177   Clark-Kennedy, A. E. *Stephen Hales* (Cambridge, 1929).

B 178   Daudin, H. *Etudes d'histoire des sciences naturelles: I, De Linné à Lamarck* (1926).

B 179   Dobell, C. *Anthony van Leeuwenhoek and his little animals* (1932).

B 180   Glass, B., Temkin, O., and Strauss, W. L. (eds.). *Forerunners of Darwin, 1745–1859* (Baltimore, 1959).

B 181   Gourlie, N. *The prince of botanists: Carl Linnaeus* (1953).

B 182   Hagberg, K. *Carl Linnaeus* (New York, 1953).

B 183   Lovejoy, A. O. *The great chain of being* (Cambridge, Mass., 1936).

B 184   'Reaumur (1683–1757)', *Revue d'histoire des sciences*, 11 (1958).

MEDICINE

B 185   d'Irsay, S. *Albrecht von Haller* (Leipzig, 1930).

GEOLOGY

B 186   Adams, F. D. *The birth and development of the geological sciences* (Baltimore, 1938).

8   Science and Technology (vol. VIII, ch. v)

General Studies

In addition to the general works already mentioned see:

A 298   Singer, C., Holmyard, E. J., et al. *A history of technology*, vol. 4 (Oxford, 1958).

Detailed Studies

B 187   Clow, A. and N. *The chemical revolution* (1952).
B 188   Dickinson, H. W. *A short history of the steam engine* (Cambridge, 1938).
B 189   Fayet, J. *La Révolution française et la science, 1789–95* (1960).
B 190   Klingender, F. D. *Art and the Industrial Revolution* (1947).
B 191   Roger, J. *Les Sciences de la vie dans la pensée française du XVIIIe siècle* (1963).

Biographies

B 192   Armitage, A. *William Herschel* (1962).
B 193   Dickinson, H. W. *James Watt, craftsman and engineer* (Cambridge, 1935).
B 194   —— *Matthew Boulton* (Cambridge, 1937).
B 195   McKie, D. *Antoine Lavoisier, Scientist, economist, social reformer* (1952).
B 196   Smeaton, W. A. *Fourcroy, chemist and revolutionary* (1962).

Intellectual Life

Many of the works on the literature and thought of the seventeenth and eighteenth centuries which are listed in the following chapter bibliographies refer to a period wider than that covered by the chapters in which they are listed. These lists on literature, thought and education should therefore be used in conjunction with one another.

9   Philosophy (vol. v, ch. iv)

Editions of the works of most of the philosophers discussed in this chapter have appeared in *Everyman's Library*. Selected texts with introduction and commentary are contained in:

B 197   Hampshire, S. *The age of reason* (New York, 1956).

There are good *Pelican* monographs, written from a modern point of view, on Spinoza, Leibniz, Hobbes, and Locke. For a survey of recent work on seventeenth-century empiricism and rationalism see:

B 198   *The Philosophical Quarterly*, April 1951, October 1952 and January 1953.

Useful general guides are:

B 199   Boas, G. *Dominant themes of modern philosophy. A history* (New York, 1957).
B 200   Bréhier, E. *Histoire de la philosophie*, vol. 2, i (4th ed., 1938).
B 201   Broad, C. D. *Ethics and the history of philosophy* (1952); containing chapters on Bacon, Locke, Leibniz and Descartes.
B 202   Cassirer, E. *Das Erkenntnisproblem* (vols. 1, 2, Berlin, 1922).
B 203   Copleston, F. *A history of philosophy*, vols. 4, 5 (1958, 1959).
B 204   James, D. G. *The life of reason. Hobbes, Locke, Bolingbroke* (1949).
B 205   Prichard, H. A. *Knowledge and perception* (Oxford, 1950); sec. 5 deals with Descartes and Locke.
B 206   Russell, B. *History of western philosophy*, book 3, part i (1946).

B 207   Sorley, W. R. *A history of English philosophy*, chs. i–vi (Cambridge, 1920).
B 208   Whitehead, A. N. *Science and the modern world*, ch. iii (Cambridge, 1926)
B 209   Willey, B. *The seventeenth-century background* (1934); containing chapters on Bacon, Descartes, Hobbes, Herbert of Cherbury, the Cambridge Platonists, Glanvill and Locke.

See also:

A 336 Burtt, E. A.

Detailed Studies

DESCARTES

B 210   Beck, L. J. *The method of Descartes, a study of the Regulae* (Oxford, 1952).
B 211   Fischer, K. *Descartes and his school* (Porter, N., ed.) (1887).
B 212   Olgiati, F. *Cartesio* (Milan, 1934); exhaustive bibliography.
B 213   Smith, N. Kemp. *New studies in the philosophy of Descartes* (1952).

SPINOZA

B 214   Parkinson, G. H. R. *Spinoza's theory of knowledge* (Oxford, 1954).
B 215   Saw, R. L. *The vindication of metaphysics, a study in the philosophy of Spinoza* (1951).

LEIBNIZ

B 216   Cohen, J. 'On the project of a universal character', *Mind*, **63** (1954); contains a good account of certain aspects of seventeenth century logical theory, particularly that of Leibniz.
B 217   Dilthey, W. 'Leibniz und sein Zeitalter', *Gesammelte Schriften*, vol. 3 (Leipzig, 1927).
B 218   Russell, B. *A critical exposition of the philosophy of Leibniz* (Cambridge, 1900).

HOBBES

B 219   Brandt, F. *Thomas Hobbes' mechanical conception of nature* (Eng. trans., 1928).

THE CAMBRIDGE PLATONISTS

B 220   Cassirer, E. *The platonic renaissance in England* (Eng. trans., Edinburgh, 1953).

LOCKE

B 221   Aaron, R. I. *John Locke* (2nd ed., Oxford, 1955).
B 222   Viano, C. A. *John Locke* (Turin, 1960).
B 223   Yolton, J. W. *John Locke and the way of ideas* (Oxford, 1956).

10   The Achievements of France in Art, Thought and Literature (vol. v, ch. xi)

General Studies

The best bibliography is:

B 224   Lanson, G. *Manuel bibliographique de la littérature française moderne* (1931).

The text of many of the writers of the period can be studied in the volumes of the series *Les grands écrivains français* (Hachette, Paris). A convenient edition of the poetry of Boileau is that published by Dent, London, 1913. The complete works of Bossuet were published in Paris in 31 vols. 1862–6; of Fénelon, in 5 vols. in Paris, 1858. As well as the above, there are many recent and critical editions of single writings by the above authors.

The fullest history of French literature is still that of:

B 225   Julleville, L. Petit de, *Histoire de la langue et de la littérature française*; vol. 5 (1897) and vol. 6 (1898) cover the Louis XIV period. This composite work is both scholarly and readable.

A very useful series of studies and short biographies, *Les Grands Écrivains français*, was published in the earlier years of this century, all by eminent scholars, but mostly without bibliographies. A similar series, of more recent date and with bibliographies, is the *Connaissance de lettres*, Hazard, P. and Jasinski, R., eds.

Monographs and detailed studies

B 226   Ashton, H. *Molière* (New York, 1930); bibliography.
B 227   Blunt, A. *Art and architecture in France 1500–1700* (1953).
B 228   Bray, R. *Molière, homme de théâtre* (1954).
B 229   Brereton, G. *Racine, a critical biography* (1951); the standard English biography; bibliography.
B 230   Brisson, P. A. B. *Les Deux Visages de Racine* (1944).
B 231   Bukofzer, M. F. *Music in the baroque era* (New York, 1947); includes an account of Lully and Couperin; bibliography.
B 232   Cherel, A. *Fénelon au XVIIIe siècle en France* (1917).
B 233   Clark, A. F. B. *Boileau and the French classical critics in England, 1660–1830* (Paris, 1925); the best account of the influence of Boileau in England.
B 234   Eustis, A. A. *Racine devant la critique française 1838–1938* (Berkeley, 1949); an interesting study of Racine's posthumous reputation in France; bibliography.
B 235   Fabre, E. *Notre Molière* (1951).
B 236   Goldmann, L. *Jean Racine dramaturge* (1956); a study of dramatic technique.
B 237   Knight, R. C. *Racine et la Grèce* (1950).
B 238   Lacratelle, P. de. *La Vie privée de Racine* (1949).
B 239   Lombard, A. *Fénelon et le retour à l'antique au XVIIIe siècle* (Neuchâtel, 1954).
B 240   Longuemare, E. *Bossuet et la société française sous le règne de Louis XIV* (1910).
B 241   Mélèse, P. *Le Théâtre et le public à Paris sous Louis XIV* (1934).
B 242   Mellers, W. *François Couperin* (London, 1950); bibliography.
B 423   Michaut, M. G. *La Jeunesse de Molière*.
B 244   —— *Les Débuts de Molière à Paris.*
B 245   —— *Les Luttes de Molière* (3 vols., 1922–5); the standard biography.

B 246   Moore, W. G. *Molière, a new criticism* (Oxford, 1957); rejects theories about Molière's intentions and concentrates on his interpretation of comedy.
B 247   Nolhac, P. de. *Histoire du château de Versailles* (1911).
B 248   Simon, A. *Molière par lui-même* (1957).
B 249   Tilley, A. A. *Molière* (Cambridge, 1921); bibliography.
B 250   Turnell, M. *The classical moment; studies of Corneille, Molière and Racine* (1946); bibliography.

11   Cultural Change in Western Europe: Tendencies in Thought and Literature (vol. VI, ch. iii (1))

General Studies

B 251   Hazard, P. *La Crise de la conscience européenne (1680–1715)* (3 vols., 1935); the only comprehensive study of European thought and literature of the period. Full bibliography.

There is relevant general and background material in:

B 252   Bury, J. B. *The idea of progress* (1920).
B 253   Cassirer, E. *The philosophy of the enlightenment* (Princeton, 1951).
A 110   Clark, G. N. *The seventeenth century* (2nd ed., Oxford, 1947).

Detailed Studies

Critical and bibliographical guidance to the various vernacular literatures is to be found in the standard national literary histories. The following list covers the major literatures, and includes introductory accounts in English where available, together with some studies, mostly recent, of special aspects:

ENGLAND

B 254   Dobrée, B. *English literature in the early eighteenth century, 1700–40* (Oxford, 1959, vol. 7 of *The Oxford history of English literature*); bibliography.
B 255   Ford, B. (ed.). *The Pelican guide to English literature. 4. From Dryden to Johnson* (Harmondsworth, 1957); a series of introductory essays on major aspects of the period, with a well arranged and comprehensive bibliography.
B 256   Sherburn, G. 'The Restoration and eighteenth century (1660–1789)', in Baugh, A. C. (ed.), *A literary History of England* (1950); very full bibliographical annotation.
B 257   Willey, B. *The eighteenth-century background* (1940).

FRANCE

A 368   Adam, A. *Histoire de la littérature française au XVIIe siècle, 5. La fin de l'école classique (1680–1715)* (1956).
B 258   Cazamian, L. *A history of French literature* (Oxford, 1955).
B 259   Havens, G. R. *The age of ideas: from reaction to revolution in eighteenth-century France* (New York, 1955).

B 260   Mornet, D. *Histoire de la littérature française classique, 1660–1700* (1940).
B 261   —— *Les Origines intellectuelles de la Révolution française, 1715–87* (1947).

Both Mornet's books have very full bibliographies.

B 262   Spink, J. S. *French free thought, from Gassendi to Voltaire* (1960).

GERMANY

B 263   Newald, R. *Die deutsche Literatur vom Späthumanismus zur Empfindsamkeit, 1570–1750* (Munich, 1951; vol. 5 of Boor, H. de, and Newald, R. *Geschichte der deutschen Literatur*); bibliography.

See also:
A 207 Robertson, J. G.

ITALY

B 264   Belloni, A. *Il Seicento* (2nd ed., Milan, 1954).
B 265   Natali, G. *Il Settecento* (2 vols., 4th ed., Milan, 1955).
These two books form vols. 4 and 5 of *Storia letteraria d'Italia*; both have full bibliographies.
B 266   Wilkins, E. H. *A history of Italian literature* (1954); bibliography.

THE NETHERLANDS

B 267   Huizinga, J. *Holländische Kultur des siebzehnten Jahrhunderts* (Cologne, 1937).
B 268   Knuvelder, G. *Handboek tot de geschiedenis der Nederlandse Letterkunde*, part ii (1610–1778) ('s-Hertogenbosch, 1948).

SPAIN

B 269   Díaz-Plaja, Guillermo (ed.). *Historia general de las literaturas hispánicas*, vols. 3 and 4 (Barcelona, 1953, 1956); bibliography.

See also:
A 205 Brenan, G.

CRITICISM AND LITERARY THEORY

B 270   Atkins, J. W. H. *English literary criticism: seventeenth and eighteenth centuries* (1951).
B 271   Gillot, H. *La Querelle des anciens et des modernes en France* (1914).
B 272   Peyre, H. *Le Classicisme français* (New York, 1942).
B 273   Sutherland, J. R. *A preface to eighteenth-century poetry* (Oxford, 1948).

See also:
B 131 Jones, R. F.

SCHOLARSHIP

B 274   Douglas, D. C. *English scholars 1660–1730* (2nd ed., 1951).

TRAVEL LITERATURE

B 275   Atkinson, G. *Les Relations de voyages du XVIIe siècle et l'évolution des idées* (1924).

B 276   Chinard, G. *L'Amérique et le rêve exotique dans la littérature française au XVIIe et au XVIIIe siècles* (1913).

B 277   Cox, E. G. *A reference guide to the literature of travel* (2 vols., Seattle, 1935, 1938); works written in, or translated into, English only.

B 278   Frantz, R. W. *The English traveller and the movement of ideas, 1660–1732* (Lincoln, Nebraska, 1934).

B 279   Martino, P. *L'Orient dans la littérature française au XVIIe et au XVIIIe siècles* (1906).

12   The Enlightenment (vol. VII, ch. V)
        Literature and Thought: The Romantic Tendency, Rousseau, Kant
        (vol. VIII, ch. III)
                            General Studies

B 280   Becker, C. *The heavenly city of the eighteenth-century philosophers* (New Haven, 1932).

B 281   Berlin, I. *The age of enlightenment* (Boston/New York, 1956); the eighteenth-century philosophers selected, with introduction and commentary.

B 282   Clive, G. *The romantic enlightenment* (New York, 1960).

B 283   Hazard, P. *La Pensée européenne au XVIIIe siècle. De Montesquieu à Lessing* (3 vols., 1946).

B 284   Lockwood, R. O. (ed.). *Carl Becker's heavenly city re-visited* (New York, 1958).

B 285   Meinecke, F. *Die Entstehung des Historismus* (2 vols., Munich, 1936).

B 286   Snyder, L. L. *The age of reason* (New York, 1955).

                            Detailed Studies

FRANCE: OUTLINES OF THOUGHT

B 287   Crocker, L. G. *An age of crisis: man and world in eighteenth-century French thought* (Baltimore, 1959).

B 288   Frankel, C. *The faith of reason: The idea of progress in the French enlightenment* (New York, 1948).

B 289   Hearnshaw, F. J. C. (ed.). *The social and political ideas of some great French thinkers of the age of reason* (1930).

B 290   Hubert, R. *Les Sciences sociales dans l'Encyclopédie* (Lille, 1923).

B 291   Leroy, M. *Histoire des idées sociales en France de Montesquieu à Robespierre* (1946).

B 292   Martin, K. *French liberal thought in the eighteenth century* (2nd ed., Mayer, J. P., ed.) (1954); good bibliography.

B 293   Morley, J. *Diderot and the Encyclopaedists* (2 vols., 1878).

B 294   Mornet, D. *La Pensée française au XVIIIe siècle* (1932).

B 295   Mousnier, R. and Legrousse, R. *Le XVIIIe siècle* (1953).

B 296   Sée, H. *Les Idées politiques en France au XVIIIe siècle* (1923).
B 297   —— *Les Idées politiques en France au XVIIIe siècle: l'évolution de la pensée politique en France au XVIIIe siècle* (1925).

For bibliographical material see: Lanson, G. *Manuel bibliographique de la littérature française* III: *XVIIIe siècle*; brought up to date by:

B 298   Giraud, J. *Manuel de bibliographie littéraire pour les XVIe, XVIIe et XVIIIe siècles françaises 1921–35* and *1936–45* (2 parts, 1939, 1956).

FRANCE: POLITICAL AND SOCIAL LIFE

B 299   Gershoy, L. *From depotism to revolution, 1763–89*, vol. 10 of *The rise of modern Europe* (William L. Langer, ed.) (New York, 1944).
B 300   Groethuysen, B. *Die Entstehung der bürgerlichen Welt- und Lebensanschauung in Frankreich* (2 vols., Halle, 1927–30).
B 301   Sagnac, P. *La Formation de la société française moderne* (2 vols. 1945–6).

The works of G. Weulersse on the Physiocrats have already been mentioned (B 122, 123, 124 and 125). For the Enlightenment as a forerunner of the French Revolution there is a good bibliography in:

B 302   Tocqueville, A. de. *L'ancien régime et la révolution*, J. P. Mayer (ed.) (2 vols., 1952–3).

OTHER COUNTRIES

B 303   Bonno, G. *La Constitution britannique devant l'opinion française: de Montesquieu à Bonaparte* (1932).
B 304   Cobban, A. *Edmund Burke and the revolt against the eighteenth century* (2nd ed., 1960).
B 305   Fletcher, F. T. H. *Montesquieu and English politics 1750–1800* (1939).
B 306   Herr, R. *The eighteenth-century revolution in Spain* (Princeton, 1958).
B 307   Pascal, R. *The German Sturm und Drang* (Manchester, 1953).
B 308   Stephen, L. *English thought in the eighteenth century* (2 vols., 1881).
B 309   Wolff, H. M. *Die Weltanschauung der deutscher Aufklärung in geschichtlichen Entwicklung* (Bern/Munich/Salzburg, 1949).

INDIVIDUAL THINKERS AND GROUPS

B 310   Brailsford, H. N. *Voltaire* (1935).
B 311   Carcasonne, E. *Fénelon: l'homme et l'œuvre* (1946).
B 312   Carré, J. R. *La Philosophie de Fontenelle* (1932).
B 313   Cassirer, E. *Kants Leben und Lehre* (Berlin, 1918).
B 314   —— *Rousseau, Kant, Goethe* (Princeton, 1945).
B 315   Chérel, A. *De Télémaque à Candide* (1933).
B 316   Delvolvé, J. *Religion, critique et philosophie chez Pierre Bayle* (1906).
B 317   Green, F. C. *Jean-Jacques Rousseau, a critical study of his life and writings* (Cambridge, 1955).
B 318   Groethuysen, B. *J.J. Rousseau* (1949).
B 319   Hubert, R. *Rousseau et l'Encyclopédie* (1928).
B 320   —— *D'Holbach et ses amis* (1928).

B 321 Lauer, R. *The mind of Voltaire* (Westminster Maryland, 1961).
B 322 Naves, R. *Voltaire: l'homme et l'œuvre* (1942); good bibliography.
B 323 Stark, W. *Montesquieu* (1960).

Historical estimates of the importance of the Enlightenment include:

B 324 Cobban, A. *In search of humanity; the role of the enlightenment in modern history* (1960).
B 325 —— *Rousseau and the modern state* (1934).
B 326 Palmer, R. R. *The age of the democratic revolution: a political history of Europe and America*, vol. 1 (Princeton, 1959); attempts a comparative view of the thirty years before 1792.
B 327 Talmon, J. L. *The origins of totalitarian democracy* (1952).

13 Educational Ideas, Practice and Institutions (vol. VIII, ch. vi)

Since a great part of the development of educational thought in this period was to be found in France, there is a preponderance in this list of books about France. Useful general studies are:

B 328 Boyd, W. *The history of western education* (7th ed. revised by King, E. J.) (1964).
B 329 Smith, P. *A history of modern culture*, vol. 2, *The enlightenment* (1934). Bibliographical articles are to be found in various numbers of the *British Journal of Educational Studies*.

Regional and national studies

B 330 Adamson, J. W. *English education, 1789–1902* (Cambridge, 1930).
B 331 Allain, E. *L'Œuvre scolaire de la révolution, 1789–1802* (1891).
B 332 'Basedow, Johann Bernhard, 1724–90', *Friedrich Manns pädagogisches Magazin* (Langensalza, 1924).
B 333 Butts, R. F. and Cremin, R. A. *A history of education in American culture* (New York, 1955).
B 334 Durkheim, E. *L'Evolution pédagogique en France* (2 vols., 1938).
B 335 Fontainerie, F. de la. *French liberalism and education in the eighteenth century* (New York, 1934); reports and documents.
B 336 Godechot, J. *Les Institutions de la France sous la révolution et l'empire* (1951).
B 337 Hippeau, C. *L'Instruction publique de la France pendant la révolution* (2 vols., 1881–3); reports and documents.
B 338 Jones, M. G. *The charity school movement: a study of eighteenth-century puritanism in action* (Cambridge, 1938).
B 339 Lefebvre, G. *La Révolution française* (rev. ed., 1951).
B 340 Mitrofanov, P. *Joseph II, seine politische und kulturelle Tätigkeit* (German trans. from Russian, Vienna, 1910).
B 341 Paulsen, F. *German education past and present* (Eng. trans., 1908).
B 342 —— *The German universities and university study* (Eng. trans., 1906); bibliography.
B 343 Picavet, F. *Les idéologues* (1890).

POLITICAL THEORY AND SOCIAL STRUCTURE

14   Political Thought (vol. v, ch. v)

General Studies

B 344   Bloch, M. *Les rois thaumaturges* (Strasburg, 1924).

B 345   Figgis, J. N. *The theory of the divine rights of kings* (2nd ed., Cambridge, 1914); still useful.

B 346   Hearnshaw, F. J. C. (ed.). *The social and political ideas of some English thinkers of the Augustan age, A.D. 1650–1750* (1928).

B 347   Strauss, L. *Natural right and history* (Chicago, 1953).

B 348   Vaughan, C. E. *Studies in the history of political philosophy before and after Rousseau*, Little, A. G. (ed.), vol. 1 (Manchester, 1925).

See also:

A 110 Clark, G. N.; A 499 Meinecke, F.; B 251 Hazard, P.

Detailed Studies

B 349   Brunschwicg, L. *Spinoza et ses contemporains* (3rd ed., 1923).

B 350   Carr, H. W. *Leibniz* (1929).

B 351   Gough, J. W. *John Locke's political philosophy* (1950).

B 352   Hartung, F. 'L'état, c'est moi', *HZ*, **169** (1949).

B 353   King, J. E. *Science and rationalism in the government of Louis XIV* (Baltimore, 1949); full references to authorities.

B 354   Lacour-Gayet, G. *L'Education politique de Louis XIV* (1898).

B 355   Mousnier, R. 'Quelques problèmes concernant la monarchie absolue', *Relazioni del X. Congresso internazionale di scienze storiche*, vol. 4 (Florence, 1955).

B 356   Sanders, E. K. *Bossuet—a study* (1921).

B 357   Strauss, L. *The political philosophy of Hobbes, its basis and its genesis* (Oxford, 1936).

B 358   Roth, L. *Spinoza* (2nd ed., 1954).

B 359   Ward, A. W. *Leibniz as a politician* (Manchester, 1911).

B 360   Wolf, E. *Grosse Rechtsdenker der deutschen Geistesgeschichte* (3rd ed., Tübingen, 1951); contains an able memoir on Thomasius.

15   The Social Foundations of States (vol. v, ch. viii)

General Studies

There do not seem to be any major works covering this subject as a whole; the best substitute is:

B 361   *Encyclopedia of the social sciences* (1930–5); many articles in which contain relevant matter.

Some of the books cited in the preceding bibliography are also useful.

For particular aspects see:

B 362 Barker, Sir. E. *The development of public services in western Europe, 1660–1930* (Oxford, 1944); a brief, but valuable, survey.

B 363 Bouthoul, G. *Traité de sociologie. Les guerres* (1951).

B 364 Koren, J. (ed.). *The history of statistics* (New York, 1918).

B 365 Sombart, W. *Der moderne Kapitalismus* (2nd ed., 2 vols. in 4 parts, Munich, 1916).

B 366 —— *The quintessence of capitalism* (Eng. trans., 1915).

See also:

A 99 Mols, R.; A 536 Clark, G. N.; A 560 Roberts, M.

Detailed Studies

Works dealing with separate countries.

FRANCE

B 367 Cole, C. W. *French mercantilism 1683–1700* (New York, 1943); this, together with A 84 and B 5 already mentioned, gives useful information on the internal conditions and social policy of France as well as on mercantile policy in a strict sense.

B 368 Normand, C. *La Bourgeoisie française au XVIIe siècle* (1908).

B 369 Roux, Marquis de. *Louis XIV et les provinces conquises* (1938); with bibliography for the several provinces as well as for general policy.

See also:

B 301 Sagnac, P.

ENGLAND

B 370 Webb, S. and B. *English local government from the revolution to the Municipal Corporations Act* (7 vols., 1906–27); although this great work begins in earnest in 1688, it is indispensable for the preceding period and covers local government in the widest sense.

In the absence of comprehensive and methodical studies of the structure of English society in the later seventeenth century the following may be used as guides to parts of the scattered literature:

B 371 Carr-Saunders, Sir A. M. *The professions* (1933).

A 1676 Clark, Sir G. N. *Science and social welfare in the age of Newton* (2nd ed., Oxford, 1949).

B 372 —— *Guide to English commercial statistics, 1696–1782* (Royal Historical Society Guides and Handbooks, no. 1, London, 1938).

This is corrected in some parts by:

B 373 Laslett, P. 'John Locke, the great recoinage, and the origins of the board of trade', *William and Mary Quarterly*, **14** (1957).

THE NETHERLANDS

The most instructive book in English is still:

B 374 Temple, Sir W. *Observations upon the united provinces of the Netherlands* (1673; latest edition Cambridge, 1932).

Two books in Dutch deserve mention as examples of method in the social study of institutions:

B 375   Elias, J. E. *Geschiedenis van het Amsterdamsche regentenpatriciaat* (The Hague, 1923); the history of a governing class based on the same author's genealogical researches.

B 376   Foekema Andreae, S. J. *De Nederlandsche staat onder de republiek* (Verhandelingen der Koninklijke Nederlandse Akademie, new ser., **68**, no. 3, Amsterdam, 1961); a study of the institutions of the republic in relation to ideas and to the social groundwork.

GERMANY

B 377   Zielenziger, C. *Die alten deutschen Cameralisten* (Berlin, 1914); deals with the aspects of German history touched on in this chapter.

16   Monarchy and Administration (vol. vii, ch. vii)

B 378   Andreas, W. *Das Theresianische Österreich und das XVIII. Jahrhundert* (Munich, 1930).

B 379   Ardascheff, P. *Les intendants de province sous Louis XVI* (1909).

B 380   —— 'Les intendants de province', *Revue d'histoire moderne et contemporaine*, **5** (1903).

Views on the powers of the intendants vary considerably. Ardascheff thinks that they could offer a good deal of resistance to the king. His views should be compared with those of B 388 Godard below.

B 381   Beidtel, I. *Geschichte der österreichischen Staatsverwaltung* (Innsbruck, 1896); difficult but most useful.

B 382   Berindoague, H. *Le Mercantilisme en Espagne* (1929).

B 383   Bickart, R. *Les Parlements et la notion de souveraineté nationale au XVIIIe siècle* (1932); a useful synthesis of 'parlementaire' political theories.

B 384   Bielfeld, J. F. von. *Institutions politiques* (The Hague, 1760); gives illuminating contemporary ideas about the strength of various monarchs. Very useful as a corrective to historical interpretations too much influenced by hindsight.

B 385   Chenon, E. *Histoire générale du droit publique et privé des origines à 1815* (1929).

B 386   Desdevises du Dézert, G. 'Les institutions de l'Espagne', *Revue Hispanique*, **70** (1927); still invaluable as an introduction to the subject.

B 387   Dussauge, A. *Etudes sur la guerre de sept ans. Le ministère de Belle-Isle* (1914).

B 388   Godard, C. *Les intendants de province sous Louis XIV* (1901).

B 389   Hintze, O. *Die Hohenzollern und ihr Werk* (5th ed., Berlin, 1915).

B 390   —— 'Preussens Entwicklung zum Rechtstaat', *Forschungen zur Brandenburgischen und Preussischen Geschichte* **32** (1920); most illuminating and thorough.

B 391   Hoetzsch, O. *Osteuropa und deutschen Osten* (Berlin, 1934).

B 392   Kaindl, R. *Geschichte der Deutschen in Ungarn* (Gotha, 1912).

B 393   Kerner, R. *Bohemia in the eighteenth century* (New York, 1932); contains useful material.

B 394   Kugelmann, K. (ed.). *Das Nationalitätenrecht des alten Österreich* (Vienna, 1934); one of the fundamental problems of old Austria.

B 395   Marczali, H. *Hungary in the eighteenth century* (Cambridge, 1910); a most readable and attractive description of Hungarian life and ideas— good historical introduction by H. W. V. Temperley.

B 396   Marion, M. *Dictionnaire des institutions de la France aux XVIIe et XVIIIe siècles* (1923).

B 397   Pagès, G. (ed.). *Etudes sur l'histoire administrative et sociale de l'ancien régime* (1938).

B 398   Pietri, F. *La Réforme de l'état au XVIIIe siècle* (1935).

B 399   Redlich, J. *Das österreichische Staats- und Reichsproblem* (2 vols., Leipzig, 1920–6).

B 400   Reissner, H. *Mirabeau und seine 'Monarchie Prussienne'* (Berlin, 1926).

B 401   Roberts, M. 'The Swedish Constitution', *Hist.*, **24** (1940); a first-class study on a subject on which little had previously been written in English.

B 402   Sacke, G. 'Adel und Bürgertum in der Regierungszeit Katharinas II von Russland', *RBPH*, **17** (1938).

B 403   Schmoller, G. F. von. *Preussische Verfassungs-, Verwaltungs- und Finanzgeschichte* (Berlin, 1921).

B 404   Schüssler, W. *Das Verfassungsproblem in Habsburger Reiche* (Stuttgart, 1918).

B 126   Small, A. W. *The Cameralists* (Chicago, 1909), already mentioned. A most useful study giving the views of the various outstanding Cameralists of the German states and Austria. Cameralism as an element in the development of German administrative ideas has been largely neglected, yet it was of considerable importance in guiding the practice of the Enlightened Despots.

B 405   Springer, K. *Grundlagen und Entwicklungziele der österreich-ungarischen Monarchie* (Vienna, 1906).

B 406   Stieda, W. F. C. *Die Nationalökonomie als Universitätswissenschaft* (Leipzig, 1906).

B 407   Tümpel, L. *Entstehung des Brandenburgisch-Preussischen Einheitsstaats im Zeitalter des Absolutismus* (Berlin, 1915).

B 408   Villiers, R. *L'Organisation du parlement de Paris et des conseils supérieurs d'après la réforme de Maupeou* (1937).

B 409   Viollet, P. *Le Roi et ses ministres pendant les derniers siècles de la monarchie* (1912).

B 410   Weber, M. *Wirtschaft und Gesellschaft im Grundriss der Sozialökonomie* (Tübingen, 1925).

See also:

A 399 Carsten, F. L.; A 400 Hartung, F.; A 1258 Fellner, T. and Kretschmayr, H.; A 1456 Konopczyński, L.

THE ART OF WAR: ARMIES
AND NAVIES

Many of the general works on naval and military history, such as the general histories of the armies and navies of the various countries, have already been mentioned in the bibliography, Section A, 17 (see p. 28), and reference should therefore also be made to that part. In most cases an independent reference is not given here to such books.

17   Armies and Navies: (vol. VI, ch. xxii)
          (1) The Art of War on Land, 1688–1721

The best available bibliographical guide is:

B 411   Pohler, J. *Bibliotheca historico-militaris* vol. I (Munich, 1890).

The best general sketches, placing the period in perspective, are:

B 412   Denison, G. T. *A history of cavalry* (1913).
B 413   Ffoulkes, C. J. *Arms and armament* (1945).
B 414   Hamley, E. D. B. *Operations of war* (7th ed., revised by Aston, G.) (Edinburgh, 1923).
B 415   Lloyd, E. M. *A review of the history of infantry* (1908).
B 416   Spalding, O. S. and others. *Warfare: a study of military methods from the earliest times* (New York, 1925); good bibliography.

Secondary authorities:

AUSTRIA

B 417   Bibl, V. *Eugen* (Vienna, 1941).
B 418   Brabant, A. *Deutsche Schlachtfelder*, vols. 1 and 2 (Dresden, 1912).
B 419   *Feldzüge des Prinzen Eugen von Savoyen* (20 vols., and atlas, Vienna, 1876–92); vol. I gives a general survey of Austrian military institutions with some data on other contemporary armies.
B 420   Frischauer, P. *Prince Eugene* (1934).

ENGLAND

B 421   Ashley, M. *Marlborough* (1939); a valuable short account.
B 422   Atkinson, C. T. *Marlborough and the rise of the British army* (1921).
B 423   Belloc, H. *The tactics and strategy of the great duke of Marlborough* (1933).
B 424   Blackmore, H. L. *British military firearms 1650–1850* (1961).
B 425   Churchill, W. S. *Marlborough. His life and times* (4 vols., 1933–8); probably the best account of the War of the Spanish Succession—valuable bibliography.
B 426   Dalton, C. *English army lists and commission registers, 1661–1714* (1892–4).
B 427   Parnell, A. *History of the War of Succession in Spain* (1888).
B 428   Walton, C. *History of the British standing army*, vol. I (1894).

FRANCE

B 429   André, L. *Michel le Tellier et Louvois* (1943).
B 430   Blomfield, Sir R. *Sebastian le Prestre de Vauban, 1623–1707* (1938).
B 431   Colin, J. *L'Infanterie dans le XVIIIe siècle* (1907).
B 432   Helevy, D. *Vauban, builder of fortresses* (1924).
B 433   Petrie, Sir C. *The marshal duke of Berwick* (1953).
B 434   Picard, E. and Jouan, R. *L'Artillerie au XVIIIe siècle* (1906).
B 435   Wilkinson, S. *The French army before Napoleon* (Oxford, 1915).

SWEDEN

B 436   Bain, R. N. *Charles XII and the collapse of the Swedish Empire* (1907).
B 437   Bengtsson, F. G. *Life of Charles XII, king of Sweden 1697–1718* (1960); probably the best modern Swedish account of the Great Northern War.
B 438   Generalstabens Krigshistoriska Avdelning, *Karl XII på Slagfältet* (4 vols., Stockholm, 1918–19).
B 439   Seitz, H. *Svärdet och Värjan som Armévapen* (Stockholm, 1955).

THE UNITED PROVINCES

B 440   Coombs, D. *The conduct of the Dutch* (Amsterdam, 1958).
B 441   Geikie, R. and Montgomery, I. A. *The Dutch barrier (1702–15)* (Cambridge, 1930).
B 442   Hoff, B. van 't. *The correspondence (1701–11) of Marlborough and Heinsius* (The Hague, 1951).
B 443   Wijn, J. W. *Het Staatsche Leger (1702–15),* part VIII (2 vols., The Hague, 1956–9).

For Russia the standard histories should be consulted.

(2) Soldiers and Civilians
General Studies

The history of successive campaigns in this period, with accounts of battles and sieges, has always received more attention than the institutional and social history of the armed forces in Europe; but useful material on the latter topic can be found in:

B 444   Babeau, A. *La Vie militaire sous l'ancien régime*, 1. *Les soldats*, 2. *Les officiers* (2 vols., 1890).
B 445   Brancaccio, N. *L'esercito del vecchio Piemonte. Gli ordinamenti* (2 vols., Rome, 1923, 1925); vol. 1 covers 1560–1814.
B 446   Jany, C. *Geschichte der königlich-preussischen Armee* (5 vols., Berlin, 1928–37); vol. 1 covers 1609–1790.
B 447   Standinger, C. *Geschichte des kurbayerischen Heeres unter Kurfürst Max II Emmanuel 1680–1726* (2 vols., Munich, 1904–5); like Jany's book, meticulous and comprehensive.

See also:

A 1326 Marsigli, L. F.

Detailed Studies

CONSCRIPTION IN FRANCE

B 448   Giraud, G. *Le Service militaire en France à la fin du règne de Louis XIV. Racolage et milice (1701–15)* (1921).

B 449   Sautai, M. *Les milices provinciales sous Louvois et Barbezieux 1688–97* (1909).

REGIMENTAL HISTORIES

There are scores of these (cf. the British Museum catalogue of printed books, under the entry 'army' of individual states), but for this period most must be used with caution. Two outstanding English works are:

B 450   Atkinson, C. T. *The South Wales Borderers 24th Foot* (Cambridge, 1937).

B 451   Murray, R. H. *History of the VIII Kings' Royal Irish Hussars* (2 vols., Cambridge, 1928).

ARMIES AND THE SOCIAL STRUCTURE

For Scandinavia and Russia the standard histories should be consulted. Italian and Spanish developments are well treated in:

B 452   Domínguez, Ortiz, A. *La sociedad española en el siglo XVIII* (Madrid, 1955).

B 453   Quazza, G. *Le riforme in Piemonte nella prima metà del settecento* (2 vols., Modena, 1957).

ARMIES OF OCCUPATION

B 454   Houtte, H. van. *Les occupations étrangères en Belgique* (2 vols., Ghent, 1930); treats the subject in detail between 1667 and 1748.

(3) Navies

General Studies

Convenient introductions are:

B 455   Graham, G. S. *Empire of the North Atlantic: the maritime struggle for North America* (1951); a thoughtful interpretation of maritime strategy.

B 456   Lewis, M. A. *A history of the British navy* (Harmondsworth, 1957).

B 457   Mahan, A. T. *The influence of sea power upon history 1660–1783* (1896); remains the classic exposition of the place of sea power in international affairs.

B 458   Tramond, J. *Manuel d'histoire maritime de la France des origines à 1815* (1947).

See also:

B 101 Richmond, Sir H.

Of the standard full-length histories which have already been mentioned, the following cover this period:

A 590   La Roncière, C. de. *Histoire de la marine française*, vols. 4–6 (1920–32).

A 596   Fernández Duro, C. *Armada Española*, vols. 5 and 6 (Madrid, 1899–1900).

For the navies of other countries see:

B 459   Jonge, J. C. de. *Geschiedenis van het Nederlandsche Zeewezen*, vols. 2–4 (Haarlem, 1859–61).

B 460   Laird Clowes, Sir W. *The royal navy. A history from the earliest times to the present day*, vols. 2–3 (1898).

B 461   Lewis, M. A. *The navy of Britain: an historical portrait* (1948).

Detailed Studies

Two most valuable books on strategic and tactical problems are:

B 462   Castex, R. V. P. *Les idées militaires de la marine du XVIIIe siècle: de Ruyter à Suffren* (1911).

B 463   Corbett, J. S. (ed.). *Fighting instructions 1530–1816* (Navy Records Society, vol. 29, 1905).

Significant developments in weapons are surveyed by:

B 464   Robertson, F. L. *The evolution of naval armament* (1921).

The following deal with administration:

B 465   Asher, E. L. *The resistance to the maritime classes: the survival of feudalism in the France of Colbert* (Berkeley/Los Angeles, 1960).

B 466   Bamford, P. W. *Forests and French sea power 1660–1789* (Toronto, 1956); interesting not only for Baltic supplies.

B 467   Clemensson, G. G. *Flottans förläggning till Karlskrona. En studie i flottstationsfrågan före år 1683* (Stockholm, 1938); important for Swedish naval administration and policy.

B 468   Ehrman, J. *The navy in the war of William III, 1689–97* (Cambridge, 1953); important for the relations between the fleet and the civil authorities and for the revolution in naval finance. Good bibliography.

B 469   Giraud, M. *Histoire de la Louisiane française* (2 vols., 1953–8—in progress). French naval and colonial administration were combined, and this is the best recent work on the period of Jérôme de Ponchartrain's ministry.

B 470   Lewis, M. A. *England's sea-officers: the story of the naval profession* (1939); studies the growth of the British officer corps.

B 471   Keevil, J. J. *Medicine and the navy, 1200–1900*, vol. 2 (1649–1714) (2 vols., Edinburgh/London, 1958); well-documented pioneer study.

B 472   Masson, P. *Les Galères de France, 1481–1781: Marseilles, port de guerre* (1938).

B 473   Tanner, J. R. *Samuel Pepys and the royal navy* (Cambridge, 1920).

See also:

B 23 Albion, R. G.

Studies of maritime operations include:

B 474   Blok, P. J. *Life of Admiral de Ruyter* (Eng. trans., 1933).

B 475   Bourne, R. *Queen Anne's navy in the West Indies* (New Haven, 1939); particularly useful for relations between naval and civil authorities.

B 476   Corbett, J. S. *England in the Mediterranean: a study of the rise and influence of British power within the straits, 1603–1713* (2 vols., 1904); standard.

B 477   Crouse, N. M. *The French struggle for the West Indies, 1665–1713* (New York, 1943).

B 478   Laloy, E. *La Révolte de Messine, l'expédition de Sicile et la politique française en Italie, 1674–8* (3 vols., 1929).

B 479   Oudendijk, J. K. *Johan de Witt en de Zeemacht* (Amsterdam, 1944).

B 480   Owen, J. H. *The war at sea under Queen Anne, 1702–8* (Cambridge, 1938).

B 481   Powley, E. B. *The English navy in the revolution of 1688* (Cambridge, 1928).

B 482   Warnsinck, J. C. M. *De Vloot van der Koning-Stadhouder 1689–90* (Amsterdam, 1934); by a great naval scholar.

See also:

A 593 Anderson, R. C.; A 595 Anderson, R. C.; B 11 Wilson, C. H.

Studies of privateering include:

B 483   Bromley, J. S. 'The Channel Island privateers in the War of the Spanish Succession', *Transactions of the Société Guernesiaise*, **14** (1950); chiefly for Guernseymen.

B 484   Little, B. *Crusoe's captain* (1960); good biography of Woodes Rogers.

B 485   Malo, H. *Les Corsaires dunkerquois et Jean Bart, 1662–1702* (1914).

B 486   —— *La Grande Guerre des corsaires: Dunkerque 1702–15* (1925).

See also:

B 18 Clark, G. N.; B 19 Clark, G. N.

The phenomenon of piracy in these years still awaits full-scale treatment, but the following offer serviceable introductions:

B 487   Dow, G. F. and Edmonds, J. H. *The pirates of the New England coast, 1630–1730* (Salem, Mass., 1923).

B 488   Kemp, P. K. and Lloyd, C. *The brethren of the coast: the British and French buccaneers in the South Seas* (1960).

B 489   Vignols, L. *Un Produit social de la guerre: flibuste et boucane* (*XVIe– XVIIIe siècles*) (1928).

18   The Armed Forces and the Art of War (vol. VII, ch. viii)
          Armed Forces and the Art of War: Armies (vol. VIII, ch. vii. 2)

General Studies

There is a lack of good general works on military organisation in the eighteenth century, and the subject is most easily studied, especially by the English reader, in works dealing with individual countries. Of works already mentioned the following cover the period:

A 531   Jähns, M. *Geschichte der Kriegswissenschaften*, vols. 2–3.

A 535   Delbrück, H. *Geschichte der Kriegskunst*, vol. 4.

The character and ethos of warfare under the *ancien régime* are nowhere better described than in:

B 490   Saxe, M. de. *Reveries; or memoirs upon the art of war* (Eng. trans., 1757).

Reference should also be made to books referred to in the earlier bibliographies of this part.

Detailed Studies

FRANCE

An excellent brief account is:

B 491   Colin, J. *L'Education militaire de Napoléon* (1901), intro. and ch. i.

On the use made of new ideas in the Napoleonic period see:

B 492   Liddell Hart, B. H. *The ghost of Napoleon* (1933).
B 493   Quimby, R. S. *The background of Napoleonic warfare* (Oxford, 1958).

On the place of the army in French society see:

B 494   Leonard, E. *L'armée et ses problèmes au XVIIIe siècle* (1958).

and also:

B 387   Dussauge, A.

PRUSSIA

B 495   Craig, G. *The politics of the Prussian army 1640–1945* (Oxford, 1955).
B 496   Dette, E. *Friedrich der Grosse und sein Heer* (Halle, 1914).
B 497   Goltz, C. von der. *Rossbach und Jena* (Berlin, 1883; French trans., Paris/Nancy, 1896).
B 498   Shanahan, W. O. *Prussian military reforms 1786–1813* (New York, 1945); the earlier parts of this are valuable for the eighteenth century.

THE ENGLISH-SPEAKING COUNTRIES

B 499   Clode, C. M. *The military forces of the crown, their administration and government* (2 vols., 1869).
B 500   Curtis, E. E. *The organisation of the British army in the American revolution* (New Haven, 1926).
B 501   Fortescue, Sir J. W. *The British army 1783–1802* (Four lectures, 1905).
B 502   Fuller, J. F. C. *British light infantry in the eighteenth century* (?1925); interesting and wide-ranging.

19   Armed Forces and the Art of War: Navies (vol. VIII, ch. vii. 1)
        Armed Forces and the Art of War: Navies (vol. IX, ch. iii (B))

General Studies

Many of the general histories have already been mentioned in earlier bibliographies in this part. The works of Admiral A. T. Mahan are still useful, particularly:

B 503   Mahan, Admiral A. T. *The influence of sea power upon the French revolution and empire* (2 vols., 1893).
B 504   —— *Sea power in its relation to the war of 1812* (2 vols., 1905).

See also:

B 505   James, W. *Naval history of Britain, 1793–1820* (6 vols., 1837); a detailed chronological account.

For the French navy see:

B 506   Chevalier, E. *Histoire de la marine française* (3 vols., 1886).

For the American navy see:

B 507   Alden, C. S. and Westcott, A. *The U.S. navy* (New York, 1943); a short textbook.

B 508   Maclay, E. S. *History of the U.S. navy* (3 vols., 1894).

The publications of the Navy Records Society, London, provide documents and valuable introductions in accessible form, which supplement or revise the general histories. For this period the following are invaluable:

B 509   Barnes, G. R. and Owen, J. H. (eds.). *Sandwich papers* (3 vols., 1932–8).
B 510   Corbett, J. S. (ed.). *Signals and instructions, 1776–96* (1908).
B 511   Corbett, J. S. and Richmond, H. W. (eds.). *Spencer papers*, (3 vols., 1913–23).
B 512   Jackson, S. (ed.). *Logs of the great sea fights, 1794–1805*, (2 vols., 1900).
B 513   Laughton, J. K. (ed.). *Letters of Lord Barham* (3 vols., 1907–11).
B 514   Perrin, W. G. and Lloyd, C. (eds.). *Keith papers* (3 vols., 1927–51).

Detailed Studies

B 515   Cook, James. *Journals* (Beaglehole, J. C., ed.) (Hakluyt Society, 1955, 1961).

A good biography of Cook is:

B 515a Carrington, A. H. *Life of Captain Cook* (1939).

B 516   Corbett, J. S. *The campaign of Trafalgar* (1910).
B 517   Dundonald, Lord. *Autobiography of a seaman* (1859).
B 518   Hampson, N. *La Marine de l'an II*, 1793 (1960).
B 519   Hecksher, E. F. *The continental system* (1922).
B 520   Lacour-Gayet, G. *La Marine militaire sous Louis XV* (1910).
B 521   —— *La Marine militaire sous Louis XVI* (1905).
B 522   Lewis, M. *A social history of the navy, 1793–1815* (1960).
B 523   Lloyd, C. and Coulter, J. L. S. *Medicine and the navy, 1715–1815* (1961).
B 524   Mackaness, G. *Life of William Bligh* (Sydney, 1931).
B 525   Mackesy, P. *The war in the Mediterranean, 1803–10* (1957).
B 526   Maclay, E. S. *History of American privateering* (New York, 1899).
B 527   Manwaring, G. and Dobree, B. *The floating republic* (1935); a study of the mutinies of 1797 which replaces:
B 528   Gill, W. C. *The Naval Mutinies of 1797* (Manchester, 1913).
B 529   Morison, S. E. *John Paul Jones* (1960).
B 530   Nelson, Lord. *Despatches and letters* (Nicolas, H., ed.) (7 vols., 1844).

The best recent biographies are:

B 531   Oman, C. *Nelson* (1947).

B 532   Warner, O. *A Portrait of Lord Nelson* (1958).
B 533   Parkinson, C. N. *War in the eastern seas, 1793–1815* (1954).
B 534   —— *Life of Lord Exmouth* (1937).
B 535   Paullin, C. D. *The navy of the American revolution* (New York, 1906).
B 536   Tucker, J. S. *Memoirs of Earl St Vincent* (2 vols., 1844).

RELIGION

Among general surveys covering the whole section (1648–1793) are:

B 537   Cragg, G. B. *The church in the age of reason 1648–1789* (Pelican history of the christian church, vol. 4, 1960).

A 1123 Préclin E. and Jarry, E. *Les luttes politiques et doctrinales aux XVIIe et XVIIIe siècles* (2 vols., *Histoire de l'église*, Fliche, A. and Martin, V., eds., 1955–6); extensive bibliographies; Roman Catholic.

B 538   Veit, L. A. *Die Kirche im Zeitalter des Individualismus, 1648 bis zur Gegenwart*, vol. 1 (Kirchengeschichte, ed. Kirsch, J. P., vol. 4/i, Freiburg i/B, 1931); good bibliographies; Roman Catholic. Particularly useful for affairs in Germany.

See also:
A 695 Müller, K.; A 889 Latourette, K. S.

20   **Church and State (vol. v, ch. vi)**

General Studies

B 539   Batten, J. Minton. *John Dury, advocate of christian reunion* (Chicago 1944); for the international and inter-confessional movement for re-union.

B 540   Ehler, S. Z. and Morrall, J. B. *Church and state through the centuries* (1954); contains translations of some of the important documents.

B 541   Hiltebrandt, P. *Die kirchliche Reunionsverhandlungen in der zweiten Hälfte des 17. Jahrhunderts: Ernst Augustus von Hannover und die katholische Kirche* (Bibliothek des preussischen historischen Instituts in Rom, **14**, 1922); on the reunion movement.

B 542   Jordan, G. J. *The reunion of the churches, a study of G. W. Leibniz and his great attempt* (1927); the reunion movement.

A 470   Mataquin, A. *Histoire de la tolérance religieuse* (1905); for the growth of toleration in various countries.

B 543   Parker, T. M. *Christianity and the state in the light of history* (1955); on the historical background of the relations of church and state.

See also:
B 251 Hazard, P.

Detailed Studies

GREAT BRITAIN

B 544   Bosher, R. S. *The making of the restoration settlement* (1951).
B 545   Cragg, G. R. *From puritanism to the age of reason* (Cambridge, 1950); useful introduction, with bibliography, to the intellectual developments.

B 546   Cragg, G. R. *Puritanism in the period of the great persecution* (Cambridge, 1957).
B 547   Mathew, D. *Catholicism in England, 1535–1935* (1936).
B 548   Russell Smith, H. F. *The theory of religious liberty in the reigns of Charles II and James II* (Cambridge, 1911).
B 549   Shaw, W. A. *A history of the English church during the civil wars and under the commonwealth* (2 vols., 1900).
B 550   Sykes, N. *From Sheldon to Secker; aspects of English church history, 1660–1768* (Cambridge, 1959).
B 551   —— *Church and state in England in the eighteenth century* (Cambridge, 1934); the first chapter is valuable for the period 1660–88.

See also:
A 475 Jordan, W. K.; A 931 Mathieson, W. L.

FRANCE

B 552   Baird, H. M. *The Huguenots and the revocation of the edict of Nantes* (2 vols., 1895); useful, but needs revision in the light of recent research.
B 553   Gazier, A. *Histoire générale du mouvement janséniste* (2 vols., 1922).
B 554   Leonard, E. G. 'Le protestantisme français au XVIIe siècle', *RH*, **200** (1948); discusses recent research.
B 555   Martimort, A. G. *Le Gallicanisme de Bossuet* (Unam Sanctam, 24, 1953); valuable for a discussion of Gallicanism in general.
B 556   Mention, L. *Documents relatifs aux rapports du clergé avec la royauté de 1682 à 1705* (2 vols., 1893, 1903).
B 557   Orcibal, J. *Louis XIV contre Innocent XI* (Bibliothèque de la société d'histoire ecclésiastique de la France, 1949); important for the 'régale' controversy.
B 558   —— *Louis XIV et les protestants* (Bibliothèque de la société d'histoire ecclésiastique de la France, 1951); a re-assessment of royal policy towards the Huguenots.
B 559   Sainte-Beuve, C. A. *Port-Royal* (3 vols., Leroy, M., ed., 1952–5).
B 560   Viénot, J. *Histoire de la réforme française de l'édit de Nantes à sa révocation* (1934).

See also:
A 935 Bremond, H.; A 938 Abercrombie, N. J.

GERMANY

B 561   Drummond, A. L. *German protestantism since Luther* (1951).
B 562   Erdmannsdörffer, B. *Deutsche Geschichte vom Westfälischen Frieden bis zum Regierungsantritt Friedrichs des Grossen, 1648–1740* (2 vols., Berlin, 1892–3); with useful sections on ecclesiastical affairs.
B 563   H. E. Feine, *Die Besetzung der Reichsbistümer vom Westfälischen Frieden bis zur Säkularisation, 1648–1803* (Kirchenrechtliche Abhandlungen, Heft 97–8, Stuttgart, 1921); for the influence of the great families.
B 564   Richardson, O. H. 'Religious toleration under the great elector and its material results', *EHR*, **25** (1910).

HOLLAND

B 565   Colie, R. L. *Light and enlightenment, a study of the Cambridge platonists and the Dutch arminians* (Cambridge, 1957); for the development of liberal theology, also valuable for England.

See also:

A 517 Nobbs, D.

SPAIN AND PORTUGAL

B 566   Almeida, F. de. *História de Igreja em Portugal*, vol. 3 (Coimbra, 1912).
B 567   Desdevises du Dézert, G. *L'Espagne de l'ancien régime* (3 vols., 1897–1904; vol. 1 revised and reprinted as 'La société espagnole au XVIIIe siècle', *Revue Hispanique*, **64** (1925); useful for the later part of the seventeenth, as well as for the eighteenth centuries.
A 1163 Lea, H. C. *A history of the inquisition of Spain* (4 vols., New York and London, 1906–7); already mentioned.

THE PAPACY AND ITALY

A 601   Pastor, L. von. *The history of the popes*, vols. 30–2.

THE SPANISH NETHERLANDS

A 53   Pirenne, H. *Histoire de Belgique*, vols. 4 and 5; deal with the Jansenist controversy.

21   Religion and the relations of church and state (vol. VI, ch. iv)

Several of the books which were mentioned in the last list also cover this chapter, and a number of the books mentioned here also cover vol. VII, ch. vi.

Great Britain

B 568   Bebb, E. D. *Nonconformity and social and economic life, 1660–1800* (1935).
B 569   Beckett, J. C. *Protestant dissent in Ireland, 1687–1780* (1948).
B 570   Bennett, G. V. *White Kennett, 1660–1728, bishop of Peterborough* (1957).
B 571   Bolton, F. R. *The Caroline tradition of the church of Ireland* (1958).
B 572   Braithwaite, W. C. *The second period of quakerism* (1919).
B 573   Carpenter, E. *The protestant bishop, Henry Compton, 1632–1713* (1956).
B 574   Clarke, T. E. S. and Foxcroft, H. C. *A life of Gilbert Burnet, bishop of Salisbury* (Cambridge, 1907).
B 575   Dudley, W. R. Bahlman. *The moral revolution of 1688* (Yale, 1957).
B 576   Every, G. *The high church party, 1688–1718* (1956).
B 577   James, F. G. *North country bishop; a biography of William Nicolson* (Yale, 1956).
B 578   Landa, L. A. *Swift and the church of Ireland* (Oxford, 1954).
B 579   Lloyd, W. A. *Quaker social history, 1669–1738* (1950).
B 580   Peare, C. O. *William Penn* (1959).
B 581   Powicke, F. J. *The Rev. Richard Baxter under the cross, 1662–91* (1927).

B 582   Sykes, N. *Edmund Gibson, bishop of London, 1669–1748* (Cambridge, 1926).

B 583   —— *William Wake, archbishop of Canterbury, 1657–1737* (2 vols., Cambridge, 1957).

B 584   Tindal Hart, A. *William Lloyd, 1627–1717* (1952).

B 585   Underwood, A. C. *A history of the English baptists* (1947).

Continental Protestantism (including Pietism)

B 586   Beyreuther, E. *Der junge Zinzendorf* (Marburg an der Lahn, 1957).

B 587   —— *Zinzendorf und die Christenheit, 1732–60* (Marburg an der Lahn, 1961).

B 588   Dodge, G. H. *The political theory of the Huguenots of the dispersion* (New York, 1947).

B 589   Grünberg, P. *Philipp Jakob Spener* (3 vols., Göttingen, 1893–1906).

B 590   Haase, E. *Einführung in die Literatur des Refuge* (Berlin, 1959).

B 591   Poland, B. C. *French protestantism and the French revolution* (Princeton, 1957).

B 592   Ritschl, A. *Geschichte des Pietismus* (3 vols., Bonn, 1880–6).

B 593   Voeltzel, R. *Vraie et fausse église selon les théologiens protestants français du XVIIe siècle* (1956).

B 594   Wernle, P. *Der schweizerische Protestantismus im 18. Jahrhundert* (3 vols., Tübingen, 1922–5).

B 595   Zeeden, E. W. *The legacy of Luther* (Eng. trans., 1954).

See also:

A 775   Wilbur, E. M.

Continental Catholicism (including Quietism and Jansenism)

B 596   Appolis, E. *Entre jansénistes et zelanti: le 'tiers parti' catholique au XVIIIe siècle* (1960).

B 597   Calvet, J. *Bossuet* (1941).

B 598   Carreyre, J. *Le Jansénisme durant la régence* (3 vols., 1923–33).

B 599   Clark, R. *Strangers and sojourners at Port Royal* (Cambridge, 1932).

B 600   Deinhardt, W. *Der Jansenismus in deutschen Landen, ein Beitrag zur Kirchengeschichte des 18. Jahrhunderts* (Munich, 1929).

B 601   Dudon, P. *Le Quiétisme espagnol: Michel Molinos, 1628–96* (1921).

B 602   Jemolo, A. C. *Il giansenismo in Italia prima della rivoluzione* (Bari, 1928).

B 603   Menéndez Pelayo, M. *História de los heterodoxos españoles*, V (*Regalismo y enciclopedia*) (Santander, 1947).

B 604   Moss, C. B. *The old catholic movement* (1949).

B 605   *Nuove ricerche storiche sul Giansenismo* (Analecta Gregoriana, **71** (Rome, 1954)); by various authors. The most important contributions refer to Italian Jansenism.

B 606   Préclin, E. *Les Jansénistes du XVIIIe siècle et la constitution civile du clergé* (1929).

B 607   Schmittlein, R. *L'Aspect politique du différend Bossuet-Fénelon* (Baden, 1954); erudite, fanatically pro-Fénelon.

B 608   Taveneaux, R. *Le Jansénisme en Lorraine* (1960); of much wider significance than the title suggests. Important for interpretation.

B 609   Thomas, J-F., *La Querelle de l'Unigenitus* (1950).

See also:

A 944 Knox, R. A.; B 311 Carcasonne, E.

Russian Orthodox Church

B 611   Koch, H. *Die russische Orthodoxie im petrinischen Zeitalter* (Breslau-
Appeln, 1929).

B 612   Lewitter, L. R. 'Peter the Great and the Polish dissenters', *SEER*, **33**
(1954).

B 613   Miliukov, P. *Outlines of Russian culture*: i. *religion and the church*
(Philadelphia, 1942).

B 614   Stupperich, R. *Staatsgedanke und Religionspolitik Peter des Grossen*
(Berlin, 1936).

See also:

A 1388 Ammann, A. M.

22   Religion (vol. VII, ch. vi)

General Studies
See:

A 601   Pastor, L. von. *History of the popes*, vols. 33–6.

B 283   Hazard, P. *La pensée européenne au XVIIIe siècle.*
Useful articles on various topics are to be found in:

A 718   *Dictionnaire de théologie catholique* (particularly on Unigenitus).

B 615   *Dictionnaire de l'archéologie et de la liturgie chrétienne.*

Detailed Studies

ENGLAND

B 616   Binns, L. E. *The early evangelicals* (1953).

B 617   Commer, D. *English dissenters in the early Hanoverian age* (1946).

B 618   Creed, J. M. and Boys Smith, J. S. *English religious thought in the
eighteenth century* (Cambridge, 1934).

B 619   Davies, G. C. B. *The early Cornish evangelists 1735–60* (1951).

B 620   Horton Davies, R. F. *Worship and theology in England: from Watts and
Wesley to Maurice, 1690–1850* (Princeton, 1961).

B 621   Southey, R. *Life of Wesley* (various editions).

B 622   Stromberg, R. L. *English religious liberalism in the eighteenth century*
(Oxford, 1954).

FRANCE

B 623   Cahen, L. *Les Querelles religieuses et parlementaires sous Louis XV* (1913).

B 624   McManners, J. *French ecclesiastical society under the ancien régime*
(Manchester, 1960).

B 625   Palmer, R. R. *Catholics and unbelievers in eighteenth-century France*
(Princeton, 1939).

THE PAPACY

B 626   Dammig, A. *Il movimento giansenista a Roma nella seconda metà del secolo XVIII* (Rome, 1945).
B 627   Heeckeren, E. de. *Correspondance de Benoît XIV* (1912).
B 628   Morelli, E. *Lettere di Benedetto XIV al Card. de Tencin*, vol. 1 (Rome, 1955).

THE POLITICS OF THE EUROPEAN STATES

23   French diplomacy and foreign policy in their European setting (vol. v, ch. ix)
        International Relations in Europe (vol. vi, ch. v)

General Studies

The most recent general survey of international relations, which has already been mentioned, is:

B 629   Zeller, G. *Histoires des relations internationales* (Renouvin, P., ed.), vol. 2 (*Les Temps modernes*, pt. ii. De Christophe Colomb à Cromwell) and vol. 3 (*Les Temps modernes*, pt. ii: De Louis XIV à 1789) (1953, 1955).

Other general surveys include:

B 630   André, L. *Louis XIV et l'Europe* (L'evolution de l'humanité, **64**, 1950).
B 631   Bourgeois, E. *Manuel historique de politique étrangère*, vol. 1: *Les origines (1610–1789)* (6th ed., 1916).
B 632   Immich, M. *Geschichte des europäischen Staatensystems von 1660 bis 1789* (Munich and Berlin, 1905).
B 633   Potemkine, V. P. *Histoire de la diplomatie* (trs. from Russian), vol. 1 (3 vols., 1946–7); a translation of the Soviet collective work.

See also:

A 1094 Platzhoff, W.

All the above contain bibliographies; those of Platzhoff, Immich and André are quite extensive.

Detailed Studies

Most of the following contain extensive bibliographical references either in the footnotes or in appendices:

B 634   Auerbach, A. *La France et le saint empire romain germanique depuis la paix de Westphalie jusqu'à la révolution française* (1912).
B 635   Baudrillart, A. *Philippe V et la cour de France* (5 vols., 1890–1901).
B 636   Chance, J. F. *George I and the Northern War* (1909).
B 637   Elzinga, S. *Het voorspel van den oorlog van 1672* (Haarlem, 1926); mainly a study of Franco-Dutch economic relations in 1660–72.
B 638   Gaedeke, A. *Die Politik Oesterreichs in der spanischen Erbfolgefrage* (2 vols., Leipzig, 1877).

B 639   Gerhard, D. *England und der Aufsteig Russlands* (Munich and Berlin, 1933).

B 640   Hatton, R. *Diplomatic relations between Great Britain and the Dutch Republic, 1714–1721* (1950).

B 641   Hippeau, C. *L'avènement des Bourbons au trône d'Espagne* (2 vols., 1875).

B 642   Klopp, O. *Der Fall des Hauses Stuart* (14 vols., Vienna, 1875–88); the scope of this study is wider than its name implies. It is really a history of international relations from 1660 to 1714, based mainly on the Vienna archives.

B 643   Landau, M. *Rom, Wien, Neapel während des spanischen Erbfolgkrieges* (Leipzig, 1885).

B 644   Legrelle, A. *La Diplomatie française et la succession d'Espagne*, (2nd ed., 6 vols., Braine-le-Comte, 1895–1900).

B 645   —— *Notes et documents sur la paix de Ryswick* (Lille, 1894).

B 646   —— *La Mission de M. de Rébenac à Madrid et la mort de Marie Louise* (1894).

B 647   Mignet, M. *Négociations relatives à la succession d'Espagne*, (4 vols. 1835–42); cover the period 1659–78; especially valuable for its extensive quotations from French diplomatic documents.

B 648   Noorden, C. F. J. von. *Europäische Geschichte im 18. Jahrhundert* (3 vols., Dusseldorf, 1870–82); extends only to 1710.

B 649   Platzhoff, W. 'Ludwig XIV, das Kaisertum, und die europäische Krisis von 1683', *HZ*, **121** (1920).

B 650   Rowen, H. H. *The ambassador prepares for war: the Dutch embassy of Arnauld de Pomponne, 1669–71* (The Hague, 1957).

B 651   Reynald, H. *Louis XIV et Guillaume III* (2 vols., 1883).

B 652   Srbik, H. von. *Wien und Versailles, 1692–7* (Munich, 1944).

B 653   Thomson, M. A. 'Louis XIV and William III, 1689–97', *EHR*, **76** (1961).

B 654   —— 'Louis XIV and the origins of the war of the Spanish succession', *TRHS*, 5th ser., **4** (1954).

B 655   —— 'Louis XIV and the grand alliance', *Bulletin of the Institute of Historical Research*, **34** (1961).

B 656   Weber, O. *Der Friede von Utrecht* (Gotha, 1891).

B 657   Zeller, G. 'Politique extérieure et diplomatie sous Louis XIV', *Revue d'histoire moderne*, **6** (1931).

See also:

A 578 Jessup, P. C. and Deák, F.; A 1096 Dickmann, F.; A 1104 Dollot, R.; A 1337 Sumner, B. H.; B 18 Clark, G. N.; B 441 Geikie, R. and Montgomery, I. A.

Collections of documents

Only a few can be mentioned here; for a comprehensive list see one of the standard bibliographies already cited. On the French side see:

A 1086 *Receuil des instructions...aux ambassadeurs de France...* (27 vols., 1884–1960); already mentioned.

A 1093 Vast, H. *Les Grandes Traités du règne de Louis XIV* (3 vols., 1893–9); already mentioned. The editor's introductory remarks contain much information on the preliminary negotiations.

On the English and the Dutch see:

B 658   Heim, H. J. van der. *Het archief van den Raadpensionarius Antonie Heinsius* (3 vols., The Hague, 1867–80); mostly letters to Heinsius (usually in Dutch,) 1689–97. These are so arranged as to be specially useful in disentangling the issues.

B 659   Hoff, B. van 't. *The correspondence, 1701–11, of...Marlborough and Anthonie Heinsius* (Utrecht, 1951); in English and French.

B 660   Japikse, N. (ed.) *Correspondentie van Willem III en...Portland* (5 vols., The Hague, 1927–37) (*Rijks geschiedkundige publicatien, kleine serie*, nos. 23, 24, 26, 27 and 28); mainly in French.

B 661   Krämer, F. J. L. *Les archives...de la maison d'Orange-Nassau* (3rd ser., 3 vols., Leiden, 1907–9); mainly long extracts from letters of William III to Heinsius (1689–1702), mostly in Dutch.

Studies of diplomatic institutions and technique:

B 662   Blaga, C. *L'Evolution de la diplomatie: idéologie, mœurs, et technique*, vol. 1 (1937); concerned mainly with the eighteenth century, but contains some information on the earlier period.

B 663   Horn, D. B. *The British diplomatic service, 1689–1789* (Oxford, 1961).

B 664   Krauske, O. *Die Entwickelung der ständigen Diplomatie* (Leipzig, 1885).

B 665   Lane, M. 'The diplomatic service under William III', *TRHS*, 4th ser., **10** (1927).

B 666   Nys, E. *Les Origines du droit international* (Brussels and Paris, 1894); deals mainly with the period from the late middle ages to Grotius.

B 667   ——— *Les Théories politiques et le droit international en France jusqu'au XVIIIe siècle* (2nd ed., Brussels and Paris, 1899).

B 668   Picavet, C. G. *La Diplomatie française au temps de Louis XIV* (1930); a comprehensive analysis of French diplomatic institutions under Louis XIV; bibliography.

B 669   Satow, E. *A guide to diplomatic practice* (2 vols., 1922); the first and second editions of this work (1922, 1927) contain much useful information for the history of international relations since the Peace of Westphalia; most of it has been omitted from subsequent editions.

B 670   Tunberg, S. (ed.). *Histoire de l'administration des affaires étrangères de Suède* (Uppsala, 1940).

24   (a) The Nine Years War, 1688–1697 (vol. VI, ch. vii)
        (b) From the Nine Years War to the Spanish Succession (vol. VI, ch. xii)
        (c) The War of the Spanish Succession in Europe (vol. VI, ch. xiii)
        (d) The Pacification of Utrecht (vol. VI, ch. xiv)

The bibliography for these chapters is covered to a considerable extent by that for vol. V, ch. ix and vol. VI, ch. v (Sec. B, **23**) which precedes it. Reference should also be made to 'The Art of War: Armies and Navies', and to the lists on such general topics as economic history. In addition the following may be found useful:

(*a, b*)

Among French works:

B 671   Beaurain, J. de. *Histoire militaire de Flandre* (2 vols., 1755) (folio ed.); is indispensable for its maps, but does not state the number of the troops: Baurain was the cartographer, and the text is by Cucé, N., marquis de Boisgelin.

B 672   Zeller, G. *L'Organisation défensive des frontières du nord et de l'est au XVIIe siècle* (1928); explains the conditions under which the armies operated.

For French military organisation:

B 673   Rousset, C. *Histoire de Louvois* (4 vols., 1862–3); though in some respects superseded, is still important.

Among the many books on *Vauban* see:

B 674   Lazard, P. *Vauban, 1633–1707* (1934); gives the best introduction.

The most important French criticisms of the campaigns are those of:

B 675   Pas, A. M. de, Marquis de Feucquières. *Mémoires* (4 vols., Paris and London, 1740).

On the British navy see:

B 676   *Dictionary of National Biography*, in which the lives contributed by [Sir] John K. Laughton are of high quality.

The standard account of the Dutch army at the end of the seventeenth century is:

A 1209   Raa, F. J. G. ten and Bas, F. de. *Het staatsche leger*, vol. 7 (The Hague, 1950).

(*c*)

GENERAL ACCOUNTS OF THE WAR OF THE SPANISH SUCCESSION

B 677   Braubach, M. *Die Bedeutung der Subsidien für die Politik im Spanischen Erbfolgekriege* (Bonn, 1923).

B 678   Pelet, J. J. G. and Vault, F. E. de. *Mémoires militaires relatifs à la succession d'Espagne sous Louis XIV* (11 vols., and atlas 1835–62); the standard work for the military operations.

B 679   Taylor, F. *The wars of Marlborough, 1702–9* (2 vols., Oxford, 1921).

MARLBOROUGH AND PRINCE EUGENE

In addition to the biographies and collections of correspondence which have already been mentioned see:

A 1318   Arneth, A. *Prinz Eugen von Savoyen* (3 vols., Vienna, 1858); already mentioned.

B 680 Coxe, W. *Memoirs of John duke of Marlborough* (2nd ed., 6 vols. and atlas, 1820).

B 681 Murray, G. (ed.). *The letters and dispatches of John Churchill 1st duke of Marlborough, from 1702 to 1712* (5 vols., 1845).

THE DUTCH REPUBLIC AND THE BARRIER

B 682 Geyl, P. 'Moderne historische apologetiek in Engeland'; 'Nederland's staatkunde in de Spaanse successie-oorlog', in *Kernproblemen van onze geschiedenis* (Utrecht, 1937); Geyl focused attention on the need to study Anglo–Dutch relations in the period and on its neglect by Dutch historians.

B 683 Hahlweg, W. 'Barriere-Gleichgewicht-Sicherheit', *HZ*, **187** (1959).

B 684 Haute, G. van den. *Les Relations anglo-hollandaises au début du XVIIIe siècle, d'après la correspondance d'Alexandre Stanhope, 1700–6* (Louvain, 1932).

B 685 Stork-Penning, J. G. *Het grote werk; vredesonderhandelingen gedurende de Spaanse successieoorlog, 1705–10* (Groningen, 1958); mainly based on new material from the Dutch archives.

THE SOUTHERN NETHERLANDS AND THE CONDOMINIUM

B 686 Kalken, F. van. *La fin du régime espagnol aux Pays-Bas* (Brussels, 1907).

B 687 Veenendaal, A. J. *Het Engels-Nederlands condominium in de zuidelijke Nederlanden tijdens de Spaanse-successie oorlog, 1706–16*, vol. 1 (Utrecht, 1945); goes down to 1709.

B 688 Veenendaal, A. J. (ed.). *Het dagboek van G. Cuper, gehouden in de zuidelijke Nederlanden in 1706* (Rijks geschiedkundige publicatien, kl. ser. 30, The Hague, 1950).

PORTUGAL AND SPAIN

B 689 Albrecht, J. *Englands Bemühungen um den Eintritt Portugals in die grosse Allianz, 1700–3* (Bremen, 1933).

B 690 Francis, A. D. 'John Methuen and the Anglo–Portuguese treaties of 1703', *Historical Journal*, **3** (1960).

B 691 Parnell, A. *The war of the succession in Spain* (1888).

B 692 Williams, B. *Stanhope: a study in eighteenth-century war and diplomacy* (Oxford, 1932).

(d)

The only modern edition of the treaties of Utrecht with commentaries and bibliographical notes is:

B 693 Davenport, F. G. *European treaties bearing on the history of the United States and its dependencies*, vol. 3 (Washington, 1934), see treaties nos. 96–107. For the treaties of Rastatt and Baden see the older collection of:

B 694 Dumont, J. *Corps universel diplomatique du droit des gens contenant un recueil des traités*, vol. 7 (of the Amsterdam ed., 1726–31).

Of the many collections of memoirs and correspondence mention may be made, on the English side, of:

B 695   Parke, G. *Letters and correspondence of the Rt. Hon. Henry St John, Lord Viscount Bolingbroke* (4 vols., 1798).

On the French side see:

B 696   Masson, F. *Journal inédit de Jean-Baptiste Colbert, Marquis de Torcy pendant des années 1709, 1710 et 1711* (1884).

General Studies

B 697   Gerard, J. W. *The peace of Utrecht* (New York, 1885).
B 698   Giraud, C. *La Paix d'Utrecht* (1847).
B 699   *Cambridge modern history*, v (Cambridge, 1908); the half-chapter by Ward, A. W.

All these are to some extent superseded by new and specialised research. It should be noted that the work frequently listed in historical bibliographies by Danvila y Burguero, A. *El congreso de Utrecht* (Madrid, 1929) is a historical novel, not a history of the peace or the congress. Of general interest are:

B 700   Fransen, P. *Leibniz und die Friedenschlüsse von Utrecht und Rastatt-Baden* (Purmerand, 1933).
B 701   Goslinga, A. *Slingelandt's efforts towards European peace* (The Hague, 1915).

Special aspects of the peace negotiations:

On the Iberian peninsula and Spanish trade see:

B 702   Conn, S. *Gibraltar in British diplomacy* (New Haven, 1942).
B 703   Gomez Molleda, F. *Gibraltar* (Madrid, 1953).
B 704   Prestage, E. *Portugal and the war of the Spanish succession* (Cambridge, 1938).

On Anglo-Dutch relations see:

B 705   Alphen, G. van. *De stemming van de Engelschen tegen de Hollanders tijdens de regeering van den Koning-Stadhouder Willem III* (Assen, 1938).

Imperial and Italian affairs have been less systematically dealt with than other subjects, but the following are relevant:

B 706   Baraudon, A. *La maison de Savoie et la triple alliance, 1713–22* (1896).
B 707   Braubach, M. *Geschichte und Abenteuer, Gestalten um den Prinzen Eugen* (Bonn, 1950).
B 708   Hantsch, H. *Reichsvizekanzler Friedrich Karl Graf von Schörnborn, 1674–1746, einige Kapitel zur politischen Geschichte Kaiser Josefs I and Karls VI* (Augsburg, 1929).

On the Dunkirk question:

B 709   Herlaut, A. P. 'La destruction du port de Dunkerque. Les conflicts diplomatiques franco-anglaises 1713–15', *RN*, 2 (1925).

B 710　Saint-Léger, P. *La question de Dunkerque et du canal de Mardyck 1709–13* (1904).

Special periods of the peace negotiations:
On Austro-French negotiations generally see:

B 711　Braubach, M. *Versailles und Wien von Ludwig XIV bis Kaunitz* (Bonn, 1952).

On the period 1705–10:

B 712　Reese, W. *Das Ringen um Frieden und Sicherheit in den Entscheidungs-iahren des Spanischen Erbfolgekrieges 1708 bis 1709* (Munich, 1933).

On the years 1710–13:

B 713　Fieldhouse, F. N. 'St John and Savoy in the war of the Spanish succession', *EHR*, **50** (1935).

B 714　Legg, L. G. W. *Matthew Prior, a study of his public career and correspondence* (Cambridge, 1921).

On the Rastatt and Baden period, 1713–14:

B 715　Landosle, H. de. 'Le congrès de Bade-en-Suisse, 1714', *Revue des questions historiques*, **97, 98** (1922, 1923).

B 716　Weber, O. 'Der Friede von Rastatt, 1714', *Deutsche Zeitung für Geschichtswissenschaft*, **8** (1890).

25　　International Relations (vol. VII, ch. ix)

The bibliographies for this chapter, and for chs. xviii, xix, and xx in the same volume (Sec. B, **26, 27, 28**) overlap considerably. A book is only mentioned once in the four lists, but the four bibliographies should be used together as a guide to the international relations of the years 1713–63. The lists on 'The Art of War' should also be used.

B 717　Arneth, A. von. *Geschichte Maria Theresias* (10 vols., Vienna, 1863–79); a classic of Austrian history.

B 718　Bain, R. N. *The pupils of Peter the Great* (1897).

B 719　Berney, A. *Friedrich der Grosse* (Tübingen, 1934).

B 720　Bourgeois, E. 'La collaboration de Saint-Simon et de Torcy. Etude critique sur les mémoires de Saint-Simon', *RH*, **87** (1905).

B 721　—— *Le secret des Farneses* (1909).

B 722　—— *Le secret de Dubois* (1910).

B 723　—— *Le secret du Régent et la politique de l'abbé Dubois* (n.d.).

These studies of French diplomacy are invaluable for the detail which they provide.

B 724　Broglie, A. de. *Frédéric II et Marie-Thérèse 1740–2* (1883).

B 725　—— *Frédéric II et Louis XV 1742–4* (1885).

B 726　—— *Marie Thérèse impératrice 1744–6* (1888).

B 727　—— *Maurice de Saxe et le Marquis d'Argenson 1746–7* (1891).

B 728　—— *La paix d'Aix la Chapelle 1748* (1891).

Another series of classic histories.

B 729　Chance, J. F. *The alliance of Hanover 1725–7* (1923).

B 730　Dupuis, V. *Le Principe d'équilibre et le concert européen depuis les traités de Westphalie* (1903).

B 731　Guglia, E. *Maria Theresia* (2 vols., Munich, 1917).

B 732　Horn, D. B. 'Saxony in the war of the Austrian succession', *EHR*, **44** (1929).

B 733　Huisman, M. *La Belgique commerciale sous l'empereur Charles VI et la compagnie d'Ostende* (1902).

B 734　Kretschmayr, H. *Maria Theresia* (Gotha, 1925).

B 735　Lodge, Sir R. *Great Britain and Prussia in the eighteenth century* (1923).

B 736　—— *Studies in eighteenth-century diplomacy 1740–8* (1930).

B 737　—— 'The first Anglo-Russian treaty, 1739–42' *EHR*, **43** (1928).

B 738　—— 'Russia, Prussia and Great Britain, 1742–4', *EHR*, **45** (1930).

B 739　—— 'Lord Hyndford's embassy to Russia, 1744–9', *EHR*, **46** (1931).

B 740　—— 'The mission of Henry Legge to Berlin, 1748', *TRHS*, 4th ser., **14** (1931).

These are based on English documentation only, and should be read with the article by:

B 741　Muret, P. 'L'histoire diplomatique au milieu du XVIIIe siècle d'après les travaux de Sir Richard Lodge', *Revue d'histoire moderne*, **7** (new ser., **1**) (1932).

B 742　Mayer, F. M. *Die Anfänge des Handels und der Industrie in Oesterreich und das orientalische Kompagnie* (Innsbruck, 1882).

B 743　Michael, W. *Englische Geschichte im 18. Jahrhundert* (5 vols., Leipzig, 1920–55); Eng. trans. of vols. 1, 2 (1936, 1939).

B 744　Muret, P. *La prépondérance anglaise* (1937); a brilliant survey of the whole period; good bibliography.

B 745　Sautai, M. *Les Préliminaires de la guerre de succession d'Autriche* (1907).

B 746　Syveton, G. *Une Cour et un aventurier au XVIIIe siècle, le baron Ripperda* (1896); still the best study of Spanish diplomacy when Ripperda was in control.

B 747　Temperley, H. W. V. 'The causes of the war of Jenkins's Ear', *TRHS*, 3rd ser., **3** (1909).

B 748　Tschuppik, K. *Maria Theresia* (Amsterdam, 1934).

B 749　Vandal, A. *Louis XV et Elisabeth de Russie* (1882).

B 750　Vaucher, P. *Robert Walpole et la politique de Fleury* (1925).

B 751　Ward, A. W. *Great Britain and Hanover* (Oxford, 1899).

B 752　Weber, O. *Der quadrupel Allianz* (Prague/Vienna/Leipzig, 1887); a classic study.

B 753　Wiesener, L. *Le Regent, l'abbé Dubois, et les Anglais* (3 vols., 1891).

B 754　Williams, B. 'The foreign policy of England under Walpole', *EHR*, **15** (1900).

See also:

A 1290 Zinkeisen, J. W., vol. 5 (1669–1774).

26   The War of the Austrian Succession (vol. VII, ch. xviii)

General Studies with a European perspective

These are few despite the vast historical literature on the war. For the background to the war see:

B 755   Wagner, F. *Kaiser Karl und die Grossen Mächte* (Stuttgart, 1938).

MILITARY STUDIES

The histories by the general staffs are fundamental:

PRUSSIA

B 756   *Die Kriege Friedrichs des Grossen* (Berlin, 1890–6, Part I and Part II, each in 3 vols.).

AUSTRIA

B 757   *Die Kriege unter der Regierung der Kaiserin-Königin Maria Theresia* (9 vols., Vienna, 1896–1914).

FRANCE

B 758   Colin, J. L. A. *Les Campagnes du maréchal de Saxe* (1900–6); deals with the campaigns of 1744 and 1745 up to and including Fontenoy.

B 759   —— *Louis XV et les jacobites: le projet de débarquement en Angleterre de 1743–4* (1901); deals with a particular phase of the war.

B 760   Pichat, H. *La Campagne du maréchal de Saxe dans les Flandres de Fontenoy à la prise de Bruxelles* (1909).

B 761   Sautai, M. *Les Débuts de la guerre de la succession d'Autriche* (1909, vol. I— no more appeared).

ENGLAND

B 762   Charteris, E. *William Augustus, duke of Cumberland, 1721–48* (1913).

B 763   Pares, R. 'American versus continental warfare 1739–63', *EHR*, 51 (1936); reprinted in Humphreys, R. A. and E. (eds.), *The historian's business and other essays* (Oxford, 1961).

B 764   Richmond, Sir H. W. *The navy in the war of 1739–48* (3 vols., Cambridge, 1920).

B 765   Skrine, H. F. *Fontenoy and Great Britain's share in the war of the Austrian succession* (1906).

For the Italian theatre see:

B 766   Wilkinson, S. *The defence of Piedmont 1742–8* (Oxford, 1927).

POLITICAL AND DIPLOMATIC STUDIES

B 767   Bédarida, H. *Parme dans la politique française au XVIIIe siècle* (1930).

B 768   Beer, A. 'Holland und der österreichische Erbfolge-Krieg', *Archiv für Österr. Geschichte*, 46 (1871).

B 769   Benedikt, H. 'Die europäische Politik des Pforte während des österreichischen Erbfolgekrieges', *Mitteilungen des Österr. Staatsarchiv*, I (1948).

B 770 Carutti, D. *Storia della diplomazia della corte di Savoia* (4 vols., Turin, 1875–80).

B 771 Coquelle, P. *L'alliance franco-hollandaise contre l'Angleterre* (1902).

B 772 Geyl, P. *Willem IV en Engeland tot 1748* (The Hague, 1924).

B 773 —— 'Holland and England in the war of the Austrian succession', *Hist.*, new ser., **14** (1929).

B 774 Karge, P. *Die russisch-österreichische Allianz von 1746* (Göttingen, 1887).

B 775 Vesme, C. B. de. *La politica mediterranea inglese nelle relazione degli inviati italiani a Londra 1741–8* (Turin, 1952).

B 776 Williams, B. *Cartaret and Newcastle* (Cambridge, 1943).

B 777 —— 'Cartaret and the so-called treaty of Hanau', *EHR*, **49** (1934).

B 778 Wilson, A. M. *French foreign policy during the administration of Cardinal Fleury* (Cambridge, Mass., 1936).

B 779 Zabala y Lera, P. *El marqués de Argensón y el pacto de familia de 1743* (Madrid, 1928).

PEACE NEGOTIATIONS

B 780 Becker, R. *Der Dresdener Friede und die Politiks Brühls* (Leipzig, 1902).

B 781 Beer, A. 'Zur Geschichte des Friedens von Aachen', *Archiv für Österr. Geschichte*, **47** (1871).

B 782 Borkovsky, E. O. *Die englische Friedensvermittlung im Jahre 1745* (Berlin, 1884).

B 783 Karg-Bebenburg, T. 'Nochmals der Nymphenburger Vertrag', *HZ*, **128** (1923).

DOCUMENTS AND MEMOIRS

B 784 *Politische Correspondenz Friedrichs des Grossen* (Droysen, J. G., Duncker, M. W., Sybel, H. C. L. von and others, eds.) (39 vols., Berlin, 1879–1925); invaluable for the mentality and actions of the Prussian king. See also his:

B 785 —— *Mémoires*, (Boutaric, E. and Campardon, E., eds.) (2 vols., Paris, 1866).

Among the many collections of documents may be mentioned:

B 786 *Archives de la maison d'Orange-Nassau* (Bussemaker, T., ed.) 4th ser., vol. 1 (Leiden, 1908).

B 787 *Österreichische Staatsverträge, England* (Pribram, A. F., ed.) vol. 1 (Innsbruck, 1907).

27 The Diplomatic Revolution (vol. VII, ch. xix)

Primary Sources

For this chapter these are clearly of the greatest importance:

B 788 Chechulin, N. D. (ed.). *Sbornik* (Archives) of the Imperial Russian Historical Society, vol. 136 (St Petersburg, 1912); provides clearest evidence of Russian aggressiveness. (See also B 1519 below.)

B 789 Khevenhüller-Metsch, R. Graf and Schlitter, H. (eds.). *Aus der Zeit Maria Theresias. Tagebuch des Fürsten Johann Josef Khevenhüller-Metsch Kaiserlichen Obersthofmeisters* (vol. 3, Vienna and Leipzig, 1910; vol. 4, Vienna/Leipzig/Berlin 1914); invaluable for the Habsburg court.

B 790   Martens, F. von (ed.). *Recueil des traîtés et conventions conclus par la Russie* (13 vols., St Petersburg, 1874–1902); includes useful documents (with a commentary) from the Russian archives.

B 791   Masson, F. (ed.). *Mémoires et lettres de François Joachim de Pierre, cardinal de Bernis* (2 vols., 1878); *ex post facto* defence of his policy by the chief French negotiator.

B 792   Schlitter, H. (ed.). *Correspondance secrète entre le comte A. W. Kaunitz-Rietberg et le baron Ignaz de Koch* (1899); documents Kaunitz's celebrated mission to France.

B 793   Volz, G. B. and Küntzel, G. (ed.). *Preussische und Österreichische Acten zur Vorgeschichte des siebenjährigen Krieges* (vol. 74 of *Publicationen aus den K. Preussischen Staatsarchiven*, Leipzig, 1899); a selection of relevant documents from Prussian and Austrian archives.

Secondary Works

B 794   Broicher, E. Ch. *Der Aufsteig der preussischen Macht von 1713 bis 1756 in seiner Auswirkung auf das europäische Staatensystem* (Köln, 1955).

B 795   Butterfield, H. *The reconstruction of an historical episode: the history of the enquiry into the origins of the Seven Years War* (Glasgow University Publications, **91**, Glasgow, 1951); argues that Russia was the real danger to European peace in the years preceding the diplomatic revolution.

B 796   Gooch, G. P. *Frederick the Great* (1947).

B 797   Horn, D. B. *Sir Charles Hanbury Williams and European diplomacy (1747–58)* (1930); an analysis of the motives and policies of the great powers.

B 798   Kaeber, E. *Die Idee des europäischen Gleichgewichts in der publizistischen Literatur vom 16. bis zur Mitte des 18. Jarhhunderts* (Berlin, 1907); analyses pamphlet literature up to 1763.

B 799   Koser, R. *Geschichte Friedrichs des Grossen* (4 vols., 6th and 7th eds., Stuttgart and Berlin, 1921–5): still the best as well as the only full-length biography; bibliography.

B 800   Küntzel, G. *Fürst Kaunitz-Rietberg als Staatsmann* (Frankfurt-on-Main, 1923); a good account of Austrian motives and policies.

B 801   Lehmann, M. *Friedrich der Grosse und der Ursprung des siebenjährigen Krieges* (Leipzig, 1894); a criticism of Frederick II which provoked a battle of the books in Germany.

B 802   Mediger, W. *Moskaus Weg nach Europa* (Brunswick, 1952); throws new light, partly from Hanoverian archives, on Russian aspirations and actions.

B 803   Nolhac, P. de. *Madame de Pompadour et la politique* (1930); shows the limitations of her influence on French policy.

B 804   Portzek, H. *Friedrich der Grosse und Hannover in ihren gegenseitigen Urteil* (Hildesheim, 1958, Veröffentlichungen der historischen Kommission für Niedersachsen, XXV, Niedersachsen und Preussen, Heft 1).

B 805   Ranke, L. von. *Zur Geschichte von Oesterreich und Preussen zwischen den Friedensschlüssen zu Aachen und Hubertusberg* (Leipzig, 1875) (Sämtliche Werke, vol. 30, reprinted and annotated, 1930); classic treatment by the greatest of German historians.

B 806   Ritter, G. *Friedrich der Grosse: ein historisches Profil* (Leipzig, 1936).

B 807   Skalweit, S. *Frankreich und Friedrich der Grosse* (Bonn, 1952); a study of French opinions on Frederick II.

B 808   Strieder, J. *Kritische Forschungen zur Österreichischen Politik vom Aachener Frieden bis zum Beginne des siebenjährigen Krieges* (Leipzig, 1906); attempts a general review of Austrian policy.

B 809   Waddington, R. *Louis XV et le renversement des alliances* (1896); still the best account of the diplomatic revolution.

28   The Seven Years War (vol. VII, ch. xx)

Printed Source Material

B 810   Pargellis, S. M. and Medley, D. J. (eds.). *Bibliography of British history: the eighteenth century, 1714–1789* (Oxford, 1951); gives the documentation for British policy.

B 811   Ozanam, D. and Antoine, M. *Correspondance secrète du comte de Broglie avec Louis XV*, vol. 1 (1956); on French diplomatic activity in central Europe, supplements the volumes of:

A 1086 *Receuil des instructions données aux ambassadeurs de France.*

Histories of the War

B 812   Corbett, Sir J. *England in the Seven Years' War* (2 vols., 1907); still valuable for English naval operations and 'navalist' theories of the war.

B 813   Gipson, L. H. *The British empire before the American revolution*, vols. 6–8, 'The great war for empire' (New York, 1946–54); effectively combines all theatres of war, enabling the student to assess problems as they presented themselves to English ministers.

B 814   Smelser, M. *The campaign for the sugar islands* (Chapel Hill, N.C., 1956).

B 815   Waddington, R. *La guerre de sept ans* (5 vols., 1899); still regarded as the most comprehensive history, though never completed.

Detailed Studies

THE STATUS OF NEUTRALS

B 816   Carter, A. C. 'The Dutch as neutrals in the seven years war', *International and Comparative Law Quarterly*, **12** (1963).

B 817   Pares, R. *Colonial blockade and neutral rights, 1739–63* (Oxford, 1938).

CHANGING ALLIANCES AND CONFLICTS OF STRATEGY

B 818   Palacio Atard, V. *El tercer pacto de familia* (Madrid, 1945); comprehensive study of Franco–Spanish relations.

B 819   Renault, F. P. *La pacte de famille et l'Amérique* (1922).

B 820   Spencer, F. 'The Anglo-Prussian breach of 1762: an historical revision', *Hist.*, **41** (1956); valuable.

ECONOMIC AND FINANCIAL ASPECTS

B 821 Eldon, C. W. *England's subsidy policy towards the continent during the Seven Years War* (Philadelphia, 1938).

B 822 Hill, S. C. *Three Frenchmen in Bengal* (1903); French accounts of economic effects of the war in India.

B 823 Jong-Keesing, E. de. *De economische crisis van 1763* (Amsterdam, 1939); traces the origin of one of the greatest credit crises of the eighteenth century.

B 824 Sutherland, L. S. *A London merchant, 1695–1774* (1933); the fortunes of a merchant who traded during the war.

B 825 —— and Binney, J. 'Henry Fox as paymaster general of the forces', *EHR*, **70** (1955).

See also:

B 87 Pares, R.; B 99 Wilson, C. H.; B 102 Pares, R.

NEGOTIATIONS AND PEACE TREATIES

B 826 Hotblack, K. 'The peace of Paris, 1763', *TRHS*, 3rd ser., **11** (1917).

B 827 Rashed, Z. E. *The Peace of Paris* (Liverpool, 1951); prints the text of the definitive treaty, and has full bibliography.

B 828 Sutherland, L. S. 'The East India Company and the peace of Paris', *EHR*, **62** (1947).

BIOGRAPHIES

Of the many biographies of Chatham see:

B 829 Robertson, C. Grant. *Chatham and the British empire* (1946).

B 830 Tunstall, W. C. B. *William Pitt, Earl of Chatham* (1938); offers a livelier interpretation, and is more readable than Robertson.

B 831 Williams, Basil, *Life of William Pitt, Earl of Chatham* (2 vols., 1913); more laudatory than Tunstall.

B 832 Ruville, A. von. *William Pitt, Earl of Chatham* (Eng. trans. 1907); more critical than Tunstall.

Other biographical studies include:

B 833 Davis, M. *Clive of Plassey* (New York, 1939).

B 834 Eyck, E. *Pitt versus Fox: father and son* (1950).

B 835 Robitaille, G. *Montcalm et ses historiens* (Montreal, 1936); an historiographical essay which also gives much information and a positive interpretation.

B 836 Tunstall, W. C. B. *Admiral Byng and the loss of Minorca* (1928).

29   European Diplomatic Relations, 1763–1790 (vol. VIII, ch. ix)

The best general treatment of the subject is again to be found in:

B 629 Zeller, G. and B 632 Immich, M.; already mentioned.

Detailed Studies

On special topics there may be added:

B 837   Aleksandrov, P. A. *Severnaya sistema* (Moscow, 1914); the only work devoted specifically to the 'northern system' of the 1760s and early 1770s.

B 838   Amburger, E. *Russland und Schweden, 1762–72* (Berlin, 1934).

B 839   Arneth, A. von. *Joseph II und Katharina von Russland: ihr Briefwechsel* (Vienna, 1869); an important collection of printed correspondence.

B 840   Beer, A. *Die erste Teilung Polens* (3 vols., Vienna, 1873); the third volume consists of printed documents.

B 841   Bemis, S. F. *The diplomacy of the American revolution* (New York, 1935); useful bibliography.

B 842   Druzhinina, E. I. *Kyuchuk-Kaïnardzhiïsky mir 1774 goda* (Moscow, 1955); deals with Russian diplomacy during the whole of the war of 1768–74.

B 843   Hanfstaengl, E. F. S. *Amerika und Europa von Marlborough bis Mirabeau; die weltpolitischen Bedeutung des belgisch-bayrischen Tauschprojekts* (Munich, 1930).

B 844   Harlow, V. T. *The founding of the second British empire, 1763–93*, vol. 1 (1952); important on the peace negotiations of 1782–3.

B 845   Madariaga, I. de. *Britain, Russia, and the armed neutrality of 1780* (New Haven and London, 1962).

B 846   Magnette, F. *Joseph II et la liberté de l'Escaut: la France et l'Europe* (Brussels, 1897).

B 847   Meng, J. J. *The comte de Vergennes: European phases of his American diplomacy* (Washington, 1932).

B 848   Ramsey, J. F. *Anglo-French relations, 1763–70: a study of Choiseul's foreign policy* (Berkeley, 1939); short but useful.

B 849   Rose, J. H. *William Pitt and national revival* (1911).

B 850   Temperley, H. W. V. *Frederick the Great and Kaiser Joseph: an episode in war and diplomacy in the eighteenth century* (1915).

B 851   Übersberger, H. *Russlands Orientpolitik in den letzten zwei Jahrhunderten*, vol. 1 (Stuttgart, 1913).

See also:

A 1371   Nolde, B., vol. 2.

THE HISTORIES OF
SEPARATE COUNTRIES
FRANCE 1648–1763

30   France under Louis XIV (vol. v, ch. x)
The Condition of France, 1688–1715 (vol. vi, ch. x)

B 852   Bourgeois, E. and André, L. *Les Sources de l'histoire de France: XVIIe siècle* (1610–1715) (8 vols., 1913–35); the most valuable single guide to printed sources.

Among the printed sources themselves the following are especially important:

B 853   Boislisle, A. de (ed.). *Mémoires des intendants sur l'état des généralités*, vol. I (1881).

B 854   Clement, P. (ed.). *Lettres, instructions et mémoires de Colbert* (10 vols., 1861–82).

B 855   Depping, G. B. (ed.). *Correspondance administrative sous le règne de Louis XIV* (4 vols., 1850–5).

See also:

B 71 Boislisle, A. M. de.

The so-called:

B 856   *Mémoires* of Louis XIV are most conveniently studied in the edition by Longnon, J. (1927).

Of primary importance for the king's political ideas and aims are:

B 857   *Oeuvres de Louis XIV: mémoires historiques et politiques* (2 vols., 1806).

Interesting accounts of the court are given by:

B 858   Saint-Maurice, Marquis de. *Lettres sur la cour de Louis XIV (1667–73)* (Lemoine, J., ed.) (2 vols., 1910–12).

B 859   Spanheim, E. *Relation de la cour de France en 1690* (Bourgeois, E., ed.) (1900).

B 860   Visconti, P. *Mémoires sur la cour de Louis XIV* (French trans.) (1909).

Comments on life in France at the height of the reign, not only in Paris, but in the provinces are to be found in:

B 861   Lough, J. (ed.). *Locke's Travels in France 1675–9* (Cambridge, 1953).

Of general secondary works see:

A 495   Préclin, E. and Tapié, V. L. *Le XVIIe Siècle*; already mentioned.

See also two volumes of the *Rise of Modern Europe* series (Langer, William L., ed.):

B 862   Nussbaum, F. L. *The triumph of science and reason 1660–85* (New York, 1953).

B 863   Wolf, J. B. *The emergence of the great powers 1685–1715* (New York, 1951). These both contain general bibliographies.

B 864   Vries, P. de. *Het beeld van Lodewijk in de franse geschiedschrijving* (Amsterdam, 1948); contains a résumé in French and provides a valuable list of works about the king from the early eighteenth century to recent years. Other works include:

B 865   Lewis, W. H. *The splendid century* (1953).

B 866   —— *The sunset of the splendid century* (1955); bibliography.

B 867   Lough, J. *An introduction to seventeenth century France* (2nd ed., 1955); elementary.

B 868   Pagès, G. *La Monarchie d'ancien régime en France (de Henri IV à Louis XIV)* (1928); although brief, still useful.

See also, for a sociological treatment:

B 301   Sagnac, P.

On France under Louis XIV:

B 869   Boissonade, P. *Colbert: le triomphe de l'étatisme* (1932).
B 870   Bertrand, L. *Louis XIV* (Eng. trans. 1928).
B 871   Gaxotte, P. *La France de Louis XIV* (1946).
B 872   Lavisse, E. *Histoire de France*, vols. 7, i, 7, ii, and 8, i cover the reign, but though detailed, their date (1907–8) reduces their usefulness.
B 873   Lewis, W. H. *Louis XIV, an informal portrait* (1959).
B 874   Mongrédien, G. *La Vie quotidienne sous Louis XIV* (1948).
B 875   Ogg, D. *Louis XIV* (1933); brief, but the standard work in English.
B 876   Saint-Léger, A. de and Sagnac, P. *Louis XIV (1661–1715)*, 3rd ed. (1949) (*Peuples et civilisations*, vol. 10).

For more specialised treatment of the period, reference should be made to the bibliographies on 'Economic and social conditions', 'Intellectual Life', 'The art of war', and 'Religion'. Very few books deal exclusively with the later part of the reign (after *c.* 1685); indeed on occasion, especially in the field of institutional history, there is no choice but to refer the reader to studies concerned only with the background to this period. For a picture of the upper levels of the central administration see:

B 877   Boislisle, A. de. 'Les conseils sous Louis XIV', in the appendices of his edition of the *Mémoires* of Saint-Simon (vols. 4–7, 1884–90).
B 878   Glasson, E. *Le Parlement de Paris, son rôle politique* (2 vols., 1901); discusses in considerable detail the crown's relations with this important body.
B 879   Mousnier, R. 'Le conseil du roy de la mort de Henri IV au gouvernement personnel de Louis XIV', *Etudes d'histoire moderne et contemporaine*, **1** (1947).

On economic problems the following monographs provide, together, a general and virtually exhaustive bibliography:

B 880   Goubert, P. *Beauvais et le Beauvaisis de 1600 à 1730* (2 vols., 1960).
B 881   Scoville, W. C. *The persecution of Huguenots and French economic development (1680–1720)* (Berkeley and Los Angeles, 1960).

Information on price movements is contained in:

B 882   Hauser, H. *Recherches et documents sur l'histoire des prix en France de 1500 à 1800* (1936), but see also:
B 883   Meuvret, J. 'Les crises des subsistences et la démographie de la France de l'ancien régime', *Population*, **1** (1946).
B 884   —— 'Histoire des prix des céréales en France dans la seconde moitié du XVIIe siècle', *Mélanges d'histoire sociale*, **5** (1944).

31   The decline of divine-right monarchy in France (vol. VII, ch. x)

Again, reference should be made to the general bibliographies in this section, particularly to 'Religion', and to the bibliography to vol. v, ch. x/vol. vi, ch. x (Sec. B, **30**) since a number of the books mentioned there also refer to this period.

Documents and contemporary commentators

B 885   Barbier, E. J. F. *Chronique de la régence et du règne de Louis XV* (1718–63) (8 vols., 1885); though Barbier gives too much consideration to rumour, he evokes a general picture of Parisian life.

B 886   Flammermont, J. *Remontrances du Parlement de Paris au XVIIIe siècle* (3 vols., 1888–98); a source of fundamental importance for the political activities and aspirations of this supreme court. The introduction is valuable, though not entirely trustworthy.

B 887   Hénault, C. J. F. *Mémoires* (1911); throws light on the activities of the parlement of Paris during the regency.

B 888   Saint-Simon, Duc de. *Mémoires* (41 vols., 1879–1928); despite his prejudices and inaccuracies, Saint-Simon's acute observation, his intimate connections with the regent and his ability as a writer make these memoirs valuable.

General Studies

B 889   Cobban, A. B. *A history of modern France*, vol. I (1957); the best short survey in English of eighteenth-century France.

B 890   Gaxotte, P. *Le siècle de Louis XV* (rev. ed., 1933); a favourable verdict on Louis XV.

B 891   Leclercq, Dom H. *Histoire de la régence* (3 vols., 1921); the most detailed narrative of the years 1715–23.

Detailed Studies

THE ARISTOCRATIC REVIVAL

B 892   Carré, H. *La Noblesse de France et l'opinion publique au XVIIIe siècle* (1920).

B 893   Ford, F. L. *Robe and sword* (Cambridge, Mass., 1953); a detailed enquiry into the changing relationship between the noblesse d'epée and the noblesse de robe from 1715 to 1748, with a useful bibliography.

THE ENLIGHTENMENT

B 894   Carcassonne, E. *Montesquieu et le problème de la constitution française au XVIIIe siècle* (1927); an excellent survey of the trends in political thought before Montesquieu.

THE 'PARLEMENTAIRE' OPPOSITION

B 895   Egret, J. 'Le procès des Jésuites devant les parlements de France', *RH*, **204** (1950).

B 896   Lacombe, B. de. *La Résistance janséniste et parlementaire au temps de Louis XV* (1949); written round the career of a magistrate in the Paris Parlement, the abbé Nigon de Berty.

See also:

B 383 Bickart, R.

ADMINISTRATIVE HISTORY

B 897   Fréville, H. *L'Intendance de Bretagne, 1689–1790* (3 vols., 1953); an important contribution to our understanding of the relations between local and central government.

B 898   Green, F. C. *The ancien régime* (Edinburgh, 1958); though intended primarily as a background for students of literature this brief outline of the structure of government and society is also useful to historians.

B 302   Tocqueville, A. de. *L'Ancien Régime et la révolution* (Mayer, J-P. and Jardin, A., eds.) (2 vols., 1952–3); a fundamental study.

RELIGION

B 899   Dedieu, J. *Histoire politique des protestants français, 1715–1794* (2 vols., 1925).

B 900   Hardy, G. *Le Cardinal de Fleury et le mouvement janséniste* (1925); though drawn from a limited number of sources, throws a valuable light on Fleury's political methods.

FINANCE AND INDUSTRY

B 901   Harsin, H. *Les Doctrines monétaires et financières en France au XVIIIe siècle* (1924).

B 902   Hyde, H. M. *John Law* (1948).

B 903   Marion, M. *Histoire financière de la France depuis 1715* (6 vols., 1914–31); a valuable introduction to a complicated subject; vol. I covers the years 1715–89.

B 904   —— *Machault d'Arnouville* (1892).

B 905   Rémond, A. *John Holker, manufacturier et grand fonctionnaire en France au XVIIIe siècle* (1946).

See also:

A 1133 Olivier-Martin, F.

FRANCE—THE REVOLUTIONARY
GENERATION TO 1793

Many of the books referred to in the bibliography to vol. VII, ch. x (Sec. B, 31) are also relevant for this period; see also the general bibliographies for this section, especially 'Economic and social conditions'.

32   Social and psychological foundations of the Revolutionary Era (vol. VIII, ch. xv)

Bibliography for so diffuse a topic must be a somewhat arbitrary selection of examples. There is a lack of works dealing with more than one nationality or social class. Much of the best writing is monographic, but social conditions and social psychology are in any case best seen at a concrete level.

General Studies

B 326   Palmer, R. R. *The age of the democratic revolution*, vol. 1 has already been mentioned. It attempts a comparative view of the thirty years before 1792 and elaborates various ideas in the present chapter. See also:

B 906   Echeverria, D. *Mirage in the west: a history of the French image of American society to 1815* (Princeton, 1957); on effects of the American Revolution in France.

B 907   Godechot, J. *La Grande Nation: l'expansion révolutionnaire de la France dans le monde 1789–1799* (2 vols., 1956); with chapters showing the susceptibility of large parts of Europe to French revolutionary expansion.

For a brief selection of recent works on national areas see:

B 908   Geyl, P. *Geschiedenis van de nederlandse stam*, vol. 3, 1751–98 (Amsterdam/Antwerp, 1959); mainly political history.

B 909   Maccoby, S. *English radicalism 1762–1785* (1955).

B 910   —— *English radicalism 1786–1832* (1955).

B 911   Valjavec, F. *Die Entstehung der politischen Strömungen in Deutschland 1770–1815* (Munich, 1951).

B 912   Valsecchi, F. *Le riforme dell'assolutismo illuminato negli stati italiani 1748–1789* (Milan, 1955).

Detailed Studies

ARISTOCRACY

B 913   Egret, J. *Le Parlement de Dauphiné et les affaires publiques dans la deuxième moitié du XVIIIe siècle* (2 vols., Paris and Grenoble, 1942) [and later writings by the same author].

A 29   Goodwin, A. (ed.). *The European nobility in the eighteenth century* (1953); containing articles by various authors on ten countries.

B 914   Rosenberg, H. *Bureaucracy, aristocracy and autocracy: the Prussian experience 1660–1815* (Cambridge, Mass., 1958).

MIDDLE CLASS

B 915 Barber, E. *The bourgeoisie in eighteenth century France* (Princeton, 1955).

B 916 Brunschwig, H. *La Crise de l'état prussien à la fin du XVIIIe siècle et la genèse de la mentalité romantique* (1947); especially illuminating on the German burgher class.

B 917 Labrousse, E. 'Voies nouvelles vers une histoire de la bourgeoisie occidentale aux XVIIIe et XIXe siècles 1700–1850', *Relazioni*, 10 congresso internazionale di scienze storiche, vol. 4 (Florence, 1955); setting forth a design for a large comparative study.

PEASANTRY

B 918 Lefebvre, G. *Les Paysans du nord et la révolution française* (new ed., Bari, 1959).

B 919 —— *La Grande Peur de 1789* (1932).

B 920 —— *Etudes sur la révolution française* (1954); a collection of the author's most important contributions to the social and economic history of the period.

B 921 Sée, H. *Esquisse d'une histoire du régime agraire en Europe aux XVIIIe et XIXe siècles* (1921); still convenient for its comprehensive view.

URBAN WORKING CLASS

Sources for working-class life are scanty before the French Revolution; see the following, which reflect light on pre-revolutionary conditions:

B 922 Rudé, G. *The crowd in the French revolution* (Oxford, 1959).

B 923 Soboul, A. *Les Sans-culottes parisiens en l'An II: mouvement populaire et gouvernement révolutionnaire 2 juin 1793–9 thermidor An II* (1958); a monumental study of popular activity and psychology.

TOWN HISTORIES

A sporadic sampling of this useful genre:

B 924 Bridenbaugh, C. *Cities in revolt: urban life in America 1743–1776* (New York, 1955).

B 925 Kleinclausz, A. J. *Histoire de Lyon* (3 vols., Lyons, 1939–52).

B 926 Patterson, A. T. *Radical Leicester: a history of Leicester 1780–1850* (Leicester, 1954).

B 927 Redford, A. *A history of local government in Manchester* (3 vols., 1939–40).

B 928 Vianello, C. A. *Il settecento milanese* (Milan, 1934).

B 929 Voelcker, H. *Die Stadt Goethes: Frankfurt-am-Main im achtzehnten Jahrhundert* (Frankfurt, 1932).

33 French administration and public finance in their European setting (vol. VIII, ch. xx)

General Studies

A number of important works on this subject have already been mentioned. Among them are:

B 396   Marion, M. *Dictionnaire des institutions de la France aux XVIIe et XVIIIe siècles.*

B 903   —— *Histoire financière de la France depuis 1715* (6 vols., vol. 1, 1715–89; vol. 2, 1789–92; vol. 3, 1792–7).

On banking and credit see:

A 123   Dillen, J. G. van. *History of the Principal Public Banks*; makes possible comparisons with other European countries.

For a broader comparison with British institutions see:

B 58   Binney, J. E. D. *British public finance and administration 1774–1792.*

The most satisfactory general work on the changes brought about by the Revolution is:

B 336   Godechot, J. *Les Institutions de la France sous la révolution et l'empire* (1951).

Monographs on French public finance include:

B 930   Bigo, R. *La Caisse d'escompte (1776–93) et les origines de la banque de France* (1928).

B 931   Bouchary, J. *Les Manieurs d'argent à Paris à la fin du XVIIIe siècle* (3 vols., 1939–43); a detailed study of the financiers.

B 932   Braesch, F. *Finances et monnaies révolutionnaires* (3 vols., Nancy and Paris, 1934–6); part 1 deals with the budget of 1790–1; part 2 with receipts and expenditures of the state in 1788–9; and part 5 with changes of currency during the revolution (parts 3 and 4 never appeared).

B 933   Villain, J. *Le Recouvrement des impots directs sous l'ancien régime* (1952).

Other useful studies are:

B 934   Harris, S. E. *The Assignats* (Cambridge, Mass., 1930).

B 935   Schnerb, R. *La Péréquation fiscale de l'assemblée constituante* (Documents inédits sur l'histoire économique de la révolution) (Clermont-Ferrand, 1936).

See also:

B 75   Mathews, G. T.

There is no general work on French public administration in the eighteenth century. Of the many books and articles on special aspects, the following may be profitably consulted:

B 936   Antoine, M. *Le Fonds du conseil d'état du roi aux archives nationales* (1955); the first fifty pages furnish an expert introduction to the royal councils and their work.

B 937   —— 'Les conseils des finances sous le règne de Louis XV', *Revue d'histoire moderne et contemporaine*, 5 (1958).

B 938   Bacquie, F. *Les Inspecteurs des manufactures sous l'ancien régime (1669–1792)* (Mémoires et documents, Hayem, J., ed.) (1927).

B 939   Biollay, L. *Le Pacte de famine. L'administration du commerce* (1885); furnishes a good history of the royal institutions which administered commerce in the eighteenth century.

B 940   McCloy, S. T. *Government assistance in eighteenth-century France* (Durham, N.C., 1946).

B 941   Masson, F. *Le Département des affaires étrangères pendant la révolution, 1787–1804* (1877).

B 942   Mention, L. *L'Armée de l'ancien régime de Louis XIV à la révolution* (1900).

B 943   Piccioni, C. *Les Premiers Commis des affaires étrangères au XVIIe et au XVIIIe siècles* (1928).

See also:

A 1128 Petot, J.

34   The Breakdown of the old régime in France (vol. VIII, ch. xxi)

A most valuable classified bibliography with an excellent index is:

B 944   Stewart, J. H. *France, 1715–1815. A guide to materials in Cleveland* (Cleveland, 1942); this is a guide to other bibliographies.

For a guide to the legislation of the period 1756–89 see:

B 945   Honoré, S. (ed.). *Actes royaux*, vol. VI. *Louis XV, Louis XVI* (*Catalogue général des livres imprimés de la bibliothèque nationale*, Paris, 1957).

There are many general surveys. The best recent works are:

B 946   Lefebvre, G. *The coming of the French Revolution* (Eng. trans., Princeton, 1947).

B 947   Sagnac, P. *La Fin de l'ancien régime et la révolution americaine* (*Peuples et Civilisations*, 12) (1941).

The political and social history of the period 1763–89 may be studied in the following works:

B 948   Allison, J. P. *Lamoignon de Malesherbes, defender and reformer of the French monarchy, 1721–94* (New York, 1938).

B 949   Carré, H. *La Fin des parlements* (1912).

B 950   Chapuisat, E. *Necker* (1938).

B 951   Dakin, D. *Turgot and the ancien régime in France* (1939).

B 952   Flammermont, J. *Le Chancelier Maupeou et les parlements* (1883).

B 953   Gomel, C. *Les Causes financières de la révolution française* (2 vols., 1892)

B 954   Goodwin, A. 'Calonne, the assembly of French notables of 1787 and the origins of the *révolte nobiliaire*', *EHR*, **61** (1946).

B 955   Labrousse, C-E. *La Crise de l'économie française à la fin de l'ancien régime et au début de la révolution*, vol. I (1944) (uncompleted).

B 956   Lavaquéry, E. *Necker: fourrier de la révolution* (1933).

B 957   Maugras, G. *Le Duc et la duchesse de Choiseul, leur vie intime, leurs amis et leur temps* (1933).

B 958   Renouvin, P. *Les assemblées provinciales de 1789* (1921).

See also:

B 397 Pagès, G. (ed.).

35   The Historiography of the French Revolution (vol. VIII, ch. xxii)

The subject of this chapter involves the whole intellectual history of
France in the nineteenth and twentieth centuries, and does not lend
itself easily to the same type of treatment as the other bibliographies in
this volume. What is attempted here is divided into two parts. The first
(Part A) consists of general works on historiography. The second (Part B)
lists the more detailed materials on the French revolution to which the
student needs to refer.

Part A

Introduction to French historiography of the nineteenth and twentieth
centuries.

B 959   Geyl, P. *Napoleon, for and against* (Eng. trans. 1949).
B 960   Gooch, G. P. *History and historians in the nineteenth century* (2nd ed.,
         1952).
B 961   Halphen, L. *L'Histoire en France depuis cent ans* (1914).
B 962   Moreau, P. *L'Histoire en France au XIXe siècle* (Etudes françaises
         fondées sur l'initiative de la société des professeurs français en Amerique,
         35e cahier) (1935).
B 963   Thompson, J. W. *A history of historical writing* (2 vols., New York, 1942).

Introductions to the historiography of the French revolution in particular.

B 964   Beik, P. H. *The French Revolution seen from the right: social theories in
         motion* (Transactions American Philosophical Society, N.S., **46** (1956)).
B 965   Farmer, P. *France reviews its revolutionary origins: social politics and
         historical opinion in the third republic* (New York, 1944); deals with
         writers after Taine.
B 966   Gottschalk, L. R. 'The French Revolution: conspiracy or circum-
         stances?', *Persecution and Liberty: essays in honour of G. Lincoln Burr*
         (New York, 1931).
B 967   Halévy, D. *Histoire d'une histoire esquissée pour le troisième cinquantenaire
         de la révolution française* (1939); a slight and provocative essay from the
         right-wing viewpoint.
B 968   Lefebvre, G. 'Les historiens de la révolution française', *Bulletin de la
         faculté des lettres de Strasbourg* (Dec. 1929, Jan. 1930); brief, just and
         masterly introduction.
B 969   Mellon, S. *The political uses of history: a study of historians in the French
         restoration* (Stanford, 1958).
B 970   Schmitt, R. E. (ed.). *Some historians of modern Europe* (Chicago, 1942);
         contains essays by J. L. Godfrey on Aulard and by F. Acomb on
         Mathiez.

Introductions to the changing pre-suppositions of historical writing:

B 971   Ariès, P. *Le Temps de l'histoire* (Monaco, 1954).
B 972   Aron, Raymond. *Introduction à la philosophie de l'histoire* (n.d.).
B 973   Febvre, L. *Combats pour l'histoire* (1953).
B 974   Marrou, H-I. *De la connaissance historique* (1956).

Part B

The more detailed materials may be divided into three groups:

(i)

The major historians of the revolution—Thiers, Mignet, Michelet, Taine, etc.

(ii)

The numerous monographs which have been produced on these historians, especially Michelet and Taine. Also the multitude of works referring to the intellectual history of France in the post-revolutionary years, such as:

B 975 Bagge, H. *Les Idées politiques en France dans la restauration* (1952).
B 976 Baldensperger, F. *Le Mouvement des idées dans l'émigration française, 1789–1815* (2 vols., 1924).
B 977 Barzun, J. *The French race* (New York, 1932).
B 978 Elboni, M. H. *French corporative theory 1789–1848* (New York, 1953).
B 979 Guyon, B. *La Pensée politique et sociale de Balzac* (1947).
B 980 Hayes, C. J. *France: a nation of patriots* (New York, 1930).
B 981 Leroy, M. *Histoire des idées sociales en France* (3 vols., 1946–54).
B 982 Tronchon, M. *La Fortune intellectuelle de Herder en France* (1920).

(iii)

The mass of critical reviews and articles devoted to histories of the French revolution, as well as the obituary notices of historians given in the *Revue historique* and most of the other learned journals.

The *Revue des Deux Mondes* contains invaluable material for the earlier historians:

B 983 Sainte-Beuve's magnificent article 'Historiens modernes de la France, IV: M. Thiers', *R.D.M.*, **9** (1845).

Aulard's journal *La Révolution française* covers the later period, and is especially valuable for a long series of articles by Aulard himself on the historians, beginning with:

B 984 Aulard, F. V. A. 'Les premiers historiens de la révolution: les deux amis de la liberté, Rabaut Saint-Etienne', *La Révolution française*, **56** (1909). The place of Aulard's journal in revolutionary studies has now been taken by *Annales historiques de la révolution française*, successively edited by Mathiez and Lefebvre, and this, of course, is a mine of information. These journals do not, however, exhaust the necessary reading of this kind. Perhaps the most important guide to Michelet's historical imagination is still:

B 985 Lanson, G. 'La formation de la méthode historique de Michelet', *Revue d'histoire moderne et contemporaine*, **7** (1905–6).

36   The Outbreak of the French Revolution (vol. VIII, ch. xxiii)
        Reform and Revolution in France: October 1789—February 1793
        (vol. VIII, ch. xxiv)

General studies of the revolution include

B 986   Aulard, F. V. A. *Political history of the French revolution* (Eng. trans.,
        4 vols., 1910).

B 987   Brinton, C. C. *A decade of revolution 1789–1799 (Rise of Modern Europe,*
        Langer, William L., ed., vol. 12), (New York and London, 1934);
        bibliography.

B 988   Göhring, M. *Die Grosse Revolution* (2 vols., Tübingen, 1948–50); the
        latest general survey in German.

B 989   Goodwin, A. *The French Revolution* (1958).

B 990   Lefebvre, G. *La révolution française* (2nd ed., 1957), (*Peuples et civilisa-
        tions,* 13); an outstanding scholarly synthesis with detailed bibliographies.

B 991   —— *La révolution française. La révolution de 1789* ('Les cours de Sor-
        bonne', Paris, n.d.).

B 992   Mathiez, A. *The French Revolution* (Eng. trans., New York, 1928).

B 993   Salvemini, G. *The French revolution 1788–1792* (Eng. trans. from Italian,
        1954).

B 994   Thompson, J. M. *The French revolution* (1953); bibliography.

Detailed Studies

SOCIAL AND ECONOMIC HISTORY AND BACKGROUND

B 995   Clough, S. B. *France, a history of national economics 1789–1939* (New
        York, 1939).

B 996   Garaud, M. *Histoire générale du droit privé français, de 1789 à 1804* (2 vols.,
        1953–9); surveys the social legislation of the revolutionary assemblies.

B 997   Labrousse, C-E. *Esquisse du mouvement des prix et des revenus en France
        au XVIIIe siècle* (2 vols., 1933).

B 998   McCloy, S. T. *The humanitarian movement in eighteenth-century France*
        (Lexington, Kentucky, 1957).

B 999   Sée, H. *La France économique et sociale au XVIIIe siècle* (1952).

See also:

B 591 Poland, B. C.

PEASANTRY AND THE LAND

B 1000 Herbert, S. *The fall of feudalism in France* (1921).

B 1001 Young, A. *Travels in France during the years 1787, 1788 and 1789*
        (Maxwell, C., ed.) (Cambridge, 1929); a lively contemporary account of
        French agricultural and economic conditions on the eve of the re-
        volution.

WORKING CLASS CONDITIONS AND MOVEMENTS IN PARIS

B 1002 Bourdin, I. *Les sociétés populaires à Paris pendant la révolution* (1937).

B 1003 Guérin, D. *La lutte des classes sous la première république* (2 vols., 1946);
        Marxist and controversial.

B 1004   Jaffé, A. *Le Mouvement ouvrier à Paris pendant la révolution française,*
         1789–1791 (1924).
B 1005   Mathiez, A. *La Vie chère et le mouvement social sous la terreur* (1927); the
         first scholarly study of the *Enragés*.

THE ARISTOCRATIC REVOLT

In addition to the general works of Goodwin (B 989), Lefebvre (B 990–1)
and Mathiez (B 992) listed above, see:

B 1006   Egret, J. *La pré-révolution française 1787–1788* (1962).

ECONOMIC CRISIS OF 1787–90

In addition to the works of Labrousse cited above (B 997) and in earlier
lists see:

B 1007   Schmidt, C. 'La crise industrielle de 1788 en France', *RH*, **157** (1908).

THE ELECTION CAMPAIGN AND THE 'CAHIERS'

B 1008   Bouloiseau, M. *Cahiers de doléances du tiers état du bailliage de Rouen*
         pour les états généraux de 1789, vol. 1 (1957).
B 1009   Champion, E. *La France d'après les cahiers de 1789* (3rd ed., 1907).
B 1010   Cochin, A. *Les sociétés de pensée et la démocratie* (1921); tendentious but
         stimulating.
B 1011   Hyslop, B. *Répertoire critique des cahiers de doléances pour les états*
         généraux de 1789 (1933).

THE STATES GENERAL OF 1789

B 1012   Braesch, F. *1789: l'année cruciale* (1941); controversial.
B 1013   Garrett, M. B. *The estates general of 1789: the problem of composition*
         and organisation (New York, 1935).
B 1014   Hutt, M. G. 'The role of the curés in the estates general of 1789',
         Journal of Ecclesiastical History, **6** (1955).

THE ARMY IN 1789

B 1015   Hartmann, L. 'Les officiers de l'armée royale à la veille de la révolu-
         tion', *RH*, **100** (1909); the most useful account for the present purpose.

THE JULY REVOLUTION IN PARIS

B 1016   Caron, P. 'Une tentative de contre-révolution en juin-juillet 1789',
         Revue d'histoire moderne, **8** (1906–7).
B 1017   Chauvet, P. *1789: L'insurrection parisienne et la prise de la Bastille*
         (1946).
B 1018   Flammermont, J. *La journée du 14 Juillet 1789* (1892).

These are all partial accounts and by no means definitive.

THE OCTOBER 'DAYS'

B 1019   Mathiez, A. 'Etude critique sur les journées des 5 et 6 octobre 1789', *RH*, **67** (1898); **68** (1898); **69** (1899).

Studies of the constitutional and diplomatic problems of France between October 1789 and 1792 include:

POLITICAL, ADMINISTRATIVE AND CONSTITUTIONAL HISTORY

The main texts of revolutionary legislation can be studied in such modern collections as:

B 1020   Cahen, L. and Guyot, R. *L'Œuvre législative de la révolution* (1913).

B 1021   Duguit, L., Monnier, H. and Bonnard, R. *Les Constitutions et les principales lois politiques de la France depuis 1789* (7th ed., 1952).

B 1022   Stewart, J. H. *A documentary survey of the French revolution* (New York, 1951); English versions of the French texts with useful introductions and bibliographies.

B 1023   Thompson, J. M. *French Revolution documents 1789–1794* (Oxford, 1933).

Other recent studies include:

B 1024   Campbell, P. *French electoral systems and elections, 1789–1957* (1958).
B 1025   Egret, J. *La Révolution des notables, Mounier et les monarchiens* (1950).
B 1026   Gooch, R. K. *Parliamentary government in France, revolutionary origins, 1789–1791* (Ithaca, 1960).
B 1027   Martin, G. *Les Jacobins* (1945).
B 1028   Palmer, R. R. *Twelve who ruled* (2nd ed., Princeton, 1959); a study of the committee of public safety.
B 1029   Sydenham, M. J. *The Girondins* (1961); destroys the view that they were a political party.
B 1030   Thompson, E. *Popular sovereignty and the French constituent assembly, 1789–91* (Manchester, 1952).

See also:

B 327 Talmon, J. L.

DIPLOMATIC RELATIONS

B 1031   Sorel, A. *L'Europe et la révolution française*, vols. 2 and 3 (9 vols., 1885–1911); provides the best survey of French foreign policy between 1789 and 1793.

See also:

B 1032   Fugier, A. *La Révolution française et l'empire napoléonien* (vol. 4 in Renouvin, P., ed., *Histoire des relations internationales* (1954)).

B 1033   Godechot, J. *La Contre-révolution: doctrine et action 1789–1804* (1961); a general survey of the forces of reaction.

B 1034   Rain, P. *La Diplomatie française de Mirabeau à Bonaparte* (1950).

Anglo-French relations are covered in:

B 1035 *Cambridge History of British Foreign Policy, 1783–1919*, Ward, A. W. and Gooch, G. P., eds. (3 vols., 1922–23) (vol. 1, Cambridge, 1922).

B 1036 Rose, J. H. *Pitt and the Great War* (1911).

B 1037 Seton-Watson, R. W. *Britain in Europe 1789–1914* (Cambridge, 1955).

For a brief selection of recent works on France's relations with other European countries see:

B 1038 Chapuisat, A. *La Suisse et la révolution française* (1945).

B 1039 Chaumié, J. *Les Relations diplomatiques entre l'Espagne et la France de Varennes à la mort de Louis XVI* (Bordeaux, 1957).

B 1040 Droz, J. *L'Allemagne et la révolution française* (1949).

B 1041 Harsin, P. *La Révolution liégoise* (Brussels, 1954).

RELIGIOUS AND ECCLESIASTICAL PROBLEMS

Recent studies of church-state relationships during the revolution, each with full bibliographies, are:

B 1042 Erdmann, K. D. *Volkssouveränität und Kirche* (Cologne, 1949).

B 1043 Latreille, A. *L'église catholique et la révolution française* (2 vols., 1946–50); Catholic in sympathy.

B 1044 Leflon, J. *La Crise révolutionnaire, 1789–1846* (*Histoire de l'église*, Fliche et Martin, eds.), vol. 20 (1949); scholarly and impartial.

For the relations of the Constituent Assembly with the Popes see:

B 1045 Hales, E. E. Y. *Revolution and Papacy 1769–1846* (1960).

B 1046 Mathiez, A. *Rome et le clergé français sous la Constituante* (1907); anti-clerical.

See also:

A 601 Pastor, L. *History of the Popes*, vol. 40.

SPAIN, PORTUGAL AND THEIR EMPIRES

For the bibliography to vol. v, ch. xv 'Spain and her Empire' see Sec. A, **41**. The bibliography to vol. iv, ch. xxiii 'The Social and Economic History of Latin America' is placed in this section in order to be in close relationship with the lists for vols. v and vi on 'Portugal and her Empire 1648–1720', since these deal primarily with Brazil.

37 **The Social and Economic History of Latin America (vol. iv, ch. xxiii)**

Bibliographies

Several bibliographical guides have already been mentioned in Section A. The most useful guide to works in English is:

B 1047 Humphreys, R. A. *Latin American History; a guide to the literature in English* (rev. ed.) (London and New York, 1958).

A far more complete general bibliography, arranged by topics and with commento io t

B 1048   Instituto panamericano de geografía e historia, Mexico City. Comisión de historia. *Programa de historia de América*. II. *Período colonial* (4 vols., Mexico City, 1953).

General Studies

The best general sketch is:

A 1013   Céspedes del Castillo, G. 'Las Indias en el siglo XVII', in Vicens Vives, J. (ed.). *Historia social y económica de España y América*, vol. iii (Barcelona, 1957); with bibliography. This does not cover Portuguese America, for which Boxer, listed below under 'Detailed Studies', is the best and most recent sketch.

The best general work in English on Latin American colonial economy is:

B 1049   Diffie, B. W. *Latin American civilization: colonial period* (Harrisburg, Pa., 1945); extensive bibliography.

Detailed Studies

Most of the social and economic history of Latin America in the seventeenth century still remains to be studied in detail and with attention to regional differences. The works cited below are the best of recent studies; almost all cover periods of time longer than the years 1610–60.

REGIONAL HISTORIES

B 1050   Arcila Farías, E. *Economía colonial de Venezuela* (Mexico City, 1946).
B 1051   Boxer, C. R. *The Dutch in Brazil, 1624–1654* (Oxford, 1957); excellent for central and northern Brazil.
B 1052   Lohmann Villena, G. *El conde de Lemos, virrey del Perú* (Madrid, 1946).
B 1053   Simpson, L. B. *Many Mexicos* (3rd ed., Berkeley, 1952).

POPULATION

B 1054   Rosenblat, A. *La población indígena y el mestizaje en América* (Buenos Aires, 1954).

THE JESUIT MISSIONS IN THE RÍO DE LA PLATA

B 1055   Graham, R. B. Cunninghame. *A vanished Arcadia: some account of the Jesuits in Paraguay, 1607–1767* (rev. ed., 1924).
B 1056   Mörner, M. *The political and economic activities of the Jesuits in the La Plata region. The Hapsburg era*, vol. 1 (Stockholm, 1953).

AGRICULTURE AND LABOUR (INCLUDING NEGRO SLAVERY)

B 1057   Arcila Farías, E. *El régimen de encomienda en Venezuela* (Seville, 1957).
B 1058   Borde, J. and Góngora, M. *Evolución de la propiedad rural en el valle del Puangue* (2 vols., Santiago, Chile, 1956).

B 1059　Freyre, G. *The masters and the slaves* (Eng. trans. from the 4th Brazilian ed.) (New York, 1946).

B 1060　Service, E. R. *Spanish-Guaraní relations in early colonial Paraguay* (Ann Arbor, 1954).

MINING

B 1061　Lohmann Villena, G. *Las minas de Huancavelica en los siglos XVI y XVII* (Seville, 1949).

B 1062　West, R. C. *The mining community in northern New Spain: the Parral mining district* (Berkeley and Los Angeles, 1949).

TRADE AND NAVIGATION

B 1063　Arcila Farías, E. *Comercio entre Venezuela y México en los siglos XVI y XVII* (Mexico City, 1950).

A 1553　Schurz, W. L. *The Manila galleon* (New York, 1939).

THE SALE OF PUBLIC OFFICE

B 1064　Parry, J. H. *The sale of office in the Spanish Indies under the Hapsburgs* (Berkeley and Los Angeles, 1953).

See also:

A 80 Borah, W. W.; A 83 Chaunu, H. and P.; A 91 Haring, C. H.; A 1742 Steward, J. H. (ed.); A 1746 Chevalier, F.; A 1772 Parry, J. H. and Sherlock, P. M.

38　　Portugal and her empire (vol. v, ch. xvi)
Portugal and her empire, 1680–1720 (vol. vi, ch. xvi)

Bibliographies

There is no general bibliographical guide for both Portugal and her empire. For Brazil see:

B 1065　Moraes, R. Borba de and Berrien, W. *Manual bibliográfico de estudos brasileiros* (Rio de Janeiro, 1949).

B 1066　Rodrigues, J. H. *Teoria da história do Brasil (introdução metodológica)* (2 vols., São Paulo, 1957).

General Studies

Of general histories of Portugal the best is:

A 1608　Peres, D. (ed.). *História de Portugal*, vol. 6 (1640–1815) (Barcelos, 1934); the chapters by J. Cortesão on the empire are particularly valuable.

B 1067　Almeida, F. de. *História de Portugal*, vols. 4 and 5 (1580–1816) (Coimbra, 1926–8); has useful bibliographies, but is naïve and prejudiced.

For general histories of Brazil see:

B 1068　Abreu, J. Capistrano de. *Capítulos de história colonial, 1500–1800* (4th ed., Rio de Janeiro, 1954).

B 1069　Calmon, P. *História do Brasil*, vols. 2 and 3 (1600–1800) (São Paulo, 1941–3).

B 1070   Calmon, P. *História social do Brasil*, vol. 1 (São Paulo, 1939).
B 1071   Varnhagon, F. A. de. *História geral do Brasil* (3rd ed., 5 vols., São Paulo, n.d.).

Detailed Studies

ECONOMIC AND SOCIAL HISTORY

B 1072   Azevedo, J. Lúcio de. *Épocas de Portugal económico* (Lisbon, 1929); not always reliable in detail but has not been superseded.
B 1073   Silbert, A. *Un Carrefour de l'Atlantique: Madère 1640–1820* (Lisbon, 1954).

See also:

B 13 Shillington, V. M. and Chapman, A. B. W.

On Brazil in particular see:

B 1074   Magalhães, B. de. *Expansão geográfica do Brasil colonial* (3rd ed., Rio de Janeiro, 1944).
B 1075   Simonsen, R. *Historia economica do Brasil 1500–1820* (2 vols., São Paulo, 1937–8).

POLITICAL AND ADMINISTRATIVE HISTORY

B 1076   Boxer, C. R. *Salvador de Sá and the struggle for Brazil and Angola* (1952); one of the best studies on the period.
B 1077   Ericeira, Conde da. *História de Portugal restaurado* (Lisbon, 1679–98); new ed. by A. Álvaro Dória (4 vols., Oporto, 1945–7); still useful for the period up to 1668.
B 1078   Leite, S. *História da companhia de Jesus no Brasil* (10 vols., Lisbon and Rio de Janeiro, 1938–50).
B 1079   Merêa, P. *O poder real e as côrtes* (Coimbra, 1923).
B 1080   Rodrigues, F. *História da companhia de Jesus na assistência de Portugal* (6 vols., Oporto, 1931–44); like Leite above, an indispensable work written from the Jesuit point of view.
B 1081   Zenha, E. *O município no Brasil 1532–1700* (São Paulo, 1948).

See also:

B 704 Prestage, E.

CULTURAL HISTORY

B 1082   Bazin, G. *L'Architecture religieuse baroque au Brésil* (2 vols., 1956–8).
B 1083   Dias, J. S. da Silva. *Portugal e a cultura europeia dos séculos XVI a XVIII* (Coimbra, 1953).

OTHER TOPICS

B 1084   Kiemen, M. C. *The Indian policy of Portugal in the Amazon region 1614–1693* (Washington, 1954).
B 1085   Lima, D. Pires de. *O Oriente e a África, desde a restauração a Pombal* (Lisbon, 1946).

See also:

A 1194 Mauro, F.; B 566 Almeida, F. de, vol. 3.

39   The Spanish Empire under foreign pressures, 1688–1715 (vol. VI, ch. xi)

The main bibliographical sources have already been mentioned in previous lists and in the parallel lists in Section A.

General Studies

Problems of old Spain. Most of the histories have been written by Castilians. Recent works stressing the viewpoint of the Aragonese realms include:

B 1086   Carrera Pujal, J. *Historia política y económica de Cataluña* (4 vols., Barcelona, 1946–7).

B 1087   Mercader, J. *El segle XVIII. Els capitans generals* (Barcelona, 1957).

B 1088   Reglà Campistol, J. *Els virreis de Catalunya* (Barcelona, 1956).

B 1089   Valls-Taberner, F. and Soldevila, F. *Historia de Cataluña* (2 vols., Madrid and Barcelona, 1955–7).

B 1090   Voltes Bou, P. *El Archiduque Carlos de Austria, rey de los Catalanes* (Barcelona, 1953).

On the question of the population of Spain see:

B 1091   Girard, A. 'Le chiffre de la population de l'Espagne', *Revue de l'histoire moderne*, **3** (1928); **4** (1929).

B 1092   —— 'La répartition de la population en Espagne', *Revue d'histoire économique*, **17** (1929).

The best general accounts of the Spanish Empire in America are:

A 1737   Haring, C. H. *The Spanish Empire in America*; already mentioned.

B 1049   Diffie, B. W. *Latin American civilization: colonial period*; already mentioned:

On particular areas see:

B 1093   Bancroft, H. H. *History of Mexico* (6 vols., San Francisco, 1883–8).

B 1094   —— *History of central America* (3 vols., San Francisco, 1883–7).

B 1095   Galdames, L. *A history of Chile* (Durham, N.C., 1941).

B 1096   Levene, *A history of Argentina* (Durham, N.C., 1937).

See also:

A 1744 Means, P. A.

Detailed Studies

ADMINISTRATIVE ORGANIZATION

B 1097   Cunningham, C. H. *The audiencia in the Spanish colonies as illustrated by the Audiencia of Manila, 1583–1800* (Berkeley, 1919).

B 1098   Lohmann Villena, G. *El corregidor de Indios en el Perú bajo los Austrias* (Madrid, 1957).

B 1099   Moore, J. P. *The cabildo in Peru under the Habsburgs* (Durham, N.C., 1954).

B 1100   Rubio Mañé, J. Ignacio. *Introducción al estudio de los virreyes de Nueva España, 1535–1746* (2 vols., Mexico, D.F., 1955–9).

NATIVE PEOPLES, THE NEGRO AND THE SLAVE TRADE

B 1101   Scelle, G. *La Traite négrière aux Indes de Castille* (2 vols., 1906).
B 1102   Tannenbaum, F. *Slave and citizen: the negro in the Americas* (New York, 1947).
B 1103   Zelinski, W. 'The historical geography of the negro population of Latin America', *Journal of negro history*, **34** (1949).

THE CHURCH AND THE MISSIONS

B 1104   Mecham, J. L. *Church and state in Latin America* (Chapel Hill, N.C., 1934).

TRADE, INDUSTRY AND MINING

B 1105   Brown, V. L. 'The south sea company and contraband trade', *AHR*, **31** (1926).
B 1106   Donnan, E. 'The early days of the south sea company', *Journal of economic and business history*, **2** (1930).
B 1107   Hussey, R. D. 'Antecedents of the Spanish monopolistic overseas trading companies (1624–1728)', *HAHR*, **9** (1929).
B 1108   Moreyra Paz-Soldán, M. *El tribunal del Consulado de Lima. Cuaderno de Juntas*, **1** (*1706–1720*); **2** (*1721–1727*) (2 vols., Lima, 1956–9).

See also:

A 1180 Hamilton, E. J.

INTERNATIONAL RIVALRIES

B 1109   Calderón Quijano, J. A. *Belice, 1663(?)–1821* (Seville, 1944).
B 1110   Chatelain, V. E. *The defenses of Spanish Florida, 1565 to 1763* (Washington, 1941).
B 1111   Dunn, W. E. *Spanish and French rivalry in the gulf region of the United States, 1678–1702* (Austin, Texas, 1917).
B 1112   Ford, L. C. *The triangular struggle for Spanish Pensacola, 1689–1739* (Washington, 1939).
B 1113   Means, P. A. *The Spanish Main, focus of envy, 1492–1700* (New York, 1935).

See also:

B 477 Crouse, N. M.

For Spain under the early Bourbon kings see bibliography Sec. B, **43** on 'Italy and the Mediterranean' below.

40   The Iberian States, 1763–1793 (vol. VIII, ch. xiii. 1)
General Studies

The main general works on the Spanish history of the period have already been mentioned, see:

A 1149   Soldevila, F. *Historia de España*, vol. 6.
B 306   Herr, R. *The eighteenth-century revolution in Spain.*
B 567   Desdevises du Dézert, G. *L'Espagne de l'ancien régime*, 3 vols.

For the histories of Portugal see:

A 1608 Peres, D. and others; B 1067 Almeida, F. de.

There are also modern histories of Portugal in English by:

A 1607   H. V. Livermore (Cambridge, 1947).
B 1114   C. E. Nowell (New York, 1952); both of which contain useful biblio-graphies.

Detailed Studies

THE BOURBONS AND THEIR GOVERNMENT

B 1115   Danvila y Collado M. *El reinado de Carlos III* (6 vols., Madrid, 1890–6); still useful source of information.
B 1116   Muriel, A. *Historia de Carlos IV* (6 vols., Madrid, 1893–5).
B 1117   Paz, Príncipe de la. *Memorias (Biblioteca de autores españoles)* (2 vols. Madrid, 1956). The memoirs of Godoy; see also the introduction by C. Seco Serrano.
B 1118   Rodríguez Casado, V. *Política interior de Carlos III* (Valladolid, 1950).
B 1119   Rousseau, F. *Règne de Charles III d'Espagne* (2 vols., 1907); also relevant for foreign policy.

THE ENLIGHTENMENT IN SPAIN

B 1120   Álvarez Requejo, F. *El conde de Campomanes. Su obra histórica* (Oviedo, 1954).
B 1121   Defourneaux, M. *Pablo de Olavide ou l'afrancesado (1725–1803)* (Paris, 1959).
B 1122   Sánchez Agesta, L. *El pensamiento político del despotismo ilustrado* (Madrid, 1953).
B 128   Sarrailh, J. *L'Espagne éclairée de la seconde moitié du XVIIIe siècle* (1954); the most complete and searching study of the subject; already mentioned.
B 1123   Shafer, R. J. *The economic societies in the Spanish world (1763–1821)* (Syracuse, N.Y., 1958).

CHURCH AND STATE IN SPAIN

B 1124   Eguia Ruíz, C. *Los Jesuítas y el motín de esquilache* (Madrid, 1947).
B 1125   Rodríguez Casado, V. 'Iglesia y estado en el reinado de Carlos III', *Estudios Americanos*, I (1948).

ECONOMIC AND SOCIAL CONDITIONS IN SPAIN

The main general works have already been mentioned. See:

A 995   Carrera Pujal, J. *Historia de la economía española.*
A 1013   Vicens Vives, J. (ed.). *Historia social y económica de España y America* (5 vols., of which vol. 4 is relevant to this period).

See also:

B 1126   Domínguez Ortiz, A. *La sociedad española en els siglo XVIII* (Madrid, 1955); valuable on classes, seigneurial jurisdiction and municipal government.

B 1127 Blart, L. *Les Rapports de la France et de l'Espagne après le pacte de famille, jusqu'à la fin du ministère du duc de Choiseul* (1915).

B 1128 Conrotte, M. *La intervención de España en la independencia de los estados unidos* (Madrid, 1920).

B 1129 Gil Munilla, O. *El río de la Plata en la política internacional. Génesis del virreinato* (Seville, 1949).

See also:

B 818 Palacio Atard, V.

PORTUGAL

B 1130 Azevedo, J. Lúcio de. *O Marquês de Pombal e a sua época* (Lisbon, 1922).

B 1131 Beirão, C. *D. Maria I, 1777–92* (Lisbon, 1934).

B 1132 Cheke, M. *Dictator of Portugal* (London, 1938).

B 1133 Macedo, J. de. *A situação económica no tempo de Pombal* (Oporto, 1951.)

ITALY AND THE MEDITERRANEAN

41   Italy after the Thirty Years War (vol. v, ch. xix)

General Studies

B 1134 Cabibbe, G. *Relazioni degli ambasciatori sabaudi, genovesi, veneti* (Istituto per gli studi di politica internazionale, Milan, 1936).

B 1135 Catalano, F. and others. *Dalla crisi della libertà agli albori dell'illuminismo: 1450–1748* (in *Storia d'Italia*, Valeri, N., ed.), vol. 2 (Turin, 1959).

B 1136 Croce, B. *Storia dell'età barocca in Italia* (3rd ed., Bari, 1953).

See also:

A 630 Visconti, A.; A 1063 Quazza, R.; A 1065 Tocco, V. di.

Detailed Studies

SAVOY

B 1137 Bulferetti, L. *Assolutismo e mercantilismo nel Piemonte di Carlo Emanuele III* (Turin, 1953).

B 1138 Carutti, D. *Il primo re di casa Savoia: Vittorio Amedeo II* (Turin, 1897).

B 1139 Pascal, A. 'Le valli valdesi negli anni del martirio e della gloria', *Bollettino della società di studi valdesi*, no. **68** (1937).

B 1140 Quazza, R. *La formazione progressiva dello stato sabaudo* (Turin, 1936).

B 1141 Viora, M. *Storia delle leggi sui Valdesi di Vittorio Amedeo II* (Bologna, 1930).

VENICE

B 1142 Cessi, R. *Storia della repubblica di Venezia* (2 vols., Milan-Messina, 1944–6).

B 1143 *La civiltà veneziana nell'età barocca* (Fondazione Cini, Florence, 1959).

B 1144   Kretschmayr, H. *Geschichte von Venedig* (3 vols., Gotha, 1905–34).
B 1145   Romanin, S. *Storia documentata di Venezia* (new ed., 3 vols., Venice, 1912).

MILAN

A 962   *Storia di Milano*, vol. 11 (Il declino spagnolo) (Fondazione Treccani, Milan, 1958); covers this period.

TUSCANY

B 1146   Himbert, G. *Seicento fiorentino* (Milan, 1930).
B 1147   Pieraccini, G. *La stirpe Medici di Cafaggiolo* (Florence, 1925).

ROME

B 1148   Papasogli, G. *Innocenzo XI* (Rome, 1956).

See also:

A 601   Pastor, L. von. *History of the Popes*, vol. 32.
B 557   Orcibal, J. *Louis XIV contre Innocent XI*.

NAPLES AND SICILY

B 1149   Croce, B. *Storia del regno di Napoli* (2 vols., Naples, 1931).
B 1150   Pepe, G. *Il mezzogiorno d'Italia sotto gli spagnoli, la tradizione storiografica* (Florence, 1952).
B 1151   Petrocchi, M. *La rivoluzione messinese del 1674* (Florence, 1954).

See also:

A 985 Coniglio, G.; A 986 Titone, V.; A 987 Titone, V.; B 478 Laloy, E.

THE LESSER STATES

B 1152   Ciasca, R. *Istruzioni e relazioni degli ambasciatori genovesi* (Rome, 1955–7).
B 1153   Pastine, O. *Genova e l'impero ottomanno nel secolo XVII* (Genoa, 1952).
B 1154   Quazza, R. *Mantova attraverso i secoli* (Mantua, 1933).
B 1155   Vitale, V. *Breviario della storia di Genova* (2 vols., Genoa, 1956).

RELIGIOUS AND CULTURAL HISTORY

B 1156   Maugain, G. *Etudes sur l'évolution intellectuelle de l'Italie de 1657 à 1750* (1909).
B 1157   Petrocchi, M. *Il quietismo italiano del seicento* (Rome, 1948).

See also:

A 948 Spini, G.; B 264 Belloni, A.; B 602 Jemolo, A. C.

42   **The Mediterranean in peace and war (vol. VI, ch. xvii)**

Reference should also be made to the bibliographies on 'Economic and Social Conditions' and on 'The Art of War'. Books on Spain and on Italy are to be found in 'Spain, Portugal and their Empires' and in the other lists of this part, including the list for vol. VII, ch. xii (Sec. B, **43**) below.

The economic background

B 1158 Beltrami, D. *Saggio di storia dell'agricoltura nella repubblica di Venezia durante l'età moderna* (Venice and Rome, 1955).

B 1159 —— *Storia delle popolazioni di Venezia dalla fine del secolo XVI alla caduta della repubblica* (Padua, 1954).

B 1160 —— 'La composizione economica e professionale della popolazione di Venezia nei secoli XVII e XVIII', *Giornale degli economisti e annali di economia*, 10 (new series), 1951.

B 1161 Braudel, F. 'L'économie de la Méditerranée au XVIIe siècle', *Cahiers de Tunisie*, 4 (1946).

B 1162 Giacchero, G. *Storia economica del settecento genovese* (Genoa, 1951).

B 1163 Luzzatto, G. *Storia economica dell'età moderna e contemporanea* (2 vols., Padua, 1950–2).

B 1164 —— *Per una storia economica d'Italia. Progressi e lacune* (Bari, 1957); bibliography.

B 1165 Meuvret, J. 'La géographie du prix des céréales et les anciennes économies européennes, prix méditerranéens, prix continentaux, prix atlantiques, à la fin du XVIIe siècle', *Revista di economia*, 4.

B 1166 —— *Les Mouvements des prix de 1661 à 1715 et leurs répercussions* (1944).

B 1167 Sella, D. 'Les mouvements longs de l'industrie lainière à Venise au XVIe et XVIIe siècles', *AESC*, 1 (1957).

B 1168 Vilar, P. 'Géographie et histoire statistique. Histoire sociale et techniques de production. Quelques points d'histoire de la viticulture méditerranéenne', *Hommage à Lucien Febvre*, vol. 1 (1953).

See also:

A 77 Braudel, F.; A 99 Mols, R.

COMMERCE

B 1169 Campos, G. 'Il commercio esterno veneziano nella seconda metà del secolo XVII secondo le statistiche ufficiali', *Archivio Veneto*, 19 (1936).

B 1170 Epstein, M. *Early history of the Levant company* (1908).

B 1171 Koenigsberger, H. G. 'English merchants in Naples and Sicily in the seventeenth century', *EHR*, 62 (1947).

B 1172 Masson, P. *Histoire des établissements et du commerce français dans l'Afrique barbaresque* (1903).

B 1173 —— *Les compagnies de Corail* (1908).

B 1174 Romano, R. *Le commerce du royaume de Naples avec la France et les pays de l'Adriatique au XVIIIe siècle* (1951).

B 1175 —— and Braudel, F. *Navires et marchandises à l'entrée du port de Livourne 1547–1611* (1951).

See also:

A 114 Bergasse, L. and Rambert, G.; A 1309 Wood, A. C.; A 1568 Foster, Sir W.; A 1663 Krishna, Bal; B 95 Paris, R.; B 121 Svoronos, N. G.

The Corsairs

B 1176 Condreau, R. *Les Corsaires de Salé* (1948).

B 1177 Fisher, G. *Barbary legend: war, trade and piracy in North Africa 1415–1830* (Oxford, 1957).

B 1178 Rossi, E. *Storia della marina del ordine di san Giovanni di Gierusalemme* (Rome and Milan, 1926).

B 1179 Salvá, J. *La orden de Malta y las acciones navales españolas contra turcos y berberiscos en los siglos XVI y XVII* (Madrid, 1944).

The Mohammedans in the Mediterranean

B 1180 Alderson, A. D. *The structure of the Ottoman dynasty* (1956).

B 1181 Ayache, A. *Le Maroc* (1958); bibliography.

B 1182 Capot Rey, R. *La Politique française et le Maghreb méditerranéen 1643–1685* (Algiers, 1935).

B 1183 Cappovin, G. *Tripoli e Venezia nel secolo XVIII* (Venice, 1943).

B 1184 Gibb, H. A. R. and Bowen, H. *Islamic society and the west* (2 parts, Oxford, 1950–7).

B 1185 Grandchamp, P. *La France en Tunisie 1577–1705* (10 vols., Tunis, 1921–37).

B 1186 Julien, Ch. A. *Histoire de l'Afrique du Nord: Tunisie, Algérie, Maroc* (revised by Le Tourneau, R.), vol. 2 (1956); bibliography.

B 1187 Lacoste, Y., Prenant, A. and Nouschi, A. *L'Algérie, passé et présent* (1960); bibliography.

B 1188 Micacchi, L. *La Tripolitania sotto il dominio dei Caramanli* (Rome, 1936).

43 **The Western Mediterranean and Italy (vol. VII, ch. xii)**

Italy

B 1189 Anzilotti, A. *Le reforme in Toscana* (Pisa, 1924).

B 1190 Bédarida, H. and others. *L'Italie au XVIIIe siècle* (1929).

B 1191 Benedikt, H. *Das Königreich Neapel unter Kaiser Karl VI* (Vienna, 1927).

B 1192 Morandi, C. 'La fine del dominio spagnuolo in Lombardia', *Archivio storico italiano*, **94** (1936).

B 1193 Pontieri, E. *Il tramonto del baronaggio siciliano* (Florence, 1943).

B 1194 —— *Il reformismo borbonico nella Sicilia* (Rome, 1945).

B 1195 Prato, G. *La vita economica in Piemonte a mezzo il secolo XVIII* (Turin, 1908).

B 1196 Pugliese, S. *Le prime strette dell'Austria in Italia* (Milan, 1932).

B 1197 Reumont, A. von. *Geschichte Toscana's seit dem Ende des florentinischen Freistaates* (2 vols., Gotha, 1876–7).

B 1198 Robiony, E. *Gli ultimi Medici e la successione al granducato di Toscana* (Florence, 1905).

B 1199 Rota, E. *Le origine del risorgimento 1700–1800* (Milan, 1938); good study of the eighteenth century, without too much preoccupation with the risorgimento.

B 1200   Schipa, M. A. *Il regno di Napoli al tempo di Carlo di Borbone* (Milan and Rome, 1923).

B 1201   Schillmann, F. *Venedig* (Leipzig and Vienna, 1933).

Spain

B 1202   Armstrong, E. *Elisabeth Farnese* (1892); excellent, thorough, objective, and based on original documents.

B 1203   Bédarida, H. *Les premiers Bourbons de Parma et l'Espagne 1731–1802* (1928).

B 1204   Bourgeois, E. (ed.). *Lettres intimes de J. M. Alberoni* (1892).

B 1205   Carrera Pujal, J. *La Barcelona del segle XVIII* (2 vols., Barcelona, 1951).

B 1206   Castagnoli, P. *Il cardinale Giulio Alberoni* (3 vols., Piacenza and Rome, 1929–32).

B 1207   Danvila, A. *Luisa Isabel de Orleans y Luis I* (Madrid, 1902).

B 1208   Harcourt Smith, S. *Cardinal of Spain: the life and strange career of Alberoni* (New York, 1944).

B 1209   Keay, C. E. *Life and manners in Madrid 1750–1800* (Berkeley, 1932); contains fascinating descriptions.

B 1210   Morel Fatio, A. (ed.). *Vida de Carlos III de Fernan-Nuñez* (2 vols., Madrid, 1898)

B 1211   Pimoden, G. de. *Louise-Elisabeth d'Orléans, reine d'Espagne 1709–1742* (1922).

B 1212   Reglá Campistol, J. and others. *Relaciones internacionales de España con Francia e Italia—siglos XV a XVIII* (Barcelona, 1951).

B 1213   Rodríguez Villa, A. *Patiño y Campillo* (Madrid, 1882).

B 1214   —— *Don Cenon de Somodevilla, el marqués de la Ensenada* (Madrid, 1878).

See also:

A 1148 Ballesteros y Beretta, A.; B 86 McLachlan, J. O.

For bibliography to vol. VIII, ch. xiii, 2, see Section C, 35.

THE BRITISH ISLES

The bibliography to vol. IV, ch. xviii has been placed here rather than in Section A since it seemed to belong most naturally with the other lists on seventeenth-century Britain.

44   The Fall of the Stuart Monarchy (vol. IV, ch. xviii)
Bibliographies

B 1215   Davies, G. (ed.). *Bibliography of British History: Stuart Period 1603–1714* (1928); the standard guide to this and to the subsequent bibliographies on Stuart history.

Reference should also be made to the bibliographies in this section on 'Religion'.

General Studies

The basic detailed general narrative is to be found in the works of S. R. Gardiner:

B 1216 *History of England 1603–42* (10 vols., 1883–4).
B 1217 *History of the great civil war* (4 vols., 1893).
B 1218 *History of the Commonwealth and protectorate* (4 vols., 1903).

These were continued by:

B 1219 Firth, C. H. *The last years of the protectorate* (2 vols., 1909).
B 1220 Davies, G. *The Restoration of Charles II 1658–60* (San Marino, 1955).
B 1221 Davies, G. *The Early Stuarts 1603–60* (2nd ed., Oxford, 1959); founded on the above but uses later work.
B 1222 Notestein, W. *The English people on the eve of colonisation 1603–1630* (New York, 1954); a masterly sketch of society and institutions.
B 1223 Wedgwood, C. V. *The King's War 1641–1647* (1958); a lively sketch, better at describing the problems of royalist leaders than those of their opponents.

The most important work by a contemporary is:

B 1224 E. Hyde, Earl of Clarendon. *The History of the rebellion and civil war in England* (the best edition is by W. D. Macray) (6 vols., Oxford, 1888).

Detailed Studies

CONSTITUTION, PARLIAMENT, POLITICAL THOUGHT

A 422 Holdsworth, W. S. *A history of English law*, vols. 4–6 (2nd ed., 1937); already mentioned, gives the most comprehensive account of the courts and the constitution.

Other studies include:

B 1225 Brunton, D. and Pennington, D. H. *Members of the Long parliament* (1953).
B 1226 Firth, C. H. *The House of Lords during the civil war* (1910).
B 1227 Hexter, J. H. *The reign of King Pym* (Cambridge, Mass., 1938).
B 1228 Pearl, V. *London and the outbreak of the Puritan revolution: city government and national politics 1625–1643* (Oxford, 1961).
B 1229 Willson, D. H. *The privy councillors in the house of commons 1604–1629* (Minneapolis, 1940).

See also:

A 508 Frank, J.; A 509 Gough, J. W.; A 510 Judson, M. A.; A 511 Pocock, J. G. A.; A 513 Zagorin, P.

FINANCE AND ADMINISTRATION

B 1230 Ashley, M. *Commercial and financial policies under the Cromwellian protectorate* (Oxford, 1934).
B 1231 Ashton, R. 'Deficit finance in the reign of James I', *Econ. HR*, 2nd ser., **10** (1957).

B 1232 Aylmer, G. E. *The King's servants* (1961); deals with the central departments and the fortunes of office-holders under Charles I.

A 140   Tawney, R. H. *Business and politics under James I* (Cambridge, 1958); already mentioned. Part i deals with Cranfield as a merchant, part ii with him as an administrator.

B 1233 Willcox, W. B. *Gloucestershire. A study in local government 1590–1640* (New Haven, 1940).

See also:

A 421 Dietz, F. C.

RELIGION

B 1234 Haller, W. A. *Liberty and reformation in the puritan revolution* (New York, 1955).

B 1235 Hill, C. *Economic problems of the church from Whitgift to the Long Parliament* (Oxford, 1956).

B 1236 Marchant, R. A. *The Puritans and the church courts in the diocese of York 1560–1642* (1960).

See also:

A 920 Haller, W. A.

BIOGRAPHIES

B 1237 Ashley, M. *The greatness of Oliver Cromwell* (1957); among the most recent lives of the protector.

B 1238 Firth, C. H. *Oliver Cromwell* (1900); still the best short life.

B 1239 Hulme, H. *The life of Sir John Eliot 1592–1632* (1957).

B 1240 Trevor-Roper, H. R. *Archbishop Laud* (1940).

See also:

A 432 Willson, D. H.; A 504 Abbott, W. C. (ed.).

SOCIAL AND ECONOMIC HISTORY

B 1241 Firth, C. H. *Cromwell's Army: a history of the English soldier during the civil wars, the commonwealth and the protectorate* (3rd ed., 1921).

B 1242 Hoskins, W. G. 'The Leicestershire farmer in the seventeenth century', *Agricultural History*, 25 (1951).

B 1243 Leonard, E. M. *The early history of English poor relief* (1900).

B 1244 Stone, L. 'The inflation of honours 1558–1641', *PP*, no. 14 (1958).

B 1245 Zagorin, P. 'The social interpretation of the English revolution', *Journal of Economic History*, 19 (1959); gives a full bibliography of the controversy about the gentry.

See also:

A 139 Supple, B. E.; A 924 Jordan, W. K.

SCOTLAND AND IRELAND

On Scotland:

A 439   Rait, R. S. *The parliaments of Scotland* (Glasgow, 1924); with bibliography.

B 1246   Brown, P. Hume. *History of Scotland* (3 vols., Cambridge, 1911); an older general work.

B 1247   Nobbs, D. *England and Scotland 1560–1707* (1952); an introductory sketch.

See in addition:

B 1248   Donaldson, G. *The Scottish prayer book of 1637* (Edinburgh, 1957).

B 1249   Mathew, D. *Scotland under Charles I* (1957).

On Ireland:

B 1250   Bagwell, R. *Ireland under the Stuarts* (3 vols., 1909–16).

B 1251   Dunlop, R. *Ireland under the Commonwealth*, (2 vols. Manchester, 1913); this is a collection of documents, but the introduction gives an excellent sketch of the whole period.

B 1252   Kearney, H. F. *Strafford in Ireland 1633–41* (Manchester, 1959); is an important recent work.

45   Britain after the Restoration (vol. v, ch. xiii)

Bibliographies

Further bibliographical information will be found in:

B 1253   Browning, A. (ed.). *English Historical Documents*, vol. 8 (1660–1714) (1953); to which reference should be made for the printed contemporary sources.

B 1254   Grose, C. L. *Select Bibliography of British History, 1660–1760* (1939). See also general bibliographies in this section on 'Religion' and 'The Politics of the European States'.

The standard modern textbook is:

B 1255   Clark, Sir G. N. *The Later Stuarts* (2nd ed., Oxford, 1956).

General accounts of the reign will be found in:

B 1256   Ranke, L. von. *History of England* (Eng. trans., 6 vols., Oxford, 1875).

B 1257   Ogg, D. *England in the reign of Charles II* (2 vols., 2nd impression, Oxford, 1956).

Detailed Studies

B 1258   Barbour, V. *Henry Bennet, earl of Arlington* (Washington, 1914); bibliography. Of particular value for Charles's foreign policy.

B 1259   Baxter, S. B. *Development of the Treasury 1660–1702* (1957); shows the importance of the Treasury in the development of the civil service and the decline of the Exchequer.

B 1260   Brown, L. F. *The first earl of Shaftesbury* (New York, 1933); bibliography. The best modern account.

B 1261   Browning, A. *Life and letters of Sir Thomas Osborne, earl of Danby, 1632–1712* (3 vols., Glasgow, 1947–51). Vol. 1 contains the standard biography, vol. 2 the letters, vol. 3 important parliamentary memoranda.

B 1262   Costin, W. C. and Watson, J. S. *Law and working of the constitution 1660–1914* (2 vols., 1952); for the documents.

B 1263   Cranston, M. W. *John Locke, a biography* (1957); bibliography. Uses the
         John Locke papers acquired by the Bodleian.
B 1264   Feiling, Sir K. G. *History of the Tory party 1640–1714* (Oxford, 1924).
B 1265   —— *British foreign policy 1660–1672* (Oxford, 1930).
B 1266   Figgis, J. N. *The divine right of Kings* (Cambridge, 1914); a brilliant
         monograph.
B 1267   Foxcroft, H. C. *Life and letters of Sir George Savile, marquis of Halifax*
         (2 vols., 1898); bibliography. One of the indispensable books for the
         period. Some corrections in a modernised version: *A Character of the
         Trimmer* (Cambridge, 1946).
B 1268   Haley, K. H. D. *William of Orange and the English opposition 1672–4*
         (Oxford, 1953); bibliography. Shows the futility of Dutch attempts to
         alter the policy of Charles II.
B 1269   Matthews, A. G. *Calamy Revised* (Oxford, 1933); a valuable account of
         the clergy who were ejected by the Act of Uniformity, 1662.
B 1270   Powicke, F. J. *The Cambridge Platonists* (1926).
B 1271   Reddaway, T. F. *The rebuilding of London after the great fire* (1940);
         bibliography. An important study.
B 1272   Schlatter, R. B. *Social ideas of religious leaders 1660–88* (1940); biblio-
         graphy. A valuable monograph based mainly on the sermons of the
         period.
B 1273   Whiting, C. F. *Studies in English puritanism 1660–88* (1931); biblio-
         graphy. Contains information about the more obscure sects.

See also:

A 434   Evans, F. M. G.

46   The English Revolution (vol. VI, ch. vi)

Since this chapter is concerned with international affairs, reference
should be made to the bibliographies on 'The Politics of the European
States'.

The British Isles

The principal bibliographies have already been listed in the preceding
chapters. A major work of contemporary history is:

B 1274   Burnet, G. *Bishop Burnet's history of his own time* (1724–34; best edition,
         Oxford, 1833).

See also:

B 1275   Foxcroft, H. C. (ed.). *A supplement to Burnet's history of my own time*
         (Oxford, 1902). Burnet was a participant in, as well as an observer of,
         the events of 1688–9. The *Supplement* contains his extant earlier drafts
         for the *History* as published.

The most detailed narrative of domestic events, which extends to 1697
(with further fragments), is:

B 1276   Macaulay, T. B. (Lord Macaulay). *The history of England, from the
         accession of James II* (5 vols., 1849–61); best edition by Sir C. H. Firth,

(6 vols., 1913–15); edition with corrections by T. F. Henderson (5 vols., 1907, reprinted 1931, etc.); general criticism, utilising later research until 1914:

B 1277 Firth, Sir C. H. *A commentary on Macaulay's History of England* (Davies, G., ed.) (1938).

Modern works include:

B 1278 Kenyon, J. P. *Robert Spencer, earl of Sunderland* (1958).
B 1279 Ogg, D. *England in the reigns of James II and William III* (Oxford, 1955).
B 1280 Thomson, M. A. *A constitutional history of England, 1642 to 1801* (1938).

Contemporary accounts of events in Scotland and in Ireland at the time of the Revolution are:

B 1281 Balfour-Melville, E. W. M. *An account of the proceedings of the estates in Scotland, 1689–90* (Scottish History Society, 1954); reprint of a London newspaper devoted to Scottish affairs, with incidental news from Ireland.

B 1282 Mesmes, J.-A de, Comte d'Avaux. *Négociations de M. le comte d'Avaux en Irlande, 1689–90* (Hogan, J., ed.) (Irish Manuscripts Commission, 1934).
Also:

B 1283 *Supplementary Volume* (Hogan, J., ed.) (Irish Manuscripts Commission, 1958).

B 1284 'Franco-Irish correspondence, December 1688–August 1691', Tate, L., ed., *Analecta Hibernica*, no. 21 (Irish Manuscripts Commission, 1959).

Other European countries

Most of the relevant books are cited in 'The Politics of the European States'. On the United Provinces two important collections of original material are:

B 1285 Müller, P. L. *Wilhelm III von Oranien und Georg Friedrich von Waldeck* (The Hague, 1873–80); contains William's surviving correspondence in 1688–9 with one of his most intimate friends.

B 1286 *Österreichische Staatsverträge: Niederlande*, vol. 1, *bis 1722* (Srbik, H. Ritter von, ed.) (Vienna, 1912).

The most substantial account of William III is:

B 1287 Japikse, N. *Prins Willem III de Stadhouder-koning* (2 vols., Amsterdam, 1930–3); full until 1689, but unsatisfactory for his reign in England.

Works on other countries which may also be mentioned are:

B 1288 Ennen, L. *Frankreich und der Niederrhein, oder Geschichte von Stadt und Kurstadt Köln seit dem 30 jährigen Kriege bis zum französischen Occupation* (Cologne, etc., 1855–6).
B 1289 Immich, M. *Papst Innocenz XI, 1676–1689* (Berlin, 1900).
B 1290 Prutz, H. 'Der Kölner Wahl und Frankreichs Friedensbruch 1688', *Historisches Taschenbuch*, 6th ser., vol. 9 (1890).

Public opinion and political thought

The works of two contemporary observers are:

B 1291   Evelyn, J. *Diary*, Beer, E. S. de (ed.) (6 vols., Oxford, 1955); reflects moderate English opinion.
B 1292   Leibniz, G. W. *Sämtliche Schriften und Briefe*, erste Reihe, Allgemeiner politischer und historischer Briefwechsel, vol. 5, 1687–90 (Deutsche Akademie der Wissenschaften, Berlin, 1954).

On political ideas:

B 1293   Gough, J. W. *The social contract* (Oxford, 1957).
B 1294   Locke, J. *Two treatises of government* (Laslett, P., ed.) (Cambridge, 1960).
B 1295   Polin, R. *La politique morale de John Locke* (1960).
B 1296   Salmon, J. H. M. *The French religious wars in English political thought* (Oxford, 1959).

See also:

B 588 Dodge, G. H.

47   The Emergence of Great Britain as a world power, 1692–1714 (vol. VI, ch. viii)

Bibliographies and general studies

The fullest bibliography for part of this period is:

B 1297   Morgan, W. T. and Morgan, C. S. *Bibliography of British history 1700–1715* (5 vols., 1934–42).

For the reign of Anne the fullest modern study is:

B 1298   Trevelyan, G. M. *England under Queen Anne*, 3 vols. of which the titles are: *Blenheim* (1930), *Ramillies* (1932), and *The peace and the protestant succession* (1934).

Reference should also be made to the bibliographies on 'Religion' and on 'The Art of War'.

Detailed Studies

B 1299   Campana de Cavelli, Marchesa. *Les Derniers Stuarts à St. Germain-en-Laye* (2 vols., 1871); the fullest account of the exiled Stuarts.
B 1300   Chapman, H. W. *Mary II, queen of England* (1953); bibliography.
B 1301   Dicey, A. V. and Rait, R. S. *Thoughts on the union between England and Scotland* (1920); the best modern account.
B 1302   Insh, G. P. *The company of Scotland trading to Africa and the Indies* (1932).
B 1303   —— (ed.). *The Darien shipping papers* (Edinburgh, 1924).
B 1304   Savidge, A. *The foundation and early years of Queen Anne's Bounty* (1955); throws much light on the social condition of the clergy.
B 1305   Sichel, W. *Bolingbroke, his life and times* (2 vols., 1901–2); a vigorously written book, with a strong Tory bias.

B 1306   Thomson, M. A. *The secretaries of state, 1681–1782* (Oxford, 1932);
          valuable for the history of this office after 1681.
B 1307   Turberville, A. S. *The House of lords in the reign of William III* (Oxford,
          1913).
B 1308   Walcott, R. *English politics in the early eighteenth century* (Cambridge,
          Mass, 1956); a study of the last parliaments of William III and the first
          parliaments of Anne from the point of view of family and party affilia-
          tions.
B 1309   Ward, Sir A. W. *The Electress Sophia and the Hanoverian succession*
          (1909).

48   England (vol. vii, ch. xi)
          The Beginnings of Reform in Great Britain (vol. viii, ch. xix)
                    Bibliographies and general studies
          The most useful bibliographical guide has already been mentioned. It
          contains a valuable classified list of recent publications:

B 810   Pargellis, S. M. and Medley, D. J. *A bibliography of British history,
          The eighteenth century, 1714–1789* (Oxford, 1951).

          Among the best general surveys of the period are two volumes of the
          Oxford History of England, Clark, Sir G. N. (ed.):

B 1310   Williams, B. *The Whig Supremacy, 1714–1760* (2nd ed., Oxford, 1962).
B 1311   Watson, J. S. *The reign of George III 1760–1815* (Oxford, 1960).

          Some general works which have already been mentioned are:

A 422   Holdsworth, W. S. *A history of English Law*, vols. 10–12 (1938).
B 743   Michael, W. *Englische Geschichte im achtzehnten Jahrhundert* (5 vols.,
          1920–55).
B 1280   Thomson, M. A. *A constitutional history of England, 1642–1801*.

          Other useful books include:

B 1312   Ashton, T. S. *An economic history of England: the eighteenth century*
          (1955); contains many references to specialised literature.
B 1313   Feiling, Sir K. G. *The second Tory party, 1714–1832* (1938).
B 1314   Overton, J. H. and Relton, F. *The English church from the accession of
          George I to the end of the eighteenth century* (1906).

          Reference should also be made to the general bibliographies in this
          section on 'Economic and social conditions', on 'The Art of war', and
          on 'Religion', and to the preceding bibliographies on the Stuart period.

                               Detailed Studies
                    POLITICAL AND CONSTITUTIONAL HISTORY
          Much of the recent work has been influenced by:

B 1315   Namier, Sir L. B. *The Structure of politics at the accession of George III*
          (2nd ed., 1957).
B 1316   —— *England in the age of the American Revolution* (1930).

On the period up to 1760:

B 1317 Carswell, J. *The south sea bubble* (1960).
B 1318 Henderson, A. J. *London and the national government* (Durham, N.C., 1945).
B 1319 Hunt, N. C. *Two early political associations* (Oxford, 1961).
B 1320 Nulle, S. H. *Thomas Pelham-Holles, duke of Newcastle; his early political career* (Philadelphia, 1931).
B 1321 Owen, J. B. *The rise of the Pelhams* (1957).
B 1322 Plumb, J. H. *Sir Robert Walpole* (2 vols., 1956, 1960).
B 1323 Realey, C. B. *The early opposition to Sir Robert Walpole, 1720–7* (Philadelphia, 1931).
B 1324 Yorke, P. C. *Life and correspondence of Philip Yorke, earl of Hardwicke, lord high chancellor of Great Britain* (3 vols., Cambridge, 1913).

There is valuable biographical material in:

B 1325 John, Lord Hervey. *Some materials towards memoirs of the reign of King George II* (Sedgwick, R., ed.) (1931).
B 1326 *Letters from George III to Lord Bute, 1756–66* (Sedgwick, R., ed.) (1939).

Much new light has been cast upon the period after 1760 by special studies, the results of which have not yet been absorbed by the general accounts. Particularly useful are:

B 1327 Brooke, J. *The Chatham administration, 1766–8* (1956).
B 1328 Christie, I. R. *The fall of Lord North's administration* (1958).
B 1329 Pares, R. *King George III and the politicians* (Oxford, 1953).
B 1330 Sutherland, L. S. *The East India company in eighteenth-century politics* (Oxford, 1952).
B 1331 —— 'The city of London in eighteenth-century politics', *Essays presented to Sir Lewis Namier* (Pares, R. and Taylor, A. J. P., eds.) (1956).

On imperial questions reference should be made to works mentioned elsewhere such as:

B 83 *Cambridge history of the British Empire*, vol. I.; B 87 Pares, R.; B 817 Pares, R.; B 844 Harlow, V. T.

ADMINISTRATIVE HISTORY

B 1332 Clark, D. M. *The rise of the British treasury: colonial administration in the eighteenth century* (New Haven and Oxford, 1960).
B 1333 Ellis, K. *The post office in the eighteenth century* (1958).
B 1334 Hoon, E. E. *The organisation of the English customs system, 1696–1786* (New York, 1938).
B 1335 Ward, W. R. *The English land tax in the eighteenth century* (1953).

ECONOMIC HISTORY

B 1336 Gayer, A. D. and others. *The growth and fluctuations of the British economy, 1790–1850* (Oxford, 1953).

B 1337 Habakkuk, H. J. 'English landownership, 1680–1740', *Econ. HR*, 1st ser., **10** (1939–40).

B 1338 Hughes, E. *North country life in the eighteenth century: the north–east 1700–50* (1952).

THE CHURCH AND UNIVERSITIES

B 1339 Elliott-Binns, L. E. *The early evangelicals* (1953).
B 1340 Green, V. H. H. *The young Wesley* (1961).
B 1341 Ward, W. R. *Georgian Oxford* (Oxford, 1958).
B 1342 Winstanley, D. A. *Unreformed Cambridge* (Cambridge, 1935).

THE NETHERLANDS

49   The Dutch Republic (vol. v, ch. xii)

A work which has already been mentioned several times gives the most recent synthesis:

A 52 *Algemene geschiedenis der Nederlanden*, Houtte, J. A. van, and others (eds.), vol. 7. It has an extensive bibliography.

B 908 Geyl, P. *Geschiedenis van de nederlandse stam*, vol. 2 (Amsterdam, 1949); gives an important new interpretation of the political history of the period.

See also:

A 115 Blok, P. J., vol. 4.; A 1204 Renier, G. J.

Two important primary sources are:

B 1343 Bontemantel, H. *De regeeringe van Amsterdam zoo in t'civiel als crimineel en militaire* (Kernkamp, G. W., ed.) (2 vols., Utrecht, 1897).

B 1344 Hop and Vivien, *Notulen gehouden ter Statenvergadering van Holland, 1671–5* (Japikse, N., ed.) (Utrecht, 1904).

Detailed Studies

DOMESTIC HISTORY

B 1345 Geddes, J. *History of the administration of John de Witt*, vol. 1 (1623–54) (The Hague, 1879).

B 1346 Geyl, P. *Democratische tendenties in 1672* (Amsterdam, 1950).
B 1347 —— *Oranje en Stuart 1641–72* (Utrecht, 1939).
B 1348 Japikse, N. *Johan de Witt* (Amsterdam, 1928).
B 1349 Kurtz, G. H. *Willem III en Amsterdam* (Utrecht, 1928).
B 1350 Lefèvre-Pontalis, A. *Vingt années de république parlementaire au XVIIe siècle. Jean de Witt, grand-pensionnaire de Hollande* (2 vols., 1884).
B 1351 Roldanus, C. W. *Coenraad van Beuningen, staatsman en libertijn* (The Hague, 1931).

See also:

B 1287 Japikse, N.

FOREIGN POLICY

B 1352   Drossaers, S. *Diplomatieke betrekkingen tusschen Spanje en de republiek der Vereenigde Nederlanden 1678–85* (The Hague, 1915).

B 1353   Elias, J. *De tweede Engelsche oorlog als keerpunt in onze betrekkingen met Engeland* (Amsterdam, 1930).

B 1354   Japikse, N. *De verwikkelingen tusschen de Republiek en Engeland van 1660–5* (Leiden, 1900).

B 1355   Krämer, F. *De Nederlandsche-Spaansche diplomatie voor den vrede van Nijmegen. Bijdrage tot de staatkundige geschiedenis der Nederlanden in het tijdperk van Willem III* (Utrecht, 1892).

B 1356   Molsbergen, E. *Frankrijk en de Republiek der Vereenigde Nederlanden 1648–62* (Rotterdam, 1902).

B 1357   Noordam, N. *De Republiek en de noordse oorlog 1655–60* (Assen, 1940).

See also:

A 1514 Kernkamp, G.; A 1600 Elias, J.

HISTORY OF THE CHURCHES

B 1358   Kühler, W. J. *Geschiedenis van de Doopsgezinden in Nederland* (2 vols., Haarlem, 1940–50).

B 1359   Reitsma, J. and Lindeboom, J. *Geschiedenis van de hervorming en de hervormde kerk der Nederlanden* (5th ed., The Hague, 1949).

B 1360   Rogier, L. J. *Geschiedenis van het Katholicisme in Noord-Nederland in de XVIe en XVIIe eeuw* (3 vols., Amsterdam, 1947).

CULTURAL HISTORY

B 1361   Busken Huet, C. *Het land van Rembrandt. Studiën over de Noord-nederlandsche beschaving in de XVIIe eeuw* (8th ed., Haarlem, 1946).

B 1362   Huizinga, J. *Nederland's beschaving in de XVIIe eeuw. Een schets* (Haarlem 1941).

B 1363   Kossmann, E. H. *Politieke theorie in het XVIIe-eeuwse Nederland* (Amsterdam, 1960).

GERMANY AND THE HABSBURG LANDS

50   The Empire after the Thirty Years War (vol. v, ch. xviii)

General Studies

The most useful introduction to the subject, which has already been mentioned, is:

A 1067   Gebhardt's *Handbuch der deutschen Geschichte* (8th ed., vol. 2, Stuttgart, 1955); in particular the following chapters:

Braubach, M. 'Vom Westfälischen Frieden bis zur Französischen Revolution'. Oestreich, G. 'Verfassungsgeschichte vom Ende des Mittelalters bis zum Ende des alten Reiches'. Treue, W. 'Wirtschafts- und Sozialgeschichte vom 16. bis zum 18. Jahrhundert'.

A general history of Germany which is still useful is:

B 1364   Lamprecht, K. *Deutsche Geschichte*, vol. 6 (Freiburg, 1904).

Important constitutional histories are:

B 1365   Bornhak, C. *Deutsche Verfassungsgeschichte vom westfälischen Frieden an* (Stuttgart, 1934).

B 1366   Feine, H. E. 'Zur Verfassungsentwicklung des Heil. Röm. Reiches seit dem Westfälischen Frieden', *Zeitschrift der Savignystiftung für Rechtsgeschichte, Germanistische Abteilung*, **52** (1932).

Detailed Studies

On specific constitutional issues see:

B 1367   Feller, H. R. *Die Bedeutung des Reiches und seiner Verfassung für die mittelbaren Untertanen und die Landstände im Jahrhundert nach dem Westfälischen Frieden* (Marburg, 1953).

B 1368   Lohmann, K. *Das Reichsgesetz vom Jahre 1654 über die Steuerpflichtigkeit der Landstände* (Bonn, 1893).

B 1369   Meinecke, Fr. 'Der Regensburger Reichstag und der Devolutionskrieg', *HZ*, **60** (1888).

See also:

A 399 Carsten, F. L.; A 400 Hartung, F.

On social and economic conditions after the war see:

B 1370   Brunner, O. *Adeliges Landleben und Europäischer Geist* (Salzburg, 1949).
B 1371   Freytag, G. *Bilder aus der deutschen Vergangenheit*, vol. 3 (Leipzig, 1867).
B 1372   Loen, J. M. von. *Der Adel* (Ulm, 1752).
B 1373   Rosenfeld, S. (ed.). *The letterbook of Sir George Etherege* (1928).
B 1374   Schnee, H. *Die Hoffinanz und der moderne Staat* (4 vols., Berlin, 1953–63); on the court Jews and their economic importance.

See also:

A 126 Elsas, M. J.; A 127 Franz, G.; A 933 Tholuck, A.; A 1262 Keyser, E.

51   The Habsburg Lands (vol. v, ch. xx)
General Studies

The two main general studies are:

B 1375   Redlich, O. *Österreichs Grossmachtsstellung in der Zeit Kaiser Leopolds I* (Gotha, 1921) (*Geschichte Österreichs*, Huber, A., ed., vol. 6); a good political history of Austria and Hungary, but neglects Bohemia as well as social and economic history.

A 1253   Hantsch, H. *Geschichte Österreichs*, vol. 2 (Graz and Vienna, 1950); a briefer and more recent narrative.

For the Austrian part of the story the following are useful:

B 1376   Fiedler, J. *Die Relationen der Botschafter Venedigs über Deutschland und Österreich im 17. Jahrhundert*, II. *K. Leopold I* (Fontes rerum austriacarum, vol. 27) (Vienna, 1867).

B 1377   Huber, A. *Österreichs diplomatische Beziehungen zur Pforte, 1658–64* (Vienna, 1898).

See also:

A 1324 Klopp, A.

For Hungary during this period, see the general histories by Sinor, Eckhardt and Kosary referred to in the bibliography, Sec. A, 25 and also:

B 1378   Lefaivre, A. *Les Magyars pendant la domination ottomane en Hongrie (1526–1722)* (2 vols., 1902).

Some of the documents relating to the Wesselényi conspiracy are in:

B 1379   *Acta conjurationis Bani P. Zrinio et com. Fr. Frangepani illustrantia* (Racki, F., ed.) (Agram, 1873).

For Bohemia during the latter half of the seventeenth century there is little available in western languages except:

B 1380   Gindely, A. *Geschichte der Gegenreformation in Böhmen* (Leipzig, 1894).
B 1381   *Relatio processus in extirpanda haeresi per regnum Bohemiae, marchionatum Moraviae et ducatum utriusque Silesiae [1661–78]* (Prague, 1893).

A newer and different approach to the subject is in:

B 1382   Klíma, A. *Čechy v období temna* [Bohemia in the age of darkness] (Prague, 1958).
B 1383   Kočí, J. *Boje venkovského lidu v období temna* [The struggles of the country folk in the age of darkness] (Prague, 1953).

52   The Rise of Brandenburg (vol. v, ch. xxiii)

General Studies

Reference should be made to the bibliographies in this section on 'Political theory and social structure' and on 'The Art of War'. The most important collection of sources is:

B 1384   *Urkunden und Actenstücke zur Geschichte des Kurfürsten Friedrich Wilhelm von Brandenburg* (20 vols., Berlin, 1864–1911); for internal development see in particular: vol. 5 (Cleves and Mark), vol. 10 (Brandenburg), vols. 15–16 (Prussia).

The most recent survey in English is:

A 1232   Carsten, F. L. *The origins of Prussia*, with bibliography.

Detailed Studies

HISTORY OF THE ARMY

B 1385   Schrötter, F. Freiherr von. *Die brandenburgisch-preussische Heeresverfassung unter dem Grossen Kurfürsten* (Staats- und socialwissenschaftliche Forschungen, vol. 11/v, Leipzig, 1892).

THE DUCHY OF PRUSSIA

B 1386   Rachel, H. *Der Grosse Kurfürst und die ostpreussischen Stände* (Staats-und sozialwissenschaftliche Forschungen, vol. 24/i, Leipzig, 1905).

CLEVES AND MARK

B 1387   Hötzsch, O. *Stände und Verwaltung von Cleve und Mark in der Zeit von 1666 bis 1697* (Urkunden und Actenstücke zur Geschichte der inneren Politik des Kurfürsten Friedrich Wilhelm von Brandenburg, vol. 2, Leipzig, 1908).

FOREIGN POLICY

B 1388   Pagès, G. *Le grand électeur et Louis XIV, 1666–88* (1905).

COLONIAL POLICY

B 1389   Schück, R. *Brandenburg-Preussens Kolonial-Politik unter dem Grossen Kurfürsten und seinen Nachfolgern (1647–1721)* (2 vols., Leipzig, 1889).

The most useful study of the great elector is:

B 1390   Philippson, M. *Der Grosse Kurfürst Friedrich Wilhelm von Brandenburg* (3 vols., Berlin, 1897–1903).

The best studies on the first king of Prussia are:

B 1391   Hinrichs, C. *Friedrich Wilhelm I König in Preussen* (Hamburg, 1941); this volume deals with the reign of Frederick William I's father.

B 1392   Hintze, O. 'Staat und Gesellschaft unter dem ersten König', *Geist und Epochen der Preussischen Geschichte* (Hartung, F., ed.) (Leipzig, 1943); a volume containing many important essays on Prussian history.

B 1393   Schrötter, R. Freiherr von. 'Das preussische Offizierkorps unter dem ersten Könige von Preussen', *Forschungen zur Brandenburgischen und Preussischen Geschichte*, **26** (1913), **27** (1914).

53   The Austrian Habsburgs (vol. VI, ch. xviii)

General Studies

The best short account of Habsburg history in this period, and in that covered by vol. VII, ch. xvii has already been mentioned:

A 1317   Uhrlitz, K. and M. *Handbuch der Geschichte Österreichs und seiner Nachbarländer Böhmen und Ungarn* (4 vols., Graz and Vienna, 1927–44); with very full bibliographies.

Some general works have already been cited in the bibliography to vol. V, ch. xx. Also useful is:

B 1394   Redlich, O. *Das Werden einer Grossmacht. Österreich von 1700 bis 1740* (Baden bei Wien and Leipzig, 1938), dealing almost exclusively with war and international politics.

See also, on administrative institutions:

A 1258   Fellner, T. and Kretschmayr, H.

Detailed Studies

DIPLOMACY AND WAR

B 1395 Berney, A. *König Friedrich I und das Haus Habsburg (1701–7)* (Munich and Berlin, 1927).

B 1396 Brunner, O. 'Österreich und die Wallachei während des Türkenkrieges von 1683–99', *Mitteilungen des österreichischen Instituts für Geschichtsforschung*, **44** (1930).

B 1397 Stelling-Michaud, S. *Saint-Saphorin et la politique de la Suisse pendant la guerre de succession d'Espagne (1700–10)* (Villette-les-Cully, 1935).

B 1398 Wendt, H. *Der italienische Kriegsschauplatz in europäischen Konflikten* (Berlin, 1936).

POLITICAL BIOGRAPHY

B 1399 Turba, G. *Reichsgraf Seilern aus Ladenburg am Necker 1646–1715* (Heidelberg, 1923).

THE NON-GERMAN LANDS OF THE DYNASTY

Two important works have already been mentioned:

A 53   Pirenne, H. *Histoire de Belgique*, vol. 5.

B 393 Kerner, R. J. *Bohemia in the eighteenth century.*

On the Hungarian lands see:

B 1400 Blanc, A. *La Croatie occidentale* (1957).

B 1401 Hengelmüller, L. *Hungary's fight for national existence, or the history of the great uprising led by Francis Rakoczi II 1703–11* (1913).

B 1402 Makkai, L. *Histoire de Transylvanie* (1946).

B 1403 Rotherberg, G. E. *The Austrian military border in Croatia (1522–1747)* (Urbana, Ill., 1960).

On Italy:

B 1191 Benedikt, H. *Das Königreich Neapel unter Kaiser Karl VI* (Vienna and Leipzig, 1927); a very detailed chronicle of politics and culture; already mentioned.

ECCLESIASTICAL HISTORY

B 1404 Coreth, A. *Pietas austriaca. Ursprung und Entwicklung Barocker Frömmigkeit in Österreich* (Munich, 1959); a concise introduction.

See also:

A 1251 Mecessennfy, G.

ECONOMIC HISTORY AND DEVELOPMENT

B 1405 Hoffmann, A. *Wirtschaftsgeschichte des Landes Oberösterreich*, vol. 1 (Linz, 1952); the best modern regional survey.

B 1406 Pantz, A. *Die Innerberger Hauptgewerkschaft 1625–1783* (Graz, 1906).

See also:

B 81 Srbik, H. von.

INTELLECTUAL HISTORY

B 1407   Brunner, O. *Adeliges Landleben und europäischer Geist. Leben und Werk Wolf Helmhards von Hohberg, 1612–88* (Salzburg, 1949); an outstanding book on central Europe in the seventeenth century.

B 1408   Coreth, A. *Österreichische Geschichtsschreibung in der Barockzeit (1620–1740)* (Vienna, 1950).

B 1409   Kann, R. A. *A study in Austrian intellectual history. From late Baroque to Romanticism* (1960); the only book on this subject in English.

B 1410   Sedlmayr, H. *Österreichische Barockarchitektur 1690–1740* (Vienna, 1930).

54   The Organisation and rise of Prussia (vol. VII, ch. xiii)

There is a good critical survey of the literature on Frederick the Great in:

B 796   Gooch, G. P. *Frederick the Great*, already mentioned.

Many of the other principal works are referred to in the bibliographies on 'Political Theory' (especially to vol. VII, ch. vii) and on 'The Politics of the European States' (especially vol. VII, ch. xix). Among older works may also be mentioned:

B 1411   Droysen, J. G. *Geschichte der preussischen Politik* (14 vols., Berlin, 1855–86).

B 1371   Freytag, G. *Bilder aus der deutschen Vergangenheit*, vol. 3 (Leipzig, 1867).

B 1412   Ranke, L. von. *Zwölf Bücher preussischer Geschichte* (Leipzig, 1874); expanded from the *Neun Bücher* of 1847–8, the first work to do justice to Frederick William I, from close study of state papers.

B 1413   Treitschke, H. von. *History of Germany in the nineteenth century* (Eng. trans., 7 vols., 1915–19).

B 1414   Winter, G. *Friedrich der Grosse* (Berlin, 1907); the best comparatively brief survey.

To these may be added, among more recent books:

B 1415   Braubach, M. *Der Aufsteig Brandenburg-Preussens 1640 bis 1815* (Freiburg-im-Breisgau, 1933); a judicial summary with good bibliography.

B 1416   Oppeln-Bronokowski, F. von. *Der Baumeister des preussischen Staates* (Jena, 1934); for Frederick William I.

On the organisation of the Prussian state, see the Prussian state papers published in the series *Acta Borussica*, especially; on general administration:

B 1417   *Behördenorganisation und allgemeine Staatsverwaltung Preussens im 18. Jahrhundert*, covering the years 1701 to 1772 in vols. 1–15 (Berlin, 1894–1936); there are valuable introductions in vol. 1 (Schmoller) and vol. 6/i (Hintze).

B 1418   W. L. Dorn. 'The Prussian bureaucracy in the eighteenth century',
          Political Science Quarterly, 46 (1931–2), with bibliography. Supple-
          ments these introductions usefully for the later years of Frederick's
          reign.

          See also:

B 1419   Hartung, F. 'Studien zur Geschichte der preussischen Verwaltung',
          Abhandlungen der preussichen Akademie, Jahrgang 1941 (Berlin, 1942).
B 1420   Hintze, O. and Skalweit, A. 'Die Wirtschaftspolitik Friedrichs des
          Grossen', *Beihefte zum militärischen Wochenblatt* (Berlin, 1911).

          and also:

          A 400 Hartung, F.

55   The Habsburg Dominions (vol. VII, ch. xvii)
                     Bibliographies and general studies

          The reign of Charles VI is one of the worst-served in Austrian history;
          reference should be also made to the bibliographies to vol. v, ch. xx and
          vol. VI, ch. xviii, Sec. B, 51, 53. For the pragmatic sanction see:

B 1421   Turba, G. *Die pragmatische Sanktion* (Vienna, 1913).

          By contrast Maria Theresa has been much written up; many of the
          principal works are referred to in the bibliographies on 'Political
          Theory' (especially to vol. VII, ch. vii) and on 'The Politics of the Euro-
          pean States' (especially vol. VII, ch. ix). The fundamental works are
          still:

B 717   Arneth, A. von. *Geschichte Maria Theresias* (10 vols.); already men-
          tioned.
B 1422   —— edition of Maria Theresa's *Correspondence* (4 vols., Vienna, 1881).

          The biographies in English are slight by:

B 1423   Bright, J. F. *Maria Theresa* (1897).
B 1424   Goldsmith, M. *Maria Theresa of Austria* (1936).

          For the central administration see the bibliographies mentioned above,
          also:

B 1425   Beidtel, J. 'Über österreichische Zustände in den Jahren 1740–92',
          Sitzungsberichte der kaiserlichen Akademie der Wissenschaften in Wien,
          Phil.-Hist. Klasse, 7–8 (1851–2).

                          Detailed Studies
                          ECONOMIC POLICY
          Most of the literature is periodical, but see:

B 1426   Eckhardt, F. *A bécsi udvar gazdasági politikája Magyarországon Mária
          Terézia korában* (Budapest, 1922).

B 1427 Fournier, A. *Maria Theresia und die Anfänge ihrer Industrie- und Handels-politik* (Leipzig, 1908).

B 1428 Pribram, C. *Geschichte der österreichischen Gewerbepolitik 1740–1860* (Leipzig, 1907).

THE BAROQUE IN AUSTRIA

B 1429 Gregor, J. *Das Wiener Barocktheater* (Vienna, 1922).

B 1430 Kralik, A. and Schlitter, H. *Wien: Geschichte der Kaiserstadt in ihrer Kultur* (Vienna, 1912).

B 1431 Riesenhuber, M. *Kirchliche Barockkunst in Österreich* (Linz, 1929).

HUNGARY

The latest work, with full bibliography is:

A 418 Hóman, B. and Szekfü, G. *Magyar történet*, vol. 4.

For the 'impopulatio' of Hungary see:

B 1432 Schünemann, K. *Bevölkerungspolitik unter Maria Theresia* (Munich, 1933).

B 1433 Szabo, J. *Ungarisches Volk* (Budapest and Leipzig, 1944).

For the Serbs of Hungary:

B 1434 Haumont, E. *La formation de la Yougoslavie* (1930).

B 1435 Schwicker, H. *Geschichte der österreichische Militärgrenze* (Vienna and Teschen, 1883).

BOHEMIA

The best narrative is in:

A 1275 *Vlastivĕda.*

For an account in a western language see:

B 1436 Denis, E. *La Bohème depuis la montagne blanche* (1930).

There is some well-written relevant material in:

B 1437 Krofta, K. *Nesmrtelný národ* (Prague, 1940); especially the second part: 'Od baroka k ostvícenství.' [From Baroque to Enlightenment.]

For the history of agriculture and the peasants:

B 1438 Krofta, K. *Dĕjiny selského stavu* (Prague, 1949).

For political history:

B 1439 Svátek, J. *Dĕjiny panování cisařovny Marie Terezie* (Prague, 1897).

56   The Habsburg possessions and Germany (vol. VIII, ch. x)
        The Reforms of Maria Theresa and Joseph II, 1763–90

The standard work on the reign of Joseph II, despite an unsatisfactory last chapter on censorship, is still:

B 340 Mitrofanov, P. von. *Joseph II, seine politische und kulturelle Tätigkeit* (2 vols., Vienna, 1910); already mentioned.

Useful short biographies, in addition to those already mentioned, are:

B 1440 Benedikt, E. *Kaiser Joseph II, 1741–90* (Vienna, 1936).
B 1441 Fejtö, F. *Un Habsbourg révolutionnaire—Joseph II* (1953).
B 1442 Gooch, G. P. *Maria Theresa and other studies* (1951).
B 1443 Lafue, P. *Marie-Thérèse, impératrice et reine* (1957).
B 1444 Leitich, A. T. *Augustissima. Maria Theresia-Leben und Werk* (Vienna, 1954).
B 1445 Padover, S. K. *The revolutionary emperor Joseph II* (1937).

DETAILED STUDIES

ADMINISTRATION

B 1446 Walter, F. *Die österreichische Zentralverwaltung* (2 vols., covering the period 1740–92, Vienna, 1938, 1951).

AGRARIAN PROBLEMS

B 1447 Grünberg, C. *Die Bauernbefreiung und die Auflösung des grundherrlich-bäuerlichen Verhältnisses in Böhmen, Mähren und Schlesien* (2 vols., Leipzig, 1893–4).
B 1448 Murr Link, E. *The emancipation of the Austrian peasant 1740–98* (New York, 1949).
B 1449 Rozdolski, R. *Die grosse Steuer- und Agrarreform Josefs II* (Warsaw, 1961).

INDUSTRY AND COMMERCE

B 1450 Grossmann, H. *Österreichische Handelspolitik mit Bezug auf Galizien in der Reformperiode 1772–90* (Studien zur Sozial- und Wirtschafts-geschichte, 10. Band) (Vienna, 1914).

ECCLESIASTICAL POLICY AND RELATIONS WITH THE PAPACY

B 1451 Frank, G. *Das Toleranzpatent Kaiser Josephs II* (Vienna, 1882).
B 1452 Kusej, R. J. *Joseph II und die äussere Kirchenverfassung Innerösterreichs* (Kirchenrechtliche Abhandlungen, nos, 49, 50) (Stuttgart, 1908).
B 1453 Maass, F. *Der Josephinismus—Quellen zu seiner Geschichte in Österreich 1760–90* (3 vols., Fontes Rerum Austriacarum, 2. Abt., 71–3 (Vienna, 1951–6).
B 1454 Wolf, A. *Die Aufhebung der Klöster in Innerösterreich, 1782–90* (Vienna, 1871).

CENSORSHIP

B 1455 Sashegyi, O. *Zensur und Geistesfreiheit unter Joseph II* (Budapest, 1958).

HUNGARY

B 1456 Krones, F. *Ungarn unter Maria Theresia und Joseph II* (Graz, 1871).
B 1457 Silagi, D. *Ungarn und der geheime Mitarbeiterkreis Kaiser Leopolds II* (Munich, 1961).

Enlightened despotism in the German territories

GENERAL STUDIES

The best general work available in English is:

B 1458 Bruford, W. H. *Germany in the eighteenth century* (1935).

Standard German works covering this period are:

B 1459 Heigel, K. Th. *Deutsche Geschichte vom Tode Friedrichs des Grossen bis zur Auflösung des alten Reiches*, vol. 1 (Stuttgart, 1899).
B 1460 Oncken, W. *Das Zeitalter Friedrichs des Grossen* (2 vols., Berlin, 1881–2).

DETAILED STUDIES

B 1461 Hartung, F. *Das Grossherzogtum Sachsen unter der Regierung Carl Augusts* (Weimar, 1923).
B 1462 Krüger, H. *Zur Geschichte der Manufakturen und der Manufaktur-arbeiter in Preussen* (Berlin, 1958).
B 1463 Ludwig, J. Th. *Der badische Bauer im 18. Jahrhundert* (Strassburg, 1896).
B 1464 Schlechte, H. *Die Staatsreform in Kursachsen 1762–3. Quellen zum kursächsichen Rétablissement nach dem siebenjährigen Krieg* (Berlin, 1958).
B 1465 Schrohe, H. *Die Stadt Mainz unter kurfürstlicher Verwaltung* (Mainz, 1920).
B 1466 Schwenke, E. *Friedrich der Grosse und der Adel* (Burg, 1911).
B 1467 Windelband, W. *Die Verwaltung der Markgrafschaft Baden zur Zeit Karl Friedrichs* (Leipzig, 1917).

The awakening of public opinion; popular opposition; repression

See also the bibliography to vol. VIII, ch. xv (Sec. B, **32**) in 'France—the revolutionary generation'.

GENERAL STUDIES

B 1468 Gooch, G. P. *Germany and the French Revolution* (1920).
B 1469 Lukács, G. *Goethe und seine Zeit* (Berlin, 1953).
B 1470 Markov, W. (ed.). *Maximilien Robespierre, 1758–1794: Beiträge zu seinem 200. Geburtstag* (Berlin, 1958); contains important studies of the influence of the French Revolution.
B 1471 Mehring, F. *Die Lessinglegende* (Berlin, 1953).
B 1472 Voegt, H. *Die deutsche jakobinische Literatur und Publizistik 1789–1800* (Berlin, 1955).

DETAILED STUDIES

B 1409 Kann, R. A. *A study in Austrian intellectual history* (1960); part II is a study of Sonnenfels.
B 1473 Philippson, M. *Geschichte des preussischen Staatswesen vom Tode Friedrichs des Grossen bis zu den Freiheitskriegen* (2 vols., Leipzig, 1880–2).

B 1474   Stulz, P. and Opitz, A. *Volksbewegungen in Kursachsen zur Zeit der französischen Revolution* (Berlin, 1956).
B 1475   Wangermann, E. *From Joseph II to the Jacobin trials* (1959).

EASTERN AND NORTHERN EUROPE

For vol. v, ch. xxi, 'The Ottoman Empire under Mehmed IV', and for vol. vi, ch. xix, 'The Retreat of Turkey 1683–1730', see Section A, **48**.

57   Russia; the beginning of westernisation (vol. v, ch. xxv)

Many general histories of Russia and similar works are to be found in the bibliography, Section A, **49**.

Two recent bibliographical surveys are:

B 1476   *Istoriya SSSR. Ukazatel' sovetskoĭ literatury za 1917–52*, vol. 1 (from the beginning to 1861) (Academy of sciences of the USSR, Moscow, 1956).
B 1477   *Verzeichnis des Schrifttums 1939–52 zur Geschichte Osteuropas und Sudosteuropas* (Forschungen zur osteuropäischen Geschichte, Berlin) (German: 1, 1954; French, Italian: 4, 1956; English: 5, 1957; American: 7, 1959).

Important printed source collections:

B 1478   Martens, F. *Receuil des traités et conventions conclus par la Russie avec les puissances étrangères*. vol. 1 (Austria, 1874); vol. 5 (Germany, 1880); vol. 10 (England, 1892) (St Petersburg).
B 1479   *Polnoe sobranie zakonov rossiĭskoĭ imperii*, vols. 1–3 (1648–99) (St Petersburg, 1830); complete collection of the imperial laws.

General Studies

B 1480   Filippov, A. N. *Uchebnik istorii russkago prava* (4th ed., Yur'ev, 1912); a textbook of the history of Russian law.
B 613   Miliukov, P. *Outlines of Russian culture* (Philadelphia, 1948); already mentioned.

Detailed Studies

B 633   Bakhrouchine, S. B. and Skazkine, S. D. 'La diplomatie au XVIIe siècle', in Potemkine, V., *Histoire de la diplomatie*.
B 1481   Konovalov, S. 'Thomas Chamberlayne's description of Russia 1631', *Oxford Slavonic Papers*, 5 (1954).
B 1482   Lewitter, L. R. 'Poland, the Ukraine and Russia in the seventeenth century', parts 1 and 2, *SEER*, 27 (1948–9).
B 1483   Loewenson, L. 'The Moscow rising of 1648', *SEER*, 27 (1948).
B 1484   Palmer, W. *The patriarch and the tsar* (1871–6).
B 1485   Petrovich, M. B. 'Juraj Križanic: a precursor of Panslavism', *American slavic and east european review*, 6 (1947).
B 1486   Rauch, G. von. 'Moskau und die europäischen Mächte des 17. Jahrhunderts', *HZ*, **178** (1954).

58   Russia under Peter the Great and the changed relations between
            East and West (vol. vi, ch. xxi)

Primary material

B 1487 *Pis'ma i bumagi Petra Velikogo* (10 vols., St Petersburg and Moscow,
        1887–1956); prints Peter's correspondence to the end of 1710.
B 1488 Lebedev, V. I. (ed.). *Reformy Petra I: sbornik dokumentov* (Moscow,
        1937); miscellaneous documents relating to the reforms as a whole.

General Studies

B 1489 Andreev, A. I. (ed.). *Petr Veliky, sbornik statei* (Moscow and Lenin-
        grad, 1947); a series of essays on various aspects of Peter's reign.
B 1490 Bogoslovsky, M. M. *Petr I. Materialy dlya biografii* (5 vols., Lenin-
        grad, 1940–8); an extremely detailed treatment which covers the reign
        only to 1700.
B 1491 Gitermann, V. *Geschichte Russlands*, vol. 2 (3 vols., Zürich, 1944).
B 1492 Kafengauz, B. B. and Pavlenko, N. I. (eds.). *Ocherki istorii SSSR;
        period feodalizma. Rossiya v pervoi chetverti XVIIIv.* (Moscow, 1954); a
        series of essays on different aspects of Peter's reign, containing much
        up-to-date factual information.
B 1493 Klyuchevsky, V. *Peter the Great* (Eng. trans. 1958); important for the
        tsar's social and administrative reforms.
B 1494 Schuyler, E. *Peter the Great, Emperor of Russia* (2 vols., 1884); out-
        dated in many ways, but still the most detailed treatment in English.
B 1495 Sumner, B. H. *Peter the Great and the emergence of Russia* (1950); an
        excellent short sketch.
B 1496 Wittram, R. *Peter der Grosse* (Berlin, 1954); a very useful short dis-
        cussion.

        Russia at the beginning of Peter's reign:

B 1497 O'Brien, C. B. *Russia under two Tsars, 1682–9: The regency of Sophia
        Alekseevna* (Berkeley, Calif., 1952).

Detailed Studies

ECONOMIC LIFE AND SOCIETY

B 1498 Gille, B. *Histoire économique et sociale de la Russie du moyen âge au XXe
        siècle* (1949); includes useful short bibliographies.
A 98   Lyashchenko, P. I. *History of the national economy of Russia* (New York,
        1949); already mentioned.
B 1499 Portal, R. *L'Oural au XVIIIe siècle* (1951).

ADMINISTRATIVE CHANGES

B 1500 Bogoslovsky, M. M. *Oblastnaya reforma Petra Velikogo* (Moscow,
        (1902).
B 1501 Voskresensky, N. A. *Zakonodatel'nyie akty Petra I*, vol. 1 (Moscow
        and Leningrad, 1945); prints the texts of many of the most important
        laws and instructions issued by Peter.

FOREIGN POLICY

B 1502   Hassinger, E. *Brandenburg-Preussen, Schweden und Russland, 1700–13* (Munich, 1953); contains a substantial bibliography.

See also:

A 1337 Sumner, B. H.; B 636 Chance, J. F.

THE ARMED FORCES

B 1503   Beskrovny, L. G. *Russkaya armiya i flot v XVIIIv.* (Moscow, 1958).

INTELLECTUAL AND RELIGIOUS LIFE

B 1504   Pekarsky, P. P. *Nauka i literatura v Rossii pri Petre Velikom*, vols. 1–2 (St Petersburg, 1862).

See the bibliography on 'Religion' (Sec. B, **21**) above.

THE UKRAINE

B 1505   Allen, W. E. D. *The Ukraine: a history* (Cambridge, 1940).
B 1506   Krupnyckyj, B. *Geschichte der Ukraine* (Leipzig, 1939).

59   Russia (vol. VII, ch. xiv)
Primary material

See the books referred to in bibliography to vol. VI, ch. xxi, and add:

B 1507   Dmietriev, S. S. and Nechkina M. V. (eds.). *Khrestomatiya po istorii SSSR*, vol. 2 (Moscow, 1949), ch. ii, pp. 131–92; miscellaneous documents on the period 1725–62.

Secondary material
CONTEMPORARY WORKS

B 1508   Hanway, J. *An historical account of the British trade over the Caspian sea* (2nd ed., 2 vols., London, 1754–5); contains a valuable description of Russia during the reign of Anna Ivanovna.
B 1509   Weber, F. C. *The present state of Russia from the year 1714 to 1720* (2 vols., 1722–3).

LATER WORKS

Two standard works have already been mentioned:

A 1350   The relevant volume of *Ocherki istorii SSSR*, the standard Soviet history, is *Rossiya vo vtoroĭ chetverti XVIII veka: chast' pervaya* (Moscow, 1957).
A 1351   Solov'ev, S. M. *Istoriya Rossii s drevneĭshikh vremen*, vols. 14–24; the classic account of the period from the accession of Peter the Great to the abdication of Peter III.
B 718   Bain, R. N. *The pupils of Peter the Great* (1897).
B 1510   —— *The daughter of Peter the Great* (1899).
B 1511   —— *Peter III Emperor of Russia* (1902).

B 1512 Bogoslovsky, M. M. *Petr Veliky i ego reforma* (Moscow, 1920).

B 1513 Kafengauz, B. B. *Vneshnyaya politika Rossii pri Petre I* (Moscow, 1942); Russian foreign policy in the reign of Peter the Great.

B 1514 Korsakov, D. A. *Votsarenie imperatritsy Anny Ioannovny* (Kazan, 1880); an account of the attempt to abolish absolute monarchy in 1730.

B 1515 Spiridonova, E. V. *Ekonomicheskaya politika i ekonomicheskie vzglyady Petra I* (Moscow, 1952); Peter's economic policy.

B 1516 Waliszewski, K. *Pierre le Grand* (2nd ed., 1897).

B 1517 —— *L'Héritage de Pierre le Grand* (1900).

B 1518 —— *La Dernière des Romanov, Elisabeth Ire* (1902).

60 Russia (vol. VIII, ch. xi)
Primary material

B 1519 *Sbornik imperatorskago russkago istoricheskago obshchestva* (the archives of the imperial Russian historical society) (St Petersburg, 1867–1915): vols. 1, 7, 10, 13, 17, 20, 23, 27, 42, 48, 51, 57, 67, 87, 97, 118, 135, 145 (correspondence and other personal papers of the Empress Catherine): vols. 4, 8, 14, 32, 36, 43, 68, 93, 107, 115, 123, 134, 144, 147 (petitions presented to the 1767 commission and records of the commission's meetings); see also B 788.

B 1520 *Pugachevshchina* (3 vols., Moscow and Leningrad, 1926–31); primary material on the rebellion of 1773–4.

B 1521 Reddaway, W. F. (ed.). *Documents of Catherine the Great: the correspondence with Voltaire and the instruction of 1767 in the English text of 1768* (Cambridge, 1931).

B 1522 Shmelev, G. N. (ed.). *Akty tsarstvovaniya Ekateriny II* (Moscow, 1907); texts of the 1775 local government statute, the city charter and the charter of the nobility.

Secondary material
CONTEMPORARY WORKS

B 1523 Catherine II, *Memoirs* (Maroger, D., ed.) (1955).

B 1524 Coxe, W. *Travels into Poland, Russia, Sweden and Denmark*, (3rd ed. vols., 1–3, 1787).

B 1525 Dashkov, E. R. Princess. *Memoirs* (Eng. trans. 1958).

B 1526 Khrapovitsky, A. V. *Dnevnik 1782–93* (St Petersburg, 1874); diary of Catherine's private secretary.

LATER WORKS

A 1350 The relevant volume of *Ocherki istorii SSSR* is *Rossiya vo vtoroĭ polovine XVIII veka* (Moscow, 1956).

B 837 Aleksandrov, P. A. *Severnaya sistema* (Moscow, 1914); an account of the operation of Panin's Northern Accord system.

B 1527 Bilbasov, V. A. *Istoriya Ekateriny vtoroĭ* (2 vols., Berlin, n.d.); a biography of Catherine up to 1764.

B 1528   Bilbasov, V. A. *Istoricheskiya monografii*, vols. 1–3 (in one vol.) (St Petersburg, 1890).

B 1529   Brückner, A. *Katharina die Zweite* (Berlin, 1883).

B 1530   Chechulin, N. D. *Vneshnyaya politika Rossii v nachale tsarstvovaniya Ekateriny II (1762–74)* (St Petersburg, 1896).

B 1531   Dityatin, I. I. *Ekaterininskaya Komissiya 1767 goda 'O sochinenii proekta Novogo Ulozheniya'* (Rostov, 1905).

B 1532   —— *Ustroĭstvo i upravlenie gorodov Rossii*, vol. 1 (St Petersburg, 1875); the only serious study of Catherine's municipal reform.

B 1533   Gautier, Yu. V. *Istoriya oblastnogo upravleniya v Rossii ot Petra I do Ekateriny II* (2 vols., Moscow and Leningrad, 1913–41); a survey of developments in provincial government during the eighteenth century.

B 1534   Gooch, G. P. *Catherine the Great and other studies* (1954).

B 1535   Semevsky, V. I. *Krest'yane v tsarstvovanie Imperatritsy Ekateriny II* (2 vols., St Petersburg, 1881–1903); the problem of serfdom in Catherine's reign.

B 1536   Thomson, G. S. *Catherine the Great and the expansion of Russia* (1947).

B 1537   Vallotton, H. *Catherine II* (7th ed., 1955).

B 1538   Waliszewski, H. *Le Roman d'une impératrice: Catherine II de Russie* (1902).

See also:

B 851   Übersberger, H.

61   Poland under the Saxon Kings (vol. VII, ch. xvi)

        (for vol. V, ch. xxiv 'Poland to the death of John Sobieski', see Sec. A, 51).

A 1406   Konopczyński, W. *Dzieje Polski nowożytnej*, vol. 2 (Warsaw, 1936, reprinted London, 1959); already mentioned, contains a detailed bibliography up to 1936. The first volume of the current *Bibliografia historii polskiej*, Baumgart, J. (ed.) appeared in 1949.

International relations

B 1539   Feldman, J. *Polska w dobie wielkiej wojny północnej 1704–9* (Kraków, 1925); the Great Northern War.

B 1540   Kalisch, J. and Gierowski, J. (eds.). *Um die polnische Krone. Sachsen und Polen während des nordischen Krieges 1700–21* (Berlin, 1962).

B 1541   Konopczyński, W. *Polska w dobie wojny siedmioletniej* (2 vols., Kraków and Warsaw, 1909, 1911); the seven years' war.

B 1542   Lewitter, L. R. 'Peter the Great and the Polish election of 1697', *Cambridge Historical Journal*, **12** (1956).

B 1543   Rostworowski, E. *O polską koronę* (Wrocław and Kraków, 1958); French policy towards Poland, 1725–33, with bibliography and summary in French.

B 1544   Skibiński, M. *Europa a Polska...1740–5* (2 vols., Kraków, 1909, 1911); the war of the Austrian succession.

Internal history

B 1545 Gierowski, J. *Rzeczpospolita w dobie upadku, 1700–40* (Wrocław, 1955); selected documents.

B 1546 Jasinski, L. *Beiträge zur Finanzgeschichte Polens im XVIII. Jahrhundert* (Posen, 1910).

B 1547 Lemke, H. *Die Brüder Załuski und ihre Beziehungen zu Gelehrten in Deutschland und Danzig* (Berlin, 1958).

B 1548 Lueck, K. *Deutsch-polnische Nachbarschaft, Lebensbilder deutscher Helfer in Polen* (3rd ed., Würzburg, 1957).

Individual biographies

B 1549 Feldman, J. *Stanisław Leszczyński* (Wrocław and Warsaw, 1948); bibliography.

B 1550 Haake, P. *August der Starke* (Berlin and Leipzig, 1927).

B 1551 Koehl, R. J. 'Heinrich Brühl: a Saxon politician of the eighteenth century', *Journal of Central European Affairs*, **14** (1954).

B 1552 Rose, W. J. *Stanislas Konarski, reformer of education in eighteenth-century Poland* (1929).

See also:

A 793 Völker, K.; A 1407 Kutrzeba, S. and Vetulani, A.; A 1408 Rutkowski, J.; A 1456 Konopczyński, L.

62   The Partitions of Poland (vol. VIII, ch. xii)

See also the bibliography on 'The Politics of the European States'.

B 1553 Askenazy, S. *Die letzte polnische Königswahl* (Göttingen, 1894).

B 1554 Dembiński, B. (ed.). *Documents relatifs à l'histoire du deuxième et troisième partages de la Pologne*, vol. 1 (Léopol, 1902) (no more published).

B 1555 Fabre, J. *Stanislas-Auguste Poniatowski et l'Europe des lumières* (1952).

B 1556 Forst-Battaglia, O. *Eine unbekannte Kandidatur auf dem polnischen Thron. Landgraf Friedrich von Hessen-Kassel und die Konföderation von Bar* (Bonn and Leipzig, 1922).

B 1557 Grossbart, J. 'La politique polonaise de la révolution française jusqu'aux traités de Bâle', *Annales historiques de la révolution française*, **6** (1929), **7** (1930).

B 1558 Haiman, M. *Kosciuszko, leader and exile* (New York, 1946).

B 1559 Horn, D. B. *British public opinion and the first partition of Poland* (Edinburgh, 1945).

B 1560 Jobert, A. *La Commission d'éducation nationale en Pologne* (Dijon, 1941).

B 1561 Kalinka, W. *Der vierjährige polnische Reichstag* (Berlin, 1896–8); obsolete but still useful.

B 1562 Kaplan, H. H. *The first partition of Poland* (New York, 1962).

B 1563 Kieniewicz, S. 'Les récentes études historiques sur la Pologne au temps des partages', *Acta Poloniae historica*, **1** (1958).

B 1564 Klotz, J. *L'Œuvre législative de la diète de quatre ans* (1913).

B 1565 Konic, C. E. L. *Comparaison des constitutions de la Pologne et de la France de 1791* (Lausanne, 1918).

B 1566 Kula, W. *Szkice o manufakturach w Polsce XVIII w.* (Warsaw, 1956); on manufactures. The English summary is not altogether reliable.

B 1567 Konopczyński, W. 'England and the first partition of Poland', *Journal of Central European Affairs*, **8** (1948).

B 1568 Leśnodorski, B. 'Le siècle des lumières en Pologne. L'état des recherches dans le domaine d'histoire politique, des institutions et des idées', *Acta Poloniae historica*, **4** (1961).

B 1569 —— 'Les partages de la Pologne. Analyse des causes et essai d'une théorie', *Acta Poloniae historica*, **8** (1963).

B 1570 Lord, R. H. *The second partition of Poland* (Cambridge, Mass., 1915).

B 1571 —— 'The third partition of Poland', *SEER*, **3** (1925).

B 1572 Lutostański, K. (ed.). *Les partages de la Pologne et la lutte pour l'indépendance* (Lausanne, 1918).

B 1573 Reddaway, W. F. 'Great Britain and Poland, 1762–72', *Cambridge Historical Journal*, **4** (1934).

B 1574 Rutkowski, J. 'Les bases économiques des partages de l'ancienne Pologne', *Revue d'histoire moderne*, **7** (1932).

B 1575 Rutkowska, M. N. *Bishop A. Naruszewicz and his 'history of the Polish nation'* (Washington, 1941).

B 1576 Wilder, J. A. *Traktat handlowy polsko-pruski z r. 1775* (Warsaw, 1937); the Prusso–Polish trade treaty of 1775. There is an appendix in French and a summary in English.

63　　Scandinavia and the Baltic (vol. v, ch. xxii)

The bibliographical aids and general histories of the various countries mentioned below cover, of course, a much longer period than this volume. Some have already been mentioned in Section A.

Bibliographies

Summaries in English, French or German of recent works by Danish, Finnish, Norwegian and Swedish historians can be found in:

B 1577 *Excerpta Historica Nordica* (published under the auspices of the International committee of the Historical Sciences). A specimen volume, ed. by U. Willers, was published in Stockholm 1950; vols. 1 and 2, covering 1950–3 and 1954–5, with P. Bagge as editor-in-chief, were published in Copenhagen in 1955 and 1959 respectively.

See also:

B 1578 Westergaard, W. 'Danish history and Danish historians', *JMH*, **24** (1952).

Reviews and review-articles of books dealing with economic and social history can be found in *The Scandinavian Economic History Review* (*SEHR*), published biennially since 1953.

General Studies

A collective work in 3 vols. in English, well illustrated and with essays dealing also with various aspects of the national histories of the five countries (Iceland is included), by individual Scandinavian historians under national headings, is:

B 1579 Bukdahl, J. and others (eds.). *Scandinavia past and present* (Copenhagen, 1959).

B 1580 Jeannin, P. *Histoire des pays scandinaves* (1956); a brief survey.

No Scandinavian historian has attempted a general treatment for the whole area in this period except at school textbook level.

National Studies

DENMARK

B 1581 Hertel, H. *Aperçu sommaire de l'agriculture en Danemark* (Copenhagen, 1925).

B 1582 Hvidfeldt, J. and others (eds.). *Danmarks historie* (2 vols., Copenhagen, 1950–1).

B 1583 Krabbe, L. *Histoire de Danemark, des origines jusqu'à 1945* (Copenhagen, 1950).

B 1584 Nielsen, A. *Dänische Wirtschaftsgeschichte* (Jena, 1933).

B 1585 La Cour, V., Fabricius, K., Hjelholt, H. and Lund, H. (eds.). *Sønderjyllands Historie fremstillet for det danske Folk*, vol. 3 (Copenhagen, 1940–2); important for Slesvig and Denmark.

B 1586 Steenstrup, J. and others. *Danmarks Riges Historie* (6 vols., Copenhagen, 1896–1907).

See also:

A 1476 Arup, E. *Danmarks Historie*; already mentioned. Excellent bibliography.

A 1479 Friis, A., Linvald, A. and Mackeprang, M. (eds.). *Schultz Danmarkshistorie. Vort Folks Historie gennem Tiderne skrevet af danske Historikere*, already mentioned. Excellent bibliography.

NORWAY

B 1587 Bull, E., Keilhau, W., Shetelig, H. and Steen, S. (eds.). *Det norske folks liv og historie gjennem tidene*, vol. 5 (*Tidsrummet 1640 til 1720*, by Steen, S.) (Oslo, 1930); the accepted authority.

B 1588 Jensen, M. *Norges historie*, vol. 2, revised. (Oslo, 1949).

B 1589 Johnsen, O. A. *Norwegische Wirtschaftsgeschichte* (Jena, 1939).

B 1590 Larsen, K. *A history of Norway* (New York, 1948).

SWEDEN

A 93 Hecksher, E. F. *An economic history of Sweden* (Cambridge, Mass., 1954).

A 1470 Andersson, I. *History of Sweden* (1955).

B 1591   Hildebrand, E. and Stavenow, L. (eds.). *Sveriges historia till våra dagar*, vol. 7 (by Hildebrand, E. and Jacobson, G.) (Stockholm, 1926), and vol. 8 (by Fåhræus, R.) (Stockholm, 1923).

B 1592   Carlson, F. F. *Sveriges historia under konungarne af pfalziska huset* (7 vols., Stockholm, 1855); an essential pioneer work in political history for the period after 1660.

B 1593   Maiander, H. (ed.). *Sveriges historia genom tiderna*, vols. 2 and 3 (Stockholm, 1948).

A 1474   Rosén, J. and Carlsson, St. *Sveriges historia*. 1. *Tiden före 1718* (Stockholm, 1962); with valuable critical bibliographies.

B 1594   Schück, A. and Almquist, H. (eds.). *Svenska folkets historia*, vols. 2–3: 1 (Stockholm, 1921–8).

FINLAND

B 1595   Hornborg, E. *Finlands hävder*, vols. 2–3 (Helsingfors, 1930–1).

B 1596   Jackson, J. H. *Finland* (2nd ed., New York, 1940).

B 1597   Jutikkala, E. *A history of Finland* (1962); a work by the leading historian of Finland.

Detailed Studies

DENMARK–NORWAY

Works in world languages in this period include:

B 1598   Friis, A. and Glamann, K. *A history of prices and wages in Denmark 1660–1800*, vol. 1 (Copenhagen, 1958); useful for economic and social history.

B 1599   Westergaard, W. *The first triple alliance* (Copenhagen, 1947); translates and edits the letters of the Danish diplomat Lindelov from London, 1668–72.

SWEDISH ADMINISTRATION OF HER TRANS-BALTIC PROVINCES

B 1600   Back, P. E. *Hertzog und Landschaft. Politische Ideen und Verfassungsprogramme in Schwedisch-Pommern um die Mitte des 17. Jahrhunderts* (Greifswald, 1955).

B 1601   Soom, A. *Der Herrenhof in Estland im 17. Jahrhundert* (Lund, 1954).

B 1602   Vasar, J. *Die grosse livländische Güterreduktion, 1676–84* (in 2 parts) (Stockholm, 1930–1).

THE SCANIAN QUESTION

B 1603   Åberg, A. *Rutger von Ascheberg* (Stockholm, 1950).

B 1604   Fabricius, K. *Skaanes Overgang fra Danmark til Sverige* (in 4 parts) (Copenhagen, 1906–58).

B 1605   Göransson, G. *Canutus Hahn* (Stockholm, 1950).

B 1606   Rosén, J. *Hur Skåne blev svenskt* (Stockholm, 1943).

THE INTRODUCTION OF ABSOLUTISM IN DENMARK–NORWAY IN 1600

B 1607   Bøggild-Andersen, C. O. *Statsomvæltningen i 1660* (Copenhagen, 1936).

B 1608　Bøggild-Andersen, C. O. *Hannibal Sehested*, 1 (Copenhagen, 1946); a biography of the Danish statesman.
B 1609　Fridericia, J. A. *Adelsvældens sidste Dage* (Copenhagen, 1894).

SWEDEN–FINLAND
For foreign policy see:

B 1610　Landberg, G. *Den svenska utrikespolitikens historia*, vol. 1: 3, *1648–97* (Stockholm 1952,); which is excellent. More detailed are:
B 1611　Fahlborg, B. *Sveriges yttre politik 1660–4* (Stockholm, 1932).
B 1612　——— *1664–1668* (Stockholm, 1949).

See also:

A 1505 Olofsson S. I.

A recent discussion about Charles X's political aims has been started by:

B 1613　Kentrschynskyj, B. 'Karl X Gustav inför krisen i öster, 1654–5', *Karol. Förb. Årsbok* (Lund, 1956).

For Charles XI's domestic reforms see:

B 1614　Ågren, S. *Karl XI:s indelningsverk för armén 1679–97* (Stockholm, 1922).
B 1615　Rystad, G. *Johan Gyllenstierna, rådet och kungamakten, studier i Sveriges inre politik 1660–80* (Lund, 1955).
B 1616　Thanner, L. 'Suveränitetsförklaringen år 1693', *Karol. Förb. Årsbok* (1954).
　　　　Christina's abdication has been much discussed; see especially:
B 1617　Olofsson, S. *Drottning Christinas tronavsägelse och trasförändring* (Stockholm, 1953).
B 1618　Weibull, C. *Drottning Christina* (Gothenburg, 1931).

For Swedish imperial administration, see, as well as the books already mentioned:

B 1619　Isberg, A. *Karl XI och den livländska adeln 1684–95* (Lund, 1953).
B 1620　Rosén, J. 'Statsledning och provinspolitik under Sveriges stormaktstid', *Scandia* (1946).

64　The Great Northern War (vol. vi, ch. xx)

Many of the relevant works have already been mentioned in other bibliographies on Eastern and Northern Europe and in general lists such as that on 'The Art of War'.

General studies of the war

B 1621　Sarauw, C. von. *Die Feldzüge Karl's XII* (Leipzig, 1881); stops at 1718.
B 1622　Schirren, C. *Zur Geschichte des Nordischen Krieges* (Stockholm, 1913); consists of posthumously collected writings by this pioneer scholar of the period.
　　　　More recently:
B 1623　Nordmann, C. *La crise du Nord au début du XVIIIe siècle* (1963); has ably put the war into a European diplomatic perspective.

A modern Russian monograph is:

B 1624   Kafengauz, B. B. *Severnaya voĭna i Nishtadtsky mir 1700–21* (Moscow, 1944).

General studies centred round particular participants in the war

SWEDEN

B 1625   Bring, S. (ed.). *Karl XII Till 200 års dagen av hans död* (Stockholm, 1918); a collective work. This should be brought up to date by articles by many specialists in *Karolinska Forbundets Årsbok* (1918–).

On foreign policy:

B 1626   Rosén, J. *Den svenska utrikespolitikens historia*, vol. 2: 1, *1697–1721* (Stockholm, 1952).

FINLAND

B 1627   Hornborg, E. *Karolinen Armfelt och kampen om Finland under stora nordiska kriget* (Helsingfors, 1953).

THE BALTIC PROVINCES

B 1628   Wittram, R. *Baltische Geschichte, Die Ostseelande* (Munich, 1954).

DENMARK

B 1629   *Bidrag til den Store Nordiske Krigs Historie* (10 vols., Copenhagen, 1899–1934); edited by Tuxen, A. P. and published by the Danish general staff, covers both military and diplomatic history.

On the war-time history of the duchies see:

B 1630   Kellenbenz, H. *Die Herzogtümer von Kopenhagener Frieden bis zur Wiedervereinigung Schleswigs, 1660–1721* (Neumünster, 1960).

POLAND, RUSSIA AND THE UKRAINE

See the bibliographies on those countries.

An article with excellent bibliographical footnotes of recent Polish work is:

B 1631   Gierowski, J. 'From Radoszkowice to Opatów—the history of the decomposition of the Stanislaw Leszczyński camp', *Poland at the XIth International Congress of Historical Sciences in Stockholm* (Warsaw, 1960).

The most recent treatment in Russian is:

B 1632   Tarle, E. V. *Severnaya voĭna i shvedskoe nashestvie na Rossiyu* (Moscow, 1958); builds on archive material, in part new, for the years 1707–9.

On the military and naval side, see:

B 1633   Tarle, E. V. 'Russky flot i vneshnyaya politika Petra I', *Sochineniya*, vol. 12 (Moscow, 1962).

B 1634   Porfir'ev, E. I. *Petr I—osnovopolozhnik voennogo iskusstva russkoĭ regulyanoĭ armii i flota* (Moscow, 1952—also in a Swedish trans., Stockholm, 1957).

Other works are:

B 802 Mediger, W. *Moskaus Weg nach Europa* (Brunswick, 1952).

On the Ukraine:

B 1635   Krupnytskyj, B. *Hetman Mazepa und seine Zeit* (Leipzig, 1942).
B 1636   Nordmann, C. *Charles XII et l'Ukraine de Mazepa* (1958).

See: TURKEY

B 1637   Tengberg, E. *Från Poltava till Bender. En studie i Karl XII's turkiska politik 1709–13* (Lund, 1953).

Biographies of Charles XII

The most scholarly work is:

B 1638   Haintz, H. *König Karl von Schweden* (3 vols., Berlin, 1958); rather old-fashioned.
B 1639   Bengtsson, F. *Charles XII of Sweden* (Eng. trans. 1957); brilliantly written, but in many ways unhistorical.
B 1640   Hildebrand, K.-G. 'Karl XII', *Svenska Män och Kvinnor*, vol. 4 (Stockholm, 1948); a brief but balanced sketch.
B 1641   —— 'Till Karl XII uppfattningens historia', *Historisk Tidskrift*, 1954 and 1955; give superb guidance to the older literature. The controversy surrounding the king's death is most easily studied, from different points of view, in:
B 1642   Jägerskiöld, S. and others. *Sanning och sägen om Karl XII:s död* (Stockholm, 1941).
B 1643   Sandklef, A. and others. *Carl XII:s död* (Stockholm, 1940).

The peace settlements of 1719–21

For the diplomacy leading up to these see:

B 1644   Jägerskiöld, S. *Sverige och Europa 1716–18* (Stockholm, 1937).
B 1645   Hartman, K. J. *Ålandska kongressen och dess förhistoria* (5 vols., Åbo, 1921–31); stimulating and controversial.

Valuable for the Russian point of view, and using new archive material is:

B 1646   Feĭgina, S. A. *Alandsky Kongress. Vneshnyaya politika Rossii v kontse severnoĭ voĭny* (Moscow, 1959).

For the final settlements see:

B 1647   Carlsson, E. *Freden i Nystad*, vol. 1 (Stockholm, 1932—the only volume to appear).
B 1648   Grönroos, H. 'England, Sverige och Ryssland 1719–21', *Historisk Tidskrift för Finland* (1931).
B 1649   Holst, W. *Fredrik I* (Stockholm, 1953).
B 1650   —— *Ulrika Eleonora* (Stockholm, 1956).
B 1651   Thanner, L. *Revolutionen i Sverige efter Karl XII:s död* (Uppsala, 1953).
B 1652   Ballantyne, A. *Lord Cartaret, a political biography 1690–1763* (1887).

B 692   Williams, B. *Stanhope. A study in eighteenth-century war and diplomacy* (1932). These last two English contributions are judged by Swedish scholars to be too uncritical in their use of the source-material, as is:

B 743   Michael, W. *Englische Geschichte im achtzehnten Jahrhundert*, vol. 2.

Administrative and other studies

B 1653   Lindeberg, G. *Svensk ekonomisk politik under den Görtzka perioden* (Lund, 1941); essential for economic policy during the Görtz years.

B 1654   Olsson, S. *Olof Hermelin* (2 vols., Stockholm, 1953); illuminating on the Swedish chancery officials.

On the army see:

B 1655   Hatton, R. M. *Captain James Jefferyes's letters from the Swedish army 1707–9* (*Historiska Handlingar*, 35: 1, Stockholm, 1953).

B 1656   Uddgren, H. E. *Karolinen Adam Ludvig Lewenhaupt* (2 vols., Stockholm, 1919, 1950).

On the navy:

B 1657   Grauers, S. *Ätten Wachtmeister genom seklerna*, vol. 2 (Stockholm, 1946).

For the relationship between Charles and his advisers see:

B 1658   Ahlström, W. *Arvid Horn och Karl XII, 1710–13* (Stockholm, 1959).
B 1659   Jonasson, G. *Karl XII och hans rådgivare, 1697–1702* (Uppsala, 1960).

65   Scandinavia and the Baltic (vol. VII, ch. xv)

General Studies

There is no adequate historical treatment of Scandinavia as a whole for the period in any of the world languages.

See:

B 1660   Hovde, B. J. *The Scandinavian countries, 1720–1865. The rise of the middle classes* (Ithaca, N.Y., 1948); the first volume is interesting for social and economic developments, while consciously ignoring political factors.

National Studies

DENMARK

B 1661   Holm, E. *Danmarks-Norges indre Historie under Enevælden 1660–1720* (2 vols., Copenhagen, 1885–6).

B 1662   —— *Danmarks-Norges Historie fra den store nordiske krigs slutning til Rigernes Adskillelse*, vols. 1–4 (Copenhagen, 1891–1902); covers the years 1720–72; of fundamental importance despite its age.

B 1663   Krumm, J. *Der schleswig-holsteinische-dänische Gesamtstaat des 18. Jahrhundert, 1721–97* (Gluckstadt, 1934).

B 1664   Olsen, A. *Danmark-Norge i det 18. Aarhundrede* (Copenhagen, 1936); analyses the relations between the two parts of the state.

NORWAY

B 1587   Bull, E. and others. *Det Norske folks liv og historie gjennem tidene*, vol. 4, *Tidsrummet 1720 til omkring 1770* (by Steen, S.) (Oslo, 1932).

SWEDEN

B 1665   Hildebrand, E. and Stavenow, L. (eds.). *Sveriges historia till våra dagar*, vol. 9 (by Stavenow, L.) (Stockholm, 1922).

B 1666   Hjärne, E. *Från Vasatiden till frihetstiden* (Stockholm, 1929).

B 1667   Malmström, C. G. *Sveriges politiska historia från Carl XII.'s död till statshvälfningen 1772* (6 vols., revised ed., Stockholm, 1893–1901); fundamental, though restricted to political and diplomatic history.

B 1594   Schück, A. and Almquist, H. (eds.). *Svenska folkets historia*, vol. 4.

B 1668   Stavenow, L. *Geschichte Schwedens 1718–72* (Gotha, 1908); covers the period in detail, but is rather old fashioned in approach.

Detailed Studies

DENMARK–NORWAY

B 1669   Friis, A. *Die Bernstorffs*, vol. 1 (Copenhagen, 1905).

B 1670   Hjelholt, H. *Inkorporationen af den Gottorpske Del af Sønderjylland i Kronen 1721* (Copenhagen, 1945).

B 1671   La Cour, V. *Mellem Brødre, Dansk-Norske problemer i det 18. Aarhundredes helstat* (Copenhagen, 1943); analyses the relations between the two parts of the state.

B 1672   Nilsson, O. *Dansk uppträdande i den svenska tronföljarefrågan 1739–43*, 4 pts. (Malmö, 1875–1905).

B 1673   Reedtz, H. C. *Répertoire historique et chronologique des traités...de Dannemarc* (Göttingen, 1826).

B 1674   Semmingsen, I. 'The dissolution of estate society in Norway', *SEHR*, 2 (1954).

SWEDEN–FINLAND

For social and constitutional history:

A 29   Roberts, M. 'Sweden', *The European nobility in the eighteenth century* Goodwin, A. (ed.) (1953).

For economic history:

B 1675   Boethius, B. 'New light on eighteenth-century Sweden', *SEHR*, 1 (1953).

B 1676   Utterström, G. 'Some population problems in pre-industrial Sweden', *SEHR*, 2 (1954).

For the political crisis of the 1740s:

B 1677   Carlsson, S. *Ståndssamhälle och ståndspersoner* (Lund, 1949); essential for the understanding of social development.

B 1678   Danielson, J. R. *Die nordische Frage in den Jahren 1746–51. Mit einer Darstellung russischer-schwedischer-finnischer Beziehungen 1740–3* (Helsingfors, 1888).

B 1679 Jägerskiöld, O. *Hovet och författningsfrågan 1760–6* (Uppsala, 1943).

B 1680 —— *Den Svenska utrikespolitikens historia*, vol. 2: 2, *1721–92* (Stockholm, 1957); essential for foreign policy and has a good bibliography.

B 1681 Lagerroth, F., Nilsson, J. E. and Olsson, R. *Sveriges Riksdag*, vol. 5, *Frihetstidens maktägande ständer 1719–72* (Stockholm, 1934); valuable for constitutional history.

THE BALTIC AND THE BALTIC COUNTRIES

B 1682 Lodge, R. 'The treaty of Abo and the Swedish succession', *EHR*, **43** (1928).

B 1683 Lybeck, O. *Öresund i Nordens historia* (Malmö, 1943).

B 1684 Senn, A. E. *The emergence of modern Lithuania* (New York, 1959).

B 1685 Svabe, A. *Histoire du peuple Letton* (Stockholm, 1953).

B 1686 Wustalu, E. *The history of the Estonian people* (1952).

See also:

A 1109 Hill, C. E.; A 1498 Hornborg, E.

EUROPE OVERSEAS: AMERICA BEFORE THE REVOLUTION: SPANISH AMERICA

(for vol. v, ch. xvii 'Europe and Asia' see Sec. A, **56**).

66 The European Nations and the Atlantic (vol. iv, ch. xxii)
Europe and North America (vol. v, ch. xiv)
France and England in North America 1689–1713 (vol. vi, ch. xv)
North America (vol. vii, chs. xxi. 2 and xxii. 2)

Many of the relevant books will be found in the earlier lists of this section, especially 'Economic and social conditions', 'The Art of War' and 'The British Isles'.

General Studies

Useful textbooks on British and French colonial expansion generally are:

B 1687 Blet, H. *Histoire de la colonisation française*, vol. 1 (1946); to 1789.

B 83 *Cambridge history of the British Empire*, vol. 1, *The old empire, from the beginnings to 1783* (1929).

B 1688 Hardy, G. *Histoire sociale de la colonisation française* (1953).

B 1689 Priestley, H. I. *France overseas through the old régime* (New York, 1939).

B 1690 Saintoyant, J. *La Colonisation française sous l'ancien régime*, vol. 1 (2 vols., 1929); to 1713.

B 1691 Williamson, J. A. *A short history of British expansion*, vol. 1 (3rd ed., 2 vols., 1945); to 1783.

Attractive outline accounts of exploration are:

B 1692 Brebner, J. B. *The explorers of North America, 1492–1806*, new ed. (1955); bibliography.

B 1693   DeVoto, B. *Westward the course of empire: the story of the exploration of North America from its discovery to 1805* (New York and London, 1953).

The following offer excellent short introductions to the general history of large regions:

B 1694   Burn, W. L. *The British West Indies* (1951).
B 1695   Creighton, D. G. *Dominion of the North: a history of Canada*, rev. ed. (1958); emphasises geography.
B 1696   Wright, L. B. *The colonial civilisation of North America, 1607–1783* (1949); bibliography.

See also:

A 1772 Parry, J. H. and Sherlock, P. M.

Valuable general surveys on a larger scale:

B 1697   Burns, Sir A. C. *History of the British West Indies* (1954).
B 1698   Jaray, G. L. *L'empire français d'Amérique, 1534–1803* (1938); bibliography.
B 1699   Jernegan, M. W. *The American colonies, 1492–1750; a study of their political, economic and social development* (New York, 1929); bibliography.
B 1700   Lower, A. R. M. *Canadians in the making: a social history of Canada* (Toronto, 1958).
B 1701   McInnis, E. *Canada: a political and social history* (New York, 1947); bibliography.
B 1702   Nettels, C. P. *The roots of American civilisation* (New York, 1938); bibliography, thoughtful all-round synthesis.

See also:

A 1770 Newton, A. P.

The following volumes of the *History of American life* series (New York), with good bibliographies, are especially useful for the settlement process and social aspects.

B 1703   Adams, J. T. *Provincial Society, 1690–1763* (1927).
B 1704   Priestley, H. I. *The coming of the white man, 1492–1848* (1929); for the French, Spanish, Dutch and Swedes.
B 1705   Wertenbaker, T. J. *The first Americans, 1607–90* (1927).

To these should be added the *New American Nation* series (New York, in progress):

B 1222   Notestein, W. *The English people on the eve of colonisation, 1603–40* (1954).
B 1706   Wright, L. B. *The cultural life of the American colonies, 1607–1763* (1957).

The fundamental syntheses on the British colonies are:

A 1767   Andrews, C. M. *The colonial period of American history* (4 vols., New Haven and Oxford, 1934–8); by the leading modern authority, includes the West Indies.

B 813   Gipson, L. H. *The British empire before the American revolution* (9 vols., 1936–56) (vols. 1–3, Caldwell, Idaho; vols. 4–9, New York).

B 1707 Osgood, H. L. *The American colonies in the seventeenth century* (3 vols., reprinted, Worcester, Mass., 1957); still important, especially for politics and religion.

B 1708 —— *The American colonies in the eighteenth century* (4 vols., New York, 1908).

There are critical bibliographies and concise editorial explanations in:

B 1709 Jensen, M. (ed.). *American colonial documents to 1776* (English Historical Documents, vol. 9, 1955).

Other selective bibliographies are:

B 1710 Handlin, O. and others. *Harvard Guide to American history* (Cambridge, Mass., 1954).

B 1711 Lanctot, G. *L'Œuvre de la France en Amérique du Nord* (Montreal and Paris, 1951); with critical commentary.

B 1712 *Readable books about early American history* (Institute of Early American History and Culture, Williamsburg, Va., rev. ed., 1960).

Much the best bibliographical coverage for the West Indies as a whole is the biennial survey:

B 1713 Debien, G. in *Revue française d'histoire d'outre-mer*, under the title 'Les travaux d'histoire sur Saint-Domingue'.

The relevant volumes of Parkman's classical narrative, *France and England in America* (1885–90, and later eds.) are listed below. See also a selection from his works:

B 1714 Parkman, F. *France and England in North America* (Morison, S. E., ed.) (1956).

Aspects of early American history are surveyed in:

B 1715 Bridenbaugh, C. *Cities in the wilderness* (New York, 1938).

B 1716 Curti, M. *The growth of American thought* (New York, 1943).

B 1717 Jernegan, M. W. *Laboring and dependant classes in colonial America* (Chicago, n.d.).

B 1718 Johnson, E. A. J. *American economic thought in the seventeenth century* (1932).

B 1719 Kraus, M. *The Atlantic civilisation: eighteenth-century origins* (Ithaca, 1949); on relations between America and Europe.

B 1720 Labaree, W. L. *Conservatism in early American history* (New York, 1948).

B 1721 Morris, R. B. *Government and labor in early America* (New York, 1946).

B 1722 Parrington, V. L. *The colonial mind, 1620–1800* (New York, 1927); penetrating, controversial, mainly New England.

B 1723 Rossiter, C. *Seedtime of the Republic: the origin of the American tradition of political liberty* (New York, 1953).

B 1724 Sachse, H. L. *The colonial American in Britain* (Madison, Wis., 1956).

B 1725 Sweet, W. W. *Religion in colonial America* (New York, 1943); bibliography.

Detailed Studies

EXPLORATION

B 1726 Delanglez, J. *Life and voyages of Louis Jolliet, 1645–1700* (Chicago, 1948).
B 1727 —— *Some La Salle journeys* (Chicago, 1938).
B 1728 Munro, W. B. *Crusaders of New France* (The Chronicles of America, New Haven, 1918).
B 1729 Nute, G. *Caesars of the wilderness* (New York, 1943).
B 1730 Parkman, F. *The discovery of the great west: La Salle* (Taylor, W. R., ed.) (New York, 1956).
B 1731 Webb, W. P. *The great plains* (New York, 1931).

THE AMERINDIANS

B 1732 Bond, R. P. *Queen Anne's American kings* (Oxford, 1952).
B 1733 Fenton, W. N. *American Indian and white relations to 1830: needs and opportunities for study* (Chapel Hill, N.C., 1957); bibliography.
B 1734 Jenness, D. *The Indians of Canada* (Ottawa, 1932).
B 1735 Kellaway, W. *The New England Company, 1649–1776* (1961); discusses missions.
B 1736 Kennedy, J. H. *Jesuit and savage in New France* (New Haven and London, 1950).
B 1737 Leach, D. E. *Flintlock and tomahawk: New England in King Philip's War* (New York, 1958); bibliography.
B 1738 Parkman, F. *The Jesuits in North America in the seventeenth century* (Boston, 1867, and later eds.); especially the introduction.
B 1739 Wissler, C. *The American Indian* (New York, 1922); both continents and the West Indies, a standard introduction.
B 1740 Wallace, P. A. W. *The white roots of peace* (Philadelphia, 1946).
B 1741 —— *Indians in Pennsylvania* (Harrisburg, Pa., 1961).

POPULATION

B 1742 Brown, R. H. *Historical geography of the United States* (New York, 1943).
B 1743 Debien, G. *Les Engagés pour les Antilles, 1634–1715* (1952); deals mainly with La Rochelle and Dieppe.
B 1744 Faust, A. B. *The German element in the United States* (2 vols., Boston, 1909); bibliography.
B 1745 Ford, H. J. *The Scotch–Irish in America* (Princeton, 1915).
B 1746 Henripin, J. *La Population canadienne au début du XVIIIe siècle: nuptialité-fécondité-mortalité infantile* (1954).
B 1747 Smith, A. E. *Colonists in bondage: white servitude and convict labor in America, 1607–1776* (Chapel Hill, N.C., 1947); includes the West Indies.
B 1748 Sutherland, S. H. *Population distribution in colonial America* (New York, 1936).

SLAVERY

B 1749 Franklin, J. H. *From slavery to freedom: a history of the American negroes* (New York, 1947); bibliography.

B 1750 Martin, G. *Histoire de l'esclavage dans les colonies françaises* (1948).

B 1751 Phillips, U. B. *American negro slavery* (New York, 1918).

B 1752 Pitman, F. W. *The development of the British West Indies, 1700–63* (New Haven, 1917); standard economic history with useful statistics.

B 1753 Westergaard, W. *The Danish West Indies under company rule, 1671–1754* (New York, 1917).

FISHERIES AND FUR TRADE

B 1754 Lounsbury, R. G. *The British fishery at Newfoundland, 1634–1763* (New Haven, 1934).

B 1755 Moloney, F. X. *The fur trade in New England, 1620–76* (Cambridge, Mass., 1931).

B 1756 Rich, E. E. *The history of the Hudson's Bay Company, 1670–1870*, vol. I (2 vols., Hudson's Bay Records Society, London, 1958–9; commercial ed. 1961).

TOBACCO AND SUGAR

B 1757 Debien, G. *Une plantation à St-Domingue: la sucrerie Galbaud du Fort, 1690–1802* (Cairo, 1941).

B 1758 Gray, L. C. *History of agriculture in the southern United States to 1860*, vol. I (2 vols., Washington, 1933).

B 1759 MacInnes, C. M. *The early English tobacco trade* (1926).

TRADE AND SHIPPING

B 1760 Bailyn, B. *The New England merchants in the seventeenth century* (Cambridge, Mass., 1955); studies the rise of a social group.

B 1761 Bailyn, B. and Bailyn L. *Massachusetts shipping, 1697–1714: a statistical study* (Cambridge, Mass., 1959).

B 1762 Hedges, J. B. *The Browns of Providence plantation. Colonial years* (Cambridge, Mass., 1952).

B 1763 Pares, R. *Yankees and Creoles: the trade between North America and the West Indies before the American revolution* (1956).

PRIVATEERING AND PIRACY

B 1764 Chapin, H. M. *Privateers, ships and sailors, 1625–1725* (Toulon, 1926).

B 1765 Newton, A. P. *The colonising activities of the English Puritans* (New Haven, 1914); on Providence Island.

INTERNATIONAL RIVALRY AND WAR

B 1766 Alvord, C. W. *The Illinois country, 1673–1818* (Springfield, Ill., 1920).

B 1767 Crane, V. W. *The southern frontier, 1670–1732* (Ann Arbor, Mich., 1929; repr. 1956); trade and diplomacy east of the Mississippi.

B 1768 Freeman, D. S. *George Washington, a biography*, vols. 1 and 2 (New York and London, 1948); deals with Washington's experiences on the western frontier.

B 1769 Frégault, G. *Iberville le conquérant* (Montreal, 1944).

B 1770 Parkman, F. *Count Frontenac and New France under Louis XIV* (Boston, 1877).

B 1771 —— *A half-century of conflict* (2 vols., Boston and London, 1892).

B 1772 Trelease, A. W. *Indian affairs in colonial New York: the seventeenth century* (Ithaca, 1960); bibliography.

B 1773 Waller, G. M. *Samuel Vetch, colonial enterpriser* (Chapel Hill, N.C., 1960); for the capture of Acadia.

FRENCH COLONIAL POLICIES

B 1774 Deschamps, H. *Les Méthodes et les doctrines coloniales de la France* (1953).

B 1775 Duchesne, A. *La Politique coloniale de la France: le ministère des colonies depuis Richelieu* (1928).

B 1776 Mims, S. L. *Colbert's West India policy* (New Haven, 1912).

See also:

A 131 Hauser, H.

ENGLISH COLONIAL POLICY

B 1777 Beer, G. L. *The origins of the British colonial system, 1578–1660* (New York, 1908).

B 1778 —— *The old colonial system*, part I: *The establishment of the system, 1660–88* (2 vols., New York, 1912).

B 1779 —— *The commercial policy of England towards the American colonies* (New York, 1948).
These are a fundamental series of studies.

B 1332 Clark, D. M. *The rise of the British treasury: colonial administration in the eighteenth century* (New Haven and Oxford, 1960); already mentioned.

B 1780 Dickerson, O. M. *American colonial government, 1696–1765* (Cleveland, 1912).

B 1781 Hall, M. G. *Edward Randolph and the American colonies, 1676–1703* (Chapel Hill, N.C., 1960).

B 1782 Knorr, K. E. *British colonial theories, 1570–1850* (Toronto, 1944).

B 1783 Labaree, L. W. *Royal government in America: a study of the British colonial system before 1783* (New Haven, 1930).

B 1784 Penson, L. M. *The colonial agents of the British West Indies* (1924).

B 1785 Thornton, A. P. *West-India policy under the Restoration* (Oxford, 1956).

INDIVIDUAL COLONIES

NEW FRANCE, ACADIA, LOUISIANA

B 1786 Brebner, J. B. *New England's outpost: Acadia before the conquest of Canada* (New York, 1927).

B 1787 Chapais, T. *The great intendant; a chronicle of Jean Talon in Canada, 1665–72* (Chronicles of Canada, vol. 6, Toronto, 1914).

B 1788   Eccles, W. J. *Canada under Louis XIV, 1663–1701* (The Canadian centenary series, vol. 3; 1964).

B 1789   Frégault, G. *La Civilisation de la Nouvelle-France 1713–44* (Montreal, 1944).

B 1790   Hammang, F. H. *The marquis de Vaudreuil: New France at the beginning of the eighteenth century*, vol. 1 (Bruges–Louvain, 1938).

B 1791   Kellogg, L. P. *The French régime in Wisconsin and the north-west* (Madison, Wis., 1925).

B 1792   Lanctot, G. *A History of Canada* (2 vols., Toronto and London, 1963–4).

B 1793   —— *L'Administration de la Nouvelle-France* (1929).

B 1794   Parkman, F. *The old régime in Canada* (Boston, 1874); for Colbert and Talon.

B 1795   Rule, J. C. 'The old régime in America: a review of recent interpretations of France in America', *William and Mary Quarterly*, **19** (1962).

B 1796   Schlarman, J. H. *From Quebec to New Orleans* (Belleville, Ill., 1929).

NEW ENGLAND

B 1797   Adams, J. T. *The founding of New England* (Boston, 1921); bibliography.

B 1798   —— *Revolutionary New England, 1691–1776* (Boston, 1923); bibliography.

B 1799   Akagi, R. K. *The town proprietors of the New England colonies, 1660–1770* (Philadelphia, 1924).

B 1800   Brockunier, S. H. *The irrepressible democrat: Roger Williams* (New York, 1940).

B 1801   Brown, R. E. *Middle-class democracy and the revolution in Massachusetts, 1691–1780* (Ithaca, 1955).

B 1802   Calder, I. M. *The New Haven colony* (New Haven, 1934).

B 1803   Fox, D. R. *Yankees and Yorkers* (New York, 1940).

B 1804   Haller, W. jr. *The Puritan frontier: town-planning in New England colonial development, 1630–60* (New York, 1951).

B 1805   Miller, P. G. *Orthodoxy in Massachusetts, 1630–50* (Cambridge, Mass., 1933).

A 226   —— *The New England mind* (2 vols., New York and Cambridge, Mass., 1939–53); already mentioned. Both are profound and sensitive works.

B 1806   Morison, S. E. *Builders of the Bay Colony* (Boston, 1930).

B 1807   —— *The intellectual life of colonial New England* (rev. ed., New York, 1956 of *The Puritan Pronaos*, New York, 1935).

B 1808   Reed, S. M. *Church and state in Massachusetts, 1691–1740* (Urbana, Ill., 1914).

B 1809   Sly, J. F. *Town government in Massachusetts* (Cambridge, Mass., 1930).

B 1810   Wertenbaker, T. J. *The Puritan oligarchy* (New York, 1947).

THE MIDDLE COLONIES

B 1811   Flick, A. C. (ed.). *History of the state of New York*, vol. 1 (10 vols., New York, 1933–7); the best modern authority, bibliography.

B 1812   Kennedy, J. H. *Thomas Dongan, governor of New York, 1682–8* (New York, 1930).

B 1813   Kessler, R. H. and Rachlis, E. *Peter Stuyvesant and his New York* (New York, 1959).
B 1814   Leder, L. H. *Robert Livingston, 1654–1728, and the politics of colonial New York*, (Chapel Hill, N.C., 1961).
B 1815   McKee, S. *Labour in colonial New York* (New York, 1935).
B 1816   Nissenson, S. G. *The patroon's domain* (New York, 1937).
B 1817   Kemmerer, D. L. *Path to freedom: the struggle for self-government in colonial New Jersey, 1703–76* (Princeton, 1940).
B 1818   Pomfret, J. H. *The province of West New Jersey, 1609–1702* (Princeton, 1956).
B 1819   —— *The province of East New Jersey, 1609–1702* (Princeton, 1962).
B 1820   Herrick, C. A. *White servitude in colonial Pennsylvania* (Philadelphia, 1926).
B 1821   Jones, R. F. *The Quakers in the American colonies* (New York, 1923).
B 1822   Lokken, R. N. *David Lloyd; colonial lawmaker* (Washington, D.C., 1959).
B 1823   Pound, A. *The Penns of Pennsylvania and England* (New York, 1932).
B 1824   Root, W. T. *The relations of Pennsylvania with the British government, 1696–1765* (Philadelphia, 1912).
B 1825   Tolles, F. B. *Meeting house and counting house: the Quaker merchants of colonial Philadelphia, 1682–1763* (Chapel Hill, N.C., 1948).
B 1826   Wertenbaker, T. J. *The founding of American civilisation: the Middle Colonies* (New York, 1938).

THE SOUTH

B 1827   Andrews, M. P. *The founding of Maryland* (New York, 1938).
B 1828   Bassett, J. S. *The constitutional beginnings of North Carolina, 1663–1729* (Baltimore, 1929).
B 1829   Craven, W. F. *The southern colonies in the seventeenth century 1607–89* (Baton Rouge, La., 1949).
B 1830   —— *The dissolution of the Virginia Company* (New York, 1932).
B 1831   Flippin, P. S. *The royal government in Virginia, 1624–1775* (New York, 1919).
B 1832   Moreton, R. L. *Colonial Virginia* (2 vols., Chapel Hill, N.C., 1960).
B 1833   Owings, D. McC. *His lordship's patronage: offices of profit in colonial Maryland* (Baltimore, 1953).
B 1834   Wallace, D. D. *Carolina: a short history* (Chapel Hill, N.C., 1951).
B 1835   —— *The history of South Carolina*, vol. 1 (3 vols., New York, 1934).
B 1836   Washburn, W. E. *The governor and the rebel: a history of Bacon's rebellion in Virginia* (Chapel Hill, N.C., 1958); differs from earlier interpretations.
B 1837   Wertenbaker, T. J. *The shaping of colonial Virginia* (New York, 1958).
B 1838   Wright, L. B. *The first gentlemen of Virginia* (San Marino, Calif., 1940).

BRITISH WEST INDIES

B 1839   Cundall, F. *The governors of Jamaica in the seventeenth century* (1936).
B 1840   Harlow, V. T. *A history of Barbados, 1625–85* (Oxford, 1926).
B 1841   —— *Christopher Codrington, 1668–1710* (Oxford, 1928).

B 1842   Ragatz, L. J. *The West Indian approach to the study of American colonial history* (1934).
B 1843   Whitson, A. M. *The constitutional development of Jamaica, 1664–1729* (Manchester, 1929).
B 1844   Wilkinson, H. C. *The adventurers of Bermuda* (2nd ed., New York, 1958).
B 1845   —— *Bermuda in the old empire, 1684–1784* (1950).
B 1846   Williamson, J. A. *English colonies in Guiana and on the Amazon, 1604–68* (Oxford, 1923).
B 1847   —— *The Caribee islands under the proprietary patents* (Oxford, 1925).

FRENCH WEST INDIES

B 1848   May, L.-P. *Histoire économique de la Martinique, 1635–1763* (1930).
B 1849   Revert, E. *La Martinique* (1949).
B 1850   Satineau, M. *Histoire de la Guadeloupe sous l'ancien régime 1635–1789* (1928).
B 1851   Vaissière, P. de. *Saint-Domingue: la société et la vie créoles sous l'ancien régime, 1629–1789* (1909).

67   Latin America (vol. VII, ch. xxi. 1)
         The Caribbean (vol. VII, ch. xxii. 1)
                          General Studies
         On Latin America in this period the most useful general works are:
A 1013   Vicens Vives, J. (ed.). *Historia social y económica de España y América*, vol. 4, already mentioned.
B 1852   Moses, B. *Spain's declining power in South America, 1730–1806* (Berkeley, 1919).

         See also:
         A 1737 Haring, C. H.
                          Detailed Studies
         Among detailed studies the best contemporary account of the administration of the Spanish possessions is contained in a secret report made to the Crown by two naval officers, subsequently translated and published in English:
B 1853   Juan, J. and Ulloa, A. de. *A voyage to South America: describing at large the Spanish cities, towns, provinces, etc. on that extensive continent* (*1758*; 5th ed., 2 vols., 1807).

         For the circumstances in which this report was compiled see:
B 1854   Whitaker, A. P. 'Antonio de Ulloa', *HAHR*, 15 (1935).

ADMINISTRATIVE DIVISIONS

B 1855   Rubio Mañé, J. I. 'Jurisdicciones del virreinato de Nueva España en la primera mitad del siglo XVIII', *Revista de Indias*, num. 25 (Madrid, 1946).

ECONOMIC DEVELOPMENTS

B 1856   Hamilton, E. J. 'Money and economic recovery in Spain under the first Bourbon, 1701–46', *JMH*, **15** (1943).

B 1857   Hussey, R. D. *The Caracas Company 1728–84* (Cambridge, Mass., 1934).

B 1107   —— 'Antecedents of the Spanish monopolistic overseas trading companies 1624–1728', *HAHR*, **9** (1929).

B 1858   Moreyra Paz-Soldán, M. *Apuntes sobre la historia de la moneda colonial en el Perú. El reglamento de la Casa de Moneda de 1755* (Lima, 1938).

B 1859   Pantaleão, O. *A penetracão comercial de Inglaterra na América española de 1713 a 1783* (São Paolo, 1946).

The Jesuit missions and their economic and political importance

B 1860   Alegre, F. J., S.J., *Historia de la Provincia de la Compañia de Jesús en la Nueva España* (4 vols., Rome, 1956–60).

B 1861   Chevalier, F. (ed.). *Instrucciones a los hermanos Jesuitas administradores de haciendas* (Mexico, 1950); documents with introduction.

See also:

B 1056 Mörner, M.

Cultural life of Spanish America

B 1862   Jiménez Rueda, J. *Historia de la cultura en México: el virreinato* (Mexico, 1950).

B 1863   Romero de Terreros, M. *El arte en México durante el virreinato* (Mexico, 1951).

Brazil

Relatively little has been written on Brazil in the first half of the eighteenth century. Some references are contained in the following general works, which deal chiefly with modern Brazil:

B 1864   Calógeras, J. P. *A history of Brazil* (Eng. trans.) (Chapel Hill, N.C., 1939).

B 1865   Normano, J. F. *Brazil, a study of economic types* (Chapel Hill, N.C., 1935).

B 1866   Oliveira Lima, M. de. *The evolution of Brazil compared with that of Spanish and Anglo-Saxon America* (Stanford, 1914).

See also:

B 1059 Freyre, G.

On more specialised topics:

B 1867   Cardozo, M. S. 'The Brazilian gold rush', *Americas*, **3** (1946).

B 1868   Manchester, A. K. 'The rise of the Brazilian aristocracy', *HAHR*, **11** (1931).

B 1869   Poppino, R. E. 'Cattle industry in colonial Brazil', *Mid-America*, **31** (1949).

See also:

B 13 Shillington, V. M. and Chapman, A. B. W.

The Caribbean

For the *Caribbean* reference should be made to the bibliography on 'North America', Sec. B, **66**, and also to the general bibliographies on 'Economic and social conditions' and on 'The Politics of the European States'.

A contemporary work which, though not first-hand, makes use of first-hand evidence is:

B 1870   *An account of the European settlements in America* (3rd ed., 2 vols., 1760).

Detailed Studies

A 1696   Donnan, E. *Documents illustrative of the history of the slave trade to America* (4 vols., Washington, 1930–5); already mentioned. Deals mostly with North America, but has some Caribbean material.

B 1106   —— 'The early days of the South Sea Company 1711–18', *Journal of Economic and Business History*, **2** (1930).

B 1871   Hart, F. R. *The siege of Havana* (Boston, 1931).

B 1872   Hildner, E. G. 'The role of the South Sea Company in the diplomacy leading to the war of Jenkins' ear, 1729–39', *HAHR*, **18** (1938).

B 1873   Nelson, G. H. 'Contraband trade under the Asiento, 1730–9', *AHR*, **51** (1945).

See also:

B 1101 Scelle, G.; B 1105 Brown, V. L.

68   **The development of the American Communities outside British rule (vol. VIII, ch. xiv)**

For bibliographical works on Latin America see 'Spain, Portugal and their empires' in this section. Reference should also be made to the preceding bibliography on 'Spanish America', Sec. B, **67**.

General Studies

For Spanish colonisation see:

B 1874   Ramos Pérez, D. *Historia de la colonización española en América* (Madrid, 1947).

For Portuguese colonisation see:

B 1875   Humboldt, A. von. *Essai politique sur le royaume de la Nouvelle-Espagne* (5 vols., 1811).

B 1876   —— *Personal Narrative of travels to the equinoctial regions of the new continent during the years 1799–1804* (Eng. trans., 7 vols., 1814–29); both are indispensable.

B 1877   Southey, R. *History of Brazil* (3 vols., 1810–19); still the most comprehensive treatment in English.

Detailed Studies

Studies dealing with the administrative reorganisation of the Spanish American empire include:

B 1878   Céspedes del Castillo, G. 'Lima y Buenos Aires. Repercusiones económicas y políticas de la creación del virreinato del Plata', *Anuario de Estudios Americanos*, **3** (Seville, 1946).

B 1879   Fisher, L. E. *The intendant system in Spanish America* (Berkeley, 1929).

B 1880   Lynch, J. *Spanish colonial administration, 1782–1810. The intendant system in the viceroyalty of the Río de la Plata* (1958).

B 1881   McAlister, L. N. *The 'Fuero Militar' in New Spain, 1764–1800* (Gainesville, Fla., 1957); deals with military reform.

B 1882   Priestley, H. I. *José de Gálvez, visitor-general of New Spain, 1765–71* (Berkeley, 1916).

For economic factors in the history of the later Spanish empire consult:

B 1883   Howe, W. *The mining guild of New Spain and its tribunal general, 1770–1820* (Cambridge, Mass., 1949).

B 1123   Shafer, R. J. *The economic societies in the Spanish world, 1763–1821* (Syracuse, N.Y., 1958).

Reference should also be made to:

B 1884   Christelow, A. 'Contraband trade between Jamaica and the Spanish Main and the free port act of 1766', *HAHR*, **22** (1942).

B 1885   —— 'Great Britain and the trades from Cadiz and Lisbon to Spanish America and Brazil, 1759–83', *HAHR*, **27** (1947).

Intellectual conditions in the Spanish American colonies are discussed in:

B 1886   Lanning, J. T. *The eighteenth-century enlightenment in the University of San Carlos de Guatemala* (Ithaca, 1956).

B 1887   Whitaker, A. P. (ed.). *Latin America and the enlightenment* (New York and London, 1942).

For the events leading up to the independence of Haiti see:

B 1888   Stoddard, T. L. *The French revolution in San Domingo* (Boston and New York, 1914).

69   The United States: American independence in its constitutional aspects (vol. VIII, ch. xvi)
          American independence in its imperial, strategic and diplomatic aspects (vol. VIII, ch. xvii)
          American independence in its American context (vol. VIII, ch. xviii)

Many books dealing with this period have already been mentioned in the preceding bibliography. Further bibliographical information will be found in:

B 1889   Bellot, H. Hale. *American history and American historians* (1952), ch. iii.

Most of the standard constitutional histories of the United States devote ample space to the revolutionary period. The following are the most useful:

B 1890   Hockett, H. C. *The constitutional history of the United States*, vol. 1 (New York, 1939).

B 1891   McLaughlin, A. C. *A constitutional history of the United States* (New York, 1955); useful opening chapter.

For the constitution-making period the indispensable source is still:

B 1892   *Records of the Federal convention of 1787* (Farrand, M., ed.) (4 vols., New Haven, 1911–37).

Also the *Federalist* papers, of which there have been many editions, by:

B 1893   Max Beloff (Oxford, 1948); the most accessible in Britain.

General Studies

General studies of parts of the period, containing useful bibliographies are the following volumes of the *New American Nation* series:

B 1894   Alden, J. R. *The American Revolution, 1775–83* (New York and London, 1954).

B 1895   Gipson, L. H. *The coming of the Revolution, 1763–75* (New York and London, 1954).

B 1896   Miller, J. C. *The Federalist era, 1789–1801* (New York and London, 1960).

Other useful books include:

B 1897   Andrews, C. M. *The colonial background of the American revolution* (revised ed., New Haven, 1931).

B 1898   Beloff, M. (ed.). *The debate on the American Revolution 1761–83* (2nd ed., 1960).

B 1899   Channing, E. *The American Revolution, 1761–89*, (A history of the United States, vol. 3, New York, 1912).

B 1900   Miller, J. C. *Origins of the American Revolution* (revised ed.) (Stanford, Calif., 1959); has an extensive bibliography.

B 1901   —— *Triumph of freedom, 1775–83* (Boston, 1948).

B 1902   Morison, S. E. (ed.). *Sources and documents illustrating the American revolution, 1764–88, and the formation of the federal constitution* (2nd ed., Oxford, 1929).

There are some brief lives of Washington:

B 1903   Cunliffe, M. *George Washington, Man and Monument* (Boston, 1958).

B 1904   Wright, E. *Washington and the American Revolution* (1957).

On a much larger scale is:

B 1768   Freeman, D. S. *George Washington, a biography* (7 vols., New York and London, 1948–57).

Detailed Studies

CONSTITUTIONAL ASPECTS

The economic interpretation of the constitution was given its classic formulation in:

B 1905 Beard, C. *An economic interpretation of the constitution of the United States* (New York, 1913). This should now be read in conjunction with:

B 1906 Brown, R. E. *Charles Beard and the constitution* (Princeton, 1956). In the Beard tradition are the two important works by Jensen:

B 1907 Jensen, M. *The articles of confederation* (Madison, 1940).

B 1908 —— *The new nation* (New York, 1950).

Of particular use for the topics they discuss and as an introduction to the sources and the abundant secondary literature are:

B 1909 Adams, R. G. *Political ideas of the American revolution* (Durham, N.C., 1922).

B 1910 Becker, C. *The declaration of independence* (New York, 1922).

B 1911 Burnett, E. C. *The continental congress* (New York, 1941).

B 1912 Douglass, E. P. *Rebels and Democrats* (Chapel Hill, N.C., 1955).

B 1913 Farrand, M. *The framing of the constitution of the United States* (New Haven, 1913).

B 1914 Guttridge, G. H. *English Whiggism and the American revolution* (Berkeley, Calif., 1942).

B 1915 McIlwain, C. H. *The American revolution. A constitutional interpretation* (New York, 1923).

B 1916 Morgan, E. S. and H. M. *The Stamp Act crisis* (Chapel Hill, N.C., 1953).

B 1917 Nevins, A. *The American states during and after the revolution* (New York, 1924).

B 1918 Ritcheson, C. *British politics and the American revolution* (Norman, Oklahoma, 1954).

B 1919 White, L. D. *The Federalists* (New York, 1948); the best single book on Washington's administration.

B 1920 Wright, B. F. *American interpretation of natural law* (Cambridge, Mass., 1931).

IMPERIAL, STRATEGIC AND DIPLOMATIC ASPECTS

Sources of colonial discontent:

B 1921 Becker, C. *The history of political parties in the province of New York* (New York, 1909).

B 1922 Dickerson, O. M. *The Navigation Acts and the American Revolution* (Philadelphia, 1951).

B 1923 Knollenberg, B. *Origin of the American revolution 1759–66* (New York, 1960).

B 1924 Morgan, E. S. *The birth of the republic 1763–89* (Chicago, 1956).

B 1925 Sydnor, C. S. *Gentlemen freeholders: political practices in Washington's Virginia* (Chapel Hill, N.C., 1952).

BRITISH COLONIAL POLICY

On this and the following sub-sections reference should also be made to the lists on 'The Politics of the European states'.

B 84   Beer, G. L. *British colonial policy, 1754–65* (New York, 1922).

B 1926   Brown, W. A. *Empire or independence: a study in the failure of reconciliation, 1774–83* (Baton Rouge, La., 1941).

B 1927   Wrong, G. M. *Canada and the American revolution, 1760–76* (New York, 1935).

MILITARY HISTORY

B 1928   Carter, C. E. 'The office of the commander-in-chief', in Morris, R. B. (ed.). *The era of the American revolution* (New York, 1939); assesses briefly the role of the British military in the West.

B 1929   Peckham, H. H. *The War of independence: a military history* (Chicago, 1958).

B 1930   Wallace, W. M. *Appeal to arms: a military history of the American revolution* (New York, 1951).

B 1931   Ward, C. L. *The war of the revolution* (2 vols., New York, 1952); the fullest modern account of the campaigns.

NAVAL HISTORY

B 1932   Allen, G. W. *A naval history of the American revolution* (2 vols., Boston, 1913).

B 1933   James, W. M. *The navy in adversity: a study of the war of independence* (London, 1926).

B 1934   Mahan, A. T. *Major operations of the navies in the war of independence* (Boston, 1913).

DIPLOMACY

B 1935   Crowin, E. S. *French policy and the American alliance of 1778* (Princeton, 1916).

B 1936   DeConde, A. *Entangling alliance: politics and diplomacy under George Washington* (Durham, N.C., 1958).

B 1937   Doniol, H. *Histoire de la participation de la France à l'établissement des États-Unis d'Amérique* (5 vols., 1886–92).

LOYALISM AND ESPIONAGE

B 1938   Bakeless, J. *Turncoats, traitors and heroes* (Philadelphia, 1959).

B 1939   Doren, C. van. *The secret history of the American revolution* (New York, 1941).

B 1940   Tyne, C. H. van. *The loyalists in the American revolution* (New York, 1929).

THE AMERICAN CONTEXT OF THE REVOLUTION

For social conditions see:

B 1941   Greene, E. B. *The revolutionary generation 1763–90* (New York, 1943).

B 1942   Jameson, J. Franklin. *The American revolution considered as a social movement* (Princeton, 1926).

B 1943   Schlesinger, A. M. sen. *Colonial merchants and the American revolution* (New York, 1918).

See also:

B 924 Bridenbaugh, C.

The best single volume on the West is:

B 1944   Abernethy, T. P. *Western lands and the American revolution* (New York, 1937).

On the role of propaganda the basic works are:

B 1945   Davidson, P. *Propaganda and the American revolution* (Chapel Hill, N.C., 1941), and:

B 1946   Schlesinger, A. M. sen. *Prelude to independence, the newspaper war on Britain, 1764–76* (New York, 1958).

The relation between voting rights and property is studied in:

B 1947   Handlin, O. and M. 'Radicals and conservatives in Massachusetts after independence', *The New England Qaurterly*, **17** (1944).

B 1948   Pole, J. R. 'Suffrage and representation in Massachusetts: a statistical note', *William and Mary Quarterly*, **14** (1957).

EUROPE OVERSEAS: ASIA AND AFRICA

For the bibliography on 'Europe and Asia' in vol. v, see Sec. A, **56**.

70   Rivalries in India (vol. VII, ch. xxiii)

General Studies

Few general studies have been published and the student has to rely on detailed monographs. The principal sources relating to the decline of Mughal rule in India are in Persian. They have been enumerated in:

B 1949   *Cambridge history of India*, vol. IV (Cambridge, 1937).

A recent work on historical geography is:

B 1950   Davies, C. Collin. *An historical atlas of the Indian peninsula* (Oxford, 1958).

The only authoritative works on the decline of the empire after 1707 are:

B 1951   Irvine, W. *Later Mughals* (Sarkar, J., ed.) (2 vols., Calcutta, 1921–2).
B 1952   Sarkar, J. *Fall of the Mughal Empire* (2 vols., Calcutta, 1932–4).

Detailed Studies

PROVINCIAL HISTORIES

B 1953   Chatterji, N. *Mir Qasim Nawab of Bengal* (Calcutta, 1935).
B 1954   Cunningham, J. D. *History of the Sikhs* (Oxford, 1918).

B 1955   Datta, K. K. *Studies in the history of the Bengal subah 1740–70* (Calcutta, 1936).
B 1956   —— *Alivardi and his times* (Calcutta, 1939).
B 1957   Gupta, H. R. *Studies in later Mughal history of the Punjab* (Lahore, 1944).
B 1958   Sinh, R. *Malwa in transition* (Bombay, 1936).
B 1959   Sinha, N. K. *Rise of the Sikh power* (Calcutta, 1946).
B 1960   Srivastava, A. L. *The first two nawabs of Oudh* (Lucknow, 1933).

THE GROWTH OF MAHRATTA POWER

B 1961   Digha, V. G. *Peshwa Bajirao I and Maratha expansion* (Bombay, 1944).
B 1962   Grant Duff, J. C. *A history of the Mahrattas* (Edwardes, S. M., ed.) (2 vols., Oxford, 1921).
B 1963   Sardesai, G. S. *New history of the Marathas*, vol. 2 (Bombay, 1948).
B 1964   Sen, S. *The administrative system of the Marathas* (Calcutta, 1925).
B 1965   —— *Military system of the Marathas* (Calcutta, 1928).
B 1966   Shejwalkar, T. S. *Panipat: 1761* (Deccan College monograph series, 1946).

ANGLO–FRENCH RIVALRY

The best works are:

B 1967   Cultru, P. *Dupleix* (1901).
B 1968   Dodwell, H. *Dupleix and Clive* (1920).
B 1969   Forrest, G. *Life of Lord Clive* (2 vols., 1918).
B 1970   Martineau, A. *Dupleix et l'Inde française* (4 vols., 1920–8).
B 1971   —— *Bussy et l'Inde française* (1935).
B 1972   Weber, M. *La compagnie française des Indes* (1908).

See also:

B 32 Kaeppelin, P.

71   **Economic relations in Africa and the far east. 2. Asia (vol. VII, ch. xxiv)**
General Studies

A useful introductory sketch is:

B 1973   Steiger, G. N., Beyer, O. and Benitez, C. *History of the Orient* (New York, 1926).

More recent outline histories of the region are:

B 1974   Eckel, P. E. *The Far East since 1500* (New York, 1947).
B 1975   Steiger, G. N. *A history of the Far East* (Boston, 1936).

For the relations of Indonesia with the remainder of South-east Asia during the period:

A 1601   Hall, D. G. E. *A history of South-east Asia* (rev. ed., 1958).

For the history of the Chinese in Indonesia and the Philippines during the period:

B 1976   Purcell, V. *The Chinese in South-east Asia* (Oxford, 1951).

Detailed Studies

CHINA

B 1977   Anson, Lord. *A Voyage round the world in the years 1740–4* (London, Everyman's Library, 1930).

B 1978   Cordier, H. *Histoire générale de la Chine*, vol. 3 (1920).

B 1979   Morse, H. B. *The international relations of the Chinese Empire*, vol. 1 (3 vols., 1910–18).

INDONESIA

B 1980   Furnivall, J. S. *Netherlands India, a study in plural economy* (Cambridge, 1944).

B 1981   Vandenbosch, A. *The Dutch East Indies* (Berkeley, 1942).

See also:

A 1606   Vlekke, B. H. M.

THE PHILIPPINES

B 1982   Barrows, D. P. *History of the Philippines* (Yonkers-on-the-Hudson, N.Y., 1924).

B 1983   Blair, E. and Robertson, J. A. *The Philippine Islands* (55 vols., Cleveland, Ohio, 1903–12); an indispensable authority containing translations of the most important Spanish books and documents.

B 1984   Forbes, W. Cameron. *The Philippine islands* (Cambridge, Mass., 1945).

72   **European Relations with Asia and Africa: Relations with Asia (vol. VIII, ch. viii. 1)**

Two works which have already been mentioned have useful bibliographies:

A 1601   Hall, D. G. E. *History of South-east Asia.*

A 1655   *Cambridge history of India*, vol. v.

Published selections of documents include:

B 1985   Forrest, G. W. (ed.). *Selections from the state papers of the Governors-General of India: Warren Hastings* (2 vols., Oxford, 1910).

B 1986   —— *Selections from the state papers of the Governors-General of India: Lord Cornwallis* (2 vols., Oxford, 1926).

B 1987   *Fort William–India House correspondence*, covering the years 1748–1800, in 21 vols. (National Archives of India, series not yet completed).

B 1988   Joshi, P. M. (ed.). *Persian records of Maratha history*, of which two volumes have so far appeared (Bombay, 1953–).

B 1989   Sarkar, J. and Sardesai, G. S. (eds.). *English records of Maratha history: Poona residency correspondence* (14 vols., Bombay, 1936–53); covering the years 1785–1818.

Detailed Studies

B 1990   Aspinall, A. *Cornwallis in Bengal* (Manchester, 1931).

B 1991   Baden-Powell, B. H. *Land systems of British India* (3 vols., Oxford, 1892).

B 1992   Choksey, R. D. *British diplomacy at the court of the Peshwas, 1786–1818* (Poona, 1951).
B 1993   Davies, C. C. *Warren Hastings and Oudh* (1939).
B 1994   Dutt, R. C. *Economic history of India under early British rule* (1906).
B 1995   Feiling, K. G. *Warren Hastings* (1954).
B 1996   Furber, H. *John Company at work* (Cambridge, Mass., 1951).
B 1997   Gleig, G. R. *Warren Hastings* (3 vols., 1841).
B 1998   Gopal, S. *Permanent settlement in Bengal and its results* (1949).
B 1999   Lovejoy, A. O. 'The Chinese origins of Romanticism', *Essays in the history of ideas* (Baltimore, 1948).
B 2000   Misra, B. B. *Central administration of the East India Company, 1773–1834* (Manchester, 1959).
B 2001   Monckton Jones, M. E. *Warren Hastings in Bengal, 1772–4* (Oxford, 1918).
B 2002   Philips, C. H. *East India Company, 1784–1834* (2nd ed., Manchester, 1961).
B 2003   Pritchard, E. H. 'Crucial years of Anglo-Chinese relations 1750–1800', *Research Studies of the State College of Washington*, vol. 4, nos. 3–4 (Pullman, Washington, 1936).
B 1963   Sardesai, G. S. *New history of the Marathas* (3 vols., Bombay, 1946–8); already mentioned above.
B 2004   Schwab, R. *La Renaissance orientale* (1950).
B 2005   Sen, S. P. *The French in India, 1763–1816* (Calcutta, 1958).
B 2006   Sinha, N. K. *Haidar Ali* (3rd ed., Calcutta, 1959).
B 2007   —— *Economic history of Bengal from Plassey to the permanent settlement*, vol. 1 (Calcutta, 1956).
B 2008   Spear, P. *Twilight of the Mughuls* (Cambridge, 1951).
B 2009   Weitzman, S. *Warren Hastings and Philip Francis* (Manchester, 1929).
B 2010   Wright, H. R. C. *East-Indian economic problems of the age of Cornwallis and Raffles* (1961).

See also:

A 1542 Hudson, G. F.; A 1666 Morse, H. B.; A 1681 Reichwein, A.; A 1686 Rowbotham, A. H.; B 844 Harlow, V. T.; B 1330 Sutherland, L. S.

73   Economic relations in Africa and the far east. 1. Africa (vol. VII, ch. xxiv)
         European relations with Asia and Africa: 2. Relations with Africa (vol. VIII, ch. viii. 2)

Reference should be made to works on 'Europe Overseas: Africa' in Section A; and, for the slave trade, to the bibliographies on 'Europe Overseas: America' and on 'Economic and social conditions' in Section B.

On the history and ethnology of the native kingdoms see:

B 2011   Cornevin, R. *Histoire des peuples de l'Afrique noire* (1962).
B 2012   Delafosse, M. *Haut-Sénégal-Niger*, 1e série (3 vols., 1912); vol. 2 deals with the history of the kingdoms of the interior.

B 2013   Johnson, S. *History of the Yorubas* (1921).

On West Africa and the slave trade a useful collection of documents, already mentioned, is:

A 1696   Donnan, E. *Documents illustrative of the history of the slave trade to America* (4 vols.).

The trade and its abolition are discussed from various viewpoints in:

B 2014   Berbain, S. *Le Comptoir français de Juda au XVIIIe siècle* (1942).
B 2015   Clarkson, T. *The history of the rise, progress and accomplishment of the abolition of the African slave-trade by the British Parliament* (2 vols., 1808); by one of the leading abolitionists.
B 2016   Coupland, Sir R. *The British anti-slavery movement* (1933).
B 2017   Edwards, B. *History...of the British colonies in the West Indies* (4th ed., 3 vols., 1807); vol. 2 contains a contemporary account of the slave trade.
B 2018   Hyde, E. E. and others. 'The Nature and profitability of the Liverpool slave trade', *Econ. HR*, 2nd ser., 5 (1953).
B 83   Martin, E. C. 'The English slave trade and the African settlements', *Cambridge history of the British Empire*, vol. I.
B 2019   Martin, G. *Nantes au XVIIIe siècle. L'ère des négriers 1714–74* (1931).
B 2020   Rinchon, D. *Les armements négriers au XVIIIe siècle* (Brussels, 1956).
B 2021   Williams, E. *Capitalism and slavery* (Chapel Hill, N.C., 1944); criticises Coupland for neglecting economic aspects.

These may be supplemented by the narratives of traders and others, including:

B 2022   Adams, J. *Sketches taken during ten voyages to Africa between the years 1786 and 1800...* (n.d. [1821]).
B 2023   Dalzel, A. *The history of Dahomey...*(1793); largely based on memoirs by the Liverpool slave-trader Robert Nelson; an important historical source, but in parts tendentious.
B 2024   Degrandpré, L. *Voyage à la côte occidentale de l'Afrique, fait dans les années 1786 et 1787* (Paris, An. IX [1801]).
B 2025   Matthews, J. *A voyage to the river Sierra Leone...*(1788).

Works studying the European settlements:

B 2026   Beaver, P. *African memoranda...* (1805); for Bulama.
B 2027   Chailley, M. *Les Grandes Missions françaises en Afrique occidentale* (Dakar 1953); for French exploration, 1639–1833.
B 2028   Cultru, P. *Histoire du Sénégal du XVe siècle à 1870* (1910).
B 2029   Delafosse, M. 'L'Afrique occidentale française', Hanotaux, G. and Martineau, A. *Histoire des colonies françaises*, vol. 4 (1931).
B 2030   Delcourt, A. *La France et les établissements français au Sénégal entre 1713 et 1763* (Mémoires de l'institut français d'Afrique noire, no. 17) (Dakar, 1952).
B 2031   Kuczynski, R. R. *Demographic survey of the British colonial empire*, vol. 1 *West Africa* (1948); for the colonisation of Sierra Leone, good bibliography.

B 2032   Martin, E. C. *The British West African settlements, 1750–1821* (1927).
B 2033   Schefer, C. (ed.). *Instructions générales données de 1763 à 1870 aux gouverneurs et ordonnateurs des établissements français en Afrique occidentale* (2 vols., 1927).
B 2034   Wadstrom, C. B. *An essay on colonisation* (1794); a useful source, but not always reliable.

SOUTH AND EAST AFRICA

B 2035   *Cambridge history of the British Empire*, vol. VIII, *South Africa*, rev. ed. (Cambridge, 1963); good bibliography.
B 2036   Marais, J. S. *Maynier and the first Boer republic* (Cape Town, n.d.).
B 2037   Sparrman, A. *A voyage to the Cape of Good Hope...1772 to 1776* (2 vols., 1785); an informative narrative of travels.
B 2038   Walker, E. A. *History of southern Africa* (3rd ed., 1957).

NORTHERN AFRICA

B 2039   Bruce, J. *Travels to discover the source of the Nile...1768–73* (3rd ed., 8 vols., Edinburgh, 1813).
B 2040   Charles-Roux, F. *France et Afrique du Nord avant 1830* (1932).
B 2041   *Proceedings of the Association for promoting the discovery of the interior parts of Africa* (London, 1790–1810).

See also:

B 1186 Julien, C. A.

SECTION C: 1793–1945

The volumes of the *New Cambridge Modern History* covered in this section are: IX (1793–1830); X (1830–70); XI (1870–98); XII (1898–1945). The book-lists for each chapter normally deal with the period of time embraced by the volume in which they appear; exceptions are noted in the synopsis. There are a few cases where particular lists overlap the general division into sections, but these are noted both in the synopsis and in the text.

Other points to note in using the bibliography are:

(1) Each entry is numbered, with a separate series of numbers for each section. The first reference to any book is to be considered the master reference, and normally only the first reference gives the full details about that work. Thereafter it appears as a number reference with the appropriate section letter added and with the author's name, e.g. B 995, Clough, S. B. Therefore, in using any list, it must be remembered that important references may be contained in these number references at the end, and these should be looked up in each case. This is particularly true of books which appear many times, such as, for the sixteenth-century chapters, F. Braudel, *La Méditerranée et le monde méditerranéen à l'époque de Philippe II.*

(2) There is a brief list of some of the chief historical bibliographies and of some of the chief historical series on pp. x–xi. In general, where a book contains a useful bibliography, this is noted in the chapter list.

(3) There are no lists on music or the visual arts, though lists have been provided for the literary chapters where this was thought appropriate. In very few other cases only has no chapter list been provided.

(4) It is assumed that English books have been published in London and French books in Paris, unless stated. Other places of publication and all dates of publication are given.

ECONOMIC AND SOCIAL CONDITIONS

1   Economic change in England and Europe, 1780–1830 (vol. IX, ch. ii)
     Economic change and growth (vol. X, ch. ii)
     Economic conditions (vol. XI, ch. ii)

General Studies

Perhaps the best general introductions for the period up to 1830 are still:

C 1   Clapham, J. H. 'Economic change', *Cambridge modern history*, vol. X (1907).

B 361   Heaton, H. 'Industrial revolution', *Encyclopaedia of the social sciences*, vol. 8 (1932). Other articles in this encyclopaedia cover all aspects of the economic history of Europe.

General studies covering a longer period of time include:

C 2   Bowden, W., Karpovich, M. and Usher, A. P. *An economic history of Europe since 1750* (New York, 1937); perhaps the best general survey, but shows its age. Excellent bibliography.

C 3   Henderson, W. O. *Britain and industrial Europe* (Liverpool, 1954).

C 4   —— *The industrial revolution on the continent* (1961).

B 1163 Luzzatto, G. *Storia economica dell'età moderna e contemporanea fino al 1950* (2 vols., Padua, 1950–2).

A 298 Singer, C. and others. *A history of technology* (Oxford, 1958); vols. 4 and 5 cover the years 1750–1900, dividing at 1850.

See also:

A 48 Clough, S. B. and Cole, C. W.; A 50 Heaton, H.

Detailed Studies

C 5   Albion, F. G. *Square-riggers on schedule* (Princeton, 1938); traces the rise and decline of the North Atlantic lines of sailing ships.

C 6   Bagehot, W. *Lombard Street* (1873); a contemporary picture.

C 7   Burn, D. L. *Economic history of steelmaking (1867–1939)* (Cambridge, 1939); a very thorough study of a basic industry in difficult times.

C 8   Cairncross, A. *Home and foreign investment 1870–1913* (Cambridge, 1953).

C 9   Carr, J. C. and Taplin, W. *A history of the British steel industry* (Oxford, 1962); should be compared with D. L. Burn above.

C 10   Conant, C. A. *A history of modern banks of issue* (New York, 1915).

C 11   Condliffe, J. B. *The commerce of nations* (1951); surveys commerce, finance and commercial policy.

C 12   Dunham, A. L. *The Anglo-French treaty of commerce of 1860* (Ann Arbor, 1930).

C 13   Feis, H. *Europe the world's banker* (New Haven, 1930); deals with movements of capital.

C 14   'Growth of banking, finance and monetary institutions', *European civilisation, its origin and development*, Eyre, E., ed., vol. 5 (Oxford, 1937).

C 15   Haber, L. F. *The chemical industry during the nineteenth century* (Oxford, 1958); views the world development of a vital industry through the eyes of a technical expert alive to general economic considerations.

C 16   Henderson, W. O. *The Zollverein* (Manchester, 1939).

C 17   Hidy, R. W. *The House of Baring in American trade and finance* (Cambridge, Mass., 1949).

C 18   Hughes, J. F. T. *Fluctuations in trade, industry, and finance 1850–60* (Oxford, 1960).

C 19   Imlah, A. H. *Economic elements in the Pax Britannica* (Cambridge, Mass., 1958).

C 20   Jenks, L. H. *The migration of British capital to 1875* (1927).

C 21   Lardner, D. *Railway economy* (1850).

C 22   Liefmann, R. *Cartels, concerns and trusts* (1932); on the problems of industrial organisation.

C 23   List, F. *The national system of political economy*, Eng. trans. (1904).

C 24   Marshall, A. *Industry and trade* (1923).
A 40   Rostow, W. W. *The process of economic growth* (Oxford, 1953); already mentioned.
C 25   Slicher van Bath, B. H. *The agrarian history of Western Europe A.D. 500–1850* (1963).
C 26   Wells, D. A. *Recent economic changes* (New York, 1889).
C 27   Wilson, C. H. *History of Unilever* (2 vols., 1954); a specific example of the way firms move from informal association into permanent union on a world scale.

See also:

B 59 Clapham, J. H.; B 105 Carr-Saunders, A. M.; B 110 Reinhard, M. E. and Armengaurd, A.

National Studies

AUSTRIA

C 28   Blum, J. *Noble landowners and agriculture in Austria, 1815–48: a study in the origins of the peasant emancipation of 1848* (Baltimore, 1948).

BELGIUM AND HOLLAND

C 29   Demoulin, R. *Guillaume Ier et la transformation économique des provinces belges* (Paris/Liége, 1938).
C 30   Wright, H. R. C. *Free trade and protection in the Netherlands 1816–30* (Cambridge, 1955).

THE CZECHS

C 31   Purs, J. *The industrial revolution in Czech lands* (Prague, 1960).

FRANCE

C 32   Cameron, R. E. *France and the economic development of Europe 1800–1914* (Princeton, 1961); the most original and recent study of France's contribution to economic growth.
C 33   Clapham, J. H. *The economic development of France and Germany 1815–1914* (4th ed., Cambridge, 1945).
C 34   Dunham, A. L. *The industrial revolution in France 1815–48* (New York, 1955).

GERMANY

C 35   Benaerts, P. *Les Origines de la grande industrie allemande* (1933).
C 36   Henderson, W. O. *The state and the industrial revolution in Prussia, 1740–1870* (Liverpool, 1958).

GREAT BRITAIN

C 37   Ashton, T. S. *The industrial revolution 1760–1830* (1949).
C 38   Clapham, J. H. *An economic history of modern Britain* (3 vols., Cambridge, 1926–38); the indispensable quantitative study.
C 39   Gayer, A. D., Rostow, W. W. and Schwartz, A. *The growth and fluctuation of the British economy, 1790–1850* (New York, 1953).

C 40 Hoffmann, W. *British industry 1700–1950* (Eng. trans.) (Oxford, 1955); considers problems of industrial growth and decay. Its conclusions and the statistical methods by which they have been reached have given rise to a considerable literature of controversy.

C 41 Lavergne, L. de. *The rural economy of England, Scotland and Ireland* (Edinburgh, 1855).

C 42 Levi, L. *History of British commerce* (1872).

C 43 Mantoux, P. *The industrial revolution in the eighteenth century* (1928).

C 44 Rostow, W. W. *British economy of the nineteenth century* (Oxford, 1948).

ITALY

C 45 Barbagallo, C. *Le origini della industria contemporanea (1750–1850)* (Perugia–Venice, 1930).

C 46 Greenfield, K. R. *Economics and liberalism in the Risorgimento: a study of nationalism in Lombardy, 1814–48* (Baltimore, 1934); concerned with the history of ideas as much as with economics, but is the only work in English on the economic history of this period.

THE UNITED STATES

C 47 Cochran, T. C. and Miller, W. *The age of enterprise* (New York, 1943).

C 48 Kirkland, E. C. *A history of American economic life* (New York, 1952).

C 49 Williamson, H. F. (ed.). *The growth of the American economy*, part iii (New York, 1951).

See also:

A 36 Lütge, F.; A 93 Hecksher, E. F.; A 98 Lyashchenko, P. I.; B 1660 Hovde, B. J.

Much definitive work on the economic history of the period has appeared in the form of articles. The following are among the most important on the latter part of the century:

From the *Economic History Review*:

C 50 Deane, P. 'Contemporary estimates of national income in the second half of the nineteenth century' (**9**, no. 3, 2nd series).

C 51 Gallagher, J. and Robinson, R. 'The imperialism of free trade' (**6**, no. 1, 2nd series).

C 52 Graham, G. S. 'The ascendancy of the sailing ship 1860–85' (**9**, no. 1).

C 53 Henderson, W. O. 'German economic penetration in the Middle East 1870–1914' (**18**, nos. 1 and 2).

C 54 Imlah, A. H. 'The British balance of payments and the export of capital 1816–1913' (**5**, no. 2, 2nd series).

C 55 Saul, S. B. 'Britain and world trade' (**7**, no. 1, 2nd series).

The *Explorations in Entrepreneurial History*, published by the Harvard Centre, contain a number of valuable articles. Those by David S. Landes, 'Anglo–German rivalry', and by John E. Sawyer, 'Entrepreneurship in periods of rapid growth: the United States', in the special volume:

C 56 *Entrepreneurship and economic growth* (1954) are specially relevant.

2   The economic map of the world: population, commerce and industries (vol. XII, ch. ii)

Reference should also be made, both for this bibliography and for that to vol. XII, ch. xviii which follows, to the parallel bibliography on economic and social conditions for vols. IX–XI above.

General Studies

A useful general sketch of economic developments in the world as a whole and in several countries during the inter-war period (with bibliography) is:

C 57   Lewis, W. A. *Economic survey, 1919–39* (1949).

Papers on the pattern of international trade, world population, war-time economic developments and industrial changes are included in:

C 58   Brown, A. J. *Applied economics* (1947).

For migration and population changes see:

C 59   Notestein, F. W. and others. *The future population of Europe and the Soviet Union* (Geneva, 1944).
C 60   Thomas, B. *Migration and economic growth* (1954); bibliography.

British economic experience is covered in:

C 61   Bowley, A. L. *Some economic consequences of the great war* (1930).
C 62   Henderson, H. D. *The inter-war years and other papers* (1955).
C 63   Loveday, A. *Britain and world trade* (1929).
C 64   Lucas, A. F. *Industrial reconstruction and the control of competition* (1937).
C 65   Pigou, A. C. *Aspects of British economic history, 1918–25* (1947).
C 66   Youngson, A. J. *The British economy, 1920–57* (1960).

For general studies of the world economic depression see:

C 67   League of Nations. *The course and phases of the world economic depression* (Geneva, 1931).
C 68   Robbins, L. C. *The great depression* (1934).
C 69   Rowe, J. W. F. *Markets and men* (1936).
C 70   Yates, P. L. *Commodity control* (1942).

Detailed Studies

The publications of the League of Nations economic secretariat are indispensable as a source of information about trade, industry and finance, particularly:

C 71   *World economic survey* (annual from 1931–2).
C 72   *Commercial policy in the inter-war period* (1942).
C 73   *Industrialisation and world trade* (1945).
C 74   *Statistical year-book of the League of Nations* (annual).
C 75   *Review of world trade* (annual).

For particular countries see:

C 76 Barger, H. and Landsberg, H. A. *American agriculture, 1899–1939* (New York, 1942).
C 77 Baykov, H. *The development of the Soviet economic system* (1947).
C 78 Guillebaud, C. W. *The economic recovery of Germany, 1933–8* (1939).
C 79 Hancock, W. K. and Gowing, M. M. *British war economy* (1949).
C 80 Hugh-Jones, E. A. and Radice, E. M. *An American experiment* (1936).
C 81 Mill, F. C. *Economic tendencies in the United States* (New York, 1932).
C 82 Peel, G. *The economic policy of France* (1937).
C 83 Richardson, J. H. *British economic foreign policy* (1936).
C 84 Rostas, L. *Comparative productivity in British and American industry* (1948).
C 85 Schumpeter, E. B. (ed.). *The Industrialisation of Japan and Manchukuo, 1930–40* (New York, 1940).

3 **Economic interdependence and planned economies (vol. XII, ch. xviii)**

General Studies

C 86 Ashley, P. *Modern tariff history. Germany—United States—France* (3rd ed., 1920); deals with tariffs up to 1914.
C 87 Ashworth, W. *Short history of the international economy 1850–1950* (2nd ed., 1962).
C 88 Hodson, H. V. *Slump and recovery 1929–37. A survey of world economic affairs* (1938).
C 89 Royal Institute of International Affairs, *The problem of international investment* (1937).
C 90 Schumpeter, J. A. *Business cycles. A theoretical, historical and statistical analysis of the capitalist process*, vol. 2 (New York, 1939).
C 91 Svennilson, I. *Growth and stagnation in the European economy* (United Nations economic commission for Europe, Geneva, 1954).
C 92 Yates, P. L. *Forty years of foreign trade. A statistical handbook…*(1959); covers the years 1913–53.

Detailed Studies

CARTELS AND BUSINESS ORGANISATIONS

C 93 Brady, R. A. *Business as a system of power* (New York, 1943).
C 94 Hexner, E. *International cartels* (1946).
C 95 Lynch, D. *The concentration of economic power* (New York, 1946); deals with corporations in the United States.
C 96 Plummer, A. *International combines in modern industry* (3rd ed., 1951).

GOVERNMENT CONTROLS IN WORLD WAR I

C 97 Beveridge, Sir W. *British food control* (1928).
C 98 Salter, J. A. *Allied shipping control. An experiment in international administration* (Oxford, 1921); both in Shotwell, J. T. (ed.). *Economic and social history of the world war* (British series).

AGRICULTURE

C 99 Masefield, G. B. *A short history of agriculture in the British colonies* (Oxford, 1950).

C 100 Royal Institute of International Affairs. *World agriculture. An international survey* (1932).

C 101 Warriner, D. *Economics of peasant farming* (1939).

C 102 Yates, P. L. *Food production in western Europe. An economic survey of agriculture in six countries* (1940).

NATIONAL ECONOMIES

BRITAIN AND THE COMMONWEALTH

C 103 Ashworth, W. *An economic history of England 1870–1939* (1960).

C 104 Hancock, W. K. *Survey of British commonwealth affairs*, vol. 2. *Problems of economic policy 1918–39*, pts. i and ii (1940, 1942).

For J. M. Keynes, see:

C 105 Keynes, J. M. *General theory of employment, interest and money* (1936).

C 106 Harrod, H. R. B. *The life of J. M. Keynes* (1951).

OTHER COUNTRIES

C 107 Bechtel, H. *Wirtschaftsgeschichte Deutschlands*, vol. 3 (Munich, 1956) (see also B 8).

C 108 Bruck, W. F. *Social and economic history of Germany from William II to Hitler* (1938).

C 109 Dobb, M. H. *Soviet economic development since 1917* (1948).

C 110 Lockwood, W. W. *The economic development of Japan. Growth and structural change 1868–1938* (Princeton, 1954).

C 111 Nathan, O. *The Nazi economic system* (Durham, N.C., 1944).

See also:

B 995 Clough, S. B.

INTELLECTUAL LIFE, LITERATURE, SCIENCE AND EDUCATION

4   Imaginative Literature (vol. x, ch. vii)
Literature (vol. xi, ch. v)

Important bibliographies are:

C 112 Bateson, F. W. *The Cambridge bibliography of English literature* (Cambridge, 1940); with a supplementary volume by Watson, G. (Cambridge, 1955).

C 113 Kosch, W. *Deutsches Literatur-Lexikon* (Berne, 1949–58).

C 114 Talvart, H. and Place, J. *Bibliographie des auteurs modernes de langue française* (1928–).

For other bibliographical material see:

C 115   Baker, E. A. *The history of the English novel*, vol. 9 (1938).
C 116   Bithell, J. *Modern German literature* (rev. ed., 1959).
C 117   Faverty, E. *The Victorian poets. A guide to research* (Cambridge, Mass., 1956).
C 118   Garten, H. F. *Modern German drama* (1959).
C 119   Ward, A. W. and Waller, A. R. (eds.). *The Cambridge history of English literature*, vols. XI–XIV (Cambridge, 1915–16).

The following works contain general material relating to the literature of the period, or to individual authors discussed in the text.

C 120   Batho, E. and Dobree, B. *The Victorians and after* (rev. ed.) (1950).
C 121   Bennett, E. K. *A history of the German novelle* (Cambridge, 1934).
C 122   Berlin, I. *The hedgehog and the fox* (1953).
C 123   Beuchat, C. *Histoire du naturalisme français* (1949).
C 124   Bewley, M. *The eccentric design* (1959).
C 125   Bourget, P. *Essais de psychologie contemporaine* (1926).
C 126   Bowra, C. M. *The heritage of symbolism* (1943).
C 127   —— *The romantic imagination* (Oxford, 1950).
C 128   Brinkmann, R. *Wirklichkeit und Illusion* (Tübingen, 1957).
C 129   Burdett, O. *The Beardsley period* (1925).
C 130   Chesterton, G. K. *The Victorian age in literature* (n.d.).
C 131   Chiari, J. *Symbolism from Poe to Mallarmé* (1956).
C 132   Cowie, A. *The rise of the American novel* (New York, 1948).
C 133   De la Mare, W. *The eighteen-eighties* (Cambridge, 1930).
C 134   Dobree, B. *The lamp and the lute* (1929).
C 135   Drinkwater, J. (ed.). *The eighteen-sixties* (Cambridge, 1932).
C 136   Du Bos, C. *Approximations* (1927).
C 137   Dumesnil, R. *L'Epoque réaliste et naturaliste* (1945).
C 138   Eliot, T. S. *From Poe to Valery* (New York, 1948).
C 139   Evans, B. Ifor. *English poetry in the later nineteenth century* (1933).
C 140   Fairchild, H. N. *Religious trends in English poetry*, vol. 4 (New York, 1957).
C 141   Foakes, R. A. *The romantic assertion, a study in the language of nineteenth-century poetry* (1958).
C 142   Forster, E. M. *Aspects of the novel* (1941).
C 143   Granville-Barker, H. *The eighteen-seventies* (Cambridge, 1929).
C 144   Heath-Stubbs, J. *The darkling plain* (1950).
C 145   Holloway, J. *The Victorian sage* (1953).
C 146   Hough, G. *The last romantics* (1949).
C 147   Jackson, H. *The eighteen-nineties* (1927).
C 148   James, H. *Notes on novelists* (1914).
C 149   Johnson, E. D. H. *The alien vision of Victorian poetry* (Princeton, 1952).
C 150   Jones, Mansell, *The background of modern French poetry* (Cambridge, 1951).
C 151   Koch, F. *Idee und Wirklichkeit* (Düsseldorf, 1956).
C 152   Lalou, R. *Histoire de la littérature contemporaine* (1924).

c 153 Lamm, M. *Modern drama* (Eng. trans.) (Oxford, 1952).
c 154 Lavrin, J. *From Pushkin to Mayakovsky* (1948).
c 155 Leavis, F. R. *The great tradition* (1948).
c 156 Lehmann, A. G. *The symbolist aesthetic* (Oxford, 1950).
c 157 Lucas, F. L. *Ten Victorian poets* (1940).
c 158 Lukács, G. *Studies in European realism* (1950).
c 159 —— *Deutsche Realisten des 19ten Jahrhunderts* (Bern, 1951).
c 160 Martino, P. *Le Naturalisme français* (1923).
c 161 Massingham, H. J. and Hugh. *The great Victorians* (1932).
c 162 Michaud, G. *Message poétique du symbolisme* (1947).
c 163 Mirsky, D. S. *A history of Russian literature* (1949).
c 164 Muir, E. *The structure of fiction* (1946).
c 165 Muschg, W. *Tragische Literaturgeschichte* (Bern, 1948).
c 166 Napler, J. *Literaturgeschichte der deutschen Schweiz* (Leipzig and Zürich, 1932).
c 167 Ortega y Gasset, J. *The dehumanisation of art and notes on the novel* (Oxford, 1948).
c 168 Praz, M. *The romantic agony* (Oxford, 1933).
c 169 —— *The hero in eclipse in Victorian fiction* (Oxford, 1956).
c 170 Quennell, P. *Baudelaire and the symbolists* (1929).
c 171 Rivière, J. *Etudes* (1924).
c 172 Sainte-Beuve, C.-A. *Causeries du lundi* (1857–75).
c 173 —— *Portraits contemporains* (n.d.).
c 174 Seurat, D. *Modern French literature, 1870–1940* (1946).
c 175 Sewell, E. *The structure of poetry* (1951).
c 176 —— *The field of nonsense* (1952).
c 177 Sitwell, E. *Introduction to prose poems from 'Les Illuminations', translated by Helen Rootham* (1932).
c 178 Steinhausen, G. *Deutsche Geistes- und Kulturgeschichte von 1870 bis zur Gegenwart* (Halle a/S. 1931).
c 179 Taine, H. *Nouveaux essais de critique et d'histoire* (1880).
c 180 Thibaudet, A. *Histoire de la littérature française de 1789 à nos jours* (1946).
c 181 Thomson, P. *The Victorian heroine* (Oxford, 1956).
c 182 Tillotson, G. *Criticism and the nineteenth century* (1951).
c 183 —— *Novels of the eighteen-forties* (Oxford, 1954).
c 184 Turnell, M. *The novel in France* (1950).
c 185 Vivier, R. *Et la poésie fut langage* (1954).
c 186 Welland, D. S. R. *The Pre-raphaelites in literature and art* (1953).
c 187 Wellek, R. *A history of modern criticism 1750–1950* (1955).
c 188 Wiese, B. von. *Das deutsche Drama* (Düsseldorf, 1958).
c 189 Willey, B. *Essays mainly on the nineteenth century* (Oxford, 1948).
c 190 —— *Nineteenth-century studies* (1949).
c 191 Wilson, E. *Axel's castle* (New York, 1931).
c 192 —— *The shock of recognition* (1956).
c 193 —— *The wound and the bow* (1952).

5   Literature, philosophy and religious thought (vol. XII, ch. vi)

The works of literature, philosophy and theology which form the subject-matter of this chapter are so numerous that only a very arbitrary selection can be given here, together with a few books of criticism and exposition. Each philosopher and theologian cited is represented by one work only, though there are naturally many others by these authors which could have been added had space permitted.

Philosophy

C 194   Alexander, S. *Space, time and deity* (2 vols., 1920).
C 195   Bergson, H. *L'Evolution créatrice* (7th ed., 1911).
C 196   Bradley, F. H. *Appearance and reality* (1893).
C 197   Gentile, G. *Theory of mind as pure act* (Eng. trans.) (1922).
C 198   Haeckel, E. *Riddle of the universe* (Eng. trans.) (1900).
C 199   Husserl, E. *Ideas: general introduction to phenomenology* (1931).
C 200   Lewis, H. D. (ed.). *Contemporary British philosophy* (1956).
C 201   Maritain, J. *Degrees of knowledge* (Eng. trans.) (1937).
C 202   Moore, G. E. *Principia Ethica* (Cambridge, 1903).
C 203   Paul. L. *The English philosophers* (1953).
C 204   Russell, B. *My philosophical development* (1959).
C 205   Ryle, G. *The revolution in philosophy* (1956).
C 206   Spengler, O. *The decline of the west* (Eng. trans.) (2 vols., 1926–8).
C 207   Toynbee, A. *A study of history* (12 vols., 1934–61).
C 208   Ward, J. *Naturalism and agnosticism* (2 vols., 1899).
C 209   Whitehead, A. N. *Process and reality* (Cambridge, 1929).
C 210   Wittgenstein, L. *Tractatus logico-philosophicus* (1922).

See also:

A 109 Weber, M.

Theology

C 211   Berdyaev, N. A. *The destiny of man* (Eng. trans.) (1937).
C 212   Bevan, E. *Symbolism and belief* (1938).
C 213   Burgh, W. G. de. *The life of reason* (1949).
C 214   Geoghegan, W. D. *Platonism in recent religious thought* (New York, 1958).
C 215   Glover, T. R. *The Jesus of History* (1917).
C 216   Gore, C. (ed.). *Lux Mundi* (1889).
C 217   Harnack, A. *History of dogma* (Eng. trans., 3rd ed.) (7 vols., 1894–9).
C 218   Headlam, A. C. *The atonement* (1935).
C 219   Horton, W. M. *Contemporary English theology: an American interpretation* (1940).
C 220   Hügel, F. Baron von. *The mystical element of religion* (2nd ed., 2 vols., 1923).
C 221   Inge, W. R. *The philosophy of Plotinus* (3rd ed., 2 vols., 1929).
C 222   Loisy, A. *L'Evangile et l'église* (1903).
C 223   Mozley, J. K. *Some tendencies in British theology* (1951).

C 224   Otto, R. *The idea of the holy* (Eng. trans.) (Oxford, 1923).
C 225   Pringle-Pattison, A. S. *Idea of God* (Oxford, 1917).
C 226   Ramsey, A. M. *From Gore to Temple* (1960).
C 227   Rashdall, H. *Theory of Good and Evil* (2 vols., Oxford, 1907).
C 228   Schweitzer, A. *The quest of the historical Jesus* (Eng. trans.) (1910).
C 229   Temple, W. *Nature, man and God* (1934).
C 230   Tennant, F. R. *Philosophical theology* (Cambridge, 1928).
C 231   Underhill, E. *Mysticism* (1911).
C 232   Webb, C. C. J. *A study of religious thought in England from 1850* (Oxford, 1933).
C 233   Wood, H. G. *Belief and unbelief since 1850* (Cambridge, 1955).

6   Science and technology (vol. IX, ch. v)

Bibliographies of the history of science and many general histories of the various sciences have already been referred to in Section A. Some other general histories are included in the bibliographies on the history of science in vols. IX–XII. The fundamental sources for the subject consist in the writings of scientists themselves, which will be found in the original treatises, in more recent collected editions of their works, or in memoirs printed in specialised periodicals and in the publications of learned societies.

General Studies

The most comprehensive general account of nineteenth-century science is:

C 234   Merz, J. T. *A history of European thought in the nineteenth century* (4 vols., Edinburgh and London, 1903–14).

For a general introduction see:

C 235   Dampier, Sir W. C. *A history of science and its relations with philosophy and religion* (4th ed., Cambridge, 1948).
C 236   Wightman, W. P. D. *Growth of scientific ideas* (Edinburgh and London, 1950).

The technology of the period is covered (with bibliographies of each topic) in a work already mentioned:

A 298   Singer, C. and others. *A History of technology*, vols. 4 and 5.

The philosophical climate of early nineteenth-century science is set out in:

C 237   Gouhier, H. *La jeunesse de Comte et la naissance du positivisme* (3 vols., 1933–41).

Detailed Studies

The history of science in its national and institutional aspects is treated in:

FRANCE

C 238   Delambre, J. and Méchain, P. *Base du système métrique* (3 vols., 1806–10).
C 239   Dupuy, P. *Le Centenaire de l'Ecole normale, 1795–1895* (1895).
C 240   Ecole polytechnique. *Livre du centenaire* (3 vols., 1894–7).

C 241   Potiquet, A. *L'Institut national de France* (1871).
C 242   Richard, C. *Le Comité de salut public et les fabrications de guerre* (1922).

See also:

B 343   Picavet, F.

GERMANY

C 243   Harnack, A. *Geschichte der königlichen preussischen Akademie der Wissenschaften zu Berlin* (2 vols., Berlin, 1900).
C 244   Schnabel, F. *Deutsche Geschichte im neunzehnten Jahrhundert*, vol. 3 (Freiburg-im-Breisgau, 1934).

ITALY

C 245   Volta, A. *Epistolaria*, ed. nazionale, (5 vols., Bologna, 1949–55); this edition of Volta's correspondence is the best source.

GREAT BRITAIN

C 246   Ashby, E. *Technology and the academics* (1958).
B 154   Lyons, H. G. *The Royal Society, 1660–1940* (Cambridge, 1944); already mentioned.

RUSSIA

C 247   Pekarsky, P. *Istoriya imperatorskoĭ akademii nauk* (2 vols., St Petersburg, 1870–3).

UNITED STATES

C 248   Hindle, B. *The pursuit of science in revolutionary America* (Chapel Hill, N.C., 1956).

7   **The Scientific movement and its influence on thought and material development (vol. x, ch. iii)**

This bibliography concentrates primarily on the pure sciences; that to vol. xi, ch. iii (Sec. C, **8**) below deals primarily with technology. For this period the histories of particular sciences and the biographies of scientists are particularly useful.

APPLIED SCIENCE

C 249   Bernal, J. D. *Science and industry in the nineteenth century* (1953).
C 250   Forbes, R. J. *Man the maker* (2nd ed., 1958).
C 251   Straub, H. *A history of civil engineering* (1952).
C 252   Taylor, F. Sherwood. *Century of science* (2nd ed., 1942); a popular account, dealing chiefly with the applications of science.

ANTHROPOLOGY AND ARCHAEOLOGY

C 253   Daniel, G. E. *A hundred years of archaeology* (1950).
C 254   Penniman, T. K. *A hundred years of anthropology* (1935).

ASTRONOMY

C 255   Clerke, A. M. *A popular history of astronomy during the nineteenth century* (4th ed., 1902).
C 256   Waterfield, R. L. *A hundred years of astronomy* (1938).

BOTANY AND ZOOLOGY

C 257 Green, J. Reynolds. *History of botany, 1860–1900* (Oxford, 1909).
C 258 Hughes, A. F. W. *History of cytology* (London and New York, 1959).

CHEMISTRY

C 259 Browne, C. A. *Source book of agricultural chemistry* (Waltham, Mass., 1944).
C 260 Leicester, H. M. and Klickstein, H. S. *Source-book in chemistry, 1400–1900* (New York, Toronto and London, 1952).
C 261 Schorlemmer, C. *Rise and development of organic chemistry* (2nd ed., Manchester, 1894).

THEORY OF EVOLUTION

C 262 Barnet, A. S. (ed.). *A century of Darwin* (1958).
C 263 Beer, Sir G. de (ed.). *Evolution by natural selection* (Cambridge, 1958); original papers by Darwin and Wallace.
C 264 Bibby, H. C. *T. H. Huxley* (1959).
C 265 Darwin, F. *Life and letters of Charles Darwin* (3 vols., 1887).
C 266 Darwin, F. and Seward, A. C. *More letters of Charles Darwin* (1903).
C 267 Drachman, J. M. *Studies in the literature of natural science* (New York, 1930).
C 268 Dupree, H. *Asa Gray* (Cambridge, Mass., 1959).

GEOLOGY

C 269 Geikie, Sir A. *Founders of geology* (2nd ed., 1905).
C 270 Gillispie, C. C. *Genesis and geology* (Cambridge, Mass., 1951).
C 271 Lyell, Sir C. *Life, letters and journals* (2 vols., 1881).

MATHEMATICS

C 272 Bell, E. T. *Men of mathematics* (New York, 1937).
C 273 Struick, D. J. *Concise history of mathematics* (New York, 1948).

MEDICINE AND PHYSIOLOGY

C 274 Bernard, C. *An introduction to the study of experimental medicine* (Eng. trans.) (New York, 1949).
C 275 Bulloch, W. *History of bacteriology* (1938).
C 276 Godlee, Sir R. J. *Lord Lister* (1917).
C 277 Long, E. R. *History of pathology* (Baltimore, 1928).
C 278 Olmsted, J. M. D. *Claude Bernard, physiologist* (2nd ed., London and New York, 1938).
C 279 —— *François Magendie* (New York, 1944).
C 280 Shryock, R. H. *Development of modern medicine* (New York, 1947).
C 281 Vallery-Radot, R. *Life of Pasteur* (Boston, Mass., 1925).

PHYSICS

C 282   Einstein, A. and Infeld, L. *Evolution of physics* (New York, 1938).
C 283   *History of the Cavendish laboratory, 1871–1910* (1910).
C 284   Maxwell, J. Clerk. *Commemoration volume* (Cambridge, 1931); valuable collection of critical essays.
C 285   Thompson, S. P. *Lord Kelvin* (2 vols., 1910).
C 286   Thomson, Sir J. J. *Recollections and reflections* (1936).
C 287   Weizsäcker, C. F. von. *World view of physics* (1952).
C 288   Wheeler, L. P. *Josiah Willard Gibbs* (New Haven, 1951).
C 289   Whittaker, Sir E. *From Euclid to Eddington* (Cambridge, 1949).
C 290   —— *History of the theories of aether and electricity:* I, *The classical theories* (2nd ed., 1951); a technical treatment.

PSYCHOLOGY

C 291   Boring, E. G. *History of experimental psychology* (New York and London, 1929).
C 292   Brett, G. S. *History of psychology* (3 vols., 1912–21).

See also:

B 180 Glass, B. and others; B 183 Lovejoy, A. O.; C 15 Haber, L. F.

8   Science and technology (vol. XI, ch. iii)

General Studies

C 293   Derry, T. K. and Williams, T. I. *A short history of technology* (Oxford, 1960).
C 294   Klemm, F. *A history of western technology* (Eng. trans.) (1959).
C 295   Mumford, L. *Technics and civilisation* (New York, 1934).
C 296   Oliver, J. W. *History of American technology* (New York, 1956).

Detailed Studies

C 297   Brown, N. and Turnbull, C. C. *A century of copper* (2 vols., 1899, 1900).
C 298   Ellis, H. *British railway history* (2 vols., 1954–9).
C 299   Gernsheim, H. and A. *History of photography* (Oxford, 1955).
C 300   Gras, N. S. B. *A History of agriculture in Europe and America* (2nd ed., New York, 1940).
C 301   McLaren, M. *The rise of the electrical industry during the nineteenth century* (Princeton, 1943).
C 302   Parsons, R. H. *The development of the Parsons steam turbine* (1936).
C 303   Passer, H. C. *The electrical manufacturers, 1875–1900* (Cambridge, Mass., 1953).
C 304   Schidrowitz, P. and Dawson, P. R. *History of the rubber industry* (Cambridge, 1952).
C 305   Williamson, H. F. and Daum, A. R. *The American petroleum industry 1859–99* (Evanston, Ill., 1959).

See also:

C 7 Burn, D. L.

9   Science and technology (vol. xII, ch. v)

Many books on science in the twentieth century, even biographies, are far too technical for the general reader. The comparatively short list which follows is intended for the reader without scientific training.

General Studies

The most useful general study of twentieth-century science, with bibliographies, is:

c 306   Taton, R. (ed.). *Histoire générale des sciences*, vol. 3, *La Science contemporaine: II, Le XXe siècle* (1964).

Other works include:

c 307   Dingle, H. (ed.). *A century of science 1851–1951* (1951).
c 308   Dunsheath, P. (ed.). *A century of technology 1851–1951* (1951).
c 309   Royal Society of Arts, *A century of British progress 1851–1951* (1951).

There are also many useful articles in the *Encyclopaedia Britannica*.

Detailed Studies

c 310   Andrade, E. N. da C. *The atom and its energy* (1947).
c 311   —— *An approach to modern physics* (1956).
c 312   Dobzhansky, T. *Genetics and the origin of species* (3rd ed., New York, 1951).
c 313   —— *Mankind evolving* (New Haven and London, 1962).
c 314   Dunsheath, P. *A history of electrical engineering* (1962).
c 315   Farber, E. *Nobel prize winners in chemistry, 1901–50* (New York, 1953).
c 316   Gibbs, F. W. *Organic chemistry to-day* (Harmondsworth, 1961).
c 317   Gibbs-Smith, C. H. *A history of flying* (1953).
c 318   Heathcote, N. H. de V. *Nobel prize winners in physics, 1901–50* (New York, 1953).
c 319   Pannekoek, A. *A history of astronomy* (1961).
c 320   Partington, J. R. *A history of chemistry*, vol. 4 (1964); the standard modern work. Technical, but contains much biographical and bibliographical detail.
c 321   Stevenson, L. G. *Nobel prize winners in medicine and physiology, 1901–50* (New York, 1953).

10   Education, and Public Opinion (vol. ix, ch. vii)
      Education and the Press (vol. x, ch. v)
      Education (vol. xi, ch. vii)

Many books on the formation of public opinion are included in the bibliographies on the respective states. Of the list which follows, the books on educational theories and institutions cover the period from the French Revolution to about 1900; those on the press extend to about 1870.

Education: General Studies

B 328 Boyd, W. *The history of western education* (7th ed., 1964); has book-lists at the chapter-ends and brief bibliography.

C 322 Cubberley, E. P. *The history of education: educational practice and progress considered as a phase of the development and spread of western civilisation* (1920).

C 323 Guex, F. *Histoire de l'instruction et de l'éducation* (2nd ed., Lausanne and Paris, 1938).

C 324 Kandel, I. L. *History of secondary education: a study in the development of liberal education* (1910); part 2 deals with the national systems of England, France, Germany, U.S.A. and with the education of girls.

C 325 —— *Comparative education* (1933); a study of systems in England, France, Germany, Italy, Russia and U.S.A.; bibliography.

C 326 Pollard, H. M. *Pioneers of popular education 1760–1850* (1956); covers both Britain and the continent.

C 327 Reisner, E. H. *Nationalism and education since 1789: a social and political history of modern education* (New York, 1925).

C 328 *Year-book of education*, published by Evans Bros. (1932–); an annual survey of different aspects of education throughout the world.

For the English reader the most useful studies of the development of education at the end of the nineteenth century in most countries of the world will be found in:

C 329 *Special reports on educational subjects*, edited by M. E. Sadler and published in nine volumes, begun by the Education Department and continued by the Board of Education (1896–1902).

See also:

A 231 D'Irsay, S. vol. 2.

Developments in different countries

GREAT BRITAIN

Two useful introductory works are:

C 330 Barnard, H. C. *A short history of English education* (2nd ed., 1961).

C 331 Knox, H. M. *Two hundred and fifty years of Scottish education 1696–1946* (Edinburgh and London, 1953).

Important contemporary works include:

C 332 Arnold, M. *A French Eton, or middle class education and the state* (London and Cambridge, 1864).

C 333 —— *The popular education of France with notices of that of Holland and Switzerland* (1861).

C 334 —— *Higher schools and universities in Germany* (1874). These give a view of continental systems as they appeared to an Englishman, and a good deal of criticism of the English situation as well.

C 335 Kay-Shuttleworth, Sir J. *Four periods of public education* (1862).

C 336   Owen, R. *A new view of society* (4th ed., 1818).
C 337   Salmon, D. (ed.). *The practical parts of Lancaster's 'Improvements' and Bell's 'Experiment'* (Landmarks in the history of Education, Cambridge, 1932).

Useful modern works:

B 330   Adamson, J. W. *English education 1789–1902* (Cambridge, 1930); already mentioned.
C 338   Altick, R. D. *The English common reader: a social history of the mass reading public 1800–1900* (Chicago, 1957).
C 339   Dobbs, A. E. *Education and social movements 1700–1850* (1919).
C 340   Lowndes, G. A. N. *The silent social revolution: an account of public education in England and Wales, 1895–1935* (Oxford, 1937).
C 341   Simon, B. *Studies in the history of education 1780–1870* (1960).

FRANCE

Useful general works:

B 334   Durkheim, E. *L'Évolution pédagogique en France*, vol. 2. *De la renaissance jusqu'à nos jours* (1938); already mentioned.
C 342   Grimaud, L. *Histoire de la liberté d'enseignement en France* (new ed., vols. 2–6) (Paris and Grenoble, 1944–); an important study of the relations between government authority and private initiative in education. These volumes cover the period between the Revolution of 1789 and the end of the July monarchy.
C 343   Liard, L. *L'Enseignement supérieur en France 1789–1893* (2 vols., 1888–94).
C 344   Weill, G. *Histoire de l'enseignement secondaire en France (1802–1920)* (1921).

On the Napoleonic period:

C 345   Aulard, A. *Napoléon Ier et le monopole universitaire* (1911).
C 346   Delfau, A. *Napoléon Ier et l'instruction publique* (1902).

On the period after 1815 and the problem of religious freedom:

C 347   Cogniot, G. *La Question scolaire en 1848 et la loi Falloux* (1948).
C 348   Johnson, D. *Guizot: aspects of French history 1787–1874* (London and Toronto, 1963).

On the system at the end of the century:

C 349   Farrington, J. E. *The public primary school system of France* (New York, 1906).
C 350   —— *French secondary schools* (1910); bibliography.

GERMANY

The works of Friedrich Paulsen already mentioned are very valuable:

A 239   *Geschichte des gelehrten Unterrichts auf den deutschen Schulen und Universitäten*, vol. 2.
B 341   *German education past and present* (Eng. trans. 1908).
B 342   *The German universities and university study* (1906); bibliography.

C 351   Cruchet, R. *Les Universités allemandes au XXe siècle* (1914).

C 352   Kerschensteiner, G. *The schools and the nation* (Eng. trans. 1914).

C 353   Lenz, M. *Geschichte der königlichen Friedrich-Wilhelms-Universität zu Berlin*, vols. 1, 2 (pt. 1) (Halle, 1910), vol. 2 (pt. 2) (Halle, 1918); contains much information on Prussian cultural life as a whole.

C 354   Lexis, W. (ed.). *Die Reform des höheren Schulwesens in Preussen* (Halle, 1902); bibliography.

C 355   Russell, J. E. *German higher schools* (New York, 1905).

C 356   Tews, J. *Ein Jahrhundert preussischer Schulgeschichte* (Leipzig, 1914); on elementary education.

Among the many accounts of German education by foreign visitors, the following are particularly valuable:

C 357   Cousin, V. *De l'instruction publique dans quelques pays de l'Allemagne et particulièrement en Prusse* (3rd ed., 1840).

C 358   Mann, H. *Report of an educational tour in Germany and parts of Great Britain and Ireland* (1846).

Other European countries:

C 359   Cousin, V. *On the state of education in Holland* (Eng. trans. 1838); an important contemporary survey.

There are some useful surveys by C. Hippeau:

C 360   *L'Instruction publique en Italie* (1875).

C 361   *L'Instruction publique dans les états du nord* (1876).

C 362   *L'Instruction publique en Russie* (1878).

C 363   Seippel, P. (ed.). *Die Schweiz im neunzehnten Jahrhundert* (Bern and Lausanne, 1899–1900), vol. 2; contains chapters on education and the press.

On the Danish peoples' high schools see:

C 364   Boje, A. and others (eds.). *Education in Denmark* (Oxford, n.d.).

There are brief lives of Bishop Grundtvig by:

C 365   Allen, E. L. *Bishop Grundtvig: a prophet of the North* (1948).

C 366   Davies, G. Nöelle. *Education for life: a Danish pioneer* (1931).

See also, on the Scandinavian countries:

B 1660 Hovde, B. J., vol. 2.

C 367   Seton-Watson, R. W. (Scotus Viator). *Racial Problems in Hungary* (1908); contains much information about education in Austria–Hungary.

C 368   Kot, S. *Five centuries of Polish learning* (Oxford, 1944).

Of the many works of the educational thinkers of the century, only very few can be mentioned here. Works available in English include:

C 369   Fichte, J. G. *Addresses to the German nation* (Eng. trans., Chicago and London, 1922).

C 370   *Froebel's chief writings on education* (Eng. trans. by S. S. F. Fletcher and J. Welton) (Educational Classics, London, 1912).

c 371   Pestalozzi, J. H. *How Gertrude teaches her children* (Eng. trans. by Holland, L. E., and Turner, F. C., 4th ed., 1907).

A recent work in English on Pestalozzi is:

c 372   Silber, K. *Pestalozzi: The Man and his work* (1960).

THE UNITED STATES

GENERAL STUDIES

c 373   Cubberley, E. P. *Public education in the United States: a study and interpretation of American educational history* (2nd ed., Boston, 1934).
c 374   Good, H. G. *History of American education* (New York, 1956).
c 375   Rugg, H. *Foundations for American education* (1947).
c 376   Thwing, C. F. *History of higher education in America* (New York, 1904).

SOME DETAILED STUDIES

c 377   Honeywell, R. J. *The Educational work of Thomas Jefferson* (Cambridge, Mass., 1931).
c 378   Jex-Blake, S. *A Visit to some American schools and colleges* (1867); a contemporary English impression by a woman visitor.
c 379   Jones, R. M. *Haverford College, a history and an interpretation* (New York, 1933).
c 380   White, A. D. *Autobiography* (2 vols., 1905).

OTHER NON-EUROPEAN COUNTRIES

c 381   Newton, A. P. *The Universities and educational systems of the British Empire* (1924).
c 382   Mackenzie, T. C. *Nationalism and education in Australia, with special reference to the state of New South Wales* (1935).
c 383   Kikuchi, Baron. *Japanese Education* (1904).
c 384   Purcell, V. *Problems of Chinese education* (1936).

On India, see the bibliography on Asia and Africa below.

Public libraries

c 385   Edwards, E. *Free town libraries, their formation, management and history; in Britain, France, Germany, and America* (1869).
c 386   Ogle, J. J. *The Free library, its history and present condition* (1897).

and also the following British and American official publications:

c 387   Return showing all the boroughs and places in the United Kingdom that have adopted the Act of 18 & 19 Vict. c. 70 and others, for establishing public libraries and museums and schools of science and art, *Parliamentary Papers*, 1870, **54**.
c 388   *Public Libraries in the United States of America* [U.S.] Department of the Interior, Bureau of Education (1876).

The Press

Two valuable general surveys are:

C 389 Chambure, Vicomte de. *A travers la presse* (1914).
C 390 Weill, G. *Le Journal* (L'évolution de l'humanité, 94) (1934).

GREAT BRITAIN

C 391 Binney Dibblee, G. *The Newspaper* (London, n.d.); a useful brief introduction.
C 392 Fox Bourne, H. R. *English newspapers. Chapters in the history of journalism*
(2 vols., 1887); a very comprehensive historical account.
C 393 Grant, J. *The Newspaper Press* (2 vols., 1871); reviews both the London
and the provincial press.

On the political background of the earlier part of the period see:

C 394 Aspinall, A. *Politics and the press c. 1780–1850* (1949).
C 395 Wickwar, W. II. *The Struggle for the freedom of the press 1819–1832*
(1928).

The story of the greatest English newspaper is told for this period in:

C 396 *The History of The Times:* vol. 1, *The Thunderer in the Making 1785–1841*
(1935); vol. 2, *The Tradition established 1841–1884* (1939).

FRANCE

C 397 Avenel, H. *Histoire de la presse française depuis 1789 jusqu'à nos jours*
(1900); a general account.
C 398 Kirwan, A. V. *Modern France: its journalism, literature and society* (1863);
gives a contemporary English impression.
C 399 Morienval, J. *Les Créateurs de la grande presse en France* (*Girardin, Ville-
messant, Millaud*) (n.d.) deals with the great entrepreneurs of the press.

GERMANY

C 400 Groth, O. *Die Zeitung. Ein System der Zeitungskunde* (4 vols., Mannheim,
1928–30).
C 401 —— *Die Geschichte der deutschen Zeitungswissenschaft* (Munich, 1948).
C 402 Salomon, L. *Geschichte der deutschen Zeitungswesens* (3 vols., Oldenburg
and Leipzig, 1900–6).

ITALY

C 403 Dresler, A. *Geschichte der italienischen Presse* (3 vols. in 1, Munich,
1933–4).

UNITED STATES

C 404 Bleyer, W. G. *Main currents in the history of American journalism* (Cam-
bridge, Mass., 1927).
C 405 Mott, F. L. *American journalism: a history of newspapers in the United
States through 250 years, 1690 to 1940* (New York, 1947).

On news agencies and the dissemination of news see:

C 406   Harlow, A. F. *Old wires and new waves. The history of the telegraph, telephone and wireless* (New York, 1936).

C 407   Rosewater, V. *History of cooperative newsgathering in the United States* (New York, 1930).

C 408   Storey, G. *Reuters' Century 1841–1951* (1951).

On printing see:

C 409   Isaacs, G. A. *The Story of the newspaper printing press* (1931).

RELIGION, SOCIAL AND POLITICAL THOUGHT AND INSTITUTIONS

11   **Religion: Church and State in Europe and the Americas (vol. IX, ch. vi)**
Religion and the relations of churches and states (vol. X, ch. iv)

General Studies

Many of the books which are cited here cover historical periods much longer than that dealt with in these chapters. An encyclopedic survey of the period, with bibliography, is provided by:

C 410   Latourette, K. S. *Christianity in a revolutionary age* (5 vols., 1959–63).

A brief account of the main themes of modern church history can be found in:

C 411   Vidler, A. R. *The Church in an age of revolution; 1789 to the present day* (Harmondsworth, 1961).

Detailed Studies

For Roman Catholic history see:

B 1044   the *Histoire de l'église* series (Fliche, A. and Martin, V., eds.), vol. 20, Leflon, J. *La Crise révolutionnaire 1789–1846* (1949), already mentioned. also:

C 412   Aubert, R. *Le Pontificat de Pie IX 1846–1878*, vol. 21 of the same series (1952). Both have detailed bibliographies.

Other useful works are:

C 413   Butler, E. C. *The vatican council* (2 vols., 1930).

C 414   Hales, E. E. Y. *Pio Nono* (1954).

C 415   Hocedez, E. *Histoire de la théologie au XIXe siècle* (3 vols., Brussels, 1947–52).

C 416   MacGregor, J. G. *The Vatican revolution* (1958).

C 417   Vidler, A. R. *Prophecy and papacy: a study of Lamennais, the Church and the revolution* (1954).

See also:

B 1043 Latreille, A.; B 1045 Hales, E. E. Y.

EASTERN ORTHODOXY

C 418 Zernov, N. *Eastern Christendom* (1961).
A 1390 Conybeare, F. C.
B 613 Miliukov, P.

PROTESTANT THEOLOGY AND BIBLICAL CRITICISM

C 419 Carpenter, J. E. *The Bible in the nineteenth century* (1903).
C 420 Dillenberger, J. *Protestant thought and natural science* (1961).
C 421 Mackintosh, H. R. *Types of modern theology: Schleiermacher to Barth* (1937).
C 422 Pfleiderer, O. *The development of theology in Germany since Kant* (1890).
C 423 Storr, V. F. *The development of English theology in the nineteenth century 1800–1860* (1913).

See also:

C 270 Gillispie, C. C.

THE DEVELOPMENT OF FOREIGN MISSIONS

A 889 Latourette, K. S. *A History of the Expansion of Christianity* (7 vols., 1938–45); already mentioned.

THE JEWS

C 424 Baron, S. *A Social and religious history of the Jews* (3 vols., New York, 1937).

NON-CHRISTIAN RATIONALISM

C 425 Robertson, J. M. *A History of freethought in the nineteenth century* (1929).

National Studies

The history of religious life in individual states is covered to a large extent in the books mentioned above. But for further study the following may be added:

GREAT BRITAIN

C 426 Carpenter, S. C. *Church and people 1789–1889* (1933).
C 427 Clark, H. W. *History of English Nonconformity* (2 vols., 1911–13); vol. 1 covers the sixteenth and seventeenth centuries to 1660, vol. 2 from 1660 to the end of the nineteenth century.
C 428 Fleming, J. R. *A History of the Church in Scotland 1843–1929* (2 vols., Edinburgh, 1927–33).

BELGIUM

C 429 Simon, A. *Le Cardinal Sterckx et son temps 1792–1867* (2 vols., Wetteren, 1950).

CANADA

C 430 Walsh, H. H. *The Christian church in Canada* (Toronto, 1956).

DENMARK

C 431   Lindhardt, P. G. *Grundtvig, an introduction* (1951).

FRANCE

C 432   Dansette, A. *Religious history of modern France* (Eng. trans., abridged, 2 vols., 1962).

C 433   Phillips, C. S. *The Church in France 1789–1907* (2 vols., 1929–36).

GERMANY

C 434   Franz, G. *Kulturkampf* (Munich, 1954); covers most of the nineteenth century up to about 1887.

C 244   Schnabel, F. *Deutsche Geschichte im 19ten Jahrhundert*, vol. 4, *Die religiösen Kräfte* (3rd ed., Freiburg, 1955).

See also:

B 561 Drummond, A. L.

ITALY

C 435   Jemolo, A. C. *Church and state in Italy: 1850–1950* (Oxford, 1960).

NORWAY

C 436   Molland, E. *Church life in Norway: 1800–1950* (Minneapolis, 1957).

SWEDEN

C 437   Wordsworth, J. *The National church of Sweden* (1911).

SOUTH AMERICA

B 1104 Mecham, J. L. *Church and state in Latin America* (Chapel Hill, N.C., 1934); already mentioned.

UNITED STATES

C 438   Smith, J. W. and Jamison, A. L. *Religion in American life* (Princeton, 1961–). Of 4 vols. planned, vols. 1–2 and 4 are now in print. Vol. 4— bound as two separate books—is a *Critical Bibliography of Religion in America*, by Burr, N. R.

C 439   Stokes, A. P. *Church and state in the United States* (3 vols., New York, 1950).

C 440   Sweet, W. W. *Religion in the development of American culture: 1765–1840* (New York, 1952).

12   **Revolutionary influences and conservatism in literature and thought (vol. IX, ch. iv)**

The primary sources are to be found in the works of the poets and writers who are dealt with in this chapter. The most important secondary sources may conveniently be grouped into the four headings which follow, though some of the books mentioned fit into more than one of the categories.

Enlightenment

C 441 Best, M. A. *Thomas Paine. Prophet and martyr of democracy* (1927).
C 442 Borries, K. *Kant als Politiker* (Leipzig, 1928).
C 443 Brailsford, H. N. *Shelley, Godwin and their circle* (1951).
C 444 Cento, A. *Condorcet e l'idea di progresso* (Florence, 1956).
C 445 Frazer, Sir J. G. *Condorcet on the progress of the human mind* (Oxford, 1933).
C 446 Friedrich, C. J. (ed.). *The Philosophy of Kant. Immanuel Kant's moral and political writings* (New York, 1949); with an introduction.
C 447 Woodcock, G. *William Godwin* (1946).

On feminism:

C 448 Campbell, G. M. V. *This shining woman. Mary Wollstonecraft Godwin* (1937).
C 449 Lacour, L. *Les Origines du féminisme contemporain. Trois femmes de la révolution* (1900); includes a study of Olympe de Gouges.

On Jewish emancipation:

C 450 Dubnow, S. *Weltgeschichte des jüdischen Volkes*, vol. 8, German trans. from Russian, Berlin, 1928).

On the abolition of the slave trade:

C 451 Coupland, Sir R. *Wilberforce* (2nd ed., 1945).
C 452 Griggs, E. L. *Thomas Clarkson. The Friend of slaves* (1936).

See also:

B 324 Cobban, A.; B 1468 Gooch, G. P.

Conservatism

GENERAL STUDIES

C 453 Barth, H. *Der konservative Gedanke* (Stuttgart, 1958).
C 454 Meinecke, F. *Weltbürgertum und Nationalstaat*, in *Werke*, vol. 5 (Munich, 1962).

DETAILED STUDIES

C 455 Bayle, F. *Les Idées politiques de Joseph de Maistre* (1945).
C 456 Canavan, F. P. *The political reason of Edmund Burke* (Durham, N.C., 1960).
C 457 Hilger, D. *Edmund Burke und seine Kritik der französischen Revolution* (Stuttgart, 1960).
C 458 Jünger, E. *Rivarol* (Frankfurt/a/M., 1956).
C 459 Mommsen, W. *Die politischen Anschauungen Goethes* (Stuttgart, 1948).
C 460 Sonntag, W. H. von. *Die Staatsauffassung Karl Ludwig von Hallers* (Jena, 1929).
C 461 Sweet, P. R. *Friedrich von Gentz. Defender of the old order* (Madison, 1941).

See also:

B 304 Cobban, A.; B 976 Baldensperger, F.

Romanticism

GENERAL STUDIES

c 462   Brinton, C. C. *The Political ideas of the English Romanticists* (Oxford, 1926).
c 463   Schenk, H. G. *Die Kulturkritik der europäischen Romantik* (Wiesbaden, 1956).
c 464   Talmon, J. L. *Political Messianism. The romantic phase* (1960).

DETAILED STUDIES

c 465   André-Vincent, P. *Les Ideés politiques de Chateaubriand* (1936).
c 466   Carnall, G. *Robert Southey and his age* (Oxford, 1960).
c 467   Colmer, J. *Coleridge, critic of society* (Oxford, 1959).
c 468   Marchand, L. A. *Byron, a biography* (3 vols., 1957).
c 469   Todd, F. M. *Politics and the poet. A study of Wordsworth* (1957).
c 470   Troyat, H. *L'Etrange Destin de Lermontov* (1952).

Social reformers and revolutionaries

GENERAL STUDIES

c 471   Cole, G. D. H. *Socialist thought. The forerunners 1789–1850* (1953).
c 472   Duroselle, J. B. *Les Débuts du catholicisme social en France 1822–70* (1957).
c 473   Gray, Sir A. *The Socialist tradition. From Moses to Lenin* (1946).
c 474   Ramm, T. *Die Grossen Socialisten als Rechts- und Sozialphilosophen*, vol. I (Stuttgart, 1955).

DETAILED STUDIES

c 475   Carcopino, C. *Les Idées sociales de Lamennais* (1942).
c 476   Cole, G. D. H. *The Life of Robert Owen* (1930).
c 477   Gide, C. *Fourier, précurseur de la co-opération* (1924).
c 478   Manuel, F. E. *The New world of Henri Saint-Simon* (Cambridge, Mass., 1956).
c 479   Prudhommeaux, J. *Icarie et son fondateur, Etienne Cabet* (1907).
c 480   Puech, J-L. *La Vie et l'œuvre de Flora Tristan* (1925).
c 481   Salis, J-R. de. *Sismondi* (1932).
c 482   Spitzer, A. B. *The revolutionary theories of Louis Auguste Blanqui* (New York, 1957).
c 483   Tchernoff, J. *Louis Blanc* (1904).
c 484   Thomson, D. *The Babeuf plot* (1947).

See also:

B 981 Leroy, M.; c 417 Vidler, A. R.

13   Liberalism and constitutional developments (vol. x, ch. viii)

General Studies

The constitutional developments in the major countries are treated in the bibliographies devoted to those countries. Some books on Belgium and on Switzerland are included in this list.

Much information can be gained from general surveys of European history such as:

c 485   Thomson, D. *Europe since Napoleon* (2nd ed., 1962).

In the relevant volumes of such major series as *The rise of modern Europe* (Langer, W. L., ed.):

c 486   Artz, F. B. *Reaction and revolution 1814–1832* (New York, 1934).
c 487   Binkley, R. C. *Realism and nationalism 1852–1871* (New York, 1935).

See also *Peuples et civilisations* (Halphen, A. and Sagnac, P., eds.):

c 488   Weill, G. *L'Eveil des nationalités 1815–1848* (1930).
c 489   Pouthas, Ch. H. *Démocraties et capitalisme 1848–1860* (3rd ed., 1961).
c 490   Hauser, H., Maurain, J., Benaerts, P. *Du libéralisme à l'impérialisme 1860–1878* (2nd ed., 1952).

Other useful general studies include:

c 491   Bowle, J. *Politics and opinion in the nineteenth century* (1954); a general survey of the political thinkers.
c 492   Brandes, G. *Main currents in nineteenth century literature* (Eng. trans., 6 vols., 1901–5).
c 493   Croce, B. *History of Europe in the nineteenth century* (Eng. trans. 1934); emphasises the role of liberalism during the century.
c 494   Rosenberg, A. *Democracy and Socialism* (Eng. trans. 1939).
c 495   Ruggiero, G. de. *History of European liberalism* (Eng. trans., Oxford, 1927); covers England, France, Germany and Italy, and has a bibliography.
c 496   Schapiro, J. S. *Liberalism and the challenge of Fascism. Social forces in England and France (1815–1870)* (New York, 1949); bibliography.

See also, on political ideas in Germany:

c 454 Meinecke, F.

Detailed Studies

On the European revolutions of the period:

c 497   *Etudes sur les mouvements libéraux et nationaux de 1830* (Comité français des sciences historiques, Paris, 1932).
c 498   Fejtö, F. (ed.). *The opening of an era. 1848. An historical symposium* (1948); covers all the countries of Europe and has an essay on the influence upon Europe of the United States.
c 499   Namier, Sir L. *1848: the revolution of the intellectuals* (Raleigh lecture on history, British academy, 1944).

C 500   Robertson, P. *Revolutions of 1848. A social history* (Princeton, 1952).
C 501   Tocqueville, A. de. *Democracy in America*. There are many editions. The
        standard English translation is by Henry Reeve (2 vols., 1875). Among
        modern studies of Tocqueville see:
C 502   Lively, J. *The social and political thought of Alexis de Tocqueville* (Oxford,
        1962).
C 503   Mayer, J-P. *Prophet of the mass age* (1939).
C 504   Pierson, G. W. *Tocqueville and Beaumont in America* (New York, 1938).

        On the contacts between America and Europe:

C 505   Bestor, A. E. *Backwoods Utopias* (Philadelphia, 1950).
C 506   Curti, M. E. *The American peace crusade 1815–1860* (Durham, N.C.,
        1929).
C 507   Holloway, M. *Heavens on earth* (1951); deals with the Utopian com-
        munities of America.
C 508   Jordan, D. and Pratt, E. J. *Europe and the American civil war* (1931).
C 509   Koht, H. *The American spirit in Europe* (Philadelphia, 1949); a general
        survey.

        On Belgium, the standard work, which has been mentioned many times,
        is:

A 53   Pirenne, H. *Histoire de Belgique*, vols. 6 [on the revolution of 1830] and
        7 (Brussels, 1926, 1932).

        Other works are:

C 510   Demoulin, R. *La Révolution de 1830* (Brussels, 1950).
C 511   Gilissen, J. *Le Régime représentatif en Belgique depuis 1790* (Brussels,
        1958).
C 512   Linden, H. vander. *Belgium. The making of a nation* (Eng. trans., Oxford,
        1920); a brief study.

        A brief recent history of Switzerland in English is:

A 1233 Bonjour, E., Offler, H. S., Potter, G. R. *A Short history of Switzerland*
        (Oxford, 1952).

        A fuller history in German is:

A 1234 Guggenbühl, G. *Geschichte der schweizerischen Eidgenossenschaft* (2 vols.,
        Zürich, 1947).

        For the Swiss constitution of 1848 see:

C 513   Bonjour, E. *Die Gründung des schweizerischen Bundesstaates* (Basel, 1948).

14   Nationalities and nationalism (vol. x, ch. ix)
                    General Studies

        The most useful bibliographical guide, containing a list of 431 books
        arranged by topics with comments on the contents, is:

C 514   Pinson, K. S. *A bibliographical introduction to nationalism* (New York,
        1935).

The best general sketch is:

C 515　Weill, G. *L'Europe du XIXe siècle et l'idée de nationalité* (L'Evolution de l'humanité, 84, 1938).

More recent books include:

C 516　Kedourie, E. *Nationalism* (1960).
C 517　Kohn, H. *Prophets and peoples: studies in nineteenth century nationalism* [J. S. Mill, Michelet, Mazzini, Treitschke, and Dostoievsky] (New York, 1946).
C 518　Kolarz, W. *Myths and realities in Eastern Europe* (1946); concerned with the ideas underlying different national movements rather than with their specific histories.
C 519　Pouthas, Ch. *Le Mouvement des nationalités en Europe dans la première moitié du XIXe siècle* (Les cours de Sorbonne, in four parts, 1946).
C 520　Shafer, B. C. *Nationalism: myth and reality* (1955).

The books by Weill, Kedourie and Shafer also contain extensive bibliographies. See also the preceding bibliography, 'Liberalism and constitutional developments' (C, **13**).

Two important essays are:

C 521　Acton, Lord. 'Nationalism', *The history of freedom and other essays* (1922).
C 522　Namier, Sir L. 'Nationality and liberty', *Avenues of history* (1952).

Detailed Studies

Accounts of national movements are to be found in the best general histories of the countries concerned. No attempt has been made here to give a comprehensive list of such books, and those included relate mainly to the smaller countries. To the books cited by Pinson may be added:

AUSTRIA

C 523　Hantsch, H. *Die Nationalitätenfrage im alten Österreich* (Vienna, 1953).
C 524　Kann, R. A. *The multinational empire: nationalism and national reform in the Habsburg monarchy 1848–1918* (2 vols., New York, 1950).

BALTIC LANDS

C 525　Bilmanis, A. *A history of Latvia* (Princeton, 1951).
C 526　Jackson, J. Hampden. *Estonia* (2nd ed., 1948).

THE CZECHS

A 798　Seton-Watson, R. W. *A history of the Czechs and Slovaks* (1943); already mentioned.

FRANCE

C 527　Martin, M-M. *La Formation morale de la France* (1949).

GERMANY

C 528 Butler, R. D'O. *The roots of National Socialism 1783–1933* (1941).
C 529 Snyder, L. L. *German nationalism: the tragedy of a people* (Harrisburg, Pa., 1952).

GREAT BRITAIN

C 530 Coupland, Sir R. *Welsh and Scottish nationalism—a study* (1954).

GREECE

C 531 Mavrogordato, J. N. *Modern Greece—a chronicle and a survey 1800–1931* (1931).

IRELAND

C 532 Gwynn, D. R. *Young Ireland and 1848* (Cork, 1949).

ITALY

C 533 Pettoello, D. *An outline of Italian civilisation* (1932).

THE JEWS

C 534 Roth, C. *A short history of the Jewish people 1600 B.C.–A.D. 1935* (1936).

PANSLAVISM

C 535 Kohn, H. *Pan-Slavism: its history and ideology* (Notre Dame, 1953).
C 536 Petrovich, M. B. *The emergence of Russian Panslavism 1856–1870* (New York, 1956).

POLAND

C 537 Frankel, H. *Poland—the struggle for power 1772–1939* (1946).

ROUMANIA

C 538 Seton-Watson, R. W. *A history of the Roumanians* (Cambridge, 1934).

RUSSIA

C 539 Rauch, G. von. *Russland: Staatliche Einheit und nationale Vielfalt* (Munich, 1953).
C 540 Seton-Watson, H. *The decline of imperial Russia 1855–1914* (1952).

SERBIA

C 541 Laffan, R. G. D. *The guardians of the gate. Historical lectures on the Serbs* (Oxford, 1918).

See also:

A 804 Kosary, D. G.; B 1628 Wittram, R.

15   Social and political thought (vol. XI, ch. iv)

General Studies

Adequate bibliographies for intellectual history are rare, and there is none for this period. But some help can be derived from:

C 542   Dolléans, E. and Crozier, M. *Mouvements ouvrier et socialiste: Chronologie et bibliographie* (1950).

C 543   Harkness, S. B. *The career of Samuel Butler, 1835–1902: a bibliography* (1955).

Trends of thought are related to events, with a useful bibliography, in:

C 544   Hayes, C. H. *A generation of materialism, 1871–1900* (New York, 1941) (*The rise of Modern Europe*, vol. 17).

General histories of the social and political thought of the period include

C 545   Soltau, R. H. *French political thought in the nineteenth century* (1931); the footnotes contain useful bibliographical data.

See also:

C 234 Merz, J. T.

Detailed Studies

DARWINISM

C 546   Dewey, J. *The influence of Darwin on philosophy* (New York, 1910).
C 547   Himmelfarb, G. *Darwin and the Darwinian revolution* (1959); useful bibliography.
C 548   Hofstadter, R. *Social Darwinism in American thought* (rev. ed., Boston, 1955); with full bibliography.

SOCIALISM AND MARXISM

C 549   Cole, G. D. H. *A history of socialist thought,* (5 vols. 1953–60). vol. 2 is on *Marxism and anarchism, 1850–1890*; vol. 3 (in 2 parts) is on *The Second International, 1889–1914.*
C 550   Diehl, K. *Über Sozialismus, Kommunismus und Anarchismus* (Jena, 1922).
C 551   Halévy, E. *Histoire du socialisme européen* (1948).

SOCIOLOGY

C 552   Hughes, H. S. *Consciousness and society: The reorientation of European social thought, 1890–1930* (1959).
C 553   Parsons, T. *The structure of social action* (New York, 1937); showing the thought common to Marshall, Pareto, Durkheim and Weber.

ROMAN CATHOLIC THOUGHT

B 540   Ehler, S. Z. and Morrall, J. B. (eds.). *Church and state through the centuries* (1954); a collection of documents, of which chs. vii and viii include relevant Papal encyclicals.

SOURCES

The major sources for intellectual history are the writings of the leading thinkers. The following list includes only the most representative works together with some biographies and monographs.

COLLECTED WORKS

C 554 Bagehot, W. *Works* (Barrington, Mrs R., ed.) (9 vols., 1915).

C 555 Butler, S. *Works* (Jones, H. F. and Bartholomew, A. T., eds.) (20 vols., 1923–6).

C 556 Dilthey, W. *Gesammelte Schriften* (12 vols., Leipzig, Berlin and Stuttgart, 1914–58).

C 557 Green, T. H. *Works* (Nettleship, R. L., ed.) (3 vols., 1885–8).

C 558 Gumplowicz, L. *Ausgewählte Werke* (4 vols., Innsbruck, 1926–8).

C 559 Jaurès, J. *Oeuvres* (Bonnafous, M., ed.) (9 vols., 1931–9); vol. 1 covers the years 1887–1903.

C 560 Marx, K. and Engels, F. *Selected Works* (2 vols., 1950). The collected editions in German, French and Russian are also available, but this selection has established itself as the handiest English collection. The full English version of Engels' *Anti-Dühring* (1878) is also available (London, 1955).

C 561 Nietzsche, F. *Gesammelte Werke* (Musarion ed.) (23 vols., Munich, 1920–9).

SEPARATE WRITINGS

C 562 Bernstein, E. *Evolutionary socialism* (Eng. trans., London and New York, 1909).

C 563 Bradley, F. H. *Ethical studies* (rev. ed., Oxford, 1927).

C 564 Chamberlain, H. S. *The foundations of the nineteenth century* (Eng. trans., 2 vols., London and New York, 1911).

C 565 Croce, B. *Historical materialism and the economics of Karl Marx* (Eng. trans. 1914); this translation, from the 2nd ed. (1906) of *Materialismo storico ed economia marxistica* omits some of the original essays.

C 566 Darwin, C. *The Descent of man* (2nd ed., 1901).

C 567 *Fabian Essays in socialism* (Jubilee ed.) (1948).

C 568 Herzl, T. *The Jewish state* (Eng. trans., 4th ed., 1946).

C 569 Kropotkin, P. A. *Mutual aid: a factor of evolution* (1902).

C 570 Marshall, A. *Principles of economics* (8th ed., 1949).

C 571 Plekhanov, G. V. *In defence of materialism* (new Eng. trans. 1947).

C 572 Renan, E. *L'avenir de la science: pensées de 1848* (1890).

C 573 Sorel, G. *Reflections on violence* (Eng. trans. 1916).

C 574 Spencer, H. *The principles of sociology* (3 vols., 1876–96).

C 575 —— *The Man* versus *the State* (1884).

BIOGRAPHIES AND MONOGRAPHS

C 576 Buthman, W. C. *The rise of integral nationalism in France* (New York, 1939).

C 577 Carr, E. H. *Michael Bakunin* (1937).

c 578   Gay, P. *The dilemma of democratic socialism* (New York, 1952); examines German 'revisionism' with reference to Bernstein, and includes useful bibliography.

c 579   Kaufmann, W. *Nietzsche: philosopher, psychologist, anti-Christ* (new ed., New York, 1956); excellent bibliography.

c 580   Mayer, G. *Friedrich Engels* (2 vols., The Hague, 1934).

c 581   Mehring, F. *Karl Marx* (Eng. trans. 1936); excellent bibliography.

16   (A) The Transformation of social life (vol. xii, ch. iii)
        (B) European civilisation in the twentieth century (vol. xii, ch. xx)

        (A)
                           General Studies

Separate national histories should be consulted for detailed developments within each country.

The League of Nations and the International Labour Organization published much material that is relevant; see especially:

c 582   Aufricht, H. *Guide to League of Nations publications: a bibliographical survey of the work of the League, 1920–1947* (New York and London, 1951).

c 583   I.L.O.: *Trente ans de combat pour la justice sociale, 1919–1949* (Geneva, 1950).

c 584   —— *International survey of social security, comparative analysis and summary of national laws* (Geneva, 1950).

On the general international growth of labour movements, see:

c 585   Laidler, H. W. *Social-economic movements: an historical and comparative survey of socialism, communism, cooperation, utopianism and other systems of reform and reconstruction* (1948).

c 586   Lorwin, L. L. *The international labor movement: history, policies, outlook* (New York, 1953).

c 587   Price, J. *The international labour movement* (R.I.I.A., London, 1945).

c 588   Sturmthal, A. *The tragedy of European labour, 1918–1939* (1944).

                           Detailed Studies

Much of the social change during this period is inseparable from economic growth and economic crisis, so the bibliographies on 'Economic and social conditions' should also be consulted.

                SOCIAL LEGISLATION AND ECONOMIC GROWTH

Material on the economic and legislative bases of social change may be found in the following:

c 589   Galenson, W. *Labor in Norway* (Cambridge, Mass., 1949).

c 590   —— *The Danish system of labor relations* (Cambridge, Mass., 1952).

c 591   Gazzetti, F. *Social welfare in Italy* (Rome, 1937).

c 592   Hall, M. P. *The Social services of modern England* (4th ed., 1959).

c 593 Hazard, J. N. *Law and social change in the U.S.S.R.* (1953).

c 594 Lorimer, F. *The population of the Soviet Union; history and prospects* (League of Nations, Geneva, 1946).

c 595 Marsh, D. C. *The changing social structure of England and Wales 1871–1951* (1958).

c 596 Rostow, W. W. and others. *The dynamics of Soviet society* (New York and London, 1953).

c 597 Seton-Watson, H. *Eastern Europe between the wars, 1918–1941* (Cambridge, 1945).

c 598 Shirer, W. L. *The challenge of Scandinavia* (1956).

c 599 Thomson, D. *Democracy in France: The third and fourth republics* (3rd ed., 1958).

c 600 Trend, J. B. *Portugal* (1957).

c 601 Warriner, D. *Land and poverty in the Middle East* (R.I.I.A., London, 1948).

REVOLUTIONARY MOVEMENTS

See also the bibliography to vol. XII, ch. iv below.

c 602 Borkenau, F. *European Communism* (1953).

c 603 Degras, J. (ed.). *The Communist international, 1919–1943*, vol. 1 (1956); a collection of documents.

c 604 Neumann, S. *Permanent revolution* (New York, 1942).

c 605 Seton-Watson, H. *The Pattern of Communist revolution: a historical analysis* (1953).

See also:

c 528 Butler, R. D'O.

THE WELFARE STATE

c 606 Benn, S. I. and Peters, R. S. *Social principles and the democratic state* (1959).

c 607 Beveridge, W. *Social insurance and allied services* (1942); the basic document for the study of the modern 'welfare state' in Britain.

c 608 Ehrmann, H. W. *French labor from popular front to liberation* (New York, 1947).

c 609 *Freedom and welfare* (Joint publication of the Scandinavian governments, Copenhagen, 1953).

c 610 Galant, H. C. *Histoire politique de la sécurité sociale française* (1955).

c 611 Mendelsohn, R. S. *Social security in the British commonwealth* (1954); comparative studies of Great Britain, Canada, Australia and New Zealand.

(B)

Any selection of books on the wide topic of European civilization in the twentieth century must be somewhat arbitrary, and controversial writing is unavoidable. The following short list indicates some of the works of reflection and generalisation which help to throw light on the trends of the first half of the century and on the changed position of Europe in the world.

c 612   Allport, G. W. *The nature of prejudice* (New York, 1954).
c 613   Arendt, H. *The human condition* (Chicago, 1958).
c 614   Aron, R. *The century of total war* (Eng. trans. 1954).
c 615   Beloff, M. *Europe and the Europeans: an international discussion* (1957).
c 616   Brogan, D. W. *The price of revolution* (1951).
c 617   Galbraith, J. K. *The affluent society* (1958).
c 618   Lewis, W. A. *The theory of economic growth* (1955).
c 619   Ortega y Gasset, J. *The revolt of the masses* (Eng. trans., new ed., New York, 1950).
c 620   Rostow, W. W. *The stages of economic growth: a non-Communist manifesto* (Cambridge, 1960).
c 621   Schapiro, J. S. *The world in crisis: political and social movements in the twentieth century* (New York, 1950).
c 622   Seton-Watson, H. *Neither war nor peace: the struggle for power in the post-war world* (1960); a wide-ranging survey of the aftermath of the second world war.
c 623   Thomson, D. and others. *Patterns of peacemaking* (1945).

17   **Political institutions in Europe: political issues and political thought (vol. XII, ch. iv)**
General Studies

There are several standard bibliographies, but none is in itself sufficient for the whole scope of this chapter. Those especially helpful are:

c 624   Gooch, G. P. *Bibliography of European history, 1918–1939* (1940).
c 625   Grandin, A. *Bibliographie générale des sciences juridiques, politiques, économiques et sociales* (1926, with subsequent annual supplements).
c 626   Hunt, R. N. C. *Books on communism* (1959); books in English, published 1945–57.
c 627   Savadjian, L. *Bibliographie Balkanique, 1920–1938* (8 vols., 1931–9).

Several standard books on aspects of the period also have up-to-date bibliographies which supplement these:

c 628   Baynes, N. H. (ed.). *The speeches of Adolf Hitler, 1922–1939* (2 vols., 1942); contains the best bibliography on German National Socialism.
c 629   Bullock, A. *Hitler: a study in tyranny* (rev. ed., 1955).
c 630   Snell, J. L. (ed.). *The Nazi revolution* (Boston, 1959).

Standard national histories usually include accounts of the country's governmental and political system. Especially useful for the themes of this chapter are those books which make comparative studies of the systems in several countries:

c 631   Bryce, J. (Viscount). *Modern Democracies* (2 vols., 1921); a pioneer classic in comparative government, including studies of France and Switzerland in 1920, as well as of the U.S.A. and the Dominions.
c 632   Chapman, B. *The profession of government: the public service in Europe* (1959); excellent bibliography.
c 633   Cobban, A. *Dictatorship: its history and theory* (1939).

c 634 Duverger, M. *Political parties* (Eng. trans., London and New York, 1954).
c 635 Ensor, R. C. K. *Courts and judges in France, Germany and England* (1933).
c 636 Headlam-Morley, A. *The new democratic constitutions of Europe* (1928).
c 637 Lakeman, E. and Lambert, J. D. *Voting in democracies* (2nd ed., 1959).
c 638 Robson, W. A. *The Civil service in Britain and France* (1956).
c 639 Rossiter, C. L. *Constitutional dictatorship: crisis government in the modern democracies* (Princeton, 1948); discusses the use of emergency powers in Germany, France, Great Britain and U.S.A.

Detailed Studies

In addition to the many works listed in the sources mentioned, the following more recent publications are relevant:

PARLIAMENTARY AND ELECTORAL SYSTEMS

c 640 Bromhead, P. A. *The House of Lords and contemporary politics, 1911–1957* (1958).
c 641 Butler, D. E. *The electoral system in Britain, 1918–1951* (1951).
c 642 Carson, G. B. jr. *Electoral practices in the U.S.S.R.* (New York, 1955).
c 643 Chester, D. N. (ed.). *The organization of British central government 1914–1956* (1957).
c 644 Eyck, E. *Geschichte der Weimarer Republik* (2 vols., Zürich, 1954–6).
c 645 Kohn, H. *Nationalism and liberty: the Swiss example* (New York, 1956).
c 646 Lidderdale, D. W. S. *The parliament of France* (rev. impression, 1954).
c 647 Rustow, D. A. *The politics of compromise: a study of parties and cabinet government in Sweden* (Princeton, 1955).
c 648 Salvatorelli, L. *Storia d'Italia nel periodo fascista* (Turin, 1956).
c 649 Schorske, C. E. *German social democracy, 1905–1917; the development of the great schism* (Cambridge, 1955).
c 650 Ullmann, R. K. and King-Hall, S. *German parliaments: a study of the development of representative institutions in Germany* (1954).

See also:

b 1024 Campbell, P.

POLITICAL ISSUES AND IDEOLOGIES

Books dealing mainly with social changes and with the rise of the 'welfare state' are listed in the bibliography to vol. XII, ch. iii (Sec. C, **16**) above; see also that for vol. X, ch. ix (Sec. C, **14**) on 'Nationalities and nationalism'.

c 651 Barghoorn, F. C. *Soviet Russian nationalism* (New York and London 1956).
c 652 Challener, R. D. *The French theory of the nation in arms, 1866–1939* (New York, 1955).
c 549 Cole, G. D. H. *A History of Socialist thought* (5 vols., 1953–60); vol. 4 covers *Communism and social democracy, 1914–1931* (2 parts); vol. 5, *Socialism and fascism, 1931–1939*.

C 653   Friedrich, C. J. and Brzezinski, Z. K. *Totalitarian dictatorship and autocracy* (Cambridge, Mass., 1957).

C 654   Hales, E. E. Y. *The Catholic church in the modern world* (London and New York, 1958).

C 655   Mack Smith, D. *Italy: a modern history* (Michigan and London, 1959); covers the whole period since 1861 with a good bibliography.

C 656   Plamenatz, J. *German Marxism and Russian communism* (1954).

C 657   Verney, D. *Parliamentary reform in Sweden, 1866–1921* (1957).

See also:

B 495 Craig, G.

THE ART OF WAR,
ARMIES AND NAVIES

Many of the general works on naval and military history have already been mentioned in the parallel parts of Sections A and B (see pp. 28, 135) and reference should therefore also be made to those parts. In most cases an independent reference is not given here to such books.

18   Navies [See Section B 19] (vol. IX, ch. iii (b))
      Armed forces and the art of war: Navies (vol. X, ch. xi)

      General Studies, covering a wider field, but including the years
      1830–70

BRITISH   MATERIAL

C 658   Abel, Sir W. *The shipwright's trade* (Cambridge, 1948).

C 659   Ballard, G. A. 'The Navy', *Early Victorian England* (Young, G. M., ed.) (2 vols., 1934).

C 660   Barnaby, Sir N. *Naval developments of the century* (1904).

C 661   Parkes, O. *The British battleship* (1957).

C 662   Robertson, F. L. *Evolution of naval armament* (1921).

C 663   Wilson, H. W. *Ironclads in action* (1896).

AMERICAN

C 664   Baxter, J. P. *The introduction of the ironclad warship* (Cambridge, Mass., 1933).

C 665   Chapelle, H. I. *History of American sailing ships* (New York, 1935).

See also:

B 23 Albion, R. G.

PERSONNEL

C 666   Fremantle, Sir E. R. *The navy as I knew it* (1904).

C 667   Napier, Sir Charles, *Life and letters of* (1917).

C 668   Robinson, C. N. *The British fleet* (1894).

C 669   Statham, E. P. *The Story of the 'Britannia'* (1904).

Detailed studies, covering mainly the period 1830–70, and mainly by
contemporary writers

BRITISH

c 670 Ballard, G. A. 'British battleships': articles, quarterly, in *The Mariner's Mirror*, **15–20** (1929–34).

c 671 Barrow, Sir J. *Navies of Great Britain and France* (1839).

c 672 Briggs, Sir J. H. *Naval administration, 1827–1892* (1897).

c 673 Busk, H. *Navies of the world* (1859).

c 674 Lindsay, W. S. *History of merchant shipping* (1876).

c 675 Plunket, E. *Past and future of the British navy* (1846).

c 676 Reed, E. J. *Our iron-clad ships* (1869).

c 677 Sharp, J. A. *Memoirs of Rear-Admiral Sir William Symonds* (1858).

AMERICAN

c 678 King, J. W. *Warships and navies of the world* (Boston, 1880).

c 679 *U.S. Naval Institute Proceedings*, **44** (1923); for the *Monitor* v. *Merrimac* action.

c 680 Very, E. W. *Navies of the world* (New York, 1880).

FRENCH

c 681 Paixhans, H. J. *Nouvelle force maritime* (1822).

c 682 —— *Expériences...sur une arme nouvelle* (1825).

19   Armed Forces and the art of war: armies (vol. IX, ch. iii (*a*))

Many books relevant to the Revolutionary and Napoleonic periods have already been mentioned in the bibliography on 'The Art of War' in Section B, **18**. No attempt is made here to list the innumerable memoirs of the soldiers of the time.

General Studies

Some general works which deal with the period are:

c 683 Nickerson, H. *The armed horde 1793–1939. A study of the rise, survival and decline of the mass army* (New York, 1940).

c 684 Vagts, A. *A history of militarism; civilian and military* (rev. ed., 1959).

On the wars themselves and their military significance:

c 685 Ballard, C. R. *Napoleon. An outline* (1924).

c 686 Dodge, T. A. *Napoleon. A history of the art of war* (4 vols., 1904–7); the most extensive English account of Napoleon's military career.

c 687 Herold, J. C. (ed. and trans.) *The mind of Napoleon. A selection from his written and spoken words* (New York, 1955); covers many subjects other than war.

c 688 Oman, Sir C. *Studies in the Napoleonic wars* (1929).

c 689 Wilkinson, S. *The Rise of General Bonaparte* (Oxford, 1930).

Detailed Studies

C 690   Becke, A. F. *Napoleon and Waterloo* (rev. ed., 1935).
C 691   Camon, H. *La Guerre napoléonienne: précis des campagnes* (3 vols., 1903–10).
C 692   Chuquet, A. M. *Les Guerres de la révolution* (11 vols., 1886–96); judged as uncritical and lacking in technical knowledge.
C 693   Godechot, J. *Les Commissaires aux armées sous le directoire* (2 vols., 1937).
C 694   Lauerma, M. *L'Artillerie de campagne française pendant les guerres de la révolution* (Annales academiae scientiarum Fennicae Ser. B, no. **96**; Helsinki, 1956).
C 695   Lefebvre de Béhaine, F. *La Défense de la ligne du Rhin* (1933).
C 696   —— *L'Invasion: décembre 1813–janvier 1814* (2 vols., 1934–5).
C 697   Phipps, R. W. *The armies of the first French republic* (5 vols., 1926–39).
C 698   Six, G. *Les Généraux de la révolution et de l'empire* (1948).

On Germany see:

C 699   Holleben, A. von and others. *Geschichte der Befreiungskrieg 1813–1815* (9 vols., Berlin, 1903–9).

On Russia see:

C 700   Jacoby, J. *Souvarov 1730–1800* (1935).
C 701   —— *Napoléon en Russie* (1939).
C 702   Tarlé, E. *Napoleon's invasion of Russia 1812* (Eng. trans. 1942).

On the British forces this period is covered in:

A 539   Fortescue, Sir John. *A History of the British army*, vols. 4–10 (published 1906–20).

See also:

C 703   Oman, Sir C. *History of the Peninsular War* (7 vols., Oxford, 1902–30).

Two briefer accounts are:

C 704   Davies, G. *Wellington and his army* (Oxford, 1954).
C 705   Oman, Sir C. *Wellington's army 1809–1814* (1912).

20   Armed forces and the art of war: armies (vol. x, ch. xii)
        The armed forces (vol. xi, ch. viii)
        Armed forces and the art of war 1. Navies; 2. Armies; 3. Air Forces (vol. xii, ch. x)
General and bibliographical Studies

The two outstanding bibliographies of military affairs before 1914 are:

B 411   Pohler, J. *Bibliotheca historico-militaris*; already mentioned.
C 706   Scharfenort, L. A. von. *Quellenkunde der Kriegswissenschaft für den Zeitraum 1740–1910* (Berlin, 1910).

Equally useful for statistical information is:

C 707   Bodart, G. *Militärhistorisches Kriegslexicon, 1618–1905* (Vienna and Leipzig, 1905).

On the two world wars see the excellent bibliographies in:

A 532   Ropp, T. *War in the modern world*; already mentioned.

For general information on military and naval organization and equipment before 1914 see:

C 708   Alten, G. von. *Handbuch für Heere und Flotte* (9 vols., Berlin, 1909–12).
C 709   Pfluck-Hartung, J. von. *Die Heere und Flotte der Gegenwart* (Berlin, 1896–1905).
C 710   Pierron, E. *Les méthodes de guerre moderne et vers la fin du XIXe siècle* (4 vols. in 7, 1886–95).

On the interwar years see:

C 711   Franke, H. *Handbuch der neuzeitlichen Wehrwissenschaften* (3 vols. in 4, Berlin, 1936).

C 712   Werner, M. *The military strength of the powers* (1939).

The most useful introductory study and bibliography for the whole period, in spite of some unevenness in the contributions, is:

C 713   Earle, E. M. (ed.). *Makers of modern strategy* (Princeton, 1943).

Detailed Studies

MILITARY SCIENCE

The main classic authorities are:

C 714   Clausewitz, C. M. von. *Hinterlassene Werke über Krieg und Kriegführung* (10 vols., Berlin, 1832–7); the most authoritative edition of his major work *Vom Kriege* is that by Werner Hahlweg (Bonn, 1952).
C 715   Colin, J. *Les Transformations de la guerre* (1912).
C 716   Engels, F. *Ausgewählte militärische Schriften* (Berlin, 1958).
C 717   Jomini, A. H. de. *Traité des grandes opérations militaires* (8 vols., 1816).
C 718   —— *Précis de l'art de guerre* (2 vols., 1855).
C 719   Lenin, V. I. *Über Krieg, Armee und Militärwissenschaft* (Berlin, 1958); a volume of selections.
C 720   Moltke, H. von. *Taktisch-strategische Aufsätze aus den Jahren 1857 bis 1871* (Berlin, 1900).
C 721   Schlieffen, A. von. *Gesammelte Schriften* (2 vols., 1897–9).

On post-war developments see the works of J. F. C. Fuller and B. H. Liddell Hart *passim*, especially:

C 722   Fuller, J. F. C. *On future warfare* (1928).
C 723   Liddell Hart, B. H. *The strategy of indirect approach* (1954).

Most of the significant documents on the development of doctrines of air war are in:

C 724   Emme, E. M. (ed.). *The Impact of air power* (Princeton, 1959).

Two important pioneer works are:

C 725   Douhet, G. *Il dominio dell'aria: saggio della guerra aerea* (Rome, 1921).
C 726   Spaight, J. M. *Air power and cities* (1930).

Among more recent works are:

C 317 Gibbs-Smith, C. H. *A history of Flying* (1953); already mentioned.
C 727 Longmore, Sir A. *From sea to sky* (1946).

NAVAL AFFAIRS

For the period before 1870 see bibliography to vol. x, ch. xi above.
Important general studies include:

C 728 Bridge, Sir C. *The art of naval warfare* (1907).
C 729 —— *Sea power and other studies* (1910).
C 730 Brodie, B. *Sea power in the machine age* (Princeton, 1941); the best survey of the whole field.
C 731 Chatfield, Lord. *The Navy and defence* (1942).
C 732 —— *It might happen again* (1947).
C 733 Colomb, P. H. *Naval warfare: its ruling principles and practice historically treated* (3rd ed., 1899).
C 734 Corbett, J. S. *Some principles of maritime strategy* (1911).
C 735 Mahan, A. T. *Naval strategy* (1911).

See also *Brassey's Naval Annual* from 1886, and the successive editions of Jane's *Fighting Ships* for technical developments.

Studies of national naval forces and of other more specialised topics include:

C 736 Charmes, G. *La Réforme de la marine* (1886).
C 737 Corbett, J. S., in *Official History of the Russo-Japanese War* (*Naval and Military*), Historical Section, Committee of Imperial Defence (3 vols., 1910–20).
C 738 —— and Newbolt, H. *Naval operations 1914–18* (5 vols., 1920–31).
C 739 Cowie, J. S. *Mines, minelayers and minelaying* (Oxford, 1949).
C 740 Crowther, J. G. and Whiddington, R. *Science at war* (His Majesty's Stationery Office, 1947).
C 741 Edwards, K. *Operation 'Neptune'* (1946).
C 742 Fayle, C. E. *War and the shipping industry* (1933).
C 743 Hubatsch, W. *Die Ära Tirpitz* (Göttingen, 1955).
C 744 —— *Der Admiralstab und die obersten Marinebehörden in Deutschland 1848–1945* (Frankfurt, 1958).
C 745 Jellicoe, Lord. *The grand fleet, 1914–16* (1919).
C 746 Kemp, P. K. *The fleet air arm* (1945).
C 747 Lipscombe, F. W. *The British submarine* (1954).
C 748 Lloyd George, D. *War Memoirs* (6 vols., 1933–6).
C 749 Marder, A. J. *British naval policy 1880–1905; the anatomy of British sea power* (1941).
C 750 —— (ed.) *Fear God and dread nought: the correspondence of Admiral of the Fleet Lord Fisher of Kilverstone* (3 vols., 1952–9).
C 751 —— *From the Dreadnought to Scapa Flow* (3 vols. to date, 1961–6).
C 752 C. B. A. Behrens, *Merchant shipping and the demands of war* (H.M.S.O., 1954).
C 753 Roskill, S. W. *The war at sea 1939–45* (4 vols., 1954).
C 754 Schüssler, W. (ed.). *Weltmachtstreben und Flottenbau* (Witten-Ruhr, 1956).

c 755   Sims, W. S. *The victory at sea* (1920).

c 756   Sprout, H. and M. *The rise of American naval power* (Princeton, 1939).

NATIONAL ARMED FORCES AND POLICY

For this the student will wish to consult the biographies and memoirs of the statesmen and senior officers concerned with defence questions, which are too numerous to be listed here. But see also:

GREAT BRITAIN

c 757   Biddulph, R. *Lord Cardwell at the war office* (1904).

c 758   Dunlop, J. K. *The development of the British army 1904–1914* (1938).

A 539   Fortescue, J. W. *History of the British Army*, vols. 11–13 (1923–30).

c 759   Johnson, F. A. *Defence by committee; the British committee of imperial defence, 1885–1959* (1960).

c 760   Liddell Hart, B. H. *The Tanks: the history of the Royal Tank Regiment and its predecessors* (2 vols., 1959).

c 761   Report of the Commissioners on the war in South Africa, Evidence and appendices, *Parliamentary Papers*, 1904, **40, 41, 42.**

FRANCE

c 762   Derrécagaix, V. B. *La Guerre moderne* (2 vols., 1885–90).

c 763   Monteilhet, J. *Les Institutions militaires de la France, 1814–1924* (1932).

c 764   Thoumas, C. A. *Les Transformations de l'armée française* (2 vols., 1887).

See also:

c 652   Challener, R. D.

GERMANY

The histories by:

A 545   E. von Frauenholz.

B 446   C. Jany already mentioned.

See also:

c 765   Castellan, G. *Le Réarmament clandestin du Reich, 1930–35* (1954).

c 766   Gordon, H. J. *The Reichswehr and the German republic, 1919–1926* (Princeton, 1957).

c 767   Ritter, G. *Staatskunst und Kriegshandwerk: das Problem des Militarismus in Deutschland* (2 vols. published, Munich, 1954, 1960).

c 768   Wheeler-Bennett, J. *The Nemesis of power: the German army in politics 1918–1945* (1956).

AUSTRIA

c 769   Jurnitschek, A. *Die Wehrreform in Österreich-Ungarn von 1866 bis 1873* (Vienna, 1873).

c 770   *Quellen zur Geschichte des K. und K. Armee aus dem Beginn des 19. Jahrhunderts....* (Vienna, 1903).

RUSSIA

C 771   Krahmer, G. *Geschichte der Entwicklung des russischen Heeres von der Thronbesteigung des Kaisers Nikolai I bis auf die neueste Zeit* (2 vols., Leipzig, 1896–7).
C 772   Liddell Hart, B. H. (ed.). *The Soviet army* (1956).
C 773   Wollenberg, E. *The Red army* (1940).

UNITED STATES

C 774   Millis, W. *Arms and Men* (New York, 1958).
C 775   Upton, E. *The military policy of the United States from 1775* (Washington, 1904).

No bibliography of individual wars is here attempted. The participants in all major conflicts between 1859 and 1918 published official histories of varying quality, usually valuable more for the source material they reprint than for their comment. The Historical Section of the German General Staff published studies of nearly every war involving a major European power, including the Boer War and the Russo–Japanese Wars, between 1859 and 1914, which are usually superior to the official histories of the countries directly concerned. They did not do so, however, for the American Civil War, for which the basic source is:

C 776   *The War of the Rebellion: a compilation of the official records of the Union and Confederate armies* (70 vols. in 128, Washington, 1880–1901).

THE POLITICS OF THE
EUROPEAN STATES

21   The Balance of power during the wars, 1793–1814 (vol. IX, ch. ix)
        The Napoleonic adventure (vol. IX, ch. xi)
        ### General Studies

C 777   Andreas, W. *Das Zeitalter Napoleons und die Erhebung der Völker* (Heidelberg, 1955); a broad analysis, emphasising war and diplomacy.
C 778   Bruun, G. *Europe and the French imperium* (New York, 1938) (*Rise of Modern Europe*, vol. 5); bibliography.
C 779   Driault, J. E. *Napoléon et l'Europe* (5 vols., 1910–27); illuminating but over-favourable to Napoleon.
C 780   Lefèbvre, G. *Napoléon* (1935) (*Peuples et civilisations*, vol. 14); the best general survey of the Napoleonic period with full bibliography.
B 1031 Sorel, A. *L'Europe et la révolution française* (9 vols., 1885–1911); still useful and impressive in its scope.
C 781   Villat, L. *La Révolution et l'empire* (1938); bibliography.

See also:

B 1032 Fugier, A.

Detailed Studies

DIPLOMACY

C 782 Buckland, C. S. B. *Metternich and the British government* (1932); Anglo-Austrian relations in the critical years 1809 to 1913.

C 783 Butterfield, H. *The peace tactics of Napoleon, 1806–1808* (Cambridge, 1929); a favourable analysis of Napoleonic statesmanship at its height.

C 784 Crouzet, F. *L'Economie britannique et le blocus continental, 1806–1813* (2 vols., 1958); an exhaustive examination of British economic strength and resiliency.

C 785 Deutsch, H. C. *The genesis of Napoleonic imperialism* (Cambridge, Mass., 1938); the development of Napoleon's aims and methods, 1801–5.

C 786 Mowat, R. W. *The Diplomacy of Napoleon* (1924); excellent summary.

C 787 Puryear, V. J. *Napoleon and the Dardanelles* (Berkeley, 1951); the eastern question in French diplomacy, 1802–15.

C 788 Robertson, W. S. *France and Latin-American independence* (Baltimore, 1939); detailed and authoritative.

See also:

B 503 Mahan, A. T.; B 1035 Ward, Sir A. W. and Gooch, G. P. (vol. 1); B 1036 Rose, J. H.

THE PERSONALITY AND IDEAS OF NAPOLEON

There are biographies by:

C 789 Fournier, A. *Napoleon I, a biography* (1911).
C 790 Kircheisen, F. *Napoleon* (Eng. trans. 1931).
C 791 Markham, F. M. H. *Napoleon* (1963).
C 792 Rose, J. H. *The Life of Napoleon I* (1922).
C 793 Thompson, J. M. *Napoleon Bonaparte, his rise and fall* (Oxford, 1952).

Other detailed studies include:

C 794 Chuquet, A. *La Jeunesse de Napoléon* (1897).
C 795 Dard, E. *Napoleon and Talleyrand* (1937).
C 796 Fisher, H. A. L. *Studies in Napoleonic statesmanship—Germany* (Oxford, 1903).
C 797 Fugier, A. *Napoléon et l'Espagne* (1930).
C 798 —— *Napoléon et l'Italie* (1947).
C 799 —— *La Révolution et l'empire napoléonien* (1954).
B 336 Godechot, J. *Les Institutions de la France sous la révolution et l'empire* (1951); already mentioned.
C 800 Gounard, P. *Les Origines de la légende napoléonienne* (1906).
C 801 Grandmaison, C. de. *L'Espagne et Napoléon* (1908).
C 802 Kohn, H. 'Napoleon and nationalism', *JMH*, **22** (1950).
C 803 Rosebery, Lord. *Napoleon, the last phase* (1900).
C 804 Savant, J. *Napoleon in his time* (1958).
C 805 Thompson, J. M. *Napoleon's letters* (Oxford, 1934).

c 806   Vandal, A. *L'Avènement de Bonaparte* (1934).
c 807   —— *Napoléon et Alexandre Ier* (1891).

See also:

B 491 Colin, J.; B 959 Geyl, P.; B 1045 Hales, E. E. Y.

22   The Final coalition and the congress of Vienna, 1813–15 (vol. IX, ch. xxiv)
        International relations, 1815–30 (vol. IX, ch. xxv)
        Bibliographies and general studies
        A good brief bibliography may be found in:

c 808   Kissinger, H. A. *A world restored: Metternich, Castlereagh and the problems of peace, 1812–22* (Boston, 1957).

Among the best of the numerous documentary sources for the Vienna Settlement are:

c 809   Angeberg, Comte d', pseud. (Leonard Jakób Borejko Chodźko), ed. *Le Congrès de Vienne et les traités de 1815* (4 vols., 1864).
c 810   Webster, Sir C. K. *British diplomacy, 1813–15* (1921).

General accounts of the diplomacy of 1814–15 may be found in Kissinger cited above, in:

B 1031 Sorel, A. *L'Europe et la révolution française*, vol. 8 already mentioned, and in:
c 811   Griewank, K. *Der Wiener Kongress und die europäische Restauration 1814–15* (rev. ed., Leipzig, 1954).
c 812   Gulick, E. V. *Europe's classical balance of power* (Ithaca, 1955); covers only the period 1805–15, but provides a firm foundation for the following years.
c 813   Nicolson, Sir H. *The Congress of Vienna, a study in allied unity: 1812–22* (1946).
c 814   Webster, Sir C. K. *The Congress of Vienna, 1814–15* (1919).

On the diplomacy of the Restoration see:

c 815   Beloff, M., Renouvin, P., Schnabel, F., Valsecchi, F. (eds.). *L'Europe du 19e et du 20e siècle: problèmes et interprétations historiques*, vols. 1–2 (1815–1870) (Milan, 1959); a composite work of wide range, useful especially for description and discussion of varying historical interpretations.
c 816   Bourquin, M. *Histoire de la sainte alliance* (Geneva, 1954); see Pirenne below c 818.
c 817   Droz, J. Genet, L. and Vidalenc, J. *L'Epoque contemporaine*, vol. 1, *Restaurations et révolutions, 1815–1871* (Clio, vol. 9.1, 1953).
c 818   Pirenne, J. H. *Histoire de la sainte alliance* (2 vols., Neuchatel, 1946); this work covers the years 1813–18, with special reference to the conception of the 'Holy Alliance' proper. Bourquin's work above uses the same title to embrace all aspects of the conservative alliance generally, in less detail and over a longer period of time (to 1825, and, summarily, to 1829 for Eastern affairs).

c 819 Schenk, H. G. *The aftermath of the Napoleonic wars: the concert of Europe —an experiment* (1947).

c 820 Temperley, H. W. V. *The foreign policy of Canning, 1822–1827* (1925).

c 821 Webster, Sir C. K. *The foreign policy of Castlereagh, 1815–1822* (1925).

See also:

B 1035 Ward, Sir A. W. and Gooch, G. P. (vol. 2).

Detailed Studies

AUSTRIA

c 822 Bertier de Sauvigny, G. de. *Metternich et son temps* (1959). The English trans. (1962) is not identical; a brilliant pen portrait, with copious extracts from Metternich's own sayings and opinions.

c 823 Coudray, H. du. *Metternich* (New Haven, 1936).

c 824 Srbik, H. Ritter von. *Metternich: der Staatsmann und der Mensch* (2 vols., Munich, 1925); an outstanding work.

c 825 Woodward, E. L. *Three studies in European conservatism* (1929); contains a helpful essay on Metternich.

See also:

c 461 Sweet, P. R.

FRANCE

c 826 Cooper, Duff. *Talleyrand* (1932).

c 827 Dupuis, C. *Le Ministère de Talleyrand en 1814* (2 vols., 1919–20); an exceptionally fine study.

c 828 Ferrero, G. *The reconstruction of Europe: Talleyrand and the Congress of Vienna, 1814–15* (Eng. trans., New York, 1941).

c 829 Houssaye, H. *1814* (1888; numerous later editions); interesting, detailed, military history.

c 830 Lacour-Gayet, G. *Talleyrand, 1754–1838* (4 vols., 1928–34).

c 831 Talleyrand, C. M. de. *Correspondance inédite du prince de Talleyrand et du roi Louis XVIII pendant le congrès de Vienne* (Pollain, G., ed.) (1881).

GREAT BRITAIN

c 832 Bryant, A. *The age of elegance 1812–22* (1950).

c 833 Renier, G. J. *Great Britain and the establishment of the kingdom of the Netherlands, 1813–15* (1930).

c 834 Webster, Sir C. K. *The Foreign policy of Castlereagh 1812–15* (1931); one of the masterpieces of research on this period.

PRUSSIA

c 835 Fournier, A. *Der Congress von Châtillon* (Vienna and Prague, 1900); first-rate treatment of early 1814.

c 836 Gebhardt, B. *Wilhelm von Humboldt als Staatsmann* (2 vols., Stuttgart, 1896–9).

B 1413 Treitschke, H. von. *History of Germany in the nineteenth century* (Eng. trans., 7 vols., London and New York, 1915–19).

RUSSIA

c 837   Knapton, E. J. *The lady of the Holy Alliance* (New York, 1939); deals with Mme. de Krüdener and her relationship with Alexander I.

c 838   Nicholas Mikhailovitch, Grand Duke. *Le Tsar Alexandre Ier* (French trans., 1931).

c 839   Waliszewski, K. *La Russie il y a cent ans; le règne d'Alexandre Ier* (3 vols., 1923–5).

SWEDEN

c 840   Scott, F. D. *Bernadotte and the fall of Napoleon* (Cambridge, Mass., 1935).

23   The System of alliances and the balance of power (vol. x, ch. x)

General Studies

c 841   Albrecht-Carrié, R. *A diplomatic history of Europe since 1815* (New York, 1958); has an excellent comprehensive bibliography.

c 842   Marriott, J. A. R. *The Eastern Question: an historical study in European diplomacy* (new ed., Oxford, 1940); still the best introduction to the subject.

c 843   Renouvin, P. *Histoire des relations internationales*, vol. 5. *Le XIX siècle*. I. *De 1815 à 1871* (1954); places European affairs in their world context.

c 844   Seignobos, C. *Histoire politique de l'Europe contemporaine* (2nd ed., 2 vols., 1924); old but still useful.

c 845   Stern, A. *Geschichte Europas seit den Verträgen von 1815 bis zum Frankfurter Frieden von 1871* (10 vols., Berlin, 1894–1924); not entirely superseded by more recent scholarship.

c 846   Taylor, A. J. P. *The Struggle for mastery in Europe, 1848–1918* (Oxford, 1954).

See also:

B 633 Potemkine, V. P. (vol. 2); B 1037 Seton-Watson, R. W.

Detailed Studies

Among the great number of special studies the following are particularly illuminating in their treatment of the varying fortunes of the European political system.

c 847   Friese, C. *Russland und Preussen vom Krimkrieg bis zum polnischen Aufstand* (Berlin, 1931).

c 848   Guichen, E. de. *La Révolution de 1830 et l'Europe* (1916).

c 849   —— *Les Grandes Questions européennes et la diplomatie des puissances sous la seconde république* (2 vols., 1925–9).

c 850   Guyot, R. *La Première Entente cordiale* (1926); a brilliantly written and perceptive study of Anglo–French relations from 1830 to 1848.

c 851   Marcks, E. 'Die europäischen Mächte und die 48er Revolution', *HZ*, **142** (1930).

c 852 Mosely, P. E. *Russian diplomacy and the opening of the Eastern Question* (Cambridge, Mass., 1934); a pioneer study.

c 853 Mosse, W. E. *The European powers and the German question* (1958).

c 854 Puryear, V. J. *International economics and diplomacy in the Near East: a study of British commercial policy in the Levant, 1834–1853* (Berkeley, 1935).

c 855 Rodkey, F. S. *The Turco-Egyptian question in the relations of England, France and Russia, 1832–1841* (Urbana, 1924).

c 856 Srbik, H. Ritter von. *Deutsche Einheit* (4 vols., Munich, 1933–42); especially valuable for Austrian policy after the Crimean war.

c 857 Taylor, A. J. P. *The Italian problem in European diplomacy, 1847–49* (Manchester, 1934).

c 858 Valsecchi, F. *Il Risorgimento e l'Europa. L'alleanza di Crimea* (Milan, 1948).

c 859 Vietsch, E. von. *Das europäische Gleichgewicht* (Leipzig, 1942).

c 860 Webster, Sir C. K. 'Palmerston, Metternich and the European system, 1830–1841', in his *Art and Practice of Diplomacy* (New York, 1962).

c 861 —— *The foreign policy of Palmerston, 1830–1841* (2 vols., 1951); a definitive work.

See also:

c 487 Binkley, R. C.

24   The Revolutions of 1848 (vol. x, ch. xv)

Reference should also be made to the bibliographies, Sec. C, **13, 14** in 'Religion, social and political thought and institutions'.

The centenary of the Revolutions of 1848 was celebrated by the publication of several collective works. Among these were:

c 862 *Recueil des actes du congrès historique du centenaire de 1848* (1948).

c 863 *Etudes d'histoire moderne et contemporaine*, vol. 2 (Société d'histoire moderne, Paris, 1948).

France: the February revolution and the second republic

Among older books are:

c 864 Renard, G. *La République de 1848. Histoire socialiste 1789–1900*, Jaurès, J. (ed.), vol. 9 (1906).

c 865 Seignobos, C. *La Révolution de 1848—Le Second Empire* (1921) (*Histoire de France contemporaine*, Lavisse, E., ed., vol. 6).

c 866 'Stern, D.' *Histoire de la révolution de 1848* (new ed., 3 vols., 1878).

On political institutions and political history see:

c 867 Bastid, P. *Doctrines et institutions politiques de la seconde république* (2 vols., 1945).

c 868 Deslandres, M. *Histoire constitutionelle de la France, de 1789 à 1870*, vol. 2 (1932).

c 869 Weill, G. *Histoire du parti républicain en France de 1814 à 1870* (2nd ed., 1928).

On the revolutionary 'days' and the social question generally:

C 870 Crémieux, A. *La Révolution de Février, Etude critique sur les journées des 21, 22, 23 et 24 février 1848* (1912).

C 871 Mackay, D. C. *The National workshops. A study in the French revolution of 1848* (Cambridge, Mass., 1933).

The centenary of the revolution has provided an occasion for the publication of many works on different aspects of its history. Among these may be mentioned:

C 872 Dautry, J. *1848 et la seconde république* (2nd ed., 1957); written from the democratic point of view.

Also two collections of official documents by Pouthas, Ch. H.

C 873 *Les Procès-verbaux du gouvernement provisoire et de la commission exécutive* (1950).

C 874 *Les Documents diplomatiques du gouvernement provisoire et de la commission exécutive* (2 vols., 1953, 1954); gives a picture of events throughout Europe.

See also, on financial affairs:

B 903 Marion, M. (vol. 3).

Germany

The history of the revolution in Germany was entirely re-interpreted by:

C 875 Valentin, V. *Geschichte der deutschen Revolution 1848–1849* (2 vols., Berlin, 1930–31). Since this stops at the end of the Frankfurt parliament it should be complemented by:

C 876 Brandenburg, E. *Die deutsche Revolution* (Leipzig, 1912).

C 877 Matter, P. *La Prusse et la révolution de 1848* (1903).

The most recent work, with up-to-date bibliography, is:

C 878 Droz, J. *Les Révolutions allemandes de 1848* (1957).

On the workers and on the democratic movements of western Germany see:

C 879 Obermann, K. *Die deutschen Arbeiter in der Revolution von 1848* (Berlin, 1953).

C 880 Repgen, K. *Märzbewegung und Maiwählen des Revolutions-Jahren 1848 in Rheinland* (Bonn, 1955).

For the policy of Bavaria see:

C 881 Döberl, M. *Bayern und die deutsche Frage in den Frankfurter Parlament* (Munich, 1922).

C 882 —— *Bayern und das preussisches Unionprojekt* (Munich, 1926).

Austria and the Habsburg Empire

For the Austrian possessions in Italy see:

C 883 Charmatz, R. *Österreichische innere Geschichte von 1848 bis 1895*, vol. 1 (Leipzig and Berlin, 1918).

C 884 Eisenmann, L. *Le Compromis austro-hongrois de 1867* (1904).

c 885   Eisenmann, L. *L'Hongrie contemporaine* (1921).

c 886   Endres, R. *Revolution in Österreich 1848* (Vienna, 1947).

c 887   Fischer, E. *Österreich 1848. Probleme der demokratischen Revolution in Österreich* (Vienna, 1946).

c 888   Friedjung, H. *Österreich von 1848 bis 1860* (2 vols., Stuttgart and Berlin, 1908, 1912).

c 889   Kiszling, R. *Die Revolution in Kaistertum Österreich 1848 bis 1849* (2 vols., Vienna, 1948).

B 399   Redlich, J. *Das Österreichische Staats- und Reichsproblem* (2 vols., Leipzig, 1920–6); vol. 1 covers the Revolutions of 1848.

c 890   Roubik, F., *Český rok 1848* (Prague, 1948).

There is no good bibliography of Schwarzenberg. For Windischgrätz see:

c 891   Müller, P. *Feldmarschall Fürst Windischgrätz: Revolution und Gegenrevolution in Österreich* (Vienna, 1934).

Italy

The most useful general work remains:

c 892   Bolton King, H. *A History of Italian Unity 1814–1871* (2 vols., 1899).

See also:

c 893   Ferrari, A. *L'Italia durante la rivoluzione 1848–1849* (Rome, 1935).

c 894   *Rassegna storica del risorgimento*, vol. 37, fasc. i–iv (Rome, 1950); contains many studies presented to the Congress of the Risorgimento, held in Rome, April 1949. On the military operations see:

c 895   *Il primo passo verso l'unità d'Italia 1848–1849* (published by the Italian general staff, Rome, 1948).

On events in Rome see:

c 896   Ghisalberti, A. M. (ed.). *Count F. C. A. Liederkerke-Beaufort; rapporti delle cose di Roma 1848–1849* (Rome, 1949); the Dutch chargé d'affaires to the Holy See.

c 897   Duff, A. B. and Degros, M. (eds.). *Rome et les états pontificaux sous l'occupation étrangère; lettres du colonel Callier, juillet 1849–mars 1850* (1950).

On Lombardy see:

c 898   Marchetti, L. *Il governo provisorio della Lombardia* (Milan, 1948); the proceedings of the Milanese government with an historical sketch.

25   The Crimean War (vol. x, ch. xviii)

Reference should also be made to the bibliographies on 'The Art of War', and on vol. x, ch. x (Sec. C, **23**) above.

General Studies

c 899   Gooch, B. D. *The new Bonapartist generals in the Crimean War* (The Hague, 1959); the war viewed from the standpoint of the French and British commanders; has a long and usefully annotated bibliography.

c 900 Henderson, G. B. *Crimean war diplomacy* (Glasgow, 1947); reprints his articles on a number of important topics from the Seymour conversations to the treaty of 2 December 1854.

c 901 Puryear, V. J. *England, Russia and the straits question* (Berkeley, 1931); has an interpretation of the Seymour conversations which has not been accepted.

c 902 Temperley, H. W. V. *England and the Near East. The Crimea* (1936).

c 903 Woodham-Smith, C. *The reason why* (1953); includes a bibliography of letters and diaries, published and unpublished.

Detailed Studies

POLITICS AND DIPLOMACY

c 904 Gorienow, S. M. *Le Bosphore et les Dardanelles* (1910); still important for the connected account of negotiations at Vienna during the war.

c 905 Kinglake, A. W. *The invasion of the Crimea* (6 vols., 1863–80); difficult to disregard since it has first-hand material; anti-French.

c 906 Tarle, E. V. *Krymskaya voĭna* (2 vols., Moscow, 1944–5); primarily a diplomatic history partly from the Russian Foreign Office papers, but has information also on discussions in the Council of State.

c 907 Zaĭonchkovsky, A. M. *Vostochnaya voĭna 1853–6* (St Petersburg, 1908–13); contains, in the second part of vol. 1 and the third part of vol. 2, documents, some of them in French.

FRANCE AND THE WAR

c 908 Bapst, E. *Les Origines de la guerre de Crimée* (1912); important for Franco–Russian relations.

c 909 Bapst, G. *Le Maréchal Canrobert* (6 vols., 1898–1913); especially vol. 3; an important source.

c 910 Rousset, C. *Histoire de la guerre de Crimée* (2 vols., 1877).

THE GERMAN POWERS

c 911 Borries, K. *Preussen im Krimkrieg* (Stuttgart, 1930).

c 912 Schlitter, H. *Aus der Regierungszeit Franz Joseph I* (Vienna, 1919); Austro–Russian relations.

GREAT BRITAIN AND THE WAR

c 913 Gillespie, F. E. *Labour and politics in England, 1850–67* (Durham, N.C., 1927); deals with English public opinion.

c 914 Knaplund, P. 'Finmark in British diplomacy 1836–55', *AHR*, **30** (1925).

c 915 Martin, B. K. *The triumph of Lord Palmerston* (1924); like Gillespie above, deals with public opinion.

26   International Relations (vol. XI, ch. xx)
       International relations, 1900–12 (vol. XII, ch. xi)
       The approach of the War of 1914 (vol. XII, ch. xii)

General Studies

Several general works, covering the years between 1870 and 1914, have already been mentioned in the bibliography to vol. X, ch. x, Sec. C, **23** above, and reference should be made to that list. Other important general works are:

c 916   Albertini, L. *The origins of the war of 1914* (Eng. trans. and ed., Oxford, 1952–7). Vol. I runs to the end of June 1914, with some neglect of Anglo–German relations and a bias to Austrian and Italian problems; the whole of vols. 2 and 3 are devoted to the next five weeks.

c 917   Baumont, M. *L'Essor industriel et l'impérialisme colonial (1878–1904)* (1937) [*Peuples et civilisations*, vol. 18].

c 918   Fay, S. B. *The origins of the world war* (2 vols., New York, 1929).

c 919   Gooch, G. P. *Before the war, studies in diplomacy* (2 vols., 1936–8).

c 920   Langer, W. L. *European alliances and alignments 1871–90* (New York, 1950); first-rate bibliography.

c 921   —— *The diplomacy of imperialism 1890–1902* (2nd ed., New York, 1952).

c 922   Mansergh, N. *The coming of the first world war 1878–1914* (1949).

c 923   Renouvin, P. *La Crise européenne et la première guerre mondiale* (1948) [*Peuples et civilisations*, vol. 19].

c 924   —— *Histoire des relations internationales.* Vol. 6. *Le XIXe siècle:* II, *de 1871 à 1914: l'apogée de l'Europe* (1955).

c 925   Renouvin, P., Préclin, E., and Hardy, G. *La Paix armée et la grande guerre (1871–1919)* (*Clio*, Paris, 1947).

c 926   Schmitt, B. E. *Triple alliance and triple entente* (New York, 1934).

c 927   —— *The coming of the war* (2 vols., New York, 1930).

Most of these books contain useful, and sometimes extensive, bibliographies. For a bibliography of works relating to European expansion overseas see:

c 928   Ragatz, L. J. *The literature of European imperialism 1815–1939* (Washington, 1944).

Documents and Memoirs

The relations of the great powers are documented in collections beginning at different dates between 1871 and 1914 which form the foundation of modern diplomatic history, such as:

c 929   Gooch, G. P. and Temperley, H. W. V. (eds.). *British documents on the origins of the war, 1898–1914* (11 vols., 1926–34).

c 930   *Documents diplomatiques français, 1871–1914* (43 vols., in 3 series, 1929–).

c 931   *Die Grosse Politik der europäischen Kabinette, 1871–1914* (40 vols., Berlin, 1924–7).

C 932   Bittner, L., Pribram, A. F. and Srbik, H. (eds.). *Österreich-Ungarns Aussenpolitik...von der bosnischen Krise 1908 bis zum Kriegsausbruch 1914* (9 vols., Vienna, 1930).

This evidence is supplemented for the years before 1914 by abundant personal records and memoirs which mostly defend national or individual policies, e.g.

AUSTRIA–HUNGARY

C 933   Conrad von Hötzendorff, Franz, Graf. *Aus meiner Dienstzeit 1906–18* (5 vols., Vienna, 1922–5).

FRANCE

C 934   Poincaré, R. *Au service de la France* (10 vols., 1926–33).

GERMANY

C 935   Bethmann-Hollweg, Th. von. *Betrachtungen zum Weltkriege* (Berlin, 1919–22); the English edition is less to be recommended.

C 936   Tirpitz, Admiral A. von. *My memoirs* (Eng. trans. 1919).

GREAT BRITAIN

C 937   Grey of Fallodon, Viscount. *Twenty-five years* (1928).

C 938   Churchill, W. S. *The world crisis* (5 vols., 1926–31).

RUSSIA

C 939   Sazonov, S. *Fateful years 1908–16* (1928).

Detailed Studies

THE BISMARCK ERA

C 940   Fuller, J. V. *Bismarck's diplomacy at its zenith* (Cambridge, Mass., 1922).

C 941   Medlicott, W. N. *The congress of Berlin and after* (1938).

C 942   Mitchel, P. B. *The Bismarckian policy of conciliation towards France, 1881–5* (Philadelphia, 1936).

C 943   Taylor, A. J. P. *Germany's first bid for colonies* (1938).

C 944   Windelband, W. *Bismarck und die europäischen Grossmächte 1879–85* (Essen, 1940).

BRITISH FOREIGN POLICY

C 945   Foot, M. R. D. *British foreign policy since 1898* (1956).

C 946   Gosses, F. *The management of British foreign policy before the first world war* (Leiden, 1948).

C 947   Lovell, R. I. *The struggle for South Africa* (New York, 1934).

C 948   Pribram, A. F. *England and the international policy of the great European powers 1871–1914* (Oxford, 1931).

See also:

B 1037 Seton-Watson, R. W.

ECONOMIC AFFAIRS

c 949   Robbins, L. C. *The economic causes of war* (1939).

See also:

c 13 Feis, H.

PUBLIC OPINION

c 950   Carroll, E. M. *French public opinion and foreign affairs* (New York, 1931).
c 951   Hale, O. J. *Publicity and diplomacy; with special reference to England and Germany 1890–1914* (New York, 1940); Anglo–German relations studied with reference to the press.

ANGLO–GERMAN RELATIONS

c 952   Anderson, P. *The background of anti-English feeling in Germany, 1890–1902* (Washington, 1939).
c 953   Meinecke, F. *Geschichte des deutsch-englischen Bündnis-problem* (Munich, 1927).
c 954   Sontag, R. J. *Germany and England, background of conflict 1848–94* (New York, 1938).
c 955   Woodward, E. L. *England and the German navy* (Oxford, 1935).

AUSTRIA–HUNGARY

c 956   Pribram, A. F. *Austrian foreign policy 1908–18* (1923).
c 957   —— *The secret treaties of Austria–Hungary* (2 vols., Cambridge, Mass., 1920–1).

TURKEY

c 958   Blaisdell, D. C. *European financial control in the Ottoman Empire* (New York, 1929).

THE BAGHDAD RAILWAY

c 959   Chapman, M. K. *Great Britain and the Baghdad railway 1888–1914* (Northampton, Mass., 1948).
c 960   Earle, E. M. *Turkey, the great powers and the Baghdad railway* (New York, 1923).
c 961   Wolfe, J. B. *The diplomatic history of the Baghdad railroad* (Columbia, Mo., 1936).

THE BOSNIAN CRISIS

c 962   Calgren, W. M. *Isvolsky und Aehrenthal vor der Bosnischen Annexionskrise* (Uppsala, 1955).
c 963   Schmitt, B. E. *The annexation of Bosnia* (Cambridge, Mass., 1937).

THE FAR EAST

c 964   Hudson, G. F. *The Far East in world politics* (2nd ed., Oxford, 1939).
c 965   Renouvin, P. *La Question d'extrême-Orient* (1946).
c 966   Treat, P. J. *The Far East, a political and diplomatic history* (New York, 1935).

EGYPT AND THE SUDAN

c 967 Giffen, M. B. *Fashoda, the incident and its diplomatic setting* (Chicago, 1930).
c 968 Mathews, J. J. *Egypt and the formation of the Anglo–French entente* (Philadelphia, 1939).

ITALY

c 969 Salvatorelli, L. *La Triplice alleanza 1877–1912* (Milan, 1939).
c 970 Serra, E. *Camille Barrère e l'intesa italo-francese* (Milan, 1950).

THE MOROCCAN CRISES

c 971 Anderson, E. N. *The first Moroccan crisis, 1904–6* (Chicago, 1930).
c 972 Barlow, P. *The Agadir crisis* (Chapel Hill, N.C., 1940).

RUSSIA

c 973 Michon, G. *L'Alliance franco-russe* (1927).
c 974 Nolde, Baron. *L'Alliance franco-russe* (1936).
c 540 Seton-Watson, H. *The decline of imperial Russia 1855–1914* (1952).
c 975 Sumner, B. H. *Tsardom and imperialism in the Far East and Middle East*, Raleigh Lecture 1940 (Oxford, 1942).
c 976 Taube, M. *La Politique russe d'avant-guerre et la fin de l'empire des Tsars (1904–17)* (1928).

THE U.S.A.

c 977 Bemis, S. F. *A diplomatic history of the United States* (1955).

THE FINAL YEARS BEFORE 1914

c 978 Helmreich, E. C. *The diplomacy of the Balkan war* (Cambridge, Mass., 1948).
c 979 Pribram, A. F. *Austria–Hungary and Great Britain, 1908–14* (1951).
c 980 Wegerer, A. von. *Der Ausbruch des Weltkrieges* (Berlin, 1939); the most thorough defence of German policy.

27   The War of 1914–18 (vol. XII, ch. xiii)

Official histories

The British histories include:

c 981 *Principal events, 1914–18* [Historical section of the committee of imperial defence; His Majesty's Stationery Office, 1922].
c 982 *France and Belgium, 1914–18*, Edmonds, Sir J. E. (11 vols.); Miles, W. (2 vols.); Falls, C. (1 vol.). [London, Macmillan, 10 vols., 1922–39: H.M.S.O., 4 vols., 1947–8].
c 983 *Transportation on the western front.* Henniker, A. M. [H.M.S.O., 1937].
c 984 *Italy.* Edmonds, Sir J. E. and Davies, H. R. [H.M.S.O., 1949].
c 985 *Gallipoli.* Aspinall-Oglander, C. F. (2 vols.) [1929, 1932].
c 986 *Egypt and Palestine.* MacMunn, Sir G. and Falls, C. (vol. 1); Falls, C. (vol. 2) [H.M.S.O., 1928, 1940].
c 987 *Macedonia.* Falls, C. (2 vols.) [H.M.S.O., 1933, 1935].

c 988 *East Africa*. Hordern, C. (vol. 1) [H.M.S.O., 1941].
c 989 *Mesopotamia*. Moberley, F. J. (4 vols.) [H.M.S.O., 1923–7].
c 990 *The merchant navy*. Hurd, Sir A. (3 vols.) [1921–9].
c 991 *War in the air*. Raleigh, Sir W. and Jones, H. A. (1 vol.); Jones, H. A. (6 vols.) [Oxford, 1922–37].
c 992 *Official history of Australia in the war of 1914–18*. (12 vols.) Bean, C. E.W. (6 vols.); Gullett, H. S. (1 vol.); and others [Sydney, 1923–42].
c 993 *New Zealand*. (4 vols. by various authors) [Auckland, etc., N.Z., 1921–3].
c 994 *The Union of South Africa and the great war* [Pretoria, 1924].

See also:

c 738 Corbett, J. S. and Newbolt, H.

For the French and German official accounts see:

c 995 *Les Armées françaises dans la grande guerre* (10 vols., Imprimerie nationale, 1930).
c 996 *Der Weltkrieg 1914 bis 1918* (14 vols., Berlin, 1925–44); for the land operations.

Other Studies

Reference should also be made to the statesmen's memoirs mentioned in the preceding bibliography.

c 997 Blake, R. (ed.). *The private papers of Douglas Haig 1914–19* (1952).
c 998 Young, F. Brett, *Marching on Tanga* (1917).
c 999 Davidson, Sir J. H. *Haig. Master of the field* (1953).
c 1000 Fayle, C. E. *Seaborne trade* (3 vols., 1920–4).
c 1001 Foch, Marshal. *Memoirs* (Eng. trans. 1931).
c 1002 Hamilton, Sir I. *Gallipoli diary* (2 vols., 1920).
c 1003 Hankey, Lord. *The supreme command 1914–18* (2 vols., 1961).
c 1004 Hoffmann, M. *War diaries and other papers* (Eng. trans. 1929).
c 1005 Ironside, Sir E. *Tannenberg* (1925).
c 1006 Joffre, Marshal. *Memoirs* (Eng. trans., 2 vols., 1932).
c 1007 Knox, Sir A. *With the Russian army* (2 vols., 1921).
c 1008 Larcher, M. *La Guerre turque dans la guerre mondiale* (1926).
c 1009 Lawrence, T. E. *Revolt in the desert* (1927).
c 1010 Robertson, Sir W. *Soldiers and statesmen* (2 vols., 1926).
c 1011 Villari, L. *The Macedonian campaign* (1922).

See also:

c 748 Lloyd George, D.

28   The Peace settlement of Versailles, 1918–33 (vol. xii, ch. xvi)

Basic works

The most comprehensive documentation of the peace conference of Paris is now:

c 1012 *The Paris peace conference 1919* (13 vols., State Dept., Washington, 1942–7), forming part of the official series of *Papers relating to the foreign relations of the United States*.

C 1013 Woodward, E. L., Butler, Rohan, and Bury, J. P. T. (eds.). *Documents on British foreign policy 1919–39* (H.M.S.O., 1946–); begins at the signature of the Treaty of Versailles in June 1919, and is in course of publication.

Among other important sources are:

C 1014 Aldrovandi-Marescotti, Count L. *Guerra diplomatica* (4th ed., Milan, 1937).
C 1015 —— *Nuovi ricordi e frammenti di diario* (2nd ed., Milan, 1938).
C 1016 Lloyd George, D. *The truth about the peace treaties* (2 vols., 1938).
C 1017 Mantoux, P. *Les Délibérations du conseil des Quatre: 24 mars-28 juin 1919* (2 vols., 1955).
C 1018 Miller, D. H. *My diary at the conference of Paris* (22 vols., New York, 1924).
C 1019 Seymour, C. *The intimate papers of Colonel House* (4 vols., 1926–8).

Much material is published in the series, *The Paris peace conference: history and documents* (Carnegie endowment for international peace). Volumes in this series include:

C 1020 Dcák, F. *Hungary at the Paris peace conference* (New York, 1942).
C 1021 Luckau, A. *The German delegation at the Paris peace conference* (New York, 1941).

Works such as those listed above are now needed to supplement the still valuable:

C 1022 Temperley, H. W. V. (ed.). *A history of the peace conference of Paris* (6 vols., 1920–4).

Two important sources for developments in the 1920s arising from the peace settlement with Germany are:

C 1023 D'Abernon, Lord. *An ambassador of peace* (3 vols., 1929–30).
C 1024 Sutton, E. *Gustav Stresemann, his diaries, letters and papers* (3 vols., 1935–40).

Particularly useful for its comprehensive bibliographies is:

C 1025 Baumont, M. *La Faillite de la paix, 1918–39* (3rd ed., 2 vols., 1951) [*Peuples et civilisations*, vol. 20].

A standard English work of general scope is:

C 1026 Gathorne-Hardy, G. M. *A short history of international affairs 1920–39* (4th ed., Royal institute of international affairs, London, 1950).

Detailed Studies

In the very large literature for the several fields in this period the following are scarcely more than examples, if outstanding ones:

C 1027 Antonius, G. *The Arab awakening* (1938).
C 1028 Baker, R. S. *Woodrow Wilson and world settlement* (3 vols., 1923).
C 1029 Bretton, H. L. *Stresemann and the revision of Versailles* (Stanford, 1953).

C 1030 Churchill, W. S. *The world crisis: the aftermath* (1929).

C 1031 Ferrell, R. H. *American diplomacy in the great depression* (1957).

C 1032 Freund, G. *Unholy alliance: Russian–German relations from the treaty of Brest Litovsk to the treaty of Berlin* (1957).

C 1033 Helbig, H. *Die Träger der Rapallo-Politik* (Göttingen, 1958); deals with the same subject as Freund.

C 1034 Hourani, A. H. *Syria and Lebanon* (R.I.I.A., Oxford, 1946).

C 1035 Jordan, W. M. *Great Britain, France and the German problem 1918–39* (R.I.I.A., Oxford, 1943).

C 1036 Keynes, J. M. *The economic consequences of the peace* (1919).

C 1037 —— *A revision of the treaty* (1922).

C 1038 Longrigg, S. H. *Syria and Lebanon under French mandate* (R.I.A.A., Oxford, 1958).

C 1039 Mantoux, E. *The Carthaginian peace* (Oxford, 1946); an answer to Keynes's brilliant polemic against the treaty of Versailles.

C 1040 Medlicott, W. N. *British foreign policy since Versailles* (1942).

C 1041 Morgan, J. H. *Assize of arms: the disarmament of Germany and her rearmament, 1919–39*, vol. I only published (1945).

C 1042 Nicolson, H. *Peacemaking 1919* (1933); a vivid evocation.

C 1043 Petrie, Sir C. *The life and letters of the right hon. Sir Austen Chamberlain* (2 vols., 1939–40).

C 1044 Rabenau, F. von. *Seeckt: aus seinem Leben, 1918–36* (Leipzig, 1940).

C 1045 Ronaldshay, Earl of. *The life of Lord Curzon* (3 vols., 1928).

29   The League of Nations (vol. XII, ch. xvii)
General Studies

The best bibliographical guide to the work of the League, already mentioned, is:

C 582 Aufricht, H. *Guide to League of Nations publications...* (New York, and London, 1951). There are also the three consecutive volumes, covering the field of international relations as a whole:

C 1046 Langer, W. L. and Armstrong, H. F. (eds.). *Foreign affairs bibliography: a selected and annotated list of books on international relations, 1919–32* (New York, 1933).

C 1047 Woolbert, R. G. (ed.). *ditto, 1932–42* (New York, 1945).

C 1048 Roberts, H. L. (ed.). *ditto, 1942–52* (New York, 1955).

The standard history of the League is:

C 1049 Walters, F. P. *A history of the League of Nations* (2 vols., 1952); comprehensive and scholarly, but lacks a bibliography.

For some of the League's own publications see 'Economic and social conditions' [Sec. C, 2].

Much relevant material is available in the double series published by the Royal institute of international affairs (London):

C 1050 *Survey of international affairs, 1920–38* (Pre-war series) Toynbee, A. J. and others (eds.).

C 1051 *Documents on international affairs, 1920–40* (Pre-war series) Wheeler-Bennett, J. W. and Heald, S. (eds.).

C 1052 *Survey of international affairs, 1939–46* (War-time series), Toynbee, A. J. and V. M. (eds.).

C 1053 *Documents on international affairs, 1939–46* (War-time series), Carlyle, M. (ed.).

The many critical studies of the diplomacy of the interwar years include:

C 1054 Carr, E. H. *The twenty years' crisis, 1919–39: an introduction to the study of international relations* (2nd ed., 1946); a classical critique.

C 1055 Dell, R. *The Geneva racket, 1920–39* (1941); a journalist's experiences and criticisms.

C 1056 Schwarzenberger, G. *Power politics: a study of international society* (2nd ed., 1951); an elaborate survey by an international lawyer, with extensive bibliography.

Detailed Studies

INTERNATIONAL ORGANISATIONS

C 1057 Azcarate, P. de. *League of Nations and national minorities; an experiment* (Washington, 1945).

C 1058 Cheever, D. S. and Haviland, H. F. jr. *Organising for peace: international organisation in world affairs* (Boston, 1954); showing how later developments benefited from League experience.

C 1059 Goodspeed, S. S. *The nature and function of international organisation* (New York and London, 1959).

C 1060 Hall, H. D. *Mandates, dependencies and trusteeship* (1948).

C 1061 Hudson, M. O. *The permanent court of international justice 1920–42* (1943).

C 1062 Macartney, C. A. *National states and national minorities* (R.I.I.A., London, 1934); useful bibliography.

C 1063 Schaper, B. W. *Albert Thomas: trente ans de réformisme social* (French trans., Assen, 1959); includes the crucial period when Thomas was director of the I.L.O.

C 1064 Shotwell, J. T. and Salvin, M. *Lessons on security and disarmament, from the history of the League of Nations* (New York, 1949).

C 1065 Wright, Q. *Mandates under the League of Nations* (Chicago, 1930); extensive bibliography.

INTERNATIONAL RELATIONS

This list indicates only standard works which describe the policies pursued by the major powers and the nature of international relations shaped by these policies. Refer also to the preceding bibliography.

C 1066 Beloff, M. *The foreign policy of Soviet Russia 1929–41* (2 vols., R.I.I.A., London, 1947–9).

C 1067 Duroselle, J. B. *Histoire diplomatique de 1919 à nos jours* (1953).

C 1068 Ferrell, R. H. *Peace in their time: the origins of the Kellogg-Briand pact* (New Haven, 1952).

C 1069 Kennan, G. F. *Soviet–American relations, 1917–20* (2 vols., Princeton, 1956–8).

C 1070 Mowat, C. L. *Britain between the wars, 1918–40* (1955); a study of the domestic forces which explain foreign policy.

C 1071 Renouvin, P. *Histoire des relations internationales,* vols. 7 and 8. *Les crises du XXe siècle:* I. *De 1914 à 1929;* II. *De 1929 à 1945* (1957–8).

C 1072 Reynolds, P. A. *British foreign policy, 1918–39* (1954).

C 1073 Wiskemann, E. *The Rome–Berlin axis: a history of the relations between Hitler and Mussolini* (1949); with useful select bibliography and note on sources.

THE HISTORIES OF
SEPARATE COUNTRIES
FRANCE

30 The Internal history of France during the wars, 1793–1814 (vol. IX, ch. x)

Many books relevant to this chapter have already been cited in Section B, **36** and reference should be made to that part. See also 'The Politics of the European States' above.

General Studies
Standard authorities are:

C 1074 Pariset, G. *La Révolution (1792–9)* (*1920*).

C 1075 —— *Le Consulat et l'empire* (1921) (vols. II and III of *Histoire de France contemporaine,* Lavisse, E., ed.).

Other useful general works:

C 1076 Godechot, J. *Les révolutions (1770–99)* (Collection 'Nouvelle Clio', 1963).

C 1077 Madelin, L. *Histoire du consulat et de l'empire* (16 vols., 1937–54).

C 1078 Mathiez, A. *La Réaction thermidorienne* (1929).

C 1079 —— *Le Directoire* (1934).

C 1080 Soboul, A. *Précis d'histoire de la révolution française* (1962).

C 1081 Tersen, E. *Napoléon* (1959).

C 1082 Thiry, J. *Napoléon Bonaparte* (1940–62; 14 vols. have appeared).

All these works contain full bibliographies.

Detailed Studies

C 1083 Anchel, R. *Napoléon et les juifs* (1928).

C 1084 Bois, P. *Les Paysans de l'Ouest* (1960).

C 1085 Bouloiseau, M., Ibanés. J., Le Moigne, Y., Perrot, J. C., Reinhard, M., Vovelle, M., *Contributions à l'histoire démographique de la révolution francaise* (Commission d'histoire économique de la révolution francaise, vol. 14, Paris, 1962).

C 1086   Durand, Ch. *Etudes sur le conseil d'état napoléonien* (1949).
C 1087   —— *Le Fonctionnement du conseil d'état napoléonien* (Gap, 1954).
C 1088   —— *Les Auditeurs au conseil d'état de 1803 à 1814* (Aix-en-Provence, 1958).
C 1089   —— *La Fin du conseil d'état napoléonien* (Aix-en-Provence, 1959).
C 1090   —— *L'Exercice de la fonction législative de 1800 à 1814* (Aix-en-Provence, 1955).
C 1091   —— *Le Régime de l'activité gouvernementale pendant les campagnes de Napoléon* (Aix-en-Provence, 1957).
C 1092   Fayet, J. *La Révolution française et la science, 1789–95* (1960).
C 1093   Francastel, A. *Le Style empire, du directoire à la restauration* (1939).
C 1094   Mazauric, Cl. *Babeuf et la conspiration pour l'égalité* (1962).
C 1095   Ponteil, F. *Napoléon Ier et l'organisation autoritaire de la France* (1956).
C 1096   —— *La Chute de Napoléon et la crise française de 1814–15* (1943).
C 1097   Reinhard, M. *Le Grand Carnot* (2 vols., 1950–2).
C 1098   Robert, D. *Les Eglises réformées en France, 1800–30* (1961).
C 1099   Tarlé, E. *La classe operaia nella rivoluzione francese* (2 vols., Rome, 1961).
C 1100   Tønnesson, K. D. *La Défaite des sans-culottes: mouvement populaire et réaction bourgeoise en l'an III* (1959).
C 1101   Walter, G. *Robespierre* (2 vols., 1950–2).

See also:
B 46 Léon, P.

31   French politics, 1814–47 (vol. IX, ch. xii)
                     General Studies

Two useful books in English are:

C 1102   Bury, J. P. T. *France 1814–1940* (3rd ed., revised, 1951).
B 889   Cobban, A. *A history of modern France*, vol. 2: *1799–1945* (1961).

General studies in French include:

C 1103   Charléty, S. *La Restauration* (1921).
C 1104   —— *La Monarchie de Juillet* (1921). (vols. 4–5 of *Histoire de France contemporaine*, Lavisse, E., ed).
C 1105   Weill, G. *La France sous la monarchie constitutionelle* (1902); still quite useful.

On the religious history of the time there are three important and scholarly biographies:

C 1106   Droulers, P. *Action pastorale et problèmes sociaux sous la monarchie de Juillet, chez Mgr d'Astro, archevêque de Toulouse* (1954).
C 1107   Limouzin-Lamothe, R. *Mgr de Quélen, archevêque de Paris* (1955–7).
C 1108   Sevrin, E. *Mgr Clausel de Montals, évêque de Chartres* (1955).

See also:
C 433 Phillips, C. S.

On the literature and ideas of the time see:

C 1109   Moreau, P. *Histoire de la littérature française,* vol. 8: *Le Romantisme* (1957), and also:

B 981   Leroy, M. (vol. 2).

Detailed Studies

C 1110   Bastid, P. *Les Institutions politiques de la monarchie parlementaire française, 1814–48* (1954).

C 1111   Chevalier, L. *Classes laborieuses et classes dangereuses* (1958); one of the most novel and provocative essays of the last decade.

C 1112   Collins, I. *The government and the newspaper press in France, 1814–81* (Oxford, 1959).

C 1113   Gille, B. *La Banque et le crédit en France, de 1815 à 1848* (1959).

C 1114   Gontard, M. *L'Enseignement primaire en France, de la revolution à la loi Guizot* (Lyons, 1959).

C 1115   Plamenatz, J. *The revolutionary movement in France, 1815–70* (1952).

C 1116   Pouthas, Ch. H. *La Population française pendant la première moitié du XIXe siècle* (1956).

C 1117   Vidalenc, J. *Le Département de l'Eure sous la monarchie constitutionnelle (1814–48)* (1952).

THE RESTORATION, 1814–30

C 1118   Artz, F. B. *France under the Bourbon restoration* (Cambridge, Mass., 1931).

C 1119   Bertier de Sauvigny, G. *La Restauration* (1955); a comprehensive synthesis, with a large selective bibliography.

C 1120   Fourcassié, E. *Villèle* (1954).

C 1121   Hall, J. R. *The Bourbon restoration* (1909).

C 1122   Leuilliot, P. *L'Alsace au début du XIXe siècle* (1959).

THE JULY MONARCHY

C 1123   Allison, J. M. S. *Thiers and the French monarchy* (Boston, 1926).

C 1124   Cuvillier, A. *Hommes et idéologies de 1840* (1956).

C 1125   Evans, D. O. *Social romanticism in France, 1830–48* (Oxford, 1951) contains a critical bibliography.

C 1126   Piscitelli, E. *Stato e chiesa sotto la monarchia di Luglio* (Rome, 1956).

C 1127   Rude, F. *Le Mouvement ouvrier à Lyon, de 1827 à 1832* (1944).

C 1128   Stoeckl, A. de. *King of the French. A portrait of Louis Philippe* (London and New York, 1957).

C 1129   Thureau-Dangin, P. *Histoire de la monarchie de juillet* (1897–1904); a seven-volume masterpiece, which is still quite valuable.

C 1130   Trannoy, A. *Le Romantisme politique de Montalembert avant 1842* (1942).

See also the bibliography, Sec. C, **24** 'The Revolutions of 1848' in 'The Politics of the European States'.

None of the books cited in this list was able to take into account:

C 1131   Rémusat, Charles de. *Mémoires de ma vie* (the first two volumes of which
          were published, 1958–9, which promises to stand out as one of the most
          remarkable contemporary sources for a period especially rich in Memoirs
          and Souvenirs.

32   The Second Empire in France (vol. x, ch. xvii)

          The fullest treatment in French is given by:

C 1132   Gorce, P. de la. *Histoire du second empire* (7 vols., 1894–1905); the work
          of a Roman Catholic historian, also:

C 1133   Ollivier, E. *L'Empire libéral* (17 vols., 1895–1915); the apologia of a
          republican who eventually supported the empire. It contains a wealth of
          documentation especially for the 1860s.

C 1134   Gorce, P. de la. *Napoléon III et sa politique* (9th ed., 1933); brief but
          illuminating.

C 1135   Dansette, A. *Napoléon III et le second empire*, vol. 1 (1961); the first of
          seven volumes to appear.

          See also:
          c 865 C. Seignobos, vol. 6. and

C 1136   C. Seignobos, vol. 7. *Le Déclin de l'empire et l'établissement de la troisième
          république* (1921) of E. Lavisse's *Histoire de France contemporaine*.

          These present an orthodox Republican view.

          Succinct and up-to-date summaries in French are:

C 1137   Blanchard, M. *Le Second Empire* (1950).
C 1138   Pradalié, G. *Le Second Empire* (1957).

          The best single volume accounts in English are:

C 1139   Bury, J. P. T. *Napoleon III and the Second Empire* (1964).
C 1140   Corley, T. A. B. *Democratic despot. A life of Napoleon III* (1961).
C 1141   Gooch, G. P. *The second empire* (1960); for various personalities.
C 1142   Guérard, A. *Napoleon III* (Cambridge, Mass., 1953).
C 1143   Thompson, J. M. *Louis Napoleon and the second empire* (Oxford, 1954).

                              Individual biographies

          For Napoleon III, in addition to the above, see:

C 1144   Simpson, F. A. *Louis Napoleon and the recovery of France 1848–56*
          (3rd ed., 1951).

          For some of the other leading figures see:

C 1145   Farat, H. *Persigny, un ministre de Napoléon III* (1957).
C 1146   Maurain, J. *Un Bourgeois français au XIXe siècle: Baroche ministre de
          Napoléon III* (1936).
C 1147   Schnerb, R. *Rouher et le second empire* (1949).
C 1148   Zeldin, T. *Emile Ollivier and the liberal empire of Napoleon III* (Oxford,
          1963).

Internal history

Valuable studies of various aspects of economic and social development are to be found in:

c 1149   Duveau, G. *La Vie ouvrière sous le second empire* (1946).
c 1150   Girard, L. *La Politique des travaux publics du second empire* (1952).
c 1151   Pinkney, D. H. *Napoleon III and the rebuilding of Paris* (Princeton, 1958).

also:

c 12 Dunham, A. L.

Authoritative works on government policy towards the church and the Republican opposition are:

c 1152   Maurain, J. *La Politique ecclésiastique du second empire* (1930).
c 1153   Tchernoff, I. *Le Parti républicain au coup d'état et sous le second empire* (1906).

Foreign policy

c 1154   Case, L. M. *French opinion on war and diplomacy during the second empire* (Philadelphia, 1954).
c 1155   Schefer, L. A. C. *La Grande Pensée de Napoléon III: les origines de l'expédition de Mexique 1858–62* (1939).
c 1156   Steefel, L. D. *Bismarck, the Hohenzollern candidature and the origins of the Franco-German war of 1870* (Cambridge, Mass., 1962).

33   The French Republic (vol. XI, ch. xi)
Bibliography and General Studies

There is no bibliography in French devoted particularly to the period 1870–1902. A useful bibliography in German is:

c 1157   *Bibliographie zur politischen Geschichte Frankreichs in der Vorkriegszeit und im Weltkrieg*, Institut für Weltpolitik (Stuttgart, 1937).

For a general treatment of the Third Republic, see:

c 1136 C. Seignobos, already mentioned.
c 1158   C. Seignobos. *L'Evolution de la troisième république* (1921) vol. 8 of E. Lavisse's *Histoire de France contemporaine*.

The best account is the more recent:

c 1159   Chastenet, J. *Histoire de la troisième république* (7 vols., 1952–63): vol. 1, *L'Enfance de la troisième, 1870–9*; vol. 2, *La République des républicains, 1879–93*; vol. 3, *La République triomphante, 1893–1906*; unfortunately it does not contain a systematic bibliography.

The best account in English is:

c 1160   Brogan, D. W. *The development of modern France* (1940).

Detailed Studies

Important works on various major themes are:

c 1161   Digeon, C. *La Crise allemande de la pensée française* (1959); a work of
first importance on the thought of the period.

c 1162   Weill, G. *Histoire du mouvement social en France* (1922); still indispensable. There is nothing comparable for the economic history of the time.

See also, on religious affairs:

c 432   Dansette, A.

On military history:

c 652   Challener, R. D.

Useful works on social history include:

c 1163   Byrnes, R. F. *Antisemitism in France. The prologue to the Dreyfus affair*
(New Brunswick, N.J., 1950).

c 1164   Dolléans, E. *Histoire du mouvement ouvrier*, vol. 2 (1948); an essay on
the philosophy of French syndicalism.

c 1165   Lefranc, G. *Histoire du mouvement syndical en France* (1937).

c 1166   Noland, A. *The founding of the French socialist party* (Cambridge, Mass.,
1956).

SPAIN

34   Spain and Portugal, 1793 to *c.* 1840 (vol. IX, ch. xvi)

General Studies

The principal general histories both of Spain and of Portugal have
already been mentioned in the relevant bibliographies of Sections A and
B. See also Section B [The histories of separate countries—Spain,
Portugal and their empires] on eighteenth-century Spain. A chronological survey of Spain in the nineteenth century is:

c 1167   Butler Clarke, H. *Modern Spain, 1815–98* (Cambridge, 1906).

On Portugal see:

c 1168   Oliveira Martins, J. P. *Portugal contemporaneo* (2 vols., Lisbon, 1881).

Detailed Studies

CHARLES IV AND THE WAR OF INDEPENDENCE

c 1169   Artola, M. *Los orígenes de la España contemporánea* (Madrid, 1959).

c 1170   Corona Baratech, C. E. *Las ideas políticas en el reinado de Carlos IV*
(Madrid, 1954).

c 1171   Fernández Almagro, M. *Orígenes del régimen constitucional en España*
(Barcelona, 1928).

c 1172   Fugier, A. *La Junta supérieure des Asturies* (1930).

C 1173 Mercader Riba, J. *Barcelona durante la ocupacíon francesa* (Madrid, 1949).

See also:

C 703 Oman, Sir C.

FERDINAND VII AND THE REVOLUTIONS OF 1820

C 1174 Comellas García-Llera, J. L. *Los primeros pronunciamentos en España* (Madrid, 1958).
C 1175 —— *Los realistas en el trienio constitucional* (Pamplona, 1958).
C 1176 D'Arriaga, J. *Historia da Revolução Portugeza de 1820* (Oporto, 1886).
C 1177 Sarrailh, J. F. *Martinez de la Rosa (1786–1862)* (Bordeaux, 1930).
C 1178 Suárez, F. *Los sucesos de la Granja* (Madrid, 1953).

THE CIVIL WAR IN SPAIN AND PORTUGAL

C 1179 Hennigsen, C. F. *Twelve months' campaign with Zumalacarregui* (2 vols., 1836).
C 1180 Luz Soriano, S. J. da. *Historia da guerra civil e do estabelecimento do governo parlamentar em Portugal* (15 vols., with documents, Lisbon, 1866–93).
C 1181 Pirala, A. *Historia de la guerra civil y de los partidos liberal y carlista* (3 vols., Madrid, 1889).
C 1182 Shaw, C. *A narrative of the war for constitutional liberty in Portugal and Spain* (2 vols., 1837).
C 1183 Suárez, F. *La crisis política del antiguo régimen en España* (Madrid, 1950).

LIBERALISM

C 1184 Burgos, J. de. *Anales del reinado de Isabel II*, vols. 1–3 (Madrid, 1850).
C 1185 Llorens Castillo, V. *Liberales y Románticos* (Mexico City, 1954).
C 1186 Sánchez Agesta, *La revolucion liberal: historia del constitucionalismo español* (Madrid, 1955).

CATALONIA

For Catalonia throughout the period see the confused work:

C 1187 Carrera Pujal, J. *Historia política de Cataluña en el siglo XIX*, vols. 1–3 (Barcelona, 1958); this is indispensable.

More thoughtful is:

C 1188 Vicens Vives, J. *Els Catalans en el segle XIX* (Barcelona, 1958).

THE ECONOMIC BACKGROUND

C 1189 Sardá, J. *La política monetaria y las fluctuaciones de la economía española en el siglo XIX* (Madrid, 1948).
C 1190 Banco de Bilbao. *Un siglo en la vida del Banco de Bilbao* (Bilbao, 1957).

ITALY

35   The Italian States 1763–93 (vol. VIII, ch. xiii. 2)
        Italy, 1793–1830 (vol. IX, ch. xv)

General Studies

There is no good general treatment of these years in English. See an old handbook:

C 1191 Vernon, H. M. *Italy from 1494 to 1790* (Cambridge, 1909); has a chapter on the eighteenth century which is still useful as a starting point.

Other summaries are:

C 1192 Berkeley, G. F-H. *Italy in the making 1815 to 1846*, vol. 1 (Cambridge, 1932).
C 1193 Whyte, A. J. *The evolution of modern Italy* (Oxford, 1950).

On the period of the French hegemony consult:

C 1194 Bourgin, G. and Godechot, J. *L'Italie et Napoléon* (*Cahiers de la révolution française*, 4, Paris, 1936); which has useful bibliographical information.

See also:

C 798 Fugier, A.

The best books covering the whole period are Italian and each contains a great deal of bibliographical information. They are:

C 1195 Candeloro, G. *Storia dell'Italia moderna* (Milan, 1958).
C 1196 Spellanzon, C. *Storia del Risorgimento e dell'unità d'Italia* (5 vols., Milan, 1936–50).

Useful as a survey of eighteenth-century printed material, although disappointingly summary, is:

C 1197 Noether, E. P. *Seeds of Italian nationalism* (New York, 1951).

Some of these books also cover the period treated in the bibliography to vol. x, ch. xxi, Sec. C, **36** below.

Detailed Studies

ECONOMIC HISTORY

C 1198 Tarle, E. V. *Le Blocus continental et le royaume d'Italie; la situation économique de l'Italie sous Napoléon Ier* (1928).
C 1199 Tremelloni, R. *Storia dell'industria italiana contemporanea. Della fine del settecento all'unità italiana* (Turin, 1947); useful bibliographical information.

See also:

C 46 Greenfield, K. R.

INDIVIDUAL STATES AND REGIONS

(arranged state by state)

c 1200 Petrocchi, M. *Il tramonto della repubblica di Venezia e l'assolutismo illuminato* (Venice, 1950).

c 1201 Valsecchi, F. *L'assolutismo illuminato in Austria e Lombardia* (2 vols., Bologna, 1931–4); useful bibliography.

a 28 Roberts, J. M. 'Lombardy', *The European nobility in the eighteenth century* (Goodwin, A., ed.) (1953).

c 1202 Pingaud, A. *Bonaparte président de la république italienne* (2 vols., 1914).

c 1203 Rath, R. J. *The fall of the Napoleonic kingdom of Italy, 1814* (New York, 1941); useful bibliography.

c 1204 Gaffarel, P. *Bonaparte et les républiques italiennes* (1895).

c 1205 Bédarida, H. *Parme et la France de 1748 à 1789* (1928).

c 1206 Zobi, A. *Storia civile della Toscana dal 1737 al 1848* (5 vols., Florence, 1850–2).

c 1207 Dufourcq, A. *Le Régime jacobin en Italie; étude sur la république romaine 1798–9* (1900).

c 1208 Acton, H. *The Bourbons of Naples (1734–1825)* (1956); useful bibliography.

c 1209 Johnston, R. M. *The Napoleonic empire in southern Italy and the rise of the secret societies* (2 vols., 1904); useful bibliography.

c 1210 Romani, G. T. *The Neapolitan revolution of 1820–1* (Evanston, 1950).

c 1211 Rosselli, J. *Lord William Bentinck and the British occupation of Sicily* (Cambridge, 1956).

c 1212 Rodolico, N. *Il popolo agli inizi del Risorgimento nell'Italia meridionale* (Florence, 1925).

c 1213 Soriga, R. *Le società segrete, l'emigrazione politica e i primi moti per l'indipendenza* (Modena, 1942).

36 Italy (vol. x, ch. xxi)

Reference should also be made to the bibliography on Italy 1763–1830, Sec. C, **35** above.

General Studies

Good bibliographies are to be found in the various chapters of:

c 1214 *Questioni di storia del Risorgimento…* (Rota, E., ed.) (Milan, 1951).

An important work of interpretation is:

c 1215 Salvatorelli, L. *Pensiero e azione del Risorgimento* (Turin, 1944).

The best general works in English are still:

c 1216 Whyte, A. J. *The political life and letters of Cavour* (1930).

See also:

c 892 Bolton King, H.; c 1192 Berkeley, G. F-H.

In Italian:

c 1196 Spellanzon, C.

Detailed Studies

C 1217 Anzilotti, A. *Gioberti* (Florence, 1922).
C 1218 Aubert, A. *Le Pontificat de Pie IX, 1846–78* (1952).
C 1219 Cavour, Carteggi di. *La liberazione del mezzogiorno* (Bologna, 1949).
C 1220 —— *Il carteggio Cavour-Nigra* (Bologna, 1929).
C 1221 —— *Cavour e l'Inghilterra* (Bologna, 1933).
C 1222 Chiala, L. *Lettere di C. Cavour* (Turin, 1887).
C 1223 Gramsci, A. *Il risorgimento* (Turin, 1949).
C 1224 Griffith, G. O. *Mazzini, prophet of modern Europe* (1932).
C 1225 Mack Smith, D. *Cavour and Garibaldi, 1860* (Cambridge, 1954).
C 1226 —— *Garibaldi, a brief life* (1957).
C 1227 Matter, P. *Cavour et l'unité italienne* (3 vols., 1925).
C 1228 Mazzini, G. *Scritti editi ed inediti di* (ed. nazionale, Menghini, M., ed. 94 vols., Imola, 1907–55).
C 1229 Omodeo, A. *Le leggenda di Carlo Alberto nella recente storiografia* (Turin, 1940).
C 1230 —— *L'opera politica del Conte di Cavour* (2 vols., Florence, 1945).
C 1231 Rive, W. de la. *Reminiscences of the life and character of Count Cavour* (1852).
C 1232 Rosi, M. (ed.). *Dizionario del risorgimento nazionale* (4 vols., Milan, 1931).
C 1233 Thayer, W. R. T. *The life and times of Cavour* (1911).
C 1234 Trevelyan, G. M. *Garibaldi's defence of the Roman Republic* (1907).
C 1235 —— *Garibaldi and the thousand* (1909).
C 1236 —— *Garibaldi and the making of Italy* (1911).

See also:

C 414 Hales, E. E. Y.; C 858 Valsecchi, F.

THE MEDITERRANEAN
AND THE NEAR EAST

37   The Near East and the Ottoman Empire, 1798–1830 (vol. IX, ch. xix)
        The Mediterranean (vol. X, ch. xvi)

        Works on the general course of war and diplomacy, and on the career of Napoleon, which includes accounts of events in the Near East, are not cited here. Nor, in general, are works cited in footnotes to the two chapters, and reference should also be made to these. Most of the books cited below contain relevant bibliographies. For older works see:

C 1237 Bengesco, G. *Essai d'une notice bibliographique sur la question d'Orient: Orient européen, 1821–97* (Brussels, 1897).
C 1238 Jovanovich, V. M. *English bibliography of the Near Eastern question* (Belgrade, 1908).

Islam and the Ottoman empire

B 1184   Gibb, H. A. R. and Bowen, H. *Islamic society and the west* (Oxford: part i, 1950; part ii, 1957); a full analysis of Islamic society and institutions (mainly in the Ottomann empire) in the eighteenth century.

C 1239   Lewis, B. *The emergence of modern Turkey* (Oxford, 1961).

C 1240   Miller, E. *The Ottoman empire and its successors, 1801–1936* (4th ed., Cambridge, 1936).

C 1241   Sykes, Sir P. M. *A history of Persia* (2 vols., 3rd ed., 1930).

Europe and the Near East

C 1242   Driault, E. *La Question d'Orient...* (7th ed., 1917); up to 1914.

C 1243   —— *La Politique orientale de Napoléon, 1806–9* (1904).

C 1244   Hoskins, H. L. *British routes to India* (New York, 1928); a scholarly work, assembling much scattered material.

C 1245   Puryear, V. J. *France and the Levant...* [1815–32] (Berkeley, 1941).

See also:

C 787 Puryear, V. J.

Egypt

C 1246   Charles-Roux, F. *L'Angleterre, l'isthme de Suez et l'Egypte au XVIIIe siècle* (1922).

C 1247   —— *Les Origines de l'expédition d'Egypte* (1910).

C 1248   —— *L'Angleterre et l'expédition française d'Egypte* (2 vols., Cairo, 1925).

C 1249   Dodwell, H. *The founder of modern Egypt* (1931); the best short account in English of the rise and career of Mehemet Ali.

C 1250   Hill, R. *Egypt and the Sudan, 1820–81* (1959).

There are numerous works on Egypt and the eastern Mediterranean between 1798 and 1833 by G. Douin, mostly published at Cairo by the Société royale de géographie d'Egypte.

The Adriatic

C 1251   Mouravieff, B. *L'Alliance russo-turque au milieu des guerres napoléoniennes* (Neuchatel, 1954); chs. iv and vii describe the Russian admiral Seniavine's activities in the Adriatic.

C 1252   Rodocanachi, E. *Bonaparte et les îles ioniennes, 1797–1816* (1899).

Roumania

C 1253   Iorga, N. *Geschichte des Rumänischen Volkes* (2 vols., Gotha, 1905).

See also:

C 538 Seton-Watson, R. W.

Bulgaria

C 1254   Hayek, A. *Bulgarien unter der Türkenherrschaft* (Berlin, 1925).

Serbia

C 1255   Yakchich, G. *L'Europe et la résurrection de la Serbie 1804–34* (2nd ed., Hamburg, 1917); full bibliography.

Greece

There are two works by eye-witnesses (who both settled in Greece) which complement each other, and which provide the best contemporary accounts in English:

C 1256   Finlay, G. *History of the Greek revolution* (2 vols., 1867) [*History of Greece*, vols. 6–8].
C 1257   Gordon, T. *History of the Greek revolution* (2 vols., 1832).
C 1258   Crawley, C. W. *The question of Greek independence, 1821–33* (Cambridge, 1930); mainly on the problem presented to British diplomacy.
C 1259   Driault, E. and L'Héritier, M. *Histoire diplomatique de la Grèce moderne*, vol. 1 (1925).
C 1260   Woodhouse, C. M. *The Greek war of independence* (1952); uses vivid material from Greek fighting men.

The Mediterranean in mid-century: the Suez Canal

For general information about Mediterranean ports, commerce, etc. (mid-twentieth century, but with some historical background) see:

C 1261   British naval intelligence division, *Geographical Handbook Series* (1942–6), which are no longer restricted in circulation—Albania, Greece, 3 vols.; Jugoslavia, 3 vols.; Syria, Tunisia, Turkey, 2 vols; Western Arabia and the Red Sea.
C 1262   *Enciclopedia Italiana* (Rome, 1929–39) is useful for ports and shipping.
C 1263   Charles-Roux, F. *L'Egypte de 1801 à 1882* (1936) [*Histoire de la nation égyptienne*, Hanotaux, G., ed., vol. 6].
C 1264   —— *L'Isthme et le canal de Suez* (2 vols., 1901).
C 1265   Hallberg, C. W. *The Suez canal, its history and diplomatic importance* (New York, 1931).
C 1266   Hitti, P. K. *History of the Arabs* (7th ed., 1960).
C 1267   Masson, P. *Les Bouches du Rhône*, vol. 9 (1922); on the commerce of Marseilles since 1789.
C 1268   Tamaro, A. *Storia di Trieste* (2 vols., Rome, 1924).

38   Rivalries in the Mediterranean, the Middle East and Egypt (vol. XI, ch. xxi)
   The Western question in Asia and North Africa 1900–45: The Near and Middle East and North Africa (vol. XII, ch. ix. 1)

For the general movements of international diplomacy see the bibliographies on 'The Politics of the European States' above.

The late nineteenth century

No comprehensive study of this area and of central Asia exists in any language, as the problems that arose in it affected the different nations involved in different ways, and historians have continued to look at the area from their own national point of view. A German account:

C 1269   J. S. Popowski, *The rival powers in central Asia* (Eng. trans. 1893); takes a more impartial view and covers a wider field than its title suggests.

A mine of information is the correspondence of the Russian ambassador in London, 1884–1902:

C 1270   Meyendorff, A. (ed.). *Correspondance diplomatique du Baron de Staal* (2 vols., 1929); which should be collated with:
C 929   Gooch, G. P. and Temperley, H. W. V. (eds.). *British documents on the origins of the war*, vols. 1 and 4.

On Anglo–Russian issues in central Asia and Persia there are two excellent British works:

C 1271   Curzon, G. N. *Russia in central Asia* (1889).
C 1272   Rawlinson, Sir H. *England and Russia in the east* (2nd ed., 1875).

A German account is:

C 1273   Hellwald, F. von. *The Russians in central Asia* (1875).

On Afghan affairs see:

C 1274   Balfour, Lady B. *Lord Lytton's Indian administration* (1899).
C 1275   Fraser-Tytler, Sir K. *Afghanistan* (Oxford, 1950); the best short account.

On Persia, two accounts by the British and by the German ministers are:

C 1276   Drummond Wolff, Sir H. *Rambling recollections* (2 vols., 1908).
C 1277   Rosen, T. *Oriental memories* (1911).

The most recent studies of Foreign Office and India Office records are:

C 1278   Greaves, R. *Persia and the defence of India* (1960).
C 1279   Thornton, A. P. 'British policy in Persia, 1858–90', pts. i–iii, *EHR*, **69** and **70** (1954–5).

On Egypt two first-hand accounts are:

C 1280   Cromer, Earl of. *Modern Egypt* (1 vol. ed., 1911).
C 1281   Malet, Sir E. *Egypt, 1879–83* (1885).

and, on sea-power in the Mediterranean, see also:

C 749 Marder, A. J.; C 750 Marder, A. J.

Still unsurpassed in polemical literature is:

C 1282   Argyll, (8th) Duke of. *The eastern question* (2 vols., 1879).

The Twentieth century

For a classified list of articles in periodicals relating to the Islamic world see:

A 1280   Pearson, J. D. *Index Islamicus 1906–55* (Cambridge, 1958).
A 1281   —— *Index Islamicus Supplement 1956–60* (Cambridge, 1962)

General surveys:

C 1283   Brockelmann, C. *History of the Islamic peoples* (1947).
C 1284   Gabrieli, F. *The Arab revival* (1961).
C 1285   Kirk, G. E. *A short history of the Middle East* (4th ed., 1957).

Selected documents:

C 1286   Hurewitz, J. C. *Diplomacy in the Near and Middle East*, vol. 2, 1914–56 (Princeton, 1956).
C 1287   Rossi, E. *Documenti sull'origine e gli sviluppi della questione araba (1875–1944)* (Rome, 1944).

Several works on particular countries are mentioned in the preceding bibliography. Among others are:

PERSIA

C 1288   Browne, E. G. *The Persian revolution of 1905–9* (Cambridge, 1910).
C 1289   Elwell-Sutton, L. P. *Modern Iran* (1941).
C 1290   Lenczowski, G. *Russia and the west in Iran, 1918–48* (Ithaca, N.Y., 1949).

TURKEY

C 1291   Lewis, G. L. *Turkey* (1955).

SYRIA AND PALESTINE

C 1292   Hitti, P. K. *Lebanon in history* (1957).
C 1293   Hurewitz, J. C. *The struggle for Palestine* (New York, 1950).
C 1294   Lammens, H. *La Syrie, précis historique* (2 vols., Beirut, 1921).
C 1295   Stein, L. *The Balfour declaration* (1961).
C 1296   Zeine, Z. N. *The struggle for Arab independence* (Beirut, 1960).
C 1297   Ziadeh, N. A. *Syria and Lebanon* (1957).

IRAQ

C 1298   Khadduri, M. *Independent Iraq: a study in Iraqi politics since 1932* (1951).
C 1299   Longrigg, S. H. *Iraq, 1900 to 1950: a political, social and economic history* (1953).

SAUDI ARABIA

C 1300   Philby, H. St J. *Sa'udi Arabia* (1955).

EGYPT AND THE SUDAN

C 1301   Colombe, M. *L'Evolution de l'Egypte* (1951).
C 1302   Holt, P. M. *A modern history of the Sudan* (1961).
C 1303   Landau, J. M. *Parliaments and parties in Egypt* (New York, 1954).
C 1304   Marlowe, J. *Anglo–Egyptian relations, 1800–1953* (1954).

NORTH AFRICA

C 1305 Le Tourneau, R. *Evolution politique de l'Afrique du Nord musulmane 1920–61* (1962).

General problems of the Near and Middle East:

C 1306 Bullard, Sir R. *Britain and the Middle East* (2nd ed., 1952).

C 1307 Howard, H. N. *The partition of Turkey: a diplomatic history 1913–23* (Norman, Oklahoma, 1931).

C 1308 Kedourie, E. *England and the Middle East: the destruction of the Ottoman empire, 1914–1921* (1956).

C 1309 Kirk, G. E. *The Middle East in the war* (2nd ed., 1953).

C 1310 Laqueur, W. Z. *Communism and nationalism in the Middle East* (1956).

C 1311 —— *The Soviet Union and the Middle East* (1959).

C 1312 Speiser, E. A. *The United States and the Near East* (Cambridge, 1950).

C 1313 Thomas, L. V. and Frye, R. N. *The United States and Turkey and Iran* (Cambridge, Mass., 1951).

BRITAIN AND THE BRITISH COMMONWEALTH

39   The United Kingdom and its world-wide interests (vol. x, ch. xiii)

General Studies

The main works are cited in the major bibliographies quoted below. The list of books which follows gives only the more recent works. The two most useful bibliographical guides, the second bringing the first up to date and adding valuable supplementary notes, are:

C 1314 Woodward, E. L. *The age of reform, 1815–70* (Oxford, 1938) (*Oxford History of England*, vol. 13).

C 1315 Young, G. M. and Handcock, W. D. (eds.). *English historical documents 1833–74* (*English Historical Documents*, Douglas, D. C., ed., vol. 12 (i), 1956).

The Cambridge history of the British empire, 8 vols. (Cambridge, 1929–59); contains excellent and comprehensive bibliographies:

C 1316 Vol. 2. *The Growth of the new empire* (1940); covers the period of this chapter.

Other recent books include:

C 1317 Edwards, R. D. and Williams, T. D. (eds.). *The great famine* (*Studies in Irish History*, Dublin, 1957); scholarly studies both of the famine and of Irish society in the mid-nineteenth century, with a good bibliography.

C 1318 Houghton, W. E. *The Victorian frame of mind, 1830–70* (New Haven and London, 1957); the attitudes and ideas of upper-class Victorians.

C 1319 Mather, F. C. *Public order in the age of the Chartists* (Manchester, 1959); on the interaction of disorder and the existing machinery of government.

C 1320   Willey, B. *More nineteenth-century studies* (1956); on 'a group of honest doubters', a sequel to:

C 190   Willey, B. *Nineteenth-century studies* (1949).

C 1321   Young, A. F. and Ashton, E. T. *British social work in the nineteenth century* (1956); a study of social workers.

See also:

c 338 Altick, R. D.

Detailed Studies

Most recent works on the period fall into the categories listed below and include, in addition to those listed by Young and Handcock, the following:

BIOGRAPHIES

C 1322   Culler, A. D. *The imperial intellect: a study of Newman's educational ideal* (New Haven and London, 1955).

C 1323   Forster, E. M. *Marianne Thornton, 1797–1887* (1956).

C 1324   Hill, W. T. *Octavia Hill* (1956).

C 1325   Johnson, L. J. *General T. Peronnet Thompson, 1783–1869* (1957).

C 1326   Jones, W. D. *Lord Derby and Victorian Conservatism* (Oxford, 1956).

C 1327   Kennedy, A. L. (ed.). *'My dear Duchess': social and political letters to the duchess of Manchester, 1858–1869* (1956).

C 1328   Mueller, I. W. *John Stuart Mill and French thought* (Urbana, Ill., 1956).

C 1329   Schoyen, A. R. *The Chartist challenge* (1958); mainly a biography of G. J. Harney.

COMMERCIAL AND BUSINESS HISTORIES

C 1330   Addis, J. P. *The Crawshay dynasty: a study in industrial organisation and development, 1765–1867* (Cardiff, 1957).

C 1331   Morris, J. H. and Williams, L. J. *The South Wales coal industry, 1841–75* (Cardiff, 1958).

C 1332   Redford, A. *Manchester merchants and foreign trade*, vol. 2, *1850–1939* (Manchester, 1956); based on the activities of the Manchester chamber of commerce.

C 1333   Whates, H. R. G. *The Birmingham Post, 1857–1957* (Birmingham, 1957); the history of a great provincial newspaper.

POLITICS AND ADMINISTRATION

C 1334   Brown, L. *The Board of Trade and the free trade movement, 1830–42* (Oxford, 1958).

C 1335   McCord, N. *The anti-corn law league, 1838–46* (1958).

C 1336   Prouty, R. *The transformation of the Board of Trade, 1830–55* (1957).

C 1337   Whyte, J. H. *The Independent Irish party, 1850–9* (Oxford, 1958).

COLONIAL DEVELOPMENTS

For India and the East see the bibliographies on Asia and Africa below:

C 1338   Diké, K. O. *Trade and politics in the Niger delta, 1830–85* (Oxford, 1956); authoritative and based on local sources.

c 1339   Eisner, G. *Jamaica, 1830–1930: a study in economic growth* (Manchester, 1959); uses modern economic methods to interpret historical developments.

c 1340   Long, A. V. *Jamaica and the new order, 1827–47* (Jamaica, 1956); a study of the transition from slavery.

40   Great Britain and the British empire (vol. XI, ch. xiv)
The British Commonwealth of Nations (vol. XII, ch. xix)
General Studies

A selection of general works includes:

c 1341   Bruce, Sir C. *The Broadstone of empire. Problems of Crown colony administration* (2 vols., 1910).

c 1342   Carrington, C. E. *The British overseas* (1950).

c 1343   Currey, C. H. *The British commonwealth since 1815* (2 vols., Sydney, 1950–1).

c 1344   Domvile-Fife, C. W. *Encyclopedia of the British empire* (3 vols., Bristol, 1924).

c 1345   Fawcett, C. B. *A political geography of the British empire* (Boston, 1933).

c 1346   Knaplund, P. *The British empire 1815–1939* (New York, 1941).

c 1347   Lucas, Sir C. P. *Historical geography of the British empire* (12 vols., Oxford, 1887–1923).

c 1348   Stewart, J. I. *An economic geography of the British empire overseas* (1933).

c 1349   Tilby, A. Wyatt. *English people overseas* (6 vols., 1908–14).

See also:

c 381 Newton, A. P.

Perhaps the best general view of the political development of the British empire into the commonwealth in the twentieth century is:

c 1350   Hancock, W. K. *Survey of British commonwealth affairs*, vol. 1, *Problems of Nationality, 1918–36* (1937). The valuable last chapter of this, 'The Law and the commonwealth', by R. T. E. Latham, has been separately published (1949).

On the economic side see also:

c 104   Hancock, W. K. *Survey of British commonwealth affairs*, vol. 2, *Problems of economic policy 1918–39*, parts i and ii: already mentioned. Interesting studies of development up to the years of their publication are:

c 1351   Hall, H. D. *The British commonwealth of nations* (1920).

c 1352   Egerton, H. E. *British colonial policy in the twentieth century* (1922).

c 1353   *The British Empire: a report on its structure and problems* (Royal institute of international affairs, London, 1937).

c 1354   Brady, A. *Democracy in the dominions* (Toronto and London, 1947); good bibliographies.

c 1355   Jennings, W. I. *The British commonwealth of nations* (1949).

c 1356   Mansergh, N. *Survey of British commonwealth affairs: problems of external policy, 1931–9* (1952).

C 1357   Mansergh, N. *Problems of wartime co-operation and post-war change, 1939–52* (1958).
These two books are very useful for the later part of the period.

On constitutional law, in addition to Latham's work noted above, see:

C 1358   Keith, A. B. *The dominions as sovereign states* (1938).
C 1359   Wheare, K. C. *The Statute of Westminster and dominion status* (3rd ed., 1947).

Useful collections of documents are:

C 1360   Dawson, R. M. (ed.). *The development of dominion status, 1900–36* (1937).
C 1361   Keith, A. B. (ed.). *British colonial policy; selected speeches and documents 1763–1917* (1948).
C 1362   —— *Speeches and documents on the British dominions 1918–31* (1932).
C 1363   Mansergh, N. (ed.). *Documents and speeches on British commonwealth affairs, 1931–52* (2 vols., 1953).

National Studies
BRITAIN

C 1364   Bonn, M. J. *Modern Ireland and her agrarian problem* (Dublin, 1906).
C 1365   Briggs, A. *Victorian people* (1954).
C 1366   Bryce, J. *Studies in contemporary biography* (1903).
C 1367   Carrothers, W. A. *Emigration from the British isles* (1929).
C 1368   Ensor, R. C. K. *England 1870–1914* (Oxford, 1936) (*Oxford history of England*, vol. 14); an excellent bibliography.
C 1369   Pelling, H. *The origins of the Labour party 1880–1900* (1954).
C 1370   Roberts, B. C. *The trades Union congress 1868–1921* (1958).
C 1371   Trevelyan, G. M. *British history in the nineteenth century and after (1782–1919)* (new ed., 1937).
C 1372   Webb, S. and B. *The history of trades unionism* (rev. ed., 1920).

See also:

c 38 Clapham, J. H.

CANADA

C 1373   Brady, A. *Canada* (New York, 1932).
C 1374   Cowan, J. *Canada's governors-general, 1867–1952* (Toronto, 1952).
C 1375   Dawson, R. M. *The government of Canada* (Toronto, 1948).
C 1376   Farr, D. M. L. *The Colonial office and Canada, 1867–87* (Toronto, 1955).
C 1377   Kennedy, W. P. M. *The constitution of Canada* (1922).
C 1378   Lower, A. R. M. *Colony to nation; a history of Canada* (Toronto, 1946).
C 1379   Soward, F. H. and others. *Canada in world affairs, the pre-war years* (Toronto, 1941).
C 1380   Wittke, C. *A history of Canada* (rev. ed., New York, 1933).

AUSTRALIA

C 1381 Crawford, R. M. *Australia* (1952).
C 1382 Greenwood, G. (ed.). *Australia: a social and political history* (Sydney, 1955).
C 1383 Hancock, W. K. *Australia* (1929).
C 1384 Hasluck, P. *The government and the people, 1939–41* (Canberra, 1952).
C 1385 Reeves, W. P. *State experiments in Australia and New Zealand* (2 vols., 1902).
C 1386 Shann, E. *An economic history of Australia* (Cambridge, 1930).

NEW ZEALAND AND THE PACIFIC

C 1387 Beaglehole, J. C. (ed.). *New Zealand and the statute of Westminster* (Wellington, N.Z., 1944).
C 1388 Martin, K. L. P. *Missionaries and annexation in the Pacific* (1924).
C 1389 Morrell, W. P. and Hall, D. O. W. *A history of New Zealand life* (1957).
C 1390 Sinclair, K. *A history of New Zealand* (1959).
C 1391 Ward, J. M. *British policy in the south Pacific (1786–1893)* (Sydney, 1948); the only detailed account of European policy in Oceania.
C 1392 Wood, F. L. W. *The New Zealand people at war: political and external affairs* (Wellington, N.Z., 1958).

SOUTH AFRICA

C 1393 Brooks, E. H. *The colour problems of South Africa* (1934).
C 1394 Hofmeyr, J. H. *South Africa* (1931).
C 1395 Keppel-Jones, A. *South Africa* (1949).
C 1396 Kiewiet, C. W. de. *A history of South Africa, social and economic* (Oxford, 1941).
C 1397 Macmillan, W. M. *Africa emergent, a survey of social, political and economic trends in British Africa* (1949).

See also:

B 2038 Walker, E. A.

EAST AND WEST AFRICA

C 1398 Crocker, W. R. *Nigeria: a critique of British colonial administration* (1936).
C 1399 Evans, I. L. *The British in tropical Africa* (Cambridge, 1929).
C 1400 Hailey, Lord (ed.). *An African survey* (2nd ed., 1956).
C 1401 Jackson, H. C. *Sudan days and ways* (1954).
C 1402 Leys, N. *Kenya* (3rd ed., 1926).
C 1403 Lugard, Lord. *The dual mandate in British tropical Africa* (2nd ed., Edinburgh and London, 1923).
C 1404 Oliver, R. *The missionary factor in East Africa* (1952).
C 1405 Perham, M. F. *Native administration in Nigeria* (1937).
C 1406 —— *Africans and British rule* (1941).
C 1407 —— *Lugard* (2 vols., 1956, 1960).
C 1408 Thomas, H. B. and Scott, R. *Uganda* (1935).

WEST INDIES

C 1409 Macmillan, W. M. *Warning from the West Indies* (1936).
C 1410 Olivier, Lord. *Jamaica the blessed island* (1936).
C 1411 Wrong, Hume. *Government of the West Indies* (Oxford, 1923).

See also:

B 1694 Burn, W. L.; B 1697 Burns, Sir A. C.

For India and the East see the bibliographies on 'Asia and Africa' below.

THE NETHERLANDS

41   The Low Countries (vol. IX, ch. xvii, A)

The main general histories, both of the Low Countries as a whole and of Belgium and of the Netherlands in particular, have already been mentioned in earlier sections. The relevant volumes are:

The Low Countries

B 908 Geyl, P. *Geschiedenis van de Nederlandse stam*, vol. 3 (1751–98).
A 52   Houtte, J. A. van and others (eds.). *Algemene Geschiedenis der Nederlanden*, vol. 8 (1748–95) and vol. 9 (1795–1840).

Belgium

A 53   Pirenne, H. *Histoire de Belgique*, vol. 5 (1648–1792) and vol. 6 (1792–1830).

The Netherlands

A 115 Blok, P. J. *History of the people of the Netherlands*, vol. 5 (New York and London, 1912).

Other works on the Netherlands are:

C 1412 Brugmans, H. (ed.). *Geschiedenis van Nederland*, vol. 6 (*1740–1813*), by Brugmans, H., and vol. 7 (*1813–49*), by Verberne, L. G. J. (Amsterdam, 1937); the latter volume deals also with Belgium under William I.
C 1413 Gosses, I. H. and Japikse, N. *Handboek tot de staatkundige geschiedenis van Nederland* (3rd ed., The Hague, 1947).

The most extensive editions of sources are:

C 1414 Colenbrander, H. T. *Gedenkstukken der algemene geschiedenis van Nederland van 1795 tot 1840* ('s Rijks Geschiedkundige Publicatiën, grote serie, 1–6, 11–13, 16, 17, 23, 25, 27, 30, 31, 37, 40, 42, 44, 46, 50, The Hague, 1905–22, 10 parts in 22 vols.); a rich collection of documentary material on general Dutch history.
C 1415 —— *Ontstaan der Grondwet* ('s Rijks Geschiedkundige Publicatiën, kleine serie, 1 and 7, The Hague, 1908–9, 2 vols.); on the founding of the kingdom and the shaping of its institutions in 1814–15.

Belgium—to 1815

C 1416   Schlitter, H. *Die Regierung Josefs II. in den Österreichischen Niederlanden* (Vienna, 1900).

C 1417   Tassier, S. *Les Démocrates belges de 1789* (Brussels, 1930).

See also:

A 55 Bindoff, S. T.; B 1041 Harsin, P.

The French dominion is dealt with by:

C 1418   Delhaize, J. *La Domination française en Belgique* (6 vols., Brussels, 1908–12); immoderately pro-French and pro-revolutionary.

C 1419   Lanzac de Laborie, L. de. *La Domination française en Belgique* (2 vols., 1895); pro-French but conservative.

C 1420   Poullet, P. *Les Institutions françaises de 1795 à 1814. Essai sur les origines des institutions belges contemporaines* (Brussels, 1907).

C 1421   Verhaegen, P. *La Belgique sous la domination française* (5 vols., Brussels, 1922–9); strong anti-French bias.

The Netherlands

C 1422   Colenbrander, H. T. *De Patriottentijd* (3 vols., The Hague, 1897–9). and a series of books for the general public by the same author, mainly based on his editions of source-material:

C 1423   Colenbrander, H. T. *De Bataafsche Republiek* (Amsterdam, 1908).

C 1424   —— *Schimmelpenninck en koning Lodewijk* (Amsterdam, 1911).

C 1425   —— *Inlijving en Opstand* (2nd ed., Amsterdam, 1941).

C 1426   —— *Vestiging van het koninkrijk* (Amsterdam, 1927).

C 1427   —— *Willem I, koning der Nederlanden* (2 vols., Amsterdam, 1931–5).

C 1428   Geyl, P. *De Patriottenbeweging* (Amsterdam, 1947).

C 1429   Heyden, M. J. M. van der. *De dageraad van de emancipatie der Katholieken* (Nymegen, 1947); the development of religious freedom for Roman Catholics.

The United Kingdom of the Netherlands

Reference should also be made to 'Economic and social conditions' and 'The Politics of the European states' above.

C 1430   Brugmans, I. J. *Statistieken van de Nederlandse nijverheid uit de eerste helft der 19e eeuw* ('s Rijks Geschiedkundige Publicatiën, gr. ser. 98–9, The Hague, 1956, 2 vols.); statistical sources for industrial history.

C 1431   Deneckere, M. *Histoire de la langue française dans les Flandres 1770–1823* (Ghent, 1954); on French cultural influences in Belgium.

C 1432   Haag, H. *Les Origines du catholicisme libéral en Belgique, 1789–1839* (Louvain, 1950); the evolution in Catholic political ideology.

C 1433   Terlinden, Ch. *Guillaume Ier, roi des Pays-Bas, et l'église catholique en Belgique* (2 vols., Brussels, 1906); deals with the political difficulties between the Dutch government and the Belgian Catholics.

GERMANY

42   German constitutional and social development, 1795–1830 (vol. IX, ch. xiii)

Prussia and the German problem, 1830–66 (vol. x, ch. xix)

General Studies

The two most useful modern textbooks are:

C 1434   Dill, M. *Germany* (Ann Arbor, 1961).
C 1435   Pinson, K. S. *Modern Germany* (New York, 1954).

A useful introduction, factual rather than analytical, is:

C 1436   Passant, E. J. *A short history of Germany, 1815–1945* (Cambridge, 1959).

See also:

B 495 Craig, G.; C 33 Clapham, J. H.

Of the general works in German see:

C 1437   Brandenburg, E. *Die Reichsgründung* (2 vols., Leipzig, 1916); a large-scale history of German unification which partly supersedes the older accounts, based mainly on the Prussian archives, of Treitschke and Sybel.

C 244   Schnabel, F. *Deutsche Geschichte im neunzehnten Jahrhundert* (4 vols. Freiburg-im-Breisgau, 1929–37); indispensable for an understanding of intellectual and religious developments.

See also:

C 454 Meinecke, F.; C 856 Srbik, H. von (for the Austrian, *grossdeutsch* viewpoint).

Detailed Studies

(a) BEFORE 1830

Important documentary collections are:

C 1438   *Die Reorganisation des preussischen Staates unter Stein und Hardenberg.* I. Teil, *Allgemeines Verwaltungs- und Behördenreform*, Winter, G. (ed.) (1931); 2. Teil, *Das preussische Heer vom Tilsiter Frieden bis zur Befreiung*, Vaupel, R. (ed.) (1938) (Publikationen aus den preussischen Staatsarchiven, **92, 93**).

C 1439   Stein, H. F. K. Freiherr vom. *Briefwechsel, Denkschriften und Aufzeichnungen* (Botzenhart, E., ed.) (7 vols., Berlin, 1931–7).

C 1440   Aris, R. *History of political thought in Germany from 1789 to 1815* (1936).

C 1441   Delbrück, H. *Das Leben des Feldmarschalls Grafen N. von Gneisenau* (2 vols., 3rd ed., Berlin, 1908).

C 1442   Ford, G. S. *Stein and the era of reform in Prussia* (Princeton, 1922).

C 1443   Lehmann, M. *Freiherr vom Stein* (3rd ed., Leipzig, 1928).

C 1444   Meinecke, F. *Das Zeitalter der deutschen Erhebung, 1795–1815* (Monographien zur Weltgeschichte, 25) (Bielefeld, 1906).

c 1445 Reiss, H. S. (ed.). *Political thought of the German romantics* (Oxford, 1955).

c 1446 Ritter, G. *Stein, eine politische Biographie* (3rd ed., Stuttgart, 1958).

c 1447 Seeley, J. R. *Life and times of Stein* (3 vols., Cambridge, 1878).

c 1448 Simon, W. M. *The failure of the Prussian reform movement* (Ithaca, N.Y., 1955).

c 1449 Stern, A. *Der Einfluss der französischen Revolution auf das deutsche Geistesleben* (Stuttgart and Berlin, 1928).

BIOGRAPHIES   (b) AFTER 1830

The best life of Bismarck in English is:

c 1450 Taylor, A. J. P. *Bismarck* (1955); a brilliant and controversial study.

Other lives include:

c 1451 Darmstaedter, F. *Bismarck and the creation of the second Reich* (1948).

c 1452 Eyck, E. *Bismarck and the German empire* (1950); a rather unsatisfactory abridgment of Eyck's masterly *Bismarck* (3 vols., Zürich, 1941–4) which is likely to remain the standard life for many years.

c 1453 Meyer, A. O. *Bismarck* (Stuttgart, 1949); contains some new material, but gives a conventional nationalist interpretation.

Other biographies include:

c 1454 Kessel, E. *Moltke* (Stuttgart, 1957).

c 1455 Meinecke, F. *Radowitz und die deutsche Revolution* (Berlin, 1913).

c 1456 Stadelmann, R. *Moltke und der Staat* (Krefeld, 1950).

SOCIAL AND POLITICAL MOVEMENTS

c 1457 Anderson, E. N. *The social and political conflict in Prussia, 1858–64* (Lincoln, Nebraska, 1954).

c 1458 Droz, J. *Le libéralisme rhénan* (1940); an important study of political movements in Prussia in the 1830s and 1840s.

c 1459 Hamerow, T. S. *Restoration, revolution, reaction* (Princeton, 1958); a valuable and original study of social and economic policy.

c 1460 Legge, J. G. *Rhyme and revolution in Germany* (1918).

See also:
c 35 Benaerts, P.

AUSTRO–PRUSSIAN RELATIONS

c 1461 Clark, C. W. *Franz Joseph and Bismarck* (Cambridge, Mass., 1934).

c 1462 Friedjung, H. *The struggle for supremacy in Germany 1859–66* (Eng. trans., abridged, 1935); an account by the leading Austrian historian of the pre-1914 generation which has not been superseded.

c 1463 Steefel, L. D. *The Schleswig-Holstein question* (Cambridge, Mass., 1932).

See also:
c 846 Taylor, A. J. P.; c 853 Mosse, W. E.

43   The Origins of the Franco-Prussian War and the remaking of Germany (vol. x, ch. xxii)

For the general background of international diplomacy see 'The Politics of the European States' above.

Collected documents:

C 1464   Bonnin, G. *Bismarck and the Hohenzollern candidature* (1957); quotes the most secret German files, essential.

C 1465   Lord, R. H. *Origins of the war of 1870* (Cambridge, Mass., 1924); German files on July 1870.

C 1466   Michaelis, H. (ed.). *Die Auswärtige Politik Preussens*, vols. 8–10 (Oldenburg, 1934–9); run from August 1866 to February 1869. No more were published.

C 1467   Oakes, Sir A. H. and Mowat, R. B. *Great European treaties of the nineteenth century* (Oxford, 1918); also includes the German constitution of 1871.

C 1468   Oncken, H. *Die Rheinpolitik Kaiser Napoleons III* (3 vols., Stuttgart, 1926).

C 1469   *Origines diplomatiques de la guerre de 1870* (29 vols., 1920–31); particularly vol. 28 on 1–15 July 1870.

C 1470   Thimme, F. (ed.). *Bismarck: Die gesammelten Werke*, vols. 6, 6A, 6B (Berlin, 1929–31); contain Bismarck's political writings from 1866 to 1871.

Detailed Studies

See also the bibliography on Germany above, and the bibliography on 'The Histories of separate countries—France' [Sec. C, **32**].

C 1471   Acton, Lord. 'The causes of the Franco–Prussian war', *Historical Essays and Studies* (1907).

C 1472   Benedetti, V. *Ma mission en Prusse* (1871).

C 1473   Bismarck, O. von. *Bismarck the man and the statesman* (2 vols., 1899); a translation of his autobiography by A. J. Butler.

C 1474   Geuss, H. *Bismarck und Napoleon III* (Cologne, 1959); the latest study.

C 1475   Knaplund, P. *Gladstone's foreign policy* (New York, 1935); on Alsace.

C 1476   Newton, Lord. *Lord Lyons: a record of British diplomacy* (2 vols., 1913).

C 1477   Sorel, A. *Histoire diplomatique de la guerre franco–allemande* (2 vols., 1875).

C 1478   Sybel, H. von. *The founding of the German empire by William I*, vols. 5–7 (Eng. trans., New York, 1891–8); written with strong prejudice and without the documents.

C 1479   Valentin, V. *Bismarcks Reichsgründung im Urteil englischer Diplomaten* (Amsterdam, n.d.).

C 1480   Wellesley, Sir V. and Sencourt, R. (eds.). *Conversations with Napoleon III* (1934); based on the Cowley papers.

44   The German Empire (vol. xi, ch. x)

                        General Studies

The most important textbooks, with useful bibliographies, are:

c 1481 Bussmann, W. *Das Zeitalter Bismarcks* (*Handbuch der deutschen Geschichte*, Just, L., ed., vol. 3, pt. 2, Konstanz, 1956).

c 1482 Frauendienst, W. *Das Deutsche Reich von 1890–1914. I: Die Kanzlerschaft Caprivi und Hohenlohe* (*Handbuch der deutschen Geschichte*, vol. 4, pt. 1, Konstanz, 1959).

c 1483 Hartung, F. *Deutsche Geschichte 1871–1919* (5th ed., Stuttgart, 1952).

The best survey, including a discussion of the general concept of modern German history, is:

c 1484 Schieder, Th. *Das Deutsche Kaiserreich von 1871 als Nationalstaat* (Cologne, 1961).

Still remarkable as one of the best-known works of the 1920s:

c 1485 Ziekursch, J. *Politische Geschichte des neuen deutschen Kaiserreichs* (3 vols., Frankfurt, 1925–30).

                        Detailed Studies

Reference should also be made to the bibliographies to vol. ix, ch. xiii and vol. x, ch. xix above, Sec. C, **42**.

DOMESTIC POLICY IN GENERAL

c 1486 Bornkamm, H. 'Die Staatsidee im Kulturkampf', *HZ*, **170** (1950).
c 1487 Heffter, H. *Die deutsche Selbstverwaltung im 19. Jahrhundert. Geschichte der Ideen und Institutionen* (Stuttgart, 1950).
c 1488 Kruck, A. *Geschichte des alldeutschen Verbandes, 1890–1939* (Wiesbaden, 1954).
c 1489 Rein, G. A. *Die Revolution in der Politik Bismarcks* (Göttingen, 1957).
c 1490 Rich, N. and Fischer, M. H. (eds.). *The Holstein papers. The Memoirs, diaries and correspondence of Friedrich von Holstein, 1837–1909* (4 vols., Cambridge, 1955–63).
c 1491 Ritter, G. *Der Schlieffenplan. Kritik eines Mythos* (Munich, 1956).
c 1492 Weber, M. *Gesammelte politische Schriften* (Winckelmann, J., ed.) (2nd ed., Tübingen, 1958).
c 1493 Zmarzlik, H. G. *Bethmann-Hollweg als Reichskanzler 1909–1914* (Düsseldorf, 1957).

See also:

c 743 Hubatsch, W.; c 767 Ritter, G.

POLITICAL PARTIES

C 1494 Bachem, K. *Vorgeschichte, Geschichte und Politik der deutschen Zentrums-partei* (9 vols., Cologne, 1927–32).

C 1495 Booms, H. *Die Deutschkonservative Partei* (Düsseldorf, 1954).

C 1496 Matthias, E. 'Kautsky und der Kautskyanismus. Die Funktion der Ideologie in der deutschen Sozialdemokratie vor dem Ersten Weltkrieg', *Marxismus-Studien*, 2. Folge (Tübingen, 1957).

C 1497 Mehring, F. *Geschichte der deutschen Sozialdemokratie* (4 vols., 4th ed., Stuttgart, 1909).

C 1498 Michels, R. *Zur Soziologie des Parteiwesens in der modernen Demokratie* (2nd ed., new impression, Conze, W., ed., Stuttgart, 1957).

C 1499 Nipperdey, Th. *Die organisation der deutschen Parteien vor 1918* (Düsseldorf, 1961).

C 1500 Ritter, G. A. *Die Arbeiterbewegung im Wilhelminischen Reich. Die Sozialdemokratische Partei und die Freien Gewerkschaften 1890–1900* (Berlin, 1959).

C 1501 Tirrell, S. R. *German agrarian politics after Bismarck's fall. The formation of the farmers' league* (New York, 1951).

BIOGRAPHICAL STUDIES

C 1502 Becker, O. *Bismarcks Ringen um Deutschlands Gestaltung* (Scharff, A., ed., Heidelberg, 1958).

C 1503 Dorpalen, A. 'Emperor Frederick III and the German liberal movement', *AHR*, 54 (1948).

C 1504 Mommsen, W. *Bismarck* (Munich, 1959).

C 1505 Muralt, L. von. *Bismarcks Verantwortlichkeit* (Göttingen, 1955).

C 1506 Rothfels, H. 'Problems of a Bismarck Biography', *Review of Politics*, 9 (1947).

Economic and social policy

C 1507 Born, U. E. *Staat und Sozialpolitik seit Bismarcks Sturz. Ein Beitrag zur Geschichte der innerpolitischen Entwicklung des Deutschen Reiches 1890–1914* (Wiesbaden, 1957).

C 1508 Rassow, P. and Born, U. E. (eds.). *Akten zur staatlichen Sozialpolitik in Deutschland 1890–1914* (Wiesbaden, 1959).

C 1509 Rothfels, H. 'Bismarck's social policy and the problem of state socialism in Germany', *Sociological Review*, 30 (1938).

C 1510 Sombart, W. *Die deutsche Volkswirtschaft im 19. Jahrhundert und im Anfang des 20. Jahrhunderts* (7th ed., Berlin, 1927).

C 1511 Stolper, G. *German economy 1870–1940* (New York, 1948).

AUSTRIA–HUNGARY
AND THE BALKANS

45   The Austrian Monarchy, 1792–1847 (vol. IX, ch. xiv)
        The Austrian Empire and its problems, 1848–67 (vol. X, ch. xx)

Bibliographical and General Studies

Several general and bibliographical works are referred to in Section B ['The Histories of separate countries—Germany and the Habsburg lands'].

Two general studies in English are:

C 1512 Kann, R. A. *The Habsburg Empire* (New York, 1957).
C 1513 Taylor, A. J. P. *The Habsburg Monarchy* (1948).

See also:

B 399   Redlich, J. *Das österreichische Staats- und Reichsproblem* (2 vols.) already mentioned; an exhaustive analysis of central measures and ideas behind them. It extends only up to 1861.

C 1514 Bibl, V. *Der Zerfall Österreichs* (2 vols., Vienna, 1922, 1924); superficial.
C 1515 —— *Die Tragödie Österreichs* (Leipzig and Vienna, 1937); has similar faults, but is more readable.

Detailed Studies

The best works on the pre-1848 period, which pay adequate attention to Hungary and the provinces, are:

C 1516 Springer, A. *Geschichte Österreichs seit dem Wiener Frieden 1809* (Leipzig, 1863).
C 1517 Wertheimer, E. *Geschichte Österreichs und Ungarns im ersten Jahrzehnte des XIX Jahrhunderts* (2 vols., Leipzig, 1884–90).

For political conditions in the 'Vormärz' period see:

C 1518 Hartig, F. *Genesis der Revolution in Österreich* (Vienna, 1850).

The only lives of Francis I (e.g. by H. von Meynert (Vienna, 1872)) are early panegyrics.

C 1519 Criste, O. *Erzherzog Carl* (3 vols., Vienna and Leipzig, 1872) is largely military.

There is nothing adequate on the Emperor Ferdinand or Kolowrat.

C 1520 Metternich's *Nachgelassene Papiere* (9 vols., Vienna, 1880–9).
C 1521 —— *Correspondence* (Leipzig, 1873–4); are chiefly of diplomatic or personal interest.

On Gentz see:

C 1522 *Briefe von und an Friedrich von Gentz* (Wittichen, F. C. (Salzer, E.), ed.) (3 vols., Munich and Berlin, 1909–32).

C 1523   Kübeck, C. F. von K. *Tagebücher* (5 vols., Vienna, 1909); gives a few glimpses behind the scenes.

See also:

c 824 Srbik, H. von.

On the Revolutions of 1848–9 and the ensuing years see bibliography on 'The Politics of the European States' [vol. x, ch. xv, Sec. C, **24**].

See also:

C 1524   Bach, M. *Geschichte der wiener Revolution im Jahre 1848* (Vienna, 1898); left-wing viewpoint.

C 1525   Bernatzik, E. (ed.). *Die österreichischen Verfassungsgesetze* (3 vols., Vienna, 1911); a collection of texts.

C 1526   Helfert, J. A. *Österreich vom Ausgang der wiener Oktoberaufstandes* (4 vols., Prague, 1869–86).

C 1527   —— *Geschichte der österreichischen Revolution* (2 vols., Freiburg-im-Breisgau, 1907–9).

C 1528   Kolmer, G. *Parlament und Verfassung in Österreich*, vol. 1 (Vienna and Leipzig, 1902).

C 1529   Redlich, J. *Kaiser Franz Josef von Österreich* (Berlin, 1928).

C 1530   Rogge, W. *Österreich von Világos bis zur Gegenwart* (3 vols., Leipzig and Vienna, 1872); a near-contemporary account.

On the central administration, see two works which have already been mentioned:

A 1258   Fellner, T. and Kretschmayr, H. *Die österreichische Zentralverwaltung.*

B 381   Beidtel, I. *Geschichte der österreichischen Staatsverwaltung*, vol. 2.

On the finances see:

C 1531   Beer, A. *Die Finanzen Österreichs im 19. Jahrhundert* (Prague, 1877).

C 1532   Fischer, E. 'Der Staatsbankerott von 1816', *Zeitschrift für Politik und Verwaltung* (1924).

On industrial and social questions; for the earlier period see:

C 1533   Engel-Jánosi, F. 'Über die Entwicklung der sozialen und staatswirtschaftlichen Verhältnisse in Deutsch-Österreich, 1815–1849', *Vierteljahrschrift für Sozial- und Wirtschaftsgeschichte*, **17** (1924).

C 1534   Slokar, J. *Geschichte der österreichischen Industrie und ihrer Forderung unter Kaiser Franz I* (Vienna, 1914).

For the later period:

C 1535   Brügel, L. *Geschichte der österreichischen Sozialdemokratie* (5 vols., Vienna, 1922–5).

C 1536   —— *Soziale Gesetzgebung in Österreich von 1848 bis 1918* (Leipzig, 1919).

C 1537   Violand, E. *Die soziale Geschichte der Revolution in Österreich* (Leipzig, 1850).

See also, on economic questions:

B 1428 Pribram, C.; B 1447 Grünberg, C.; c 28 Blum, J.

On Hungary the latest detailed account, with rich bibliographies, is:

A 418   Hóman, V. and Szekfű, G. *Magyar történét*, vol. 5 by G. Szekfű.

For histories of Hungary in English see Section A, **25**. There are also two works by Horváth:

C 1538   Horváth, M. *25 Jahre aus der Geschichte Ungarns, 1823–1848* (2 vols., Leipzig, 1867).

C 1539   —— *Geschichte des Unabhängigkeitskrieges in Ungarn 1848–1849* (3 vols., Budapest, 1872).

There is no adequate biography of either Szechenyi or Kossuth.

For the absolutist period in Hungary see:

C 1540   Berzeviczy, A. *Az absolutismus kora Magyarországon 1849–1865* (4 vols., Budapest, 1922–32).

For the negotiation of the Compromise of 1867 see:

C 1541   Wertheimer, E. *Graf Julius Andrassy* (3 vols., Stuttgart, 1910–13).

For the Hungarian Nationalities Law see:

C 1542   Ferenczi, Z. *Deák Élete*, vol. 3 (Budapest, 1904).
C 1543   Nagy, J. *A nemzetiségi törvény a magyar Parlament elött* (Budapest, 1930); a useful pamphlet.

See also, on Transylvania and the Rumanian question:

B 1402   Makkai, L.

NATIONAL MOVEMENTS IN GENERAL AND PANSLAVISM

C 1544   Fischel, A. *Das österreichische Sprachenrecht* (Brünn, 1890).
C 1545   —— *Materialen zur Sprachenfrage in Österreich* (Brünn, 1902); useful collection of documents.
C 1546   —— *Der Panslawismus* (Stuttgart and Berlin, 1918).
C 1547   Geist-Lányi, P. *Das Nationalitätenproblem auf dem Reichstag zu Kremsier* (Munich, 1920); an excellent short analysis.
C 1548   Kerner, R. J. (ed.). *Slavic Europe* (Cambridge, Mass., 1918).

THE SOUTHERN SLAVS

C 1549   Wendel, H. *Aus dem Südslawischen Risorgimento* (Gotha, 1921).
C 1550   —— *Der Kampf der Südslawen um Freiheit und Einheit* (Frankfurt, 1925).

GALICIA

C 1551   Sala, M. von. *Geschichte des polnischen Aufstandes im Jahre 1846* (Vienna, 1867).

THE CZECHS

A 798   Seton-Watson, R. W. *A history of the Czechs and Slovaks*; already mentioned.

Works in Czech include:

C 1552   Bokeš, F. *Dejiny slovenska a slovákov* (Bratislava, 1946); the large part concerns the period after 1790.
C 1553   Černý, J. M. *Boj za právo* [1848–1867] (2 vols., Prague, 1893).

C 1554   Kazbunda, K. *České hnutí roku 1848* (Prague, 1929).

C 1555   *Přehled Československých Dějin. Díl I: Do roku 1848* (Československá Akademie Věd, Prague, 1958); pp. 581–770 relates to the period 1790–1848. Typical Marxist collective work, but valuable, if judiciously used, for social, economic and cultural history.

C 1556   Kramář, K. and Tobolka, Z. *Dějiny české politiky nové doby* (Prague, 1909).

C 1557   Tobolka, K, *Politieké dějiny československého národa od r. 1848 až do dnešní doby* (4 vols. Prague, 1932–).

46   Austria-Hungary, Turkey and the Balkans (vol. XI, ch. xii)

Although studies of special aspects are numerous, there is no definitive history of this phase of Austro–Turkish relations or of the political development of south-east Europe in its broader historical setting. The first two sections below deal with the more domestic aspects of Austrian and Turkish history; the third with the international crises. See also the bibliographies on 'The Politics of the European States', and Sec. C, **14, 38, 45** above.

Austria-Hungary

A useful general study is:

C 1558   May, A. J. *The Hapsburg monarchy, 1867–1914* (Cambridge, Mass., 1951).

Works on aspects and individuals:

C 1559   Auerbach, B. *Les Races et les nationalités en Autriche–Hongrie* (1917).

C 1560   Charmatz, R. *Geschichte der auswärtigen Politik Österreichs im XIXten Jahrhundert*, vol. 2 (Leipzig, 1919).

C 1561   Diner-Denes, J. *La Hongrie, Oligarchie-Nation-Peuple* (1927).

C 1562   Molisch, P. *Geschichte der deutsch-nationalen Bewegung in Österreich* (Jena, 1926).

A 797   Thomson, S. Harrison. *Czechoslovakia in European history* (Princeton, 1953).

Turkey

C 1563   Engelhardt, E. *La Turquie et le Tanzimat* (1882, 1884).

C 1564   Hayek, A. *Bulgariens Befreiung und staatliche Entwicklung unter seinem ersten Fürsten* (Munich, 1939).

C 1565   Midhat Bey, Ali Haydar. *The life of Midhat Pasha* (1903).

C 1566   Odysseus [Sir Charles Elliot]. *Turkey in Europe* (2nd ed., 1902).

C 1567   Ramsaur, E. E. *The young Turks* (Princeton, 1957).

C 1568   Sarkissian, A. D. *History of the Armenian question to 1885* (Urbana, 1938).

C 1569   Sax, K. von. *Geschichte des Machtverfalls der Türkei* (Vienna, 1913).

C 1570   Skendi, S. *Albania* (1957).

C 1571   Toynbee, A. J. 'The modern West and Islam', *A study of history*, vol. 8 (1954).

C 1572   White, W. W. *The process of change in the Ottoman empire* (Chicago, 1937).

The Eastern Question

C 904   Gorienow, S. M. *Le Bosphore et les Dardanelles* (1910).

C 1573   —— *La Question d'Orient à la veille du traité de Berlin, 1870–1876* (1948).

C 1574   Harris, D. *A diplomatic history of the Balkan crisis of 1875–1878: the first year* (Stanford, 1936); *Britain and the Bulgarian horrors* (Chicago, 1939).

C 1575   Jelavich, C. *Tsarist Russia and Balkan nationalism: Russian influence in the internal affairs of Bulgaria and Serbia, 1879–1886* (Berkeley, 1958).

C 1576   Lee, D. E. *Great Britain and the Cyprus convention* (Cambridge, Mass., 1934).

C 1577   Medlicott, W. N. *Bismarck, Gladstone and the concert of Europe* (1956).

C 1578   Rupp, G. H. *A wavering friendship, 1876–1878* (Cambridge, Mass., 1941).

C 1579   Sosnosky, T. von. *Die Balkanpolitik Österreich-Ungarns seit 1866* (Stuttgart, 1913, 1914).

C 1580   Stojanovic, M. N. *The great powers and the Balkans, 1875–1878* (1937); a useful short survey.

C 1581   Sumner, B. H. *Russia and the Balkans, 1870–1880* (Oxford, 1937); bibliography.

EASTERN AND NORTHERN EUROPE

47   **Russia, 1789–1825 (vol. IX, ch. xviii)**
     Russia in Europe and Asia (vol. X, ch. xiv)

Primary material and contemporary sources

Documentary material is published in appendices to the following histories of the period:

C 1582   Nicholas Mikhailovitch, Grand Duke. *L'Empereur Alexandre I* (2 vols., St Petersburg, 1912) [A different edition is referred to in 'The Politics of the European States', Sec. C, **22**].

C 1583   —— *Le Comte Paul Stroganov* (3 vols., Paris, 1905).

C 1584   Schiemann, Th. von. *Zur Geschichte der Regierung Paul und Alexander I* (Berlin, 1906).

C 1585   —— *Geschichte Russlands unter Kaiser Nikolaus I* (4 vols., Berlin, 1904–19).

C 1586   Shil'der, N. K. *Imperator Aleksandr Pervy* (4 vols., St Petersburg, 1897–8).

C 1587   —— *Imperator Nikolaĭ Pervy* (St Petersburg, 1903); very full, but to 1831 only.

C 1588   Tatishchev, S. S. *Imperator Aleksandr II* (2 vols., St Petersburg, 1913).

Informative contemporary works:

C 1589   Custine, Marquis A. de. *La Russie en 1839* (2 vols., 1843).

C 1590   Czartoryski, Prince A. *Mémoires et correspondance avec l'empereur Alexandre I* (2 vols., 1847).

C 1591   Haxthausen, Baron A. von. *Studien über die inneren Zustände, das Volks-leben und insbesondere die ländlichen Einrichtungen Russlands* (3 vols., Hanover, 1847); there is a less complete English trans.: *The Russian Empire, its people, institutions, resources* (1856).
C 1592   Herzen, A. *My Past and thoughts* (Eng. trans. 1924–7).
C 1593   Karamzin, N. M. *Memoir on ancient and modern Russia* (Eng. trans., Cambridge, Mass., 1959).
C 1594   Mackenzie Wallace, D. *Russia* (1877).
C 1595   Radishchev, A. N. *A Journey from St Petersburg to Moscow* (Eng. trans., Cambridge, Mass., 1958).
C 1596   Schuyler, E. *Turkestan* (1877).
C 1597   Storch, H. F. von. *Tableau historique et statistique de l'empire de Russie à la fin du XVIIIe siècle* (French trans. of German ed., Basle, 1801).
C 1598   Tooke, W. *View of the Russian empire during the reign of Catherine the second to the close of the 18th century* (3 vols., 1800).
C 1599   Tourgueniev, N. *La Russie et les Russes* (3 vols., 1847).
C 1600   Vigel, F. F. *Zapiski* (2 vols., Moscow, 1928).

See also:

B 1521 Reddaway, W. F. (ed.); B 1525 Dashkov, Princess.

General Studies

B 1491   Gitermann, V. *Geschichte Russlands* (3 vols., Zürich, 1944); vol. 3. The appendix contains some documentary material of general interest.
C 1601   Kornilov, A. A. *Modern Russian History* (2 vols., New York, 1924); still perhaps the most practical survey in English.

See also:

C 540 Seton-Watson, H.

Detailed Studies
THE PERIOD UP TO 1825

C 1602   Klochkov, M. V. *Ocherki pravitel'stvennoĭ deyatel'nosti vremeni Pavla I* (St Petersburg, 1916).
C 1603   Lang, D. M. *The first Russian radical* (1959); on Radishchev.
C 1604   Larivière, C. de. *Catherine II et la révolution française* (1895).
C 1605   Mazour, A. G. *The First Russian revolution* (Berkeley, 1937); deals with the Decembrist conspiracy.
C 1606   Mel'gunov, S. *Dela i lyudi aleksandrovskogo vremeni* (Berlin, 1923).
C 1607   Raeff, M. *Michael Speransky* (The Hague, 1957).

See also:

C 839 Waliszewski, K.

AGRARIAN AND INDUSTRIAL HISTORY

C 1608   Blum, J. *Lord and peasant in Russia* (Princeton, 1961).

C 1609   Engelmann, J. *Die Leibeigenschaft in Russland* (Leipzig, 1884); still the best proportioned book on Russian serfdom.

C 1610   Khromov, P. A. *Ekonomicheskoe razvitie Rossii v xix–xx vekakh* (Russian state publishing house, 1950).

A 98   Lyashchenko, P. I. *History of the national economy of Russia to 1917* (New York, 1949); already mentioned; fuller than this imperfect English translation is the Russian edition, *Istoriya narodnogo khozyaïstva S.S.S.R.* (2 vols., Moscow, 1952), an indispensable work.

B 1499   Portal, R. *L'Oural au XVIIIième siècle* (1957).

C 1611   Pypin, A. N. *Obshchestvennoe dvizhenie v Rossii pri Aleksandre I* (St Petersburg, 1901).

C 1612   Robinson, G. T. *Rural Russia under the old regime* (New York, 1938); the standard work in English. Thorough but imperfectly digested and arranged.

C 1613   Semevsky, V. I. *Krestyansky vopros v Rossii v XVIII i pervoï polovine XIX veka* (St Petersburg, 1888).

THE REFORMS

C 1614   Leroy-Beaulieu, A. *L'Empire des Tsars et les Russes* (3 vols., 1881–9).

C 1615   Mosse, W. E. *Alexander II and the modernisation of Russia* (1958).

CENSORSHIP AND POLICE

C 1616   Lemke, M. K. *Ocherki po istorii russkoï tsenzury* (St Petersburg, 1904).

C 1617   Riasanovsky, N. V. *Nicholas I and official Russian nationality* (Berkeley, 1960).

REVOLUTIONARY MOVEMENTS

C 1618   Carr, E. H. *Michael Bakunin* (1937).

C 1619   Venturi, F. *Roots of revolution: a history of the populist and socialist movements in 19th century Russia* (Eng. trans. 1960); a comprehensive study up to 1881.

CULTURE AND POLITICAL THOUGHT

C 1620   Hare, R. G. *Pioneers of Russian thought* (1951).

C 1621   Schelting, A. von. *Russland und Europa* (Bern, 1948).

See also:

B 613 Miliukov, P.

THE REGIONS OF THE EMPIRE

C 1622   Lang, D. M. *The last years of the Georgian monarchy* (New York, 1957).

RUSSIA IN ASIA

c 1623 Baddeley, J. A. *The Russian conquest of the Caucasus* (1908).
c 1624 Kennan, G. *Siberia and the exile system* (2 vols., New York, 1891).
c 1625 Pierce, R. A. *Russian central Asia 1867–1917* (Berkeley, 1960).
c 1626 Raeff, M. *Siberia and the reforms of 1822* (Seattle, 1956).

48   Russia (vol. XI, ch. xiii)

Many books relevant to this chapter are mentioned in the bibliography above. Reference should also be made to 'The Politics of the European States', and to the bibliographies, Sec. C, **14, 45, 46.**

General Studies

The relevant chapters in:

A 1341 Florinsky, M. T. *Russia: a history and an interpretation*, 2 vols., already mentioned, are of outstanding value.

An excellent introductory sketch of the reign of Nicholas II is:

c 1627 Charques, R. *The twilight of imperial Russia* (1958); bibliography. There is, however, nothing corresponding for the reign of Alexander III.

Detailed Studies

FOREIGN POLICY AND ASIAN EXPANSION

Among the numerous works dealing with Russia's relations with the other European powers, special mention may be made of:

c 1628 Langer, W. L. *The Franco–Russian alliance, 1890–4* (Cambridge, Mass., 1929); bibliography.

On expansion in the Far East:

c 1629 Romanov, B. A. *Russia in Manchuria, 1892–1906* (Eng. trans., Ann Arbor, 1952); the work of a Soviet scholar.
c 1630 Malozemoff, A. *Russian far eastern policy, 1881–1904* (Cambridge, Mass., 1959); gives perhaps too uncritical a view of Tsarist policy.
c 1631 Zabriskie, E. H. *American–Russian rivalry in the Far East: a study in diplomacy and power politics, 1895–1914* (Philadelphia, 1946).

DOMESTIC POLITICS

Essential reading for the period 1892–1906 is:

c 1632 *The memoirs of Count Witte* (Eng. trans. 1921); a much abridged version of the original.

Witte's controversial character and achievements are assessed in several articles by T. H. von Laue:

c 1633 Laue, T. H. von. 'Count Witte and the Russian revolution of 1905', *American Slavic and E. European Review*, **17** (1958).

C 1634 Laue, T. H. von 'The Industrialization of Russia in the writings of S. Witte', *Ibid.*, **10** (1951).

C 1635 —— 'Factory inspection under the Witte system, 1892–1903', *Ibid.*, **19** (1960).

C 1636 —— 'A Secret memorandum on the industrialization of imperial Russia', *JMH*, **26** (1954).

C 1637 —— 'The High cost and the gamble of the Witte system', *Journal of Economic History*, **13** (1953).

C 1638 —— 'The Witte system in mid-passage, 1896–9', *Jahrbücher für die Geschichte Osteuropas*, N.F., **8** (1960).

On Pobedonostsev, see F. Steinmann's introduction to:

C 1639 Steinmann, F. and Hurwicz, E. *Konstantin Petrowitsch Pobjedonoszew, der Staatsmann der Reaktion unter Alexander III* (vol. II of *Quellen und Aufsätze zur russischen Geschichte*) (Königsberg, 1933)

C 1640 Pobedonostsev, K. P. *Reflections of a Russian statesman* (Eng. trans. 1898).

Two conservative officials have given their views on Russian political developments towards the end of the period covered:

C 1641 Gurko, V. I. *Features and figures of the past: government and opinion in the reign of Nicholas II*, Wallace Sterling, J. E. and others (eds.) (Stanford, 1939).

C 1642 Kokovtsov, V. N. *Out of my past: the Memoirs...* Fisher, H. H. (ed.) (Stanford and London, 1935).
These two books are publications no. 14 and 6 respectively of the Hoover War Library.

Two contrasting studies of Russian liberalism are:

C 1643 Fischer, G. *Russian liberalism: from gentry to intelligentsia* (Cambridge, Mass., 1957) (Harvard University Russian Research Center studies, no. 30).

C 1644 Leontovitsch, V. *Geschichte des Liberalismus in Russland* (Frankfurt, 1957) (Frankfurter Wissenschaftliche Beiträge: Kultur-wissenschaftliche Reihe, Bd. 10).

THE LATER PERIOD OF AGRARIAN SOCIALISM

C 1645 Billington, J. H. *Mikhailovsky and Russian populism* (Oxford, 1958).

C 1646 Treadgold, D. W. *Lenin and his rivals: the struggle for Russia's future* (1955); dealing with the period 1898–1905.

THE MARXIST SOCIALISTS

C 1647 Martov, L. *Geschichte der russischen Sozialdemokratie...* (Berlin, 1926); a Menshevik account.

C 1648 Schapiro, L. B. *A History of the Communist party of the Soviet Union* (1960).

C 1649 Wolfe, B. D. *Three who made a revolution* (1956); highly readable biographies of Lenin, Stalin and Trotsky (up to 1914).

POLITICAL AND SOCIAL THOUGHT

C 1650   Masaryk, T. G. *The spirit of Russia*, trans. from German by E. and C. Paul, 2nd ed., with additional chapters and bibliographies by T. Slavicki... (London and New York, 1955); retains its usefulness despite its age.

C 1651   Simmons, E. J. (ed.). *Continuity and change in Russian and Soviet thought* (Cambridge, Mass., 1955); contains a number of valuable articles.

There is no satisfactory work on the abortive revolution of 1905–7.

C 1652   Anweiler, O. 'Die russische Revolution von 1905', *Jahrbücher für die Geschichte Osteuropas*, N.F. 3 (1955); is a brief factual account, which has value.

SOCIAL AND ECONOMIC PROBLEMS

The all-important agrarian issue may be studied in:

C 1653   Owen, L. A. *The Russian peasant movement, 1906–7* (1937).
C 1654   Pavlovsky, G. *Agricultural Russia on the eve of the Revolution* (1930); which corrects some common misconceptions.
C 1655   Treadgold, D. W. *The great Siberian migration: government and peasant in resettlement from emancipation to the first world war* (Princeton, 1957).

For the economy as a whole, see:

B 1498   Gille, B. *Histoire économique et sociale de la Russie du moyen âge au XXe siècle* (1949); bibliography. An astonishingly compact work, sound in its approach.

On the question of penetration by foreign capital:

C 1656   Crihan, A. *Le Capital étranger en Russie* (1934).

On the situation of the working class before 1905, see:

C 1657   Goebel, O. *Der Entwicklungsgang der russischen Industriearbeiter bis zur I. Revolution* (Leipzig and Berlin, 1920) (Quellen und Studien des Osteuropas-Instituts in Breslau, Abt. I, Heft 4).

ECCLESIASTICAL HISTORY

C 1658   Curtiss, J. S. *Church and state in Russia: the last years of the empire, 1900–17* (New York, 1940); an excellent and objective study of the Russian Orthodox church.

EDUCATION

In the absence of a really satisfactory account, reference should be made to:

C 1659   Hans, N. A. *History of Russian education policy, 1701–1917* (1931).

THE NATIONAL MINORITIES

This aspect of the history of the Russian empire has as yet been relatively little studied. The following works are useful:

On Russian Poland:

c 1660 Feldman, J. *Geschichte der politischen Ideen in Polen seit dessen Teilungen, 1795–1914* (Munich and Berlin, 1917); now somewhat dated.
c 1661 Rose, W. J. *The rise of Polish democracy* (1944).

On Russian Jewry:

c 1662 Greenberg, L. S. *The Jews in Russia* (2 vols., New Haven, 1944, 1951).

On the Baltic Lands:

c 1663 Kruus, H. *Grundriss der Geschichte des estnischen Volkes* (trans. from Estonian, Tartu, 1932).
c 1664 Schybergson, M. G. *Politische Geschichte Finnlands, 1809–1919* (trans. from Swedish, Gotha and Stuttgart, 1925).

On the Ukraine:

c 1665 Krupnyckyj, B. *Geschichte der Ukraine von den Anfängen bis zum Jahre 1920* (Berlin, 1943).

On Transcaucasia:

c 1666 Manvelichvili, A. *Histoire de Géorgie* (1951).
c 1667 Pasdermadjian, H. *Histoire de l'Arménie* (1949).

49   The Russian Revolution (vol. XII, ch. xiv)

This brief bibliography consists entirely of accounts by actors and by eye-witnesses representing every political view-point of any consequence.

c 1668 Bunyan, J. and Fisher, H. H. *The Bolshevik Revolution 1917–18: documents and materials* (Stanford, 1934).
c 1669 Buchanan, Sir G. *My Mission to Russia* (1923).
c 1670 Chernov, V. *The Great Russian revolution* (New Haven, 1936).
c 1671 Denikin, A. I. *The Russian turmoil* (1922).
c 1672 Kerensky, A. *The Crucifixion of liberty* (1934).
c 1673 Lenin, V. I. *Collected works*, vols. 20–21 (London, n.d.).
c 1674 Lockhart, R. H. Bruce. *Memoirs of a British agent* (1932).
c 1675 Miliukov, P. N. *Istorya vtoroĭ russkoĭ revolyutsii* (Sofia, 1921).
c 1676 Paléologue, M. *La Russie des Tsars pendant la grande guerre*, vol. 3 (1929).
c 1677 Price Philips, M. *My Reminiscences of the Russian Revolution* (1921).
c 1678 Reed, J. *Ten days that shook the world* (1934).
c 1679 Sadoul, J. *Notes sur la révolution bolchevique* (1919).
c 1680 Stalin, J. V. *The October revolution* (1936).
c 1681 Steinberg, I. *Als ich Volkskommissar war* (Munich, 1929).
c 1682 Sukhanov, N. N. *The Russian revolution 1917* (1955).
c 1683 Trotsky, L. D. *History of the Russian revolution*, vols. 1–3 (1932–3).

50   Scandinavia (vol. IX, ch. xviii B.)

The large-scale national histories in the Scandinavian languages have already been mentioned in the parallel bibliographies in Section B. The volumes relating to this period of some of these histories are:

B 1593   Maiander, H. (ed.). *Sveriges historia genom tiderna*, vols. 3 and 4 (Stockholm, 1948).

A 1479   Friis, A., Linvald, A. and Mackeprang, M. (eds.). *Schultz Danmarkshistorie*, vol. 4 (Copenhagen, 1942).

B 1587   *Det norske folks liv og historie gjennem tidene*; vol. 7 by S. Steen and vol. 8 by W. Keilhau (Oslo, 1933, 1929).

Other major works in Scandinavian languages are:

C 1684   Höjer, T. *Carl XIV Johan* (3 vols., Stockholm, 1939, 1943, 1960).

C 1685   Steen, S. *Det Frie Norge*, vols. 1–5 (Oslo, 1951–62).

Of the books which are available in English, several general histories have already been mentioned in Section B. Among these is:

B 1660   Hovde, B. J. *The Scandinavian countries 1720–1865* (2 vols., Ithaca, N.Y., 1948); a widely based analytical survey.

Other works include:

C 1686   Birch, J. H. S. *Denmark in history* (1938).

C 1687   Derry, T. K. *A Short history of Norway* (1957).

C 1688   Gjerset, K. *History of Iceland* (1923).

C 1689   Lauring, P. *A History of the kingdom of Denmark* (Copenhagen, 1960); translated from Danish.

C 1690   Stefansson, J. *Denmark and Sweden with Iceland and Finland* (1916); by an Icelander.

C 1691   Stomberg, A. A. *A History of Sweden* (1932).

C 1692   Toyne, S. M. *The Scandinavians in history* (1948); very slight on this period.

THE AMERICAS

51   The United States and the Old World, 1794–1828 (vol. IX, ch. xxii)

Useful collections of source material for American history are:

C 1693   Commager, H. S. (ed.). *Documents of American History* (4th ed., New York, 1948); a good selection of documents, mainly from official sources.

C 1694   Hofstadter, R. *Great Issues in American history: a documentary record* (2 vols., New York, 1958); prints materials from non-official as well as official sources and concentrates on points of controversy.

General Studies

C 1695   Adams, Henry. *History of the United States during the administrations of Jefferson and Madison* (9 vols., 1891–92).

A condensed version of this is:

c 1696   *The formative years* (Agar, H., ed., 2 vols., 1948).
c 1697   Adams, John Quincy. *Diary 1794–1845* (Nevins, A., ed., New York, 1928); an important contemporary record.
c 1698   McMaster, J. B. *History of the people of the United States from the Revolution to the Civil War* (8 vols., 3rd ed., 1883–1913); vols. 2–5 cover the years 1790–1830. Makes use of newspaper and other contemporary periodical sources.

There are volumes in two major series of historical works:

c 1699   Krout, J. A. and Fox, D. R. *The Completion of independence 1790–1830* (New York, 1944) (*A History of American Life*, Schlesinger, A. M. and Fox, D. R., eds., vol. 5).
c 1700   Nye, R. B. *The Cultural life of the new nation* (1960) (*New American Nation* series, Commager, H. S. and Morris, R. B., eds.).

Detailed Studies

AMERICA AND THE OUTSIDE WORLD

c 1701   Allen, H. C. *Great Britain and the United States* (1954); bibliography. The non-diplomatic portion of this has been re-published in a revised form, together with a shorter version of the rest, as:
c 1702   *The Anglo–American relationship since 1783* (1960).
c 1703   Bemis, S. F. *John Quincy Adams and the foundations of American foreign policy* (New York, 1956).
c 1704   Burt, A. L. *The United States, Great Britain and British North America from the revolution to the establishment of peace after the war of 1812* (New Haven, 1940).
c 1705   Hansen, M. L. *The Atlantic migration, 1607–1860* (Cambridge, Mass., 1945).
c 1706   Perkins, D. *A History of the Monroe doctrine* (Boston, 1955).
c 1707   Pratt, J. W. *Expansionists of 1812* (New York, 1925).
c 1708   Thistlethwaite, F. *The great experiment* (Cambridge, 1955); interprets American history as the formation, through migration, of a new society.
c 1709   —— *The Anglo–American connection in the early nineteenth century* (Philadelphia, 1959).

POLITICAL AND ADMINISTRATIVE HISTORY

c 1710   Beard, C. A. *Economic origins of Jeffersonian democracy* (New York, 1915).
c 1711   Beveridge, A. J. *Life of John Marshall* (4 vols., Boston, 1916–19).
c 1712   Bowers, C. G. *Jefferson and Hamilton. The struggle for democracy in America* (New York, 1926).
c 1713   Brant, I. *James Madison* (6 vols., Indianapolis, 1941–61).
c 1714   Dangerfield, G. *The era of good feelings* (1953).
c 1715   Dauer, M. J. *The Adams federalists* (Baltimore, 1953).
c 1716   Schachner, N. *Alexander Hamilton* (New York, 1957).

C 1717   Shachner, N. *Thomas Jefferson* (New York, 1957).
C 1718   Walters, R. *Albert Gallatin. Jeffersonian financier and diplomat* (New York, 1957).
C 1719   Warren, C. *The Supreme court in United States history* (rev. ed., 2 vols., Boston, 1937); vol. 1 covers the years 1789–1835.
C 1720   White, L. D. *The Jeffersonians. A study in administrative history 1801–1829* (New York, 1951).
C 1721   Wiltse, C. M. *The Jeffersonian tradition in American democracy* (Chapel Hill, N.C., 1935).

WESTWARD EXPANSION AND SECTIONALISM

C 1722   Billington, R. A. *Westward expansion. A history of the American frontier* (New York, 1949).
C 1723   Bond, B. W. *The civilization of the old north-west...1788–1812* (New York, 1949).
C 1724   Buley, R. C. *The old north-west; pioneer period 1815–1840* (2 vols., Indianapolis, 1950).
C 1725   Sydnor, C. S. *The development of southern sectionalism 1819–1848* (Baton Rouge, 1948) (*A history of the South*, Coulter, E. M. and Stephenson, W. H., eds., vol. 5).
C 1726   Whitaker, A. P. *The Mississippi question 1795–1803* (New York, 1939).

ECONOMIC HISTORY

C 1727   Morison, S. E. *The Maritime history of Massachusetts 1783–1860* (Boston, 1941).
C 1728   Nettels, C. P. *The emergence of a national economy 1775–1815* (New York, 1962).
C 1729   Gates, P. W. *The farmer's age: agriculture 1815–1860* (New York, 1960).
C 1730   Taylor, G. R. *The Transportation revolution 1815–1860* (New York, 1951).

These are vols. 2–4 of *The Economic history of the United States*, David, H. and others (eds.).

52   National and sectional forces in the United States (vol. x, ch. xxiii)

General Studies

C 1731   Deusen, G. G. van. *The Jacksonian Era 1828–1848* (New York, 1948); excellent bibliography.
C 1732   Nevins, A. *Ordeal of the Union* (2 vols., New York, 1947).
C 1733   —— *The Emergence of Lincoln* (2 vols., New York, 1950). These provide the foremost history of the period 1848–60.
C 1734   Schlesinger, A. M. jr. *The Age of Jackson* (Boston, 1945).

Detailed Studies

THE JACKSONIAN PERIOD 1828–1848

C 1735   Bassett, J. S. *Life of Andrew Jackson* (2 vols., New York, 1911); more a history of Jackson's presidency than a biography.

C 1736   Bemis, S. F. *John Quincy Adams and the Union* (New York, 1956).
C 1737   Deusen, G. G. van. *Life of Henry Clay* (Boston, 1937).
C 1738   Fuess, C. M. *Daniel Webster*, (2 vols. Boston, 1930).
C 1739   Hammond, B. *Banks and politics in America from the Revolution to the Civil War* (Princeton, 1957).
C 1740   James, M. *Life of Andrew Jackson* (2 vols. in 1, Indianapolis, 1938).
C 1741   Turner, F. J. *The United States, 1830–1850: the nation and its sections* (New York, 1935).
C 1742   Wiltse, C. M. *John C. Calhoun* (3 vols., Indianapolis, 1944–51).

WESTWARD EXPANSION AND THE SECTIONAL CRISIS, 1845–1861

C 1743   Beveridge, A. J. *Abraham Lincoln, 1809–1858* (2 vols., Boston, 1928).
C 1744   Billington, R. A. *The far western frontier, 1830–1860* (New York, 1956).
C 1745   Craven, A. O. *The Coming of the Civil War* (rev. ed., Chicago, 1957).
C 1746   —— *The Growth of southern nationalism, 1848–1861* (Baton Rouge, 1953).
C 1747   Donald, D. *Charles Sumner and the coming of the Civil War* (New York, 1960).
C 1748   Filler, L. *The crusade against slavery, 1830–1860* (New York, 1960); excellent bibliography.
C 1749   Nichols, R. F. *The disruption of American democracy* (New York, 1948).
C 1750   Potter, D. M. *Lincoln and his party in the secession crisis* (New Haven, 1942).
C 1751   Randall, J. G. *Lincoln the President* (4 vols., New York, 1945–55).
C 1752   —— *Lincoln the liberal statesman* (1947); essays.
C 1753   Rhodes, J. F. *History of the United States from the compromise of 1850 to...1877* (7 vols., New York, 1893–1906).
C 1754   Stampp, K. M. *The peculiar institution: slavery in the ante-bellum South* (New York, 1956).
C 1755   —— *And the war came: the North and the secession crisis* (Baton Rouge, 1950).
C 1756   Smith, J. H. *The War with Mexico* (2 vols., New York, 1919); the classic account.

See also:

B 1751 Phillips, U. B.

53   The American Civil War (vol. x, ch. xxiv)

The literature on the war is so vast as almost to defy listing or classification. This list attempts to name only those books which have been recognized as standard. Most of them contain detailed bibliographies.

General Studies

The best general treatments are:

C 1757   Fish, C. R. *The American Civil War* (New York, 1937).
C 1758   Randall, J. G. *The Civil War and reconstruction* (Boston, 1937).

More recent books, the first parts of planned multi-volume works, are:

C 1759 Foote, S. *The Civil War: a narrative: Fort Sumter to Perryville* (New York, 1958).

C 1760 Nevins, A. *The War for the union: the improvised war, 1861–1862* (New York, 1959).

Other, general accounts dealing with one section or another, include:

C 1761 Catton, B. *This hallowed ground* (New York, 1956); the North at war.

C 1762 Coulter, E. M. *The confederate states of America, 1861–1865* (Baton Rouge, 1950).

C 1763 Dowdey, C. *The land they fought for* (New York, 1955); the confederacy.

C 1764 Eaton, C. *A history of the southern confederacy* (New York, 1954).

C 1765 Henry, R. S. *Story of the confederacy* (rev. ed., Indianapolis, 1957).

Detailed Studies

ECONOMIC DEVELOPMENTS

C 1766 Fite, E. D. *Social and industrial conditions in the North during the Civil War* (New York, 1910).

C 1767 Ramsdell, C. W. *Behind the lines in the southern confederacy* (Baton Rouge, 1944).

DIPLOMACY

C 1768 Adams, E. D. *Great Britain and the American Civil War* (new ed., New York, 1957).

C 1769 Monaghan, J. *Diplomat in carpet slippers* (Indianapolis, 1945); Lincoln and northern diplomacy.

C 1770 Owsley, F. L. *King Cotton diplomacy* (rev. ed., Chicago, 1959).

POLITICS

C 1771 Hendricks, B. J. *Statesmen of the lost cause* (Boston, 1939); the Confederate cabinet.

C 1772 —— *Lincoln's War cabinet* (Boston, 1946).

C 1773 Williams, T. H. *Lincoln and the Radicals* (Madison, Wis., 1941).

STRATEGY AND COMMAND

C 1774 Fuller, J. F. C. *The Generalship of Ulysses S. Grant* (1929).

C 1775 Maurice, Sir F. *Statesmen and soldiers of the Civil War* (Boston, 1926).

C 1776 Vandiver, F. *Rebel brass* (Baton Rouge, 1956); the confederate command system.

C 1777 Williams, T. H. *Lincoln and his generals* (New York, 1952).

MILITARY ACCOUNTS

C 1778 Catton, B. *Mr Lincoln's army* (New York, 1951).

C 1779 —— *Glory road* (New York, 1952).

C 1780 —— *A Stillness at Appomattox* (New York, 1954).

These deal with the Northern army of the Potomac.

c 1781   Freeman, D. S. *R. E. Lee* (4 vols., New York, 1934–5).
c 1782   —— *Lee's lieutenants* (3 vols., New York, 1942–4).
c 1783   Henderson, G. F. R. *Stonewall Jackson and the American Civil War* (2 vols., 1898).
c 1784   Horn, S. F. *The Army of Tennessee* (rev. ed., Norman, Okla., 1953); the confederate army in the western theatre.
c 1785   Sandburg, C. *Abraham Lincoln: the war years* (4 vols., New York, 1939).
c 1786   Thomas, B. P. *Abraham Lincoln* (New York, 1952).
c 1787   West, R. S. *Mr Lincoln's navy* (New York, 1957).
c 1788   Williams, K. P. *Lincoln finds a general* (5 vols., New York, 1949–59).

See also:

c 508 Jordan, D. and Pratt, E. J.

54   The United States (vol. XI, ch. xviii)

General Studies

c 1789   Oberholzer, E. P. *A history of the United States since the Civil War* (5 vols., New York, 1917–37).
c 1753   Rhodes, J. F. *History of the United States from the compromise of 1850*, already mentioned, continued as *History of the United States from Hayes to McKinley* (New York, 1919) and *The McKinley and Roosevelt Administrations* (New York, 1922).

Both retain their value as full-scale histories of the period, though requiring amplification and modification at many points.

In *The New American Nation* series:

c 1790   Faulkner, H. U. *Politics, reform and expansion 1890–1900* (New York, 1959).

Detailed Studies

THE POLITICAL SYSTEM

c 1791   Bryce, Lord. *The American Commonwealth* (2 vols., New York and London, 1882 and several later eds.).
c 1792   Wilson, Woodrow. *Congressional government* (New York, 1885; new ed., 1957).

These are classic studies which remain of primary importance.

c 1793   Josephson, M. *The Politicos* (New York, 1938); readable and well-informed, but his judgment should not be accepted without consulting some of the collections of letters and papers, reminiscences and modern biographies, such as:
c 1794   Hesseltine, W. B. *Ulysses S. Grant: politician* (New York, repr. 1957).
c 1795   Nevins, A. *Grover Cleveland* (New York, 1932).
c 1796   Williams, C. R. (ed.). *R. B. Hayes: diary and letters* (5 vols., Columbus, Ohio, 1922–6).

Political corruption in municipal government may be studied in:

c 1797   Steffens, L. *The Shame of cities* (New York, repr. 1957).
c 1798   —— *Autobiography* (New York, 1931).
c 1799   Zink, H. *City bosses in the United States* (Durham, N.C., 1930).

An administrative history, with many illuminating sidelights on political practices, is:

c 1800   White, L. D. *The Republican era* (New York, 1958).

ECONOMIC HISTORY

c 47   Cochran, T. C. and Miller, W. *The age of enterprise* (New York, 1943).
c 1801   Dewey, D. R. *Financial history of the United States* (10th ed., New York, 1928).
c 1802   Kirkland, E. C. *Industry comes of age* (New York, 1961).

THE SOCIAL SYSTEM

c 1803   Commons, J. R. and others. *History of Labor in the United States* (4 vols., New York, 1918–35).
c 1804   Nevins, A. *The emergence of modern America, 1865–98* (New York, 1927).
c 1805   Schlesinger, A. M. sen. *The rise of the city* (New York, 1938).
c 1806   Ulman, L. *The rise of the national trade union: the development and significance of its structure, governing institutions, and economic policies* (Cambridge, Mass., 1955).

RECONSTRUCTION

c 1807   Beale, H. K. *The critical year* (New York, repr. 1958).
c 1808   Beale, H. K. (ed.). *Diary of Gideon Welles* (3 vols., New York, 1960); a new edition with many emendations.
c 1809   Kendrick, B. B. *The journal of the committee of fifteen on reconstruction* (New York, 1914); an essential source document for congressional policy with a valuable commentary.
c 1810   Stryker, L. P. *Andrew Johnson: a study in courage* (New York, 1937).

All the above works are hostile, in some cases bitterly hostile, to Congress; a different point of view is represented in:

c 1811   Brodie, F. *Thaddeus Stevens: scourge of the south* (New York, 1959).
c 1812   McKitrick, E. *Andrew Johnson and reconstruction* (Chicago, 1960).
c 1813   Sharkey, R. P. *Money, class and party: an economic study of civil war and reconstruction* (Baltimore, 1959).

Sharply contrasted views of the south during reconstruction are presented by:

c 1814   Coulter, E. M. *The South during reconstruction* (Baton Rouge, 1947).
c 1815   Daniels, J. *Prince of carpetbaggers* (Philadelphia and New York, 1958)

THE SOUTH AFTER RECONSTRUCTION

c 1816   Cash, W. B. *The mind of the south* (New York, repr., 1954); a brilliant and provocative interpretation.

c 1817   Santis, V. P. de. *Republicans face the southern question: the new departure, 1877–97* (Baltimore, 1959).

c 1818   Woodward, C. V. *Reunion and reaction: the compromise of 1877 and the end of reconstruction* (Boston, 1951).

c 1819   —— *Origins of the new South* (Baton Rouge, 1951).

THE WEST AND AGRARIAN RADICALISM

c 1820   Hicks, J. R. *The populist revolt* (Minneapolis, 1931).

c 1821   Hofstadter, R. *The age of reform* (New York, 1956).

c 1822   Shannon, F. A. *The farmer's last frontier* (*The Economic History of the United States*, vol. 5) (New York, 1945).

THE AMERICAN MIND IN THE LATER NINETEENTH CENTURY

c 1823   Commager, H. S. *The American Mind* (New York, 1950).

c 1824   Dorfman, J. *The economic mind in American civilization*, vol. 3 (New York, 1949).

See also:

B 1716 Curti, M.; c 548 Hofstadter, R.

55   The United States and the old world (vol. xi, ch. xxiv)
                        General Studies

See, on the diplomatic side:

c 1825   Bemis, S. F. and Griffin, G. G. (eds.). *Guide to the Diplomatic history of the United States, 1775–1921* (Washington, D.C., 1935).

There are also several other useful works by Bemis:

c 977   Bemis, S. F. *A Diplomatic History of the United States*, already mentioned.

c 1826   —— *A Short history of American foreign policy and diplomacy* (New York, 1959).

c 1827   Bemis, S. F. (ed.). *The American secretaries of state and their diplomacy*, vols. 7 and 8 (New York, 1928) and vol. 9 (New York, 1929).

The study of migration history is developing rapidly at present. The most recent survey is:

c 1828   Jones, M. A. *American immigration* (Chicago, 1960).

The student should also consult:

c 1829   Thistlethwaite, F. 'Migration from Europe overseas in the nineteenth and twentieth centuries', *Rapports* of the XIth International Historical Congress, 5 (Stockholm, 1960), pp. 32–60, which contains note references to a great body of material.

Further studies on emigration are:

C 1830   Handlin, O. *The Uprooted* (Boston, 1952).
C 1831   Hansen, M. L. *The Immigrant in American history* (Cambridge, Mass., 1942); a series of germinal essays, collected and edited by A. M. Schlesinger.
C 1832   Higham, J. *Strangers in the land. Patterns of American Nativism, 1860–1925* (New Brunswick, N.J., 1955); bibliography.

There is no general study of the European attitude to the United States, nor, for that matter, of the American attitude to Europe, though on the latter see:

C 1833   Kohn, H. *American nationalism. An interpretative essay* (New York, 1957).

Detailed Studies

American relations with other powers may be studied in the following:

GREAT BRITAIN

C 1834   Campbell, A. E. *Great Britain and the United States, 1895–1903* (1960).

See also:

C 1701 Allen, H. C.; C 1702 Allen, H. C.

GERMANY

C 1835   Vagts, A. *Deutschland und die Vereinigten Staaten in der Weltpolitik* (1935).

RUSSIA

C 1836   Bailey, T. A. *America faces Russia. Russian–American relations from early times to our day* (Ithaca, 1960); bibliography.
C 1837   Williams, W. A. *American–Russian relations, 1781–1947* (New York, 1952).

SPAIN

C 1838   Chadwick, F. E. *The relations of the United States and Spain. Diplomacy* (New York, 1909).
C 1839   Freidel, F. *The splendid little war* (Boston, 1958); deals graphically with the Spanish–American war.

CANADA

C 1840   Brebner, J. B. *North Atlantic triangle. The interplay of Canada, the United States and Great Britain* (New Haven, 1945).
C 1841   Callahan, J. M. *American foreign policy in Canadian relations* (New York, 1937).
C 1842   Tansill, C. C. *Canadian–American relations, 1871–1911* (New Haven, 1943).

MEXICO

C 1843   Callahan, J. M. *American foreign policy in Mexican relations* (New York, 1932).

For various aspects of American foreign relations see:

c 1844 Alstyne, R. W. van. *The Rising American Empire* (Oxford, 1960).
c 1845 Beale, H. K. *Theodore Roosevelt and the rise of America to world power* (Baltimore, 1956).
c 1846 Bemis, S. F. *The Latin American policy of the United States* (New York, 1943).
c 1847 Dulles, F. R. *America's rise to world power 1898–1954* (1955); (*New American Nation* Series) the first chapters are introductory and deal with the earlier period. Bibliography.
c 1848 Griswold, A. W. *The far eastern policy of the United States* (New York, 1943).
c 1849 Perkins, D. *The Monroe doctrine 1867–1907* (Baltimore, 1937).
c 1850 Pratt, J. W. *America's colonial experiment* (New York, 1950).

Material on the cultural links between the United States and Europe in the later nineteenth century is sparse, but, in addition to the books by H. C. Allen cited above, the following may be mentioned:

c 1851 Heindel, R. H. *The American impact on Great Britain, 1898–1914* (Philadelphia, 1940).
c 1852 Pelling, H. *America and the British left* (1956).

56 The United States of America (vol. XII, ch. vii)
General Studies

A useful general narrative is:

c 1853 Dulles, F. R. *The United States since 1865* (*The University of Michigan history of the world*, Ann Arbor, 1959).

Several volumes cover this period, with elaborate bibliographies, in the major historical series:

A History of American Life, vols. 11–13:

c 1854 Faulkner, H. U. *The quest for social justice 1898–1914* (New York, 1959).
c 1855 Slosson, P. W. *The great crusade and after 1914–1928* (New York, 1930).
c 1856 Wecter, D. *The age of the great depression 1929–1941* (New York, 1956).

The New American Nation series:

c 1857 Mowry, G. E. *The era of Theodore Roosevelt 1900–1912* (New York, 1958).
c 1858 Link, A. S. *Woodrow Wilson and the progressive era* (New York, 1954).
c 1847 Dulles, F. R. *America's rise to world power 1898–1954*; already mentioned.

Detailed Studies
ECONOMIC HISTORY

The period is covered in vols. 7–9 of *The Economic History of the United States*, David, H. and others, eds.

c 1859 Faulkner, H. U. *The decline of Laissez Faire 1897–1917* (New York, 1951).

C 1860   Soule, G. *Prosperity decade. From war to depression 1917–1929* (New York, 1947).
C 1861   Mitchell, B. *Depression decade. From new era through new deal 1929–1941* (New York, 1947).

SOCIAL HISTORY

C 1862   Lynd, R. S. and H. M. *Middletown. A study in contemporary American culture* (New York and London, 1929).
C 1863   —— *Middletown in transition. A study in cultural conflicts* (New York and London, 1937).
C 1864   Myrdal, G. (with the assistance of R. Sterner and A. Rose). *An American Dilemma. The Negro problem and modern democracy* (2 vols., New York, 1944).
C 1865   *Recent social trends in the United States. Report of the President's research committee on social trends*, with foreword by Herbert Hoover (2 vols., New York, 1933).
C 1866   Taft, P. *The A.F. of L. in the time of Gompers* (New York, 1957).
C 1867   —— *The A.F. of L. From the death of Gompers to the merger* (New York, 1959).

FOREIGN POLICY

Reference should be made to the preceding bibliographies.
C 1868   Langer, W. L. and Gleason, S. E. *The challenge to isolation* (New York, 1952).
C 1869   —— *The undeclared war 1940–1941* (1953).
C 1870   Tansill, C. C. *Back door to war. The Roosevelt foreign policy 1933–1941* (Chicago, 1952).

BIOGRAPHIES

C 1871   Blum, J. M. *The Republican Roosevelt* (Cambridge, Mass., 1954).
C 1872   Freidel, F. *Franklin D. Roosevelt. The apprenticeship: The Ordeal: The Triumph* (3 vols., Boston, 1952, 1954, 1956).
C 1873   Hoover, H. *Memoirs* (3 vols., 1952).
C 1874   —— *State papers* (Myers, W. S., ed.) (Garden City, N.Y., 1934).
C 1875   Link, A. S. *Wilson. The road to the White House: The new freedom* (Princeton, 1947, 1956).
C 1876   Pringle, H. F. *Theodore Roosevelt* (1932).
C 1877   —— *The life and times of William Howard Taft* (2 vols., New York, 1939).
C 1878   Pusey, M. J. *Charles Evans Hughes* (2 vols., New York, 1951).
C 1879   Roosevelt, F. D. *Public papers and addresses* (Rosenman, S. I., ed.) (13 vols., New York, 1939–50).
C 1880   Roosevelt, Theodore. *Letters* (Morison, E. E. and others, eds.) (8 vols., Cambridge, Mass., 1951–4).
C 1881   —— *Works* (24 vols., New York, 1923–6).
C 1882   Schlesinger, A. M. jr. *The age of Roosevelt. The crisis of the old order: The triumph of the new deal* (2 vols., Boston and London, 1957, Boston, 1958).

c 1883   Sherwood, R. E. *Roosevelt and Hopkins. An intimate history* (1948).
c 1884   Stimson, H. L. (and Bundy, McG.) *On active service in peace and war* (1949).
c 1885   Walworth, A. *Woodrow Wilson. American prophet* (2 vols., 1958).
c 1886   Wilson, Woodrow. *Public papers* (Baker, R. S. and Dodd, W. E. eds.) (6 vols., Garden City, N.Y., 1925–7).

57   **The Emancipation of Latin America (vol. IX, ch. xxiii)**
         General Studies

For bibliographies see the parallel book-lists in Sections A and B and the list on 'Spain, Portugal and their empires' in Section B. See also on the period of this chapter:

c 1887   Humphreys, R. A. 'The Historiography of the Spanish–American revolutions', *HAHR*, **36** (1956).

General introductions to this period include:

c 1888   Robertson, W. S. *Rise of the Spanish–American republics as told in the lives of the liberators* (New York and London, 1918).

Also, though less comprehensive in scope:

c 1889   Humphreys, R. A. *Liberation in South America, 1806–27. The career of James Paroissien* (1952).

On the action of Bolívar and San Martín see:

c 1890   Masur, G. *Simón Bolívar* (Albuquerque, New Mexico, 1948); the best biography of the great northern 'liberator' in any language.
c 1891   Mitre, B. *Historia de San Martín y de la emancipación sudamericana* (4 vols., Buenos Aires, 1888–9); an Argentine classic, many times reprinted.
c 1892   Piccirilli, R. *San Martín y la política de los pueblos* (Buenos Aires, 1957).

Source materials available in English include:

c 1893   Webster, Sir C. K. (ed.). *Britain and the independence of Latin America, 1812–30. Select documents from the foreign office archives* (2 vols., 1938); which is supplemented by:
c 1894   Humphreys, R. A. (ed.). *British consular reports on the trade and politics of Latin America, 1824–26* (1940).
c 1895   Manning, W. R. (ed.). *Diplomatic correspondence of the United States concerning the independence of the Latin American nations* (3 vols., New York, 1925).
c 1896   Lecuna, V. and Bierck, H. A. (eds.). *Selected writings of Bolívar* (2 vols., New York, 1951).

Detailed Studies

REGIONAL STUDIES

THE DISSOLUTION OF THE OLD VICEROYALTY OF THE RÍO DE LA PLATA

C 1897 Arnade, C. W. *The Emergence of the republic of Bolivia* (Gainesville, Fla., 1957).

C 1898 Levene, R. *Ensayo histórico sobre la revolución de mayo y Mariano Moreno* (3 vols., 2nd ed., Buenos Aires, 1925).

C 1899 Piccirilli, R. *Rivadavia y su tiempo* (2 vols., Buenos Aires, 1943).

C 1900 Street, J. *Artigas and the emancipation of Uruguay* (Cambridge, 1959).

THE ESTABLISHMENT OF BRAZILIAN INDEPENDENCE

C 1901 Manchester, A. K. *British pre-eminence in Brazil: its rise and decline* (Chapel Hill, N.C., 1933); and the contemporary work:

C 1902 Armitage, J. *The History of Brazil* (2 vols., 1836).

NORTHERN SOUTH AMERICA

C 1903 Bushnell, D. *The Santander regime in Great Colombia* (Newark, Delaware, 1954).

C 1904 Robertson, W. S. *The Life of Miranda* (2 vols., Chapel Hill, N.C., 1929)

MEXICO

C 1905 Castillo Ledón, L. *Hidalgo. La vida del héroe* (2 vols., Mexico, 1948–9).

C 1906 Robertson, W. S. *Iturbide of Mexico* (Durham, N.C., 1952).

SPECIAL ASPECTS

C 1907 Belaunde, V. A. *Bolívar and the political thought of the Spanish American revolution* (Baltimore, 1938); opens up the field of political ideas.

C 1908 Griffin, C. C. 'Economic and social aspects of the era of Spanish–American independence', *HAHR*, **29** (1949); discusses the havoc wrought by the revolutionary wars on the one hand and the stimulus afforded by world trade on the other.

C 1909 Hasbrouck, A. *Foreign legionaries in the liberation of Spanish South America* (New York, 1928); mostly concerned with northern South America.

DIPLOMATIC HISTORY

On British policy consult:

C 1910 Kaufmann, W. W. *British policy and the independence of Latin America, 1804–1828* (New Haven, 1951).

See also:

C 820 Temperley, H. W. V.; C 821 Webster, Sir C. K.

On the policy of the United States:

C 1911   Perkins, D. *The Monroe doctrine, 1823–1826* (Cambridge, Mass., 1927).
C 1912   Rippy, J. F. *Rivalry of the United States and Great Britain over Latin America, 1808–1830* (Baltimore, 1929).
C 1913   Whitaker, A. P. *The United States and the independence of Latin America, 1800–1830* (Baltimore, 1941).

On French policy:

C 788   Robertson, W. S. *France and Latin American independence* (Baltimore, 1939); already mentioned.

On the Panama congress of 1826:

C 1914   Lockey, J. B. *Pan Americanism: its beginnings* (New York, 1920).

58   The States of Latin America (vol. x, ch. xxv)
          The States of Latin America (vol. xi, ch. xix)

For bibliographical aids, apart from those mentioned above, see two articles in the *Hispanic American Historical Review*.:

C 1915   Barager, J. R. 'The Historiography of the Río de la Plata area since 1830', **39** (1959).
C 1916   Stein, S. J. 'The Historiography of Brazil, 1808–1889', **40** (1960).

General Studies

C 1917   Humphreys, R. A. *The Evolution of modern Latin America* (New York, 1946); an excellent brief sketch which emphasises the history of the larger countries and of the major themes.
B 1866   Oliveira Lima, M. de. *The Evolution of Brazil, compared with that of Spanish and Anglo–Saxon America* (Stanford, 1914); one of the few comparative essays; already mentioned.
C 1918   Williams, M. W. *The People and politics of Latin America* (Boston, 1930); one of the most accurate surveys of Latin American history. It deals country by country with the period since independence.

Some general surveys of particular themes:

C 1919   Bain, H. F. and Reed, T. T. *Ores and industries in South America* (New York, 1934); deals chiefly with mining.
C 1920   Brady, G. S. and Long, W. R. *The Railways of South America* (in 3 parts) (Washington, 1926–30); the co-author has also published works on railways in Mexico and Central America.
C 1921   Crawford, W. R. *A Century of Latin American thought* (Cambridge, Mass., 1944); an introduction to the social and political ideas of representative nineteenth century figures.
C 1922   Jones, C. F. *The Commerce of South America* (Boston, 1928).
C 1923   Kirstein, L. *The Latin American collection of the museum of modern art* (New York, 1943); a pioneer sketch.

C 1924   Rippy, J. F. *Latin America and the industrial age* (New York, 1947);
describes the advent of modern technology in mining, transport, com-
munications, and public utilities.

C 1925   Wythe, G. *Industry in Latin America* (New York, 1945); though chiefly
devoted to a later period is very useful.

See also:

B 1104 Mecham, J. L.

Individual countries and regions:

C 1926   Basadre, J. *Historia de la república de Perú* (Lima, 1949).
C 1927   Bellegarde, D. *La nation haitien* (1938).
C 1928   Chapman, C. E. *History of the Cuban republic* (New York, 1927).
C 1929   Galdames, L. *A History of Chile* (Eng. trans., Chapel Hill, N.C., 1951).
C 1930   Guerra y Sánchez, R. *Manual de historia de Cuba* (Havana, 1938).
C 1931   Haring, C. H. *Empire in Brazil. A new world experiment with monarchy*
(Cambridge, Mass., 1958).
C 1932   Kirkpatrick, F. A. *A History of the Argentine Republic* (Cambridge,
1931).
C 1933   Munro, D. G. *The Five republics of Central America* (New York, 1918).
C 1934   Parkes, H. B. *A History of Mexico* (rev. ed., Boston, 1950).
C 1935   Priestley, H. I. *The Mexican nation, a history* (New York, 1924).
C 1936   Schoenrich, O. *Santo Domingo* (New York, 1918).
C 1937   Warren, H. G. *Paraguay. An informal history* (Norman, Okla., 1959).

To these should be added three notable achievements of twentieth-
century historiography:

C 1938   Encina, F. *Historia de Chile desde la prehistoria hasta 1891* (20 vols.,
Santiago, 1941–52).
C 1939   Gil Fortoul, J. *Historia constitucional de Venezuela* (2nd ed., rev., 3 vols.,
Caracas, 1930).
C 1940   Levene, R. (ed.). *Historia de la nación argentina desde los orígines hasta
la organización definitiva en 1862* (10 vols., Buenos Aires, 1936–42).

Detailed Studies

ARGENTINA

C 1941   Bunkley, A. W. *The life of Sarmiento* (Princeton, 1952).
C 1942   Burgin, M. *The economic aspects of Argentine federalism, 1820–1852*
(Cambridge, Mass., 1946); a fundamental study.
C 1943   Cady, J. F. *Foreign intervention in the Río de la Plata, 1838–50* (Phila-
delphia, 1929); examines British, French and United States diplomacy.
C 1944   Quesada, E. *La época de Rosas* (Buenos Aires, 1898); a classic of
Argentine historiography, many times reprinted.
C 1945   Sarmiento, D. F. *Life in the Argentine republic in the days of the tyrants:
or civilization and barbarism* (translated by Mrs Horace Mann, 1868); a
famous tract for the times, first published in 1845.

BRAZIL

c 1946 Hill, L. F. 'The abolition of the African slave trade to Brazil', *HAHR*, 11 (1931).

c 1947 Marchant, A. 'A New portrait of Mauá the banker; a man of business in nineteenth-century Brazil', *ibid.*, **30** (1950).

c 1948 Stein, S. J. *Vassouras. A Brazilian coffee county, 1850–1900* (Cambridge, Mass., 1957).

c 1949 Williams, M. W. *Dom Pedro the magnanimous, second emperor of Brazil* (Chapel Hill, N.C., 1937); the best biography of the scholar-emperor.

CHILE AND PERU

c 1950 Davis, W. C. *The Last conquistadores: the Spanish intervention in Peru and Chile, 1833–1866* (Athens, Ga., 1950).

c 1951 Donoso, R. *Las ideas políticas en Chile* (Mexico, 1946).

c 1952 Stewart, Watt. *Henry Meiggs, Yankee Pizarro* (Durham, N.C., 1946).

c 1953 —— *Chinese bondage in Peru. A history of the Chinese coolie in Peru, 1849–1874* (Durham, N.C., 1951).

PARAGUAY

c 1954 Box, P. H. *The origins of the Paraguayan war* (Urbana, Ill., 1930); a masterly analysis.

CENTRAL AMERICA

c 1955 Scroggs, W. O. *Filibusters and financiers: the story of William Walker and his associates* (New York, 1916); a standard work.

c 1956 Williams, M. W. *Anglo–American isthmian diplomacy, 1815–1915* (Washington, 1916); in need of revision, but still valuable.

MEXICO

c 1957 Beals, C. *Porfirio Díaz, dictator of Mexico* (Philadelphia, 1932).

c 1958 Callcott, W. H. *Church and state in Mexico, 1822–57* (Durham, N.C., 1926).

c 1959 Corti, E. C. *Maximilian and Charlotte of Mexico* (Eng. trans., 2 vols., New York, 1928); the major diplomatic study.

c 1960 Roeder, R. *Juárez and his Mexico* (2 vols., New York, 1947); the best biography, not annotated.

c 1961 Scholes, W. V. *Mexican politics during the Juárez regime, 1855–72* (Columbia, Mo., 1957).

See also:

c 1756 Smith, J. H.

CUBA

c 1962 Mañach, J. *Martí, apostle of freedom* (Eng. trans., New York, 1950).

59   Latin America, 1899–1949 (vol. xii, ch. viii)

General Studies

The best contemporary guide to the Latin American countries is:

c 1963   Davies, H. (ed.). *The South American handbook* (London, Trade and Travel publications, published annually).

Among the very numerous general descriptions and general histories in the twentieth century, the following call for special mention:

c 1964   Arciniegas, G. *The state of Latin America* (New York, 1952).
c 1965   Bernstein, H. *Modern and contemporary Latin America* (Philadelphia, 1952); a convenient popular general history.
c 1966   Bryce, J. *South America: observations and impressions* (rev. ed., New York, 1914).
c 1967   García Calderón, F. *Latin America, its rise and progress* (Eng. trans. 1913); a pioneer work by a Peruvian scholar.
c 1968   *The Republics of South America* (Royal Institute of International Affairs, Oxford, 1937); a comprehensive and penetrating report by a study group.

Detailed Studies

POLITICAL, ECONOMIC, CULTURAL

c 1969   Azevedo, E. *Brazilian culture* (New York, 1950).
c 1970   Hanson, S. G. *Economic development in Latin America* (Washington, 1951).
c 1971   Henríquez-Ureña, P. *Literary currents in Hispanic America* (Cambridge, Mass., 1945); a brilliant survey of the whole field of arts and letters.
c 1972   Ireland, G. *Boundaries, possessions and conflicts in South America* (Cambridge, Mass., 1938).
c 1973   —— *Boundaries, possessions and conflicts in central and north America and the Caribbean* (Cambridge, Mass., 1941).
c 1974   Jones, C. L. *The Caribbean area since 1900* (New York, 1936).
c 1975   Munro, D. G. *The United States and the Caribbean area* (Boston, 1934).
c 1976   Normano, J. F. *The struggle for South America: economy and ideology* (1931); a penetrating account of developments between the two world wars.
c 1977   Putnam, S. *Marvelous journey. A survey of four centuries of Brazilian writing* (New York, 1948).
c 1978   Scott, J. B. (ed.). *The international conferences of American states, 1889–1928* (New York, 1931).
c 1979   —— the *First Supplement, 1933–40* (Washington, 1940).
c 1980   Stuart, G. H. *Latin America and the United States* (New York, 1955).
c 1981   Whitaker, A. P. *The United States and South America: the northern republics* (Cambridge, Mass., 1948).
c 1982   —— *The Western hemisphere idea: its rise and decline* (Ithaca, 1954).

ARGENTINA

c 1983 Hanson, S. G. *Argentine meat and the British market* (Stanford, 1938).
c 1984 Jefferson, M. *Peopling the Argentine pampa* (New York, 1926).
c 1985 Martinez, A. B. and Lewandowski, M. *The Argentine in the twentieth century* (1911).
c 1986 Rennie, Y. F. *The Argentine republic* (New York, 1945).
c 1987 Whitaker, A. P. *The United States and Argentina* (Cambridge, Mass., 1954).
c 1988 —— *Argentine upheaval: Perón's fall and the new regime* (New York, 1956).
c 1989 Wilgins, A. C. (ed.). *Argentina, Brazil and Chile since independence* (Washington, D.C., 1935).

BRAZIL

c 1990 Lowenstein, K. *Brazil under Vargas* (New York, 1942).
c 1991 Smith, T. L. *Brazil, people and institutions* (Baton Rouge, 1954).

See also:
B 1864 Calógeras, J. P.; B 1865 Normano, J. F.

CHILE

c 1992 Ellsworth, P. T. *Chile, an economy in transition* (New York, 1945).
c 1993 McBride, G. M. *Chile, land and society* (New York, 1936).

MEXICO

c 1994 Chine, H. F. *The United States and Mexico* (Cambridge, Mass., 1953).
c 1995 Cosío Villegas, D. (ed.). *Historia moderna de México* (7 vols., Mexico, 1955–); a large, co-operative, authoritative study.
c 1996 *The economic development of Mexico. Report of the combined Mexican working party* (International bank for reconstruction and development, Baltimore, 1953).
c 1997 Whetten, N. L. *Rural Mexico* (Chicago, 1948); a detailed study of the agrarian revolution.
c 1998 Whitaker, A. P. (ed.). *Mexico to-day* (Philadelphia, 1940); a collection of informative essays by Mexican and North American writers.

ASIA AND AFRICA

60 Relations with South and South-East Asia (vol. IX, ch. xx)
India 1840–1905 (vol. XI, ch. xv)
The Western question in Asia and North Africa, 1900–45: India (vol. XII, ch. ix. 2)

General Studies

The most useful bibliographical guide to both manuscript and printed work is to be found in:

A 1655 *Cambridge History of India*, vols. V and VI (Cambridge, 1929, 1932).

Shorter bibliographies of printed works will be found at the relevant chapter ends of :

c 1999   *Oxford history of India* (3rd ed., Oxford, 1958).

THE PERIOD 1800–40

This list includes books on Ceylon and South-east Asia as well as on British India.

Published selections of documents:

c 2000   Firminger, W. K. (ed.). *Fifth report from the select committee of the House of Commons on the affairs of the East India company dated 28th July, 1812* (3 vols., Calcutta, 1917–18).

c 2001   Martin, M. (ed.). *Despatches, minutes and correspondence of the marquess Wellesley* (5 vols., 1836–7).

c 2002   Mendis, G. C. (ed.). *Colebrooke–Cameron papers. Documents on British colonial policy in Ceylon, 1796–1833* (2 vols., Oxford, 1956).

c 2003   *Selections of papers from the records at the East-India House, relating to the revenue, police, and civil and criminal justice under the [East India] Company's Governments in India* (4 vols., 1820–6).

c 2004   Sharp, H. (ed.). *Selections from educational records*, part i, *1789–1839* (Calcutta, 1920).

Detailed Studies

c 2005   Ascoli, F. D. *Early revenue history of Bengal and the fifth report, 1812* (Oxford, 1917).

c 2006   Ballhatchet, K. A. *Social policy and social change in western India, 1817–30* (1957).

c 2007   Bastin, J. *Native policies of Sir Stamford Raffles in Java and Sumatra* (Oxford, 1957).

c 2008   Basu, P. *Oudh and the East India Company, 1785–1801* (Lucknow, 1943).

c 2009   Bose, N. S. *The Indian awakening and Bengal* (Calcutta, 1960).

c 2010   Embree, A. *Charles Grant and British rule in India* (1962).

c 2011   Glasenapp, H. von. *Das Indienbild deutscher Denker* (Stuttgart, 1960).

c 2012   Gleig, G. R. *Life of Sir Thomas Munro* (3 vols., 1830).

c 2013   Greenberg, M. *British trade and the opening of China* (Cambridge, 1951).

c 2014   Gupta, P. C. *Baji Rao II and the East India Company, 1796–1818* (Oxford, 1939).

c 2015   Mills, L. A. *Ceylon under British rule* (1933).

c 2016   Parkinson, C. N. *Trade in the eastern seas, 1793–1813* (Cambridge, 1937).

B 533   —— *War in the eastern seas, 1793–1815* (1954).

c 2017   Pieris, P. E. *Tri Sinhala, the last phase, 1796–1815* (Cambridge, n.d.).

c 2018   Roberts, P. E. *India under Wellesley* (1929).

c 2019   Silva, C. R. de. *Ceylon under the British occupation, 1795–1833* (Colombo, 1953).

c 2020   Stokes, E. *The English Utilitarians and India* (Oxford, 1959).

BRITISH INDIA AFTER 1840

Standard works covering this period are:

A 1655   *The Cambridge history of India*, vols. V and VI.
C 2021   Majumdar, R. C. (ed.). *The History and Culture of the Indian people* (Bombay, 1961), vol. 9 (*The British domination*).

Shorter summaries are:

C 2022   Dodwell, H. H. *A sketch of the history of India 1858–1918* (1925).
C 2023   Mazumdar, R. C., Raychaudhuri, H. C., Datta, K. K. *An advanced history of India*, part iii (1946).
C 1999   *The Oxford history of India*, part iii by T. G. P. Spear (3rd ed., 1958).
C 2024   Chirol, Sir V. *India* (1926).
C 2025   Wint, G. *The British in Asia* (1947).

Two recent collections of documents are:

C 2026   Gwyer, Sir M. and Appadorai, A. *Speeches and documents on the Indian constitution 1921–47* (2 vols., 1957).
C 2027   Philips, C. H. (ed.). *The evolution of India and Pakistan 1858 to 1957: select documents* (1962).

THE DEVELOPMENT OF INDIA UNDER BRITISH RULE

ADMINISTRATION

C 2028   Strachey, Sir J. *India, its administration* (1911).

CONSTITUTION

C 2029   Coupland, Sir R. *Report on the constitutional problems in India*, parts i–iii (1942–3).
C 2030   —— *India. A restatement* (1945).
C 2031   Ilbert, Sir C. *The government of India: an historical survey* (1922).
C 2032   Keith, A. B. *Speeches and documents on Indian policy 1750–1921* (2 vols., 1922).
C 2033   —— *A constitutional history of India 1600–1935* (1936).

THE VICEROYS AND THEIR RULE

C 2034   Arnold, E. *Dalhousie's administration of British India* (2 vols., 1861).
C 2035   Fraser, L. *India under Curzon and after* (1911).
C 2036   Gopal, S. *The Viceroyalty of Lord Irwin 1926–31* (Oxford, 1957).
C 2037   Hardinge of Penshurst, Lord. *My Indian years 1910–16* (1948).
C 2038   Mary, Countess of Minto. *India, Minto and Morley 1905–10* (1934).

See also:

C 1045 Ronaldshay, Earl of., vol. 2.

THE SERVICES

C 2039   O'Malley, L. S. S. *The Indian civil service* (1937).
C 2040   Woodruff, P. *The men who ruled India*, vol. 2, *The guardians* (1954).

LOCAL SELF-GOVERNMENT

C 2041   Tinker, H. *Foundations of local self-government in India, Pakistan and Burma* (1954).

THE MUTINY OF 1857

C 2042   Holmes, T. R. E. *History of the Indian mutiny* (5th ed., 1904).
C 2043   Sen, S. N. *1857* (1957).

FOREIGN POLICY

C 2044   Kaye, J. W. *History of the war in Afghanistan* (3 vols., 4th ed., 1878).
C 2045   Prasad, Bisheshwar. *The foundations of India's foreign policy*, vol. 1, 1860–82 (1956).

See also:

c 1272 Rawlinson, Sir H.

THE FRONTIER

C 2046   Davies, C. C. *The problem of the north-west frontier* (Cambridge, 1932).

EDUCATION

C 2047   Mayhew, A. *The education of India* (1926).
C 2048   Trevelyan, C. E. *The education of the people of India* (1838).

ECONOMIC DEVELOPMENT

C 2049   Anstey, V. *The economic development of India* (4th ed., 1952).
C 2050   Buchanan, R. H. *Development of capitalist enterprise in India* (New York, 1934).
C 2051   Gadgil, D. R. *The industrial evolution of India* (1934).
C 2052   Knowles, L. C. A. *Economic development of the British overseas empire* (1924).
C 2053   Misra, B. B. *The Indian middle classes: their growth in modern times* (1961).

THE PEOPLES AND CULTURES OF INDIA

C 2054   O'Malley, L. S. S. (ed.). *Modern India and the West* (1941); a useful series of studies.

RELIGION

C 2055   Farquhar, J. N. *Modern religious movements in India* (New York, 1918).
C 2056   Richter, J. *History of missions in India* (1908).

THE INDIAN STATES

C 2057   Lee-Warner, Sir W. *The Native states of India* (1911).

THE PANJAB

B 1954   Cunningham, J. D. *History of the Sikhs* (1918); already mentioned.
C 2058   Singh, K. *The Sikhs* (1953).

INDIANS OVERSEAS

c 2059   Kondapi, C. *Indians overseas, 1838–1949* (Delhi, 1953).

INDIAN NATIONAL MOVEMENTS

c 2060   Andrews, C. F. and Mukerji, G. *The rise and growth of the Congress in India* (1938).
c 2061   Banerjea, Sir S. N. *A nation in making* (1925).
c 2062   Brecher, M. *Nehru, a political biography* (1959).
c 2063   Desai, A. R. *Social background of Indian nationalism* (Bombay, 1948).
c 2064   Gandhi, M. K. *An autobiography* (2nd ed., Ahmedabad, 1940).
c 2065   Nanda, B. R. *Mahatma Gandhi: a biography* (1958).
c 2066   Nehru, Jawaharlal. *An autobiography* (1936).
c 2067   —— *The discovery of India* (3rd ed., 1957).
c 2068   Sitaramayya, P. *The history of the Indian national congress* (2 vols., Bombay, 1946–7).
c 2069   Smith, W. R. *Nationalism and reform in India* (New Haven, 1938).
c 2070   Tahmankar, D. V. *Lokamanya Tilak* (1956).
c 2071   Tendulkar, D. G. *Mahatma. Life of Mohandas Karamchand Gandhi* (8 vols., Bombay, 1951–4).

On the Muslims see:

c 2072   Bolitho, H. *Jinnah, creator of Pakistan* (1954).
c 2073   Graham, G. F. I. *The life and work of Syed Ahmed Khan* (Edinburgh, 1885).
c 2074   Qureshi, I. H. *The Muslim community of the Indo–Pakistan subcontinent (610–1947)* (The Hague, 1962); the later chapters deal with the Muslim revival of the nineteenth century.
c 2075   Symonds, R. A. *The making of Pakistan* (3rd ed., 1957).

On the ending of British rule see:

c 2076   Lumby, E. W. R. *The transfer of power in India 1945–7* (1954).
c 2077   Menon, V. P. *The transfer of power in India* (1957).

61   **The Far East (vol. X, ch. xxvi)**
         China (vol. XI, ch. xvi)
         Japan (vol. XI, ch. xvii)
         The Western question in Asia and North Africa, 1900–45: South-east Asia (vol. XII, ch. ix. 3)

General histories of the Far East are listed below; for books on the Far East in international politics in the late nineteenth and twentieth centuries, see the bibliographies to vol. XI, ch. xxiii and vol. XII, ch. xv (Sec. C, **62**) below.

General histories

c 2078   Clyde, P. H. *The Far East: a history of the impact of the West on eastern Asia* (3rd ed., New York, 1958); the most used account.

C 2079   Michael, F. H. and Taylor, G. E. *The Far East in the modern world*
         (New York, 1956); the only survey to use recent studies of Asian
         specialists. Includes South-east Asia.
C 2080   Peffer, N. *The Far East. A modern history* (Ann Arbor, 1958).
C 2081   Vinacke, H. M. *A history of the Far East in modern times* (6th ed., New
         York, 1959); useful bibliographies at chapter ends. Includes South-east
         Asia.

China

SOURCE MATERIAL

C 2082   Hertslet, Sir E. (ed.). *Treaties etc. between Great Britain and China and
         between China and foreign powers* (3rd ed., 2 vols., 1908).
C 2083   Ssu-yü Teng and Fairbank, J. K. *China's response to the West: a docu-
         mentary survey 1839–1923* (Cambridge, Mass., 1954).

CONTEMPORARY ACCOUNTS

C 2084   Elgin, [8th] Earl of. *Letters and journals* (Walrond, T., ed.) (1872).
C 2085   Williams, S. Wells. *The middle kingdom* (rev. ed., 2 vols., 1883).

GENERAL STUDIES

C 2086   Cordier, H. *Histoire des relations de la Chine avec les puissances occiden-
         tales, 1860–1902* (3 vols., 1901–3); the best general work on China's
         relations with the West.
C 2087   Dulles, F. R. *China and America. The story of their relations since 1784*
         (Princeton, 1946).
C 2088   Li Chien-Nung. *The political history of China 1840–1928* (Eng. trans.,
         Princeton, 1956); bibliography.
C 2089   Hughes, E. R. *The invasion of China by the western world* (1937); on
         cultural and religious contacts.

On extraterritoriality in China and Japan see:

C 2090   Keeton, G. W. *The development of extraterritoriality in China* (2 vols.,
         1928).
C 2091   Jones, F. C. *Extraterritoriality in Japan* (New Haven, 1931).

The period to the end of the Taiping rebellion:

C 2092   Boardman, E. P. *Christian influence upon the ideology of the Taiping
         rebellion 1851–64* (Madison, Wisc., 1952).
C 2093   Bonner-Smith, B. and Lumby, W. R. (eds.). *The second China war
         1856–60* (Navy Records Society, 1954).
C 2094   Costin, W. C. *Great Britain and China 1833–60* (Oxford, 1937).
C 2095   Fairbank, J. K. *Trade and diplomacy on the China coast: the opening of
         the treaty ports 1842–54* (2 vols., Cambridge, Mass., 1953).
C 2096   Fox, G. *British admirals and Chinese pirates 1832–69* (1940).
C 2097   Hail, W. J. *Tsêng Kuo-Fan and the Taiping rebellion* (New Haven, 1927).
C 2098   Taylor, G. E. 'The Taiping rebellion: its economic background and
         social theory', *Chinese Social and Political Science Review*, **16** (1932–3).

c 2099   Waley, A. *The opium war through Chinese eyes* (1958).
c 2100   Wright, S. F. *Hart and the Chinese customs* (Belfast, 1950); deals with the early days of the inspectorate of customs.

See also:

c 2013 Greenberg, M.

The later nineteenth century:

For the reign of the empress dowager see:

c 2101   Bland, J. O. P. and Backhouse, E. *China under the empress dowager* (1910); reflects the point of view of the period. Contains the well-known translation of the 'diary of Ch'ing Shan', now known to be spurious.

A more recent work, using Chinese sources, for the internal history of the years 1862–74, valuable for the whole period, is:

c 2102   Wright, M. C. *The last stand of Chinese conservatism* (Stanford, 1957).

For biographies of well-known Chinese of the period, with much information on the general history, based on Chinese sources, see:

c 2103   Hummel, A. W. (ed.). *Eminent Chinese of the Ch'ing period* (2 vols., Washington, 1943).
c 2104   Chiang, S. T. *The Nien rebellion* (Seattle, 1954); deals with the aftermath of the Taiping rebellion and the restoration of internal peace.

For the Boxer rebellion see:

c 2105   Fleming, P. *The siege at Peking* (1959); full account of the siege of the legations and their relief, using eyewitness accounts and official sources.
c 2106   Tan, C. C. *The Boxer catastrophe* (New York, 1955).
c 2107   Thomson, H. C. *China and the powers* (1902); an eyewitness account of the campaign to relieve the legations and concessions at Tientsin.
c 2108   Weale, P. *Indiscreet letters from Peking* (1906); an eyewitness account of the siege of the legations. Entertaining, not wholly reliable, and rather malicious.
c 2109   Wu Yung. *The flight of an empress* (1906); a Chinese official's eyewitness account of the flight of the court from Peking.

Japan

The end of the Tokugawa period:

CONTEMPORARY ACCOUNTS

c 2110   Alcock, Sir R. *The capital of the tycoon. A narrative of three years' residence in Japan* (2 vols., 1863).
c 2111   Cosenza, M. E. (ed.). *The complete journal of Townsend Harris, first American consul and minister to Japan* (2nd ed., Rutland, Vt., 1959.)

MODERN STUDIES

c 2112   Beasley, W. G., trans. and ed. *Select documents on Japanese foreign policy 1853–68* (1955).
c 2113   Beasley, W. G. *Great Britain and the opening of Japan 1834–58* (1951).

C 2114   Craig, A. M. *Chōshū in the Meiji restoration* (Cambridge, Mass., 1961).
C 2115   Gubbins, J. H. *The progress of Japan 1853–71* (Oxford, 1911); with appendix of documents.
C 2116   Jansen, M. B. *Sakamoto Ryoma and the Meiji restoration* (Princeton, 1961).
C 2117   Keene, D. *The Japanese discovery of Europe* (1952).
C 2118   Sansom, G. *A History of Japan 1615–1867* (1964).
A 1546   —— *The Western world and Japan,* which has already been mentioned, traces Japan's political and cultural relations with the West to the end of the nineteenth century.
C 2119   Walworth, A. *Black ships off Japan: the story of Commodore Perry's expedition* (New York, 1946).

THE MEIJI ERA

General works dealing extensively with this period are:

C 2120   Allen, G. C. *A short economic history of modern Japan 1867–1937* (1946).
C 2121   Beasley, W. G. *The modern history of Japan* (1963).
C 2122   Borton, H. *Japan's modern century* (New York, 1955).
C 2123   Scalapino, R. A. *Democracy and the party movement in pre-war Japan* (Berkeley and Los Angeles, 1953); a detailed political history of the period after 1868. Valuable bibliography of works in Japanese.

See also:

C 110 Lockwood, W. W.

Works dealing specifically with the second half of the nineteenth century include:

C 2124   Beckmann, G. M. *The making of the Meiji constitution. The oligarchs and the constitutional development of Japan, 1868–91* (Lawrence, 1957); including translations of some important contemporary memoranda on constitutional issues.
C 2125   Fujii, Jintarō. *Outline of Japanese history in the Meiji era* (Eng. trans., Tokyo, 1958); a cultural history, part of a series entitled *Japanese culture in the Meiji era,* of which ten volumes had appeared by 1960. Other volumes deal with such subjects as religion, thought, customs, literature etc. The treatment is detailed, but uneven in quality.
C 2126   Ike, Nobutaka. *The beginnings of political democracy in Japan* (Baltimore, 1950); a study of early political parties.
C 2127   McLaren, W. W. *A political history of Japan during the Meiji era: 1867–1912* (1916).
C 2128   —— *Japanese government documents* (Transactions of the Asiatic Society of Japan, vol. 42, part i, Tokyo, 1914); a volume of translations of documents chiefly concerning the political, constitutional and administrative history of the Meiji period.
C 2129   Norman, E. H. *Japan's emergence as a modern state* (I.P.R. Inquiry series, New York, 1940); an analysis of political and economic problems of the period 1850–1900. Valuable bibliography of works in Japanese.

C 2130 Ōkuma, S. (ed.). *Fifty years of new Japan* (2 vols., 1910).
C 2131 Smith, T. C. *Political change and industrial development in Japan: government enterprise 1868–80* (Stanford and London, 1955).
C 2132 Wilson, R. A. *Genesis of the Meiji government in Japan 1868–71* (Berkeley and Los Angeles, 1957); a study of administration and of the abolition of the feudal system.

South-east Asia

Useful bibliographies are:

C 2133 Embree, J. F. and Dotson, L. O. *Bibliography of the peoples and cultures of mainland South-east Asia* (Cambridge, Mass., 1950).
C 2134 Kennedy, R. *Bibliography of Indonesian peoples and cultures* (rev. ed., 2 vols., New Haven, 1955).
C 2135 *Selected bibliography of the Philippines* (Philippine studies programme, University of Chicago) (New Haven, 1956).

Modern works:

C 2136 Allen, G. C. and Donnithorne, A. G. *Western enterprise in Indonesia and Malaya* (1957); bibliography.
C 2137 Bauer, P. T. *The Rubber industry: a study in competition and monopoly* (Cambridge, Mass., 1948).
C 2138 Blumberger, J. Th. P. *De communistische Beweging in Nederlandsch Indië* (Haarlem, 1928).
C 2139 Bousquet, G. H. *Dutch colonial policy through French eyes* (New York, 1940).
C 2140 Brock, J. O. M. *The economic development of the Netherlands Indies* (New York, 1942).
C 2141 Cady, J. F. *A history of modern Burma* (Ithaca, 1958); bibliography.
C 2142 Christian, J. L. *Modern Burma* (1942); bibliography.
C 2143 Devillers, P. *Histoire du Viet-Nam de 1940 à 1952* (1952).
C 2144 Emerson, R. *Malaysia; a study in direct and indirect rule* (1937).
C 2145 Furnivall, J. S. *Colonial policy and practice, a comparative study of Burma and Netherlands India* (Cambridge, 1948); bibliography.
C 2146 Grunder, G. A. and Livezey, W. *The Philippines and the United States* (Norman, Okla., 1951).
C 2147 Hall, D. G. E. *Burma* (3rd ed., 1960).
C 2148 Jacoby, E. *Agrarian unrest in South-east Asia* (New York, 1949).
C 2149 Kahin, G. McT. (ed.). *Governments and politics of South-east Asia* (Ithaca, 1959); bibliography.
C 2150 Kalaw, T. M. *The Philippine revolution* (Manila, 1925).
C 2151 Le Thanh Koi. *Le Viet-Nam* (1955).
C 2152 Mills, L. A. *British rule in eastern Asia* (1942).
C 2153 Nguyen-Ai-Quoc. (Ho Chi Minh). *Le Procès de la colonisation française* (1926).
C 2154 Priestley, H. I. *France overseas, a study of modern imperialism* (New York, 1938).
C 2155 Robequain, C. *The economic development of French Indo-China* (1940).

C 2156   Vella, W. *The impact of the West on government in Thailand* (Berkeley and Los Angeles, 1955).
C 2157   Winstedt, Sir R. *Malaya and its history* (1948).
C 2158   Worcester, D. C. *The Philippines, past and present* (New York, 1930).

See also:

A 1601 Hall, D. G. E.; B 1980 Furnivall, J. S.; B 1981 Vandenbosch, A.; B 1984 Forbes, W. Cameron; C 2041 Tinker, H.

62   Expansion in the Pacific and the Scramble for China (vol. xi, ch. xxiii)
         The Pacific in the First World War and in the Settlement (vol. xii, ch. xv)

International relations in the Pacific in the late nineteenth and twentieth centuries really form part of the general problems of world politics. Reference should therefore be made, particularly for the First World War and the peace settlement, to the bibliographies on 'The Politics of the European States' above.

General Studies

General studies of national and international politics in the Far East include:

C 2159   Morse, H. B. and MacNair, H. F. *Far Eastern international relations* (Boston, 1931); on Chinese external relations.
C 2160   MacNair, H. F. and Lach, D. *Modern Far Eastern international relations* (2nd ed., New York, 1955); external relations with an emphasis on the American role.

See also:

B 1979 Morse, H. B.; C 964 Hudson, G. F.; C 965 Renouvin, P.

EUROPEAN AND AMERICAN EXPANSION AT THE END OF THE NINETEENTH CENTURY

C 2161   Dennett, T. *Americans in Eastern Asia: a critical study of the policy of the United States with reference to China, Japan and Korea in the nineteenth century* (repr. New York, 1963); the most exhaustive account based on government documents.
C 2162   Hinsley, F. H. 'British foreign policy and colonial questions, 1895–1904', *Cambridge history of the British Empire*, vol. iii; a brief survey.
C 2163   Hubbard, G. E. *British Far Eastern policy* (New York, 1943); a standard work.
C 2164   Kiernan, E. V. G. *British diplomacy in China 1880–5* (Cambridge, 1939).
C 2165   McCordock, R. S. *British Far Eastern policy 1894–1900* (New York, 1931).

C 2166 Townsend, M. E. and Peake, C. H. *European colonial expansion since 1871* (New York, 1941).

See also:

C 1391 Ward, J. M.

Detailed Studies

C 2167 Ariga, N. 'Diplomacy', *Japan by the Japanese* (Stead, A., ed., New York, 1904); an unusually frank account of Japanese policy by a contemporary.

C 2168 Ellison, J. W. *Opening and penetration of foreign influence in Samoa to 1880* (Corvallis, Or., 1938).

C 2169 Ennis, T. E. *French policy and developments in Indo-China* (Chicago, 1936).

C 2170 Gordon, D. C. *The Australian frontier in New Guinea 1870–85* (New York, 1951); the Australian struggle against the Germans.

C 2171 Masterman, S. *The origins of international rivalry in Samoa 1845–84* (Stanford, 1934); the clash of German, British and American interests.

C 2172 Power, T. F. *Jules Ferry and the renaissance of French imperialism* (New York, 1944).

C 2173 Pratt, J. W. *Expansionists of 1898: the acquisition of Hawaii and the Spanish islands* (Baltimore, 1936).

C 2174 Ryden, G. H. *The foreign policy of the United States in relation to Samoa* (New York, 1933); good on American aspects of Samoan policy.

C 2175 Tsiang, T. F. 'Sino–Japanese diplomatic relations 1870–94', *Chinese Social and Political Science Review*, **17** (1933); the only account to make use of Chinese records.

The First World War and the peace settlement

Many of the documentary collections and historical works which have been referred to in 'The Politics of the European States' above contain information on this subject, such as:

C 1013 Woodward, E. L. and Butler, Rohan (eds.). *Documents on British foreign policy 1919–39*, 1st ser., vols. 5 and 6 (1919).

C 1012 *The Paris peace conference 1919. Papers relating to the foreign relations of the United States.*

C 1022 Temperley, H. W. V. (ed.). *A history of the peace conference of Paris* (6 vols.).

C 992 Bean, C. E. W. (ed.). *Official history of Australia in the war of 1914–18*, of which the relevant volumes are: vol. 9: Jose, A. W. *The royal Australian navy, 1914–18* (4th ed., Sydney, 1937); vol. 10: Mackenzie, S. S. *The Australians at Rabaul: the capture and administration of the German possessions in the southern Pacific* (4th ed., Sydney, 1937).

DETAILED STUDIES

New Zealand's involvement in the war is interestingly discussed in the biography of Sir Francis Bell, who was a member of the New Zealand Cabinet throughout the period:

C 2176   Stewart, W. D. *The Right Hon. Sir Francis H. D. Bell...his life and times* (Wellington, 1937).

On the international politics of the Far East during the period (and see also the bibliographies on the United States above):

C 2177   Curry, R. W. *Woodrow Wilson and Far Eastern policy, 1913–21* (New York, 1957).
C 2178   Fifield, R. H. *Woodrow Wilson and the Far East: the diplomacy of the Shantung question* (New York, 1952).
C 2179   La Fargue, T. E. *China and the world war* (Stanford, 1937).
C 2180   Morley, J. W. *The Japanese thrust into Siberia, 1918* (New York, 1957).
C 2181   Vinson, J. C. *The parchment peace: the United States Senate and the Washington conference, 1921–2* (Athens, Ga., 1955).
C 2182   Whiting, A. S. *Soviet policies in China, 1917–24* (New York, 1954).

63   **Europe's economic and political relations with Tropical Africa (vol. IX, ch. xxi)**
         The Partition of Africa (vol. XI, ch. xxii)

Many works which are relevant to this period have already been referred to in the bibliographies on Africa in Sections A and B, and in the bibliography on Britain and the British Commonwealth in Section C. A few standard works are again cited here, but reference should be made to those parts as well.

There is no general history of tropical Africa on any scale, but the relevant chapters of:

C 2183   Oliver, R. and Fage, J. D. *A short history of Africa* (Harmondsworth, 1962); give a useful outline and have helpful bibliographies.

The main general works on the activities of the relevant European powers have already been mentioned, such as:

B 2035   *Cambridge history of the British Empire*, vol. VIII [South Africa].
C 1316   *Cambridge history of the British Empire*, vol. II.
A 1697   Duffy, J. *Portuguese Africa.*
B 2029   Hanotaux, G. and Martineau, A. *Histoire de colonies françaises* (6 vols.).
C 2154   Priestley, H. I. *France overseas, a study of modern imperialism.*

Europe and Africa before 1870

Aspects of the European approach to Africa are discussed in:

C 2184   Boahen, A. Adu. 'The African association, 1788–1805', *Transactions of the Historical Society of Ghana*, 5 (1961).

C 2185   Boahen, A. Adu. *Britain, the Sahara and the Western Sudan, 1788–1861*
(Oxford Studies in African Affairs, Oxford, 1964).

C 2186   Coupland, Sir R. *Kirk on the Zambezi* (Oxford, 1928): ch. i.

C 2187   Curtin, P. D. *The Image of Africa: British ideas and action, 1780–1850*
(Madison, Wisc., 1964).

C 2188   Groves, C. P. *The planting of Christianity in Africa;* the standard
history of missionary activities, of which vols. 1 (1948) and 2 (1954) are
relevant, and which contain full references to sources.

C 2189   Hallett, R. 'The European approach to the interior of Africa in the
eighteenth century', *Journal of African History*, **4** (1963).

C 2190   Mellor, G. R. *British imperial trusteeship, 1783–1850* (1951); which also
deals with the suppression of the slave trade.

C 2191   Newbury, C. W. *British policy towards West Africa: select documents,*
vol. 1, 1783–1874 (Oxford, 1963).

C 2192   Perham, M. and Simmons, J. *African discovery* (1942).

For the slave trade and its suppression see:

C 2193   Kuczyinski, R. R. *Population movements* (1936)—an estimate of volume.

C 2194   Lloyd, C. *The navy and the slave trade* (1948).

The following are important for West Africa:

C 2195   Metcalfe, G. E. *Maclean of the Gold Coast* (1962).

C 2196   Newbury, C. W. *The Western slave coast and its rulers* (Oxford, 1961);
useful bibliographies.

For Faidherbe, apart from his own writings, see:

C 2197   Delavignette, R. 'Faidherbe', *Les Techniciens de la colonisation,
XIXe–XXe siècles* (Julien, Ch.-A., ed.) (1947).

For East Africa see:

C 2198   Coupland, R. *The exploitation of East Africa, 1856–90* (1939).

Livingstone is best studied in his own writings, but a useful introduction
is:

C 2199   Simmons, J. *Livingstone and Africa* (London, 1955).

The literature of South African history is enormous (see *Cambridge
history of the British Empire*, vol. VIII), but particular mention should
be made of:

C 2200   Walker, E. A. *The great trek* (1934).

The Partition of Africa

Reference has already been made at the beginning of this list to other
bibliographies. For the international diplomacy of the time, 'The
Politics of the European States' should also be consulted.

GENERAL STUDIES

C 2201   Hertslet, Sir E. *The map of Africa by treaty* (3rd ed., 3 vols., 1909).

C 2202   Lucas, Sir C. *The partition and colonisation of Africa* (Oxford, 1922).

C 2203   Robinson, R., Gallagher, J. and Denny, A. *Africa and the Victorians. The official mind of imperialism* (1961).

C 2204   Woolf, L. *Empire and commerce in Africa. A study in economic imperialism* (1920).

For the indigenous cultures of Africa see:

C 2205   Baumann, H. and Westermann, D. *Les peuples et les civilisations de l'Afrique* (1948).

DETAILED STUDIES

C 2206   Aydelotte, W. O. *Bismarck and British colonial policy. The problem of south-west Africa 1883–5* (Philadelphia, 1937).

C 2207   Brunschwig, H. *Mythes et réalités de l'impérialisme colonial français 1871–1914* (1960).

C 2208   —— *L'Expansion allemande outre-mer du XVe siècle à nos jours* (1957).

C 2209   Cambon, H. *Histoire de la régence de Tunis* (1948).

C 2210   Cook, A. N. *British enterprise in Nigeria* (Philadelphia, 1948).

C 2211   Crowe, S. E. *The Berlin west African conference 1884–5* (1942).

C 2212   Kiewiet, C. W. de. *The imperial factor in South Africa* (Cambridge, 1937).

C 2213   Delebecque, J. *Vie du Général Marchand* (12th ed., 1936).

C 2214   Flint, J. E. *Sir George Goldie and the making of Nigeria* (1960).

C 2215   Hanna, A. J. *The beginnings of Nyasaland and north-eastern Rhodesia 1859–95* (Oxford, 1956).

C 2216   Headlam, C. (ed.). *The Milner papers; South Africa 1897–9* (1931); *South Africa 1899–1905* (1933).

C 2217   Holt, P. M. *The Mahdist state in the Sudan 1882–1902* (1952).

C 2218   Hornik, M. P. *Der Kampf der Grossmächte um den Oberlauf des Nil* (Vienna, 1948).

C 2219   Oliver, R. *Sir Harry Johnston and the scramble for Africa* (1957).

C 2220   Poel, J. van der. *The Jameson Raid* (Cape Town, 1951).

C 2221   Raphael, L. A. C. *The Cape-to-Cairo dream. A study in British imperialism* (New York, 1936).

C 2222   Roberts, S. H. *The history of French colonial policy 1870–1925* (repr. 1963).

C 2223   Rudin, H. R. *Germans in the Cameroons 1884–1914* (1938).

C 2224   Shibeika, M. *British policy in the Sudan 1882–1902* (1952).

C 2225   Townsend, M. E. *The rise and fall of Germany's colonial empire 1884–1918* (New York, 1930).

See also:

C 1280 Cromer, Earl of; C 2172 Power, T. F.

INDEX

NOTE   Periods: A = 1493–1648
                       B = 1648–1793
                       C = 1793–1945

Names of authors are not indexed.

Personal names (in their accepted English forms) are of those of whom there are biographies or studies. These names are usually not included in the cross-references.

· The entries following the name of a leading country refer to general and political histories.

The generally used name is given: e.g. 'Marlborough, Duke of' is so indexed and not as 'Churchill, John'.

To avoid frequent repetition of long lists of countries, the cross-references are limited to those that are closely relevant.